PROFESSIONAL
UNIFIED COMMUNICATIONS DEVELOPMENT
WITH MICROSOFT® LYNC™ SERVER 2010

PROFESSIONAL

Unified Communications Development with Microsoft® Lync™ Server 2010

PROFESSIONAL

Unified Communications Development with Microsoft® Lync™ Server 2010

George Durzi
Michael Greenlee

Wiley Publishing, Inc.

Professional Unified Communications Development with Microsoft® Lync™ Server 2010

Published by
Wiley Publishing, Inc.
10475 Crosspoint Boulevard
Indianapolis, IN 46256
www.wiley.com

ISBN: 978-0-470-93903-1
ISBN: 978-1-118-11650-0 (ebk)
ISBN: 978-1-118-11396-7 (ebk)
ISBN: 978-1-118-11397-4 (ebk)

Manufactured in the United States of America

10 9 8 7 6 5 4 3 2 1

For general information on our other products and services please contact our Customer Care Department within the United States at (877) 762-2974, outside the United States at (317) 572-3993 or fax (317) 572-4002.

Wiley also publishes its books in a variety of electronic formats. Some content that appears in print may not be available in electronic books.

Library of Congress Control Number: 2011926919

To my wife Amy, my parents Victor and Juliette, and my siblings Mark and Tamara. I love you.

—George

To my father.

—Michael

ABOUT THE AUTHORS

GEORGE DURZI is a Principal Consultant at Clarity Consulting, where he works with clients to implement solutions based on various Microsoft tools and technologies. George started working with Lync as part of a project for the Microsoft Developer and Platform Evangelism team to build and deliver developer training content for early adopters of Lync and Exchange. George is active in the Chicago software development community, helping to organize and speaking at events in the region. George was born in Lebanon, raised in the United Arab Emirates, and moved to the United States to attend college. To this day, some American pop culture references completely elude him.

MICHAEL GREENLEE works for Clarity Consulting, where he manages implementations of Clarity Connect, a contact center and customer care platform native to Microsoft Lync. Michael has worked with the Unified Communications Managed API since 2008, when it was still referred to by the code name OOTY, and his blog about Lync development is widely read within the Lync developer community. Born and raised on the tropical island of New Jersey, Michael is fluent in several languages, including American English, Canadian English, and British English.

CREDITS

ACKNOWLEDGMENTS

I'D LIKE TO THANK CHRIS MAYO FOR PRESENTING the opportunity to write this book, and Ryan Powers for telling me "If you get an opportunity to write a book, you figure out a way to make it happen," when I was agonizing over whether this was something I wanted to do. Various people on the Lync team were incredibly helpful throughout the process, providing guidance and taking the time to meet in person to make sure that the content was the best that it could be. I'd like to thank Albert Kooiman, Marcelo Ivan Garcia, Chris Schindler, Stephane Taine, Nick Fish, Ajay Soni, Bahram Chehrazy, Yiu-Ming Leung, and Julio Lins for all of their help. Thanks to Rebecca Laszlo for being a great non-fictitious, fictitious user. Thanks to Jon Rauschenberger (our technical editor) for being a great mentor. Thanks to Clarity Consulting for supporting us as we worked on this book and providing the opportunity to be involved in projects which something like this could come out of. Finally, thanks to my lovely wife Amy for being patient as every minute of my free time was consumed by this and various other activities.

—GEORGE

MANY OF THE EXPLANATIONS AND CONCEPTS in this book originated in conversations I had with others who were working with the Lync APIs. Talking to these people and getting their feedback on the book helped immeasurably in deciding how to say what we wanted to say. I'd like to thank all of these folks who contributed in this way, including Peter Miller, Dan Gardiner, Marshall Harrison, Curtis Swartzentruber, Oscar Newkerk, Hui Liu at Computer-Talk, and Lav Pathak. I'd also like to thank Ahmed Stewart for reviewing several of the UCMA chapters on short notice for technical accuracy, and Stephane Taine, Dalibor Kukoleca, K. Ganesan, and Ganesh Sridharan for explaining details of the Lync APIs as this book was coming together. Jon Rauschenberger (our technical editor) introduced me to Unified Communications development, and his vision of the Lync APIs as a revolutionary tool that changes the game of communications development first got me excited about this topic. Without that, this book (or at least my chapters!) would not have been written. Finally, I'd like to say thanks to my wife for her support, patience, and shoulder rubs during the writing of this book.

—MICHAEL

CONTENTS

INTRODUCTION

RATHER THAN SIMPLY REPLACING PHONES and instant messages, Microsoft Lync, Microsoft's Unified Communications platform, makes communicating in completely new ways possible. Lync users can see whether a contact is available and where he or she is located before reaching out. After a user has decided to contact someone, he can choose between a variety of methods, including audio, video, and instant message, depending on the situation, or even combine them all. Users can even send context along with a communication, so that the person on the other end does not need to scramble for old emails or account details before the conversation can begin.

Once of the most distinctive things about Lync, though, is how easy it is to extend. Conventional telephony platforms tend to be difficult to customize, and require learning esoteric development platforms or hiring expensive consultants. The Lync development platform described in this book allows developers to build custom solutions for Lync in a fraction of that time using the familiar and widely used .NET platform. This makes Lync perfect for building a custom communications solution for your organization.

This book explains in detail how to write custom client and server applications for Lync.

WHO THIS BOOK IS FOR

This book is intended primarily for readers ages 3 and up who are doing custom development to extend Microsoft Lync, either on the client side or the server side. Readers are expected to have a working familiarity with C# and the .NET Framework 3.5, and at least a very rudimentary understanding of Microsoft Lync and what it does. Newcomers to the Lync platform can ramp up slowly with the introductory material in Chapters 1 and 6, whereas those who are already familiar with Lync development or who worked with the development platform in Office Communications Server 2007 will find plenty of advanced material throughout the book.

Readers who are interested primarily in building custom server applications to extend Lync can begin with Chapter 6 after a brief dip into Chapter 1, and return to Chapters 2–5 later. Readers who have been tasked with building custom client applications for Lync can read Chapters 1–5 in order. Finally, those who are already somewhat familiar with Lync development and are desperate to solve a knotty server-side development problem may want to skip to Chapter 13, which covers troubleshooting.

Readers who are hungry are advised to have a snack before beginning, because this book does not contain any food.

WHAT THIS BOOK COVERS

This book describes in detail how to extend Lync through custom development. It covers both client-side development using the Lync 2010 Software Development Kit (SDK), and custom server application development using the Unified Communications Managed API (UCMA) SDK and the Unified Communications Managed API Workflow SDK. Rather than rehash the API documentation and detail every single feature of the Lync development platform, this book attempts to explain in depth what the authors feel are the most commonly used areas of functionality. Readers will finish the chapters in this book not only understanding the big picture of what can be done with Lync development, but also the real-world practices that make life easier for a Lync developer. Last, but not least, a thorough examination of this book will reveal the meaning of the word *octothorpe*.

HOW THIS BOOK IS STRUCTURED

Aside from **Chapter 1**, which explains what Lync is all about and how the development platform works, the book is roughly divided into two sections. Chapters 2–5 cover client-side development, while Chapters 6–14 cover server-side development.

Chapter 2 explains how to use the Lync controls to embed Lync client features into WPF and Silverlight applications.

Chapter 3 introduces the Lync 2010 Managed API, which allows developers to perform Lync client operations, such as initiating calls or monitoring the presence of contacts, from within other applications.

Chapter 4 describes how you can use the Lync controls and the Lync Managed API to create "contextual conversations," where information relevant to the topic is sent along with the communication.

Chapter 5 discusses the UI Suppression feature in the Lync Managed API, which allows the standard Lync client interface to be hidden and Lync client operations managed through custom development.

Chapter 6 is the first of the server-side development chapters, and introduces the Unified Communications Managed API (UCMA).

Chapter 7 explains how to build the skeleton of a UCMA application, which can connect to a Lync server.

Chapter 8 describes how to use UCMA to initiate, accept, monitor, and control two-party calls.

Chapter 9 discusses the presence capability in Lync and how to manipulate it through UCMA.

Chapter 10 talks about using UCMA to perform contact list operations on behalf of Lync users.

Chapter 11 introduces conferencing: how to create, join, modify, and manipulate conferences, either for traditional conference call scenarios or for specialized applications such as call center or billing systems.

Chapter 12 describes some of the advanced features in UCMA, which allow applications to control media, including playing and recording audio, manipulating the flow of media between conference participants, and dealing with tones.

Chapter 13 explains some of the fundamentals of troubleshooting custom server applications for Lync, delving into some details of messaging in the process.

Chapter 14 covers the UCMA Workflow SDK, which allows developers to build interactive voice and messaging applications quickly with a graphical designer.

WHAT YOU NEED TO USE THIS BOOK

To derive the most benefit from this book, the authors recommend having access to a functioning Lync environment, with at least one free application server on which to test server applications. To derive maximum enjoyment from this book, a sense of humor is also recommended.

The Lync 2010 SDK (for client-side development) and the UCMA 3.0 SDK (for server-side development) will be necessary to try out any of the code discussed in this book. The chapters contain details on finding and installing these SDKs. In order to install and use the SDKs, readers will also need Visual Studio 2008 SP1 or a later version.

CONVENTIONS

To help you get the most from the text and keep track of what's happening, we've used a number of conventions throughout the book.

> *Boxes with a warning icon like this one hold important, not-to-be-forgotten information that is directly relevant to the surrounding text.*

> *The pencil icon indicates notes, tips, hints, tricks, or asides to the current discussion.*

As for styles in the text:

➤ We *italicize* new terms and important words when we introduce them.

➤ We show keyboard strokes like this: Ctrl+A.

➤ We show filenames, URLs, and code within the text like so: `persistence.properties`.

➤ We present code in two different ways:

```
We use a monofont type with no highlighting for most code examples.
We use bold to emphasize code that is particularly important in the present
context or to show changes from a previous code snippet.
```

SOURCE CODE

As you work through the examples in this book, you may choose either to type in all the code manually, or to use the source code files that accompany the book. All the source code used in this book is available for download at www.wrox.com. When at the site, simply locate the book's title (use the Search box or one of the title lists) and click the Download Code link on the book's detail page to obtain all the source code for the book. Code that is included on the website is highlighted by the following icon:

Available for download on Wrox.com

Listings include the filename in the title. If it is just a code snippet, you'll find the filename in a code note such as this:

Code snippet filename

 Because many books have similar titles, you may find it easiest to search by ISBN; this book's ISBN is 978-0-470-93903-1.

After you download the code, just decompress it with your favorite compression tool. Alternatively, you can go to the main Wrox code download page at www.wrox.com/dynamic/books/download .aspx to see the code available for this book and all other Wrox books.

ERRATA

We make every effort to ensure that no errors are in the text or in the code. However, no one is perfect, and mistakes do occur. If you find an error in one of our books, like a spelling mistake or faulty piece of code, we would be very grateful for your feedback. By sending in errata, you may save another reader hours of frustration, and at the same time, you will be helping us provide even higher quality information.

To find the errata page for this book, go to www.wrox.com and locate the title using the Search box or one of the title lists. Then, on the book details page, click the Book Errata link. On this page, you can view all errata that has been submitted for this book and posted by Wrox editors. A complete book list, including links to each book's errata, is also available at www.wrox.com/misc-pages/booklist.shtml.

If you don't spot "your" error on the Book Errata page, go to www.wrox.com/contact/techsupport.shtml and complete the form there to send us the error you have found. We'll check the information and, if appropriate, post a message to the book's errata page and fix the problem in subsequent editions of the book.

P2P.WROX.COM

For author and peer discussion, join the P2P forums at p2p.wrox.com. The forums are a web-based system for you to post messages relating to Wrox books and related technologies and interact with other readers and technology users. The forums offer a subscription feature to email you topics of interest of your choosing when new posts are made to the forums. Wrox authors, editors, other industry experts, and your fellow readers are present on these forums.

At http://p2p.wrox.com, you can find a number of different forums that will help you, not only as you read this book, but also as you develop your own applications. To join the forums, just follow these steps:

1. Go to p2p.wrox.com and click the Register link.

2. Read the terms of use and click Agree.

3. Complete the required information to join, as well as any optional information you want to provide, and click Submit.

4. You will receive an email with information describing how to verify your account and complete the joining process.

 You can read messages in the forums without joining P2P, but to post your own messages, you must join.

After you join, you can post new messages and respond to messages other users post. You can read messages at any time on the Web. If you want to have new messages from a particular forum emailed to you, click the Subscribe to this Forum icon by the forum name in the forum listing.

For more information about how to use the Wrox P2P, be sure to read the P2P FAQs for answers to questions about how the forum software works, as well as many common questions specific to P2P and Wrox books. To read the FAQs, click the FAQ link on any P2P page.

1

Building Communications Solutions with Microsoft Lync Server 2010

Information workers rely heavily on two inherently inefficient technologies — email and the telephone — to perform their day-to-day job duties. If you've ever been buried in email and can only dream of achieving "inbox zero," you recognize the limitations of email as a productivity tool. When you email someone, he is probably not sitting at his desk anxiously awaiting your email and chomping at the bit to helpfully respond. Occasionally, you might receive someone's out of office notification in response to your email and realize that you probably won't get a real response for a few days. The same goes for the traditional phone: you don't know whether or not the person you are trying to reach is available to pick up your call; you end up playing voicemail tag until you finally get in touch with him or her.

Even entertaining the possibility that email and the phone are going anywhere would be naive; however, both could use a complementary technology to increase their usefulness and streamline the process of communicating and collaborating with others. Instead of calling people without knowing whether they are available, how about knowing their availability and the best way to contact them before placing the call? Instead of emailing a document back and forth with changes, how about starting an application sharing session and collaborating on the document in real time? Wouldn't it be great if you knew what an incoming call was about before you even picked it up? Or if you could pick up that call anywhere, not just at your desk?

Microsoft Lync Server 2010 — the successor to Office Communications Server — provides instant messaging, voice and video calling, online meeting, and application sharing capabilities that integrate with the tools that information workers use every day: Microsoft Office and SharePoint. When working with a Word document in SharePoint, you can see the edits that someone else who is editing the document at the same time has made and use Microsoft Lync to start an audio or instant message conversation with him to discuss the edits. Because you can see peoples' presence in various Office applications, SharePoint, and your custom-developed applications, you know whether they are actually available before contacting them.

As a Private Branch Exchange (PBX) replacement, Microsoft Lync Server 2010 can double as your phone system, enabling you to make phone calls directly from the Microsoft Lync client running on your desktop or laptop. You are no longer tethered to that hunk of plastic sitting at your desk; you can receive a call on whatever device you happen to be connected from, wherever you are. Your ability to receive calls at a certain number no longer depends on your proximity to the physical phone attached to that number.

If you have an Internet connection and a headset, that's all you need! This is what happens when telephony moves from being a hardware solution to a software one.

Have you begun thinking of the types of communications features that you can build into your applications? After a brief introduction of the functionality available in the Microsoft Lync Server 2010 product, this chapter gives you a developer-centric overview of the types of communications solutions that you can build on top of it.

You'll learn about the Lync software development kit (SDK), which includes the Lync controls that you can use to integrate Lync functionality such as presence and click-to-call into your applications. The Lync SDK also includes the Lync API; a brand-new, managed API for building communications-enabled applications. Finally, the chapter shows you how the Unified Communications Managed API 3.0 (UCMA 3.0) and the Unified Communications Managed API 3.0 Workflow SDK (UCMA 3.0 Workflow SDK) are used to build server-side communications solutions such as automatic call distributors, conferencing solutions, Interactive Voice Response (IVR) systems, and virtual personal assistants.

LYNC PRODUCT OVERVIEW

So, what is Lync? Microsoft Lync Server 2010 is the successor to Office Communicators Server, and Live Communications Server before that. Although most people might be familiar with Lync as an enterprise instant messaging solution, it's a lot more than that when you take advantage of all the features it has to offer.

Lync adds value to the Microsoft applications that you use every day: Office and SharePoint. It provides a unified communication and collaboration experience across Office and SharePoint, providing the same way to start an instant message, audio call, or desktop sharing session with a contact regardless of the application you are working in. The new Lync client (the replacement for Microsoft Communicator) enables you to connect with people within your organization by allowing you to perform a skills search to find coworkers with a particular skill. The Lync skills search queries users' My Sites for skills that they have indicated expertise in.

Lync provides a built-in conferencing solution that you can use to schedule and host online meetings with contacts both inside and outside your organization. Online meetings are easy to create by scheduling them in Outlook, or by selecting a list of contacts in Lync and starting an ad-hoc meeting. For users outside your organization who don't have the Lync client installed, the Lync Web App — the successor to LiveMeeting — enables them to join your online meeting and participate in your application sharing session. Attendees can dial in to a conference call, or have the Lync Web App call them back on a number they provide. A new conference lobby experience allows presenters and the meeting organizers to exercise more control over the online meeting by notifying them when people outside the organization join the meeting and providing them with the option to admit these visitors (or not) into the meeting.

This book is not geared to people responsible for architecting, deploying, and administering Microsoft Lync Server 2010 in an enterprise environment; however, the following is a brief overview of the new features available to administrators.

The Microsoft Lync Server 2010 Control Panel is a new Silverlight-based tool for administering a Lync deployment; it includes functionality to:

- ➤ Manage users
- ➤ Manage the various servers in the Lync topology
- ➤ Configure instant messaging and presence
- ➤ Create and maintain voice dialing plans
- ➤ Configure conferencing
- ➤ Monitor the quality of service in the deployment
- ➤ Adjust bandwidth utilization

Administrators can alternatively use PowerShell to execute management scripts in the topology. The Lync Server Management Shell provides an experience that Exchange and SharePoint administrators are already familiar with from managing their environments using PowerShell.

Now that you know a little bit about the functionality offered by Microsoft Lync Server 2010, it's time to learn about the development tools that you use to build communications functionality into your applications.

BUILDING COMMUNICATIONS APPLICATIONS WITH THE LYNC SDK

The Lync 2010 SDK includes the Lync controls, a set of Silverlight and Windows Presentation Foundation (WPF) controls that you can use to integrate functionality found in the Lync client directly into your applications.

The SDK also includes the Lync application programming interface (API), a brand-new, managed API for building custom communications solutions. The Lync API is intended to replace the IMessenger and UCC APIs available with Office Communications Server 2007 R2. The IMessenger API was easy to get started with, but was fairly limited in functionality; it was also a little cumbersome to troubleshoot because it used COM interoperability to interact with the running instance of Communicator on the user's machine.

The UCC API was very difficult to get started with in comparison, but it provided the most power and functionality if you wanted to build a Communicator replacement. Unlike the UCC API, the Lync API requires the Lync client to be running — it reuses the connection that the client has established with the Lync infrastructure. You can configure the Lync client to run in UI Suppression mode — where its user interface is invisible to the user — enabling you to build custom communications clients previously only possible when using the UCC API.

Integrating Lync Functionality into Your Applications Using the Lync Controls

Think of the Lync client as being built out of LEGO blocks, each providing a specific piece of functionality such as showing the presence of contacts, organizing contacts into groups, and interacting with contacts by starting instant message or phone conversations. The Lync controls separate the functionality in Lync clients into individual controls that developers can drag and drop into their Windows Presentation Foundation (WPF) or Silverlight applications.

The Lync controls include a control to show the presence of a contact; for example, the presence of an account manager in a CRM system. Controls are also available to easily start an instant message or audio conversation with that contact at the click of a button. with no additional code required.

A set of other controls provides functionality for managing contact lists; for example, to integrate the user's Lync contact list into an application. You can also use custom contact lists to create and display an ad-hoc list of contacts, such as the account team for a client in a CRM application. Additional controls are available to search for contacts and display the results. Controls are also available to set the current user's presence, personal note, and location.

Due to their obvious dependence on user interface elements of the Lync client, the Lync controls are not available in UI Suppression mode.

Integrating Lync functionality into applications using the Lync controls allows users to launch communications directly from the application that they are working in without needing to switch to the Lync client. The Lync controls are available in WPF and Silverlight and are extremely easy to use; you only need to drag and drop the appropriate controls into the application, and they work without the need for any additional code.

Integrating Communications into Your Applications Using the Lync API

The Lync API object model exposes extensibility points that allow developers to build applications that interact with the running instance of the Lync client. You can use the Lync API to programmatically sign a user into the Lync client and handle events for changes in its state. You can also start a conversation, add participants, handle conversation and participant events, and add contextual data to the conversation.

You can use the Lync API to create subscriptions on attributes of contacts in your contact list; for example, to track when the availability of a particular contact changes. The Lync API also provides functionality to modify attributes of users signed in to Lync, such as changing their presence or publishing a personal note or location.

Like the IMessenger API, the Lync API includes automation: the ability to start conversations in different modalities (such as instant message or audio/video) with a very small amount of code. The functionality in automation simply invokes the necessary Lync user interface elements, such as a Lync conversation that includes the Application Sharing modality so that a user can share her desktop with another user. Because it is dependent on Lync user interface elements, the functionality in automation is not available when the Lync client is running in UI Suppression mode.

In conjunction with the Lync controls, you can use the Lync API to easily add communications functionality into Silverlight, WPF, and Windows Forms applications. For example, you can spruce up a customer relationship management (CRM) application by integrating presence and click-to-call functionality, allowing users to accomplish their work without needing to switch back and forth between the application and the Lync client.

Working with Lync UI Suppression

When the Lync client is configured to run in UI Suppression mode, its interface is completely hidden from the user. Applications that use Lync UI Suppression are responsible for recreating those user interface elements from scratch. The Lync API with Lync running in UI Suppression mode is the recommended development pattern for applications you would have previously built with the UCC API.

Lync UI Suppression requires that the Lync client is installed on the user's machine; this eliminates the complexity of managing the connectivity of the application back to the Lync server infrastructure. In UI Suppression, you use the Lync API to replicate some of the functionality available in the Lync client, such as signing users into Lync, retrieving their contact list, and starting and responding to conversations in different modalities.

When working with UI Suppression, you interact with conversations at the modality level — activating individual modalities manually, creating conversations, adding participants, and disconnecting the modalities when the conversation is completed. For example, you can build a Silverlight instant messaging client that provides a completely customized user interface for instant message conversations. In this case, you would be responsible for recreating application functionality and user interface elements such as a contact list and conversation window. You would work directly with the instant message modality, creating a conversation, connecting the modality, sending instant message text to participants, notifying participants when someone is typing, and delivering the instant message text to the participants in the conversation.

Using the Lync API with Lync running in UI Suppression mode, you can build compelling Lync-replacement solutions such as a custom instant messaging client, or a dedicated audio/video conferencing solution.

Adding Context to Conversations

The context of a conversation refers to the subject or topic of the conversation; the Lync API provides some mechanisms for embedding context directly into a conversation, allowing the participants to immediately know what a new conversation is about.

A great example of adding context to a conversation is the "Reply by IM" feature in Microsoft Outlook that allows you to respond to an email message using Lync. The message recipient sees the subject of the original email message in the incoming conversation notification window (also known as the toast) and as the title of the conversation window. When the person receives the instant message, she knows right away what you are contacting her about.

The Lync API introduces the concepts of Launch Link context and Lync Extensibility Window context that you can use to enhance the communications capabilities of your applications by embedding context into the conversations started by the application.

Launch Link context allows conversation recipients to launch applications directly from the Lync conversation window. For example, you select a customer account when working with a CRM application; after selecting the account, you can see the account manager's presence and are able to start an instant message or audio conversation with her directly from the application. The conversation that the account manager receives contains a link that she can use to launch the CRM application directly from the conversation window. The contextual data payload supplied with the conversation also includes information about the particular account that you are contacting her about. The user can launch the CRM application and automatically load the customer account record in question.

Lync Extensibility Window context allows you to host Silverlight or Web applications in the Lync conversation window. When a person receives a conversation that includes Lync Extensibility Window context, the Lync conversation window expands to host the specified Silverlight or Web application. The application hosted in the Lync conversation window enhances the conversation by providing additional services to it not available in the out-of-the-box Lync experience.

Launch Link and Lync Extensibility Window context are often combined to provide an end-to-end contextual conversation experience to the user. For example, a developer working in Visual Studio can highlight a section of code — using a Visual Studio add-in — and learn which team member authored that section of code. The Lync controls are used to show the team member's presence and, if she is available, start a conversation with her. When she receives the conversation, you can use Lync Extensibility Window context to display the section of code in question in a Silverlight application hosted in the Lync conversation window. If the developer needs to modify the code, you can use Launch Link context to include a launch link in the Lync conversation that allows her to start Visual Studio and automatically open the project containing the code.

You can build two main types of applications to run in the Lync conversation window. The first is a companion application, such as a translation application that provides two-way translation of an instant message conversation. This type of application interacts with the conversation but doesn't depend on it for startup parameters; the user can start this application as needed from the Lync conversation window. The other type of application depends on the conversation it is hosted in to provide the necessary startup parameters; for example, when a customer service agent in a call center receives a call, a Silverlight application automatically loads in the Lync conversation window and uses the caller's phone number to look up the customer record and display information, such as the recent order history to the agent.

The contextual conversation functionality provided by Launch Link context and Lync Extensibility Window context allows you to inject contextual data into conversations, providing for a richer and more efficient conversation experience that ensures that participants always have access to the contextual application data that they need.

BUILDING COMMUNICATIONS SOLUTIONS WITH THE UNIFIED COMMUNICATIONS MANAGED API SDK

The Unified Communications Managed API SDK includes the Unified Communications Managed API (UCMA) and the Unified Communications Managed API Workflow SDK (UCMA Workflow SDK) that are used to build middle-tier communications solutions such as automatic call distributors, IVR (Interactive Voice Response) systems, and virtual personal assistants.

UCMA is the most mature of the APIs in Microsoft Lync Server 2010 and its predecessors. In Office Communications Server 2007, UCMA 1.0 simply provided an abstraction over the Session Initiation Protocol (SIP) while providing limited collaboration functionality to developers. In Office Communications Server 2007 R2, UCMA 2.0 added presence, conferencing, media, and workflow and collaboration functionality, finally establishing Microsoft as a player in the software telephony space and enabling developers to build software to power high-volume call centers.

In Microsoft Lync Server 2010, UCMA 3.0 builds upon the functionality in UCMA 2.0 to make developing and deploying these types of applications much easier. It also adds functionality that enables some advanced call center scenarios such as supervisor monitoring and coaching.

Building Communications Solutions with UCMA

Although the Lync SDK is used to integrate communications functionality into applications that run on the client, UCMA is typically used to build communications applications that run on the server; for example, hosted in Internet Information Services (IIS), exposed through Windows Communication Foundation (WCF), or running in a Windows Service. A UCMA application is usually a long-running process such as an automatic call distributor used to handle and distribute incoming calls in a call center. Users interact with the UCMA application via an endpoint that can either be a contact in Lync, such as `sip:HelpDesk@fabrikam.com`, or simply a phone number. The user can start a Lync call, instant message with the UCMA application contact or dial the phone number associated with the application.

Consider the following scenario where Contoso, a fictitious company, uses a UCMA-based application to run its call center operations.

When customers call Contoso's customer service phone number, the UCMA application picks up the calls and guides callers through a workflow, such as one built with the UCMA Workflow SDK, to gather information from them such as the reason for their call, their account number, and so on. After the workflow gathers the necessary information from the callers, it places them on hold and searches for an agent with the right skills to assist them. Customers remain on hold until an agent becomes available; the UCMA application tracks all the agents' Lync presence so it knows when an agent becomes available again to handle a call.

When an agent picks up calls, he or she already knows a lot about the callers based on the information they provided. An Agent Dashboard application hosted in the Lync conversation window can display information about the caller such as order history or any open customer service tickets that require attention. The agent can use this information to provide better service to the customer.

An application such as the customer service Agent Dashboard is built using the Lync SDK, including the Lync controls and the Lync API. The UCMA application interacts with the Agent Dashboard using the Context Channel, a new feature in UCMA 3.0 that provides a channel across which a UCMA application and Lync SDK application can send information to each other. For example, if the agent realizes that he needs to consult another agent to help with the call, he can issue an "escalate" command from the Agent Dashboard application. The command is sent across the context channel to the UCMA application, which knows how to process it and look for another available agent with the necessary skills to assist with the call.

Part of a supervisor's duties in Contoso's customer service department is to monitor the performance of agents and coach them on how to provide better service to customers. The supervisor can launch a Supervisor Dashboard application that shows a list of all active calls. The supervisor selects a call to silently join, allowing him to monitor the call without the knowledge of either the customer or agent. The new audio routes functionality in UCMA 3.0 enables developers to build routes across which audio can travel in a conference, effectively controlling who can hear what. When the supervisor is monitoring a call, audio flows to her from the conference but doesn't flow back in, allowing her to listen in to a call without being heard. If the supervisor needs to provide coaching to the customer service agent, an audio route is established from the supervisor to the agent, allowing her to "whisper" to the agent without the customer hearing any of the conversation.

UCMA 3.0 includes several other enhancements that are covered in more detail later in the book, including an easier development experience for working with presence and conferences, and a feature known as auto-provisioning, which greatly simplifies the process of managing the plumbing and configuration information required to run a UCMA application.

Building Workflow Solutions with the UCMA Workflow SDK

You use the UCMA Workflow SDK to build communications-enabled workflow solutions such as IVR systems and virtual personal assistants. You typically use an IVR system to gather information from a caller such as the customer account number and reason for the call before connecting him or her to a live agent. A virtual personal assistant, on the other hand, provides services to the caller such as the ability to reserve a conference room from a mobile phone.

For a more concrete example, consider this scenario. In the legal industry, potential cases need be vetted for any conflicts of interest that could prevent the firm from being able to take on the case. This process is referred to as *new matter intake*, and each potential case is called a *matter*. Most law firms have software in place to streamline this process; however, such a solution can be extended to provide users with the ability to call in and check on the status of a new matter.

For example, an attorney could place a call to the New Matter Intake application contact in Microsoft Lync from her mobile phone. Using text-to-speech technology, the IVR prompts the attorney to enter her identification PIN and validates her identity. The IVR can then execute code to access the database, retrieve a list of outstanding matters for that attorney, and prompt her to select one. After the attorney selects a matter, the IVR can again access the database to identify the conflicts attorney assigned to the matter. The IVR can now check the presence of the conflicts attorney, and if he is available, ask the caller whether she wants to be transferred. The IVR can then perform a blind transfer of the call and disconnect itself from the call.

The UCMA 3.0 Workflow SDK enables developers to visually construct communications-enabled workflows by dragging workflow activities onto a design service, arranging and connecting them to form the workflow solution. You can construct workflows to accept audio or instant message calls, or both.

In the case of audio calls, input from the user can be in the form of *dual-tone multi-frequency (DTMF)* tones (choosing an option by entering its corresponding number using the phone's keypad), speech recognition, or both. The text-to-speech engine, available in 26 different languages, converts text to prompts that the caller hears during different activities of the workflow. You can also substitute professionally recorded audio prompts to give the IVR a more polished feel.

The previous attorney example represents an incoming communications workflow; however, developers can also build outgoing communications workflows. For example, a person might receive an automated call from the Service Desk asking him to rate his experience with a ticket he recently opened. The communications workflow can ask him several questions, such as his satisfaction with how the ticket was handled, and then save the results of the survey to a database when the call is completed.

Workflows are a critical part of a communications solution, allowing the software to provide services to a caller and only transferring the call to a live customer service agent — the comparatively more expensive resource — if necessary and only after providing the agent with all the relevant information about the caller.

SUMMARY

The development tools available in Microsoft Lync Server 2010 not only enable you to integrate communications features into your applications, they also enable you to build a whole new type of communication-centric application that can be the backbone of your business. In the next chapter, you will learn about the Lync controls that are available in the Lync SDK. You use the Lync controls to easily integrate functionality found in the Lync client directly into your applications.

2

Integrating Microsoft Lync Functionality into Your Applications

WHAT'S IN THIS CHAPTER?

➤ Setting up your development environment to work with the Lync controls

➤ Working with the Lync controls in WPF and Silverlight

➤ Starting conversations from the Lync controls

➤ Extending the Lync controls by creating a new control template

Using the Lync controls, you can integrate functionality from the Microsoft Lync 2010 client into your Windows Presentation Foundation (WPF) and Silverlight applications. Think of the Lync client as being built out of Lego blocks, each providing a specific piece of functionality such as showing the presence of contacts, organizing contacts into groups, and interacting with contacts by starting instant messaging or audio conversations. The Lync controls make this functionality available in WPF and Silverlight controls that you can use in your applications.

The Lync controls include individual controls to show the presence of contacts; for example, the presence of an account manager for a client in a Customer Relationship Management (CRM) application. Controls are also available to easily start an instant message or audio conversation with that contact at the click of a button — with no additional code required.

A set of other controls provides functionality for managing contact lists; for example, to integrate the user's Lync contact list into an application. You can also create custom contact lists and use them to display an ad-hoc list of contacts, such as the entire account team for a client in a CRM application. Additional controls are available to search for contacts and display the results. Controls are also available to set the current user's presence, personal note, and location.

Integrating Lync functionality into applications using the Lync controls enables end users of the application to launch communications directly from the application in which they are working without needing to switch to Lync. The Lync controls are available in WPF and Silverlight and are extremely easy to use; you only need to drag and drop the appropriate controls into the application, and they work with little to no additional code.

All the code shown in this chapter is available as part of a companion WPF project that you can download at Wrox.com.

SETTING UP YOUR DEVELOPMENT ENVIRONMENT

This section describes how to set up your development environment to use Visual Studio or Expression Blend to integrate the Lync controls into your WPF and Silverlight applications.

Requirements for Developing with the Lync Controls

Before you install the Microsoft Lync 2010 SDK and start developing with the Lync controls, take a moment to ensure that you have the right prerequisites installed and configured in your development environment.

Microsoft Lync 2010

The user's machine must have Lync installed and running in order to use the Lync controls. Lync acts as an "endpoint" for the controls, providing a communications channel between the controls and the Microsoft Lync Server 2010 infrastructure. When used in an application, the Lync controls are automatically associated with the identity of the user currently signed in to Lync.

If Lync is not running — or if the user is not signed in — the Lync controls are disabled and appear grayed out.

Visual Studio Support

Visual Studio 2008 SP1 and Visual Studio 2010 are officially supported for developing applications with the WPF Lync controls. You can use the WPF controls in both C# and Visual Basic .NET applications targeting either .NET Framework 3.5 SP1 or .NET Framework 4.

The Silverlight Lync controls are only supported in Visual Studio 2010 and Silverlight 4. You can use the Silverlight controls in both C# and Visual Basic .NET applications targeting .NET Framework 4.

Expression Blend Support

Expression Blend 3 and Expression Blend 4 are officially supported for developing applications with the WPF Lync controls. The Silverlight Lync controls are only officially supported in Expression Blend 4.

Silverlight Tools and Support

The Lync controls are only supported in Silverlight 4. Be sure to install the Silverlight 4 Tools for Visual Studio before beginning development.

If the appropriate Silverlight tools are not installed in your development environment, you will not be able to use the Visual Studio Silverlight project templates that are available with the Lync SDK.

When working with the Silverlight Lync controls, be sure to add the web site that hosts the Silverlight application to the user's Trusted Sites collection in the security settings in Internet Explorer.

The Silverlight Lync controls are not supported in Silverlight applications running in out-of-browser mode.

Installing the Lync Controls

The Lync controls are installed as part of the Microsoft Lync 2010 SDK, which also includes the Microsoft Lync 2010 Managed API (which Chapter 3 covers in detail).

The installer deploys the necessary assemblies for Silverlight and WPF, some sample applications, and Visual Studio project templates.

The Microsoft Lync 2010 SDK is installed to `C:\Program Files (x86)\Microsoft Lync\SDK`.

Assemblies

The Microsoft Lync 2010 SDK installation directory contains an `Assemblies` folder where you can find assemblies compiled for Silverlight and WPF. If you're not using the Visual Studio project templates that are available with the SDK, you should reference the assemblies from this location.

A good practice is to include the necessary assemblies in a `lib` folder in your Visual Studio solution and reference them directly from there. This is particularly useful if you are using Microsoft Team Foundation Server — or any other build automation software — to perform automated builds of your application because you don't need to install the Microsoft Lync 2010 SDK directly on the build server.

Lync SDK Redistributable

When building a custom software application that uses the Lync SDK, you can't assume that users will have the SDK already installed on their machine. You can package the Microsoft Installer (MSI) file for the Lync SDK Redistributable with your application's installer, and then install it on the user's machine as part of the application's installation process.

The redistributable is available by default at `C:\Program Files (x86)\Microsoft Lync\SDK\ Redist\LyncSdkRedist.msi`.

Visual Studio Project Templates

After installing the Microsoft Lync 2010 SDK, you will be able to create a *Lync Silverlight Application* or *Lync WPF Application* project in Visual Studio as shown in Figure 2-1.

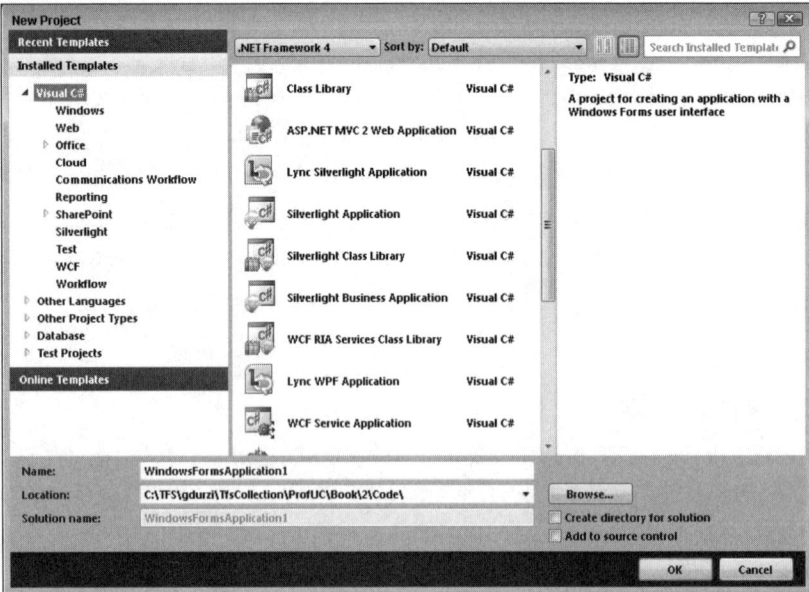

FIGURE 2-1

These Visual Studio project templates provide a great starting point for integrating the Lync controls into your applications. The project templates take care of adding the appropriate references to the Lync controls assemblies, declaring the XAML namespace references to the Lync controls, and laying out a `PresenceIndicator` control on the project's main page, as shown in Figure 2-2.

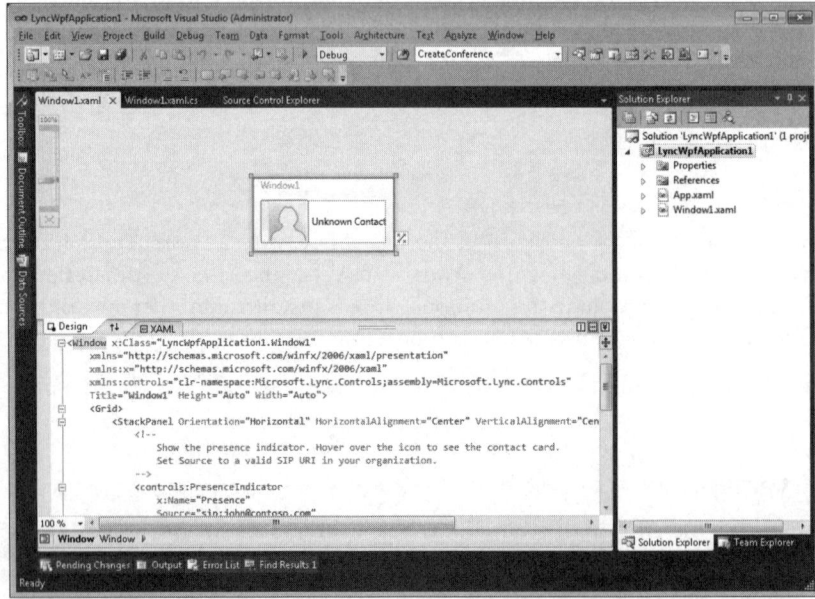

FIGURE 2-2

Setting Up Your Visual Studio Project Manually

If you have an existing Silverlight or WPF application that you need to integrate the Lync controls into, you won't have the luxury of being able to create your project from the Lync Silverlight Application or Lync WPF Application Visual Studio project templates. In that case, the following describes how to integrate the Lync controls into an existing Silverlight or WPF project.

Adding References to the Lync Controls

You can find all the assemblies for the Microsoft Lync 2010 SDK by default at `C:\Program Files (x86)\Microsoft Lync\SDK\Assemblies`. Assemblies for WPF and Silverlight are available in separate folders.

 The assemblies for WPF are contained in a folder called `Desktop`.

Add references to the following assemblies:

➤ Microsoft.Lync.Controls.dll

➤ Microsoft.Lync.Controls.Framework.dll

➤ Microsoft.Lync.Utilities.dll

➤ Microsoft.Office.Uc.dll (only for WPF applications)

Be sure to also add a reference to Microsoft.Lync.Model.dll if you need to use the Microsoft Lync 2010 API in your application. The Lync controls expose objects from the `Microsoft.Lync.Model` namespace; for example, a contact list contains a list of `Microsoft.Lync.Model.Contact` objects. You will only be able to interact with these objects in code if you add a reference to Microsoft.Lync.Model.dll.

Declaring XAML Namespaces

In the pages that you intend to use the Lync controls, add the following XAML namespace declaration:

Available for download on Wrox.com

```
xmlsn:controls="clr-namespace:Microsoft.Lync.Controls;
assembly=Microsoft.Lync.Controls"
```

Code snippet LyncControls\MainWindow.xaml

With this XAML namespace declaration in place, you can use the `controls:` prefix to use the Lync controls in a Silverlight or WPF application; for example, `<controls:PresenceIndicator .../>.`

WORKING WITH THE LYNC CONTROLS

The Lync controls include controls for displaying presence of contacts, working with lists of contacts, searching for contacts, modifying the current user's presence properties, and starting conversations. You can integrate the controls into your Silverlight or WPF applications to provide Lync functionality to your users directly from within the applications.

When you use the Lync controls in a Silverlight application, an ActiveX control is used to provide an automation bridge between the controls and Lync. ActiveX is obviously only supported in Internet Explorer. Unfortunately, this means that the Lync controls are currently only supported in Silverlight applications running in Internet Explorer.

You can also attach context to the controls that start conversations, allowing you to include contextual application data that gets passed to the conversation. For example, you can specify text that will appear in the toast (the notification window that appears on the bottom right of the screen when you receive a conversation invitation) that the recipients see when they receive a conversation invitation. You learn about the basic scenarios in this chapter; Chapter 4 covers contextual conversations in much more detail.

The code accompanying this chapter contains a WPF application that demonstrates the various Lync controls. The application shown in Figure 2-3 is divided into sections highlighting controls in the areas of presence, contacts, and communications.

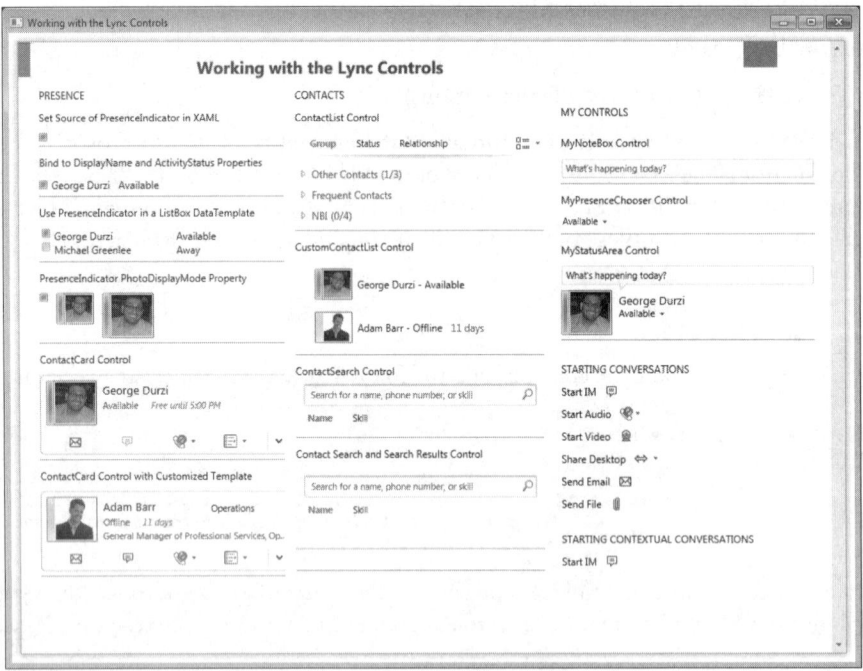

FIGURE 2-3

Displaying Presence

You use the `PresenceIndicator` and `ContactCard` controls to display the presence and contact card information for a contact. Both of these controls expose a `Source` property representing the

Session Initiation Protocol (SIP) URI of the contact that they will be bound to; for example, `sip:adamb@fabrikam.com`.

You can set the `Source` property explicitly in XAML, through binding, or in the code behind.

You can also set the `Source` property to a tel URI representing a telephone contact; for example, `tel:+13125551212`. Although doing this doesn't make much sense for the `PresenceIndicator` control, it's useful for the `ContactCard` control because you would be able to place a call to the tel URI from the control.

The PresenceIndicator Control

The `PresenceIndicator` control is often referred to as the "tic-tac." It is a graphical representation of a contact's presence. This section describes the various ways to connect the PresenceIndicator control to a contact to display its presence.

The Source Property

To connect the `PresenceIndicator` control to a contact, set its `Source` property in the XAML to the SIP URI of the contact.

```
<controls:PresenceIndicator Source="sip:georged@fabrikam.com" />
```

Code snippet LyncControls\MainWindow.xaml

You can also set the `Source` property of the `PresenceIndicator` in code behind. In this case, you don't need to set the `Source` property in XAML. However, you must give the `PresenceIndicator` control a `Name` so you can refer to it from the code behind.

```
<controls:PresenceIndicator x:Name="presenceIndicator" />
```

Set the `Source` property in the code behind of the page.

```
presenceIndicator.Source = "sip:georged@fabrikam.com";
```

You can also set the `Source` property in the XAML through binding. This is useful if the `PresenceIndicator` control is in the data template of an items control such as a `DataGrid` or `ListBox`, or if the value for `Source` is being populated from another property in the page's data context.

In the following example, `AccountManagerSIPUri` represents the SIP URI of the contact to which the `PresenceIndicator` control will be bound. In this case, `AccountManagerSIPUri` is a property of the `DataContext` of the page containing the `PresenceIndicator` control.

```
<controls:PresenceIndicator x:Name="presenceIndicator"
        Source="{Binding AccountManagerSIPUri}" />
```

DisplayName and ActivityStatus Properties

You can bind other properties of the `PresenceIndicator` control to properties of other controls on your page, as shown in Figure 2-4. For example, you can bind the `DisplayName` property to the `Text` property of a `TextBlock`.

```
<TextBlock Text="{Binding DisplayName,
    ElementName=presenceIndicator}" />
```

FIGURE 2-4

Code snippet LyncControls\MainWindow.xaml

You can also bind the `ActivityStatus` property to the `Text` property of a `TextBlock`.

```
<TextBlock Text="{Binding ActivityStatus,
    ElementName=presenceIndicator}" />
```

Code snippet LyncControls\MainWindow.xaml

Using the PresenceIndicator Control in a ListBox DataTemplate

Here's an example of using the `PresenceIndicator` control and the properties it exposes in an items control such as a `ListBox`.

In WPF and Silverlight, you can define a `DataTemplate` for items in controls such as the `ListBox` or `DataGrid`, giving you complete control over how the items are displayed in the control.

Define a `DataTemplate` that contains a grid with three columns. The `PresenceIndicator` control is bound to the default property of the data source using the `Source="{Binding}"` syntax. The `Text` property of the two `TextBlock` elements is bound to the `DisplayName` and `ActivityStatus` property of the `PresenceIndicator` control.

```
<ListBox x:Name="accountManagers" BorderThickness="0">
    <ListBox.ItemTemplate>
        <DataTemplate>
            <Grid>
                <Grid.ColumnDefinitions>
                    <ColumnDefinition Width="*"/>
                    <ColumnDefinition Width="150"/>
                    <ColumnDefinition Width="75"/>
                </Grid.ColumnDefinitions>
                <controls:PresenceIndicator Source="{Binding}"
                    x:Name="accountManagerPresence" Grid.Column="0" />
                <TextBlock Text="{Binding DisplayName,
```

```
                              ElementName=accountManagerPresence}"
                              Grid.Column="1" Margin="5,0,10,0"/>
                <TextBlock Text="{Binding ActivityStatus,
                              ElementName=accountManagerPresence}"
                              Grid.Column="2"/>
            </Grid>
        </DataTemplate>
    </ListBox.ItemTemplate>
</ListBox>
```

Code snippet LyncControls\MainWindow.xaml

Create a list of strings containing the SIP URIs of the contacts to display in the list, and set the `ItemsSource` property of the `ListBox` to the list of SIP URIs.

```
var contacts = new List<string>()
{
    "sip:georged@fabrikam.com",
    "sip:michaelg@fabrikam.com"
};
accountManagers.ItemsSource = contacts;
```

Code snippet LyncControls\MainWindow.xaml.cs

Because the `ListBox` is simply bound to a `List<string>`, you don't need to specify a property to bind to when setting the `Source` property of the `PresenceIndicator` control. Instead, use the default binding syntax of `Source="{Binding}"`. If you were binding the `ListBox` to a more complex list, such as a `List<AccountManager>`, you would need to specify the property of the `AccountManager` class to bind the `Source` property of the `PresenceIndicator` control to; for example, `Source="{Binding AccountManagerSIPUri}"`.

The PhotoDisplayMode Property

You can set the `PhotoDisplayMode` property of the `PresenceIndicator` control to choose how to display the contact's profile photo if he or she has one.

The `PhotoDisplayMode` property of the `PresenceIndicator` can be set to:

➤   Hidden

➤   Large

➤   Small

The default value for `PhotoDisplayMode` is `Hidden`. Figure 2-5 shows the `PresenceIndicator` control with the `PhotoDisplayMode` set to `Hidden`, `Small`, and `Large`.

FIGURE 2-5

SETTING PROFILE PHOTOS FOR CONTACTS

A domain administrator can set the profile photo for contacts in Microsoft Lync by setting the `thumbnailPhoto` property of the user's Active Directory object using a PowerShell script.

The `thumbnailPhoto` property in Active Directory expects a base 64–encoded string of the user's profile photo. Note that the profile photo must be less than 100KB in size.

You can write a PowerShell script to set the user's `thumbnailPhoto` property. The following PowerShell script accepts three parameters: the user's first and last name, and the path to the image to use as a profile photo.

The script attempts to locate the user in Active Directory using the first name, last name, and LDAP path to where his or her account is stored (make sure to modify this to match your environment).

The script then encodes the image, applies the encoded string to the `thumbnailPhoto` property, and finally commits the changes to Active Directory.

Available for download on Wrox.com

```powershell
$firstName  = $args[0]
$lastName   = $args[1]
$profilePic = $args[2]
$ldapPath   = $args[3]

$objDomain = [ADSI]""
$dn = $objDomain.distinguishedname # returns a formatted DN

[string]$fullName = [string]$firstName
                    + " " + [string]$lastName

$user = [ADSI]("LDAP://cn="+$fullName+","
    +$ldapPath)

[byte[]]$file = Get-Content $profilePic -Encoding Byte
$user.Properties["thumbnailPhoto"].Clear()
$user.Properties["thumbnailPhoto"].Add
    ([System.Convert]::ToBase64String($file))
$user.CommitChanges()
```

Code snippet SetUserProfilePhoto.ps1

Here's an example of calling SetUserProfilePhoto.ps1 to set a user's thumbnail photo in Active Directory. In this example, the user is in the `users` organizational unit of the `fabrikam.com` domain in Active Directory:

```powershell
.\SetUserProfilePhoto.ps1 "George", "Durzi", "gdurzi.png",
    "ou=users,dc=fabrikam,dc=com"
```

Before you can see the contact's profile photo in Lync, you must run two PowerShell cmdlets in the Lync Server Management Shell to update the user database and address book:

Available for download on Wrox.com

```
$fqdn = $args[0]
Update-CsUserDatabase $fqdn
Update-CsAddressBook $fqdn
```

Code snippet UpdateUserDatabaseAndAddressBook.ps1

where $fqdn is the fully qualified domain name of the Lync Server front-end server; for example, cs-se.fabrikam.com.

According to the Lync Server Management Shell documentation, the Update-CsUserDatabase PowerShell cmdlet forces the backend database to clear itself and re-read all the user-related information from Active Directory. The Update-CsAddressBook cmdlet forces Lync Server to sync immediately with Active Directory — Lync Server otherwise syncs with Active Directory every five minutes.

HoverAction and SingleClickAction Properties

If you hover over the PresenceIndicator control, the default behavior is to show the ContactCard control for the contact to whom the PresenceIndicator control is bound.

You can control this behavior by setting the HoverAction and SingleClickAction properties of the PresenceIndicator control:

➤ None

➤ ShowContactBrief

➤ ShowContactDetails

If you want to override the default behavior and only show the ContactCard control when the user clicks the PresenceIndicator control, set HoverAction to None, and SingleClickAction to either ShowContactBrief or ShowContactDetails:

```
<controls:PresenceIndicator Source="sip:georged@fabrikam.com"
        SingleClickAction="ShowContactBrief" HoverAction="None"/>
```

The ContactCard Control

The ContactCard control is a composite control that shows a contact's presence and provides click-to-communicate functionality for starting conversations with the contact.

The default behavior of the `PresenceIndicator` control is to display the `ContactCard` control for the contact when hovering over the presence tic-tac. However, you can use the `ContactCard` control independently from the `PresenceIndicator` control:

```
<controls:ContactCard Source="sip:georged@fabrikam.com" />
```

Code snippet LyncControls\MainWindow.xaml

If the contact with whom the control is associated has a personal note set in Microsoft Lync, the note appears at the top of the control, as shown in Figure 2-6.

The IsExpanded Property

You can expand the `ContactCard` control to display other information about the contact. When you expand the control using the expander toggle button, the details container contains two tabs: Contact and Organization.

FIGURE 2-6

The Contact tab displays contact information such as department, phone numbers, email address, upcoming calendar availability, and location. The Organization tab displays information about the contact's organizational hierarchy such as to whom he or she reports.

By default, the `ContactCard` loads with the `IsExpanded` property set to `false`. You can set the `IsExpanded` property to `true` to display the details container when the control loads, as shown in Figure 2-7.

The SelectedTabIndex Property

When the `ContactCard` control is expanded, the `SelectedTabIndex` property represents the index of the tab that is currently active.

Setting `IsExpanded` to `true` and `SelectedTabIndex` to `1` loads the `ContactCard` control with the details container expanded and Organization tab active.

FIGURE 2-7

Working with Contact Lists

The Lync controls include two controls for working with lists of contacts: `ContactList` and `CustomContactList`. You can use the `ContactList` control to integrate the user's Lync contact list into your WPF or Silverlight application. The `CustomContactList` is suitable for displaying an ad-hoc or application-specific list of contacts, such as the sales team contacts for a customer account in a CRM system.

The ContactList Control

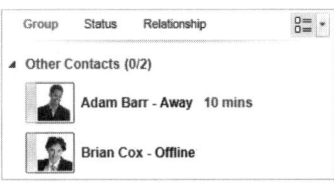

The `ContactList` control represents the current user's Microsoft Lync contact list. The `ContactList` control shown in Figure 2-8 does not expose a `Source` property; it will always display the contact list control for the user who is signed in to Lync.

FIGURE 2-8

```
<controls:ContactList />
```

Code snippet LyncControls\MainWindow.xaml

You can configure the `ContactList` control similarly to how you can configure your contact list in Lync; for example, you can customize how contacts are laid out in the list.

The ContactLayoutView Property

You can set the `ContactLayoutView` property of the `ContactList` control to either `OneLine` or `TwoLines`.

Setting `ContactLayoutView` to `OneLine` displays the contact's presence tic-tac, name, and availability on one line, as shown in Figure 2-9.

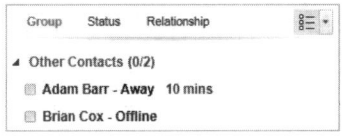

When you set `ContactLayoutView` to `TwoLines`, the `PresenceIndicator` control that is a part of the list item's data template appears with its `PhotoDisplayMode` property set to

FIGURE 2-9

`Large`. The contact's name and availability are displayed on one line, and the contact's personal note (if it's set) is displayed on the next line.

The ShowFriendlyName Property

Setting the `ShowFriendlyName` property of the `ContactList` control to `false` displays the SIP URI of the contact instead of his or her friendly name.

The ShowFrequentContacts Property

Set the `ShowFrequentContacts` property of the `ContactList` control to `false` to hide the Frequent Contacts group from the list.

The GroupViewBySetting Property

You can set the `GroupViewBySetting` property of the `ContactList` control to `Groups`, `Relationship`, or `Status`, allowing you to set the method by which the contacts in the list are grouped.

The ShowPivotBar Property

The `ShowPivotBar` property of the `ContactList` control is set to `true` by default, allowing you to toggle displaying the contacts in the list by Group, Status, or Relationship.

The pivot bar also enables you to customize the ContactList control, effectively allowing you to set the GroupViewBySetting, ContactLayoutView, ShowFrequentContacts, and ShowFriendlyName properties of the control directly in the UI.

The SelectedContactUri Property

The SelectedContactUri property of the ContactList control is a read-only property that you can use to retrieve the SIP URI of contact who is selected in the list.

The CustomContactList Control

The CustomContactList control enables you to display an ad-hoc list of contacts in your application. The contacts in the list don't necessarily have to be in the current user's Lync contact list. For example, if you want to show all the contacts in the account team for a particular client in a CRM application, you can use the CustomContactList control to display the list of contacts.

You can create the CustomContactList control and corresponding CustomContactListItem elements declaratively in XAML:

Available for
download on
Wrox.com

```
<controls:CustomContactList>
    <controls:CustomContactListItem Source="sip:georged@fabrikam.com"/>
    <controls:CustomContactListItem Source="sip:michaelg@fabrikam.com"/>
</controls:CustomContactList>
```

Code snippet LyncControls\MainWindow.xaml

The contacts are added to the custom contact list, as shown in Figure 2-10.

Alternatively, you can set the ItemsSource property of the CustomContactList control to a List<string> representing the contacts to show in the control. In this case, the XAML for the CustomContactList control doesn't contain any CustomContactListItem elements.

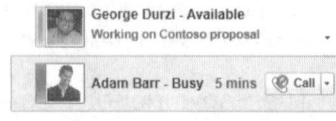

FIGURE 2-10

```
<controls:CustomContactList x:Name="customContactList" />
```

In the code-behind for the page, set the ItemsSource property of the CustomContactList control to a List<string> containing the SIP URIs of the contacts to display in the list.

```
var accountTeam = new List<string>()
{
    "sip:georged@fabrikam.com",
    "sip:michaelg@fabrikam.com",
};
customContactList.ItemsSource = accountTeam;
```

Control Properties

The `CustomContactList` control exposes some of the same properties as the `ContactList` control such as `ContactLayoutView` and `ShowFriendlyName`.

The `ContactList` and `CustomContactList` controls are based on the `ListBox` control, so they expose all the properties you would expect a `ListBox` to have. For example, you can set the `SelectionChanged` event to execute logic each time the user selects an item in the list.

```
<controls:CustomContactList x:Name="accountManagers"
        SelectionChanged="customContactList_SelectionChanged"/>
```

In this simple example, the code in the `SelectionChanged` event loads the clients belonging to the selected account manager.

```
private void customContactList_SelectionChanged(object sender,
    SelectionChangedEventArgs e)
{
    LoadClients((accountManagers.SelectedItem as Contact).Uri);
}
```

The value of `SelectedItem` is an object of type `Microsoft.Lync.Model.Contact`.

CustomContactList Versus ListBox and DataTemplate

You saw earlier how to use a `ListBox` with a custom `DataTemplate` to display a list of contacts and their presence. How is this different from using the `CustomContactList` control? Not much actually, except that the `CustomContactList` control does a lot of the work for you by already defining the `DataTemplate` for the items to show in the list.

For each contact in the list, the `CustomContactList` control shows the contact's presence, name, activity status, and also provides a click-to-call button to start calls with the contact. Double-clicking a contact in the list starts an instant messaging conversation with the contact. The `CustomContactList` control also handles some of the styling for you, such as the font styling and hover states of the items in the list.

If you want absolute control of how your contacts appear in the `CustomContactList`, you have two options: Start from scratch with a `ListBox` and custom `DataTemplate`, or use Expression Blend 4 to customize the various `DataTemplates` that the `CustomContactList` control exposes.

You learn how to create a new control template for the Lync Controls in the "Extending the Lync Controls with Expression Blend 4" section later in this chapter.

Searching for Contacts

To replicate the contact search functionality available in Lync, simply add the `ContactSearch` control to your application. Use the `ContactSearchInputBox` and `ContactSearchResultList` controls if you need to split up the search and results functionality, or if you need to add additional search filters to the search results.

The ContactSearch Control

The `ContactSearch` control replicates the contact search functionality in Microsoft Lync. It allows you to search for contacts by name or skill. Search results appear under the search input box, as shown in Figure 2-11.

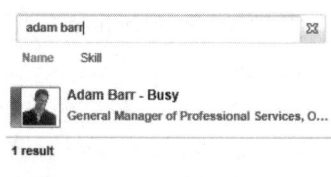

FIGURE 2-11

```
<controls:ContactSearch />
```

Available for download on Wrox.com

Code snippet LyncControls\MainWindow.xaml

The MaxResults Property

You use the `MaxResults` property to limit the number of search results returned by the `ContactSearch` control.

The SearchType Property

The `SearchType` property sets the default mode of the `ContactSearch` control, specifying whether to search for contacts by Name or Skill. The default value of `SearchType` is Name. When `SearchType` is set to Skill, the `ContactSearch` control performs a search for contacts by skill unless the user changes the search type by clicking on Name in the control.

When performing a Skill search, Microsoft Lync uses the SharePoint search web service to search for users whose Ask Me About property in their My Site matches the search criteria.

An administrator must configure Microsoft Lync Server 2010 to know the URL of the SharePoint search service and People Results page. This is done by running the following PowerShell script in the Lync Server Management Shell:

Available for download on Wrox.com

```
$SearchInternalURL       = $args[0]
$SearchCenterInternalURL = $args[1]
Set-CsClientPolicy -SPSearchInternalURL $SearchInternalURL
                   -SPSearchCenterInternalURL
                   $SearchCenterInternalURL
```

Code snippet ConfigureSkillSearch.ps1

where `SPSearchInternalURL` *is the internal URL of the SharePoint search service, and* `SPSearchCenterInternalURL` *is the internal URL of the SharePoint search people results page; for example:*

```
.\ConfigureSkillSearch
    "http://sps2010/sites/search/_vti_bin/search.asmx"
    "http://sps2010/sites/Search/Pages/peopleresults.aspx"
```

> *To enable the skill search functionality when the user is connected to Lync from outside the corporate network, you can use the* Set-CsClientPolicy *PowerShell cmdlet to set the values of* SPSearchExternalURL *and* SPSearchCenterExternalURL *to the corresponding externally accessible URLs.*
>
> *Note that a skill search is performed using the identity of the user who is running Lync — the user should thus be able to access the URLs specified in* SPSearchInternalURL, SPSearchCenterInternalURL, SPSearchExternalURL, *and* SPSearchCenterExternalURL.

ContactSearchInputBox and ContactSearchResultList Controls

If you want more control over contact search functionality in your application, you can use the ContactSearchInputBox and ContactSearchResultList controls to separate the search input and results functionality, as shown in Figure 2-12.

To connect the ContactSearchResultList control to a ContactSearchInputBox control, bind the ItemsSource and ResultsState properties of the ContactSearchResultList control to the Results and SearchState properties of the ContactSearchInputBox control that will be supplying the search results.

FIGURE 2-12

Available for download on Wrox.com

```
<controls:ContactSearchInputBox x:Name="contactSearchInputBox" />
<controls:ContactSearchResultList x:Name="contactSearchResultList"
    ItemsSource="{Binding Results, ElementName=contactSearchInputBox,
                  Mode=OneWay}"
    ResultsState="{Binding SearchState,
                   ElementName=contactSearchInputBox,
                   Mode=OneWay}" />
```

Code snippet LyncControls\MainWindow.xaml

ContactSearchInputBox exposes some of the same properties as ContactSearch, such as MaxResults and SearchType. The control also exposes a SearchTextInput property that, if specified, immediately executes a search with the criteria being the value of the property.

```
<controls:ContactSearchInputBox x:Name="contactSearchInputBox"
        SearchTextInput="Rebecca Laszlo" />
```

When the ContactSearchResultList control is bound to a ContactSearchInputBox control, it is only visible if the ContactSearchInputBox control returns any search results. Make sure to account for this in your layout.

When you separate the contact search functionality in your application between the `ContactSearchInputBox` and `ContactSearchResultList` control, you can filter the search results before they are rendered by the `ContactSearchResultList` control. This is useful if you need to add additional criteria to the search; for example, to limit the search results to contacts from a particular department, or to contacts who have a specific title.

The Lync SDK documentation has a great example of using this technique to filter the search results based on `Microsoft.Lync.Model.ContactInformationType`; for example, by Title, Department, or Availability. Take a look at the Lync SDK documentation for the complete source code of the solution.

The solution uses a custom control called `AdvancedSearch` to display a series of checkboxes and textboxes to provide additional search criteria:

```
<CheckBox x:Name="cbTitle"
    Content="Title"
    Unchecked="OnSearchStateChanged" Checked="OnSearchStateChanged" />
<TextBox x:Name="tbTitle"
    IsEnabled="{Binding IsChecked, ElementName=cbTitle, Mode=OneWay}"
    LostFocus="OnSearchStateChanged"/>
```

The results list is filtered (by executing the `OnSearchStateChanged` handler) when the checkbox is checked/unchecked or when the value in the textbox changes. For example, when the user checks the Title checkbox, the search results will be filtered to only include contacts whose value for `Microsoft.Lync.Model.ContactInformationType.Title` matches the text in the Title search criteria textbox.

You can implement your own `AdvancedSearch` control that provides the capability to search using other properties.

The `AdvancedSearch` control exposes the same Dependency properties as the `ContactSearchResultList` control: `SearchType`, `SearchState`, and `Results`. The control also exposes a `FilteredResults` property that contains the filtered search results.

Most importantly, instead of being bound to the `ContactSearchInputBox` control, the `ContactSearchResultList` control is bound to the `AdvancedSearch` control:

```
<local:AdvancedSearchControl
    x:Name="advancedSearch"
    Results="{Binding Results, ElementName=input, Mode=OneWay}"
    SearchType="{Binding SearchType, ElementName=input, Mode=OneWay}"
    SearchState="{Binding SearchState, ElementName=input,
                Mode=OneWay}" />

<controls:ContactSearchInputBox x:Name="input" />

<controls:ContactSearchResultList
    x:Name="searchResults"
    ItemsSource="{Binding FilteredResults, ElementName=advancedSearch,
                Mode=OneWay}"
```

```
ResultsState="{Binding SearchState, ElementName=advancedSearch,
               Mode=OneWay}"
SearchType="{Binding SearchType, ElementName=advancedSearch,
               Mode=OneWay}" />
```

In the `OnSearchStateChanged` handler, the `AdvancedSearch` control iterates through every `SearchResult` item (an object of type `Microsoft.Lync.Model.Contact`) in the `Results` collection and compares the contact's Title to the search criteria. A contact is only added to the results collection if it matches the search criteria.

The `FilteredResults` property of the `AdvancedSearch` control is an instance of `SearchResultCollection` containing the filtered search results.

Displaying Information about the Current User

The "My" controls are a set of controls that allow the user who is currently signed in to Lync to view and update information about himself such as his personal note and presence. These controls don't expose a `Source` property because they're only intended to be used by the current user. You can't use these controls to set a user's personal note or presence on his behalf.

The MyNoteBox Control

Users can use the `MyNoteBox` control to change their personal note from within your application, as shown in Figure 2-13. When users change their personal note in the `MyNoteBox` control, their new personal note is also shown in Lync, and vice versa.

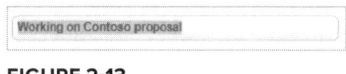

FIGURE 2-13

Available for download on Wrox.com

```
<controls:MyNoteBox />
```

Code snippet LyncControls\MainWindow.xaml

Use the `PersonalNote` property to get the text of the user's personal note.

The MyPresenceChooser Control

Users can use the `MyPresenceChooser` control to change their presence from within your application, as shown in Figure 2-14. When a user changes their presence using the `MyPresenceChooser` control, their new presence is also shown in Lync, and any of the other Lync controls that display the presence of users. Changing presence in Lync also sets the user's presence in the `MyPresenceChooser` control.

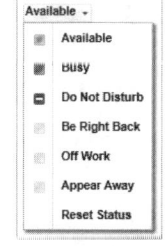

FIGURE 2-14

Available for download on Wrox.com

```
<controls:MyPresenceChooser />
```

Code snippet LyncControls\MainWindow.xaml

Use the `AvailabilityState` property to get the user's presence. The `AvailabilityState` property is of type `ContactAvailability`; an enumeration of valid availability states.

The MyStatusArea Control

The `MyStatusArea` is a composite control made up of a
`MyNoteBox` and a `MyPresenceChooser` control. It exposes the
`PersonalNote` and `ContactAvailability` properties that
the `MyNoteBox` and `MyPresenceChooser` controls expose. When
you add it to an application, the logged-in users can use it to
change their availability and set their personal note, as shown
in Figure 2-15.

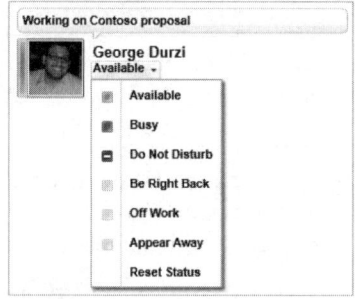

FIGURE 2-15

Available for download on Wrox.com

```
<controls:MyStatusArea />
```

Code snippet LyncControls\MainWindow.xaml

The control also exposes a `PhotoDisplayMode` property similar to the `PresenceIndicator` control
that you can use to control how the contact photo is rendered.

Starting Conversations

The `StartInstantMessagingButton`, `StartAudioCallButton`, `StartVideoCallButton`,
`ShareDesktopButton`, `SendEmailButton`, and `SendFileButton` controls provide
click-to-communicate functionality to start conversations and interact with contacts. All of
these controls expose a `Source` property that you can set to the SIP URI of a contact.

The StartInstantMessagingButton Control

Use the `StartInstantMessagingButton` control to start an instant message with the
contact specified in the `Source` property, as shown in Figure 2-16.

FIGURE 2-16

Available for download on Wrox.com

```
<controls:StartInstantMessagingButton Source="sip:adamb@fabrikam.com" />
```

Code snippet LyncControls\MainWindow.xaml

The StartAudioCallButton Control

Use the `StartAudioCallButton` control to start an audio call with the
contact specified in the `Source` property, as shown in Figure 2-17.

FIGURE 2-17

Available for download on Wrox.com

```
<controls:StartAudioCallButton Source="sip:adamb@fabrikam.com" />
```

Code snippet LyncControls\MainWindow.xaml

The `StartAudioCallButton` control exposes the various phone numbers that the contact to
whom it is bound to has published, just as you would see in Lync. You can start an audio call
to the contact's mobile phone number, or simply start a Lync call.

The StartVideoCallButton Control

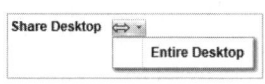

FIGURE 2-18

Use the `StartVideoButton` control to start a video call with the contact specified in the `Source` property, as shown in Figure 2-18.

```
<controls:StartVideoCallButton Source="sip:adamb@fabrikam.com" />
```

Code snippet LyncControls\MainWindow.xaml

The ShareDesktopButton Control

Use the `ShareDesktopButton` control to start a desktop sharing session with the contact specified in the `Source` property, as shown in Figure 2-19.

FIGURE 2-19

```
<controls:ShareDesktopButton Source="sip:adamb@fabrikam.com" />
```

Code snippet LyncControls\MainWindow.xaml

When starting a desktop sharing session with the `ShareDesktopButton` control, you can select the area of your monitor to share.

The SendEmailButton Control

Use the `SendEmailButton` control to start composing a new email to the contact specified in the `Source` property, as shown in Figure 2-20.

FIGURE 2-20

The SendFileButton Control

Use the `SendFileButton` control to send a file to the contact specified in the `Source` property, as shown in Figure 2-21. A file chooser dialog box appears after the user clicks the `SendFileButton` control to allow him or her to select the file to send.

FIGURE 2-21

Starting Contextual Conversations from the Lync Controls

The context of a conversation refers to the topic of the conversation. Context is usually established at the beginning of an audio call or instant message; for example, "Do you have time to discuss the General Industries account?" The back-and-forth involved in establishing the conversation's context can be wasteful: "I'd like to check on the status of the request so we can get started with the case."; "Hang on, let me open the CRM application and pull up the General Industries account so I can check on the status."

Throughout this book, you learn about the different ways to streamline this process by injecting context into conversations. This section shows you how to add context to conversations initiated from the Lync controls. Later chapters show you more complex ways to attach context to a conversation, such as the ability to host a Silverlight application in the Lync conversation window.

What does it mean to attach context to the Lync controls? Suppose you're building a new Customer Relationship Management (CRM) application in Silverlight. Using the `PresenceIndicator`, you added functionality to be able to see the presence of the account manager for a particular client. You also used the `StartInstantMessagingButton` and `StartAudioCallButton` controls to enable users to start a conversation with the account manager directly from the application.

By attaching context to the `StartInstantMessagingButton` and `StartAudioCallButton` controls, you can enable users to launch a conversation with the account manager *about the particular account*.

Attaching Context to the Lync Controls Using ConversationContextualInfo

When an instance of `ConversationContextualInfo` is attached to one of the Lync controls, the context described by the properties exposed by `ConversationContextualInfo` is attached to conversations initiated from the control.

Subject

Suppose that in the example of the CRM application, if the user is on the Account Detail page, you would like the subject of any conversations started from the page to be the name of the account.

Define a static resource that's accessible to the page, for example in `Page.Resources`:

Available for download on Wrox.com

```
<Page.Resources>
    <controls:ConversationContextualInfo x:Key="contextualInfo"
        Subject="General Industries" />
</Page.Resources>
```

Code snippet LyncControls\MainWindow.xaml

where General Industries is the name of the account currently loaded in the application. The `Subject` is hardcoded for simplicity; you will typically use binding to set its value; for example, `Subject="{Binding AccountName}"`.

You can now attach the instance of `ConversationContextualInfo` to a Lync control such as the `StartInstantMessagingButton` control:

Available for download on Wrox.com

```
<controls:StartInstantMessagingButton Source="sip:adamb@fabrikam.com"
    ContextualInformation="{StaticResource contextualInfo}"/>
```

Code snippet LyncControls\MainWindow.xaml

where `sip:adamb@fabrikam.com` is the SIP URI of the account manager. This is again hardcoded for simplicity; you will typically use binding to set its value; for example, `Source="{Binding AccountManagerSIPURI}"`.

When the user starts a conversation with the account manager from that page, the toast window that the conversation recipient sees will contain a custom toast string with the name of the account, as shown in Figure 2-22.

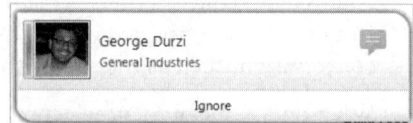

FIGURE 2-22

As shown in Figure 2-23, the subject of the conversation window will also be the name of the account.

You can also attach the instance of `ConversationContextualInfo` to a Lync control in the code behind of the page. Create an instance of `ConversationContextualInfo` and set the `Subject` property to the account name:

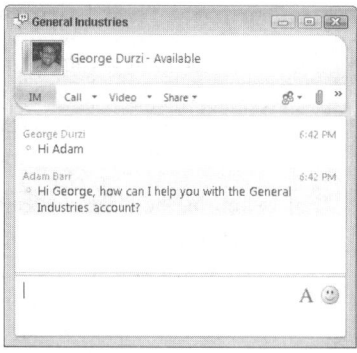

```
var contextInfo = new ConversationContextualInfo()
{
    Subject = accountName
};
```

FIGURE 2-23

Set the `ContextualInformation` property of `StartInstantMessagingButton` control to `contextInfo`:

```
startIMAccountManager.ContextualInformation = contextInfo;
```

ContextualLink

Specifying the `ContextualLink` property of `ConversationContextualInfo` also embeds a link into the conversation, as shown in Figure 2-24.

```
var contextInfo = new ConversationContextualInfo()
{
    Subject = accountName,
    ContextualLink = "http://crm.fabrikam.com/Account/" + accountName
};
```

Lync notifies the user that a contextual link has been provided with the conversation; it also warns the user not to click the link if it appears suspicious. Chapter 4 shows you how to securely embed a contextual link into a conversation so that no warning text appears.

ApplicationId and ApplicationData

You may have noticed that `ConversationContextualInfo` exposes two more properties: `ApplicationId` and `ApplicationData`. You use these properties to specify that a *contextual application package* is attached to the conversation. You learn about contextual application packages in Chapter 4.

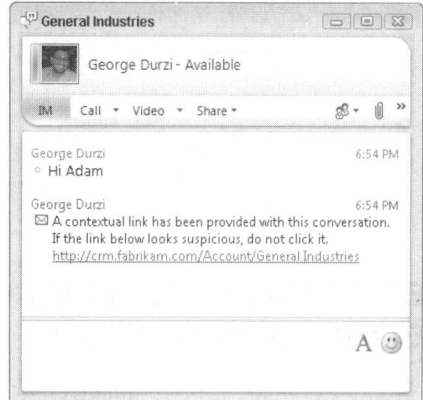

FIGURE 2-24

Lync Controls That Support ContextualInformation

You can attach an instance of `ConversationContextualInfo` to any Lync control that exposes a `ContextualInformation` property. In a composite Lync control such as the `ContactCard` control, the value of the `ContextualInformation` property cascades down into any of the contained controls that expose the `ContextualInformation` property.

For example, the `ContactControl` contains other Lync controls that can be used to start a conversation, such as the `StartInstantMessagingButton` and `StartAudioCallButton` controls. When you set the `ContextualInformation` property of the `ContactCard` control, the context is then also attached to the `StartInstantMessagingButton` and `StartAudioCallButton` controls.

The same applies to any of the Lync controls that display lists of contacts, such as the `ContactList` and `ContactSearch` controls. Starting a conversation with a contact who is listed in those controls attaches the context described in `ContextualInformation` to the conversation.

The following Lync controls expose the `ContextualInformation` property:

➤ ContactCard

➤ ContactList

➤ ContactSearch

➤ ContactSearchResultList

➤ CustomContactList

➤ ScheduleMeetingButton

➤ SendEmailButton

➤ SendFileButton

➤ ShareDesktopButton

➤ StartAudioCallButton

➤ StartInstantMessagingButton

➤ StartVideoCallButton

EXTENDING THE LYNC CONTROLS WITH EXPRESSION BLEND 4

You can apply some limited styling to the Lync controls in XAML, but if you need to make more extensive changes to one of the controls, you must extend the underlying control template. This section shows you how to use Microsoft Expression Blend 4 to create a new control template for the Lync controls.

You're already familiar with the `ContactCard` control; now take a look at a simple example of extending the `ContactCard` control, shown in Figure 2-25, to also show the contact's department in addition to his or her title.

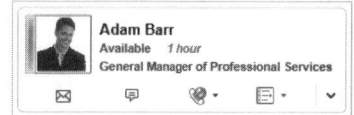

FIGURE 2-25

Creating a Copy of the Control Template

To create a new control template for the `ContactCard` control, you will first use Blend to create a copy of the existing control template and instruct the instance of the `ContactCard` control to use the new template. You can leave the new control template in the XAML, or you can put it in a Resource dictionary so that all instances of the `ContactCard` control in your application can reference it and take advantage of the customizations and improvements that you will make.

Launch Expression Blend 4 and open an existing project into which you've already integrated the `ContactCard` control. The Lync SDK doesn't include Visual Studio project templates for Blend; you can create a Lync WPF Application project in Visual Studio 2010, save it, and open it in Blend.

Locate the `ContactCard` control on the design surface and select it. In the Objects and Timelines window, right-click the `ContactCard` control and select Edit Template ⇨ Edit a Copy, as shown in Figure 2-26.

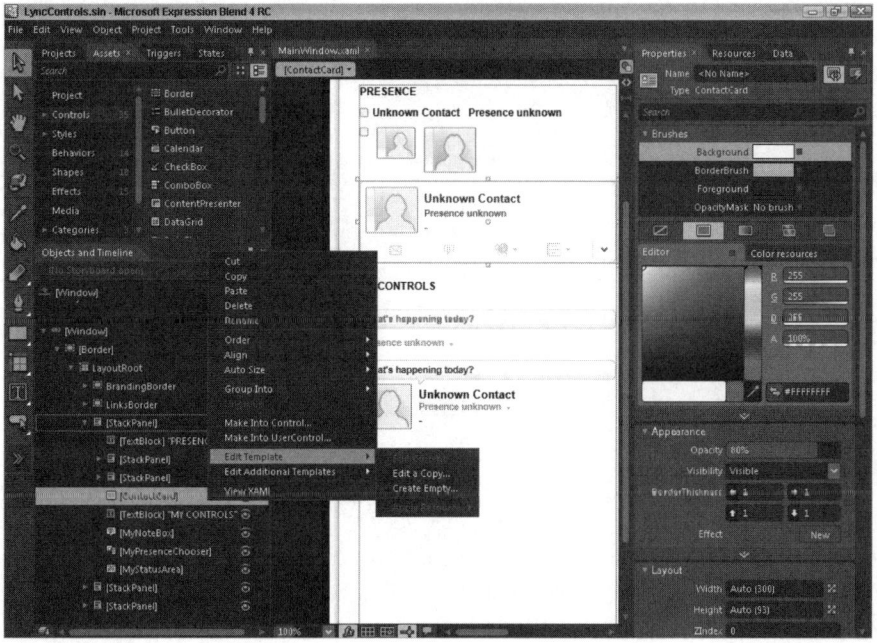

FIGURE 2-26

As shown in Figure 2-27, you will now be prompted to choose where to save the new control template resource. You can choose:

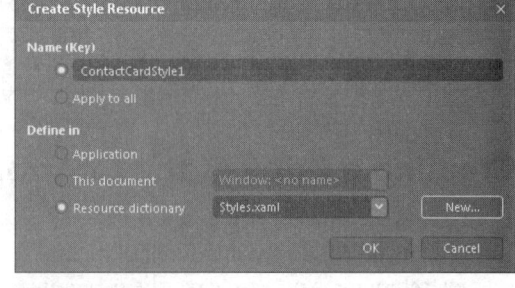

➤ Application (The resource will be created in your application's `App.xaml` file.)

➤ This document (The resource will be created in a Resources section of the window or page; for example, in `<Window.Resources>`.)

FIGURE 2-27

➤ Resource dictionary (The resource will be created in an existing or new resource dictionary.)

For this exercise, choose Resource dictionary to add the new control template to a new or existing Resource dictionary in your application. This is much better than adding the generated control template into the XAML in the page because other instances of the `ContactCard` control in your application will be able to use the new control template by simply referencing it from the Resource dictionary.

Examining the Control Template

The new control template is now available as a custom style in the application's Resource dictionary. Open the Resource dictionary and examine the XAML that was generated for the `ContactCardStyle1` style.

```
<Style x:Key="ContactCardStyle1"
    TargetType="{x:Type controls:ContactCard}" .../>
```

Code snippet LyncControls\Assets\ContactCard.xaml

The `Style` element has a `Key` property specifying a unique name for the style, and a `TargetType` property indicating that it can only be applied to items of type `ContactCard`.

The `ContactCard` control now has a `Style` attribute that points to the newly created `ContactCardStyle1` style.

```
<controls:ContactCard Source="sip:adamb@fabrikam.com"
    Style="{DynamicResource ContactCardStyle1}" />
```

Code snippet LyncControls\\MainWindow.xaml

Switch back to the resource dictionary and spend some time looking through the XAML that was generated for `ContactCardStyle1` — it's really long! You can see the various parts that make up the control template for the `ContactCard` control; for example, `PART_NoteContainer` contains the XAML for the section of the control that displays the user's personal note.

The style contains different templates for displaying information about the different types of contacts that the ContactCard control can be bound to. For example, if the Source property of the ContactCard control is set to a tel URI such as tel:+13125551212, the control is rendered using ContactCardBriefTelephoneDataTemplate, not the ContactCardBriefPersonDataTemplate.

Modifying the Control Template

If you take a closer look at the ContactCardStyle1 style, you'll notice that it includes multiple data templates. The ContactCard control is flexible enough to be connected to a SIP URI, a tel URI, a distribution list, and even an application contact that is associated with a Unified Communications Managed API (UCMA) application. The ContactCard control renders using a different data template depending on the type of contact that it is connected to. For example, you can't start an instant message with a telephone number, so the data template for a tel URI contact doesn't include a StartInstantMessagingButton control.

When extending or modifying any of the Lync control templates, be sure to modify the data template for the appropriate type of contact. In this example, you're displaying the contact's department in the ContactCard control next to his title, so you need to modify the control template for a person, not a telephone, distribution list, or application contact. In the ContactCard control, the data template for a person has a key of ContactCardBriefPersonDataTemplate.

Locate the <DataTemplate x:Key="ContactCardBriefPersonDataTemplate"> line in the style definition and examine the data template. Inside the Grid element, you can see the various pieces that make up this section of the control: the availability icon, the contact's name, the amount of time he has been idle (if applicable), and his title.

Insert the following code in the grid's content to display the contact's Department in a smaller font to the right of his name.

```
<Microsoft_Lync_Controls_Internal:TruncatedTextBlock
    Grid.Row="0" Grid.Column="2" Grid.ColumnSpan="3" Margin="0,0,42,0"
    VerticalAlignment="Bottom" HorizontalAlignment="Right"
    Text="{Binding PresenceItems.Department, Mode=OneWay}"
    Foreground="{Binding GlobalTextColor_Black,
            Source={StaticResource ControlColors}}"
    Style="{StaticResource GlobalTruncatedTextSizeStyle.Medium}"
    AutomationProperties.AutomationId="Department">
    <ToolTipService.ToolTip>
        <ToolTip Style="{StaticResource DefaultToolTipStyle}"
                Content="{Binding PresenceItems.Department}" />
    </ToolTipService.ToolTip>
</Microsoft_Lync_Controls_Internal:TruncatedTextBlock>
```

Code snippet LyncControls\Assets\ContactCard.xaml

When you run the application, the ContactCard control that is using the ContactCardStyle1 style will now show the contact's Department to the right of his name, as shown in Figure 2-28.

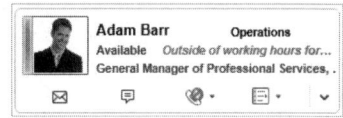

FIGURE 2-28

The Lync controls for WPF and Silverlight were designed to add functionality into your applications that is consistent with the look and feel of Lync. When extending the controls, keep in mind that your users are expecting behavior that is consistent with their experience when using Lync. In the authors' opinion, if you need to drastically change how one of the Lync controls functions, you're better off just building your own control — you have access to all the tools that you would need to do so.

SUMMARY

Using the Lync controls, you can easily add Lync functionality such as presence, contact lists, and contact search to your WPF and Silverlight applications. You can also use the controls to start contextual conversations with contacts directly from your applications.

The next chapter shows you how to use the Microsoft Lync 2010 Managed API to programmatically integrate communications functionality into your applications, such as managing groups, subscribing to the presence of contacts, and starting contextual conversations.

3

Building Communications Clients with the Microsoft Lync 2010 Managed API

WHAT'S IN THIS CHAPTER?

➤ Integrating Communications into Your Applications Using the Microsoft Lync 2010 Managed API

➤ Managing Conversations

➤ Publishing and Subscribing to Presence Items

➤ Automating the Running Instance of Microsoft Lync

➤ Managing Contacts and Groups

The Microsoft Lync 2010 Managed API is a new API that is available as part of the Microsoft Lync 2010 SDK. You can use the Lync Managed API in your application to interact with the running instance of the Lync client, manage groups and contacts, start conversations, and publish and subscribe to contact presence items. The Lync API requires a running instance of the Lync client; it uses the endpoint provided by the Lync client as the connection back to the Lync Server infrastructure.

The Lync API fits somewhere in between the IMessenger and Unified Communications Client (UCC) APIs that shipped with Office Communications Server 2007 R2. Although it was relatively easy to get started with, the IMessenger API was fairly limited in functionality. It also used COM to interact with an instance of Microsoft Communicator, making for an unpleasant development experience, especially when it came to handling and troubleshooting COM exceptions. The UCC API was very difficult to get started with in comparison, but provided the most power and functionality if you wanted to build a Communicator replacement. When developing with the UCC API, you were responsible for managing the endpoint and its ability to handle calls, which could be confusing if you were running Communicator alongside a custom client built with the UCC API.

The Lync API is intended to replace both the IMessenger and UCC APIs. The advantages that the Lync Managed API has over the IMessenger API are obvious: It provides a lot more functionality and a much better development experience. However, how the Lync Managed API can replace the UCC API to build custom communications clients might be a little less clear. When you build a communications client with the UCC API, you are responsible for creating all the user interface items such as conversation windows, notifications, replicating features such as location and E911 support, and so on. You are essentially building a communications client intended to replace the Lync client; you don't even need to have the Lync client installed.

The Lync 2010 client can run in UI Suppression mode, where its UI is completely hidden from the user. Using the Lync Managed API in conjunction with UI Suppression enables you to build a custom communications client while still taking advantage of the benefits of programming with the Lync Managed API, such as the ability to reuse the Lync endpoint to connect to the Lync Server infrastructure. However, similar to developing with the UCC API, you are responsible for developing all the UI components of the communications client when the Lync client is in UI Suppression mode. In Chapter 5, you learn about using UI Suppression to build custom communications clients.

The code accompanying this chapter includes a Windows Presentation Foundation (WPF) application, shown in Figure 3-1, that highlights the functionality available in the Lync API. The application monitors various events that the Lync API can subscribe to, such as creating and removing conversations and contacts, and subscribing to the properties of contacts such as their presence. The application also uses the Automation functionality of the Lync API to easily start conversations in different modalities, and to dock the Lync conversation window into the application.

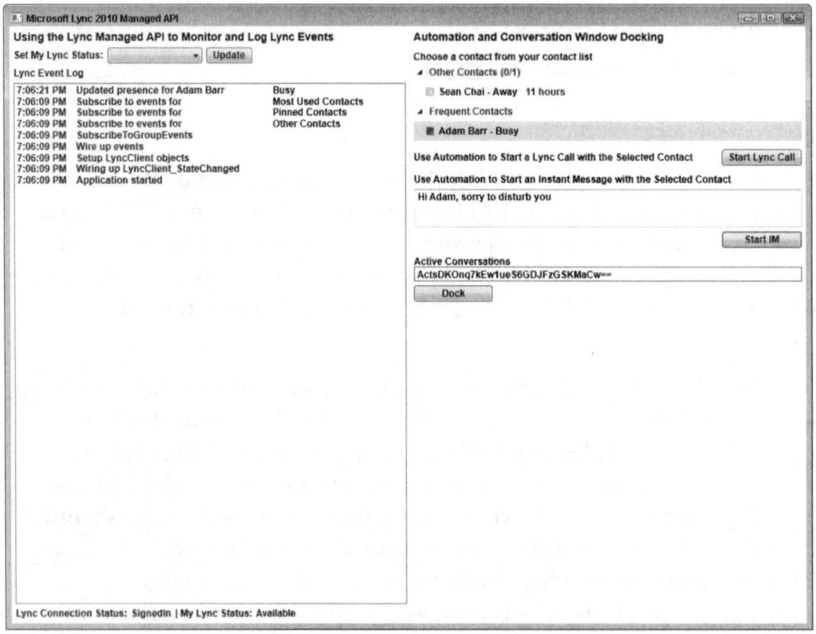

FIGURE 3-1

GETTING STARTED WITH THE LYNC 2010 MANAGED API

In this section you learn about setting up your development environment to work with the Lync API. Applications use the Lync API to interact with the running instance of the Lync client — a concept reiterated throughout this chapter. The Lync API reuses the connection that the running instance of the Lync client has to the Lync infrastructure, making for a much easier development experience where you are not responsible for maintaining this connection or the underlying logic of starting and participating in conversations across the connection. You learn how to use the Lync API so that your application can connect to the running instance of the Lync client and manage changes in its state.

Setting Up Your Development Environment

The Lync API is installed as part of the Microsoft Lync 2010 SDK, which also includes the Lync controls. In a default installation, the Lync SDK is installed at `C:\Program Files (x86)\ Microsoft Lync\SDK`.

Microsoft Lync 2010

The Lync client must be installed in order for you to programmatically interact with it using the Lync API. The user doesn't necessarily have to be initially signed in to the Lync client to start; you can use the Lync API to programmatically sign in the current user.

Visual Studio Support

Visual Studio 2008 SP1 and Visual Studio 2010 are officially supported for developing applications with the Lync API. You can use the Lync API in.NET applications targeting either .NET Framework 3.5 SP1 or .NET Framework 4.

The Lync API for Silverlight is only supported in Visual Studio 2010 and Silverlight 4. You can use the Lync API in Silverlight applications targeting .NET Framework 4.

Assemblies

You can find the Lync API assemblies in `C:\Program Files (x86)\Microsoft Lync\SDK\ Assemblies`, where different assemblies are available for WPF (and Windows Forms) and Silverlight applications. When adding the necessary references, make sure to add them from the correct folder.

Add references to the following assemblies:

➤   Microsoft.Lync.Model.dll

➤   Microsoft.Lync.Utilities.dll

Interacting with the Running Instance of the Lync Client

When integrating communications features into your application using the Lync API, you are responsible for managing the lifecycle of the Lync client. If the Lync client is not signed in, you can use the Lync API to sign in to the running instance. Your application must also react accordingly when the state of the Lync client changes; for example, the user signs out or loses network connectivity and is disconnected. In this section, you learn how to sign in to the running instance of the Lync client and wire up the necessary events so that your application can handle changes in the state of the Lync client.

Signing into the Lync Client Instance

To access functionality exposed by the Lync API throughout your application, add a module level of type `LyncClient` representing the running instance of the Lync client, as shown in the following:

```
private Microsoft.Lync.Model.LyncClient _lyncClient;
```

Code snippet LyncEventsLogger\Window1.xaml.cs

You can now access the running instance of the Lync client throughout the application; for example, to sign in or out, wire up event handlers for changes in the state of the Lync client, and access other features such as Automation.

Getting a Handle to the Running Instance of the Lync Client

When your application loads, you can get a reference to the running instance of the Lync client by calling the static `GetClient` method of the `Microsoft.Lync.Model.LyncClient` class. Set the module level variable `_lyncClient` to the return value of the `GetClient` method. Be sure to wrap the call to `GetClient` in a try/catch block as shown in the following code; an exception is raised if the Lync client is not installed or not running.

```
try
{
    _lyncClient = Microsoft.Lync.Model.LyncClient.GetClient();
}
catch
{
    MessageBox.Show(
        "Microsoft Lync is not running.",
        "Error",
        MessageBoxButton.OK,
        MessageBoxImage.Error);

    Close();
}
```

Code snippet LyncEventsLogger\Window1.xaml.cs

Signing In with the Current User's Credentials

After checking that the Lync client is installed and running on the user's machine, the next step is to programmatically sign the user into Lync. Signing in the user programmatically has the same effect as the user signing in by interacting directly with the Lync client.

Call BeginSignIn on the instance of LyncClient to sign into the running instance of the Lync client, as shown in the following code. The BeginSignIn method takes in userUri, domainAndUsername, and password parameters to sign in a user with specific credentials. Passing in null for these parameters will sign in the user who is currently logged into Windows.

```
_lyncClient.BeginSignIn(
    null,
    null,
    null,
    result =>
    {
        if (result.IsCompleted)
        {
            _lyncClient.EndSignIn(result);

            LogEvent("SignInCallback", "Signing in to Lync");
            InitializeClient(); // Setup application logic
        }
        else
        {
            LogEvent("SignInCallback", "Count not sign in to Lync");
        }
    },
    "Local user signing in" as object);
```

Code snippet LyncEventsLogger\Window1.xaml.cs

Alternatively, you can specify credentials for the user to sign in as the following:

```
_lyncClient.BeginSignIn(
    "adamb@fabrikam.com",
    "fabrikam\\adamb",
    "pass@word1",
    ...
```

As with most other operations in the Lync API, BeginSignIn is an asynchronous operation that implements the IAsyncResult pattern. You can use a lambda expression to handle the callback inline or specify a callback function that will execute when the sign-in process is completed. If you prefer not to use a lambda expression, define a callback function that will execute when the operation is complete, and set the callback function as the callback parameter of the BeginSignIn method:

```
_lyncClient.BeginSignIn(
    null,
    null,
    null,
    SignInCallback,
    "Local user signing in" as object);
```

Define a callback method following the `IAsyncResult` pattern; for example, the `SignInCallback` method accepts a parameter of type `IAsyncResult`, which you can use to check the status of the operation:

```
void SignInCallback(IAsyncResult ar)
{
    if (ar.IsCompleted)
    {
        ...
    }
}
```

 After signing in successfully to the running instance of the Lync client, you can define other Lync API objects that your application will use. Encapsulating this logic into its own function is useful; you never know how many times the current user will sign in and out of Lync while using your application. You will have to react to these state changes and re-create any objects that your application is using; for example, to create instances of the `ConversationManager` *and* `ContactManager` *objects.*

Managing the Lifecycle of the Lync Client

Applications using the Lync API are responsible for managing the lifecycle of the `LyncClient` instance and reacting accordingly. For example, if your application subscribes to the presence of some contacts, those subscriptions are lost when the Lync client signs out; your application needs to re-create them when the connection to the Lync client is reestablished.

Checking the State of the Lync Client

The `LyncClient` class exposes a `State` property that you can use to check the state of the running instance of the Lync client. The `ClientState` enum represents the various states that the client can be in:

➤ `Invalid`

➤ `Uninitialized`

➤ `SignedOut`

➤ `SigningIn`

➤ `SignedIn`

➤ `SigningOut`

➤ `ShuttingDown`

➤ `Initializing`

When the application starts, it can check to see whether the current user is signed in to the Lync client — the `State` property of `LyncClient` is not equal to `ClientState.SignedIn`. If the user is not signed in, you can use the Lync API to programmatically sign them in.

Handling Changes in the State of the Lync Client

The `StateChanged` event of `LyncClient` is raised when the state of the Lync client changes; for example, from `ClientState.SignedIn` to `ClientState.SigningOut` and then `ClientState.SignedOut` when the user signs out or is disconnected. The `StateChanged` event fires immediately when you sign into the Lync client; you must wire up the event handler for the `StateChanged` event beforehand if you want your application to execute any custom logic when the user signs in.

Wire up the `StateChanged` event of `LyncClient` and specify an event handler that will be called when the state of the Lync client changes.

```
_lyncClient.StateChanged +=
    new EventHandler<ClientStateChangedEventArgs>
        (LyncClient_StateChanged);
```

Code snippet LyncEventsLogger\Window1.xaml.cs

The instance of `ClientStateChangedEventArgs` in the `StateChanged` event handler exposes `OldState` and `NewState` properties representing the previous and current state of the Lync client. You can use that information to perform application logic specific to the state of the Lync client; for example, to clean up any Lync API–related application resources when signing out:

```
void LyncClient_StateChanged
    (object sender, ClientStateChangedEventArgs e)
{
    switch (e.NewState)
    {
        case ClientState.SigningOut:
            Cleanup();
            break;
    };


    ...


    UpdateMyAvailability();
    UpdateMyConnectionStatus(e.NewState.ToString());
}
```

Code snippet LyncEventsLogger\Window1.xaml.cs

The `StateChanged` event handler is also an ideal place from which to globally update the current user's availability and connection status in the application. For example, the application can implement a visual cue representing the current status of the Lync client.

WORKING WITH CONVERSATIONS

The Lync API provides functionality that your application can use to manage and interact with conversations. For example, it can track when conversations are started and closed and when participants join and leave them. You can also use the Lync API to create conversations and to join a conference.

The Lync API provides two ways to programmatically start conversations. You can use the `Automation` class to automate the running instance of the Lync client (just like the IMessenger API) and start conversations in various modalities. You can also interact directly with the `ConversationManager` class and manually create a conversation, add modalities to the conversation, and invite participants.

The `Automation` class is the quickest way to start conversations using the least code, while the `ConversationManager` class is a more manual method that involves a little more code. However, regardless of the method used to start a new conversation, you use the events and classes exposed by the `ConversationManager` class to track the conversation throughout its lifecycle.

In Chapter 5, you learn about working with the Lync API when the Lync client is running UI Suppression mode and its user interface is invisible to the user. `Automation` *is not available in UI Suppression mode because it relies on Lync user interface elements to start new conversations, so you need to use the* `ConversationManager` *to start conversations. When the Lync client is not running in UI Suppression mode, you can simply use* `Automation` *to create conversations instead of dealing with the complexity of creating conversations with the* `ConversationManager`*.*

Chapter 5 details using the `ConversationManager` *to start conversations. This chapter will instead focus on using* `Automation` *to start conversations, and then using the* `ConversationManager` *to interact with and track the lifecycle of the conversations.*

Starting Conversations with Automation

Lync Automation provides the simplest way of starting conversations because it completely leverages the Lync user interface and is very easy to program with. Lync Automation automates the running instance of the Lync client, invoking the appropriate user interface elements based on the type of conversation that is started. With a very small amount of simple code, you can start conversations in different modalities such as instant message, audio, video, application sharing, and file transfer.

In this section, you learn about initializing the `Automation` object so that you can use it to start conversations throughout the application. You also learn how to start conversations in different modalities, and finally get a handle to the conversation that was created.

Getting Started with Automation

To integrate the functionality available in the `Automation` class into your application, you initialize an instance of the class after the application has programmatically signed in to the running instance of the Lync client.

Define a module-level instance of the `Microsoft.Lync.Model.Extensibility.Automation` class in your application to take advantage of the Lync Automation functionality in the Lync API:

```
private Microsoft.Lync.Model.Extensibility.Automation _automation;
```

Code snippet LyncEventsLogger\Window1.xaml.cs

After initializing the `LyncClient` object, set `_automation` to the return value of the static `GetAutomation` function in the `LyncClient` class:

```
_automation = LyncClient.GetAutomation();
```

Code snippet LyncEventsLogger\Window1.xaml.cs

With the `Automation` object initialized, you can easily start conversations in different modalities using the `BeginStartConversation` method.

Starting Conversations Using Automation

Starting conversations using Lync Automation follows a simple pattern:

1. Create a list of participants to invite to the conversation.

2. Create a set of automation modality settings to attach to the conversation. These settings will vary, depending on whether you are dealing with instant messaging, desktop sharing, transferring files, using video, and so on.

3. Start the conversation.

4. Handle the callback.

Using this pattern, you can start conversations in different modalities including instant message, audio, video, application sharing, and file transfer.

Creating the Participant List

You can create a `List<string>` containing the SIP URIs of the contacts to invite to the conversation; for example:

```
var participants = new List<string>();
participants.Add("sip:georged@fabrikam.com");
participants.Add("sip:adamb@fabrikam.com");
```

Alternatively, if you are using a Lync control such as the `ContactList` or `CustomContactList` control, those controls expose a `SelectedContactUris` property that returns the SIP URIs of the contacts selected by the user; for example:

```
<controls:ContactList x:Name="myContactList"
    ContactLayoutView="OneLine" ShowPivotBar="False" />

...

var participants = myContactList.SelectedContactUris;
```

Defining Automation Modality Settings

The `BeginStartConversation` method accepts a `contextData` parameter of type `Dictionary <AutomationModalitySettings, object>` representing the various automation modality settings to start the conversation with. Table 3-1 shows the values for the `AutomationModalitySettings` enum.

TABLE 3-1: AutomationModalitySettings Enum

ENUM	DESCRIPTION	VALUE
SharedDesktop	Specifies the conversation will share a desktop.	An integer that specifies the desktop ID.
SharedMonitor	Specifies the conversation will share a monitor.	An integer that specifies the monitor ID.
SharedProcess	Specifies the conversation will share a process.	An integer that specifies the process.
SharedWindow	Specifies the conversation will share a window.	An hWnd that specifies the window handle.
ApplicationData	Specifies the conversation will share data.	A string that specifies the application data.
ApplicationId	Specifies the application ID used to initiate the contextual conversation.	A GUID that specifies the application ID.

ENUM	DESCRIPTION	VALUE
ContextualLink	Specifies the URL shared by the conversation.	A string that specifies the URL.
ToastString	Specifies the string to be displayed on the toast.	A string displayed on the custom toast.
DataObjectFor FileTransfer	Specifies the conversation will pass a file.	An IDataObject that contains the drag-and-drop file object.
FileHistoryLink	Specifies the history file for the conversation.	A string that specifies the file path.
FileIsShared	Specifies whether or not the file passed in the conversation is shared.	A Boolean value that specifies whether the file is shared.
FilePathToTransfer	Specifies the path to the file shared in the conversation.	A string that specifies the file path.
FirstInstantMessage	Specifies the text of the first IM in the conversation.	A string that specifies the message text.
OutlookEntryId	Specifies the ID of the Outlook message shared in the conversation.	A string that specifies the message ID.
PreviousConversation	Specifies the previous conversation shared in the current conversation.	A string that specifies the message.
SendFirstInstant MessageImmediately	Specifies whether or not the IM text is sent immediately.	A Boolean value that specifies whether the IM text is sent immediately.
StartConferenceBy CallingMeAt	Specifies the phone number to open the conference.	A string that specifies the phone number.
Subject	Specifies the subject line for the conversation.	A string that specifies the subject text.
ParentWindow	Specifies the hWnd for the parent window of the conversation window.	An hWnd that specifies the window handle.

Lync SDK documentation

When starting conversations of different modalities, you must create and set the automation modality settings specific to that modality. Table 3-2 shows the automation modalities defined in the `AutomationModalities` enum paired up with automation modality settings from the `AutomationModalitySettings` enum.

TABLE 3-2: Pairing AutomationModalities and AutomationModalitySettings

AUTOMATIONMODALITIES	AUTOMATIONMODALITYSETTINGS
ApplicationSharing	SharedDesktop, SharedMonitor, SharedProcess, SharedWindow
Audio	StartConferenceByCallingMeAt
FileTransfer	DataObjectForFileTransfer, FileHistoryLink, FileIsShared, FilePathToTransfer
InstantMessaging	ApplicationData, ApplicationId, ContextualLink, FileHistoryLink, FirstInstantMessage, OutlookEntryId, SendFirstInstantMessageImmediately, ToastString
Video	ApplicationData, ApplicationId, ContextualLink, OutlookEntryId, ParentWindow, StartConferenceByCallingMeAt, ToastString, Subject

Lync SDK documentation

If the modality of the conversation is not paired up appropriately with a set of automation modality settings, the call to `BeginStartConversation` will throw an exception. As you can see, automation modality settings can apply to multiple modalities.

In Chapter 4, you learn how to use the `ApplicationData`, `ApplicationId`, and `ContextualLink` enum values to start contextual conversations using Lync Automation.

Instant Messaging

For an instant messaging conversation, you can set the text for the first instant message and specify whether it should be sent immediately to the participants after starting the conversation.

```
var contextData = new Dictionary<AutomationModalitySettings, object>();

contextData.Add(
    AutomationModalitySettings.FirstInstantMessage,
    instantMessageText.Text);

contextData.Add(
    AutomationModalitySettings.SendFirstInstantMessageImmediately,
    true);
```

As shown in Figure 3-2, the text is added to the instant message and sent immediately to all the participants.

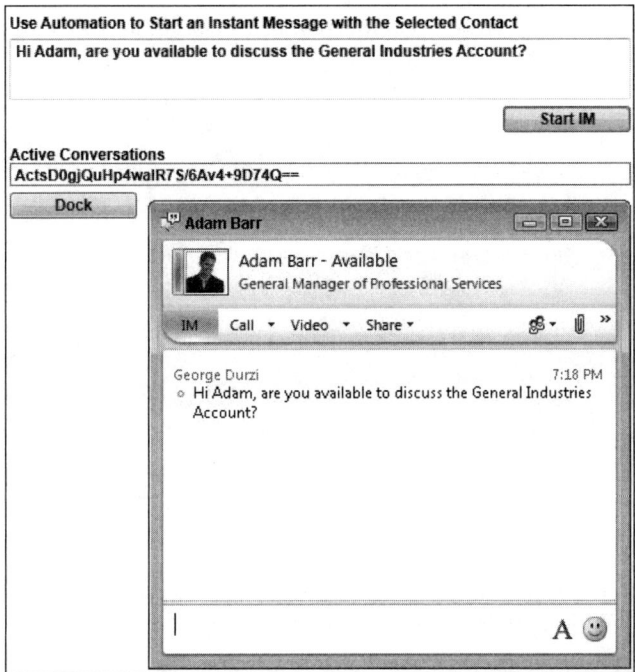

FIGURE 3-2

Desktop Sharing

To invite participants to a desktop sharing session, add the `SharedDesktop` enum to the application modality settings property bag:

```
var contextData = new Dictionary<AutomationModalitySettings, object>();
contextData.Add(AutomationModalitySettings.SharedDesktop, true);
```

As shown in Figure 3-3, a desktop sharing conversation is started among the participants in the conversation.

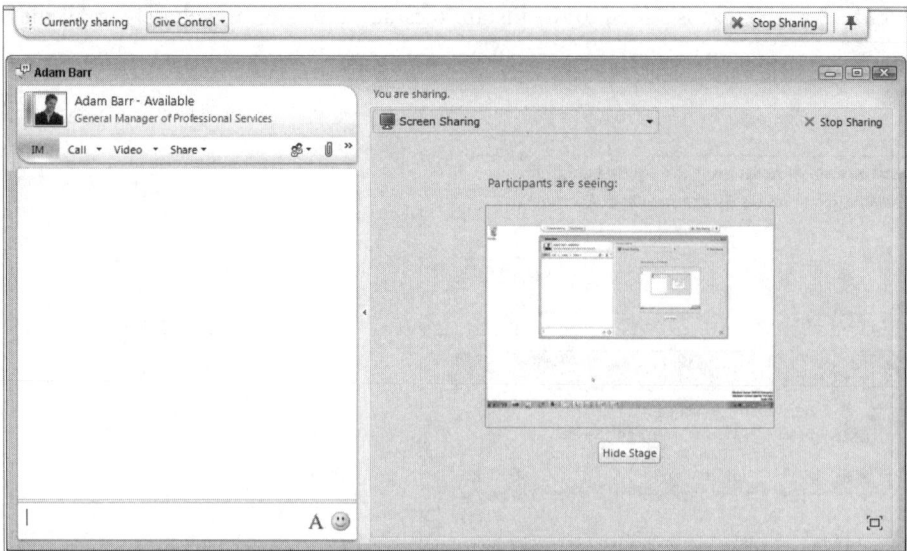

FIGURE 3-3

File Transfer

To transfer a file to the participants in the conversation, add the `FilePathToTransfer` and `FileIsShared` enumerations to the automation modality settings property bag:

```
var contextData = new Dictionary<AutomationModalitySettings, object>();

contextData.Add(
    AutomationModalitySettings.FilePathToTransfer,
    fileTransferPath.Text);

contextData.Add(
    AutomationModalitySettings.FileIsShared,
    true);
```

You can use a file transfer dialog to capture the path of the file to share. As shown in Figure 3-4, a file transfer request for the specified file is sent to the participants in the conversation.

Audio and Video

You don't need to set any specific `Automation ModalitySettings` to start a simple audio or video conversation. You can simply pass `null` to the `contextData` parameter of the `BeginStartConversation` function.

FIGURE 3-4

Starting a Conversation

To start a conversation of a given modality with the specified automation modality settings, call the BeginStartConversation method of the Automation object, specifying the modality, participants, automation modality settings, a callback to execute when the conversation is started, and if necessary, an object representing the state of the asynchronous operation:

```
if (!String.IsNullOrEmpty(imText.Text))
{
    // Specify some simple context to add to the conversation
    var contextData =
        new Dictionary<AutomationModalitySettings, object>();

    // Specify the text of the first instant message
    contextData.Add(
        AutomationModalitySettings.FirstInstantMessage,
        imText.Text);

    // Specify that the message should be sent immediately.
    contextData.Add(
        AutomationModalitySettings.SendFirstInstantMessageImmediately,
        true);

    _automation.BeginStartConversation(
        AutomationModalities.InstantMessage,
        myContactList.SelectedContactUris,
        contextData,
        StartConversationCallback,
        _automation);
}
```

Code snippet LyncEventsLogger\Window1.xaml.cs

Pass _automation as the state of the asynchronous function call. When handling the conversation callback, you will use this to get a handle to the ConversationWindow instance created as a result.

You can also combine modalities; for example, to send an instant message to a contact inviting him or her to a desktop sharing session. In this case, separate the automation modalities passed in to the BeginStartConversation method with a | character:

```
var contextData = new Dictionary<AutomationModalitySettings, object>();

contextData.Add(
    AutomationModalitySettings.FirstInstantMessage,
    imText.Text);

contextData.Add(
    AutomationModalitySettings.SendFirstInstantMessageImmediately,
    true);

contextData.Add(
    AutomationModalitySettings.SharedDesktop,
```

```
        true);

    _automation.BeginStartConversation(
        AutomationModalities.InstantMessage
            | AutomationModalities.ApplicationSharing,
        myContactList.SelectedContactUris,
        contextData,
        StartConversationCallback,
        _automation);
```

Handling the Conversation Callback

In the conversation callback, first check whether the asynchronous operation was completed successfully. Cast the `AsyncState` property of the `IAsyncResult` into an `Automation` object and call its `EndStartConversation` function.

```
    void StartConversationCallback(IAsyncResult ar)
    {
        if (ar.IsCompleted)
        {
            var conversationWindow =
                ((Automation)ar.AsyncState).EndStartConversation(ar);

            var conversation = conversationWindow.Conversation;

            ...
        }
    }
```

Calling `EndStartConversation` returns a `ConversationWindow` object for the conversation that was just created. Later in this section, you learn how to use this to dock the conversation window into the WPF application. You can also get a handle to the `Conversation` object for the new conversation via the `Conversation` property of the `ConversationWindow` object.

Getting Started with the ConversationManager

After creating a conversation, you use an instance of the `Microsoft.Lync.Model` `.ConversationManager` class to interact with the conversation. For example, you can wire up events for the conversation or add and remove participants. This section covers how to manage a new conversation throughout its lifecycle by handling changes in the conversation's state and monitoring properties of the conversation.

To access the functionality available in the `ConversationManager`, define a module-level instance of the class in your application.

```
    private Microsoft.Lync.Model.ConversationManager _conversationManager;
```

Code snippet LyncEventsLogger\Window1.xaml.cs

After your application has initialized the instance of `LyncClient`, use its read-only `ConversationManager` property to get a reference to an instance of `ConversationManager` for the running instance of the Lync client.

```
_conversationManager = _lyncClient.ConversationManager;
```

Code snippet LyncEventsLogger\Window1.xaml.cs

With the `ConversationManager` initialized, your application can now manage conversations in the running instance of the Lync client.

ConversationManager Events

Use the `ConversationAdded` and `ConversationRemoved` events to track when conversations are added or removed from the `Conversations` collection of the `ConversationManager` object. These events are raised regardless of how the conversations were created or closed; for example, programmatically by the application, or by the user in the Lync client. Wire up the event handlers for the `ConversationAdded` and `ConversationRemoved` events:

```
_conversationManager.ConversationAdded +=
    new EventHandler<ConversationManagerEventArgs>
        (Conversations_ConversationAdded);

_conversationManager.ConversationRemoved +=
    new EventHandler<ConversationManagerEventArgs>
        (Conversations_ConversationRemoved);
```

Code snippet LyncEventsLogger\Window1.xaml.cs

The instance of `ConversationManagerEventArgs` in the event handler for the `ConversationAdded` and `ConversationRemoved` events provides access to the `Conversation` object responsible for raising the event. You can use `e.Conversation` to access properties of the conversation such as its modalities, and also to wire up various conversation events:

```
void Conversations_ConversationAdded(
    object sender, ConversationManagerEventArgs e)
{
    LogEvent("Conversation added",
        String.Format("Current conversations: {0}",
        _conversationManager.Conversations.Count));

    e.Conversation.ParticipantAdded +=
        new EventHandler<ParticipantCollectionChangedEventArgs>
            (Conversation_ParticipantAdded);

    e.Conversation.ParticipantRemoved +=
        new EventHandler<ParticipantCollectionChangedEventArgs>
```

```
                    (Conversation_ParticipantRemoved);
    }

void Conversations_ConversationRemoved(
    object sender, ConversationManagerEventArgs e)
{
    LogEvent("Conversation removed",
        String.Format("Current conversations: {0}",
        _conversationManager.Conversations.Count));
    }
```

Code snippet LyncEventsLogger\Window1.xaml.cs

Wire up an event handler for the `ParticipantAdded` and `ParticipantRemoved` events of the conversation to track when people join and leave the conversation. You will learn about other events that the `Conversation` class exposes later in this section.

Figure 3-5 illustrates how the companion WPF application tracks conversations as they are started and closed.

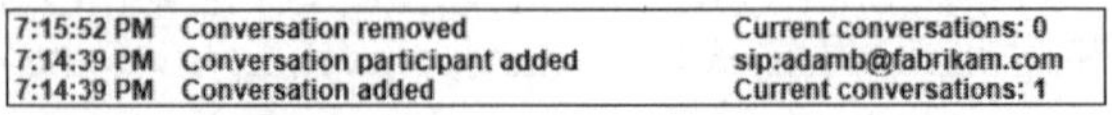

7:15:52 PM	Conversation removed	Current conversations: 0
7:14:39 PM	Conversation participant added	sip:adamb@fabrikam.com
7:14:39 PM	Conversation added	Current conversations: 1

FIGURE 3-5

Conversation Properties

After a conversation is created, you have access to its various properties. These properties enable you to work with things such as the participants in the conversation, its modalities, and the conversation's state.

➤ **Modalities:** A Lync conversation can have multiple modalities such as instant message or audio. The `Modalities` property is of type `Dictionary<ModalityTypes, Modality>`; the dictionary key gives you access to the instance of the `Modality` if it is present in the conversation. You can get access to the underlying `Modality` object for a particular conversation modality as follows:

```
var instantMessageModality =
    conversation.Modalities[ModalityTypes.InstantMessage]
```

In Chapter 5, you will learn how to interact with the modalities in a conversation; for example to programmatically add the instant messaging modality to a conversation to send an instant message.

➤ **Participants:** The `Participants` collection is a `List<Participant>` representing everybody in the conversation.

➤ **Properties:** The `Properties` property is a `Dictionary<ConversationProperty, Object>` that contains other attributes of the conversation not available as first-level properties. Table 3-3 shows the values of the `ConversationProperty` enum. You can access the properties shown in Table 3-3 as follows:

```
var conversationId = conversation.Properties[ConversationProperty.Id]
```

➤ **SelfParticipant:** The `SelfParticipant` property of the `Conversation` class is a shortcut to the participant in the conversation who is the user currently signed in to Lync.

➤ **State:** The `State` of the conversation is represented by the `ConversationState` enum; the valid states of a conversation are

- ➤ `Inactive`
- ➤ `Active`
- ➤ `Parked`
- ➤ `Terminated`

TABLE 3-3: ConversationProperty Enum

NAME	DESCRIPTION
Id	The conversation identifier.
Subject	The conversation subject.
Importance	The conversation importance level.
TransferredBy	If this conversation originated through a transfer, then the ID of the conversation that originated transfer.
Replaced	If this conversation is or has ever been in conference, the conference focus URI it is connected to or will reconnect to.
ConferencingUri	If this conversation is or has ever been in conference, the conference focus URI it is connected to or will reconnect to.
RepresentedBy	If this conversation is affected by boss or admin retargeting, this provides the representation details.
ConferenceInviter RepresentationInfo	If this conference conversation is affected by boss or admin retargeting, this provides the representation details.
FollowUp	The conversation follow-up flag.
ConferenceAccepting Participant	If this conference conversation is answered by another party, this provides the party's contact object.
AcceptanceState	The acceptance state (from the local point of view) of this conversation.
IsUsbConversation	Indicates whether the conversation is a USB conversation.
AutoTerminateOnIdle	Indicates whether the conversation will implicitly terminate when the last modality session becomes inactive.

continues

TABLE 3-3 *(continued)*

NAME	DESCRIPTION
ConferenceEscalation Progress	Indicates the progression of escalation to conference.
ConferenceEscalationResult	Indicates the result code of escalation to conference.
ConferencingInvitedModes	Mask with bits set corresponding to invited types.
Inviter	Contact for the party that sent the invite to the conversation.
ConferencingLocked	Flag corresponding to whether the conference is currently locked.
ConferencingFirst InstantMessage	If the IM message was sent with a conference invite, the simple text of the value of it (string).
ConferenceAccess Information	Conference access information detailing accessibilty mechanisms for this conference. (ConferenceAccessInfo).
ConferencingAccessType	Indicates the current access type of the conference.
CallParkOrbit	The orbit used to retrieve a parked call.
ConferenceDisclaimer	Disclaimer title and body.
ConferenceDisclaimer Accepted	Set when the user accepts the conference disclaimer.
ConferenceTerminate OnLeave	Terminate conference when terminating the conversation.
IsBeingRecorded	The conversation is being recorded by at least one participant.

Lync SDK Documentation

Conversation Events

The Conversation class exposes the following events that you can wire up event handlers for when a conversation is created:

➤ ActionAvailabilityChanged

➤ ContextDataReceived

➤ ContextDataSent

➤ ConversationContextLinkClicked

➤ InitialContextReceived

- ➤ InitialContextSent

- ➤ ParticipantAdded

- ➤ ParticipantRemoved

- ➤ PropertyChanged

- ➤ StateChanged

The ContextDataReceived, ContextDataSend, ConversationContextLinkClicked, InitialContextReceived, and InitialContextSend event are used to work with contextual application data in contextual conversations. You learn about contextual conversations and their related events in Chapter 4.

This section focuses on the ParticipantAdded, ParticipantRemoved, PropertyChanged, and StateChanged events that are raised when participants join or leave a conversation, or when a property or the state of the conversation changes.

ParticipantAdded and ParticipantRemoved

The ParticipantAdded and ParticipantRemoved events are raised when participants join and leave a conversation. These events are raised when a participant either is programmatically added to the conversation or joins by accepting a conversation invitation in the Lync client:

Available for download on Wrox.com

```
void Conversation_ParticipantAdded(object sender,
    ParticipantCollectionChangedEventArgs e)
{
    if (e.Participant.Contact.Uri !=
        (sender as Conversation).SelfParticipant.Contact.Uri)
    {
        LogEvent("Conversation participant added",
                e.Participant.Contact.Uri);
    }
}

void Conversation_ParticipantRemoved(object sender,
    ParticipantCollectionChangedEventArgs e)
{
    if (e.Participant.Contact.Uri !=
        (sender as Conversation).SelfParticipant.Contact.Uri)
    {
        LogEvent("Conversation participant removed",
                e.Participant.Contact.Uri);
    }
}
```

Code snippet LyncEventsLogger\Window1.xaml.cs

The ParticipantCollectionChangedEventArgs object in the event handler exposes the Contact object for the Participant that was added or removed from the conversation. In this example, the application checks first whether the participant responsible for raising the event is not the user who is signed in to the running instance of the Lync client.

Figure 3-6 shows how the companion WPF application tracks participants as they join and leave a conversation.

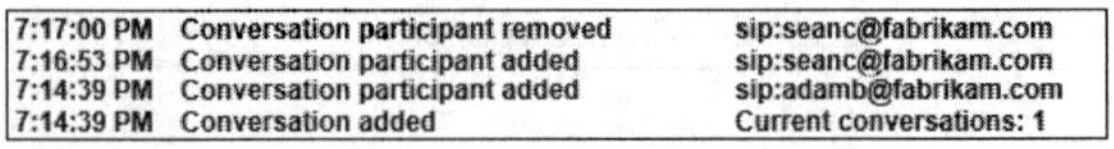

7:17:00 PM	Conversation participant removed	sip:seanc@fabrikam.com
7:16:53 PM	Conversation participant added	sip:seanc@fabrikam.com
7:14:39 PM	Conversation participant added	sip:adamb@fabrikam.com
7:14:39 PM	Conversation added	Current conversations: 1

FIGURE 3-6

PropertyChanged

You can use the `PropertyChanged` event to track changes of any of the items in the `Properties` property of the conversation:

```
e.Conversation.PropertyChanged +=
    new EventHandler<ConversationPropertyChangedEventArgs>
    (Conversation_PropertyChanged);

...

void Conversation_PropertyChanged(
    object sender, ConversationPropertyChangedEventArgs e)
{
    if (e.Property == ConversationProperty.Subject)
    {
        // do something
    }
}
```

The `ConversationPropertyChangedEventArgs` object in the event handler exposes the property responsible for raising the event. You can check for the property that changed and perform custom logic accordingly; for example, you can monitor the `IsBeingRecorded` property of an audio conversation to be notified if any of the participants begins recording the conversation.

StateChanged

You can use the `StateChanged` event to track changes in the state of a conversation:

```
e.Conversation.StateChanged +=
    new EventHandler<ConversationStateChangedEventArgs>
    (Conversation_StateChanged);

...

void Conversation_StateChanged(object sender,
ConversationStateChangedEventArgs e)
{
    LogEvent("Conversation state changed",
        String.Format("{0} => {1}",
            e.OldState,
            e.NewState));
}
```

The `ConversationStateChangedEventArgs` object in the event handler exposes both the `OldState` and `NewState` of the conversation, as well as access to its `Properties` property.

Tracking the state of the conversation is useful if you need to enable or disable functionality in your application based on the state of the application. For example, if the conversation state changes from `Active` to `Terminated`, you can disable user interface elements that allow the user to add a new participant to the conversation.

Managing Participants

You can manually add and remove participants in a conversation using the `AddParticipant` and `RemoveParticipant` methods of the `Conversation` object. When a participant joins the conversation, the `Conversation.ParticipantAdded` event is raised. Similarly, when a participant leaves or is removed from a conversation, the `Conversation.ParticipantRemoved` event is raised.

```
conversation.AddParticipant(
    _contactManager.GetContactByUri("sip:seanc@fabrikam.com"));
```

You can also use the `Add` method of the `Participants` collection of the `Conversation` object to add a `Participant` object to the collection. However, using `Conversation.AddParticipant` to add a new participant to a conversation is easier because it accepts a `Contact` object instead of a `Participant` object — instantiating a `Contact` object using `ContactManager.GetContactByUri` or `Group.TryGetContact` is easier than instantiating a `Participant` object because the `Participant` class doesn't define a constructor.

To remove a participant from a conversation, you first must identify them in the `Participants` collection in the `Conversation` object:

```
conversation.RemoveParticipant(conversation.Participants.Where(
        p => p.Contact.Uri == "sip:seanc@fabrikam.com")
            .FirstOrDefault());
```

Docking the Lync Conversation Window in a WPF Application

Conversation window docking enables you to dock the Lync conversation window directly into your WPF application. Using conversation window docking, you can integrate the Lync conversation window into your application or build a custom communications client that supports tabbed conversations.

This section will walk you through integrating conversation window docking into your application, starting by adding the necessary references into your application in order to integrate Windows Forms controls into a WPF application, performing the conversation window docking, and handling events raised by the conversation window after it is docked.

1. Begin by adding the following assembly references to your application:

   ➤ System.Windows.Forms

   ➤ WindowsFormsIntegration

   These assemblies provide access to the Windows Forms `Panel` object that the conversation window is docked in, and to some necessary supporting objects such as `WindowInteropHelper`.

2. Add the following namespace declarations to the XAML in the window in the application where you will dock the conversation window:

```
xmlns:interop="clr-namespace:System.Windows.Forms.Integration;
    assembly=WindowsFormsIntegration"
xmlns:forms="clr-namespace:System.Windows.Forms;
    assembly=System.Windows.Forms"
```

Code snippet LyncEventsLogger\Window1.xaml

3. Add a `WindowsFormsHost` control to the XAML; this will contain the Windows Forms `Panel` to dock the conversation window in:

```
<interop:WindowsFormsHost x:Name="windowsFormsHost">
<forms:Panel x:Name="windowsFormsPanel"></forms:Panel>
</interop:WindowsFormsHost>
```

Code snippet LyncEventsLogger\Window1.xaml

4. Define the `FocusWindow` and `ResizeWindow` delegates that the application will use to handle the `NeedsAttention` and `NeedsSizeChanged` events of the `ConversationWindow` object:

```
private delegate void FocusWindow();
private delegate void ResizeWindow(Size resizeTo);
private WindowInteropHelper _windowHelper;
private Int32 _handle;
```

Code snippet LyncEventsLogger\Window1.xaml.cs

5. Create an instance of `WindowInteropHelper` and an `Int32` representing the handle of the conversation window. In the application window's `Loaded` event handler, prep the instance of `WindowInteropHelper`:

```
void Window1_Loaded(object sender, RoutedEventArgs e)
{
    ...

    _windowHelper = new WindowInteropHelper(this);
    _handle = _windowHelper.Handle.ToInt32();
}
```

Code snippet LyncEventsLogger\Window1.xaml.cs

6. Now you will implement the `ConversationWindow` event handlers. In the callback for the `BeginStartConversation` method, get a handle to the `ConversationWindow` object created for the new conversation and wire up event handlers for the `NeedsSizeChange` and `NeedsAttention` events of the window as shown in the following snippet. If your application will manage multiple conversation windows, you can also maintain a list of active conversation windows in order to be able to dock a certain window in the application. The companion WPF application also maintains an `ObservableCollection` `<string>` of active conversation IDs to display in the application.

```
void StartConversationCallback(IAsyncResult ar)
{
    if (ar.IsCompleted)
    {
        conversationWindow =
            ((Automation)ar.AsyncState).EndStartConversation(ar);

        Dispatcher.Invoke(new Action(() =>
        {
            _activeConversationWindows.Add(
                conversationWindow.Conversation.Properties
                    [ConversationProperty.Id].ToString(),
                conversationWindow);

            _activeConversationIds.Add(
                conversationWindow.Conversation.Properties
                    [ConversationProperty.Id].ToString());
        }));

        ...

        _conversationWindow.NeedsSizeChange +=
            new EventHandler<ConversationWindowNeedsSizeChangeEventArgs>
                (ConversationWindow_NeedsSizeChange);

        _conversationWindow.NeedsAttention +=
            new EventHandler<ConversationWindowNeedsAttentionEventArgs>
                (ConversationWindow_NeedsAttention);
    }
}
```

Code snippet LyncEventsLogger\Window1.xaml.cs

7. You can now use the `Dock` and `Undock` methods of the `ConversationWindow` object to dock and undock the conversation window in the WPF application. When calling the `Dock` method, provide the handle of the `WindowsFormsHost` control containing the Windows Forms `Panel` control to dock the conversation window in:

```
void dockConversationWindow_Click(object sender, RoutedEventArgs e)
{
    if (activeConversations.SelectedItem != null)
    {
        var conversationWindow = _activeConversationWindows
```

```
            [activeConversations.SelectedItem.ToString()]
                as ConversationWindow;

    if (conversationWindow.Width != -1
        && conversationWindow.Height != -1
        && conversationWindow.Left != -1
        && conversationWindow.Top != -1)
    {
        if (!_isDocked)
        {
            dockConversationWindow.Content = "Undock";
            if (_handle != 0)
            {
                conversationWindow.Dock(windowsFormsHost.Handle);

                startIM.IsEnabled = false;
                startLyncCall.IsEnabled = false;
            }
        }
        else
        {
            dockConversationWindow.Content = "Dock";
            conversationWindow.Undock();
        }
        _isDocked = !_isDocked;
    }
    else
    {
        dockConversationWindow.Content = "Dock";

        conversationWindow.Undock();

        _isDocked = false;
        startIM.IsEnabled = true;
        startLyncCall.IsEnabled = true;
    }
  }
}
```

Code snippet LyncEventsLogger\Window1.xaml.cs

Before docking the conversation window, check that the conversation window exists by verifying that its Height, Width, Left, and Top properties are not equal to –1.

As shown in Figure 3-7, the conversation window is docked into the WPF application. The chrome for the conversation window is removed.

FIGURE 3-7

WORKING WITH CONTACTS AND GROUPS

The Lync API provides functionality that your application can use to interact with the current user's groups and contacts in Lync. For example, you can subscribe to events that are raised when a contact is added or removed from a group, when a contact's presence changes, or when a property of the contact changes.

Getting Started with the ContactManager

You can use an instance of the `Microsoft.Lync.Model.ContactManager` class in your application to interact with the current user's Lync groups and contacts. To access the functionality available in the `ContactManager`, define a module-level instance of the class in your application:

```
private Microsoft.Lync.Model.ContactManager _contactManager;
```

Available for download on Wrox.com

Code snippet LyncEventsLogger\Window1.xaml.cs

After your application has initialized the instance of LyncClient, use its read-only ContactManager property to get a reference to an instance of ContactManager for the running instance of the Lync client:

```
_contactManager = _lyncClient.ContactManager;
```

Available for download on Wrox.com

Code snippet LyncEventsLogger\Window1.xaml.cs

With the `ContactManager` initialized, you are ready to configure its events and interact with the current user's Lync groups and contacts.

ContactManager Events

To interact with the current user's groups and the contacts contained with them, start by wiring up event handlers for the `ContactManager` instance's `GroupAdded` and `GroupRemoved` events:

Available for download on Wrox.com

```
_contactManager.GroupAdded +=
    new EventHandler<GroupCollectionChangedEventArgs>
        (ContactManager_GroupAdded);

_contactManager.GroupRemoved +=
    new EventHandler<GroupCollectionChangedEventArgs>
        (ContactManager_GroupRemoved);
```

Code snippet LyncEventsLogger\Window1.xaml.cs

The `GroupAdded` and `GroupRemoved` events are raised when a group is added or removed from the `ContactManager`'s `Groups` collection, as shown in the following code. This happens when a user creates or deletes a group directly in the Lync client, or it happened when the user signed in to the Lync client and his existing groups and contacts were initialized. Figure 3-8 illustrates these events occurring when the user signs into the Lync client when starting up the companion WPF application.

7:07:15 PM	Group added	Most Used Contacts
7:10:40 PM	Group added	Pinned Contacts
7:10:40 PM	Group added	Other Contacts

FIGURE 3-8

Available for download on Wrox.com

```
void ContactManager_GroupAdded
    (object sender, GroupCollectionChangedEventArgs e)
{

    LogEvent("Group added", e.Group.Name);
}

void ContactManager_GroupRemoved
    (object sender, GroupCollectionChangedEventArgs e)
{
    _contactSubscriptions.Remove(e.Group.Name);

    LogEvent("Group removed", e.Group.Name);
}
```

Code snippet LyncEventsLogger\Window1.xaml.cs

You will learn later in this section about creating subscriptions for properties of contacts that are members in groups. When a group is removed from the user's collection of groups, you should also remove any subscriptions that were created for the group.

Group Events

With the application initialized and the supporting objects created, you can now iterate through the `Groups` collection of the `ContactManager` instance and wire up events for the groups in the collection.

Iterate through the `Groups` collection, verifying that the group is not null, and wire up event handlers for the `ContactAdded` and `ContactRemoved` events of each group:

```
foreach (var group in _contactManager.Groups)
{
    if (group != null && !String.IsNullOrEmpty(group.Name))
    {
        group.ContactAdded +=            new EventHandler<GroupMemberChangedEventArgs>
                (Group_ContactAdded);
        group.ContactRemoved +=
            new EventHandler<GroupMemberChangedEventArgs>
                (Group_ContactRemoved);

        LogEvent("Subscribe to events for ", group.Name);

        SubscribeToGroup(group);
    }
}
```

Code snippet LyncEventsLogger\Window1.xaml.cs

Similar to the `GroupAdded` and `GroupRemoved` events of the `ContactManager` class, the `ContactAdded` and `ContactRemoved` events are raised when the user adds or removes contacts in the Lync client, and also when the `LyncClient` instance signs in and initializes the current user's existing groups.

Creating Contact Subscriptions

The `Microsoft.Lync.Model.ContactSubscription` class provides functionality to subscribe to changes in the properties of a group of contacts; for example, changes in their availability, location, or personal note.

To create a new contact subscription, call `CreateSubscription` on the `ContactManager` object in your application. You then must define the attributes of the contact that the application will subscribe to changes in; this is defined by the `ContactInformationType` enum. Create a `List<ContactInformationType>` and add to it the values of `ContactInformationType` to track. Finally, call the `Subscribe` method of the `ContactSubscription` object to create the subscription:

```
var subscription = _contactManager.CreateSubscription();

// Choose the types of presence changes to listen for
var contactInformationTypes =
    new List<ContactInformationType>()
        {
            ContactInformationType.Availability,
            ContactInformationType.Activity
        };

subscription.Subscribe(
```

```
        ContactSubscriptionRefreshRate.Low,
        contactInformationTypes);

    _contactSubscriptions.Add(group.Name, subscription);
```

Code snippet LyncEventsLogger\Window1.xaml.cs

ContactInformationType Enum

The `ContactInformationType` enum represents the many attributes of a `Contact` object that your application can subscribe to. Table 3-4 shows some of the most commonly used values of the `ContactInformationType` enum.

TABLE 3-4: ContactInformationType Enum

NAME	DESCRIPTION
Availability	Contact availability. Value type is `AvailabilityType`enum.
ActivityId	A token describing current contact activity.
LocationName	The name of a contact's location.
Activity	A contact's current activity (for example, on the phone, in a meeting, or available).
DisplayName	Display name of a contact.
PrimaryEmailAddress	The primary e-mail address.
HomePageUrl	The contact's homepage URL.
Photo	A contact's photo.
DefaultNote	The default note, shown if no other note is set.
PersonalNote	A personal note.
OutOfficeNote	An out-of-office note.
ContactType	Contact's type. Value type is `ContactPresentityType`enum.

Lync SDK Documentation

ContactSubscriptionRefreshRate Enum

The `ContactSubscription.Subscribe` method accepts a subscription refresh rate defined by the `ContactSubscriptionRefreshRate` enum to specify how often the subscription should be refreshed. Table 3-5 shows the values for the `ContactSubscriptionRefreshRate` enum.

TABLE 3-5: ContactSubscriptionRefreshRate Enum

NAME	DESCRIPTION
Low	The caller needs infrequent refreshing of contact data.
High	The caller needs frequent refreshing of contact data.

Lync SDK Documentation

> *Set the contact subscription refresh rate based on the individual requirements of your application, keeping in mind that overhead is involved in maintaining a large number of contact subscriptions, especially when the application is subscribed to a large number of* ContactInformationType *values for the contacts in the subscription.*

Contact Events

The contact subscription alone doesn't provide a mechanism for your application to handle the events that are raised when one of the ContactInformationType values for a particular contact in the subscription changes. To track changes in the properties of contacts in a group, wire up the ContactInformationChanged event for each contact in the group:

Available for download on Wrox.com

```
foreach (var contact in group)
{
    contact.ContactInformationChanged +=
        new EventHandler<ContactInformationChangedEventArgs>
            (Contact_ContactInformationChanged);
}
```

Code snippet LyncEventsLogger\Window1.xaml.cs

You can use the instance of ContactInformationChangedEventArgs in the handler for the ContactInformationChanged event to discover which ContactInformationType values caused the event to be raised, as shown in the following snippet. This is useful if you are subscribing to multiple ContactInformationType values and need to handle each slightly differently.

Available for download on Wrox.com

```
void Contact_ContactInformationChanged
    (object sender, ContactInformationChangedEventArgs e)
{
    if (_lyncClient != null)
    {
        if (e.ChangedContactInformation.Contains
            (ContactInformationType.Activity))
```

```
        {
            LogEvent(String.Format(
                "Updated presence for {0}",
                (sender as Contact).GetContactInformation
                    (ContactInformationType.DisplayName).ToString()),
                (sender as Contact).GetContactInformation
                    (ContactInformationType.Activity).ToString());
        }
    }
}
```

Code snippet LyncEventsLogger\Window1.xaml.cs

Query the `ChangedContactInformation` list to check whether it contains a specific `ContactInformationType`. The event sender is a `Contact` object; use the `Contact` `.GetContactInformation` method to get the value of a specific `ContactInformationType` for the contact that caused the event to be raised; for example, his display name. Figure 3-9 illustrates how the companion WPF application displays changes in contacts' presence.

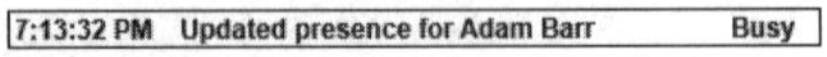

| 7:13:32 PM | Updated presence for Adam Barr | Busy |

FIGURE 3-9

You can also use the `GetContact` method of `ContactManager` to get a `Microsoft.Lync.Model` `.Contact` object for a contact given a SIP URI:

```
var contact = _contactManager.GetContactByURI("sip:adamb@fabrikam.com");
```

If you provide an invalid contact SIP URI to the `GetContactByURI` method, the return value will be null. Always check to verify that the returned `Contact` object is not null before proceeding.

Adding and Removing Groups

The `ContactManager` provides functionality for maintaining the groups in the current user's Lync groups list, allowing your application to programmatically add and remove contacts from the user's contact list. You can also use the Lync API to add or remove existing contacts from a group, or add new contacts to the user's contact list and assign them to a group.

You can use the `ContactManager` to add and remove groups from the current user's groups in Lync. When a group is added or removed, the operation raises the `GroupAdded` or `GroupRemoved` events of the `ContactManager` object.

Adding a Group

Use the `BeginAddGroup` and `EndAddGroup` methods of `ContactManager` to add a new distribution group or custom group to the current user's Lync groups. The following code creates a new custom group called My Group in the current user's Lync groups:

```
_contactManager.BeginAddGroup(
    "My Group",
    result =>
    {
```

```
        _contactManager.EndAddGroup(result);

        SubscribeToGroup(contactManager.Groups.Where
            (g => g.Name == "My Group").FirstOrDefault());
    },
    null);
```

You can create a contact subscription for the group as soon as it is created. The group is obviously empty at first, but the necessary event handlers are in place to subscribe to changes in contact properties as contacts are added to the group.

Email distribution lists defined in your organization's Active Directory can also be added as groups in Lync. For example, if your organization has a distribution group called Employees that contains all the employees in the company, adding it as a group in Lync instead of adding the individual employees as contacts is very convenient.

Removing a Group

To remove a group from the user's list of groups in Lync, use the `BeginRemoveGroup` and `EndRemoveGroup` methods of the `ContactManager` class. The `BeginRemoveGroup` only accepts a `Group` object representing the group to remove; you have to query the `Groups` collection exposed by the `ContactManager` to find the group by name:

```
_contactManager.BeginRemoveGroup(
    _contactManager.Groups.Where(g => g.Name == "My Group")
        .FirstOrDefault(),
    result =>
    {
        _contactManager.EndRemoveGroup(result);
    },
    null);
```

If the group being removed is not empty, the contacts in the group are automatically moved into the Other Contacts group.

Adding and Removing Contacts

Contacts must be added or removed from the group in which they are contained. When a contact is added or removed from a group, the group's `ContactAdded` or `ContactRemoved` events are raised.

Adding Contacts

To add a contact to a group, call the `Add` method on the `Group` object and provide the `Contact` object to add. Use the `ContactManager` object's `GetContactByURI` method to get a `Contact` object given a SIP URI:

```
group.BeginAddContact(
_contactManager.GetContactByURI("sip:adamb@fabrikam.com"),
    result =>
```

```
    {
        _group.EndAddContact();
    },
    null);
```

Removing Contacts

To remove a contact from a group, call the `Remove` method on the `Group` object and provide the `Contact` object to remove:

```
group.BeginRemoveContact(
    _contactManager.GetContactByURI("sip:adamb@fabrikam.com"),
    result =>
    {
        _group.EndRemoveContact();
    },
    null);
```

When you remove a contact from a group, it is moved to the Other Contacts group, but not deleted from the user's Lync contact list. To permanently remove a contact from the user's Lync contact list, use the `ContactManager` object's `BeginRemoveContactFromAllGroups` method.

```
_contactManager.BeginRemoveContactFromAllGroups(
    _contactManager.GetContactByURI("sip:adamb@fabrikam.com"),
    result =>
    {
        _contactManager.EndRemoveContactFromAllGroups(result);
    },
    null);
```

Using TryGetContact

The `ContactCollection` property of a `Group` exposes a `TryGetContact` method that you can use to query the collection of contacts in a group for a particular contact. The `TryGetContact` method returns a Boolean value indicating whether or not the contact exists in the group; if it does, the resulting `Contact` object is populated into the method's `outcontact` parameter:

```
Group group = _contactManager.Groups.Where
(g => g.Name == "My Group").FirstOrDefault();

Contact contact = null;

if (group.TryGetContact("sip:adamb@fabrikam.com", out contact))
{
    group.BeginRemoveContact(
        contact,
        result =>
        {
            group.EndRemoveContact(result);
        },
        null);
}
```

INTERACTING WITH THE SELF CONTACT

An instance of the `Microsoft.Lync.Model.Self` class represents the user signed into the running instance of the Lync client. You can use the `Self` class to set the current user's presence, publish his personal note, or set other presence information such as his location.

To get started, define a module level `Self` object in your application:

Available for download on Wrox.com

```
private Microsoft.Lync.Model.Self _self;
```

Code snippet LyncEventsLogger\Window1.xaml.cs

After your application has initialized the instance of `LyncClient`, use its read-only `Self` property to get a reference to an instance of `Self` for the current user:

Available for download on Wrox.com

```
_self = _lyncClient.Self;
```

Code snippet LyncEventsLogger\Window1.xaml.cs

Using the `Self` class, you can publish presence items for the user currently signed in to the running instance of the Lync client. For example, you can set their presence or personal note. You can also wire up events to handle when any of these presence items change. For example, you can update the user's location in your application when it changes in the Lync client.

Publishing Self Presence Items

As shown in Figure 3-10, you can update the current user's presence directly from the application by selecting the appropriate presence in the drop-down list and clicking the Update button to publish the user's presence.

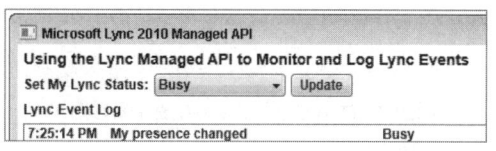

FIGURE 3-10

You can programmatically change the user's availability, status, and other properties defined by the `PublishableContactInformationType` enum. To publish a set of presence items for the user, your application should:

➤ Create a list of presence items to publish

➤ Publish the list of presence items

Setting Publishable Contact Information

The `PublishableContactInformationType` enum defines the publishable attributes of a contact; these include:

➤ `Availability`

➤ `ActivityId`

➤ CustomStatusId

➤ Location

➤ PersonalNote

➤ DisplayPhoto

➤ PhotoUrl

To publish contact information for the Self contact, create a List<KeyValuePair<Publishable ContactInformationType, object>> to store a list of key value pairs of the attributes of the contact to publish:

Available for
download on
Wrox.com

```
var contactInformation =
new List<KeyValuePair<PublishableContactInformationType, object>>();
```

Code snippet LyncEventsLogger\Window1.xaml.cs

Add each contact information item to the list of attributes to publish. In the companion WPF application, the drop-down list defines the numerical value for each presence state; for example, 3500 represents Available. Add PublishableContactInformationType.Availability to the list, and set its value to the presence selected in the drop-down list:

Available for
download on
Wrox.com

```
contactInformation.Add(
    new KeyValuePair<PublishableContactInformationType, object>(
        PublishableContactInformationType.Availability,
        Convert.ToInt32((status.SelectedValue as ComboBoxItem).Tag)));
```

Code snippet LyncEventsLogger\Window1.xaml.cs

Publishing the Presence Items

Call BeginPublishContactInformation to publish the items defined in the list:

Available for
download on
Wrox.com

```
_self.BeginPublishContactInformation(
    contactInformation,
    result => _self.EndPublishContactInformation(result),
    "Updating my status");
```

Code snippet LyncEventsLogger\Window1.xaml.cs

As shown in Figure 3-11, the user's updated presence is immediately reflected in the Lync client.

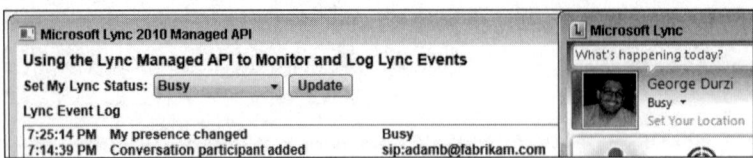

FIGURE 3-11

Subscribing to Self Presence Events

The Self class exposes the Contact object for the current user; you can use that to wire up an event handler for the ContactInformationChanged event of the contact:

```
_self.Contact.ContactInformationChanged += new
    EventHandler<ContactInformationChangedEventArgs>
    (Self_ContactInformationChanged);
```

Code snippet LyncEventsLogger\Window1.xaml.cs

The ContactInformationChanged is raised when an application using the Lync API updates a contact information item, or when the user himself updates his presence, personal note, or location in the Lync client.

The ChangedContactInformation property of the instance of ContactInformationChanged EventArgs in the ContactInformationChanged event handler contains a collection of contact information items that have changed. You can query the collection for a particular contact information item and perform custom logic for that item:

```
void Self_ContactInformationChanged
    (object sender, ContactInformationChangedEventArgs e)
{
    // This event can be triggered by the application itself
    //     and also by Lync
    //   Always use Dispatcher.Invoke to execute on the UI thread
    //
    if (_lyncClient != null)
    {
        this.Dispatcher.Invoke(
            DispatcherPriority.Input,
            new Action(() =>
            {
                var contact = sender as Contact;

                if (e.ChangedContactInformation.Contains
                (ContactInformationType.PersonalNote))
                {
                    LogEvent("My personal note changed",
                        contact.GetContactInformation
(ContactInformationType.PersonalNote) == null? "n/a" :
contact.GetContactInformation
(ContactInformationType.PersonalNote).ToString());
                }

                if (e.ChangedContactInformation.Contains
                (ContactInformationType.Activity))
                {
                    LogEvent("My presence changed",
                        contact.GetContactInformation
```

```
                              (ContactInformationType.Activity).ToString());

                 UpdateMyAvailability();
             }
         }));
    }
  }
```

Code snippet LyncEventsLogger\Window1.xaml.cs

As shown in Figure 3-12, changes in the current user's presence or personal note are captured and logged in the companion WPF application.

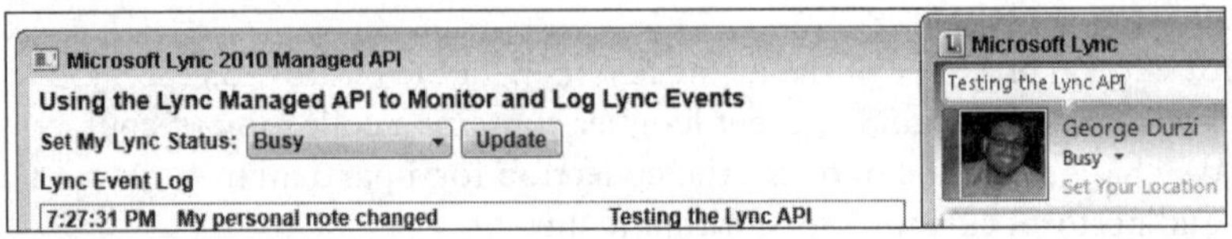

FIGURE 3-12

SUMMARY

Using the Lync API, you can interact with the running instance of the Lync client to manage groups and contacts, conversations, and their participants. The Automation capabilities of the Lync API are used to easily start conversations of different modalities and to integrate the Lync conversation window into your application by docking the conversation window into a Windows Forms Panel control.

In the next chapter, you will learn about more advanced features of the Lync API that are used to add context to conversations. Context in conversations enables all the participants in a conversation to immediately know what the conversation is about. You will learn how to start contextual conversations that provide contextual links, launch applications, and use the Lync extensibility window to host a Silverlight application directly in the Lync conversation window.

Adding Context
to Conversations

The context of a conversation is typically established at the beginning of a call or instant message; for example, "Do you have time to talk about the General Industries account?" The back and forth involved in establishing context can be wasteful as everybody in the conversation slowly gets on the same page, with the conversation sometimes going like this:

> "Hi Sean, do you have time to talk about the General Industries account?"

> "Give me a minute; let me open the CRM application. "OK, here we go . . . What about the General Industries account?"

> "I have a question about the 2010 sales figures."

> "OK, hang on; let me pull those up . . . What about the sales figures?"

Using the Lync SDK, you can build functionality into your communications-enabled applications to streamline this process and enable the participants in the conversation to immediately know what the call or instant message they are receiving is about.

A great example of this capability is the Reply by IM feature in Outlook, which allows you to reply to any email in your mailbox with an instant message. The email subject appears in the toast window that the recipient sees; the subject also appears as the title of the Lync conversation window itself. The Lync SDK provides several mechanisms to inject this context directly into the Lync conversation. The simplest of these is Simple Link context, which allows you to embed a link into a conversation that is initiated from the Lync controls or programmatically by the Lync API. You saw in Chapter 2 how to start contextual conversations that include Simple Link context from the Lync controls using the `ConversationContextualInfo` class.

Launch Link context allows you to launch applications from within a Lync conversation, and also send contextual application data back and forth between communications-enabled applications. For example, when working with a customer relationship management (CRM) application, you can start a conversation with the account manager for a particular client directly from the application. When he receives the conversation invitation, not only does he know what you are calling about, but he can open the CRM application directly from the Lync conversation and automatically load the account. Using Launch Link context, you can launch any application and provide the necessary launch parameters to it. The catch is that the application in question must be able to process the parameters provided to it, either by the ability to accept and process command line arguments, or through a plug-in mechanism where you can use the Lync API to allow the application to process contextual data in incoming conversations.

Lync Extensibility Window context allows you to host Silverlight applications in the Lync conversation window. For example, when a customer call is routed to an agent in a call center, a Silverlight application displaying information about the customer is available to the agent directly in the Lync conversation window. The agent can easily access the necessary customer information such as the reason for the call or the customer's order history without needing to open a separate application.

The `ConversationContextualInfo` class is central to the ability to start contextual conversations. A subset of the Lync controls exposes a `ConversationContextualInfo` property that you can set in order to start contextual conversations from the controls. Also, when starting a conversation using `Automation` or manually via the Lync API, you can provide an instance of `ConversationContextualInfo` to add context to the conversation.

The companion solution for this chapter includes a Fabrikam CRM Windows Presentation Foundation (WPF) application (shown in Figure 4-1) that includes built-in communications features. Users can browse accounts, account team contacts, and start contextual conversations with account team members. The application uses Lync Extensibility Window context to display a mini version of the Fabrikam CRM application to conversation recipients. The conversation recipients can also use Launch Link context to launch the full Fabrikam CRM application from the Lync conversation window if they choose to. In this chapter, you learn how to integrate contextual conversation functionality similar to the Fabrikam CRM application into your own application using Launch Link and Lync Extensibility Window context.

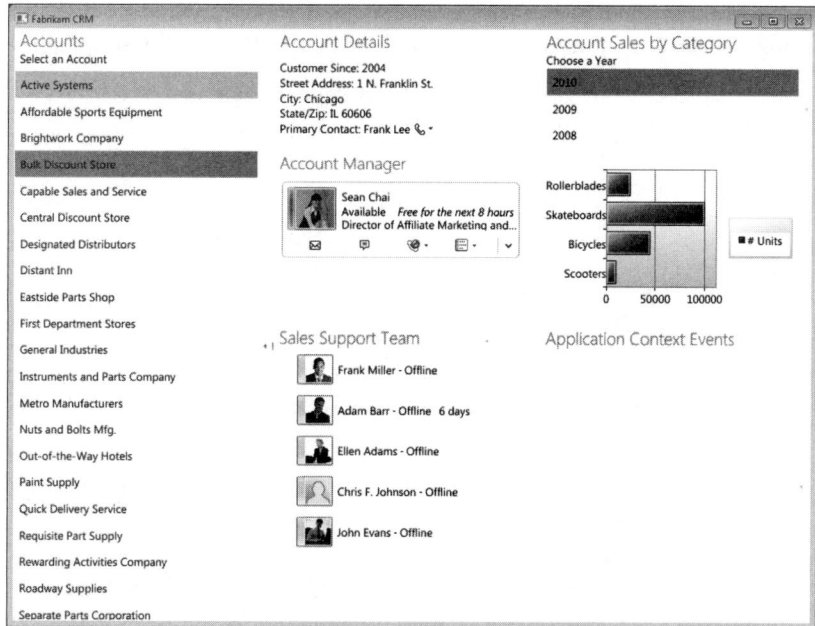

FIGURE 4-1

LAUNCHING APPLICATIONS FROM LYNC CONVERSATIONS

In this section, you learn to start a contextual conversation that includes Launch Link context from the Lync controls and using `Automation`. You also learn about the different ways to register contextual conversation components so that they are trusted by the Lync Server infrastructure.

Registering a Contextual Application Package for Launch Link Context

To start an application that includes Launch Link context from a Lync conversation, you must provide some details about the application such as the path to its executable and any parameters that that it will start with. You then must compile this information into a contextual application package and register it with the Lync Server infrastructure. A contextual application package has some other properties such as a GUID representing a unique ID for the contextual application, as well as the application name.

Later in this chapter, you learn about combining Launch Link context and Lync Extensibility Window context into a single contextual application package.

Deploying a Contextual Application Package for Lync Launch Link Context to the Registry using Install Registration

Deploying a contextual application package to the user's registry hive is referred to as Install Registration. When deploying a contextual application package to the registry, the package must be installed in the registry of every user who will use the application. You have several ways to deploy contextual application packages into the registry; for example, during the setup process of the application, manually using code, by an administrator, or with an Active Directory Group Policy.

To use Install Registration to deploy a contextual application package in the registry, create a Windows registry file to deploy the registry entries:

```
Windows Registry Editor Version 5.00

[HKEY_CURRENT_USER\Software\Microsoft\Communicator\ContextPackages]
[HKEY_CURRENT_USER\Software\Microsoft\Communicator\ContextPackages\
    {6B7BACE8-3968-4A1E-9BB5-F4BD666E36FB}]
"Name"="Fabrikam CRM"
"Path"="C:\\Program Files\\FabrikamCRM\\Fabrikam.CRM.WPF.exe"
"Parameters"="%AppData%"
"InstallLink"="https://register.fabrikam.com/Default.aspx
    ?ApplicationId={6B7BACE8-3968-4A1E-9BB5-F4BD666E36FB}"
```

Code snippet Fabrikam.CRM.WPF\PackageRegistration_Launch.reg

The syntax used in the `PackageRegistration_Launch.reg` file isn't specific to Lync; you use the Windows Registry Editor to deploy entries to the Windows registry. The first line of the file specifies the version of the Windows Registry Editor version; for example, Windows Registry Editor Version 5.00. The next two lines refer to the location in the registry to which contextual application packages are deployed.

As shown in Figure 4-2, the contextual conversation components are written to the registry at `HKEY_CURRENT_USER\Software\Microsoft\Communicator\ContextPackages`. A sub-key is created in this location for every installed contextual application package; the GUID representing the unique ID for the application is used as the registry sub-key.

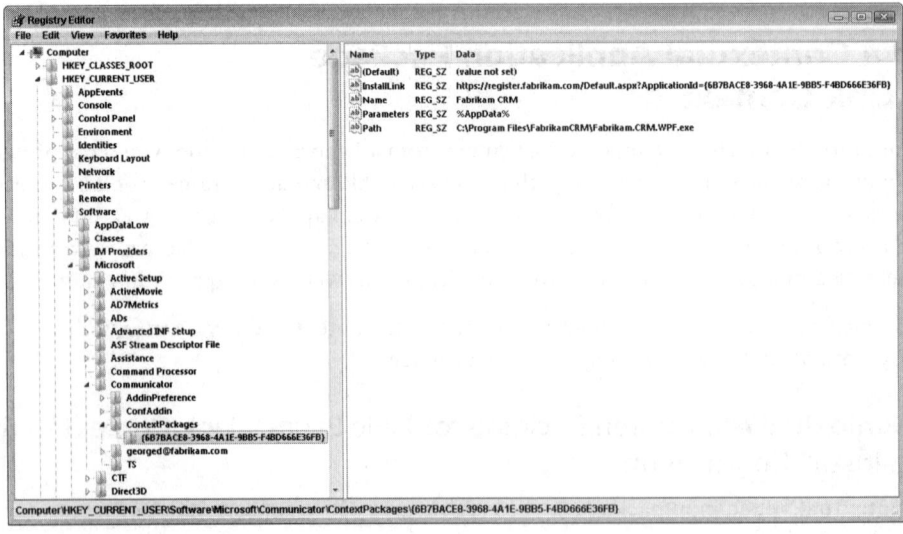

FIGURE 4-2

When creating a contextual application package for Launch Link context using Install Registration, you must define the settings shown in Table 4-1 in the package.

TABLE 4-1: Contextual Application Package Settings for Launch Link Context

SETTING	DESCRIPTION	NOTES
Name	The name of the contextual application package.	
Path	The location where the application is installed — the path to its executable.	
Parameters	Parameters to pass to the application when launching it from a Lync conversation window.	Set this to %AppData%. Size limit is 2kB.
InstallLink	If the user doesn't have the contextual application package installed, he can browse to this URL — if specified — to install it.	Optional. Developer is responsible for implementing install logic.

As noted in Table 4-1, the size limit for the %AppData% parameter is 2kB; this is plenty of space to pass a delimited set of startup parameters, or even a simple XML structure that your application can deserialize into an instance of some class and consume.

Install Registration can present some deployment challenges to an organization, particularly when it comes to modifying the details of a contextual application package that has already been deployed to users in the organization. However, the advantage of this approach is that the contextual application package persists in the registry regardless of whether or not the user is signed in to Lync, and also doesn't need to be redeployed whenever the user starts the application.

Later in this chapter, you will learn about additional settings you can use during Install Registration to enable Lync Extensibility Window context in the contextual application package.

Launching Applications Using Launch Link Context

When receiving a conversation that contains Launch Link context, a message such as the one shown in Figure 4-3 appears in the Lync conversation window.

The message notifies the user that the conversation he is in contains some embedded context. The application name — from the Name attribute used during Install Registration — also appears in the message. The user can click the link to launch the application.

If the user receives a conversation with embedded context, but doesn't have the necessary contextual application package deployed on his computer, he will see a message similar to the one shown in Figure 4-4 notifying him that he doesn't have the necessary contextual application package installed to process the context in the conversation. If you specified the `InstallLink` parameter in the contextual application package, the user will also see a link pointing him to a web page where you can implement some custom logic for installing the contextual application package on his computer.

If you attempt to open the contextual application without installing the contextual application package, you will see a warning similar to the one in Figure 4-4 letting you know that the contextual application is not installed or registered with Lync.

FIGURE 4-3

You can use Launch Link context to start any application that can process the parameters provided in the contextual conversation payload. For example, you can start the Fabrikam CRM application and provide a command line argument for the customer account to load in the application. In this case, the Fabrikam CRM application understands how to process command line arguments. Not all applications might have this functionality; if you didn't write the application yourself to start with (or have access to its source), you should explore whether it offers any extensibility or plug-in mechanism to allow you to add the Lync API code necessary to handle application context.

FIGURE 4-4

You can also launch native Windows and Office applications such as Internet Explorer and Microsoft Word. These applications can process command line arguments; for example, you can launch Internet Explorer from the Run menu or from a command prompt using the following syntax:

```
iexplore.exe http://crm.fabrikam.com/account/234
```

In this case, you can deploy the contextual application package to launch `iexplore.exe` or `winword.exe` and then programmatically provide the command line parameters. In this example, you don't need to provide the full path to `iexplore.exe` or `winword.exe` because the PATH environment variable already contains the full path to the executables for these applications.

Setting Conversation Contextual Info for Launch Link Context

To start a contextual conversation that uses Launch Link context, you first use the `ConversationContextualInfo` class to define the context data. You can then attach the instance of `ConversationContextualInfo` to one of the Lync controls capable of starting conversations, or use it to start a conversation using `Automation`.

Start by creating an instance of `ConversationContextualInfo` and set its `Subject`, `ApplicationId`, and `ApplicationData` properties.

```
var context = new ConversationContextualInfo();
context.Subject = account.AccountName;
context.ApplicationId = _applicationGuid;
context.ApplicationData = String.Concat
    ("AccountId:", account.Id.ToString());
```

Code snippet Fabrikam.CRM.WPF\MainWindow.xaml.cs

The string specified in `Subject` will appear in the toast window notifying the conversation recipients of the new conversation, and also as the title of the Lync conversation window. `ApplicationId` represents the GUID of the contextual application package, and `ApplicationData` is the data that will be passed to the application.

Adding Launch Link Context to the Lync Controls

To attach the context to any Lync control capable of starting a conversation, you set its `ContextualInformation` property to the instance of `ConversationContextualInfo`. For example, in the Fabrikam CRM application, the `ContactCard` Lync control is embedded into the application, as shown in Figure 4-5, and used to start conversations with the account manager for an account.

When you set the `ContextualInformation` property of the `ContactCard` Lync control to the instance of `ConversationContextualInfo`, all conversations started from the `ContactCard` Lync control will contain the context defined in the instance of `ConversationContextualInfo`.

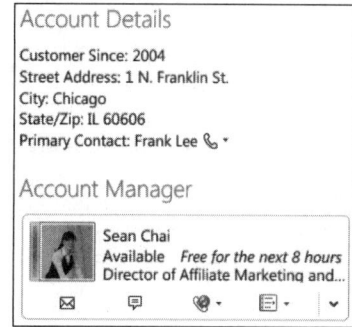

FIGURE 4-5

```
accountManager.ContextualInformation = context;
```

Code snippet Fabrikam.CRM.WPF\MainWindow.xaml.cs

The `ContactCard` control is a composite control in that it contains other Lync controls capable of starting conversations. When you set the `Contextual Information` property of the `ContactCard` control — or any composite Lync control — all the embedded controls will inherit the context. For example, the `ContextualInformation` details attached to the `ContactCard` Lync control will cascade down to the instances of the `StartInstantMessagingButton` and `StartAudioCallButton` controls embedded in the control.

In Chapter 3, you also learned how to easily start a conversation using the `Automation` class. To make those conversations contextual, simply set the instance of `ConversationContextualInfo` as the `contextData` parameter of the `Automation.BeginStartConversation` method:

```
_automation.BeginStartConversation(
    AutomationModalities.Audio,
    myContactList.SelectedContactUris,
    context,
    StartConversationCallback,
    _automation);
```

Setting and Retrieving Command Line Arguments for Application Context

To enable your application to process command line parameters, you must define a format that the parameters should be in and implement a mechanism for processing the parameters that are supplied.

In the Fabrikam CRM application, the logic to process command line arguments is implemented in the `Application_Startup` event in `App.xaml.cs`. This implementation was adapted from an MSDN article; it first checks for the presence of any command line parameters, verifies that they are in the correct format, and then puts them in a `Hashtable` of parameters that is available throughout the application.

```
// http://msdn.microsoft.com/en-us/library/ms743714(VS.85).aspx

public static Hashtable CommandLineArgs = new Hashtable();

private void Application_Startup(object sender, StartupEventArgs e)
{
    if (e.Args.Length == 0) return;

    // Parse command line args for args in the following format:
    //    /argname:argvalue /argname:argvalue /argname:argvalue ...
    string pattern = @"(?<argname>\w+):(?<argvalue>\w+)";
    foreach (string arg in e.Args)
    {
        var match = Regex.Match(arg, pattern);

        // If match not found, command line args are improperly formed.
        if (!match.Success)
            throw new ArgumentException
                ("The arguments are improperly formed.
                 Use argname:argvalue.");

        // Store command line arg and value
        CommandLineArgs[match.Groups["argname"].Value]
            = match.Groups["argvalue"].Value;
    }
}
```

Code snippet Fabrikam.CRM.WPF\App.xaml.cs

In the `Loaded` event of the application's `Mainpage.xaml.cs`, you can check the command line arguments collection for a particular argument and perform the appropriate logic. In the Fabrikam CRM application, if the `AccountId` parameter is provided, the application will load that account.

```
void MainWindow_Loaded(object sender, RoutedEventArgs e)
{
    accountList.ItemsSource = _accounts;

    try
    {
        _lyncClient = Microsoft.Lync.Model.LyncClient.GetClient();

        if (App.CommandLineArgs.Count > 0
            && App.CommandLineArgs["AccountId"] != null)
        {
            LoadSelectedAccount(
                Convert.ToInt32(App.CommandLineArgs["AccountId"]));
        }

        InitializeLyncClient();
    }
    catch (Exception)
    {
        throw;
    }
}
```

Code snippet Fabrikam.CRM.WPF\MainWindow.xaml.cs

Registering a Contextual Application Package for Lync Launch Link Context at Runtime Using Runtime Registration

An alternative approach to deploying a contextual application package to the registry is to use the Lync API to register the contextual application package at runtime with the Lync infrastructure. This is called Runtime Registration. Note, though, that Runtime Registration does not replace Install Registration; it can be either used on its own or to complement Install Registration. However, when used alone, Runtime Registration doesn't offer all the capabilities of Install Registration for contextual application packages that use Launch Link context. For example, you can't launch an application from the Lync conversation window without having first registered the contextual application package using Install Registration.

Runtime Registration allows your contextual application to receive and process context when it is already running. For example, if you are already running the Fabrikam CRM application and receive a contextual conversation request in Lync from a coworker with a question about another account, Runtime Registration allows your application to process the context provided in the conversation and load that account. In this section, you learn how the Fabrikam CRM application uses Runtime Registration to register itself in the Lync registration pool.

In Install Registration, the contextual application package is deployed permanently to the Windows Registry; however, when using Runtime Registration the application registration only exists in the Lync registration pool until the user signs out of Lync, or the application registration is explicitly removed in code, or garbage is collected.

You typically will use both Install Registration and Runtime Registration to enable the users to use Launch Link context to start an application directly from a Lync conversation window, and then be able to process application context if the application is already running.

When you use both Install Registration and Runtime Registration, any settings in the Runtime Registration of the contextual application package will override their Install Registration equivalents until the application registration is removed.

When an application starts, use the `ApplicationRegistration` class to perform Runtime Registration for a contextual application package. Use the `CreateApplicationRegistration` static method of the `LyncClient` class to create an instance of `ApplicationRegistration`. You only need to provide the application GUID and name to the `CreateApplicationRegistration` method. Finally, call the `AddRegistration` method on the `ApplicationRegistration` object to complete the registration.

Available for
download on
Wrox.com

```
private ApplicationRegistration _applicationRegistration;

...

_applicationRegistration =
    _lyncClient.CreateApplicationRegistration(
        _applicationGuid,
        _applicationName);

_applicationRegistration.AddRegistration();
```

Code snippet Fabrikam.CRM.WPF\MainWindow.xaml.cs

Use the `RemoveRegistration` method to remove the application registration from the Lync registration pool.

Available for
download on
Wrox.com

```
void MainWindow_Unloaded(object sender, RoutedEventArgs e)
{
    _applicationRegistration.RemoveRegistration();
}
```

Code snippet Fabrikam.CRM.WPF\MainWindow.xaml.cs

Later in this section, you learn about using the `SetExtensibilityWindowProperties` method of the `ApplicationRegistration` class to add Lync Extensibility Window context to the contextual application package using Runtime Registration.

Processing Application Context at Runtime

When using the `ApplicationRegistration` class to perform Runtime Registration for the contextual application package, your application can process context data when it is already running. Because the application is running, you must use a mechanism other than processing command line arguments during start up in order to process the context provided with the conversation.

Contextual data will arrive as part of an incoming conversation, so your application must wire up the `ConversationAdded` event of the instance of the `ConversationManager` class. To process the context in the `ConversationAdded` event handler, wire up the `ConversationContextLinkClicked` or `InitialContextReceived` events of the conversation.

> *The* `ConversationContextLinkClicked` *or* `InitialContextReceived` *events of the conversation are only available if you are able to handle the* `Conversation` `Added` *event in your application. If you used Launch Link context to launch the application for the first time from the Lync conversation window, your application won't handle the* `ConversationAdded` *event because it wasn't even running when the conversation was created.*

Based on the experience that you intend to present to the users of the application, you might choose not to implement both the `ConversationContextLinkClicked` and `InitialContextReceived` events.

The `ConversationContextLinkClicked` event is only raised when the user clicks the launch link inside the Lync conversation window. On the other hand, the `InitialContextReceived` event is raised even before the conversation recipient opens the conversation window for the incoming conversation. If your application is only implementing the `InitialContextReceived` event, you can present a choice to the user — for example in a modal pop-up window — letting her know that she is receiving incoming application context and allow her to accept or decline it.

Available for download on Wrox.com

```
void ConversationManager_ConversationAdded
    (object sender, ConversationManagerEventArgs e)
{
    e.Conversation.ConversationContextLinkClicked +=
        new EventHandler<InitialContextEventArgs>
        (Conversation_ConversationContextLinkClicked);

    e.Conversation.InitialContextReceived +=
        new EventHandler<InitialContextEventArgs>
        (Conversation_InitialContextReceived);
}
```

Code snippet Fabrikam.CRM.WPF\MainWindow.xaml.cs

InitialContextReceived

The `InitialContextReceived` event is raised when your application first receives contextual application data in an incoming conversation. This event is raised even as the recipients in the conversation are just seeing the incoming toast for the conversation. Use the `InitialContextReceived` event if your application needs to handle contextual application data without intervention from the user, or if you want to allow the user to choose whether he or she wants to accept the incoming context.

The contextual application data is accessible through the instance of `InitialContextEventArgs`. Your application can potentially receive contextual application data from multiple contextual applications, so be sure to use the `ApplicationId` property of `InitialContextEventArgs` to ensure that you are handling contextual application data from the expected contextual application.

The application data accessible in the `InitialContextReceived` event is similar to context passed to the application using the `%AppData%` parameter of the contextual application package during launch; its size limit is thus also 2kB.

```
void Conversation_InitialContextReceived
    (object sender, InitialContextEventArgs e)
{
    Dispatcher.Invoke(
        DispatcherPriority.Input,
        new Action(() =>
        {
            Debug.Assert(e.ApplicationData != null,
            "Initial Context Received: " + e.ApplicationData);

            int accountId = Convert.ToInt32
            (e.ApplicationData.Split(new char[] { ':' })[1]);
            LoadSelectedAccount(accountId);
        }));
}
```

Code snippet Fabrikam.CRM.WPF\MainWindow.xaml.cs

When working with the `InitialContextReceived` *and* `ConversationContextLinkClicked` *events, the authors noticed that the* `InitialContextReceived` *event is sometimes raised multiple times for a single conversation. Be sure to account for this, especially if you are doing any sort of setup logic as part of the* `InitialContextReceived` *event.*

ConversationContextLinkClicked

The `ConversationContextLinkClicked` event is only raised when the user clicks the launch link visible in the Lync conversation window. Use the `ConversationContextLinkClicked` event if your application should only take action on the contextual application data if the user clicks the launch link in the Lync conversation window.

Similar to the `InitialContextReceived` event, the contextual application data is also accessible through an instance of `InitialContextEventArgs`. This is also considered to be initial contextual data, so it is subject to the 2kB size limitation.

You would likely implement similar business logic in the `InitialContextReceived` and `ConversationContextLinkClicked` events. Choosing between them comes down to the application experience that you must present to the users of the application.

```
void Conversation_ConversationContextLinkClicked
    (object sender, InitialContextEventArgs e)
{
    Dispatcher.Invoke(
        DispatcherPriority.Input,
        new Action(() =>
        {
            int accountId = Convert.ToInt32
                (e.ApplicationData.Split(new char[] { ':' })[1]);
            LoadSelectedAccount(accountId);
        }));
}
```

Code snippet Fabrikam.CRM.WPF\MainWindow.xaml.cs

Passing Contextual Data Back and Forth between Conversation Participants

After creating and sending the initial contextual application data to the participants in a conversation, you now programmatically send additional contextual application data back and forth between the participants in a conversation. You can even reset the context and send new initial contextual application data.

Consider a CAD application implemented in WPF: The users of the application can interact with a model by rotating it or zooming in to an area of interest. Those actions in the application can be packaged up and sent to the other participants as contextual application data — allowing them to all see the same thing.

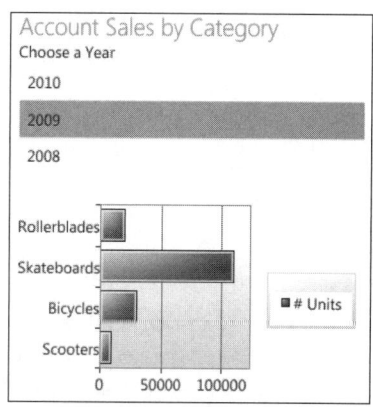

In the Fabrikam CRM application, after initiating a contextual conversation with the account manager for the selected account, you can now browse the sales data for recent years. The year selected to run the report for is passed back and forth as the context of the conversation and the chart is automatically loaded with the report data, as shown in Figure 4-6.

FIGURE 4-6

BeginSendContextData

You use `Conversation.BeginSendContextData` to inject additional application context data into the conversation. In the Fabrikam CRM application, when a user selects a different account or a different year to show the chart data for, the application injects the application context into the active conversation. Every time the user chooses a new year, the context data is sent again to the recipient. You can use this mechanism to allow users to send application context data back and forth.

> *Unlike initial context, you can send a significantly larger application context payload using* `BeginSendContextData`*: 64kB. This is sufficient for sending an XML structure representing much more complex application context, or even a serialized object that you can deserialize on the receiving side.*

To send contextual application data using `Conversation.BeginSendContextData`, you must specify the following:

➤ The GUID representing the ID of the contextual application package

➤ A string representing the type of data being sent; for example, text/plain

➤ The contextual application data to send

Available for download on Wrox.com

```
private void accountList_SelectionChanged
(object sender, SelectionChangedEventArgs e)
{
    if (accountList.SelectedItem != null)
    {
        if (_conversation != null)
        {
            _conversation.BeginSendContextData(
                _applicationGuid,
                "text/plain",
                String.Concat("AccountId:",
                    ((Account)accountList.SelectedItem).Id),
                result => { _conversation.EndSendContextData(result); },
                null);
        }
    }
}
```

Code snippet Fabrikam.CRM.WPF\MainWindow.xaml.cs

On the sender side, calling the `BeginSendContext` method raises the `ContextDataSent` event. On the receiver side, it raises the `ContextDataReceived` event. You can add custom business logic in the `ContextDataSent` and `ContextDataReceived` events to take action on the context data that was sent or received; for example, to log it. The Fabrikam CRM logs context events, as shown in Figure 4-7.

Application Context Events
7:22:25 PM ConversationRemoved
7:22:35 PM ConversationAdded
7:22:35 PM InitialContextReceived
7:22:36 PM InitialContextReceived
7:22:43 PM ConversationContextLinkClicked
7:22:46 PM ConversationRemoved

FIGURE 4-7

BeginSendInitialContext

You learned in the previous section how to handle initial application context using the `InitialContextReceived` event; this event is raised when a contextual conversation is started manually in code or when initial context is injected into the conversation using `Conversation.BeginSendInitialContext`. You can use `BeginSendInitialContext` multiple times; for example, to change the subject of the conversation when you choose a new account in the Fabrikam CRM application.

To send application context to a conversation using `BeginSendInitialContext`, you first must create a `List<KeyValuePair<ContextType, object>>` representing the context data to pass to the operation. To this list, add the GUID representing the ID of the contextual application package and the contextual application data to send.

Available for download on Wrox.com

```
private void accountList_SelectionChanged
    object sender, SelectionChangedEventArgs e)
{
    if (accountList.SelectedItem != null)
    {
        if (_conversation != null)
        {
            var contextData =
                new List<KeyValuePair<ContextType, object>>();

            contextData.Add(new KeyValuePair<ContextType, object>
                (ContextType.ApplicationId, _applicationGuid));

            contextData.Add(new KeyValuePair<ContextType, object>
                (ContextType.ApplicationData,
                 String.Concat("AccountId:",
                 ((Account)accountList.SelectedItem).Id)));

            _conversation.BeginSendInitialContext(
                contextData,
                result =>
                {
                    _conversation.EndSendInitialContext(result);
                },
                null);
        }

    ...
    }
```

Code snippet Fabrikam.CRM.WPF\MainWindow.xaml.cs

On the sender side, calling the `BeginSendInitialContext` method will raise the `InitialContextSent` event. On the receiver side, it will raise the `InitialContextReceived` event.

 Regardless of how it is sent, initial context is always limited to 2kB.

HOSTING SILVERLIGHT APPLICATIONS IN THE LYNC CONVERSATION EXTENSIBILITY WINDOW

Lync Extensibility Window context allows you to host Silverlight applications in the Lync conversation window. The Silverlight application can be a utility application such as a translator, or a mini version of an application that the user can also launch from the Lync conversation window using Launch Link context.

When used in conjunction with Launch Link context, Lync Extensibility Window context is a powerful mechanism that you can use to pass initial context to a conversation. For example, in the Fabrikam CRM application, you can embed the Account Sales by Category chart into a Silverlight application that runs in the Lync conversation window. When someone receives the conversation that includes that context, the specified Silverlight application loads in the conversation window. This visual context is more useful than just setting the title of the conversation window; it provides additional information to streamline getting all the contacts in the conversation on the same page. If they need to, the contacts can also use the Launch Link embedded in the conversation to launch the full version of the application.

When used alone, Lync Extensibility Window context is useful for applications that are only intended to run in the Lync conversation window. A great example of this is an Agent Dashboard that call center agents use for all customer calls. The Agent Dashboard Silverlight application can be defined in a contextual application package that also sets itself as a default context package — meaning that it is used for all incoming calls that don't include embedded context. Agents in the call center will receive calls from customers; the Agent Dashboard can do a reverse-lookup on the customer's phone number and load his customer profile, allowing the agent to provide him with personalized service without having to open a separate application.

You have several options for registering a contextual application package that uses Lync Extensibility Window context. The method you choose depends on several factors such as:

➤ Will the application receive parameters from the conversation it is hosted in? A Silverlight application hosted in the Lync Extensibility Window may rely on some startup parameters in order to load. For example, in the Fabrikam CRM application, the Silverlight application needs to know the customer for which to display the sales chart.

➤ Should the user be able to manually start the application from the Lync menu? A companion application such as a conversation translator application may interact with the active conversation, but it doesn't expect any startup parameters from it. This type of application can be launched manually from the Lync conversation window's context menu.

➤ Will the application be used in a contextual application package that also uses Launch Link context? Choosing to combine Launch Link context and Lync Extensibility Window context in the same contextual application package affects how you can register the contextual application package.

Now you will explore how to register a contextual application package for Lync Extensibility Window context using install registration, starting the contextual conversation, and retrieving the contextual application data supplied to the conversation. Then you will look at how to register a contextual application package for Lync Extensibility Window context at runtime using runtime registration. After examining both options, you will be ready to consider which registration method is most suitable for your application.

Working with Lync Extensibility Window Context Using Install Registration

When using install registration to deploy a contextual application package that uses Lync Extensibility Context, the application settings are deployed to the user's Lync hive in the Windows registry. Adding Lync Extensibility Window context to a contextual application package is just a matter of adding the appropriate settings to the package, as shown in Table 4-2.

TABLE 4-2: Contextual Application Package Settings for Lync Extensibility Window Context

SETTING	DESCRIPTION	NOTES
Name	The name of the contextual application package.	
Parameters	Parameters to pass to the Silverlight application.	Optional. Only required if the application needs to receive startup parameters from the conversation it is hosted in. Set this to `%AppData%`. Size limit is 2kB.
InstallLink	If the user doesn't have the contextual application package installed, she can browse to this URL — if specified — to install it.	Optional. Developer is responsible for implementing install logic.
InternalURL	An internally accessible URL to the website that hosts the Silverlight application.	
ExternalURL	An externally accessible URL to the website that hosts the Silverlight application.	Lync will automatically determine which URL to open.
ExtensibilityWindowSize	The size of the extensibility window embedded into the Lync conversation window.	Default value is 0. 0 = small (300 x 200 pixels). 1 = medium (400 × 600 pixels). 2 = large (800 x 600 pixels).
DefaultContextPackage	Specifies whether the contextual application package is the default context package for the user.	Default is 0 / No.

The Fabrikam CRM application combines Launch Link context and Lync Extensibility Window context in the same contextual application package. Users will see the Silverlight application specified in the `InternalURL` and `ExternalURL` settings embedded in the Lync conversation window; they will also be able to launch the application specified by the `Path` setting directly from the Lync conversation window, as shown in the following code.

```
Windows Registry Editor Version 5.00

[HKEY_CURRENT_USER\Software\Microsoft\Communicator\ContextPackages]
[HKEY_CURRENT_USER\Software\Microsoft\Communicator\ContextPackages\
    {6B7BACE8-3968-4A1E-9BB5-F4BD666E36FB}]
"Name"="Fabrikam CRM"
"Path"="C:\\Program Files\\FabrikamCRM\\Fabrikam.CRM.WPF.exe"
"Parameters"="%AppData%"
"InstallLink"="http://register.fabrikam.com?ApplicationId=
    {6B7BACE8-3968-4A1E-9BB5-F4BD666E36FB}"
"InternalURL"="http://crm.fabrikam.com/Default.aspx"
"ExternalURL"="https://crm.fabrikam.com/Default.aspx"
"ExtensibilityWindowSize"=dword:00000000
"DefaultContextPackage"=dword:00000000
```

Code snippet Fabrikam.CRM.WPF\PackageRegistration_Launch.reg

> *You can optionally combine Launch Link context and Lync Extensibility Window context into the same contextual application package by combining the necessary settings from Table 4-1 and Table 4-2 into the one contextual application package. In the section "Install Registration, Runtime Registration, or Both?", you learn about scenarios where you would combine Launch Link context and Lync Extensibility Window context into the same contextual application package.*

When you deploy a contextual application package that includes Lync Extensibility Window context to the registry using Install Registration, the user can start the associated contextual application directly from a context menu in a Lync conversation window, as shown in Figure 4-8.

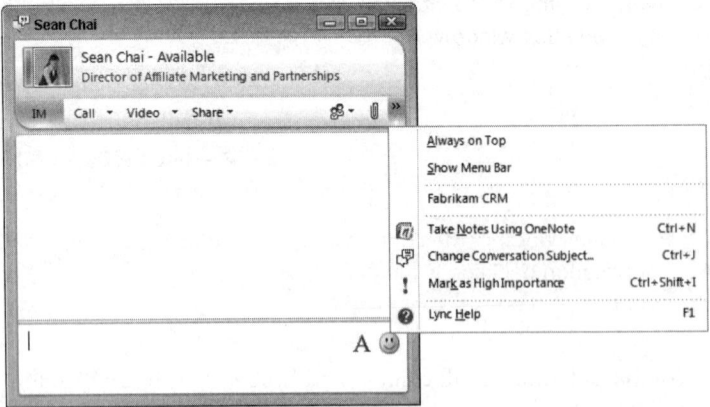

FIGURE 4-8

This is useful for utility applications such as a translator application that don't expect startup parameters from the conversation. However, if a user manually starts a Lync Extensibility Window context application that requires a startup parameter, make sure your application uses defensive coding techniques to alert the user that the application doesn't have all the information it needs in order to start. Otherwise, your users will see the ugly JavaScript error handling alert pop out of the Silverlight application in the Lync conversation window.

Keep your application's expected user experience in mind when choosing between Install Registration and Runtime Registration to deploy the application's contextual application package. Consider whether or not you want users to be able to start the application from the context menu of a Lync conversation window.

When the contextual application package is deployed to the user's Lync registry hive, new contextual conversations can access this information and launch the Silverlight application in the Lync conversation window. Now you will learn how to start a contextual conversation using the Lync Extensibility Window context.

Starting a Contextual Conversation with Lync Extensibility Window Context

Starting a contextual conversation with Lync Extensibility Window context is exactly the same as starting one that includes Launch Link context; create an instance of `ConversationContextualInfo` and set its `Subject`, `ApplicationId`, and `ApplicationData` properties, as shown in the following code:

Available for download on Wrox.com

```
var context = new ConversationContextualInfo();
context.Subject = account.AccountName;
context.ApplicationId = _applicationGuid;
context.ApplicationData = String.Concat
    ("AccountId:", account.Id.ToString());
```

Code snippet Fabrikam.CRM.WPF\MainWindow.xaml.cs

When the user receives a conversation that includes Lync Extensibility Window context, the Silverlight application specified in the contextual application package is immediately loaded in the Lync conversation window, as shown in Figure 4-9.

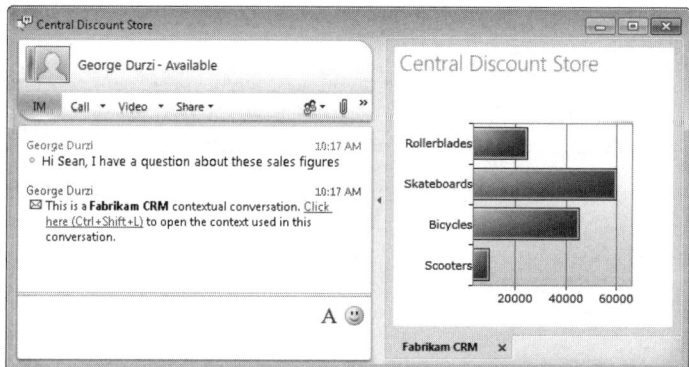

FIGURE 4-9

The Silverlight application specified in the contextual application package is only loaded for the contacts on the recipient side of the conversation, but not the person who initiated the conversation.

> *Notice how the Silverlight version of the Fabrikam CRM application shown in Figure 4-9 is loaded in its own tab in the extensibility window in the Lync conversation. This enables the scenario where one Silverlight application is loaded automatically by a contextual application package, and the user can launch another one manually from the context menu in the Lync conversation window.*

Unless you are building a simple companion Silverlight application that will run in the Lync conversation window, the application will likely need to receive and process some startup parameters when the conversation is initiated. Next you will learn how to process the contextual application data supplied to the Silverlight application running in the Lync conversation window.

Retrieving Contextual Application Data from the Silverlight Application

To access the contextual application data from a Silverlight application running in the Lync conversation window, you first must get access to the `Conversation` object that is hosting the application. You can get access to this hosting conversation in the `Loaded` event handler of the `Page`.

To get the hosting conversation, call `LyncClient.GetHostingConversation()` and cast the resulting object as a `Conversation` object. After checking that the conversation is not null, you can get the application data by calling the `GetApplicationData` method of the `Conversation` instance and providing the GUID of the contextual application package as a parameter.

```
Accounts _accounts = new Accounts();

string _appData = String.Empty;
string _applicationGuid = "{6B7BACE8-3968-4A1E-9BB5-F4BD666E36FB}";

public Page()
{
    InitializeComponent();
    this.Loaded += new RoutedEventHandler(Page_Loaded);
}

void Page_Loaded(object sender, RoutedEventArgs e)
{
    Conversation conversation = null;
    conversation = LyncClient.GetHostingConversation() as Conversation;

    if (conversation != null)
    {
        _appData = conversation.GetApplicationData(_applicationGuid);

        this.Dispatcher.BeginInvoke(
            new Action(() =>
        {
```

```
        int accountId = Convert.ToInt32
            (_appData.Split(new char[] { ':' })[1]);
        Account account =
            _accounts.Where(a => a.Id == accountId).First();

        this.accountName.Text = account.AccountName;

        ((BarSeries)accountSalesChart.Series[0]).ItemsSource =
            account.GetSalesByYear(DateTime.Now.Year);
    }));
  }
}
```

Code snippet Fabrikam.CRM.Silverlight\Page.xaml.cs

The Default Context Package

When starting a contextual conversation and specifying an instance of `ConversationContextualInfo`, you are explicitly telling Lync to load a specific Silverlight application in the conversation window. What if you need a certain Silverlight application to always load for every conversation that the user receives? A contextual application package can be set as the default context package for the user, meaning it is processed for every conversation that the user receives. When installing a contextual application package using Install Registration, you can set the `DefaultContextPackage` attribute to 1 to indicate that the contextual application package is the default context package for the user.

 A user can only have one default context package. A contextual application package can only be set as the default context package using Install Registration.

A default context package is only useful for contextual application packages that include Lync Extensibility Window context, such as an Agent Dashboard application that customer service agents in a call center would be using. In this case, you might want to load a Silverlight CRM application in the Lync extensibility window for every incoming call. The CRM application could do a reverse lookup on the phone number in the incoming call, and if the number points to an existing customer, open the customer's record in the application.

To enforce this behavior for every incoming call, you can register a default context package on every customer service agent's computer. When the agent receives a call with no context specified — such as a call from a customer — the contextual application defined in the default context package is automatically loaded.

Working with Lync Extensibility Window Context at Runtime Using Runtime Registration

Runtime Registration enables you to set the properties for Lync Extensibility Window context at runtime using the `ApplicationRegistration` class instead of using Install Registration. Keep in mind, though, that the experience for the user is going to be different, particularly because the application responsible for creating the application registration must already be running.

Later, in the "Install Registration, Runtime Registration, or Both?" section, you will learn about choosing the registration method most suitable for your application.

You can still use Install Registration to register a contextual application package containing settings specific to Lync Extensibility Window context, such as `InternalURL`, `ExternalURL`, and `ExtensibilityWindowSize`. However, these settings are overridden by the registration created at runtime using `ApplicationRegistration`.

Creating Application Registration

After creating an instance of `ApplicationRegistration`, you can call its `SetExtensibilityWindowProperties` method to set the `InternalURL`, `ExternalURL`, and `ExtensibilityWindowSize` properties:

```
_applicationRegistration =
    _lyncClient.CreateApplicationRegistration(
        _applicationGuid,
        _applicationName);

_applicationRegistration.SetExtensibilityWindowProperties(
    "http://crm.fabrikam.com/Default.aspx",
    "https://crm.fabrikam.com/Default.aspx",
    ConversationWindowExtensionSize.Small);

_applicationRegistration.AddRegistration();
```

Retrieving Contextual Data in the Silverlight Application

When using Install Registration to define a contextual application package that includes Lync Extensibility Window context, you saw how to get access to the hosting conversation and call the `GetApplicationData` method of the `Conversation` instance to get the application data that was passed into the application.

When you're using Runtime Registration alone, this approach won't work. The call to `GetApplicationData` will throw a security exception because of a security mechanism dictating that only the application that performed the application registration — the WPF application that launched the conversation — can access the application data.

The workaround for this issue is to modify the application registration to pass `%AppData%` to the Silverlight application as a querystring parameter:

```
_applicationRegistration =
    _lyncClient.CreateApplicationRegistration(
        _applicationGuid,
        _applicationName);
```

```
_applicationRegistration.SetExtensibilityWindowProperties(
    "http://crm.fabrikam.com/Default.aspx?data=%AppData%",
    "https://crm.fabrikam.com/Default.aspx?data=%AppData%",
    ConversationWindowExtensionSize.Small);

_applicationRegistration.AddRegistration();
```

In the Silverlight application, instead of using `Conversation.GetApplicationData` to get the application data, grab it from the querystring parameter:

```
_appData = System.Windows.Browser.HtmlPage.Document.QueryString["data"];
```

Manually Opening the Extensibility Window

To manually open the extensibility window from the application, you must subscribe to the `ConversationAdded` event of the `ConversationManager` and open it from there. To get a handle to the conversation window in the `ConversationAdded` event handler, call the `Automation.GetConversationWindow` method and pass in the `Conversation` instance as a parameter. You can then call the `BeginOpenExtensibilityWindow` method on the conversation window and provide the GUID of the contextual application to open in the extensibility window.

```
void ConversationManager_ConversationAdded
(object sender, ConversationManagerEventArgs e)
{
    Automation automation = LyncClient.GetAutomation();
    ConversationWindow window =
        automation.GetConversationWindow(e.Conversation);

    window.BeginOpenExtensibilityWindow(
        _applicationGuid,
        result => { window.EndOpenExtensibilityWindow(result); },
        null);

    ...
}
```

There is no overload for `BeginOpenExtensibilityWindow` that allows you to also specify application data to pass in. This dictates the type of Silverlight application that you can run in the Lync extensibility window if you choose to open it manually, especially if your Silverlight application expects some startup parameters.

Security Requirements for Lync Extensibility Window Context

You must add the website hosting a Silverlight application that is intended to run in the Lync conversation window to the Trusted Sites collection for every user. The easiest way to do this is using an Active Directory Group Policy.

During development, you will most likely be using Visual Studio's built-in web server so your application will be accessible at a URL such as `http://localhost:5454/Default.aspx`. In this case, you only need to add `http://localhost` to the Trusted Sites collection on your development machine.

If the website hosting the Silverlight application is not in the user's Trusted Sites collection, the Lync API code will throw an `AutomationServerException` with a detail message of "Client is not trusted."

Install Registration, Runtime Registration, or Both?

How should you register your contextual application packages — do you use Install Registration, Runtime Registration, or both? As with any good software development question, the answer is: It depends! It all comes down to how users will interact with the application as defined by the contextual application package.

Table 4-3 shows some common scenarios for using contextual application packages and the registration method you should choose for each. You might realize that your requirements may be a combination of those shown in Table 4-3. In that case, combining Install Registration and Runtime Registration for the contextual application package will give you the flexibility you need.

TABLE 4-3: Choosing a Contextual Package Registration Method

REQUIREMENT	CHOOSE
The contextual application package needs to be set as a Default Context Package.	Install Registration
Users should be able to launch an application and pass startup parameters to it from a Lync conversation window.	Install Registration
Users should be able to pass context to an application that is already running.	Runtime Registration
Users should be able to start a Silverlight application in the Lync extensibility window from the context menu of a Lync conversation window.	Install Registration
Users should not be able to start a Silverlight application in the Lync extensibility window from the context menu of a Lync conversation window.	Runtime Registration
A Silverlight application running in the Lync extensibility window needs to receive startup parameters in order to function.	Install Registration
A Silverlight application running in the Lync extensibility window does not need to receive startup parameters in order to function.	Runtime Registration

SUMMARY

The Lync API includes new functionality to allow you to start contextual conversations from the Lync controls or using `Automation`. This functionality gives you the ability to build new applications — or extend existing ones — to take advantage of the contextual conversation features available in the Lync API. You can use these features to allow users to launch applications directly from the Lync conversation window, and to also host Silverlight application in the extensibility window or a Lync conversation window.

In the next chapter, you will learn about working with the Lync API at a lower level. Instead of starting conversations from the Lync controls or using `Automation`, you will work with the underlying conversation modality. This will allow you to build communications clients that don't rely on the Lync interface being visible to the user. You will learn how to put the Lync user interface in UI Suppression mode to hide it from the user.

Building Custom Communications Clients with Lync UI Suppression

WHAT'S IN THIS CHAPTER?

➤ Suppressing the Lync Client User Interface

➤ Building Custom Communications Solutions with Lync UI Suppression

➤ Working with the Instant Message Modality

➤ Working with the Audio and Video Channels in the Audio Video Modality

In Microsoft Lync Server 2010, the Microsoft Lync 2010 Managed API is intended to replace both the IMessenger and UCC APIs that were available with Microsoft Office Communications Server 2007 R2. The case for replacing the IMessenger API is easy to make because although it is easy develop with, it is extremely limited in functionality. In OCS 2007 R2, the UCC API was the tool of choice for building completely custom communications clients; however, the API is difficult to get started with because the developer is responsible for managing the connectivity of the communications client back to the OCS 2007 R2 infrastructure.

As you learned in Chapters 3 and 4, the Lync API combines the ease of use of the IMessenger API and the rich functionality provided by the UCC API. However, a common requirement for building custom communication clients is to replace the Lync user interface with your own. In Lync 2010, you can suppress the Lync user interface and replace it with your own, enabling you to build a custom communications client such as a communications kiosk or a custom conference room control system, while still taking advantage of the ease of developing with the Lync API — specifically not having to deal with programming the connectivity of the custom client back to the Microsoft Lync 2010 Server infrastructure.

Lync UI Suppression requires that the Lync client is installed on the user's machine. You use the Lync API to replicate some of the functionality available in the Lync client, such as the ability to sign the user into Lync and start conversations.

In this chapter, you learn how to configure and build communications clients that use Lync UI Suppression. You also learn about the tradeoffs you make when putting the Lync client into UI Suppression mode, such as the inability to use automation or the Lync controls in your solution. When building solutions that work with Lync UI Suppression, you will work with conversations at the individual modality level. You learn to work with the instant messaging modality and both the audio and video channels of the `AudioVideo` modality to programmatically create conversations from scratch.

This chapter includes two companion projects that take advantage of Lync UI Suppression:

➤ A simple Silverlight instant messaging client

➤ A custom WPF audio video communications client

WORKING WITH LYNC UI SUPPRESSION

When developing an application that uses Lync in UI Suppression mode, understanding the tradeoffs that you're making is important; for example, you are responsible for creating custom versions of almost the entire Lync client user interface. Additionally, your application has to programmatically sign the user into the Lync client using a custom login interface that you are also responsible for creating.

With the exception of the `VideoWindow` control that is used to render video, all the user interface elements of the Lync client are not visible when it is running in UI Suppression mode. The `VideoWindow` control is only available when running in UI Suppression mode. Later in this chapter, you learn how to access the `VideoWindow` when working with conversations that use the `AudioVideo` modality.

The Lync controls are not available when the Lync client is running in UI Suppression mode; they are automatically grayed out and disabled. You must create your own custom versions of controls such as the `PresenceIndicator` and `ContactList`.

`Automation` is also unavailable when running in UI Suppression mode. `Automation` provides an extremely easy way of starting conversations in different modalities; however, it relies exclusively on Lync user interface elements such as the conversation window. Later in this chapter, you will learn about creating conversations at the modality level and building the necessary user interface elements to support them.

This section walks you through configuring the Lync client to run in UI Suppression mode, and programmatically signing the user in to the Lync client using a custom sign-in interface.

> *Both WPF and Silverlight applications can interact with the Lync client when it is running in UI Suppression mode.*

Configuring Lync UI Suppression

Lync UI Suppression mode is configured in the registry. When the Lync client is put into UI Suppression mode, it affects every user on the machine. Lync UI Suppression mode can't be configured on a per-user basis. To put Lync into UI Suppression mode, you must create and set a registry key called UISuppressionMode in the appropriate location in the Windows registry depending on whether you're running the 32-bit or 64-bit version of the Lync client.

> *When the Lync client is configured to run in UI Suppression mode on a machine that is shared by multiple users, it affects every user on the machine.*

Configuring UI Suppression on 32-bit Machines

To configure the 32-bit version of the Lync client to run in UI Suppression mode, create a key called UISuppressionMode in HKEY_LOCAL_MACHINE\SOFTWARE\Microsoft\Communicator and set its value to 1.

Alternatively, create and run a Windows registry script to create and set the appropriate registry entry:

Available for download on Wrox.com

```
Windows Registry Editor Version 5.00

[HKEY_LOCAL_MACHINE\SOFTWARE\Microsoft\Communicator]
"UISuppressionMode"=dword:00000001
```

Code snippet Registry\32-bit\EnableUISuppressionMode.reg

To disable UI Suppression mode, set the UISuppressionMode registry key value back to 0.

Available for download on Wrox.com

```
Windows Registry Editor Version 5.00

[HKEY_LOCAL_MACHINE\SOFTWARE\Microsoft\Communicator]
"UISuppressionMode"=dword:00000000
```

Code snippet Registry\32-bit\DisableUISuppressionMode.reg

Configuring UI Suppression on 64-bit Machines

Configuring Lync UI Suppression mode on a 64-bit machine is identical to configuring it on a 32-bit machine except for the location in the registry where the UISuppressionMode key is created. To configure the 64-bit version of the Lync client to run in UI Suppression mode, create a key called

`UISuppressionMode` in `HKEY_LOCAL_MACHINE\SOFTWARE\Wow6432Node\Microsoft\Communicator` and set its value to 1.

Alternatively, create and run a Windows registry script to create and set the appropriate registry entry:

```
Windows Registry Editor Version 5.00

[HKEY_LOCAL_MACHINE\SOFTWARE\Wow6432Node\Microsoft\Communicator]
"UISuppressionMode"=dword:00000001
```

Code snippet Registry\64-bit\EnableUISuppressionMode.reg

To disable UI Suppression mode, set the `UISuppressionMode` registry key value back to 0.

```
Windows Registry Editor Version 5.00

[HKEY_LOCAL_MACHINE\SOFTWARE\Wow6432Node\Microsoft\Communicator]
"UISuppressionMode"=dword:00000000
```

Code snippet Registry\64-bit\DisableUISuppressionMode.reg

Interacting with the Lync Client Process

When Lync is configured to run in UI Suppression mode, your application has to initialize the Lync client process, sign the user in, and perform any necessary startup logic. Multiple applications that use Lync could also be running on the machine and may have already initialized the Lync client process and signed the user in. As part of its startup logic, your application must check the state of the Lync client process and act accordingly. This section walks you through the necessary startup logic that your application has to implement when Lync is running in UI Suppression mode.

Initializing the Lync Client Process

When Lync is configured to run in UI Suppression mode, users aren't able to start the Lync client as they typically would — from the Windows Start menu. Nothing happens if the user attempts to launch the Lync client manually. Your application is responsible for initializing the Lync client process by calling the `BeginInitialize` method of the `LyncClient` class; this starts the `Communicator.exe` process. In Figure 5-1, you can see the `Communicator.exe` process running in the Windows Task Manager, but the Lync client is nowhere to be seen because its user interface is suppressed.

After getting a handle to the `LyncClient` object by calling `LyncClient.GetClient()`, wire up handlers for the `StateChanged` and `CredentialRequested` events. The Lync client process raises the `StateChanged` event when its state changes, and the `CredentialRequested` event when it doesn't have the necessary credentials to sign the user in.

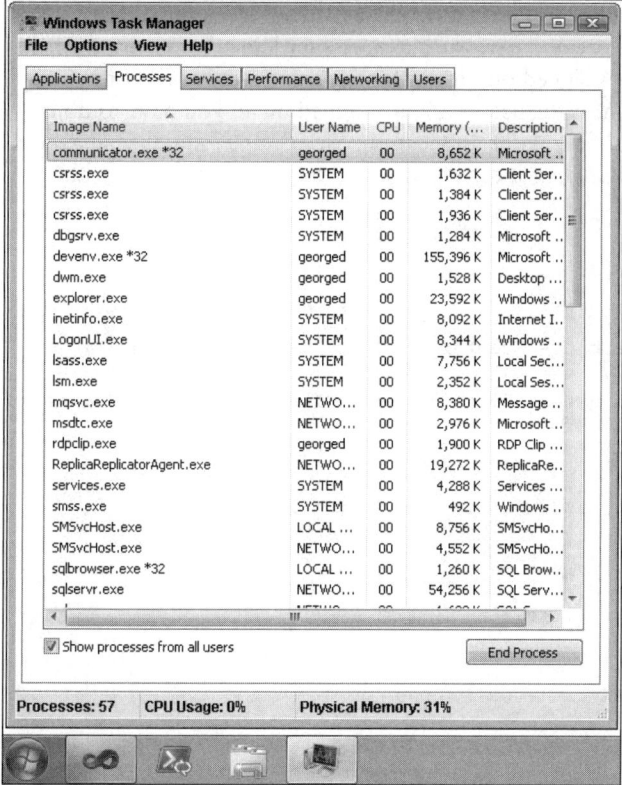

FIGURE 5-1

You can then check whether the Lync client is configured to run in UI Suppression mode by checking the InSuppressedMode property of the LyncClient object. After checking whether the Lync client is running in UI Suppression mode, your application has to determine whether to initialize the Lync client process. If the state of the Lync client is ClientState.Unitialized, you must call LyncClient .BeginInitialize to initialize and start the Lync client process. Calling BeginInitialize will prompt the Lync client process to start and its state to change; for example, from ClientState .Unitialized to ClientState.Initializing — your application will respond to these state changes in the StateChanged event handler.

> *Your application should maintain a Boolean flag to denote whether it was responsible for initializing the Lync client process. As part of its shutdown process, the application shouldn't sign out of or terminate the Lync client process if it wasn't responsible for initializing it in the first place.*

As you can see in the following code, if the Lync client process has already been initialized by another application, you must check its state and perform the necessary logic. For example, if the process is already initialized but the user is signed out, it display a pop-up window that the user can use to enter his credentials and sign in. If the user is already signed in, all you have to do is perform the application startup logic specific to your application; for example, initialize instances of `ConversationManager` and `ContactManager` that your application will use to work with conversations and contacts.

```
_lyncClient = LyncClient.GetClient();

_lyncClient.StateChanged +=
    new EventHandler<ClientStateChangedEventArgs>(LyncClient_StateChanged);
_lyncClient.CredentialRequested +=
    new EventHandler<CredentialRequestedEventArgs>(LyncClient_CredentialRequested);

if (_lyncClient.InSuppressedMode)
{
    if (_lyncClient.State == ClientState.Uninitialized)
    {
        try
        {
            _lyncClient.BeginInitialize(
                result =>
                {
                    if (result.IsCompleted == true)
                    {
                        _lyncClient.EndInitialize(result);
                        _myAppInitializedLync = true;
                    }
                },
                null);
        }
        catch (Exception)
        {
            throw;
        }
    }
    else
    {
        if (_lyncClient.State == ClientState.SignedOut)
        {
            ShowSignInPopUpWindow();
        }
        else if (_lyncClient.State == ClientState.SignedIn)
        {
            PerformApplicationStartupLogic();
        }
    }
}
```

Code snippet SilverlightIMClient\Page.xaml.cs

Signing In to the Lync Client

When Lync is running in UI Suppression mode, your application can sign in a user by calling the `LyncClient.BeginSignIn` method and providing the credentials of the user. The application can collect the user's credentials using a custom form such as the one shown in Figure 5-2.

If the application is intended to always sign in using a specific user's credentials, you can hardcode the credentials to use when calling the `LyncClient.BeginSignIn` method. For example, in a kiosk application used to look up and dial employees in a company directory, you can create a domain account such as "Front Desk" for the application, and sign in to Lync using that account's credentials.

Sign In to Lync

SIP URI: (e.g.: sip:adamb@fabrikam.com

sip:georged@fabrikam.com

Domain and User Name: (e.g: fabrikam\adamb

fabrikam\georged

Password:

•••••••••

OK

FIGURE 5-2

When capturing the user's credentials using a custom login form such as the one shown in Figure 5-2, you need a mechanism to pass those credentials back to the application's main form to use them to call the `LyncClient.BeginSignIn` method. The Silverlight IM Client application available with this chapter uses an implementation of a loosely coupled notification mechanism available in the MVVMLight toolkit for the Model-View-ViewModel (MVVM) software development pattern to notify the application of a sign in attempt. You can implement your own notification mechanism to allow different windows in your application to send messages to each other.

The application defines a `SignInAttemptNotification` class that exposes properties for the user's SIP URI, domain and username, and password:

Available for
download on
Wrox.com

```
public class SignInAttemptNotification : NotificationMessage
{
    public string SipUri { get; set; }
    public string DomainUserName { get; set; }
    public string Password { get; set; }

    public SignInAttemptNotification() : base(string.Empty) { }

    public SignInAttemptNotification(
        string sipUri, string domainUserName, string password)
        : base(string.Empty)
    {
        this.SipUri = sipUri;
        this.DomainUserName = domainUserName;
        this.Password = password;
    }
}
```

Code snippet SilverlightIMClient\Notifications\SignInAttemptNotification.cs

When a user enters his credentials into the custom login form and clicks OK, the application broadcasts a notification of type `SignInAttemptNotification` as shown in the following code:

```
private void OKButton_Click(object sender, RoutedEventArgs e)
{
    if ((!String.IsNullOrEmpty(this.sipUri.Text))
    && (!String.IsNullOrEmpty(this.domainUserName.Text))
    && (!String.IsNullOrEmpty(this.password.Password)))
    {
        this.DialogResult = true;

        Messenger.Default.Send<SignInAttemptNotification>(
            new SignInAttemptNotification(
                this.sipUri.Text,
                this.domainUserName.Text,
                this.password.Password));
    }
}
```

Code snippet SilverlightIMClient\SignInPopUpWindow.xaml.cs

In this loosely typed architecture, subscribers can subscribe to notifications of a particular type and define a handler that will execute when they receive a notification of that type:

```
Messenger.Default.Register<SignInAttemptNotification>
    (this, Notification_SignInAttempt);
```

Code snippet SilverlightIMClient\Page.xaml.cs

When the application receives a notification of type `SignInAttemptNotification`, you can call `LyncClient.BeginSignIn` and sign in the user with the credentials specified in the notification:

```
public void Notification_SignInAttempt(SignInAttemptNotification notification)
{
    if ((!String.IsNullOrEmpty(notification.SipUri))
    && (!String.IsNullOrEmpty(notification.DomainUserName))
    && (!String.IsNullOrEmpty(notification.Password)))
    {
        _lyncClient.BeginSignIn(
            notification.SipUri,
            notification.DomainUserName,
            notification.Password,
            result =>
            {
                if (result.IsCompleted)
                {
                    _lyncClient.EndSignIn(result);
                    PerformApplicationStartupLogic();
                }
            },
```

```
                        "Local user signing in" as object);
            }
    }
```

Code snippet SilverlightIMClient\Page.xaml.cs

The `CredentialRequested` event is raised if your application calls `LyncClient.BeginSignIn` with null or invalid values for the SIP URI, domain and username, and password parameters. In the handler for the `CredentialRequested` event, you can check for the type credentials that are being requested and direct the user again to the login form for him to enter the correct credentials:

```
void LyncClient_CredentialRequested(object sender, CredentialRequestedEventArgs e)
{
    if (e.Type == CredentialRequestedType.SignIn)
    {
        ShowSignInPopUpWindow();
    }
}
```

Code snippet SilverlightIMClient\Page.xaml.cs

Performing Application Startup Logic

After completing the sign-in process, your application can perform application-specific startup logic such as creating instances of `Self`, `ConversationManager`, and `ContactManager` to enable it to interact with the signed in user's conversations, groups, and contacts. This is also an ideal place to wire up other event handlers that your application will work with, such as those for the `ConversationAdded` and `ConversationRemoved` events:

```
void PerformApplicationStartupLogic()
{
    _conversationManager = _lyncClient.ConversationManager;
    _contactManager = _lyncClient.ContactManager;
    _self = _lyncClient.Self;

    _conversationManager.ConversationAdded +=
        new EventHandler<ConversationManagerEventArgs>
            (ConversationManager_ConversationAdded);
    _conversationManager.ConversationRemoved +=
        new EventHandler<ConversationManagerEventArgs>
            (ConversationManager_ConversationRemoved);

    this.MyContacts = new List<Contact>();

    foreach (var group in _contactManager.Groups)
    {
        foreach (var contact in group)
        {
```

```
            if (!this.MyContacts.Contains(contact))
            {
                this.MyContacts.Add(contact);
            }
        }
    }
}
```

Code snippet SilverlightIMClient\Page.xaml.cs

Signing Out Of or Shutting Down the Lync Client Process

If your application was responsible for initializing the Lync client process as part of its startup logic, its shutdown logic should also sign out the logged-in user. Your application doesn't necessarily have to call `LyncClient.BeginShutdown` to shut down the Lync client process — the process will automatically terminate if it is no longer being used and all references to it have been released. You can verify this by looking for the `Communicator.exe` process in the Windows Task Manager after your application has shut down and released any references to the Lync client process.

In a Silverlight application such as the Silverlight IM Client application, there isn't a good extensibility point to automatically perform any signout and shutdown logic when the user closes the browser or navigates away from the Silverlight application. The `LyncClient.BeginSignOut` and `LyncClient.BeginShutdown` operations are asynchronous; you shouldn't block the UI thread in a Silverlight application and attempt to execute these operations synchronously in an event such as `Application.Exit`.

However, in a .NET or WPF application, you can subscribe to the `Dispatcher.ShutdownStarted` event in a window and add logic in the event handler to sign out of the Lync process as part of the application's shutdown process. You should disconnect the event handlers for the `LyncClient .StateChanged` and `LyncClient.CredentialRequested` events to prevent them from firing as the application is signing out of the Lync client process.

```
void Dispatcher_ShutdownStarted(object sender, EventArgs e)
{
    if (_lyncClient != null)
    {
        _lyncClient.StateChanged -=
            new EventHandler<ClientStateChangedEventArgs>
                (LyncClient_StateChanged);
        _lyncClient.CredentialRequested -=
            new EventHandler<CredentialRequestedEventArgs>
                (LyncClient_CredentialRequested);

        if (_myAppInitializedLync && _lyncClient.State == ClientState.SignedIn)
        {
            _lyncClient.BeginSignOut(SignOutCallback, null);
        }
    }
}

void SignOutCallback(IAsyncResult ar)
{
    if (ar.IsCompleted)
    {
```

```
        if (ar.IsCompleted == true)
        {
            _lyncClient.EndSignOut(ar);
            _lyncClient = null;
        }
    }
}
```

In a .NET or WPF application, the easiest approach is to simply sign out of the Lync client process before shutting down the application. You should only do this if the application was responsible for initializing the process in the first place. No need exists to explicitly shut down the Lync client process; it automatically terminates when all references to it are released.

WORKING WITH THE INSTANT MESSAGE MODALITY

You learned in Chapter 3 how to easily start conversations using the `Automation` class. To start a conversation using `Automation`, simply specify the modality of the conversation, the participants, any context data to be embedded in the conversation, a callback function that will execute when the asynchronous operation completes, and some asynchronous state value:

```
_automation.BeginStartConversation(
AutomationModalities.InstantMessage,
    myContactList.SelectedContactUris,
    contextData,
    StartConversationCallback,
    _automation);
```

As you can see from the preceding code, starting a conversation using `Automation` is extremely easy to do; however, calling `Automation.Begin StartConversation` immediately brings up a new Lync conversation window for the conversation that was just created. When working with Lync in UI Suppression mode, `Automation` is not available because it relies on user interface elements from the Lync client in order to function. Calling `LyncClient.GetAutomation` when the Lync client is running in UI Suppression mode will throw a `ClientNotFoundException`, as shown in Figure 5-3.

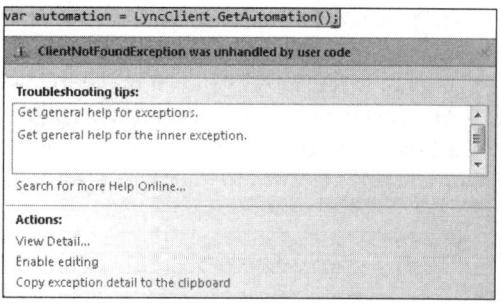

FIGURE 5-3

Applications that need to send and receive instant messages when the Lync client is running in UI Suppression mode need to work directly with the Instant Message modality. In this section, you learn how to programmatically create a new conversation, add participants to the conversation, and interact with the Instant Message modality for each participant in the conversation.

The Lync client doesn't necessarily have to be running in UI Suppression mode for your application to work directly with the Instant Message modality. However, when the Lync user interface is not suppressed, using the Lync controls or Automation *instead to start conversations is a lot easier.*

The code accompanying this chapter includes a Silverlight IM Client application that displays a list of the user's contacts, as shown in Figure 5-4. The user selects a contact from the list with whom to start an instant message conversation; the application then launches a custom conversation window for the new conversation.

After selecting a contact with whom to start a conversation, the application programmatically creates a new conversation and adds the selected contact as a participant in the conversation. However, the contact doesn't see the new conversation toast window until you send the first instant message. Afterwards, you can engage in a back-and-forth instant message conversation. The application also implements behavior similar to the Lync client where a participant in the conversation is notified when the other participant is composing a message.

Creating a New Conversation and Adding Participants

To allow the user to engage in multiple instant message conversations at the same time, the Silverlight IM Client application maintains a list of active conversation IDs in a module-level `ObservableCollection<string>`, as shown in the following code. The application uses this collection to keep track of all the active conversations and to broadcast instant messages it receives to the correct conversation window based on the conversation ID.

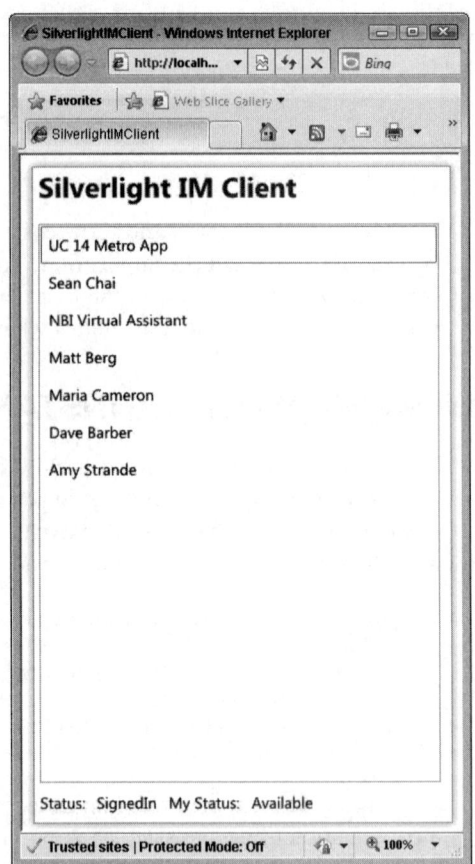

FIGURE 5-4

```
private ObservableCollection<string> _activeConversationIds =
new ObservableCollection<string>();
```

Code snippet SilverlightIMClient\Page.xaml.cs

As part of its startup logic, the application creates an instance of the `ConversationManager` class and wires up handlers for its `ConversationAdded` and `ConversationRemoved` events:

```
_conversationManager = _lyncClient.ConversationManager;

_conversationManager.ConversationAdded +=
    new EventHandler<ConversationManagerEventArgs>
        (ConversationManager_ConversationAdded);
_conversationManager.ConversationRemoved +=
```

```
new EventHandler<ConversationManagerEventArgs>
    (ConversationManager_ConversationRemoved);
```

Creating a New Conversation

When the user clicks a contact with whom to start a conversation, the application calls the AddConversation method on the instance of ConversationManager, causing its ConversationAdded event to fire.

The application should first verify that the contact is not offline before starting a new conversation. You can create a new conversation with a contact who happens to be offline and even add that person as a participant in a conversation; however, the Lync API will throw an exception when you attempt to send an instant message to a contact who is offline:

```
void MyContacts_SelectionChanged(object sender, SelectionChangedEventArgs e)
{
    var contact = (Contact) contactList.SelectedValue;

    if ((ContactAvailability)contact.GetContactInformation
        (ContactInformationType.Availability)
        != ContactAvailability.Offline)
    {
        _conversationManager.AddConversation();
    }
}
```

In the handler for the ConversationAdded event, add the ID of the new conversation to the collection of active conversation IDs. The Conversation object for the new conversation is accessible from the ConversationManagerEventArgs in the event handler; you can then get the ID of the new conversation from its properties collection.

Adding a Participant to the Conversation

After wiring up the ParticipantAdded and StateChanged events of the new conversation, the Silverlight IM Client application adds the selected contact as a participant in the conversation and then launches the conversation window for the new conversation:

```
void ConversationManager_ConversationAdded
    (object sender, ConversationManagerEventArgs e)
{
    _activeConversationIds.Add(
        e.Conversation.Properties[ConversationProperty.Id].ToString());

    e.Conversation.ParticipantAdded +=
        new EventHandler<ParticipantCollectionChangedEventArgs>
            (Conversation_ParticipantAdded);
```

```
e.Conversation.StateChanged +=
    new EventHandler<ConversationStateChangedEventArgs>
        (Conversation_StateChanged);

if (e.Conversation.CanInvoke(ConversationAction.AddParticipant))
{
    e.Conversation.AddParticipant((Contact)contactList.SelectedValue);

    var conversationWindow = new ConversationWindow(
        e.Conversation.Properties[ConversationProperty.Id].ToString(),
        e.Conversation.Participants);

    conversationWindow.Show();
}
}
```

Code snippet SilverlightIMClient\Page.xaml.cs

The `Conversation` class exposes a `CanInvoke` method that you can use to check whether you can invoke a particular action on the conversation. The available actions are represented by the `ConversationAction` enum whose values are

➤ `Merge`

➤ `Park`

➤ `AddParticipant`

➤ `RemoveParticipant`

If the `CanInvoke` check for `ConversationAction.AddParticipant` returns `true`, add the selected contact as a participant in the conversation. To add a participant to the conversation, you must supply a `Contact` object to the `AddParticipant` method; the item's source for the contact list is a `List<Contact>` so you can simply pass in the selected value from the ListBox. Alternatively, you can use the `ContactManager.GetContactByUri` method to get a `Contact` object given a SIP URI.

In a Lync conversation window like the one shown in Figure 5-5, you can see the list of participants in the conversation by clicking the People Options button in the conversation window toolbar and selecting Show Participant List. Next to each participant are icons representing the modalities that can be used in the conversation. In Figure 5-5, the instant message icon is enabled to indicate that the participants are engaged in an instant message conversation; the icons for the other modalities are grayed out because those modalities aren't currently active in the conversation.

When working with conversations programmatically, the modalities in the conversation are accessible at either the conversation or participant level; for example,

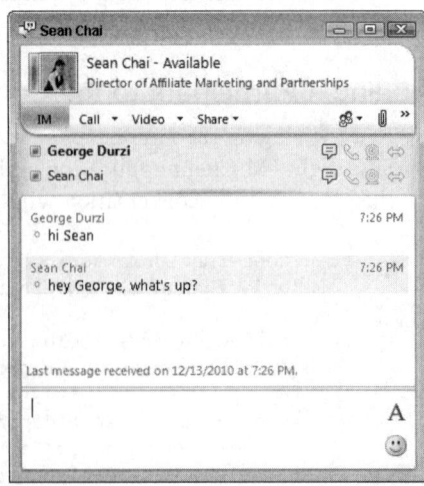

FIGURE 5-5

`Conversation.Modalities` or `Participant.Modalities`. The Silverlight IM Client application works with the Instant Message modality at the participant level. Calling `Conversation` `.AddParticipant` will cause the `ParticipantAdded` event to be fired; the `ParticipantAdded` event handler is where you wire up events specific to the Instant Message modality for that participant such as `InstantMessageReceived` and `IsTypingChanged`.

In the `ParticipantAdded` event handler, check first to verify that the participant being added is not the user who is currently signed in to Lync. You can then verify that the conversation includes the Instant Message modality by checking for the `ModalityTypes.InstantMessage` key in the `Modalities` dictionary that the `Conversation` class exposes. You can then wire up the event handlers for the `InstantMessageReceived` event and the `IsTypingChanged` event. The `InstantMessageReceived` event is raised when an instant message is received from that participant. The `IsTypingChanged` event is raised when the participant begins composing a message in the conversation window:

Available for download on Wrox.com

```
void Conversation_ParticipantAdded
    (object sender, ParticipantCollectionChangedEventArgs e)
{
    if (e.Participant.IsSelf == false)
    {
        if (((Conversation)sender).Modalities
            .ContainsKey(ModalityTypes.InstantMessage))
        {
            var imModality = e.Participant.Modalities
                [ModalityTypes.InstantMessage] as InstantMessageModality;

            imModality.InstantMessageReceived +=
                new EventHandler<MessageSentEventArgs>
                    (InstantMessageModality_InstantMessageReceived);

            imModality.IsTypingChanged +=
                new EventHandler<IsTypingChangedEventArgs>
                    (InstantMessageModality_IsTypingChanged);
        }
    }
}
```

Code snippet SilverlightIMClient\Page.xaml.cs

 The `InstantMessageModality` class inherits from the `Modality` base class; the `Modality` class exposes a `BeginConnect` method that you use to connect to a specific modality in a conversation. Unlike with the `AudioVideo` modality, you do not need to call `BeginConnect` to begin working with the `InstantMessageModality` — the modality is automatically accepted and usable as soon as you retrieve it from the `Modalities` collection of the `Conversation` or `Participant` object.

Note that the `ConversationWindow` *control is a custom control provided with the sample code in this chapter. It is not an official control in the Lync API.*

Sending Instant Messages

The Silverlight IM Client application implements a simple conversation window, as shown in Figure 5-6. The conversation window displays the name of the contact with whom you are having an instant message conversation, a history of the individual messages in the conversation, and a textbox to compose and send the message text.

Implementing a Custom Instant Message Class

The conversation window includes a ListBox that contains all the messages in the instant message conversation. The individual instant messages are represented by the `InstantMessage` class; this simple class exposes properties representing the date and time that the message was sent, who it was sent by, and the contents of the message:

FIGURE 5-6

Available for
download on
Wrox.com

```
public class InstantMessage
{
    public DateTime DateTimeSent { get; set; }
    public string Author { get; set; }
    public string MessageText { get; set; }

    public InstantMessage(
        DateTime dateTimeSent,
        string author,
        string messageText)
    {
        this.DateTimeSent = dateTimeSent;
        this.Author = author;
        this.MessageText = messageText;
    }
}
```

Code snippet SilverlightIMClient\Model\InstantMessage.cs

Implementing an Instant Message Notification Mechanism

The conversation window also needs to implement a notification mechanism to communicate with the underlying application to

➤ Notify the other participant in the conversation that the user is composing an instant message

➤ Send an instant message

➤ Receive notifications that the other participant is composing an instant message

➤ Receive an instant message

The Silverlight IM Client application uses the loosely coupled notification mechanism available in the MVVMLight toolkit to broadcast and process these notifications — this is implemented in the InstantMessageNotification class. The notification class exposes a ConversationId property to specify the conversation that the notification is intended for, a value of the Direction enumeration to specify whether the notification is incoming or outgoing, a Boolean to indicate whether the participant is in the process of composing a message, and an instance of InstantMessage containing the message being sent or received.

```
public enum Direction
{
    Incoming = 0,
    Outgoing
};

public class InstantMessageNotification : NotificationMessage
{
    public string ConversationId { get; set; }
    public Direction Direction { get; set; }
    public string Author { get; set; }
    public bool Composing { get; set; }
    public InstantMessage Message { get; set; }

    public InstantMessageNotification() : base(string.Empty) { }

    public InstantMessageNotification(
        string conversationId,
        string author,
        Direction direction,
        bool composing) : base(string.Empty)
    {
        this.ConversationId = conversationId;
        this.Author = author;
        this.Direction = direction;
        this.Composing = composing;
    }

    public InstantMessageNotification(
        string conversationId,
        string author,
        Direction direction,
```

```
            bool composing,
            InstantMessage message)
    : this(conversationId, author, direction, composing)
        {
            this.Message = message;
        }
```

Code snippet SilverlightIMClient\Notifications\InstantMessageNotification.cs

When the user is composing an instant message in the conversation window, the window broadcasts a notification letting the other participant know that the user is typing, as shown in Figure 5-7.

When the user presses the Enter key, the conversation window broadcasts a notification containing the text of the instant message. Because the user has completed typing, the notification also specifies that he is no longer composing the message:

FIGURE 5-7

Available for
download on
Wrox.com

```
void messageText_KeyDown(object sender, KeyEventArgs e)
{
    var messageAuthor = _lyncClient.Self.Contact.GetContactInformation
(ContactInformationType.DisplayName).ToString();

    if (e.Key == Key.Enter)
    {
        if (!String.IsNullOrEmpty(messageText.Text.Trim()))
        {
            var instantMessage = new InstantMessage(
                dateTimeSent: DateTime.Now,
                author: messageAuthor,
                messageText: messageText.Text.Trim());

            Messenger.Default.Send<InstantMessageNotification>(
                new InstantMessageNotification(
                    conversationId: this.ConversationId,
                    author: instantMessage.Author,
                    direction: Notifications.Direction.Outgoing,
                    composing: false,
                    message: instantMessage));

            this.Messages.Add(instantMessage);

            messageText.Text = string.Empty;
            messages.GetScrollHost().ScrollToBottom();
        }
    }
    else
    {
        Messenger.Default.Send<InstantMessageNotification>(
```

```
new InstantMessageNotification(
    conversationId: this.ConversationId,
    author: messageAuthor,
    direction: Notifications.Direction.Outgoing,
    composing: true));
}
```

Code snippet SilverlightIMClient\ConversationWindow.xaml.cs

The `Page` class in the Silverlight IM Client application subscribes to notifications of type `InstantMessageNotification` and executes the `Notification_InstantMessageComposing` handler when it receives a matching notification.

Available for download on Wrox.com

```
Messenger.Default.Register<InstantMessageNotification>(this,
    Notification_InstantMessagingComposing);
```

Code snippet SilverlightIMClient\Page.xaml.cs

When the application processes the notification, the first thing it needs to do is find the conversation that the notification is referring to — the application must make sure to send message composition notifications and instant messages to the appropriate conversation.

After retrieving the `InstantMessageModality` from the `Modalities` of the `Conversation`, the application checks the value of `Composing` in the `InstantMessageNotification` instance to determine whether the participant is in the process of composing an instant message.

As shown in the following code, if `Composing` is `false`, and the notification is for an outgoing instant message, the application calls the `InstantMessageModality.BeginSendMessage` method to send the instant message text packaged in the notification to the appropriate conversation. If `Composing` is `true`, the application calls the `InstantMessageModality.BeginSetComposing` method to notify the other participants in the conversation that the user is still typing.

Available for download on Wrox.oom

```
public void Notification_InstantMessagingComposing
(InstantMessageNotification notification)
{
    if (notification.Direction == Direction.Outgoing)
    {
        var conversation = _conversationManager.Conversations.Where(
            c => c.Properties[ConversationProperty.Id].ToString()
                == notification.ConversationId).FirstOrDefault();

        if (conversation != null)
        {
            var imModality = conversation.Modalities
                [ModalityTypes.InstantMessage] as InstantMessageModality;

            if (notification.Composing == false
                && !String.IsNullOrEmpty(notification.Message.MessageText))
            {
                imModality.BeginSendMessage(
                    notification.Message.MessageText,
```

```
                    sendMessageResult =>
                    {
                        imModality.EndSendMessage(sendMessageResult);
                    },
                    null);
            }

            if (imModality.CanInvoke(ModalityAction.SetIsTyping))
            {
                imModality.BeginSetComposing(
                    notification.Composing,
                    composingResult =>
                    {
                        imModality.EndSetComposing(composingResult);
                    },
                    null);
            }
        }
    }
}
```

Code snippet SilverlightIMClient\Page.xaml.cs

Receiving Instant Messages

In addition to displaying the history of instant messages between participants in the conversation, the custom conversation window in the Silverlight IM Client application notifies the user when other participants in the conversation are typing. When the remote participant finishes typing and sends the instant message, the application displays the message in the conversation window.

Processing Composition Notifications from Remote Participants

The `IsTypingChanged` changed event of the `InstantMessageModality` is raised when a remote participant in the conversation is in the process of composing an instant message. The instance of `IsTypingChangedEventArgs` in the `IsTypingChanged` event handler exposes an `IsTyping` property that indicates whether the remote participant is still typing. When the Silverlight IM Client application handles the `IsTypingChanged` event, it broadcasts an `InstantMessageNotification` to notify the other participants in the conversation if the participant that raised the event is still typing:

```
void InstantMessageModality_IsTypingChanged
(object sender, IsTypingChangedEventArgs e)
{
    var imModality = sender as InstantMessageModality;

    if (imModality != null)
    {
        Messenger.Default.Send<InstantMessageNotification>(
            new InstantMessageNotification(
                conversationId: imModality.Conversation.Properties
                    [ConversationProperty.Id].ToString(),
                author: imModality.Participant.Contact.GetContactInformation
```

```
                        (ContactInformationType.DisplayName).ToString(),
                    direction: Notifications.Direction.Incoming,
                    composing: e.IsTyping));
        }
    }
```

Code snippet SilverlightIMClient\Page.xaml.cs

The `ConversationWindow` control in the Silverlight IM Client application subscribes to notifications of type `InstantMessageNotification` and executes the `Notification_InstantMessageComposing` handler when it receives a matching notification:

Available for download on Wrox.com

```
Messenger.Default.Register<InstantMessageNotification>(this,
    Notification_InstantMessagingComposing);
```

Code snippet SilverlightIMClient\ConversationWindow.xaml.cs

When the `ConversationWindow` control processes the `InstantMessageNotification`, it checks whether the notification indicates that the remote participant is composing an instant message. If so, it displays a status message, as shown in Figure 5-8, to let the user know that the remote participant is typing.

The `ConversationWindow` control itself broadcasts and subscribes to notifications of type `InstantMessageNotification`; when processing an `InstantMessageNotification`, check the notification direction to ensure that the `ConversationWindow` processes only incoming notifications. If the notification includes an instant message, the application adds it to the `Messages` collection and displays it in the conversation window:

FIGURE 5-8

Available for download on Wrox.com

```
public void Notification_InstantMessagingComposing
(InstantMessageNotification notification)
{
    if (this.ConversationId == notification.ConversationId
        && notification.Direction == Direction.Incoming)
    {
        if (notification.Composing)
        {
            status.Text = String.Format("{0} is typing", notification.Author);
        }
        else
        {
            status.Text = string.Empty;
```

```
              if (notification.Message != null)
              {
                  this.Messages.Add(notification.Message);
              }
          }
      }
  }
```

Code snippet SilverlightIMClient\ConversationWindow.xaml.cs

Receiving Instant Messages from Remote Participants

When the participant finishes typing and sends the instant message, the `InstantMessageReceived` event of the `InstantMessageModality` is raised. The text of the instant message is available in the `Text` property of the instance of `MessageSentEventArgs` in the event handler. The application broadcasts a notification of type `InstantMessageNotification` that includes an instance of `InstantMessage` containing the instant message text.

```
void InstantMessageModality_InstantMessageReceived
(object sender, MessageSentEventArgs e)
{
    var imModality = sender as InstantMessageModality;

    if (imModality != null)
    {
        string author = imModality.Participant.Contact.GetContactInformation
                        (ContactInformationType.DisplayName).ToString();

        var instantMessage = new InstantMessage(
            dateTimeSent: DateTime.Now,
            author: author,
            messageText: e.Text);

        Messenger.Default.Send<InstantMessageNotification>(
            new InstantMessageNotification(
                conversationId: imModality.Conversation.Properties
                    [ConversationProperty.Id].ToString(),
                author: author,
                direction: Direction.Incoming,
                composing: false,
                message: instantMessage));
    }
}
```

Code snippet SilverlightIMClient\Page.xaml.cs

Terminating Instant Message Conversations

The Silverlight IM Client application can support simultaneous instant message conversations in multiple instances of the `ConversationWindow` control. When the user closes a conversation window, the application should also terminate the conversation in the window. When the user closes a conversation window in the Silverlight IM Client application, the ConversationWindow_ Unloaded event of the ConversationWindow control is raised. In the handler for the ConversationWindow_Unloaded event, the application broadcasts a notification of type ConversationRemovedNotification to notify any subscribers to this notification type that the conversation should be terminated:

```
void ConversationWindow_Unloaded(object sender, RoutedEventArgs e)
{
    Messenger.Default.Send<ConversationRemovedNotification>(
        new ConversationRemovedNotification(this.ConversationId));
}
```

Code snippet SilverlightIMClient\ConversationWindow.xaml.cs

The Silverlight IM Client application subscribes to notifications of type ConversationRemoved Notification. In the handler for the notification, the application disconnects any modalities in the conversation that are not disconnected. When all the modalities in a conversation are disconnected, the state of the conversation changes to ConversationState.Terminated. On every iteration through the modalities of the conversation, the application checks to ensure that conversation has not been terminated. When all the modalities of the conversation are disconnected, the conversation is automatically terminated and its properties become inaccessible — the Lync API will throw an exception if the application tries to access the Modalities collection of the conversation after it has been terminated.

```
public void Notification_ConversationRemoved
(ConversationRemovedNotification notification)
{
    var conversation = _conversationManager.Conversations.Where(
        c => c.Properties[ConversationProperty.Id].ToString()
            == notification.ConversationId).FirstOrDefault();

    if (conversation != null)
    {
        foreach (var modalityKey in conversation.Modalities.Keys)
        {
            if (conversation.State != ConversationState.Terminated)
            {
                if (conversation.Modalities[modalityKey] != null)
                {
                    if (conversation.Modalities[modalityKey].State
                        != ModalityState.Disconnected)
                    {
                        conversation.Modalities[modalityKey].BeginDisconnect(
                            ModalityDisconnectReason.None,
                            result =>
                            {
                                conversation.Modalities[modalityKey]
                                    .EndDisconnect(result);
                            },
```

```
                          null);
                   }
              }
         }
         else
              break;
      }
   }
}
```

When all the modalities in the conversation are disconnected and its state changes to `ConversationState.Terminated,` the `ConversationManager.ConversationRemoved` event is immediately raised. In the event handler for the `ConversationRemoved` event, the application removes the conversation from the collection of active conversations it is maintaining:

```
void ConversationManager_ConversationRemoved
(object sender, ConversationManagerEventArgs e)
{
    this.Dispatcher.BeginInvoke(
        new Action(() =>
            {
                _activeConversationIds.Remove(
                    e.Conversation.Properties[ConversationProperty.Id].ToString());
            }));
}
```

WORKING WITH THE AUDIOVIDEO MODALITY

Working with the Audio Video modality in a conversation is quite different than working with the Instant Message modality because Lync does all the heavy lifting after your application connects to the modality. In the previous section, you learned how to use the Instant Message modality to send messages to participants in the conversation, and to broadcast message-composing notifications so that participants know when someone else is composing an instant message. There is no such concept when working with the Audio Video modality; after you connect the audio, video, or both channels of the modality, audio and video automatically flow between the participants in the conversation. Unlike when composing an instant message, you are not responsible for capturing the audio or video and sending it to the other participants — all of that is taken care of automatically by Lync.

Another key difference between the Instant Message and Audio Video modalities is that you have to explicitly connect to the Audio Video modality in the conversation. You will recall that in the Silverlight IM Client application in the previous section, the Instant Message modality is automatically accepted by all the participants in the conversation and connected as soon as it is retrieved from the conversation's `Modalities` collection. When working with the Audio Video modality, your application has to connect to the modality before it is able to use it and access its audio and video channels.

The code that accompanies this chapter includes a WPF Kiosk application, shown in Figure 5-9, that demonstrates working with the Audio Video modality and its audio and video channels. The application demonstrates how to start audio and video calls and how to perform simple call control functionality with the Audio Video modality.

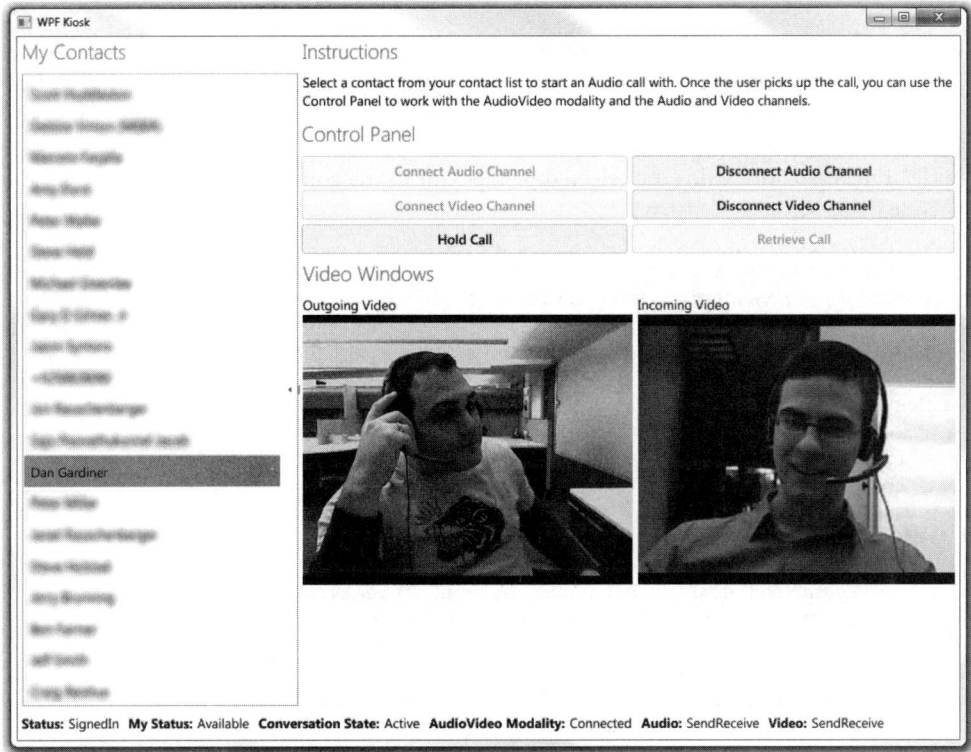

FIGURE 5-9

Starting Audio and Video Conversations

To start an audio conversation with a contact, the application creates a new conversation, adds a participant to the conversation, and then connects to the Audio Video modality of the conversation. The audio channel of the Audio Video modality is automatically started after the connection is established. After the application connects to the Audio Video modality, you can access the individual audio and video channels to start or stop them.

The WPF Kiosk application displays a list of the user's contacts; after selecting one of these contacts, the application verifies that the contact is available before adding a conversation to the ConversationManager instance available in the application.

Available for
download on
Wrox.com

```
var contact = (Contact)contactList.SelectedValue;

if ((ContactAvailability)contact.GetContactInformation
(ContactInformationType.Availability) != ContactAvailability.Offline)
{
    _conversationManager.AddConversation();
}
```

Code snippet WPFKiosk\Window1.xaml.cs

Adding a conversation to the `ConversationManager` instance causes the `ConversationManager`
`.ConversationAdded` event to fire. In the handler for the `ConversationAdded` event, the application
wires up handlers for the conversation's `ParticipantAdded` and `StateChanged` events. The
application also gets a handle to the Audio Video modality and wires up its `ModalityStateChanged`
event. Finally, the application adds the selected participant to the conversation, as shown in the
following code.

Available for
download on
Wrox.com

```
void ConversationManager_ConversationAdded
(object sender, ConversationManagerEventArgs e)
{
_conversation = e.Conversation;

    e.Conversation.BeginSetProperty(
        ConversationProperty.AutoTerminateOnIdle,
        false,
        result => { e.Conversation.EndSetProperty(result); },
        null);

    e.Conversation.ParticipantAdded +=
        new EventHandler<ParticipantCollectionChangedEventArgs>
            (Conversation_ParticipantAdded);

    e.Conversation.StateChanged +=
        new EventHandler<ConversationStateChangedEventArgs>
            (Conversation_StateChanged);

    if (e.Conversation.Modalities.ContainsKey(ModalityTypes.AudioVideo))
    {
        _avModality = e.Conversation.Modalities[ModalityTypes.AudioVideo]
                    as AVModality;

        _avModality.ModalityStateChanged +=
            new EventHandler<ModalityStateChangedEventArgs>
                (AVModality_ModalityStateChanged);
    }

    if (e.Conversation.CanInvoke(ConversationAction.AddParticipant))
    {
        this.Dispatcher.BeginInvoke(
            new Action(() =>
            {
```

```
                        e.Conversation.AddParticipant((Contact)contactList.SelectedValue);
                    }));
            }
        }
```

Later in this chapter, you learn how to distinguish between an outgoing and incoming conversation in the ConversationAdded event.

Understanding the AutoTerminateOnIdle Conversation Property

The WPF Kiosk application also sets the AutoTerminateOnIdle property of the new conversation to false. The AutoTerminateOnIdle property indicates whether the conversation will terminate when all of its modalities are no longer active. In conversations created by the Lync client, the AutoTerminateOnIdle property of the conversation is set to false by default; this allows the conversation to remain active as long as the Lync conversation window is open.

```
e.Conversation.BeginSetProperty(
    ConversationProperty.AutoTerminateOnIdle,
    false,
    result => { e.Conversation.EndSetProperty(result); },
    null);
```

When the Lync client is running in UI Suppression mode, new conversations are created with the AutoTerminateOnIdle property set to true by default. In the WPF Kiosk application, this causes the conversation to automatically terminate if the Audio Video modality becomes inactive. Setting the AutoTerminateOnIdle property of the conversation to false when in UI Suppression mode ensures that the application can still access the conversation and its properties after the Audio Video modality is no longer active. This allows the application to restart the audio or video channels of the modality because the conversation is not in a terminated state.

If a conversation contains both the Instant Message and Audio Video modalities, it will only terminate when both of the modalities become inactive. Setting the AutoTerminateOnIdle property to true ensures that the underlying conversation never enters a terminated state, allowing the application to connect to either modality again as needed. Note that in this case, when the application shuts down, it needs to explicitly terminate any active conversations by calling the End method of the conversation.

```
void Dispatcher_ShutdownStarted(object sender, EventArgs e)
{
    if (_conversation != null)
    {
        if (_conversation.State != ConversationState.Terminated)
        {
            _conversation.End();
        }
    }

    ...
}
```

Connecting to the Audio Video Modality

Like the Instant Message modality, the Audio Video modality is accessible either at the conversation or participant level. The WPF Kiosk application works with the Audio Video modality at the conversation level, and initially connects to it when a participant joins the conversation. You can connect to the Audio Video modality as long as the conversation itself is not in a terminated state and at least one other participant is in the conversation other than the logged-in user. The WPF Kiosk application also demonstrates how to disconnect from and reconnect to the audio and video channels in the Audio Video modality of the conversation.

To connect to the Audio Video modality, call the `BeginConnect` method on the `AVModality` object. In the asynchronous callback for the operation, wire up an event handler for the `ActionAvailability Changed` event of the `AVModality` class. You can now also get a handle to the `AudioChannel` and `VideoChannel` in the modality and wire up a hander for their `StateChanged` events.

Available for
download on
Wrox.com

```csharp
void Conversation_ParticipantAdded
(object sender, ParticipantCollectionChangedEventArgs e)
{
    if (e.Participant.IsSelf == false)
    {
        try
        {
            if (_avModality.CanInvoke(ModalityAction.Connect))
            {
                _avModality.BeginConnect(
                    result =>
                    {
                        _avModality.EndConnect(result);

                        _avModality.ActionAvailabilityChanged +=
                            new EventHandler
                                <ModalityActionAvailabilityChangedEventArgs>
                                (AVModality_ActionAvailabilityChanged);

                        _audioChannel = _avModality.AudioChannel;
                        _audioChannel.StateChanged +=
                            new EventHandler<ChannelStateChangedEventArgs>
                                (AudioChannel_StateChanged);

                        _videoChannel = _avModality.VideoChannel;
                        _videoChannel.StateChanged +=
                            new EventHandler<ChannelStateChangedEventArgs>
                                (VideoChannel_StateChanged);
                    },
                    null);
            }
        }
        catch (Exception)
        {
            throw;
        }
    }
}
```

Code snippet WPFKiosk\Window1.xaml.cs

When the Audio Video modality is connected, the audio channel is immediately started and an audio call is placed to the participant, as shown in Figure 5-10.

FIGURE 5-10

To disconnect the Audio Video modality in a conversation, call the `AVModality.BeginDisconnect` method and specify a value of the `ModalityDisconnectReason` enum.

Available for download on Wrox.com

```
if (_avModality.CanInvoke(ModalityAction.Disconnect))
{
    _avModality.BeginDisconnect(
        ModalityDisconnectReason.None,
        disconnectResult => { _avModality.EndDisconnect(disconnectResult); },
        null);
}
```

Code snippet WPFKiosk\Window1.xaml.cs

The `ModalityDisconnectReason` enum describes the reason for disconnecting the modality; its values include:

➤ `None`

➤ `Timeout`

➤ `Busy`

➤ `NotAcceptableHere`

➤ `Decline`

➤ `DeclineEverywhere`

➤ `ReplyOther`

Later in this section, you learn how to use the `ModalityDisconnectReason` enum to handle incoming calls that use the Audio Video modality.

Tracking Changes in the State of the Audio Video Modality

You can track changes in the state of the Audio Video modality in the handler for the `ModalityState Changed` event. The WPF Kiosk application uses the value of `ModalityStateChangedEventArgs .NewState` in the `ModalityStateChanged` event handler to display the current status of the Audio Video modality.

```
void AVModality_ModalityStateChanged
(object sender, ModalityStateChangedEventArgs e)
{
    this.Dispatcher.BeginInvoke(
        new Action(() =>
        {
            this.AudioVideoModalityStatus = e.NewState.ToString();
        }));
}
```

Code snippet WPFKiosk\Window1.xaml.cs

The valid states for the Audio Video modality are defined by the `ModalityState` enum; its values include:

- ➤ Disconnected
- ➤ Connecting
- ➤ Notified
- ➤ Joining
- ➤ ConnectingToCaller
- ➤ Connected
- ➤ Suspended
- ➤ OnHold
- ➤ Forwarding
- ➤ Transferring

Understanding Modality Actions

As the state of the Audio Video modality changes, different actions become available on the modality. These actions are defined by the `ModalityAction` enum and include the following values:

- ➤ Connect
- ➤ Disconnect
- ➤ SetProperty

➤ Hold

➤ Retrieve

➤ Forward

➤ RemoteTransfer

➤ ConsultAndTransfer

➤ SendInstantMessage

➤ SetIsTyping

➤ SetAudioEndpoint

➤ Accept

➤ Reject

➤ LocalTransfer

You can check whether an action is currently available on the modality by calling the `CanInvoke` method and specifying the `ModalityAction` to check for; for example:

```
if (_avModality.CanInvoke(ModalityAction.Connect))
    _avModality.BeginConnect( ...
else
    Console.Writeline("Can't connect to AVModality.");
```

 You should always use `CanInvoke` *to check whether a particular action is availability on the modality before performing the action. If the action is not available, you should notify the application and take an alternative action.*

The `Modality.ActionAvailabilityChanged` event is raised when the availability of a particular action on the modality changes. In the handler for the `ActionAvailabilityChanged` event, the WPF Kiosk application checks for the availability of certain actions and updates its user interface accordingly. The `ModalityActionAvailabilityChangedEventArgs` class exposes `Action` and `IsAvailable` properties that you can use to check whether a particular action is available.

Available for
download on
Wrox.com

```
void AVModality_ActionAvailabilityChanged(object sender,
ModalityActionAvailabilityChangedEventArgs e)
{
    this.Dispatcher.BeginInvoke(
        new Action(() =>
        {
            switch (e.Action)
            {
                case ModalityAction.Connect:
                    this.CanConnectAudioChannel = e.IsAvailable;
                    this.CanConnectVideoChannel = e.IsAvailable;
                    break;
```

```
                        case ModalityAction.Disconnect:
                            this.CanDisconnectAudioChannel = e.IsAvailable;
                            this.CanDisconnectVideoChannel = e.IsAvailable;
                            break;
                        case ModalityAction.Hold:
                            break;
                        case ModalityAction.Retrieve:
                            break;
                        case ModalityAction.Forward:
                            break;
                        case ModalityAction.RemoteTransfer:
                            break;
                        case ModalityAction.ConsultAndTransfer:
                            break;
                    };
                }));
    }
```

Code snippet WPFKiosk\Window1.xaml.cs

Starting the Audio Channel

You can start the audio channel manually by calling the `AudioChannel.BeginStart` method. This is useful when the Audio Video modality is still connected but the audio channel has been disconnected.

Various actions are available on the channel; these actions are defined by the `ChannelAction` enum and include the following values:

➤ Start

➤ Stop

➤ SendDtmf

Before starting the audio channel, you should use the `CanInvoke` method to check whether you can invoke the appropriate action on the channel.

```
void ConnectAudioChannel_Click(object sender, RoutedEventArgs e)
{
    if (_audioChannel.CanInvoke(ChannelAction.Start))
    {
        _audioChannel.BeginStart(
            result =>
            {
                _audioChannel.EndStart(result);
            },
            null);
    }
}
```

Code snippet WPFKiosk\Window1.xaml.cs

In the handler for the `AudioChannel.StateChanged` event, you can examine the state of the audio channel and enable or disable specific functionality in the application accordingly. The state of both the audio and video channels is represented by the `ChannelState` enum, whose values include:

➤ Connecting

➤ Notified

➤ Send

➤ Receive

➤ SendReceive

➤ Inactive

The WPF Kiosk application uses the state of the audio channel to enable and disable the buttons to control the audio and video channels of the Audio Video modality. For example, if the audio channel is in a `ChannelState.Connecting` state, the application doesn't allow the user to attempt to start the channel again.

Available for
download on
Wrox.com

```csharp
void AudioChannel_StateChanged(object sender, ChannelStateChangedEventArgs e)
{
    this.Dispatcher.BeginInvoke(
        new Action(() =>
        {
            switch (e.NewState)
            {
                case ChannelState.SendReceive:
                    this.CanDisconnectAudioChannel = true;
                    this.CanConnectVideoChannel =
                        _videoChannel.State == ChannelState.None ? true : false;
                    this.CanDisconnectVideoChannel = !this.CanConnectVideoChannel;
                    break;
                case ChannelState.Send:
                case ChannelState.Receive:
                case ChannelState.Notified:
                case ChannelState.Connecting:
                    this.CanConnectAudioChannel = false;
                    this.CanDisconnectAudioChannel = false;
                    this.CanConnectVideoChannel = false;
                    this.CanDisconnectVideoChannel = false;
                    break;
                case ChannelState.Inactive:
                    this.CanConnectAudioChannel = true;
                    this.CanDisconnectAudioChannel = false;
                    break;
                default:
                    break;
            };

            this.AudioChannelStatus = e.NewState.ToString();
        }));
}
```

Code snippet WPFKiosk\Window1.xaml.cs

The audio and video channels of the Audio Video modality are closely related; for example, the audio channel is automatically started when the video channel starts. Because the video functionality available from the video channel depends on the state of the audio channel, the WPF Kiosk application uses the handler for the `AudioChannel.StateChanged` event to enable or disable user interface elements used to control the video channel.

Call Control with the Audio Video Modality

The Audio Video modality provides simple call control functionality that includes the ability to:

➤ Place a call on hold and later retrieve it

➤ Send DTMF tones to a call

➤ Transfer a call

Actions taken on the Audio Video modality of a conversation can affect the Instant Message modality if it is also active in the conversation; for example, a conversation that includes both the Instant Message and Audio Video modality can be placed on hold or transferred.

Placing a Call on Hold

When issuing the `AVModality.BeginHold` command, the Instant Message modality is also put on hold if it is active in the conversation. If both the audio and video channels of the Audio Video modality active, they are placed on hold. To place a call on hold, first use `CanInvoke` to ensure that you can invoke the `Hold` modality action on the call, and then call the `AVModality.BeginHold` method to place the call on hold.

```
private void HoldCall_Click(object sender, RoutedEventArgs e)
{
    if (_avModality.CanInvoke(ModalityAction.Hold))
    {
        _avModality.BeginHold(
            result => { _avModality.EndHold(result); },
            null);
    }
}
```

Code snippet WPFKiosk\Window1.xaml.cs

When the call is placed on hold, a message is displayed to the participant in the Lync conversation window, as shown in Figure 5-11.

When a call is placed on hold:

➤ The state of the Audio Video modality changes to `OnHold`.

➤ The state of the audio channel changes to `Inactive`.

➤ If it is started, the state of the video channel also changes to `Inactive`.

FIGURE 5-11

To retrieve a call from hold, first use `CanInvoke` to ensure that you can invoke the `Retrieve` modality action on the call, and then call the `AVModality.BeginRetrieve` method to retrieve the call.

```
private void RetrieveCall_Click(object sender, RoutedEventArgs e)
{
    if (_avModality.CanInvoke(ModalityAction.Retrieve))
    {
        _avModality.BeginRetrieve(
            result => { _avModality.EndRetrieve(result); },
            null);
    }
}
```

Code snippet WPFKiosk\Window1.xaml.cs

When a call is retrieved from hold:

➤ The state of the Audio Video modality changes back to `Connected`.

➤ The state of the audio channel changes to `SendReceive`.

➤ If it was previously started, the state of the video channel changes to `Send`, `Receive`, or `SendReceive`, depending on its previous state.

Sending DTMF Tones

A custom communications application that uses Lync UI Suppression mode needs to provide an alternate mechanism for the user to send DTMF tones to a call. For example, a communications kiosk that allows a user to look up and dial employees in a company directory may require the user to use a number keypad to enter the extension to dial.

The number keypad in the Lync conversation window is not available in UI Suppression mode; the application needs to implement a custom number keypad control, and a mechanism to send DTMF tones to the audio channel of the Audio Video modality in the call.

You can implement a custom number keypad control that sends the DTMF tone to the audio channel of the call when the user presses a key on the keypad. After verifying that you can invoke the `SendDtmf` action on the audio channel, use the `AudioChannel.BeginSendDtmf` method to send a DTMF tone to the audio channel representing the key that the user pressed on the keypad:

```
if (_audioChannel.CanInvoke(ChannelAction.SendDtmf))
{
    _audioChannel.BeginSendDtmf(
        numericKeypad.PressedKey,
        result => { _audioChannel.EndSendDtmf(result); },
        null);
}
```

Working with Video

The Audio Video modality includes a video channel that you can use to broadcast and receive video from other participants. The video channel of the Audio Video modality relies heavily on the audio channel; the audio for the video channel is broadcast to all participants in the conversation via the audio channel. When starting the video channel of the Audio Video modality, the audio channel is started automatically if it isn't already. If the audio channel is stopped, the video channel is also stopped if it was previously started.

To start the video channel, first check whether you can invoke the `Start` channel action, and then call `VideoChannel.BeginStart`:

```csharp
void ConnectVideoChannel_Click(object sender, RoutedEventArgs e)
{
    if (_videoChannel.CanInvoke(ChannelAction.Start))
    {
        _videoChannel.BeginStart(
            result =>
            {
                _videoChannel.EndStart(result);
            },
            null);
    }
}
```

Code snippet WPFKiosk\Window1.xaml.cs

After the video channel is started, its status changes to `Send` and the recipient in the conversation sees the video you are broadcasting. If the recipient begins broadcasting video, the status of the video channel changes to `SendReceive` to indicate that you are sending and also receiving video across the video channel of the Audio Video modality.

To track changes in the state of the video channel, wire up a handler for its `StateChanged` event. In the handler for the `StateChanged` event, you can check the state of the video channel and display a `VideoWindow` control for incoming video, outgoing video, or both. The `VideoWindow` control is only available when Lync is running UI Suppression mode.

> *The `VideoWindow` control is not a Lync control; it is a native Win32 control, and is available in the `Microsoft.Lync.Model.Conversation.AudioVideo` namespace. Recall that the Lync controls are not available when Lync is running in UI Suppression mode.*

Calling `VideoChannel.CaptureVideoWindow` control returns an instance of the `VideoWindow` control representing the video being broadcast by the user currently signed in to Lync. Calling `VideoChannel.RenderVideoWindow` returns an instance of the `VideoWindow` control for the video being broadcast by the other participant in the conversation.

```csharp
void VideoChannel_StateChanged
(object sender, ChannelStateChangedEventArgs e)
{
    this.Dispatcher.BeginInvoke(
```

```
                new Action(() =>
                {
                    this.VideoChannelStatus = e.NewState.ToString();

                    if ((e.NewState == ChannelState.Send
                        || e.NewState == ChannelState.SendReceive)
                        && _videoChannel.CaptureVideoWindow != null)
                    {
                        ShowVideo(windowsFormsPanelOutgoingVideo,
                            _videoChannel.CaptureVideoWindow);
                    }

                    if ((e.NewState == ChannelState.Receive
                        || e.NewState == ChannelState.SendReceive)
                        && _videoChannel.RenderVideoWindow != null)
                    {
                        ShowVideo(windowsFormsPanelIncomingVideo,
                            _videoChannel.RenderVideoWindow);
                    }

                }));
    }
```

Code snippet WPFKiosk\Window1.xaml

Because the `VideoWindow` control is a native Win32 control, you need to host it in a Windows Forms Panel control that is inside a `WindowsFormsHost` control in the XAML.

Available for
download on
Wrox.com

```
<TextBlock>Outgoing Video</TextBlock>
<interop:WindowsFormsHost x:Name="windowsFormsHostOutgoingVideo">
<forms:Panel x:Name="windowsFormsPanelOutgoingVideo"/>
</interop:WindowsFormsHost>

<TextBlock>Incoming Video</TextBlock>
<interop:WindowsFormsHost x:Name="windowsFormsHostIncomingVideo">
<forms:Panel x:Name="windowsFormsPanelIncomingVideo"/>
</interop:WindowsFormsHost>
```

Code snippet WPFKiosk\Window1.xaml.cs

To show the `VideoWindow`, you need to place it in a Windows Forms Panel control, and then set its position and style.

Available for
download on
Wrox.com

```
// From AudioVideoConversation sample application in Lync SDK
void ShowVideo(System.Windows.Forms.Panel videoPanel, VideoWindow videoWindow)
{
    //Win32 constants:               WS_CHILD | WS_CLIPCHILDREN | WS_CLIPSIBLINGS;
    const long lEnableWindowStyles = 0x40000000L | 0x02000000L | 0x04000000L;
    //Win32 constants:               WS_POPUP| WS_CAPTION | WS_SIZEBOX
    const long lDisableWindowStyles = 0x80000000 | 0x00C00000 | 0x00040000L;
    const int OATRUE = -1;

    try
```

```
    {
        //sets the properties required for the native video window to draw itself
        videoWindow.Owner = videoPanel.Handle.ToInt32();
        videoWindow.SetWindowPosition(0, 0, videoPanel.Width, videoPanel.Height);

        //gets the current window style to modify it
        long currentStyle = videoWindow.WindowStyle;

        //disables borders, sizebox, close button
        currentStyle = currentStyle & ~lDisableWindowStyles;

        //enables styles for a child window
        currentStyle = currentStyle | lEnableWindowStyles;

        //updates the current window style
        videoWindow.WindowStyle = (int)currentStyle;

        //updates the visibility
        videoWindow.Visible = OATRUE;
    }
    catch (Exception exception)
    {
        throw(exception);
    }
}
```

Code snippet WPFKiosk\Window1.xaml.cs

The WPF Kiosk application renders incoming and outgoing video, as shown in Figure 5-12.

FIGURE 5-12

Handling Incoming Audio and Video Conversations

An application that works with Lync running in UI Suppression mode may need to provide the user with an interface to initiate and receive instant message and audio or video calls. This section describes how to handle incoming instant message and audio or video conversations.

Evaluating the Direction of the Conversation

The `ConversationManager.ConversationAdded` event is raised by an outgoing or incoming conversation; however, the event doesn't expose a way of checking the direction of the new conversation. Instead, you must rely on checking the status of the individual modalities in the conversation.

Recall that the Instant Message modality is automatically accepted by all the participants in a conversation; so when checking the state of the Instant Message modality in the `ConversationAdded` event, the conversation is incoming if the state of the Instant Message modality is `Connected`.

The Audio Video modality is not automatically accepted by the participants in the conversation; so the conversation is incoming if the state of the Audio Video modality is `Notified`.

```
void ConversationManager_ConversationAdded
    (object sender, ConversationManagerEventArgs e)
{
    _conversation = e.Conversation;

    _isIncomingAVConversation = false;

    if (_conversation.Modalities.ContainsKey(ModalityTypes.AudioVideo)
        && _conversation.Modalities[ModalityTypes.AudioVideo].State
        == ModalityState.Notified)
    {
        _isIncomingAVConversation= true;
    }

    ...
    if (_isIncomingAVConversation)
    {
        ...
    }
}
```

Code snippet WPFKiosk\Window1.xaml.cs

Working with Audio and Video Devices

If the state of the Audio Video modality is `Notified`, you have to explicitly handle and accept the incoming call. However, before accepting the call, you must ensure that the user has the necessary audio or video hardware available to handle the call.

The `LyncClient` class exposes a `DeviceManager` class that you can use to query the audio and video devices that are installed on the user's machine. The `DeviceManager` class exposes an `ActiveAudioDevice` and `ActiveVideoDevice` property that allows you to get a handle to the active audio or video device on the machine. If an active audio device is present, call `AVModality.Accept` to accept the incoming call, and `AVModality.BeginConnect` to connect to the Audio Video modality.

If no active audio device is present, call `AVModality.Reject` to reject the call; you need to also provide a `ModalityDisconnectReason` — in this case, use `NotAcceptableHere` to indicate that the user doesn't have the hardware required to accept the incoming call.

```
void ConversationManager_ConversationAdded
(object sender, ConversationManagerEventArgs e)
{

    ...

    if (_isIncomingAVConversation)
    {
        if (_lyncClient.DeviceManager.ActiveAudioDevice != null)
        {
            if (_avModality.CanInvoke(ModalityAction.Connect))
            {
                _avModality.Accept();
                _avModality.BeginConnect(
                    result => { _avModality.EndConnect(result); },
                    null);
            }
        }
        else
        {
            _avModality.Reject(ModalityDisconnectReason.NotAcceptableHere);

            throw new Exception("No active audio device.");
        }
    }

    ...

}
```

Code snippet WPFKiosk\Window1.xaml.cs

If you also need to ensure that the user has an active video device before accepting the call, verify that `LyncClient.DeviceManager.ActiveVideoDevice` is not null.

The `DeviceManager` class also exposes `AudioDevices` and `VideoDevices` collections that contain a list of `Microsoft.Lync.Model.Device.Device` objects. You can iterate through the collections to get or set the active audio or video device if more than one audio or video device is on the user's machine.

SUMMARY

When running the Lync client in UI Suppression mode, you can build a new class of communications applications that don't rely on the Lync user interface to provide communications capabilities. UI Suppression mode gives you the ability to build such applications without having to work with a lower level API such as the UCC API; the Lync client is still the user endpoint that connects to the Microsoft Lync Server 2010 infrastructure — its user interface is just not visible.

When the Lync client is running in UI Suppression mode, you have to start conversations at the individual modality level because `Automation` and the Lync controls are not available. Using the Lync API, you can work with the Instant Message and Audio Video modalities to create conversations; add participants; and start instant message, audio, or video calls.

The next chapter introduces you to building server-side communications applications with the Unified Communications Managed API 3.0 (UCMA). Unlike the Lync API, UCMA applications are typically long-running processes hosted in a Windows or Windows Communications Foundation (WCF) service. UCMA applications can be used to run back office operations such as help desks, call centers, or virtual personal assistants.

Introduction to the Unified Communications Managed API

WHAT'S IN THIS CHAPTER

➤ Building server-side Lync applications with UCMA

➤ Working with Session Initiation Protocol

➤ Using basic UCMA classes

➤ Applying coding best practices for UCMA applications

➤ Deploying UCMA applications

Think of Microsoft Lync Server 2010 as a sort of technological iceberg. On the surface, it is a revolutionary enterprise voice and unified communications platform that makes powerful communication capabilities easy and inexpensive to deploy in organizations of any size. Dig a bit deeper, and you find that it has fantastic integration with other Microsoft products, such as Exchange, Outlook, SharePoint, the Office suite, Dynamics CRM, and others.

This integration capability alone would make Lync Server 2010 a compelling product. But many people are unaware of the enormous range of customization that is possible with the server-side extensibility platform that is built into Lync Server. The Unified Communications Managed API, commonly known as UCMA, is the large and powerful chunk of Lync Server 2010 that is usually hidden below the surface.

Using this API, developers can build communication-enabled applications that can facilitate special communication scenarios such as automatic call distribution for contact centers, interactive voice response applications, call monitoring and billing solutions, middle-tier communications clients, and many others. Even better, UCMA provides a layer of abstraction over the complexities of connection management and messaging, so that developers can concentrate on solving business problems.

The following chapters attempt to take you on progressively deeper dives below the water to see the full extent of the customization that you can accomplish with Lync Server using UCMA.

Each chapter, besides describing generally what a UCMA feature can do, pulls back the layers of abstraction to show you what happens under the surface in Session Initiation Protocol (SIP) messages when a UCMA operation is executing. The chapters also show UCMA capabilities as much as possible in context, so that you can understand how they can fit into the real-world applications you may need to develop.

UCMA 3.0 is the current version of the API that ships with Lync Server 2010. Throughout the following chapters, the authors highlight features that are new in UCMA 3.0, for the benefit of readers who have experience building applications using previous versions of the API.

This chapter initiates you into the wonderful world of UCMA, beginning with a short overview of Session Initiation Protocol, the language spoken by Lync Server 2010, and then a sort of whirlwind tour of what UCMA applications can do and some key points of development and deployment.

WHAT IS A UCMA APPLICATION?

In theory, you could create server-side applications that interact with Lync Server by opening a TCP connection with the server yourself in code, constructing the necessary SIP messages manually, line by line, listening for the responses, and parsing them. This would be a bit like building a new telephone from spare parts every time you want to make a phone call.

As an example, here are the individual low-level steps you would need to go through, even in the simplest case, to initiate an audio call:

1.   Send an `INVITE` request to the proxy server for the target user agent.

2.   Include some SDP (Session Description Protocol) in the message body to negotiate how media should be sent back and forth.

3.   Receive a `100 Trying` message from the proxy server.

4.   Receive a `180 Ringing` message from the proxy server after the call is ringing to the user you are calling.

5.   Receive a `200 OK` when the user has answered the call.

6.   Look at the SDP in the `200 OK` and decide whether the media parameters are acceptable.

7.   Send an `ACK` message to acknowledge the `200 OK`.

8.   Begin sending audio media in Real-Time Transport Protocol (RTP) format to the other user agent.

9.   Begin receiving audio media in RTP format from the other user agent.

What Does UCMA Do?

The Unified Communications Managed API, also known as UCMA, saves you all of this trouble by abstracting away all the messy details of SIP signaling, so that the entire sequence of messages that two user agents exchange to initiate an audio call becomes a single asynchronous method like this one:

```
// Start the call.
_call.BeginEstablish(OnEstablishCompleted, null);
```

This saves your intellectual energy for the code that is specific to the scenario you are trying to enable or the other components with which you want to integrate your call control code.

UCMA adds this level of abstraction by means of a collection of classes that handle the various aspects of unified communications. The actual SIP signaling goes on under the covers. These high-level classes make diving right into unified communications development easy.

Server-side Uses

The primary purpose of UCMA is to allow developers to build server-side Unified Communications applications that extend Lync Server. These fall into two general categories: middle-tier client applications and highly available multi-user services.

The Lync Web App (formerly known as Communicator Web Access) is a great example of a middle-tier client application. This type of application acts as a sort of proxy for clients, allowing users to perform Lync operations through an interface that is hosted on a server rather than a client application on the user's PC. A middle-tier client could be a web application, a web service, a voice-activated application, or even something else entirely.

The other common use of UCMA is to provide services that extend Lync in some way to many users at once. An example is conference recording: With UCMA, a developer can easily create an application with a Lync contact that users can invite to conferences to have them recorded. UCMA takes care of needs such as high availability, resiliency, and connection pooling so that developers do not need to reinvent each of these capabilities for every new application.

Client-side Uses

UCMA can work in conjunction with the client-side extensibility APIs, discussed in the previous chapters, to dynamically provide a wide variety of types of context to users in the Lync client.

Also, UCMA can simulate a large number of clients for load-testing purposes.

Finally, although UCMA is primarily intended as a server-side API, building some types of client-side applications with this API is possible, as long as the UCMA runtime is installed on every computer that will run the application.

 Unlike previous versions of the API, UCMA 3.0 supports only the 64-bit versions of Windows. There is no 32-bit version of the UCMA 3.0 SDK available.

Integration with Non-Microsoft SIP Platforms

Lync Server 2010 and UCMA 3.0 can interoperate with other SIP platforms in certain cases. UCMA 3.0 applications can route two-party audio calls to and from an IP-PBX or gateway if its SIP domain is configured as a trusted SIP domain for the application's collaboration platform. Audio is the only supported modality; interoperation with instant messaging and conferencing is not supported.

SESSION INITIATION PROTOCOL IN BRIEF

To initiate and control calls and other communication sessions, Microsoft Lync Server uses a somewhat extended version of the *Session Initiation Protocol*, commonly known as SIP. SIP is one of the three relatively standard protocols that are used in Internet telephony and in other unified communications solutions. The others are *H.323*, which is the oldest of the three protocols, and *IAX*, which is specific to the open-source VoIP (Voice over Internet Protocol) platform *Asterisk*.

SIP is defined in RFC 3261, a so-called Request for Comments document written by the Internet Engineering Task Force (IETF). It was intended to standardize the initiation of VoIP calls across different platforms, and it allows interoperation between servers and devices from different vendors. Although Lync Server adds a number of its own Microsoft-specific features to SIP, forming what you can think of as a SIP dialect, Lync Server 2010 and UCMA 3.0 supports interoperation with non-Microsoft SIP platforms for basic voice calls.

 Although SIP plays many important roles in communication sessions, it does not carry the actual audio for voice calls. For this purpose, Lync Server uses another protocol, Real-time Transport Protocol (RTP), discussed later.

A number of excellent books cover the Session Initiation Protocol in great detail, so the authors won't attempt to rehash those in their entirety here. However, several SIP concepts are important to a full understanding of how Lync Server works behind the scenes.

SIP User Agents

In SIP-based communications, the senders and recipients are known as *user agents*, or UAs for short. During each SIP transaction, one endpoint acts as the server (the *user agent server*, or UAS) and the other acts as the client (the *user agent client*, or UAC). Generally speaking, any SIP endpoint can act at different times as both a client and a server, just as any normal phone can both send and receive calls.

In Lync Server, the Communicator application acts as a user agent on an individual PC. SIP phones and voicemail boxes are also user agents, and nearly any UCMA application you build will need to function as a user agent (or multiple user agents). In fact, if it had a TCP/IP connection to the Lync Server domain and spoke proper SIP, your nose hair trimmer could register with the server as a user agent and send and receive SIP messages.

Although sending messages to one another directly is entirely possible for user agents, they need to know the exact network location of the target user agent to do this. To relieve individual user agents of the burden of keeping track of each other user agent and following its every move, SIP introduces two other roles: the proxy and the registrar.

SIP Proxies and Registrars

In Lync Server, the SIP proxy and the SIP registrar are alter egos; although they have different names and different (though related) roles, they are performed by the same server. In a nutshell, the registrar receives a message from a user agent telling its current location, and stores this information in a directory. The proxy receives incoming communication requests that are intended for a specific user agent, optionally authenticates the requestor, looks up its location and registration status in the directory, and either denies the request, responds that the recipient is not available, or routes the request.

Registration

Imagine a busy lawyer with a thriving international law practice. This lawyer, although she travels frequently and is difficult to reach, is lucky enough to have a top-notch secretary who knows her travel schedule and her important contacts down to the letter. Because she is too busy to field unsolicited calls from photocopier salesmen, Jane (the lawyer) never gives out any of her phone numbers or email addresses. Instead, anyone who needs to reach her calls the secretary.

Whenever she arrives in a new location, Jane sends a message from her phone to her secretary (let's call her Roxanne, or Roxie for short) saying, for instance, "Arrived Slovakia. Send calls to Ljubljana office until 1pm EST."

While she is still around, she sends a regular update so the secretary knows she is still available: "Still in Ljubljana. Send calls here until 2pm EST."

If she gets on a plane and won't be able to take any calls, Jane sends a message to "sign off," so the secretary knows not to send her any more calls.

Jane might even give her secretary multiple places to reach her: "Arrived. Send calls to Beirut office or Lebanese cell number."

This is more or less how SIP registration works in Lync Server. Every user agent that wants to receive communication requests and other messages from the proxy server is responsible for registering with the SIP registrar (in this case, the front-end server) by means of a REGISTER message. The message specifies the user agent's current IP address along with some other information on its status.

The Proxy

Every day, hundreds of calls come in for Jane. Before she sends a call anywhere, Roxie asks a few questions to determine the caller's identity. She politely rebuffs any unwanted callers, be they photocopier salesmen, competitors fishing for information, or neurotic ex-lovers, telling them, in a gentle but firm voice, "403 Forbidden," which is SIP for "I'm sorry, she's not available. I'll let her know you called."

To those wrong number callers who hesitantly ask whether they've reached Jane's Drains and Sinks, Roxie calmly says, "404 Not Found," sending them on their way.

Sometimes the caller is someone Jane would want to speak with, but she is on a plane and can't take calls. In these cases, Roxie can either ask the caller to call back, or send the call along to Jane's voicemail box.

Finally, if an important call comes in and Jane has registered with Roxie saying she is available, Roxie lets the caller know she is trying to put the call through to Jane, and rings all the phones Jane has registered. If Jane answers one of the phones, Roxie puts the call through.

Roxie is doing basically what a SIP proxy server does. The proxy server (which is the front-end server in Lync Server) receives SIP requests for user agents, authenticates the clients if necessary, and then proxies the request to the destination as well as the response back to the client.

SIP Methods and Responses

The foundation of SIP is defined in RFC 3261, which includes six standard SIP methods. When SIP was originally conceived, it was meant for the much more specific purpose of initiating VoIP calls, and it has gradually been applied to other communications functions such as presence, multi-modal communication sessions, sending instant messages, and conferencing, necessitating extensions to the original specification. On top of this, Lync Server adds a few of its own proprietary extensions to the SIP protocol.

SIMPLE is a protocol that was devised to handle the new functions of presence management and instant messaging that were not supported by the original SIP protocol. Lync Server uses SIMPLE as part of its own brand of SIP; you may see the term SIP/SIMPLE to describe this pairing. SIMPLE, in case you are curious, stands for "SIP for Instant Messaging and Presence Leveraging Extensions," which is a mouthful, especially if you read out SIP as separate words. Reciting it in a deep voice can be effective at warding off anyone who challenges your technical knowledge, as well as feral animals.

Although Lync Server treats its own SIP progeny and the ones it adopted from the RFCs perfectly equally, knowing which MS-SIP features are proprietary is useful. These features are highlighted as they come up in discussions of SIP operations.

SIP Methods in Lync Server

Table 6-1 shows all the standard SIP methods that are supported by Lync Server.

TABLE 6-1: Standard SIP Methods Supported By Lync Server

METHOD NAME	PURPOSE	WHERE DEFINED
INVITE	Requests a SIP signaling session with another user agent.	RFC 3261
ACK	Acknowledges a request or response from another agent.	RFC 3261
CANCEL	Requests the cancellation of a SIP request that has already been sent before it is accepted by the remote user agent.	RFC 3261
BYE	Requests the termination of a SIP signaling session that is in progress.	RFC 3261
REGISTER	Requests that the SIP registrar register the user agent's current network location so that requests coming from other user agents can be routed.	RFC 3261
OPTIONS	Requests information on the capabilities of a SIP server.	RFC 3261
SUBSCRIBE	Requests ongoing notification of a specified type of events, such as presence changes.	RFC 3265
NOTIFY	Informs subscribers that an event has occurred.	RFC 3265
MESSAGE	Carries some type of message, which can be either text or another content type, to another user agent.	RFC 3428
INFO	Carries a session control message that does not change the session state to another user agent.	RFC 2976
REFER	Requests the other user agent in an existing session to issue a new SIP INVITE to a specific user agent (generally for a transfer).	RFC 3515

Any SIP-enabled device should support at least the methods defined in RFC 3261, and many support the methods defined in the other RFCs. The methods shown in Table 6-2, however, are very rarely supported by SIP platforms other than Lync Server.

TABLE 6-2: SIP Methods Specific to Lync Server

METHOD NAME	PURPOSE
BENOTIFY	Informs subscribers that an event has occurred without requiring any response.
SERVICE	Requests a service provided by the server.

UCMA 3.0 provides access in some way to each of the SIP methods described here, and we will discuss how the methods work in a bit more detail in later chapters.

SIP Responses in Lync Server

Most SIP methods (the one significant exception being BENOTIFY) require the recipient to send a response back to the sender. These responses are very similar to the standard HTTP responses, although they have different meanings in the SIP world. Each one begins with a three-digit response code, with the first digit between 1 and 6, followed by a short plain-text description of the response.

Table 6-3 shows some of the more common SIP response codes used by Lync Server.

TABLE 6-3: Common SIP Responses

SIP STATUS CODE	ENGLISH TRANSLATION
100 Trying	I'm trying to route your request.
180 Ringing	It's ringing, and we're waiting for the user to accept.
183 Session Progress	Something's changed, but we're still waiting for the user to accept.
200 OK	Okay, I accept your call.
202 Accepted	Got your message. (MESSAGE requests don't require a SIP session to be created, so there's no 200 OK.)
301 Moved Permanently	Update your address book.
302 Moved Temporarily	This user is taking calls somewhere else for a while.
400 Bad Request	I didn't understand your request.
401 Unauthorized	I need you to authenticate before you can register.
403 Forbidden	"I'm sorry, Dave. I'm afraid I can't do that."
404 Not Found	No such user.
407 Proxy Authentication Required	I need you to authenticate before you can send requests.
408 Request Timeout	The user couldn't send a response fast enough.
480 Temporarily Unavailable	Can't take your call right now.
481 Call/Transaction Does Not Exist	You're telling me to do something with a call that doesn't exist or already ended.
484 Address Incomplete	This isn't a valid SIP address.
486 Busy Here	The user is already on a call at this particular network location.

SIP STATUS CODE	ENGLISH TRANSLATION
488 Not Acceptable Here	This user can't do what you're asking for.
500 Server Internal Error	Something's wrong with the server.
503 Service Unavailable	The proxy server is down or not available.
504 Server Timeout	I was trying to reach another server and it didn't respond.
603 Decline	I don't want to take your call.

You can perform almost any operation in UCMA 3.0 without using these codes at all, but you will find them in exception details and in the response data from call control operations if you inspect it under a powerful microscope. There's certainly no need to memorize the codes, but a basic familiarity with what they mean and which ones are bad news will take you a long way in some of the trickier troubleshooting situations.

If you want to be cool and cutting-edge, consider answering your phone with the words "200 OK." It's very trendy, and, paired with a stylish hat, will get you into some of the most exclusive clubs.

How Is Lync Server Different from Other Platforms?

At this point, you may be wondering what differentiates Lync Server 2010 from other SIP-based communications platforms. This question has many answers, including some concerning call quality, security, and the like, but from the perspective of what you can do with the Unified Communications Managed API, you can take note of a few features as they come up later in this chapter: multi-modal communication sessions, enhanced presence, and powerful conferencing capabilities.

One noteworthy technical feature that distinguishes Lync from most SIP-based telephony platforms is that Lync uses TCP to transmit SIP messages, while most other platforms use UDP. This is important to keep in mind when integrating Lync applications with other SIP platforms.

UCMA BASIC CONCEPTS

This section serves as a sort of primer on the fundamentals of the Unified Communications Managed API. The classes and concepts described here come up frequently in the following chapters on UCMA, and so spending a bit of time understanding them before delving in to the various capabilities of UCMA is worthwhile.

The Collaboration Platform

The foundation of any UCMA application is an instance of the `CollaborationPlatform` class, which manages connections with Lync Server, as well as other resources that are shared between all the user agents created by the application.

Any application that will use the UC Managed API must have an instance of the `CollaborationPlatform` class. Depending on the purpose of the application, it will use either `ClientPlatformSettings`, `ProvisionedApplicationPlatformSettings`, or `ServerPlatformSettings` to supply the configuration values for the collaboration platform.

Chapter 7 goes into the details of creating and configuring a collaboration platform and describes the steps in starting it up.

Client Platforms

Although UCMA is primarily a server-side API, one situation in which it can be useful is for building client-side applications. To load-test server applications, having many clients connected to the application at once is usually necessary. This is difficult to do with Communicator, because each instance of Communicator allows only one user to be signed in. A collaboration platform initialized with `ClientPlatformSettings` can use only user endpoints and cannot perform any trusted operations. However, it can be used in an application without any provisioning (that is, objects do not need to be created in the Lync central management store for the application).

Server Platforms

By far the majority of UCMA applications use a server platform, which allows them to perform trusted operations. To initialize the collaboration platform with `ServerPlatformSettings`, your application must have its own trusted application object in the central management store (see Chapter 7 for details). Unlike client platforms, server platforms have the option of using transport layer security (TLS) for all SIP signaling rather than ordinary TCP, as long as the server on which the application runs has a certificate that it can use to authenticate itself to Lync Server. Using TLS is a good idea in almost all cases for security reasons.

Endpoints

The network endpoints that UCMA applications use for their user agents are represented in code by instances of the `UserEndpoint` or the `ApplicationEndpoint` class, which, with the assistance of some other related classes, handle all operations that concern a single user agent. The individual endpoints are tied to the collaboration platform, which can have any number of endpoints associated with it.

Although the terms represent slightly different concepts, UCMA developers use the term endpoint *more or less interchangeably with* user agent *when talking about unified communications applications. In this book you'll mostly see the terms* Lync Server endpoints *or just* endpoints *during discussions about the specifics of UCMA code.*

In theory, a UCMA application can run without any endpoints, but it would not be able to serve any useful purpose, because the application would have no SIP user agents with which to send or receive messages. Therefore, any useful UCMA application will, when starting up, initialize and establish at least one user endpoint or application endpoint. Each class is appropriate for a somewhat different type of UCMA application.

When to Use a UserEndpoint

The `UserEndpoint` class allows an application to perform communication operations on behalf of a single Lync Server user (a User object in Active Directory). When established, the user endpoint always registers with Lync Server and retrieves presence and contact information for the specified user. Through the `UserEndpoint` class, you can perform contact and contact group operations as well as publish a presence using a presence grammar (both of which are covered in later chapters), but because the user endpoint represents a single user, an application cannot use it to perform trusted operations such as impersonating another Lync Server user.

Acting on Behalf of One or More Users

The `UserEndpoint` class is best suited for an application that acts on behalf of a number of different existing users simultaneously. Some common examples are

➤ Load testing applications

➤ Voice mail systems

➤ Web-based client applications (like Communicator Web Access)

Contact and Group Operations

Because contact lists are only available for full-fledged Lync users (not server application contacts) any application that performs contact list operations must use the `UserEndpoint` class.

Presence Publishing Using Grammars

Publishing presence information for a user is simplified by the `UserEndpoint` class, because it can take advantage of grammar-based presence publication, which automatically assigns access control information and instance IDs to presence elements.

The user endpoint is not as robust in recovering from connection failures as the application endpoint, so it is less appropriate for server applications that must be highly available. When a user endpoint loses connectivity with Lync Server, it attempts to re-register with Lync Server once, but if this attempt fails it gives up and makes no further attempts to recover the connection. Applications that must weather temporary losses of connectivity should use the application endpoint.

When to Use an Application Endpoint

The `ApplicationEndpoint` class is meant for highly available server applications that provide a service to many different users simultaneously. Because it does not represent an individual user, it has a separate identity defined by a `Contact` object in Active Directory.

Automated Communications Services

Common examples of applications for which the `ApplicationEndpoint` class is appropriate include:

➤ Interactive voice response (IVR) systems

➤ Automatic call distributors

➤ Message broadcasting or alert applications

➤ Conference recording services

Impersonation and Other Trusted Operations

Because an application endpoint is automatically trusted by Lync Server, it is able to "impersonate" any individual user in order to perform communications operations on behalf of that user. The trust relationship also frees the endpoint from the connection throttling that is normally imposed on endpoints by Lync Server.

Providing Services to a Conference

The application endpoint's trusted status with Lync server allows it to perform conference operations that would otherwise be restricted to conference leaders, as well as some special operations that cannot be performed at all through the Lync client. It can also join conferences as a trusted participant; in this state, it is not shown in the conference roster and has the same rights as a conference leader.

The `ApplicationEndpoint` class is able to load-balance connections across several front-end servers. In addition, it is more persistent than the `UserEndpoint` class in recovering connectivity with Lync Server. When an application endpoint loses its connection to Lync Server, it goes into the `Reestablishing` state and tries to regain its connection with the server until it succeeds, regardless of how long it remains without a connection.

Application endpoints are not able to perform any contact operations, nor can they publish presence with a presence grammar. Applications that need to do either of these should use the `UserEndpoint` class.

Conversations and Calls

In theory, an adventurous developer with plenty of time to spare could build a .NET application that acts as a SIP user agent without using UCMA at all. It would need to open and manage the necessary TCP connections on its own, receive incoming connections, build SIP messages to send to other user agents, and parse incoming SIP messages, extracting the necessary information from the headers and the message body.

In most cases, however, the repetitive steps of establishing a connection, building SIP messages with the proper headers, and keeping track of SIP session state would be a distraction from the more varied business logic that needs to go into complex unified communications applications.

UCMA 3.0 takes those low-level signaling responsibilities off of developers' hands, so that they can concentrate on the higher-level functions of the application, while allowing access to technical details such as SIP headers, signaling, and media negotiation where finer-grained control is necessary.

Communication Between Local and Remote Endpoints

Just as the `UserEndpoint` and `ApplicationEndpoint` classes abstract away the low-level details of maintaining a SIP user agent, the `Conversation` class abstracts away the signaling required to establish a SIP dialog with another user agent. Between Lync Server endpoints, a `Conversation` can consist of multiple modalities, with each modality represented by a `Call` object.

WHAT IS A MODALITY?

One of the features of "unified communications" platforms such as Lync Server is that they support a number of different forms of communication. These typically include audio, video, and instant messaging. Lync Server also supports application sharing and web sharing. Each of these forms of communication is known as a *modality*.

A `Call` object represents a single SIP signaling session (with a single modality) between the application and a remote user agent. The `Call` class itself is abstract, so an application must use one of the modality-specific subclasses, such as `InstantMessagingCall` or `AudioVideoCall`.

Figure 6-1 shows the relationship between endpoints, conversations, and calls in UCMA.

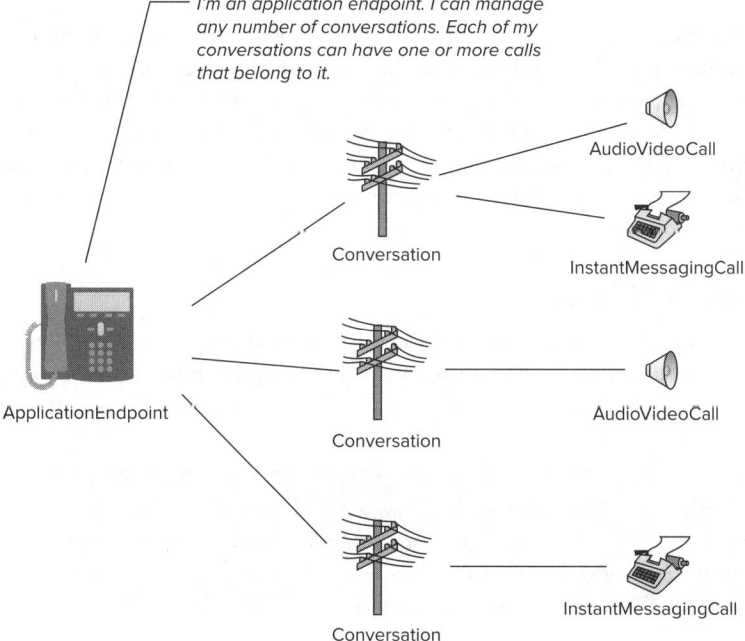

I'm an application endpoint. I can manage any number of conversations. Each of my conversations can have one or more calls that belong to it.

AudioVideoCall

Conversation

InstantMessagingCall

ApplicationEndpoint

AudioVideoCall

Conversation

InstantMessagingCall

Conversation

FIGURE 6-1

Conversation Objects Provide a Layer of Abstraction

The different functions of the `Conversation` and `Call` classes are a common source of confusion for developers new to UCMA 3.0. Which one is responsible for doing what can often be unclear at first when you are establishing a new instant messaging session or audio call from an application.

In two-party communication, the `Conversation` object holds together all the calls to a single remote endpoint. Through its associated `ConferenceSession` instance, it also handles signaling with a conference focus to join a conference for multi-party communication.

Visualizing `Conversation` and `Call` may help, as shown in Figure 6-2. You can think of the `Conversation` object as a larger pipe between two endpoints that contains one smaller pipe, a `Call` instance, for each modality.

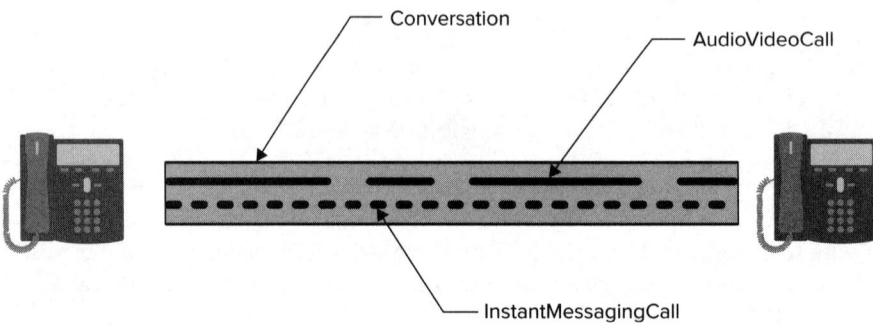

FIGURE 6-2

Another easy way to understand the `Conversation` class is to think of the conversation windows in the Communicator application. Generally anything that would occur in a single window in Communicator is handled by a single instance of the `Conversation` class in UCMA 3.0. Two-party instant message and audio calls with a single other user can be handled with one instance of `Conversation`, just as they would require only one window in Communicator. To create a second instant message call with a different user, however, you require a new `Conversation`, just as you would need a new window in Communicator.

Call Objects Represent Types of Media

A `Conversation` alone is not enough to start communicating with another endpoint. Actually establishing a signaling session and negotiating media exchange is the responsibility of the subclasses of `Call`.

 In Lync Server terms, any communication session, whether or not it involves audio, is referred to as a call. Throughout this book, consider audio, instant message, and application sharing sessions alike as calls.

Establishing a call has three major components: the SIP signaling, the media negotiation (using SDP), and the media delivery (via RTP). Each of these responsibilities is handled by a separate class. Table 6-4 shows the responsibilities of these three classes.

TABLE 6-4: Abstract Base Classes Involved in Call Establishment

CLASS	RESPONSIBILITY
Call	SIP signaling
MediaProvider	SDP media negotiation
MediaFlow	Media delivery

Each modality has a set of subclasses derived from these three base classes. Table 6-5 shows the subclasses for audio/video calls and for instant messaging calls.

TABLE 6-5: Subclasses of Call, MediaProvider, and MediaFlow

BASE CLASS	AUDIO/VIDEO SUBCLASS	INSTANT MESSAGING SUBCLASS
Call	AudioVideoCall	InstantMessagingCall
MediaProvider	AudioVideoProvider	InstantMessagingProvider
MediaFlow	AudioVideoFlow	InstantMessagingFlow

There is also a set of subclasses for the application sharing modality, with names following the same pattern.

Generally, unless you extend UCMA 3.0 to handle a new modality, you will not need to deal directly with the MediaProvider subclasses. The Call subclasses use their corresponding media providers to perform media negotiation at the appropriate point in call establishment.

The MediaFlow subclasses also do much of their work behind the scenes. They provide an abstraction for the flow of media back and forth between the participants in a call. These classes expose APIs that allow an application to manipulate the media for the call. For instant messaging calls, this can include, for example, sending and receiving individual instant messages. For audio calls, UCMA 3.0 provides several helper classes, such as Player and Recorder, that allow an application to easily send audio to a call or process audio that it receives from a call. You can read about these classes in detail in Chapter 12.

The `Call` object itself is responsible for signaling, which includes just about anything that affects the state of the call. To establish, accept, terminate, or transfer a call, for instance, you must call methods on the `Call` object. Chapter 8 covers all of these call control APIs.

Conferencing

Many SIP-based communication platforms extend SIP in some way to support conference calling. Lync Server makes use of some extensions to SIP based on the framework described in RFC 4353 to handle multi-party communication sessions, or conferences. Microsoft's version of this conferencing protocol is known as C3P (Centralized Conference Control Protocol). A conference in Lync Server is any communication session (whether instant message, audio, web sharing, or something else) in which having more than two participants is possible.

SIP Sessions with Multiple Remote Endpoints

A SIP signaling session can only have two participating endpoints: the user agent server and the user agent client. To get around this limitation, Lync Server introduces two server roles, the conference focus and the multipoint control unit, which manage conferences by handling multiple sessions at once — one with each conference participant — and route the media from each participating endpoint to all the others.

A number of UCMA classes deal with conferences. These can be divided roughly into three categories:

➤ The `ConferenceServices` class handles conference scheduling and management. `ConferenceServices` is accessible through a property on the `ApplicationEndpoint` or `UserEndpoint` instance.

➤ The `ConferenceInvitation` class allows an application to invite remote users to a conference. The application must create a new instance of `ConferenceInvitation` for each remote user who is to be invited.

➤ The `ConferenceSession` class represents a communication channel with a conference focus, and handles joining the conference. `ConferenceSession` also handles sending commands to the conference focus to perform conference operations such as removing a participant. It is associated with `McuSession` objects, each of which represents a communication channel with an MCU. These expose methods to send commands to the MCU.

The Conference Focus Manages the Roster

The conference focus is a Lync Server role that acts as a sort of traffic cop for SIP signaling in conferences. Whenever a conference is created, the focus creates a new conference focus session that represents that conference. Endpoints that want to join the conference send a SIP INVITE message to the conference focus along with some additional information that specifies which conference they want to join. Depending on the conference admission policy (who is allowed to join under what circumstances) the focus either admits them or forbids them to join.

The focus keeps track of which modalities are included in the conference, how long it is scheduled to last, which participants are designated as leaders, and who is to be invited to the conference. Conference leaders can send commands to the focus to invite additional participants or to terminate the conference.

Multipoint Control Units Mix the Media

While the conference focus manages the conference as a whole and its participants, multipoint control units, or MCUs, handle the routing of media from each participant to the others in the conference. A separate MCU exists for each modality, because the routing works differently for each one.

Trusted conference participants can send commands to an audio MCU to manipulate the routing of media. See Chapter 12 for details.

Collaboration is the term used for the capabilities in Lync Server that enable you to keep track of other users and whether they are available for conversations, as well as control which other users can see the same information about you.

The collaboration features in Lync Server fall into two general categories: presence and contact lists. Each of these has a chapter devoted to it later in the book. For now, the following sections introduce some basic concepts that can help you to understand the presence and contact list APIs in UCMA 3.0, so that they will make sense to you when they come up in later chapters.

Enhanced Presence

The essential idea behind presence is simple and clever. With a conventional telephone, you have no way to tell whether the person you are about to call is available to talk, or even near a phone. There is also no particularly good way to determine which number (home, office, mobile) will be the best to call. This leads to situations such as "phone tag" where two people repeatedly miss each other's phone calls.

Presence-enabled communication platforms alleviate this problem by allowing users to publish "presence" information that shows whether they are available on one or more communication devices (whether a phone, computer, or something else) and whether they are in a position to answer incoming communications. At a minimum, users can generally be "Available," "Busy," or "Away."

Some platforms, such as Lync Server, allow users to publish a number of different categories of information, such as location, contact details, customized status notes, and calendar information. These things give others even more context to use as they decide whether and how to contact the user.

Some protocols, such as Extensible Messaging and Presence Protocol (XMPP), which is used by Google Chat, have built-in support for presence. The plain vanilla variety of SIP, unfortunately, does not have any presence support. Lync Server accordingly uses a popular SIP extension called SIP/SIMPLE that introduces some new headers and message types into standard SIP to support presence operations.

What Is Enhanced Presence?

The presence mechanism in Lync Server is known as *enhanced presence*. It is "enhanced" because it has a number of features that go above and beyond the basic concept of presence. These features include:

➤ Multiple "categories" of presence information, including state, calendar data, contact card, and location

➤ Support for multiple points of presence — more than one endpoint publishing presence information for a single user

➤ Access control lists that allow users to limit who can see what presence information

➤ Interruption control — the Do Not Disturb status allows users to block incoming communications

Presence Categories

Lync Server has five built-in presence categories, which are shown in Table 6-6. All the standard presence information is contained in these categories.

TABLE 6.6: Built-in Presence Categories

CATEGORY	PURPOSE
State	Indicates how available the user is for communications, and whether the user is in a call or conference.
contactCard	Contains contact details for the user.
calendarData	Contains data from Exchange on the user's availability during the day.
Services	Indicates what communication capabilities (such as audio, instant messaging, or application sharing) the user can currently support.
routing	Indicates where calls to the user should be routed (forwarding or simultaneous-ring details).
note	Holds a plain-text status note that is usually entered by the user in Communicator.

In addition to these, with a bit of tinkering, defining custom presence categories to hold other types of information on the user is possible.

Presence Aggregation

Lync Server allows users to be logged in from more than one place. That is to say, a user can have multiple endpoints with his or her SIP URI connected to Lync Server at the same time. Each of these endpoints can publish its own presence information. For instance, one of the endpoints could be a computer that publishes an "Away" state when the user hasn't moved the mouse for 20 minutes.

Another could be a SIP-enabled phone that publishes a "Busy" state when the phone is "off the hook." If the user picks up the phone and makes a long call, neglecting the computer for some time, the phone might publish a "Busy" state to Lync Server while the computer publishes an "Away" state. For Lync Server to come up with a single, consistent presence state to make available to other users, it needs to combine all of these various inputs in a process called *presence aggregation*.

Lync Server mixes together four types of state when calculating an aggregated presence that will determine the color of the user's presence indicator. These states are shown in Table 6-7.

TABLE 6-7: Types of State in Lync Server

STATE TYPE	DESCRIPTION
User state	The presence selected by the user in Communicator or another client.
Phone state	Whether the user is in an audio call or conference at the moment.
Machine state	Whether the user is active at the machine associated with this endpoint (for example, whether the mouse has been moved recently).
Calendar state	The user's availability according to his or her Exchange calendar.

Lync Server collects these four types of information from all the available sources and looks at when each one was published to determine an aggregate presence state.

Presence Containers for Access Control

In Communicator, users have the option of putting a contact into an access control list such as "Team," "Company," or "Public" to indicate how much of the user's presence information should be available to that contact. Within Lync Server, these access control lists are managed using *presence containers*.

You can think of a presence container as a box for pieces of presence information that is restricted to certain users. When Lync Server stores a user's presence, it associates each piece of information with one or more of the presence containers. Other users only get the presence information in the containers they have access to.

Each user has a different set of presence containers. So, for instance, Deborah might publish her location details to the Team and Personal containers, whereas Reginald only publishes them to the Personal container. Likewise, Deborah might give Reginald access to her Team container, whereas Adela gives Reginald access to her Company container.

Presence Queries and Subscriptions

A Lync Server endpoint has two options for learning about the presence of a specific user. To check a user's presence on a one-time or intermittent basis, an endpoint can query Lync Server to find out the current presence of one or more users. If an endpoint needs to be notified of a user's every presence update, it can register a *presence subscription* with Lync Server for one or more users. Thereafter, whenever Lync Server receives a presence update for one of those users (the *subscription targets*), it sends the subscriber a notification of the new presence.

Because multiple points of presence can exist for a single user, each endpoint needs a way to find out about presence updates that are triggered by other endpoints for the same user. Lync Server allows an endpoint to subscribe to its own ("local") presence, so that it finds out about any presence updates published by other endpoints for the same user.

Automatic Presence Publishing in UCMA

When registering with Lync Server, you can configure both user endpoints and application endpoints to automatically publish certain pieces of presence information. In the case of an application endpoint, this is an "automaton" presence that is designed to remain on the server for a long period of time without expiring. For user endpoints, it is simply an initial presence publication to be provided to the server on registration.

Local Presence and Remote Presence

UCMA provides separate APIs to handle *local presence* and *remote presence*. Local presence is the presence of the application or the user on whose behalf it is acting; a UCMA application can use the `LocalOwnerPresence` class to publish presence updates and receive notifications of presence changes made by other endpoints representing the same user.

Remote presence is the presence of any other Communications Server user. Access to remote presence operations is through instances of the `RemotePresenceView` class. This class maintains up-to-date presence information on one or more other users, which are referred to as the *subscription targets*. Performing a one-time query of a user's presence through the `RemotePresenceServices` object associated with an endpoint is also possible.

Contact List and Contact Group Operations in UCMA

Because a user may sign in to Lync Server from any instance of Communicator, or from a web client, storing information on contacts locally would be problematic — the contact list would be different depending on where the user signed in. Instead, Lync Server maintains a contact list for each user at the server level. Endpoints can retrieve this information from Lync Server and can make modifications to the server-side contact list by sending SIP messages with a particular type of XML content.

Lync Server also allows you to place the contacts into contact groups for ease of lookup.

The `ContactGroupServices` property on the `UserEndpoint` class references an object through which you can make changes to the contact list that belongs to the endpoint owner.

Application endpoints do not have contact lists associated with them, and so the `Application Endpoint` class does not have the `ContactGroupServices` property.

UCMA DEVELOPMENT PRACTICES

A number of best practices exist for development with the UC Managed API that will come up in subsequent chapters. Having a general understanding of these before diving into UCMA code is helpful, so this section briefly explains some of the common practices you will see in UCMA 3.0 applications. When you encounter them later in sample code, they will be familiar.

Asynchronous Programming

Perhaps the most important thing to know as you begin developing with UCMA is that most of its methods execute asynchronously. There are two primary reasons for this. The first is that most UCMA operations involve sending SIP messages to a remote endpoint and awaiting responses, so quite a bit of waiting can be involved. The second is that, to take advantage of the full processing power of multiple CPUs, the UCMA runtime queues these operations and executes them using a pool of worker threads.

The Begin/End Pattern

The asynchronous programming model used by UCMA is the Begin/End pattern. Each operation is initiated by a `BeginMethodName` method, such as `BeginEstablish`. The `BeginMethodName` method queues the operation for execution on a worker thread managed by the UCMA runtime. The last two parameters of any `BeginMethodName` method are always `userCallback` (which takes an optional callback delegate) and `state` (which takes an optional object containing context about the operation).

The `BeginMethodName` method returns an object that implements the `IAsyncResult` interface. This object gives the application visibility to the status of the asynchronous operation.

Each operation with a `BeginMethodName` method also has a corresponding `EndMethodName` method (for example, `EndEstablish`). The `EndMethodName` method waits on the completion of the asynchronous operation if it has not yet completed, and then throws any exceptions that occurred on the calling thread.

CHAINING BEGIN AND END METHODS

You might be tempted, especially when writing test code, to simply chain together the `Begin` and `End` methods for an asynchronous operation, in effect making it synchronous, as in the following line of code:

```
call.EndEstablish(call.BeginEstablish(null, null));
```

This approach is not *always* a bad thing, but that's just about the best thing to say about it. It's strongly discouraged in any code that might be used in a production environment. Asynchronous operations in UCMA, although they are designed to finish eventually, are not 100 percent guaranteed to complete, so calling them in this way could very rarely cause a thread to block endlessly. Blocking threads also can have a negative impact on performance if an application does it too often or for too long.

In summary, chaining `Begin` and `End` methods occasionally to keep coding easy when testing a new feature won't hurt anything, but steer clear of it whenever possible in any code you plan to use in a production application.

Callback Methods

If you supply a callback delegate when calling Begin*MethodName*, the UCMA runtime will call that delegate after the asynchronous operation finishes executing. The callback method must take a single parameter, an instance of IAsyncResult. When the UCMA runtime executes the callback method, it passes in the IAsyncResult instance that represents this operation. You can use that instance to call the End*MethodName* method.

 Always calling the End*MethodName* *method for whatever operation you are performing within the callback method is important. If you skip this step, you will miss any exceptions that were thrown during the asynchronous operation.*

The following code snippet shows what this pattern looks like in code. Don't worry too much about the AudioVideoCall class for now; the important thing to note is how the Begin/End pattern works.

```
void EstablishCall(AudioVideoCall call)
{
    // Queue the asynchronous operation.
    // This will return immediately and the
    // operation will execute on a worker thread.
    call.BeginEstablish(OnCallEstablishCompleted, call);
}

private void OnCallEstablishCompleted(IAsyncResult result)
{
    // Retrieve a reference to the call object from
    // the AsyncState property.
    AudioVideoCall call = (AudioVideoCall)result.AsyncState;

    // Complete the operation and throw
    // any exceptions that occurred.
    call.EndEstablish(result);
}
```

Notice how the callback method retrieves the AudioVideoCall object from the AsyncState property on the IAsyncResult instance. Whatever is passed into the state parameter on Begin*MethodName* is stored in this AsyncState property for later retrieval. The code simply needs to cast it to its original type in order to use it.

Lambda Expressions as Callbacks

At times, the aforementioned method of keeping track of state across the stages of the asynchronous operation can feel clunky and inconvenient. Thankfully, an alternative exists. Instead of defining the callback method separately and passing it into the Begin*MethodName* method as a delegate, you can simply pass an anonymous delegate or lambda expression as the callback delegate. The following code snippet demonstrates this:

```
void EstablishCall(AudioVideoCall call)
{
    // Queue the asynchronous operation.
    // This will return immediately and the
    // operation will execute on a worker thread.
    call.BeginEstablish(result =>
        {
            // Complete the operation and throw
            // any exceptions that occurred.
            call.EndEstablish(result);
        },
        null // No need for the state parameter.
    );
}
```

The compiler creates a closure, so that the local variables from the EstablishCall method are essentially still in scope in the callback. This allows for much more concise code, particularly when the callback needs to work with a number of state objects.

 Avoiding blocking the thread that is executing a callback method is best. These threads are UCMA worker threads. Other operations will continue even if a worker thread is blocked in a callback, but no other events or callbacks on the same object will be invoked until the thread is released.

Exception Handling

Proper exception handling is an often tedious but always crucial part of UCMA development. Thankfully, UCMA keeps things easy by throwing exceptions in a very consistent way.

Begin*MethodName* methods can throw the following types of exceptions:

➤ InvalidOperationException

➤ ArgumentException

➤ ArgumentNullException

Assuming you are careful about your arguments, catching InvalidOperationException is generally only necessary when calling Begin*MethodName* methods.

End*MethodName* methods throw nothing but subclasses of RealTimeException. The RealTimeException type is defined in the Microsoft.Rtc.Signaling namespace, and is used exclusively for errors that occur during asynchronous UCMA operations.

Catching RealTimeException whenever you're calling an End*MethodName* method is important. By default, the UCMA runtime does not have any handling of its own for exceptions that occur when it is executing a callback. If you do not catch these exceptions, your application may crash or become unstable. For the same reason, catching any exceptions that may be thrown by any other code that is executed in callback methods is important.

The following code snippet illustrates catching exceptions on both ends of the asynchronous operation.

```
try
{
    call.BeginEstablish(result =>
        {
            try
            {
                // Complete the operation and throw
                // any exceptions that occurred.
                call.EndEstablish(result);
            }
            catch (RealTimeException ex)
            {
                // Catch and log exceptions.
                Console.WriteLine(ex);
            }
        },
        null
    );
}
catch (InvalidOperationException ioex)
{
    // Catch and log exceptions.
    Console.WriteLine(ioex);
}
```

This does, admittedly, make the code a bit longer and more cumbersome, but it is important for keeping UCMA applications working reliably.

As a last resort for handling any exceptions that are thrown in callbacks and not handled, UCMA provides a static class called UnhandledExceptionManager. By setting the VerifyAndIgnore UnhandledThreadPoolException static property to a delegate with the correct method signature, you can define your own handling for otherwise unhandled exceptions thrown in callbacks.

The following code shows how to register a delegate for unhandled thread pool exceptions.

```
UnhandledExceptionManager.VerifyAndIgnoreUnhandledThreadPoolException =
    HandleUnhandledException;
```

A negligently simple handler method might look like the following:

```
private bool HandleUnhandledException(Exception ex,
    System.Threading.WaitCallback method, object state)
{
    // Log the exception.
    Console.WriteLine(ex);

    // Return true to tell UCMA to ignore the exception.
    return true;
}
```

The first parameter passed to the handler method is the exception that was thrown, so that it can be logged or inspected. The other two parameters should be ignored. The handler can return `false` to rethrow the exception (probably causing the application to crash) or `true` to have UCMA ignore it.

> *UCMA endpoints can automatically recover from brief connection failures by re-registering with Lync Server. While these reconnection attempts do not cause exceptions to be thrown, the UCMA application sometimes needs to do some cleanup afterwards. Events such as* `RepublishingRequired` *can notify the application of these conditions. Chapters 7 and 9 discuss these events in more detail.*

DEPLOYING A UCMA APPLICATION

During development and initial testing, nothing is wrong with running a UCMA application on the server you are using for development. When deploying an application, however, giving it a dedicated server is best. This is particularly important if the application handles audio, video, or other media at all. Problems will usually arise if more than one media stack is active on a single physical server.

Where to Deploy

You may be able to run a UCMA application successfully on the same server as other Lync server roles, but hosting UCMA applications on separate application servers is best. This is especially important for UCMA applications that handle real-time media such as audio. Hosting a UCMA application on a server that also hosts a Lync server role such as the audio/video MCU will generally lead to performance problems and poor audio quality.

To host a UCMA application, your application server must have a number of things:

➤   Connectivity with Lync Server

➤   If your application will use mutual TLS, a certificate whose subject name is the fully qualified domain name (FQDN) of the application server, issued by a CA that is trusted by Lync Server

➤   The UCMA 3.0 runtime

Your application must also be configured with the following:

➤   A trusted application

➤   A service ID with permission to access the certificate store, if your application is using TLS to connect to Lync Server

Deployment Tips

Setting up an application server for a UCMA application takes a number of steps that are not obvious and bear mentioning. These steps are often the culprit when a UCMA application works fine in debugging but will not run on the application server.

Certificates

To use mutual transport-layer security (MTLS) when communicating with Lync Server, which is highly recommended, a UCMA application must have access to a certificate in the local computer store. This certificate must be issued by a certificate authority that is trusted by Lync Server, and its subject name must be the fully qualified domain name of the application server.

If this certificate is not installed or the application does not have sufficient permissions to access it, a `TlsException` will be thrown on startup.

Depending on your configuration, you may be able to request the certificate from the Certificates snap-in in Microsoft Management Console on the application server. Alternatively, you can issue the certificate elsewhere, move it to the application server, and import it through the Certificates snap-in.

Permissions

For a UCMA application to function properly, it should be run in the context of an account that is a member of the RTCComponentsUniversalServices group in Active Directory. The recommended approach is to add the computer account to this group, and then run the UCMA application as a Network Service. Alternatively, you can create a new Active Directory identity for the UCMA application, and add it to the RTCComponentsUniversalServices group.

If the application is using mutual transport-layer security (TLS), as mentioned earlier, it must have adequate permissions to access the certificate in the local computer certificate store that it will use to authenticate with Lync Server. You can confirm this by right-clicking on the certificate in the Certificates management console and selecting All Tasks ⇨ Manage Private Keys.

Load-Balanced Applications

You can deploy UCMA applications in a load-balanced topology if they are provisioned accordingly. Chapter 7 covers the necessary provisioning process in detail.

UCMA supports both hardware and DNS load balancing.

SUMMARY

This chapter introduced the Unified Communications Managed API, what you can do with it, and some of the fundamentals required to begin developing with the API and deploying applications. It also discussed the Session Initiation Protocol (SIP) and how Lync Server uses it to control communication sessions.

The next chapter goes a bit deeper into the API, showing how to build a simple UCMA application, initialize and clean up basic components such as the collaboration platform and endpoints, and provision the necessary Active Directory objects to get a UCMA application running on the server.

7

Starting Up and Shutting Down a UCMA Application

WHAT'S IN THIS CHAPTER

➤ Provisioning applications in Active Directory

➤ Starting up a UCMA application

➤ Shutting down a UCMA application

➤ Draining calls

➤ Troubleshooting startup and shutdown

A bit of preparation is required before you can run an application written with the Unified Communications Managed API (UCMA). Although building a simple communications service takes a matter of minutes, you must take a few steps in your code to set the stage for whatever communication operations you will perform. Also, before your application can actually run, connect to Lync Server, and interact with the server or other endpoints, you must provision some objects to represent it in Active Directory.

This chapter describes the steps required to set up a server to run UCMA applications, and explains how to write the basic startup and shutdown code which forms the foundation of any UCMA application.

PROVISIONING AN APPLICATION

Each server-side UCMA application is represented by a trusted application object in the Lync Central Management Store (a repository that contains topology and configuration data for Lync Server). The properties of this object provide the configuration settings for the

`CollaborationPlatform` object in UCMA code. In addition, just as any Lync Server user must exist as a `User` object in Active Directory, any application endpoint must correspond to an Active Directory `Contact` object. This object is the source of the settings for an `ApplicationEndpoint` object in the application's code.

Unified Communications developers usually refer to this process of creating Active Directory objects for a UCMA service as *provisioning an application.*

Client-side UCMA applications, which use the `ClientPlatformSettings` object to provide configuration for the collaboration platform, do not require any provisioning. However, applications of this variety never amount to much, because they are limited to user endpoints and consequently cannot perform any trusted operations. They can often be found roaming the streets late at night, mumbling to no one in particular about their bitter fate.

Active Directory itself does not provide a user interface for creating these objects. Rather than leave users to struggle helplessly with WMI commands, the developers of the UC Managed API SDK created some tools to make this provisioning process easier. The UCMA 2.0 SDK, which was associated with Office Communications Server 2007 R2, had a tool called `ApplicationProvisioner.exe`, a Windows Forms application that provided a graphical user interface for these provisioning operations. For Lync Server 2010, these have been replaced with a set of Windows PowerShell cmdlets.

Before sitting down to write code for a new UCMA application, you generally want to begin with a cup of tea, some light stretching, and a short session of application provisioning with these handy and easy-to-use PowerShell cmdlets.

Creating a Trusted Application Pool

Before provisioning a trusted application and endpoint for your UCMA application, you must configure the server that the application will run on to host a trusted application pool. You can create a trusted application pool using the Lync Topology Builder — a new Silverlight-based management tool for administering your Lync Server deployment — or using the PowerShell cmdlets. In this section, you learn how to create a trusted application pool using the PowerShell cmdlets.

Before creating a UCMA trusted application pool, you must configure a Windows server to run UCMA applications on. You can host UCMA 3.0 applications on a server running Windows Server 2008 or Windows Server 2008 R2.

The UCMA 3.0 SDK is now only supported on 64-bit operating systems, so start with a Windows Server 2008 (64-bit) or Windows Server 2008 R2 server that is fully patched and joined to the domain.

If you're going to be doing development on this machine, you should also install Visual Studio 2010. Visual Studio 2010 is a required prerequisite for installing the UCMA 3.0 SDK, which includes the necessary Visual Studio project templates.

Installing the UCMA 3.0 SDK

The UCMA 3.0 SDK includes the necessary components that allow you to run and develop UCMA applications on a Windows server. Your environment for developing UCMA applications differs from typical .NET development environments in that you have to perform development tasks on a server machine that has been configured to connect to an existing Lync Server environment. The first step in configuring a Windows server to run UCMA applications is to install the UCMA 3.0 SDK.

Download the UCMA 3.0 SDK and run `UcmaSdkSetup.exe` to start the installation process. As shown in Figure 7-1, the installer verifies that the necessary prerequisites are available and prompts you to proceed if they are.

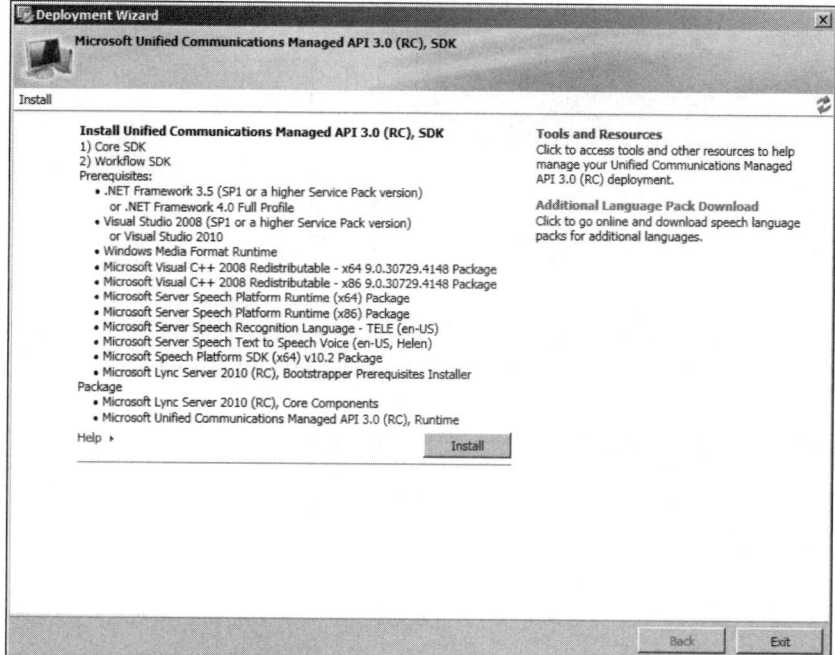

FIGURE 7-1

The installer also installs the Windows Media Format Runtime and prompts you to reboot before continuing.

Install the UCMA 3.0 SDK to the default location, as shown in Figure 7-2.

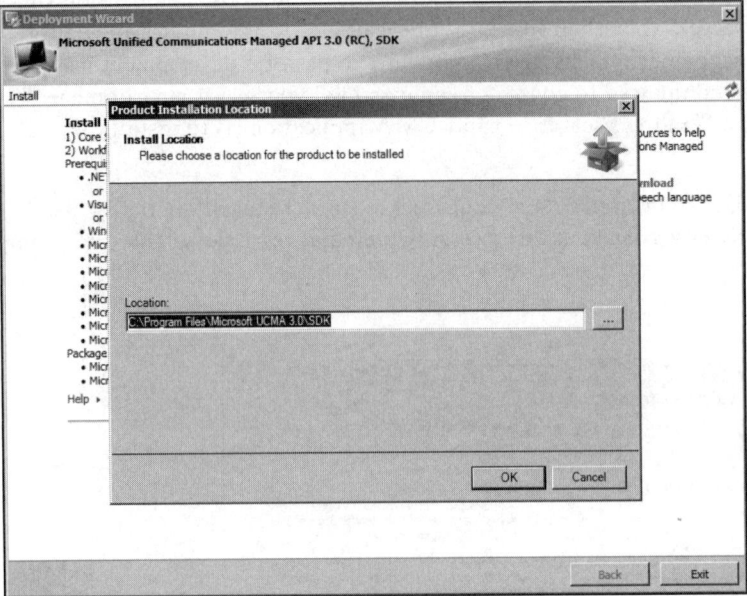

FIGURE 7-2

As shown in Figure 7-3, the installer informs you after the installation is complete. It also provides some handy links for downloading additional language packs and tools and resources.

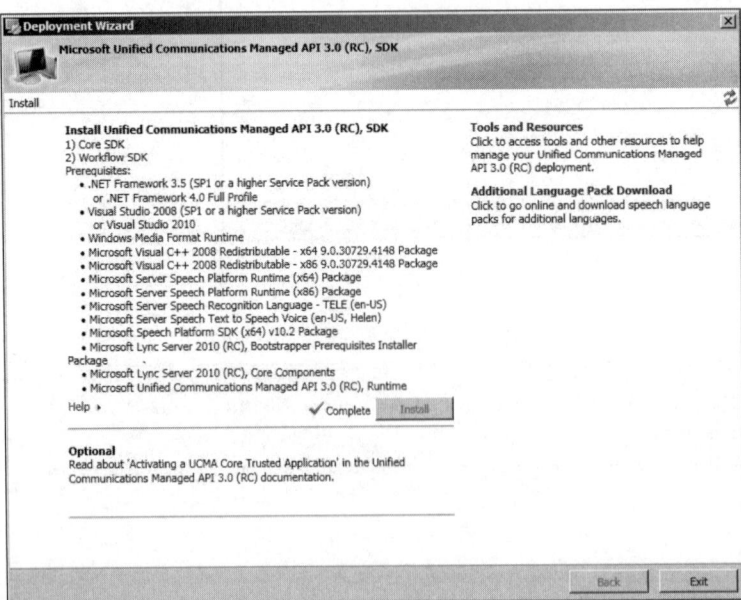

FIGURE 7-3

Installing the Lync Server 2010 Core Components

The UCMA 3.0 SDK installation also installs additional tools that you can now use to configure the server to host a Lync local management store. The local management store is a local SQL Server Express database containing information about provisioned applications. The central management store runs on the front-end server in the Lync topology and syncs to each application server's local management store.

Why do you care about this as a developer? If you did any development in UCMA 2.0, recall all the pieces of information you had to provide to your application in order to start the `CollaborationPlatform` for the trusted application. You had to specify a Globally Routable User Agent URI (GRUU), port, certificate, trusted application name, and trusted application contact name. UCMA 3.0 introduces the concept of *auto-provisioning* where your application only needs to know the UCMA application's application ID; for example, `urn:application:contactcenter`. The UCMA runtime queries the local management store using the application ID to get all the other necessary pieces of information such as the GRUU, port, and certificate.

To install the Lync Server 2010 core components and configure a local management store, browse to `C:\Program Files\Microsoft Lync Server 2010\Deployment` and run the following command:

```
Bootstrapper.exe /BootstrapLocalMgmt /MinCache
```

As shown in Figure 7-4, the command checks for the necessary prerequisites and installs the Lync Server 2010 core components.

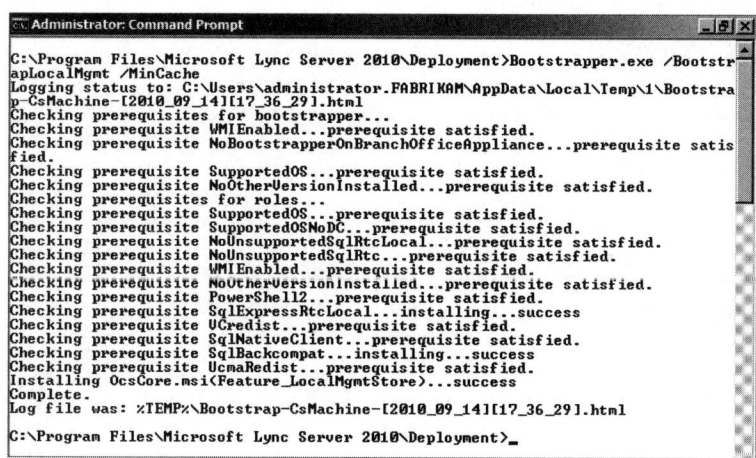

FIGURE 7-4

Using PowerShell to Create a Trusted Application Pool

After the Lync Server 2010 core components are installed, you will see a new program group called Microsoft Lync Server 2010. Expand this program group and run the Lync Server Management

Shell. The Lync Server Management Shell provides an environment to run the Lync PowerShell cmdlets against the Lync Server environment.

Use the `New-CsTrustedApplicationPool` cmdlet to create a new trusted application pool. The cmdlet requires you to specify the fully qualified domain name of the registrar and also the site ID. To get these pieces of information, run the `Get-CsSite` and `Get-CsService` cmdlets and take note of the registrar name and site ID, as follows:

```
Get-CsSite

Get-CsService -Registrar
```

Run the `New-CsTrustedApplicationPool` cmdlet and specify the name of the trusted application pool, the registrar, and the site ID:

```
New-CsTrustedApplicationPool -Identity <fqdn> -Registrar <registrar> -Site <site>
```

Figure 7-5 shows the `New-CsTrustedApplicationPool` cmdlet being used to create a trusted application pool called `appsrv2.fabrikam.com` using the `cs-se.fabrikam.com` registrar and the `fabrikam.com` site ID.

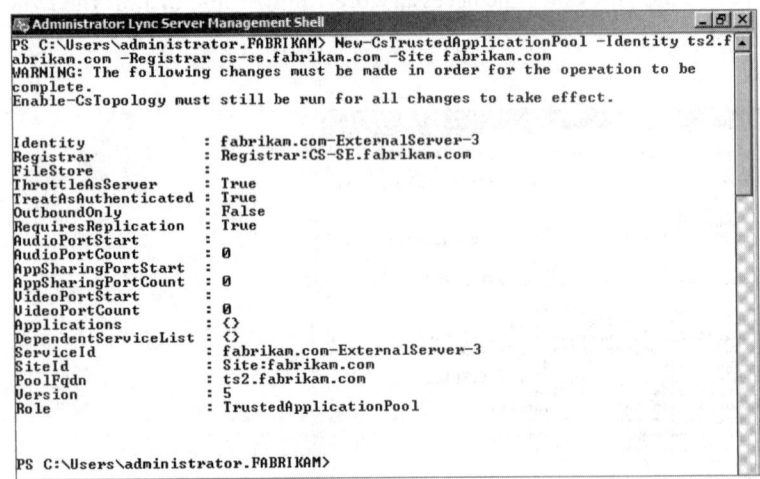

FIGURE 7-5

As prompted by the output of the `New-CsTrustedApplicationPool` cmdlet, run the `Enable-CsTopology` cmdlet to complete the operation. According to the UCMA 3.0 SDK documentation, this creates the necessary entries in Active Directory for the trusted service:

```
Enable-CsTopology
```

To check that the trusted application pool was created properly and added to the Lync topology, run the `Get-CsTopology` cmdlet and examine its output:

```
(Get-CsTopology -AsXml).ToString() > Topology.xml
```

`Topology.xml` contains the details for the entire Lync topology; look for a Cluster node for the trusted application pool that was just created:

```xml
<Cluster Fqdn="appsrv2.fabrikam.com" RequiresReplication="true"
  RequiresSetup="true">
  <ClusterId SiteId="fabrikam.com" Number="5" />
  <Machine OrdinalInCluster="1" Fqdn="appsrv2.fabrikam.com">
    <NetInterface InterfaceSide="Primary"
        InterfaceNumber="1" IPAddress="0.0.0.0" />
  </Machine>
</Cluster>
```

Configuring Management Store Replication

Now that you have created a UCMA 3.0 trusted application pool on the server, the next step is to configure replication from the central management store to the new local management store.

Run the `Enable-CsReplica` cmdlet as shown in the following code snippet to enable the Replica service on the server. The Replica service is responsible for replicating changes in the central management store to all local management store databases in the topology.

```
Enable-CsReplica
```

The Replica service is now installed on the server, but it hasn't done anything yet. You can verify this by running the `Get-CsManagementStoreReplicationStatus` cmdlet to check the replication status of the servers in the topology, as follows:

```
Get-CsManagementStoreReplicationStatus
```

You can see in Figure 7-6 that the `UpToDate` property of the new server is still `False`.

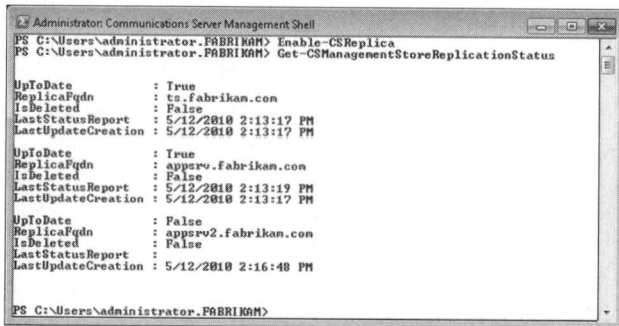

FIGURE 7-6

Force replication to start by running the `Invoke-CsManagementStoreReplicationStatus` cmdlet, as follows:

```
Invoke-CsManagementStoreReplicationStatus
```

As shown in Figure 7-7, this cmdlet has no output; it just starts the replication process to replicate the central management store database to all the local management store databases in the topology.

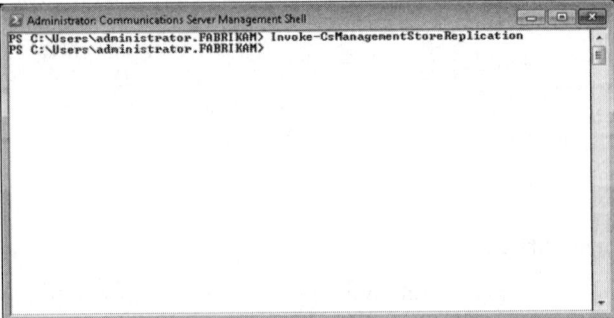

FIGURE 7-7

Replication takes some time; use the `Get-CsManagementStoreReplicationStatus` cmdlet to check the status of the replication:

```
Get-CSManagementStoreReplicationStatus
```

As shown in Figure 7-8, the `UpToDate` property of the new server is `True` when replication has completed, meaning that the local management store is in synch with the central management store.

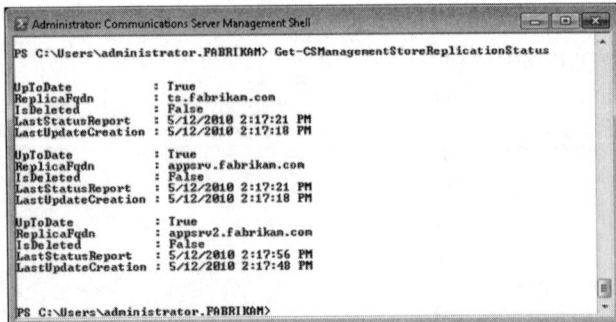

FIGURE 7-8

Requesting and Setting a New Certificate for the Server

The application server is now hosting a UCMA 3.0 trusted application pool and is replicating back and forth between the local management store on the server and the central management store on the registrar server. The final step in the process is to request a new certificate from the domain certificate authority and set it on the server. This allows the Lync server infrastructure to recognize and trust the application server as a component of the Lync topology.

Use the `Request-CsCertificate` cmdlet to request a new certificate. Use the `-New` switch to specify that this is a new certificate, and the `-Type` switch to specify that this will be the default certificate on the server, as shown in the following snippet. Also provide the path to the certificate authority.

```
Request-CSCertificate -New -Type default
    -CA <Domain Controller FQDN>\<Certificate Authority> -Verbose
```

Here is an example:

```
Request-CSCertificate -New -Type default -CA dc.fabrikam.com\FabrikamCA -Verbose
```

Set the `-Verbose` switch of the cmdlet to get detailed output from the cmdlet, such as the `Thumbprint` of the new certificate.

Use the `Set-CsCertificate` cmdlet to set the certificate and specify its type and thumbprint:

```
Set-CsCertificate -Type Default -Thumbprint <Thumbprint>
```

There is no output if the `Set-CsCertificate` cmdlet runs successfully.

Creating a Trusted Application

The steps you take to provision your application are generally the same from application to application. For any UCMA server-side application, you must provision a trusted application using the `New-CsTrustedApplication` cmdlet. If the application uses only user endpoints, no other provisioning is necessary. If it uses any application endpoints, then you must provision a contact object for each application endpoint using the `New-CsTrustedApplicationEndpoint` cmdlet.

To begin, open the *Lync Server Management Shell* from the Start menu on any server where it has been installed. The Lync Server Management Shell is a Windows PowerShell console that automatically connects to Lync Server in your domain and loads the various cmdlets that you can use to manage Lync Server.

To run the cmdlets, you must be logged in as a user who is a member of the `RTCUniversalServerAdmins` group in Active Directory and also a local administrator on the server.

 Unified Communications development is much like a first date in that many of the things you want to do require special permissions. Provisioning, for instance, requires you to have administrative privileges on both the local machine and on the server where Lync Server is running. If you have any issues with the Management Shell, check that you are running it with administrator permissions.

Creating a Trusted Application

The cmdlet for creating a new trusted application has the fairly unsurprising name of New-CsTrustedApplication. To create a trusted application, type this cmdlet into Management Shell and press Enter.

> *To encourage laziness, Lync Server Management Shell allows you to type the first few letters of a cmdlet and press Tab to auto-fill the rest of the name. You can press Tab again to cycle through the options.*

As shown in Figure 7-9, you are prompted for a number of required parameters:

➤ **ApplicationId:** This is a name for your trusted application. You will use this later to refer to it when configuring your collaboration platform. For ease of reference, choose a descriptive name such as Percival or Bartholomew.

➤ **TrustedApplicationPoolFqdn:** This is the fully qualified domain name of the trusted application pool you created on your application server.

➤ **Port:** This is a listening port number for your application. The application will listen for incoming SIP traffic from Lync Server on this port. Choosing a high-numbered port that is unlikely to conflict with other services is usually easiest.

> *It is important to ensure that the listening port you choose is opened on the local firewall for the application server, so that other servers can send messages to the application successfully on that port.*

```
Administrator: Lync Server Management Shell
PS C:\Users\michaelg> New-CsTrustedApplication

cmdlet New-CsTrustedApplication at command pipeline position 1
Supply values for the following parameters:
ApplicationId: startup.sample
TrustedApplicationPoolFqdn: ts.fabrikam.com
Port: 14000
WARNING: The following changes must be made in order for the operation to be
complete.
Enable-CsTopology must still be run for all changes to take effect.


Identity                   : ts.fabrikam.com/urn:application:startup.sample
ComputerGruus              : {ts.fabrikam.com sip:ts.fabrikam.com@fabrikam.com;
                             gruu;opaque=srvr:startup.sample:JcX-H-6MF1OoTmHB0x
                             0BpAAA}
ServiceGruu                : sip:ts.fabrikam.com@fabrikam.com;gruu;opaque=srvr:
                             startup.sample:JcX-H-6MF1OoTmHB0x0BpAAA
Protocol                   : Mtls
ApplicationId              : urn:application:startup.sample
TrustedApplicationPoolFqdn : ts.fabrikam.com
Port                       : 14000
LegacyApplicationName      : startup.sample
```

FIGURE 7-9

Alternatively, you can specify all the parameters at once:

```
New-CsTrustedApplication -ApplicationId startup.sample
    -TrustedApplicationPoolFqdn ts.fabrikam.com -Port 14000
```

 *If you need help with a cmdlet, you can enter the cmdlet name followed by -?
for an explanation of its usage and syntax.*

Viewing a Trusted Application

To look up the details for a trusted application after creating it, use the Get-CsTrustedApplication
cmdlet. The simplest way to use this cmdlet is to supply the Identity parameter, which is composed of:

applicationPoolFqdn/urn:application:*applicationName*

For instance, to look up the MyUC14App trusted application, enter:

```
Get-CsTrustedApplication -Identity ts.fabrikam.com/urn:application:startup.sample
```

The result is a number of details on the application, as shown in Figure 7-10.

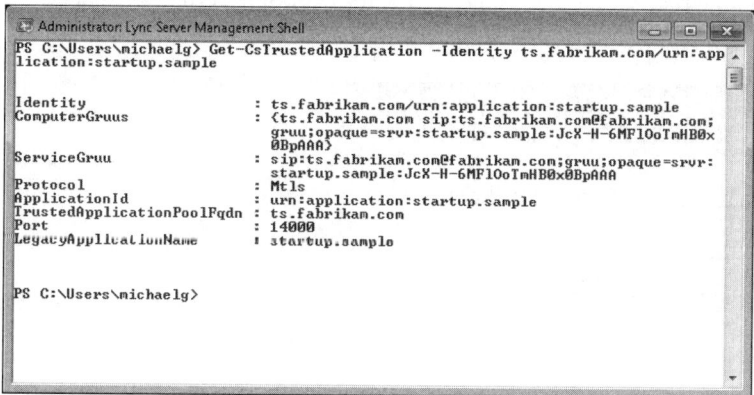

FIGURE 7-10

You can also express the same command by entering the application ID and the fully qualified
domain name of the trusted application pool separately:

```
Get-CsTrustedApplication -ApplicationId urn:application:startup.sample
    -TrustedApplicationPoolFqdn ts.fabrikam.com
```

The result is exactly the same.

Finally, if the application ID is unknown, you can list details on all trusted applications by entering only the following:

```
Get-CsTrustedApplication
```

This retrieves all trusted applications that have been created. Because the list is often quite long, the output can be sent to a file using a command like the following:

```
Get-CsTrustedApplication > C:\applications.txt
```

Creating a Trusted Application Endpoint

After you've created the trusted application, the next step is to create one or more endpoints with which the application can send and receive calls and other communications, publish and subscribe to presence, and perform other Lync Server operations.

To create an endpoint for a trusted application, use the `New-CsTrustedApplicationEndpoint` cmdlet. Include the following parameters, as shown in Figure 7-11.

- ➤ **ApplicationId:** The name of the application in the form `urn:application:name`.

- ➤ **TrustedApplicationPoolFqdn:** The fully qualified domain name of the trusted application pool associated with the trusted application.

- ➤ **SipAddress:** The SIP URI that the new endpoint should use, in the form `sip:user@domain`.

- ➤ **DisplayName:** The name that should be displayed for this endpoint in the Lync client.

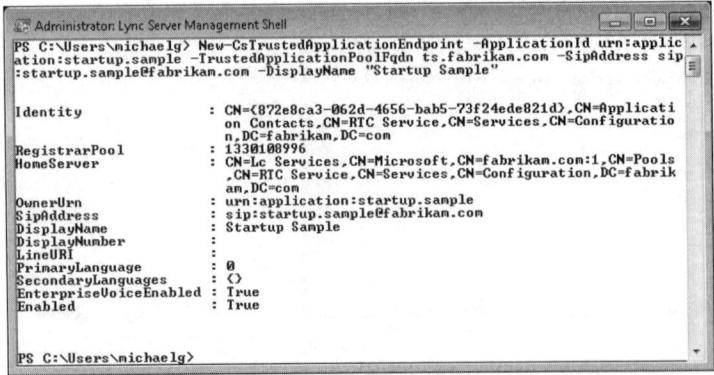

FIGURE 7-11

Viewing a Trusted Application Endpoint

To retrieve the details for a previously created trusted application endpoint, use the `Get-CsTrustedApplicationEndpoint` cmdlet, with the SIP URI of the endpoint as the `Identity` parameter, as shown in Figure 7-12.

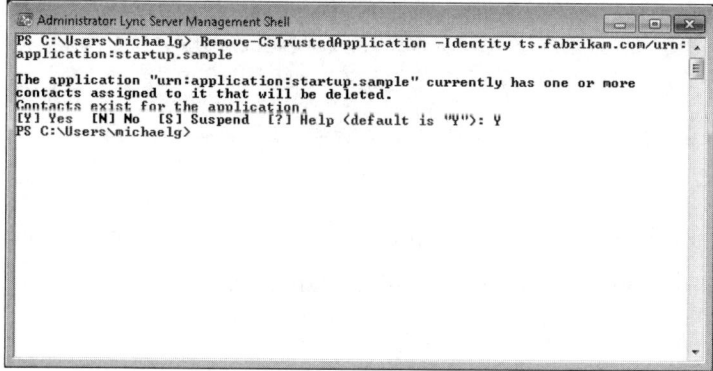

```
Administrator: Lync Server Management Shell

PS C:\Users\michaelg> Get-CsTrustedApplicationEndpoint -Identity sip:startup.sam
ple@fabrikam.com

Identity                : CN={872e8ca3-062d-4656-bab5-73f24ede821d},CN=Applicati
                          on Contacts,CN=RTC Service,CN=Services,CN=Configuratio
                          n,DC=fabrikam,DC=com
RegistrarPool           : CS-SE.fabrikam.com
HomeServer              : CN=Lc Services,CN=Microsoft,CN=fabrikam.com:1,CN=Pools
                          ,CN=RTC Service,CN=Services,CN=Configuration,DC=fabrik
                          am,DC=com
OwnerUrn                : urn:application:startup.sample
SipAddress              : sip:startup.sample@fabrikam.com
DisplayName             : Startup Sample
DisplayNumber           :
LineURI                 :
PrimaryLanguage         : 0
SecondaryLanguages      : <>
EnterpriseVoiceEnabled  : True
Enabled                 : True


PS C:\Users\michaelg>
```

FIGURE 7-12

As with trusted applications, retrieving the whole list as a file by entering something like the following is possible:

```
Get-CsTrustedApplicationEndpoint > C:\endpoints.txt
```

This creates a file called endpoints.txt, which contains details on every trusted application endpoint that has been configured.

Deleting Applications and Endpoints

To remove a trusted application that has been configured previously, use the Remove-CsTrustedApplication cmdlet. Like Get-CsTrustedApplication, you can run this cmdlet with just the Identity parameter, as in the following example:

```
Remove-CsTrustedApplication -Identity
    ts.fabrikam.com/urn:application:startup.sample
```

If any endpoints exist for this trusted application, the cmdlet will ask for confirmation that these should be deleted. After you confirm this, the application and endpoint(s) will be deleted, as shown in Figure 7-13.

```
Administrator: Lync Server Management Shell

PS C:\Users\michaelg> Remove-CsTrustedApplication -Identity ts.fabrikam.com/urn:
application:startup.sample

The application "urn:application:startup.sample" currently has one or more
contacts assigned to it that will be deleted.
Contacts exist for the application.
[Y] Yes  [N] No  [S] Suspend  [?] Help (default is "Y"): Y
PS C:\Users\michaelg>
```

FIGURE 7-13

To remove a trusted application endpoint without affecting the rest of the application, use `Remove-CsTrustedApplicationEndpoint`. In this case, the `Identity` parameter should be the SIP URI of the endpoint, as shown here:

```
Remove-CsTrustedApplicationEndpoint -Identity sip:startup.sample@fabrikam.com
```

STARTING UP AND SHUTTING DOWN WITH EXPLICIT SETTINGS

The first order of business in starting any UCMA application is to create an instance of `CollaborationPlatform` and start it up. All the other UCMA classes depend on the collaboration platform in order to operate.

Simply starting up the collaboration platform and establishing an endpoint by itself does not really accomplish anything useful, so the code in this chapter will be less exciting than in some of the subsequent ones. At the same time, you must perform these same steps for every single UCMA application you develop.

Because the setup and teardown code is essentially the same in every UCMA application, having a sort of test harness that you can use for trying things out in UCMA is handy. The next few sections describe how to build a test harness application, and then go into more detail on the various methods of starting up and shutting down.

A UCMA Test Harness

Whenever you do any UCMA development in Visual Studio, assuming you are using transport-layer security (TLS) for the connection with Lync Server (almost always a good idea), you must run Visual Studio with administrator rights so that your application can access the certificate store when you are debugging. You can do this by right-clicking on Visual Studio and selecting Run as administrator.

 If you forget to start Visual Studio with administrator rights and then try to debug a UCMA application, the UCMA runtime will throw a `TlsException` when you try to start your collaboration platform with TLS enabled. The exception is thrown because the process needs access to the local certificate store to retrieve the certificate private key, which it uses for TLS. See Chapter 13 for more details on this.

After starting Visual Studio, follow these steps to create a project for a basic UCMA application:

1. Create a new C# class library project. This project will contain the UCMA code for your application. You can call it `StartupShutdown`, or, if you prefer, `Samuel`.

2. Go to the Solution Explorer, right-click on your project, and choose Add Reference. Add a reference to the `Microsoft.Rtc.Collaboration` assembly, which has everything you will need for core UCMA development.

3. Return to the Solution Explorer, right-click on the project, and choose Add Reference again. Add a reference to `System.Configuration`, which you will use to get your trusted application information from an `App.config` file.

4. Now add a second project to your solution. This one should be a console application project (`StartupShutdown.Console`, if you like). After creating this project, right-click on it in the Solution Explorer and choose Add Reference. Switch to the Project tab and add a reference to the `StartupShutdown` project.

Building the Test Harness Class

The next step is to create a class which will handle startup and shutdown of the collaboration platform and endpoint. In larger applications, these responsibilities may be split into several classes.

Add a code file called `ApplicationEndpointStarter.cs` to your UCMA project. This class will eventually handle starting up the collaboration platform and a single application endpoint. You can modify this class to try out different methods of initialization and startup.

To begin building the `ApplicationEndpointStarter` class, add the following `using` statements to the code file. `Microsoft.Rtc.Collaboration` is the namespace for UCMA 3.0 Core, which you may see referred to as the collaboration API. `Microsoft.Rtc.Signaling` is the namespace for the lower-level signaling API (originally UCMA 1.0) on which UCMA 3.0 is built. The other two namespaces will come in handy later.

```
using Microsoft.Rtc.Collaboration;
using Microsoft.Rtc.Signaling;
using System.Threading;
using System.Configuration;
```

Code snippet StartupShutdown\ApplicationEndpointStarter.cs

Next, add a couple of instance variables to your class to hold references to the `CollaborationPlatform` object and the `ApplicationEndpoint` object:

```
using System;
using Microsoft.Rtc.Collaboration;
using Microsoft.Rtc.Signaling;
using System.Threading;
using System.Configuration;

namespace Wrox.ProfessionalUC.Chapter7
{
    public class ApplicationEndpointStarterManualSettings
```

```
    {
        CollaborationPlatform _collaborationPlatform;
        ApplicationEndpoint _appEndpoint;
    }
}
```

Code snippet StartupShutdown\ApplicationEndpointStarter.cs

Adding Logging and Certificate Helper Classes

The application needs some way of logging what it is doing. Add another code file to your project called ILogger.cs. This will be an interface that the ApplicationEndpointStarter class can use to post log messages.

The interface will define three methods: one that takes only a string as a parameter, another that also takes an exception, and another that takes a string plus a list of parameters.

Enter the following code into the new file for the ILogger interface:

```
using System;

namespace StartupShutdown
{
    public interface ILogger
    {
        void Log(string message);

        void Log(string message, Exception ex);

        void Log(string message, params object[] arg);
    }
}
```

Code snippet StartupShutdown\ILogger.cs

Having a more robust logging framework later on might be useful, but for now logging to the console window should be sufficient. Create a new code file, ConsoleLogger.cs, which will contain an implementation of ILogger that logs all messages to the console window:

```
using System;

namespace StartupShutdown
{
    public class ConsoleLogger : ILogger
    {
        public void Log(string message)
        {
            Console.WriteLine(message);
        }

        public void Log(string message, Exception ex)
```

```
            {
                Console.WriteLine(message, ex);
            }

            public void Log(string message, params object[] arg)
            {
                Console.WriteLine(message, arg);
            }
        }
    }
```

Code snippet StartupShutdown\ConsoleLogger.cs

Before returning to `ApplicationEndpointStarter`, create one more helper class. This one is a static class that does nothing but retrieve a private key from the local machine certificate store. This is the certificate that the application needs in order to authenticate with Lync Server for mutual TLS.

Call the new code file `CertificateHelper.cs`, and add the following code. The `GetLocalCertificate` method opens the local machine certificate store and iterates through the collection of certificates, returning the first one it finds whose subject name matches the fully qualified domain name of the local machine, and which has a private key.

Available for download on Wrox.com

```
using System.Net;
using System.Security.Cryptography.X509Certificates;

namespace StartupShutdown
{
    internal static class CertificateHelper
    {
        internal static X509Certificate2 GetLocalCertificate()
        {
            // Get a reference to the local machine certificate store and
            // open it in read-only mode.
            X509Store store = new X509Store(StoreLocation.LocalMachine);
            store.Open(OpenFlags.ReadOnly);

            // Get a reference to the collection of certificates in the store.
            X509Certificate2Collection certificates = store.Certificates;

            // Find the first certificate whose name is the
            // FQDN of the local machine.
            foreach (X509Certificate2 certificate in certificates)
            {
                if (certificate.SubjectName.Name.ToUpper().Contains
                    (Dns.GetHostEntry("localhost").HostName.ToUpper())
                    && certificate.HasPrivateKey)
                {
                    return certificate;
```

```
                }
            }

            return null;
        }
    }
}
```

 Notice that the code uses the ToUpper *method to make the comparison between the certificate subject name and the host name case-insensitive. Make sure you don't forget this step, because the two will not necessarily match case.*

Returning to the ApplicationEndpointStarter class, add another instance variable to hold a reference to an instance of ILogger, along with a constructor that takes an ILogger instance as a parameter and stores it in the instance variable.

```
public class ApplicationEndpointStarter
{
    CollaborationPlatform _collaborationPlatform;
    ApplicationEndpoint _appEndpoint;

    ILogger _logger;

    public ApplicationEndpointStarter(ILogger logger)
    {
        _logger = logger;
    }
}
```

Starting the Collaboration Platform with Explicit Settings

The class needs an entry point for starting the UCMA application; this will be the Start method. Go ahead and add it to your class as follows:

```
public void Start()
{
```

To start up the collaboration platform, your application needs a number of settings: the trusted application name, the GRUU, and the listening port. Those can come from the App.config file.

It also needs the host name of the server on which the application will be running, which you can determine using System.Net.Dns.

> ## GRUUs
>
> A GRUU, contrary to initial impressions, is not a mythical beast or the noise you make when Lync calls won't connect because of a complex certificate issue. GRUU stands for Globally Routable User Agent URI, and a GRUU is a URI that is assigned uniquely to a user agent and can be used to route SIP messages to that user agent from any user agent client with Internet connectivity.
>
> Each Lync user has a SIP URI that can be used to route communications to that user. However, a user can be signed in from multiple locations, in which case the SIP URI does not uniquely identify an endpoint, or user agent. Communications sent to that SIP URI will be routed ("forked") to all the registered endpoints for that user.
>
> Each of these endpoints has a different GRUU associated with it, which allows the endpoints to be uniquely identified with a URI.
>
> A trusted application is identified by a GRUU because it is configured for a specific server and so messages intended for it are always directed to the same location.

Available for download on Wrox.com

```
// Get the trusted application settings from App.config.
string applicationName = ConfigurationManager.AppSettings["applicationName"];
string localhost = System.Net.Dns.GetHostEntry("localhost").HostName;
int listeningPort =
    int.Parse(ConfigurationManager.AppSettings["listeningPort"]);
string gruu = ConfigurationManager.AppSettings["gruu"];
```

Code snippet StartupShutdown\ApplicationEndpointStarter.cs

A ServerPlatformSettings object will hold all of these settings for the initialization of the collaboration platform:

Available for download on Wrox.com

```
// Create a settings object.
ServerPlatformSettings settings = new ServerPlatformSettings(
    applicationName,
    localhost,
    listeningPort,
    gruu,
    CertificateHelper.GetLocalCertificate()
);
```

Code snippet StartupShutdown\ApplicationEndpointStarter.cs

Using the `ServerPlatformSettings` object, create a new instance of `CollaborationPlatform` and store a reference to it in the `_collaborationPlatform` instance variable:

```
// Create a new collaboration platform with the settings.
_collaborationPlatform = new CollaborationPlatform(settings);
```

Code snippet StartupShutdown\ApplicationEndpointStarter.cs

Finally, call `BeginStartup` on `_collaborationPlatform` in order to start up the platform:

```
// Start the platform as an asynchronous operation.
_collaborationPlatform.BeginStartup(OnPlatformStartupCompleted, null)
}
```

Code snippet StartupShutdown\ApplicationEndpointStarter.cs

At this point, the UCMA runtime will begin starting the collaboration platform and initiating a connection to Lync Server. It will do this on a worker thread, so execution of the `Start` method will finish right away, while the startup operation continues in the background.

ASYNCHRONOUS METHODS IN UCMA

Most methods in UCMA are asynchronous, and use the *Begin/End pattern* for asynchronous operations. This means that you call a `Begin` method (for example, `BeginStartup`) to queue up the asynchronous operation for execution by a worker thread.

In addition to any other method-specific parameters, the `Begin` method takes two additional parameters, usually at the end of the parameter list: `asyncCallback` and `state`. The `asyncCallback` parameter takes a delegate that represents a callback method that executes when the operation concludes. The `state` parameter can be any object that should be made available to the callback method when it is called.

The worker thread performs the operation in the background, and when it finishes, it calls the callback method, which must take a single parameter, a reference to an `IAsyncResult`. The callback method must call the corresponding `End` method (for example, `EndStartup`), passing in the `IAsyncResult`, to finish the operation and throw any exceptions on the application thread.

The object that was passed in as the state parameter, if any, is accessible in the `IAsyncResult.AsyncState` property (and must be cast to its original type).

Turning these operations synchronous is actually quite possible by stringing together the `Begin` and `End` methods, but this is a bit like trying to catch the tooth fairy at work by staying awake all night, and is highly discouraged. The reason is

> that some of the operations are quite long-running (a good example is establishing a call, which can take a few seconds or more if the recipient does not answer right away), and it's not absolutely guaranteed that they will always finish.
>
> Along those same lines, throwing unhandled exceptions or blocking for long periods of time in the callback methods are also not good ideas. There is only one worker thread for each major UCMA object (`CollaborationPlatform`, `ApplicationEndpoint`, `UserEndpoint`, `Conversation`, and so on), and if you block it, no other operations can be processed for that object.

The compiler will be complaining right about now that there is no such method as `OnPlatform StartupCompleted`, so go ahead and add that in as well. This method does little more than cleanly finish the asynchronous operation, but this is always an important step.

As mentioned in Chapter 6, always catching `RealTimeException` when calling any `End` method in UCMA is a good practice. This prevents any exceptions from bubbling back up to the UCMA runtime and crashing your application or causing unpredictable behavior.

```
private void OnPlatformStartupCompleted(IAsyncResult result)
{
    try
    {
        // Finish the startup operation.
        _collaborationPlatform.EndStartup(result);

        _logger.Log("Collaboration platform started.");
    }
    catch (RealTimeException ex)
    {
        _logger.Log("Platform startup failed: {0}", ex);
    }
}
```

Code snippet StartupShutdown\ApplicationEndpointStarter.cs

Establishing an Application Endpoint

After the collaboration platform starts up, the application must establish an endpoint. Add a new method, `EstablishEndpoint`, to your class to do this:

```
private void EstablishApplicationEndpoint()
{
```

Code snippet StartupShutdown\ApplicationEndpointStarter.cs

Retrieve the configuration for the application endpoint from `App.config`. The standard port for TLS is 5061; if for whatever reason your Lync Server deployment uses a different TLS port, you can switch the value of the `tlsPort` variable.

```
string contactUri = ConfigurationManager.AppSettings["contactUri"];
string proxyServerFqdn = ConfigurationManager.AppSettings["proxyServerFqdn"];
int tlsPort = 5061;
```

Code snippet StartupShutdown\ApplicationEndpointStarter.cs

Use these settings to create an instance of `ApplicationEndpointSettings`, and set the `UseRegistration` property on the settings object to `true`. This causes the application endpoint to register with Lync Server, which it would not do by default.

```
ApplicationEndpointSettings settings =
        new ApplicationEndpointSettings(contactUri, proxyServerFqdn, tlsPort);
```

Code snippet StartupShutdown\ApplicationEndpointStarter.cs

Initialize a new instance of `ApplicationEndpoint`, passing in the reference to your collaboration platform and the newly created `ApplicationEndpointSettings`. Store a reference to the new endpoint in `_appEndpoint`.

```
_appEndpoint = new ApplicationEndpoint(_collaborationPlatform, settings);
```

Code snippet StartupShutdown\ApplicationEndpointStarter.cs

Whenever the `ApplicationEndpoint` class changes state, it calls the `StateChanged` event. Add an event handler for `StateChanged` so that you can watch the state changes as they occur.

```
_appEndpoint.StateChanged +=
        new EventHandler<LocalEndpointStateChangedEventArgs>(
        _appEndpoint_StateChanged);
```

Code snippet StartupShutdown\ApplicationEndpointStarter.cs

Finally, call `BeginEstablish` to establish the endpoint.

```
    _logger.Log("Establishing application endpoint...");

    _appEndpoint.BeginEstablish(OnApplicationEndpointEstablishCompleted, null);
}
```

Code snippet StartupShutdown\ApplicationEndpointStarter.cs

Now create the callback method, `OnApplicationEndpointEstablishCompleted`. In addition to calling `EndEstablish`, it also sends some details on the endpoint to the log, just so you can see that it is really established.

Available for
download on
Wrox.com

```
private void OnApplicationEndpointEstablishCompleted(IAsyncResult result)
{
    try
    {
        _appEndpoint.EndEstablish(result);

        _logger.Log("Application endpoint established.");
        _logger.Log("Contact URI: {0}", _appEndpoint.OwnerUri);
        _logger.Log("Endpoint URI: {0}", _appEndpoint.EndpointUri);
    }
    catch (RealTimeException ex)
    {
        _logger.Log("Application endpoint establishment failed: {0}", ex);
    }
}
```

Code snippet StartupShutdown\ApplicationEndpointStarter.cs

The application should begin establishing the endpoint only after the collaboration platform is fully started up. Go back to the `OnPlatformStartupCompleted` callback method and add a line of code to call `EstablishCompleted` after the startup operation finishes.

Available for
download on
Wrox.com

```
private void OnPlatformStartupCompleted(IAsyncResult result)
{
    try
    {
        // Finish the startup operation.
        _collaborationPlatform.EndStartup(result);

        _logger.Log("Collaboration platform started.");

        EstablishApplicationEndpoint();
    }
    catch (RealTimeException ex)
    {
        _logger.Log("Platform startup failed: {0}", ex);
    }
}
```

Code snippet StartupShutdown\ApplicationEndpointStarter.cs

Also, add the event handler for `ApplicationEndpoint.StateChanged`. This can simply log the state change.

Available for
download on
Wrox.com

```
private void _appEndpoint_StateChanged(object sender,
    LocalEndpointStateChangedEventArgs e)
{
```

```
        _logger.Log("Application endpoint state changed from {0} to {1}",
            e.PreviousState,
            e.State);
    }
```

Code snippet StartupShutdown\ApplicationEndpointStarter.cs

Shutting Down the Platform and Endpoint Cleanly

Now that the platform and endpoint are both set up and started, it's time to shut everything down. Add a public ShutDown method to the class, which kicks off the shutdown process by terminating the application endpoint.

Available for download on Wrox.com

```
public void ShutDown()
{
    _logger.Log("Terminating application endpoint...");

    _appEndpoint.BeginTerminate(OnApplicationEndpointTerminateCompleted, null);
}
```

Code snippet StartupShutdown\ApplicationEndpointStarter.cs

As you can see, the shutdown process is more or less the reverse of startup; the first step is to terminate the endpoint, and after the endpoint is terminated the application can shut down the platform.

> *Exiting a UCMA application without properly shutting down the collaboration platform can cause memory leaks, because unmanaged resources may not be released correctly. You needn't worry about it too much during debugging if your application crashes a few times without shutting down cleanly, but ensuring that a clean shutdown always occurs in any production application is important.*

The callback for the endpoint termination can finish the asynchronous operation and then begin shutting down the collaboration platform.

Available for download on Wrox.com

```
private void OnApplicationEndpointTerminateCompleted(IAsyncResult result)
{
    try
    {
        _appEndpoint.EndTerminate(result);

        _logger.Log("Application endpoint terminated.");

        ShutDownPlatform();
    }
    catch (RealTimeException ex)
```

```
        {
            _logger.Log("Application endpoint termination failed: {0}", ex);
        }
    }

    private void ShutDownPlatform()
    {
        _logger.Log("Shutting down platform...");

        _collaborationPlatform.BeginShutdown(OnPlatformShutdownCompleted, null);
    }
```

Code snippet StartupShutdown\ApplicationEndpointStarter.cs

Last but not least, the callback method for the platform shutdown calls the EndShutdown method and writes one final log message:

```
    private void OnPlatformShutdownCompleted(IAsyncResult result)
    {
        try
        {
            _collaborationPlatform.EndShutdown(result);

            _logger.Log("Platform shut down.");
        }
        catch (RealTimeException ex)
        {
            _logger.Log("Platform shutdown failed: {0}", ex);
        }
    }
```

Code snippet StartupShutdown\ApplicationEndpointStarter.cs

Adding Wait Handles for Startup and Shutdown

The UCMA code is complete and ready to be run. One more addition to the code will make things easier for the host console application. When the console application calls the Start method on the ApplicationEndpointStarter, having a way for it to wait until the startup has finished before moving on to the shutdown process will be helpful. Add two ManualResetEvent instance variables to the class. These function as wait handles for startup and for shutdown.

```
// A wait handle for startup and one for shutdown.
// They are set to unsignaled to start.
ManualResetEvent _startupWaitHandle = new ManualResetEvent(false);
ManualResetEvent _shutdownWaitHandle = new ManualResetEvent(false);
```

Code snippet StartupShutdown\ApplicationEndpointStarter.cs

Return to the `OnApplicationEndpointEstablishCompleted` and add a line of code (indicated in bold) to signal the startup wait handle:

```
private void OnApplicationEndpointEstablishCompleted(IAsyncResult result)
{
    try
    {
        _appEndpoint.EndEstablish(result);

        _logger.Log("Application endpoint established.");
        _logger.Log("Contact URI: {0}", _appEndpoint.OwnerUri);
        _logger.Log("Endpoint URI: {0}", _appEndpoint.EndpointUri);

        _startupWaitHandle.Set();
    }
    catch (RealTimeException ex)
    {
        _logger.Log("Application endpoint establishment failed: {0}", ex);
    }
}
```

Code snippet StartupShutdown\ApplicationEndpointStarter.cs

Add a corresponding line of code (indicated in bold) to the `OnPlatformShutdownCompleted` callback method:

```
private void OnPlatformShutdownCompleted(IAsyncResult result)
{
    try
    {
        _collaborationPlatform.EndShutdown(result);

        _logger.Log("Platform shut down.");

        _shutdownWaitHandle.Set();
    }
    catch (RealTimeException ex)
    {
        _logger.Log("Platform shutdown failed: {0}", ex);
    }
}
```

Code snippet StartupShutdown\ApplicationEndpointStarter.cs

Now add two more public methods to the class. Each one will block until its respective wait handle has been signaled.

```
public void WaitForStartup()
{
    _startupWaitHandle.WaitOne();
}
```

```
public void WaitForShutdown()
{
    _shutdownWaitHandle.WaitOne();
}
```

Code snippet StartupShutdown\ApplicationEndpointStarter.cs

Building the Console Application

With your starter class complete, you can open the `Program.cs` file in your console application
project and add some code to initialize and run your `ApplicationEndpointStarter` class:

Available for
download on
Wrox.com

```
static void Main(string[] args)
{
    ApplicationEndpointStarter sample =
        new ApplicationEndpointStarter (new ConsoleLogger());

    sample.Start();
    sample.WaitForStartup();

    System.Console.WriteLine("Hit enter to stop");
    System.Console.ReadLine();

    sample.ShutDown();
    sample.WaitForShutdown();

    System.Console.WriteLine("Hit enter to exit");
    System.Console.ReadLine();
}
```

Code snippet StartupShutdown\Program.cs

Running the Test Harness

All that's left is to add an `App.config` file to the console application project, containing the settings
you referenced in the startup code:

Available for
download on
Wrox.com

```
<configuration>
  <startup>
    <supportedRuntime version="v2.0.50727"/>
  </startup>
  <appSettings>
    <add key="applicationName" value="startup.sample"/>
    <add key="gruu" value="<your trusted application's gruu>"/>
    <add key="listeningPort" value="<your trusted application's listening port>"/>
    <add key="contactUri" value="<contact for your application>"/>
    <add key="proxyServerFqdn" value="<CS server FQDN>"/>
  </appSettings>
</configuration>
```

Code snippet StartupShutdown\App.config

With that in place, go ahead and run your application. Assuming everything is configured properly, you should see something like this in the console window:

```
Starting collaboration platform...
Collaboration platform started.
Establishing application endpoint...
Application endpoint state changed from Idle to Establishing
Application endpoint state changed from Establishing to Established
Application endpoint established.
Contact URI: sip:startup.sample.app@fabrikam.com
Endpoint URI: sip:appsrv.fabrikam.com@fabrikam.com;gruu;opaque=srvr:startup.samp
le:lodROR5GXVeJton_2mjypwAA
Hit enter to stop
```

After you press Enter, the shutdown code runs:

```
Terminating application endpoint...
Application endpoint state changed from Established to Terminating
Application endpoint state changed from Terminating to Terminated
Application endpoint terminated.
Shutting down platform...
Platform shut down.
Hit enter to exit
```

Congratulations. You've just successfully run a simple, but complete, UCMA application.

LOADING TRUSTED APPLICATION SETTINGS AUTOMATICALLY

Given how simple the steps are to get a UCMA application up and running, you may have felt that the most difficult part of the process was copying the GRUU correctly into the App.config file. For those of you who found this irritating, and particularly those who suffered through this step many times with the previous version of the API, UCMA 2.0, glad tidings are here. UCMA 3.0 introduces a feature, usually referred to as "auto-provisioning," which allows your application to automatically load all of those troublesome alphanumeric hemorrhages without the need for you to enter them anywhere in configuration or code. All that you need to provide in order for this to work is the application ID from your trusted application, which you may remember looks something like this:

```
urn:application:maximillian
```

Applications that use one or more application endpoints can also automatically discover settings for all application endpoints that are provisioned for that trusted application by means of an event on the CollaborationPlatform class. These two approaches often go together, but can just as easily be used separately, so that automatically loading settings for a collaboration platform and then manually entering settings for an application endpoint are perfectly possible.

Starting a Collaboration Platform with ProvisionedApplicationPlatformSettings

Loading provisioning settings automatically when starting a collaboration platform is as simple as using an instance of `ProvisionedApplicationPlatformSettings` to provide settings when initializing the `CollaborationPlatform` object.

`ProvisionedApplicationPlatformSettings` takes two parameters:

➤ `applicationUserAgent` is the identifier for the application that will appear in SIP messages in the `User-Agent` header. It doesn't have much effect on your application's behavior, but could be useful if you look at the SIP messages for debugging.

➤ `applicationId` is an ID of the form `urn:application:something` that you created for your trusted application when provisioning it.

Modified to use `ProvisionedApplicationPlatformSettings`, the `Start` method in the test harness application would look like this:

```
public void Start()
{
    // Get the application ID from App.config.
    string applicationUserAgent = "maximillian";
    string applicationId =
        ConfigurationManager.AppSettings["urn:application:maximillian"];

    // Create a settings object.
    ProvisionedApplicationPlatformSettings settings =
        new ProvisionedApplicationPlatformSettings(applicationUserAgent,
            applicationId);

    // Create a new collaboration platform with the settings.
    _collaborationPlatform = new CollaborationPlatform(settings);

    _logger.Log("Starting collaboration platform...");

    // Start the platform as an asynchronous operation.
    _collaborationPlatform.BeginStartup(OnPlatformStartupCompleted, null);
}
```

Nothing else in the code needs to change in order for the application to use auto-provisioning for the collaboration platform.

Discovering Application Endpoints Automatically

UCMA can also retrieve provisioning information automatically for application endpoints. There is no `ProvisionedApplicationEndpointSettings`; instead, there is a method on the `CollaborationPlatform` class called `RegisterForApplicationEndpointSettings`, which takes an event handler. In the test harness application, this could go just after the line of code that initializes the collaboration platform:

```
public void Start()
{
    // Get the application ID from App.config.
    string applicationUserAgent = "maximillian";
    string applicationId =
        ConfigurationManager.AppSettings["urn:application:maximillian"];

    // Create a settings object.
    ProvisionedApplicationPlatformSettings settings =
        new ProvisionedApplicationPlatformSettings(applicationUserAgent,
            applicationId);

    // Create a new collaboration platform with the settings.
    _collaborationPlatform = new CollaborationPlatform(settings);

    _collaborationPlatform.RegisterForApplicationEndpointSettings(
        OnApplicationEndpointSettingsDiscovered);

    _logger.Log("Starting collaboration platform...");

    // Start the platform as an asynchronous operation.
    _collaborationPlatform.BeginStartup(OnPlatformStartupCompleted, null);
}
```

UCMA calls the handler delegate supplied to this method once for each application endpoint associated with the trusted application. The event arguments contain a reference to an instance of ApplicationEndpointSettings, which you can use to initialize the new ApplicationEndpoint object.

Here is what an event handler might look like. Because this application only needs a single application endpoint, the event handler keeps track of how many endpoints the application has already discovered, and uses only the first one. (If the application were designed to use multiple endpoints, the handler could initialize each one and store them in a collection or another object.)

```
private void OnApplicationEndpointSettingsDiscovered(object sender,
    ApplicationEndpointSettingsDiscoveredEventArgs args)
{
    // Keep track of how many endpoints we've found
    // so that we only take one.
    Interlocked.Increment(ref _endpointsDiscovered);

    if (_endpointsDiscovered > 1)
    {
        // We've already found an endpoint
        // and we don't need another one. Sorry!
        return;
    }

    _appEndpoint = new ApplicationEndpoint(_collaborationPlatform,
        args.ApplicationEndpointSettings);

    _appEndpoint.BeginEstablish(OnApplicationEndpointEstablishCompleted, null);
}
```

After the application has a reference to the `ApplicationEndpointSettings` object, the process of establishing the endpoint is exactly the same as if you initialized the settings manually.

Note that the number of times the event handler runs depends on how many application endpoints are provisioned for the trusted application. For this reason, code that uses auto-discovery of application endpoints should not depend on finding a certain number of them if it can be avoided, or at least should gracefully handle conditions where the wrong number of endpoints has been provisioned.

PREPARING ENDPOINTS FOR AN APPLICATION

Chapter 6 introduces the concept of endpoints and offers some guidance for choosing between user endpoints and application endpoints. This section describes how to configure settings for an instance of `ApplicationEndpoint` or `UserEndpoint` to fit the needs of the UCMA application.

Using ApplicationEndpoint for Services

As mentioned in Chapter 6, the `ApplicationEndpoint` class is most suited to highly available Lync services that do not act on behalf of specific users, such as "bots" or interactive voice response systems.

The settings for an instance of `ApplicationEndpoint` are supplied in the form of an `ApplicationEndpointSettings` object. When an application uses auto-provisioning, the settings object is provided when an application endpoint is discovered; otherwise, it must be created from scratch using the constructor. In either case, the properties on the settings object can be changed to customize the other settings.

`ApplicationEndpointSettings` has a number of these properties, which control the behavior of the endpoint. Table 7-1 covers some of the more commonly used ones.

TABLE 7-1: Properties of ApplicationEndpointSettings

PROPERTY	DESCRIPTION
`AutomaticPresencePublicationEnabled`	If this is `true`, UCMA automatically publishes an initial presence state for the endpoint when it starts up.
`EndpointUserAgent`	Determines what text will appear in the User-Agent SIP header for messages from this endpoint.
`IsDefaultRoutingEndpoint`	If this is `true`, UCMA routes any messages that are sent to the application but are not matched with any specific endpoint to this endpoint. For example, messages where the destination URI is the GRUU of the application rather than a SIP URI will go to the endpoint in this case.

continues

TABLE 7-1 *(continued)*

PROPERTY	DESCRIPTION
`MaxRegisterRetries`	Determines how many times the endpoint tries to register with Lync Server before giving up.
`Presence`	Used to set the presence information that will be published on endpoint startup if automatic presence publication is enabled. See Chapter 9 for details.
`PresenceBasedScreeningDisabled`	In short, when set to `false` this allows endpoints to use the Do Not Disturb presence to block incoming messages. In order for this property to work, the `UseRegistration` property must also be `true`.
`UseRegistration`	If `true`, this property tells the endpoint to register with Lync Server. The default is `false`, because application endpoints are not required to register. This must be `true` if the endpoint will be publishing presence updates that expire when the endpoint "signs out of Lync," as opposed to persistent presence states, which never expire.

ENDPOINT TYPE AND SUBTYPE

Two other properties on `ApplicationEndpointSettings` control how the endpoint is treated by other Lync endpoints: `EndpointType` and `EndpointSubtype`.

`EndpointType` has four possible values: `User`, `Application`, `Gateway`, and `Conference`. Normally, only the first two will be of any use for a UCMA application. They control how calls are routed in a multi-modal conversation. If the endpoint type is `Application`, any modalities that are added to a conversation with this endpoint must be routed to exactly the same endpoint, and not to another endpoint owned by the same user (that is, with the same SIP URI). On the other hand, if the endpoint type is `User`, any calls for modalities that are added are routed to all endpoints representing that user — so that a user can pick up the audio on a phone while typing IM messages on the computer, for example.

The default value is almost always appropriate for this property.

The `EndpointSubtype` property gives further detail on what purpose the endpoint serves (if it belongs to the `Application` category), with values of `None`, `Principal`, `MessageTaker`, `Attendant`, and `Information`. Normally this can be left at the default value of `Attendant`.

To change these values, call the `SetEndpointType` method on `ApplicationEndpointSettings`.

`UserEndpoint` has the same properties, but does not allow them to be modified.

Most applications that use `ApplicationEndpoint`, being intended as highly available services, do not need to make changes to their presence state, and simply need to appear as available in the contact lists of potential users. For these applications, UCMA makes publishing a persistent presence state that does not expire possible.

In UCMA 3.0, publishing this type of presence on application startup is quite easy. Chapter 9 describes how to modify the `ApplicationEndpointSettings` object to do this.

Using UserEndpoint for Clients

The `UserEndpoint` class, as discussed in Chapter 6, is best for applications that act on behalf of Lync users or provide a client interface of some kind for them. Instances of this class are configured with a `UserEndpointSettings` object.

There is no automatic endpoint discovery for user endpoints, as there is for application endpoints, because user endpoints are not associated with specific applications. To create an instance of `UserEndpointSettings`, use the constructor, passing in the same three parameters as for an instance of `ApplicationEndpointSettings`:

```
UserEndpointSettings settings =
        new UserEndpointSettings(contactUri, proxyServerFqdn, tlsPort);
```

`UserEndpointSettings`, like `ApplicationEndpointSettings`, has a number of additional properties that you may set to control the endpoint's behavior; Table 7-2 lists some of these.

TABLE 7-2: Properties of UserEndpointSettings

PROPERTY	DESCRIPTION
AutomaticPresencePublicationEnabled	If true, causes UCMA to automatically publish presence for the endpoint on startup, as described in Chapter 9.
Credential	Contains the credentials that will be used to sign in to Lync Server as the user represented by the endpoint. When the endpoint is part of a trusted application, the credential is not necessary, and Lync Server will allow the application to register as any user.
EndpointUserAgent	Determines what text appears in the User-Agent SIP header for messages from this endpoint.
MaxRegisterRetries	Determines how many times the endpoint tries to register with Lync Server before giving up.

continues

TABLE 7-2 *(continued)*

PROPERTY	DESCRIPTION
Presence	Used to set the presence information that will be published on endpoint startup if automatic presence publication is enabled. See Chapter 9 for details.
PresenceBasedScreeningDisabled	Set this to `true` to allow other users to send messages to this endpoint even when the presence state is Do Not Disturb.

As with application endpoints, UCMA 3.0 can automatically publish presence information for a user endpoint on startup. Chapter 9 describes this mechanism in more detail.

SHUTTING DOWN WITHOUT DROPPING CALLS

Inevitably, performing some sort of maintenance on a UCMA server application becomes necessary at some point. If the application handles many communications, shutting it down without interrupting any calls or chat sessions that are in progress is important.

UCMA 3.0 introduces a draining feature which makes taking down services for maintenance in this way easy. An application that is being drained waits for all currently active communication sessions to conclude, while rejecting any new incoming ones. If the application is load balanced, Lync automatically redirects incoming calls to an active instance of the application.

After all calls have terminated, the draining operation completes and UCMA calls the callback method, at which point the application can continue with shutdown. Because the draining is not considered complete until all calls finish on their own, this process can potentially take quite a long time. In some cases, application developers may wish to use a `Timer` object or some other mechanism to force shutdown after a certain period of time if the draining has not concluded.

 Both application endpoints and user endpoints can take advantage of the draining capability in UCMA 3.0.

Telling an endpoint to begin draining is simple: Call the `BeginDrain` method on the endpoint object, as the following code demonstrates:

```
public void Drain()
{
    _logger.Log("Draining endpoint.");
```

```
    try
    {
        _appEndpoint.BeginDrain(OnDrainingCompleted, null);
    }
    catch (InvalidOperationException ioex)
    {
        _logger.Log("Failed draining endpoint.", ioex);
    }
}

private void OnDrainingCompleted(IAsyncResult result)
{
    try
    {
        _appEndpoint.EndDrain(result);

        // Begin terminating the endpoint, etc.
    }
    catch (RealTimeException rtex)
    {
        _logger.Log("Failed draining endpoint.");
    }
}
```

Code snippet Draining\DrainingSample.cs

After `BeginDrain` and the corresponding `EndDrain` method are called, any subsequent calls into the endpoint are declined. The UCMA runtime invokes the callback method (`OnDrainingCompleted` in the preceding example) after all active calls have completed. At this point, the application can call the `BeginTerminate` method on the endpoint to start the shutdown process.

TROUBLESHOOTING STARTUP AND PROVISIONING

As touched upon previously, Unified Communications development requires quite a bit more environment setup than better-known development platforms such as, say, ASP.NET. With Visual Studio and perhaps a SQL Server Express instance, a single developer can write, run, and debug an ASP.NET website on the local machine, without any other special setup. Running a UCMA application, on the other hand, requires quite a few complex dependencies. Lync Server must be deployed and configured on the network, the UCMA application must be able to connect to it, and any number of misconfigurations can prevent the application from even starting up. At times, starting a server-side application for Lync Server on an unfamiliar environment can feel like an insurmountable task requiring superhuman endurance.

Because startup and shutdown are so uniform between different UCMA applications, most of the problems that developers encounter with the startup code can be traced to one of a handful of underlying causes. With experience, unified communications developers begin to notice the patterns and recognize certain common issues when they occur, but those who are just starting out can find themselves using up hours of debugging time on identifying the same issues over and over.

For each of the common symptoms, having a circuit of things to check can help. More often than not, by trying the common fixes one by one, you can quickly resolve issues with the collaboration platform or endpoints.

The common issues fall into two large categories: difficulties with provisioning a trusted application or application endpoint, and errors encountered while trying to start a UCMA application.

Troubleshooting a Trusted Service

Lync Server in its simplest configurations still requires a fairly complex server architecture, and developers who do not have a background in configuring Lync Server may find the application provisioning process challenging at first. This section covers some common issues that can arise during application provisioning and how to resolve them.

Fixing Insufficient Permissions Errors in Provisioning

To run the PowerShell cmdlets that create or modify trusted application pools and trusted applications, a user must be a domain administrator. Trying to run one of these cmdlets without the necessary permissions results in an error much like the one shown in Figure 7-14.

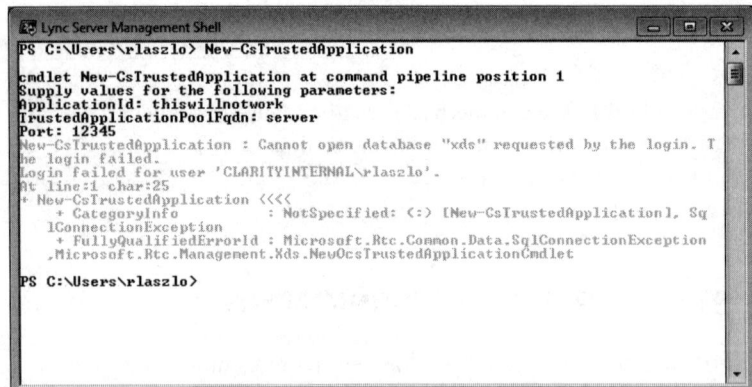

FIGURE 7-14

A user who is a member of the RTCUniversalServerAdmins group in Active Directory and who is also a local administrator on the application server can create and modify trusted application endpoints.

Fixing a Missing Trusted Application Pool

Because each trusted application object is tied to a specific server, simply moving a UCMA application to another server and running it with the same provisioning settings is not possible. In fact, a close inspection of the GRUU reveals that the server name is incorporated into the GRUU so that identifying which server a particular trusted application is associated with is fairly easy.

Preparing a new server for a UCMA application requires creating a new trusted application pool and trusted application using the PowerShell cmdlets described in the section "Provisioning an Application" earlier in this chapter.

If you attempt to create a trusted application on a server that is not part of a trusted application pool, the PowerShell cmdlet will fail with an error message, as shown in Figure 7-15.

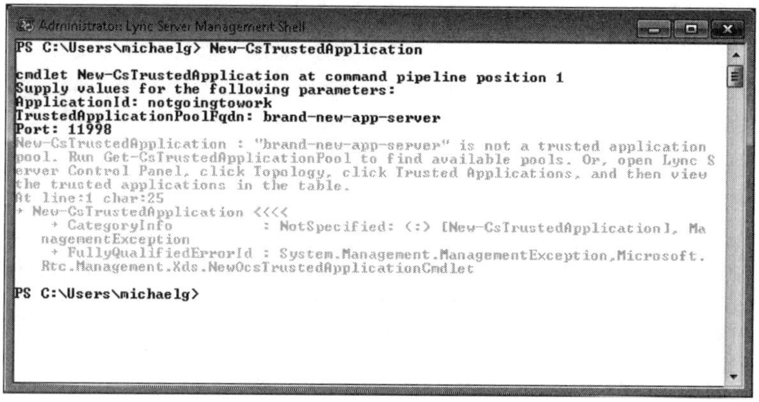

FIGURE 7-15

In this case, either creating a new trusted application pool or, if the application is load balanced, running `New-CsTrustedApplicationComputer` to add a new server to the existing application pool is necessary.

Troubleshooting Errors on Startup

An application can run into errors either on starting the collaboration platform or while establishing endpoints. Most of the issues that come up during these actions have to do with the provisioning settings for the application and can be resolved by double-checking these settings for various common errors.

Dealing with a Failed to Listen on Any Address and Port Supplied Message

If a UCMA application tries to start up a collaboration platform using the same provisioning settings as another UCMA application that is already running, it will fail with a `ConnectionFailureException` with the message "Failed to listen on any address and port supplied." Having another instance of the application running is the most common reason for this somewhat confusing exception message. This can be particularly bewildering if the other process is running in the context of another user on the same server. If an application fails to start with this exception, check for other UCMA applications running on the server using the same trusted application. See Chapter 13 for more advice on troubleshooting this problem.

Troubleshooting TLS Exceptions

Using transport-layer security (TLS) for the connection with Lync Server whenever possible is recommended for any server-side application. For an application to use TLS, however, it must authenticate with Lync Server using a certificate. If an application throws a `TlsException` on startup, chances are it does not have a certificate to use for TLS.

The simplest explanation in these cases is that a valid certificate was never installed on the server where the application is running. The certificate must be in the local machine store, in the Personal folder, and its subject name must be the fully qualified domain name (FQDN) of the application server.

If such a certificate is not installed on the application server, you must install it. Refer to the instructions in the previous chapter on installing certificates trusted by Lync Server on an application server.

If the certificate is installed, the possibility exists that the application cannot access it because it does not have sufficient permissions. This happens most often because developers forget to open Visual Studio with administrator rights (by right-clicking on Visual Studio and selecting Run as administrator). When running with administrator permissions, the Visual Studio process will have no trouble accessing the certificate store and retrieving the certificate to use for TLS.

If the application is being run by a service account, the service account must be granted read permissions on the private key for this certificate. The easiest way to do this is through the Certificates snap-in in Microsoft Management Console, by right-clicking on the certificate and selecting All Tasks ⇨ Manage Private Keys.

See Chapter 13 for more details.

Fixing Failures with Auto-Provisioning

The section "Configuring Management Store Replication" earlier in this chapter describes how to configure replication from the master Central Management Store into the local management store replica on the application server. If this step is not completed on the application server, auto-provisioning using `ProvisionedApplicationSettings` will not work properly. If a UCMA application will not start using auto-provisioning on a new server but works fine with manual provisioning, likely this step has been missed. See the section "Configuring Management Store Replication" earlier in this chapter for step-by-step instructions.

SUMMARY

In this chapter, you have learned how to provision and build a functioning UCMA application that brings up a Lync endpoint and shuts down cleanly. You have also learned how to drain endpoints to shut down without interrupting communications.

The next chapter covers one of the most important and fundamental topics in UCMA: how to establish, accept, and control two-party communication sessions.

8

Two-Party Call Control with UCMA

WHAT'S IN THIS CHAPTER

➤ Managing calls

➤ Working with media flows

➤ Monitoring call state

➤ Using quality of service metrics

➤ Retrieving call information

➤ Call parking

Managing communication sessions is the bread and butter of the Unified Communications Managed API (UCMA). Every form of communication supported by Lync — audio, video, instant messaging, application sharing — can be reduced to an SIP signaling session plus some sort of transfer of media. In UCMA parlance, these communications are known as *calls* and are represented by Call objects in code.

This chapter describes how applications can set up, manage, and tear down communication sessions using the various call control APIs in UCMA.

PLACING OUTBOUND CALLS WITH UCMA

Establishing an outbound call from the application to a remote endpoint is one of the most common tasks with UCMA. The three main steps in placing an outbound call in code are:

1. Creating the Conversation

2. Creating the Call

3. Establishing the Call asynchronously

The next few sections describe each of these steps in gruesome detail, explaining the process for performing each operation in code and delving into the SIP signaling that happens behind the scenes during the call establishment. The code snippets are taken from sample applications that are available on this book's website at www.wrox.com.

The following code shows a class that places an outbound instant messaging call to a remote endpoint.

```csharp
using System;
using System.Configuration;
using System.Threading;
using Microsoft.Rtc.Collaboration;
using Microsoft.Rtc.Collaboration.AudioVideo;
using Microsoft.Rtc.Signaling;

namespace TwoPartyCallControl
{
    public class OutboundInstantMessagingCallSample : ISampleComponent
    {
        ApplicationEndpoint _appEndpoint;
        InstantMessagingCall _imCall;
        string _destinationSipUri;

        // A wait handle for startup and one for shutdown.
        // They are set to unsignaled to start.
        ManualResetEvent _startupWaitHandle =
            new ManualResetEvent(false);
        ManualResetEvent _shutdownWaitHandle =
            new ManualResetEvent(false);

        ILogger _logger;

        public OutboundInstantMessagingCallSample(
            ApplicationEndpoint endpoint, ILogger logger)
        {
            _appEndpoint = endpoint;
            _logger = logger;
        }

        public void Start()
        {
            Console.Write("Enter destination URI: ");
            _destinationSipUri = Console.ReadLine();

            EstablishCall();
        }

        private void EstablishCall()
        {
            // Create a new Conversation.
            Conversation conversation = new Conversation(_appEndpoint);

            // Create a new IM call.
```

```
        _imCall = new InstantMessagingCall(conversation);

        try
        {
            // Establish the IM call.
            _imCall.BeginEstablish(_destinationSipUri,
                new CallEstablishOptions(),
                result =>
                {
                    try
                    {
                        // Finish the asynchronous operation.
                        _imCall.EndEstablish(result);
                    }
                    catch (RealTimeException ex)
                    {
                        // Catch and log exceptions.
                        _logger.Log("Failed establishing IM call",
                            ex);
                    }
                },
                null
            );
        }
        catch (InvalidOperationException ioex)
        {
            _logger.Log("Failed establishing IM call", ioex);
        }
    }

    public void Stop()
    {
        // Terminate the IM call if necessary.

        if (_imCall.State != CallState.Terminating &&
            _imCall.State != CallState.Terminated &&
            _imCall.State != CallState.Idle)
        {
            try
            {
                _imCall.BeginTerminate(ar =>
                {
                    try
                    {
                        _imCall.EndTerminate(ar);
                    }
                    catch (RealTimeException rtex)
                    {
                        _logger.Log("Failed terminating IM call.",
                            rtex);
                    }
                },
                null);
            }
            catch (InvalidOperationException ioex)
```

```
              {
                  _logger.Log("Failed terminating IM call.", ioex);
              }
          }
      }
  }
}
```

Code snippet TwoPartyCallControl\OutboundInstantMessagingCallSample.cs

The section of the code that actually creates and initiates the outgoing call is highlighted in bold. Notice that placing the call takes only a few lines of code. This is because UCMA is performing some sleight of hand. When you call the `BeginEstablish` method, UCMA handles an entire SIP handshake — a complex sequence of SIP messages to initiate the call — behind the scenes on your behalf.

To handle the sending and receiving of SIP messages and the other activities involved in communicating with Lync Server, the UCMA runtime creates and manages a pool of worker threads that it uses to perform its communication operations in the background.

As a developer, you can easily just sit back and enjoy the magic show without needing any knowledge of the underlying SIP messaging or what it means. However, if you build applications of moderate to high complexity with UCMA, you will eventually face situations where understanding the inside of the black box is important.

So, although each of the operations discussed in this chapter consists of only a few lines of code, the chapter also covers the messaging that happens in each case below the surface.

Preparing an Outbound Call Using UCMA Objects

The first step in establishing a new outbound call is creating the necessary UCMA objects: an instance of `Conversation` and one or more `Call` objects.

Every Lync communication session handled by UCMA must start with a `Conversation` object. The `Conversation` object is associated with one or more `Call` objects and has a couple of functions: It allows for multi-modal communication sessions by tying together `Call` objects (and under the covers, SIP signaling sessions) of different modalities, and also provides access to the conferencing APIs in UCMA for `Call` objects that are involved in a conference.

MULTI-MODAL COMMUNICATION

A multi-modal communication session is a conversation that includes, for instance, audio and instant message, or instant message and application sharing, at the same time — a single conversation where more than one communication method is in play.

In the Lync client, you can easily make a conversation multi-modal by adding new modalities (audio, video, instant messaging, application sharing) within a conversation window that is already open.

The `Conversation` object alone is not sufficient to establish a communication session. Along with the conversation, you must create at least one instance of `AudioVideoCall`, `InstantMessagingCall`, or some other class that derives from the `Call` abstract class. You can then call the `BeginEstablish` method on this object to start the asynchronous operation that establishes the call.

Initializing UCMA Conversation and Call Objects

Creating a new instance of `Conversation` and one of the `Call` subclasses can be quite simple. In its simplest form, it looks like the code in the following snippet.

Available for download on Wrox.com

```
// Create a new Conversation.
Conversation conversation = new Conversation(_endpoint);

// Create a new IM call.
InstantMessagingCall imCall = new InstantMessagingCall(conversation);
```

Code snippet TwoPartyCallControl\OutboundInstantMessagingCallSample.cs

For two-party calls, these two objects, the `Conversation` and the `Call` objects, are usually initialized together, because a `Conversation` object by itself is about as useful as a bicycle tire without a bicycle. Conferences work a bit differently, as you will see in Chapter 11.

The simplest constructor for `Conversation` takes only a reference to an endpoint. The endpoint you provide will be the one that initiates the communication session, so if the application has established multiple endpoints you must pass a reference to the endpoint you want to place the call or send the instant message.

Another constructor for `Conversation` takes a `ConversationSettings` object as a second parameter. This object has properties that enable you to specify a subject and priority for the conversation. These will be associated with the Lync communication session and be visible in the Lync conversation window if the other participant is using the Lync client.

The constructors for `InstantMessagingCall` and `AudioVideoCall` always take a reference to a `Conversation` object.

Impersonating a User

Application endpoints, shady characters that they are, have the ability to impersonate any user when initiating a communication session. Using impersonation, a single application endpoint can manage Lync communication sessions on behalf of a number of different users.

Impersonation is often useful for applications that broker calls between users. As an example, a "click to call" application can place a call to User B on behalf of User A and then transfer the call to User A's mobile phone. By impersonating User A in the outgoing call, the application can make it appear that User A is actually placing the call.

To impersonate a user when initiating a communication session, call the `Impersonate` method on the `Conversation` object. The `Impersonate` method takes three parameters: the impersonated user's SIP URI, display name, and tel URI. The latter two parameters can be null.

The following code snippet shows how to impersonate a user:

```
// Create a new Conversation.
Conversation conversation = new Conversation(_endpoint);

// Impersonate a user.
conversation.Impersonate("sip:aldous@wrox.com",
"tel:+15555551212",
    "Aldous");

// Create a new IM call.
InstantMessagingCall imCall = new InstantMessagingCall(conversation);
```

You can add the highlighted line of code into the `OutboundInstantMessagingCallSample` class shown earlier to see how impersonation works.

An interesting thing about impersonation is that the impersonated user does not have to be a real Lync user. Your application can make up a fake SIP URI, fake display name, and everything short of a fake moustache, and the conversation will still work fine.

Keep in mind that impersonation operates at the level of a single `Conversation` object. Any outgoing communications you initiate using this `Conversation` or its associated `Call` objects after calling `Impersonate` will come from the impersonated SIP URI. The impersonation will not apply to any new `Conversation` objects you create.

Establishing a Two-Party Call with BeginEstablish

After the necessary objects are initialized, you can place the outgoing call using the `BeginEstablish` and `EndEstablish` methods on the `Call` object. In UCMA, the process is more or less the same whether the call is an `InstantMessagingCall`, an `AudioVideoCall`, or some other `Call` subclass, although the parameters are slightly different for some of the overloads of `BeginEstablish`. In the underlying SIP messaging, however, some significant differences exist, as discussed next.

Establishing an Instant Messaging Call

The following code snippet establishes an outgoing instant message call, catching exceptions at both the beginning and end of the asynchronous operation.

```
try
{
    // Establish the IM call.
    imCall.BeginEstablish(_destinationSipUri,
        new CallEstablishOptions() /* this could also just be null */,
        result =>
```

```
        {
            try
            {
                // Finish the asynchronous operation.
                imCall.EndEstablish(result);
            }
            catch (RealTimeException ex)
            {
                // Catch and log exceptions.
                _logger.Log("Failed establishing IM call", ex);
            }
        },
        null
    );
}
catch (InvalidOperationException ioex)
{
    _logger.Log("Failed establishing IM call", ioex);
}
```

Code snippet TwoPartyCallControl\OutboundInstantMessagingCallSample.cs

In this case, the first parameter of `BeginEstablish` is the SIP URI to which the call is being directed. The second parameter is a `CallEstablishOptions` object, which allows you to specify custom MIME parts, SIP headers, and some other options for the SIP `INVITE` message that is sent to the remote endpoint. If you have no options to specify, this parameter can be null.

OMITTING THE DESTINATION SIP URI

One of the overloads of `BeginEstablish` leaves out the parameter for the destination SIP URI. You should use this overload and let UCMA determine the destination in two cases. The first case is when the call belongs to a `Conversation` object that already has another call (for another modality) established. In this case, UCMA already knows the SIP URI for the remote user and you do not need to supply it again. The second case is when the call and its associated `Conversation` object are for a conference. Chapter 11 covers this situation in more detail.

When the application calls `BeginEstablish`, an entire SIP drama unfolds behind the curtains. Figure 8-1 shows the storyline in a nutshell.

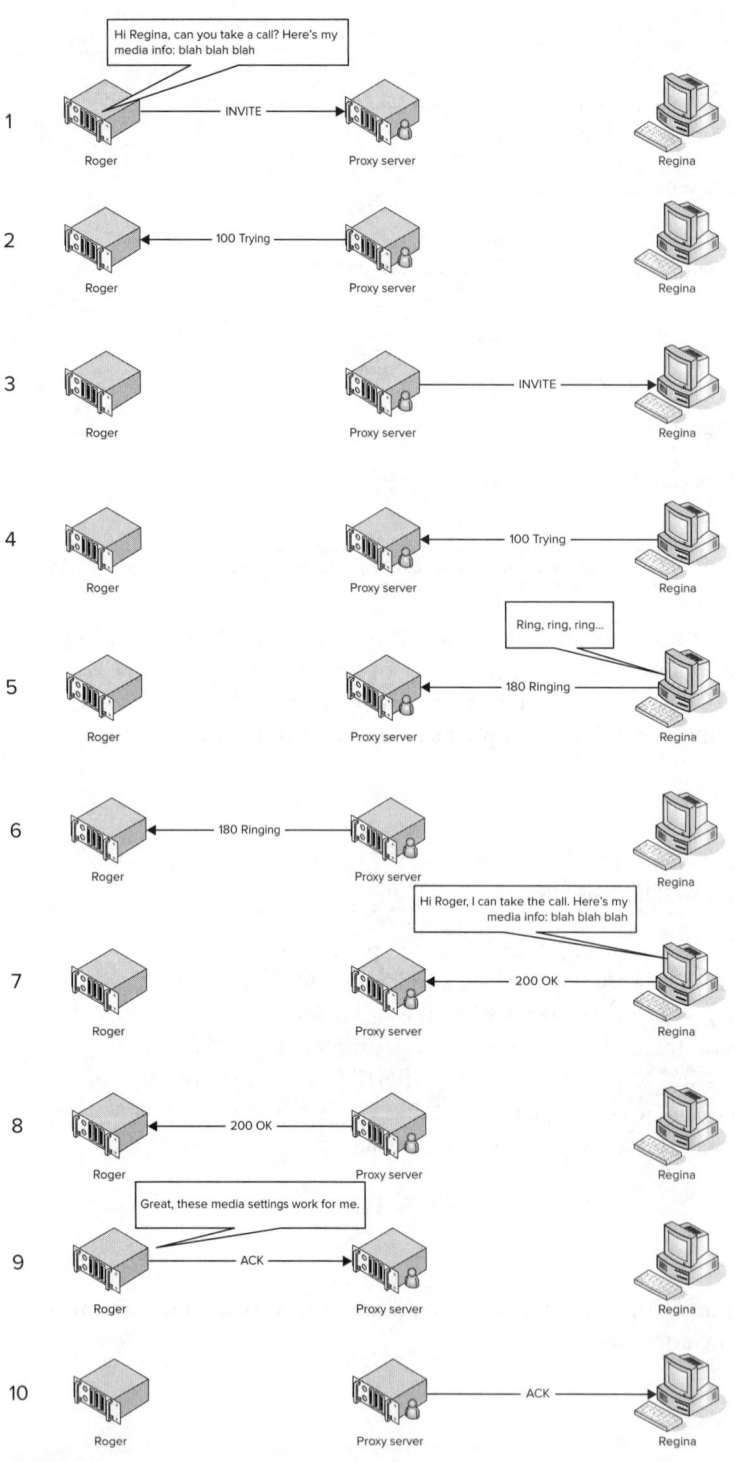

FIGURE 8-1

First, the UCMA endpoint (Roger in the diagram) sends a SIP INVITE request to the SIP proxy, which for Lync is the Front End or Director server role, for the destination (remote) endpoint. The SIP INVITE for an instant messaging call looks something like this:

```
INVITE sip:regina@wrox.com SIP/2.0
From: "Roger"<sip:roger@wrox.com>;epid=5CA655BF4D;
    tag=69cb34c4e9
To: <sip:regina@wrox.com>
CSeq: 4 INVITE
Call-ID: 82ee5000-876e-45e7-b03e-7d0795e47785
MAX-FORWARDS: 70
VIA: SIP/2.0/TLS 192.168.0.40:51762;branch=z9hG4bKfbe1f9cc
CONTACT: <sip:ts.wrox.com@wrox.com;gruu;opaque=srvr:
    outbound.sample:jRw31iBwA16ogIm8s~CA
    XN68AAA>;automata;actor="attendant";text;audio;video;image
CONTENT-LENGTH: 146
EXPIRES: 600
PRIORITY: Normal
SUPPORTED: ms-dialog-route-set-update
SUPPORTED: timer
SUPPORTED: ms-delayed-accept
SUPPORTED: ms-sender
SUPPORTED: gruu-10
USER-AGENT: RTCC/4.0.0.0 maximillian
CONTENT-TYPE: application/sdp
ALLOW: ACK
P-ASSERTED-IDENTITY: "Roger"<sip:roger@wrox.com>
Content-ID: ed829ac4-2119-4fb6-a003-7f8b4f25aa4f
Ms-Conversation-ID: 98fbb0767c774e629f215886a75501de
Session-Expires: 1800
Min-SE: 90
Allow: CANCEL,BYE,INVITE,MESSAGE,INFO,SERVICE,
    OPTIONS,BENOTIFY,NOTIFY,UPDATE
Message-Body: v=0
o=- 727625166 727625166 IN IP4 67.104.203.240
s=session
t=0 0
m=message 5060 sip null
a=accept-types:text/plain application/ms-imdn+xml
```

Contained in the body of the INVITE is a Session Description Protocol (SDP) message, which describes the media transfer arrangement the calling endpoint is proposing. In the example above, the SDP message begins with v=0. This is generally quite simple for instant messaging calls, and somewhat more complex for audio/video or application sharing calls. In the media negotiation (or Offer/Answer) process, this SDP content is the "offer," and it comes into play if the receiving endpoint accepts the call.

The proxy server, on receiving the INVITE, sends a 100 Trying response back to the initiating endpoint. It then attempts to pass the INVITE along to the destination. This is step 2 in Figure 8-1.

The destination endpoint may respond with a failure response, but if it does not, it sends its own 100 Trying to the proxy server. It follows this up with a 180 Ringing response, indicating that the call is ringing and that the user, if any, is being notified. These are steps 3–5 in Figure 8-1.

The proxy server passes the `180 Ringing` response back to the initiating endpoint (step 6 in Figure 8-1).

If the destination endpoint accepts the call (step 7 in Figure 8-1), it eventually responds with a `200 OK`, which the proxy again passes back to the calling endpoint. The `200 OK` may also have more SDP in its body. This section of SDP is the "answer," and is generally based on the initial media "offer" as well as the receiving endpoint's own capabilities.

A typical `200 OK` response for an instant messaging call looks something like this:

```
SIP/2.0 200 OK
From: "Roger"<sip:roger@wrox.com>;epid=55E8B5E4B4;
    tag=b3a32f5933
To: <sip:regina@wrox.com>;epid=330747cef7;tag=f4daaba013
CSeq: 5 INVITE
Call-ID: e05acebe-c668-4203-92df-b967d3f2c54a
Via: SIP/2.0/TLS 192.168.0.20:5061;branch=z9hG4bK4ED93107.
    08B41FBE4FF11978;branched=TRUE;ms-internal-
info="baZ0rPfy5Z9RCA7VIWpYkS5rqgJJcIpGljf4ANfA8v3ga-H7QIEvWV9wAA"
Via: SIP/2.0/TLS 192.168.0.40:51953;branch=z9hG4bKcf182b6;
    ms-received-port=51953;ms-received-cid=14E00
Record-Route: <sip:CS-SE.fabrikam.com:5061;transport=tls;
    opaque=state:T:F:Ci.R400;lr;
    ms-route-sig=aaaw2xtSBHscf6ZTaMnR-KwzRPaTSB73rYfwAgq0_ujK2-
H7QIzkdb4QAA>;tag=6B86779D25FF4920F0F73855F9486523
Contact: <sip:regina@wrox.com;opaque=user:
    epid:HDBxNZHKnV2aRq0Ta5HnuAAA;gruu>
User-Agent: UCCAPI/4.0.7457.0 OC/4.0.7457.0 (Microsoft Lync 2010 (RC))
Supported: ms-sender
Supported: histinfo
Supported: ms-safe-transfer
Supported: ms-dialog-route-set-update
Allow: INVITE, BYE, ACK, CANCEL, INFO, MESSAGE, UPDATE,
    REFER, NOTIFY, BENOTIFY
Supported: ms-conf-invite
Proxy-Authorization: TLS-DSK qop="auth",
    realm="SIP Communications Service", opaque="5049DE55",
    targetname="CS-SE.wrox.com", crand="3656df38",
cnum="64", response="0e68db68b1dfb3131ea2262e6e227ae1036b4bfa"
Content-Type: application/sdp
Content-Length: 265
Message-Body: v=0
o=- 0 0 IN IP4 192.168.0.40
s=session
c=IN IP4 192.168.0.40
t=0 0
m=message 5060 sip sip:regina@wrox.com
a=accept-types:text/plain multipart/alternative
    image/gif text/rtf text/html application/x-ms-ink
    application/ms-imdn+xml text/x-msmsgsinvite
```

Notice that although the `200 OK` is sent from the receiving endpoint to the initiating endpoint, the `To` and `From` headers have the same SIP URIs as in the `INVITE`. This is true for the other responses as well. So, in the `200 OK`, the `To` header has the SIP URI of the call recipient and the From header has the SIP URI of the caller.

Finally, assuming it accepts the receiving endpoint's media negotiation answer, the calling endpoint acknowledges the 200 OK with an ACK message (step 9 in Figure 8-1), like the following one:

```
ACK sip:regina@wrox.com;opaque=user:epid:
    HDBxNZHKnV2aRq0Ta5HnuAAA;gruu SIP/2.0
From: <sip:roger@wrox.com>;epid=EF1E6F9EFD;tag=be20a45d39
To: <sip:regina@wrox.com>;epid=330747cef7;tag=fd97fb2043
CSeq: 4 ACK
Call-ID: 672fa237-1e0b-4b50-bb43-6eae35651a7c
MAX-FORWARDS: 70
VIA: SIP/2.0/TLS 192.168.0.40:51982;branch=z9hG4bK063f5e3
ROUTE: <sip:CS-SE.wrox.com:5061;transport=tls;opaque=state:T:F;lr>
CONTENT-LENGTH: 0
SUPPORTED: ms-dialog-route-set-update
USER-AGENT: RTCC/4.0.0.0 maximillian
Message-Body: -
```

The SIP handshake is now complete, and the endpoints can begin to send media back and forth.

Establishing an Audio/Video Call

The code to establish an AudioVideoCall looks nearly identical to the equivalent for an InstantMessagingCall, as you can see in the following code snippet.

```
try
{
    // Establish the A/V call.
    avCall.BeginEstablish(_destinationSipUri,
        new CallEstablishOptions() /* this could also just be null */,
        result =>
        {
            try
            {
                // Finish the asynchronous operation.
                avCall.EndEstablish(result);
            }
            catch (RealTimeException ex)
            {
                // Catch and log exceptions.
                _logger.Log("Failed establishing A/V call", ex);
            }
        },
        null
    );
}
catch (InvalidOperationException ioex)
{
    _logger.Log("Failed establishing A/V call", ioex);
}
```

However, the SIP handshake is somewhat different, particularly when it comes to media negotiation. Here is an example of an INVITE message for an outgoing audio call:

```
INVITE sip:regina@wrox.com SIP/2.0
From: "Roger"<sip:roger@wrox.com>;
    epid=968F0DB62C;tag=8d9bdb997
To: <sip:regina@wrox.com>
CSeq: 4 INVITE
Call-ID: 0fd4e971-b834-49e7-9b3e-ea7a8dbae674
MAX-FORWARDS: 70
VIA: SIP/2.0/TLS 192.168.0.40:51918;branch=z9hG4bK88f54bc8
CONTACT: <sip:ts.wrox.com@fabrikam.com;gruu;opaque=srvr:
    outbound.sample:jRw31iBwA16ogIm~CA
    8sXN68AAA>;automata;actor="attendant";text;audio;video;image
CONTENT-LENGTH: 2912
EXPIRES: 600
PRIORITY: Normal
SUPPORTED: Replaces
SUPPORTED: ms-dialog-route-set-update
SUPPORTED: timer
SUPPORTED: 100rel
SUPPORTED: gruu-10
USER-AGENT: RTCC/4.0.0.0 maximillian
CONTENT-TYPE: multipart/alternative;
    boundary=7AXOlKeopsdkNyOEOZ1H0bmi6VtsOuBK
ALLOW: ACK
P-ASSERTED-IDENTITY: "Roger"<sip:roger@wrox.com>
Ms-Conversation-ID: 4a974820c5d64c1bba324de4a6a75e2b
ms-endpoint-location-data: NetworkScope;ms-media-location-type=Intranet
Session-Expires: 1800
Min-SE: 90
Allow: CANCEL,BYE,INVITE,MESSAGE,INFO,SERVICE,OPTIONS,
    BENOTIFY,NOTIFY,PRACK,UPDATE
Message-Body: --7AXOlKeopsdkNyOEOZ1H0bmi6VtsOuBK
Content-Type: application/sdp
Content-ID: 8ceb5037-b55f-432f-a7bc-df853d9b55f8
Content-Disposition: session;handling=optional;ms-proxy-2007fallback
v=0
o=- 1 0 IN IP4 192.168.0.40
s=session
c=IN IP4 192.168.0.40
b=CT:3000000
t=0 0
m=audio 22148 RTP/SAVP 112 111 0 8 116 4 13 118 97 101
c=IN IP4 192.168.0.40
a=rtcp:22149
a=candidate:/uVXmZpmEYTjeY3jMHTk/ZYjBjxZHIRxK8G3fxXcDk0 1
    vPaqkFeIhmlAG1R1vkCrrw UDP~CA
    0.830 67.104.203.240 24976
a=candidate:/uVXmZpmEYTjeY3jMHTk/ZYjBjxZHIRxK8G3fxXcDk0 2
    vPaqkFeIhmlAG1R1vkCrrw UDP~CA
    0.830 67.104.203.240 24977
a=candidate:V47grZeFck6d9zBHNQLSA0p5psZniTDCmrE3KJ0/bhM 1
```

```
    TkNrw7Xy0YhonPtxIWVcTQ UDP~CA
    0.840 192.168.0.40 22148
a=candidate:V47grZeFck6d9zBHNQLSA0p5psZniTDCmrE3KJ0/bhM 2
    TkNrw7Xy0YhonPtxIWVcTQ UDP~CA
    0.840 192.168.0.40 22149
a=label:main-audio
a=cryptoscale:1 client AES_CM_128_HMAC_SHA1_80
    inline:Do9MxY1Pp2C+bek0JDLhU7eVbCjg0nSdAJYYmQDH|2^31|1:1
a=crypto:2 AES_CM_128_HMAC_SHA1_80
    inline:GMGAJ5f0SitIUSEQxJ5IcKrm9vFYBW1I1vzVSFLW|2^31|1:1
a=crypto:3 AES_CM_128_HMAC_SHA1_80 inline:
    O361O0LhqMUHi3V1FROwpvlrwvgHfvWfomtqT5Me|2^31
a=rtpmap:112 G7221/16000
a=fmtp:112 bitrate=24000
a=rtpmap:111 SIREN/16000
a=fmtp:111 bitrate=16000
a=rtpmap:0 PCMU/8000
a=rtpmap:8 PCMA/8000
a=rtpmap:116 AAL2-G726-32/8000
a=rtpmap:4 G723/8000
a=rtpmap:13 CN/8000
a=rtpmap:118 CN/16000
a=rtpmap:97 RED/8000
a=rtpmap:101 telephone-event/8000
a=fmtp:101 0-16,36
```

The SDP message for an audio INVITE is quite a bit longer. The primary indication that this INVITE is for a different modality is contained in the line which begins with m=audio. This line indicates that the SDP describes an audio media session. The SDP message also contains information on where the audio stream should be sent, possible audio codecs, and various other details on the audio media. Chapter 13 provides some more detail on interpreting these messages for troubleshooting purposes.

The 200 OK response to an audio INVITE is, again, quite a bit longer than the equivalent for an instant messaging call. Here is a typical 200 OK response for an audio call:

```
SIP/2.0 200 OK
From: "Roger"<sip:roger@wrox.com>;
    epid=EF1E6F9EFD;tag=be20a45d39
To: <sip:regina@wrox.com>;epid=330747cef7;tag=fd97fb2043
CSeq: 4 INVITE
Call-ID: 672fa237-1e0b-4b50-bb43-6eae35651a7c
ms-application-via: cs-qms.wrox.com_rtc;
    ms-server=CS-SE.wrox.com;~CA
    ms-pool=CS-SE.wrox.com;
    ms-application=51FB453D-5B9F-45df-83B4-ADD1F7E604A8
P-Asserted-Identity: <sip:regina@wrox.com>
Via: SIP/2.0/TLS 192.168.0.40:51982;branch=z9hG4bKdf621f0;
    ms-received-port=51982;~CA
    ms-received-cid=15900
Record-Route: <sip:CS-SE.wrox.com:5061;transport=tls;
    opaque=state:T:F;lr>
Contact: <sip:regina@wrox.com;opaque=user:
    epid:HDBxNZHKnV2aRq0Ta5HnuAAA;gruu>
```

```
User-Agent: UCCAPI/4.0.7457.0 OC/4.0.7457.0 (Microsoft Lync 2010 (RC))
Supported: histinfo
Supported: ms-safe-transfer
Supported: ms-dialog-route-set-update
Allow: INVITE, BYE, ACK, CANCEL, INFO, UPDATE, REFER,
    NOTIFY, BENOTIFY, OPTIONS
Session-Expires: 720;refresher=uac
ms-accepted-content-id: 8a5ccd25-a87c-4ef2-855f-71d7556e2724
ms-client-diagnostics: 51007;reason="Callee media connectivity diagnosis
info";CalleeMediaDebug="audio:ICEWarn=0x80000,
    LocalSite=192.168.0.40:32354,~CA
    RemoteSite=192.168.0.40:29746,PortRange=1025:65000,LocalLocation=2,~CA
    RemoteLocation=2,FederationType=0"
ms-endpoint-location-data: NetworkScope;ms-media-location-type=Intranet
Supported: replaces
Content-Type: application/sdp
Content-Length: 1068
Message-Body: v=0
o=- 0 0 IN IP4 192.168.0.40
s=session
c=IN IP4 192.168.0.40
b=CT:99980
t=0 0
m=audio 32354 RTP/SAVP 112 111 0 8 116 4 97 13 118 101
a=ice-ufrag:8GWb
a=ice-pwd:bevuz8JIwIHtbiXcW8hfx3jp
a=candidate:1 1 UDP 2130706431 192.168.0.40 32354 typ host
a=candidate:1 2 UDP 2130705918 192.168.0.40 32355 typ host
a=candidate:2 1 UDP 2130705919 67.104.203.240 14850 typ host
a=candidate:2 2 UDP 2130705406 67.104.203.240 14851 typ host
a=candidate:3 1 TCP-ACT 1684798463 192.168.0.40 32354 typ
    srflx raddr 192.168.0.40~CA
    rport 32354
a=candidate:3 2 TCP-ACT 1684797950 192.168.0.40 32354 typ
    srflx raddr 192.168.0.40~CA
    rport 32354
a=crypto:2 AES_CM_128_HMAC_SHA1_80
    inline:dvEqb8qZOWmEoep2FG0uo2caL++9wLCpZya7JueK|2^31|1:1
a=maxptime:200
a=rtpmap:112 G7221/16000
a=fmtp:112 bitrate=24000
a=rtpmap:111 SIREN/16000
a=fmtp:111 bitrate=16000
a=rtpmap:0 PCMU/8000
a=rtpmap:8 PCMA/8000
a=rtpmap:116 AAL2-G726-32/8000
a=rtpmap:4 G723/8000
a=rtpmap:97 RED/8000
a=rtpmap:13 CN/8000
a=rtpmap:118 CN/16000
a=rtpmap:101 telephone-event/8000
a=fmtp:101 0-16
```

Like the audio INVITE, this 200 OK message contains a large block of SDP in its message body, describing the call recipient's answer to the media options proposed by the caller. Again, Chapter 13 describes in more detail how to interpret these messages.

Supplying an Initial Message

When establishing an instant messaging call, you can determine the message that appears in the pop-up box in the recipient's Lync client by supplying an initial message, or *toast message*. The toast message is the text that the recipient should see when being notified of the incoming instant message. It is usually taken from the first message in the conversation, and is passed in as a parameter to the BeginEstablish method in the form of a ToastMessage object. You can create the ToastMessage object with a string body or, if you choose, with another content type.

The following code snippet shows how to initiate an instant messaging call with a toast message.

Available for
download on
Wrox.com

```
// Create a new IM call.
InstantMessagingCall imCall = new InstantMessagingCall(conversation);

try
{
    ToastMessage toast = new ToastMessage("Good day");

    // Establish the IM call.
    imCall.BeginEstablish(_destinationSipUri,
        toast,
        new CallEstablishOptions(),
        result =>
        {
            try
            {
                // Finish the asynchronous operation.
                imCall.EndEstablish(result);
            }
            catch (RealTimeException ex)
            {
                // Catch and log exceptions.
                _logger.Log("Failed establishing IM call", ex);
            }
        },
        null
    );
}
catch (InvalidOperationException ioex)
{
    _logger.Log("Failed establishing IM call", ioex);
}
```

Code snippet TwoPartyCallControl\ToastMessageSample.cs

UCMA applications that receive instant messaging calls can access the toast message content on the incoming call.

HOW DO YOU CHANGE THE POP-UP TEXT FOR AN AUDIO CALL?

Developers often wonder whether any way exists to supply a toast message for an `AudioVideoCall`. Although toast messages only work with `InstantMessagingCall`, a way does exist to change the text that appears in the incoming audio call popup in Lync — changing the conversation subject. (Incidentally, this also works with conference invitations.)

To do this, create a `ConversationSettings` object when first initializing the UCMA objects for your call. Set the `Subject` property on the `ConversationSettings` object to whatever text you want to appear in the call popup. Then use this `ConversationSettings` object as a parameter for the `Conversation` constructor.

The Lync client will display the conversation subject in the incoming call popup.

Specifying Custom Headers

For one reason or another, you may one day find that you need to manually add a certain SIP header to the `INVITE` message for a new call — or to the SIP message for some other UCMA operation.

Most of the asynchronous operations in UCMA have a sidekick, an options object that allows you to specify extra information about the operation. In the case of `BeginEstablish`/`EndEstablish`, for example, this options object is `CallEstablishOptions`. These options objects have a `Headers` property that is a collection of `SignalingHeader` objects. For any custom header you want to add to the SIP message UCMA will generate for the operation, you can create a new `SignalingHeader` object with the name and value of the header and add it to the options object, which you can then pass in with the `BeginOperation` method.

Here is an example:

```
// Create a SignalingHeader object for the custom header.
SignalingHeader myHeader =
    new SignalingHeader("Polygraph-Result", "Lying");

// Create a new CallEstablishOptions instance and
// add the custom header to the Headers collection.
CallEstablishOptions options = new CallEstablishOptions();
options.Headers.Add(myHeader);
```

This code creates a custom signaling header and adds it to the `CallEstablishOptions` object. This object can then be passed as a parameter to `BeginEstablish`.

For establishing calls, you also have the option of providing custom MIME content for the SIP `INVITE` message using the `CustomMimeParts` property of `CallEstablishOptions`.

HANDLING INCOMING CALLS AND MESSAGES WITH UCMA

Adept as it is at starting conversations, a UCMA application is equally capable of receiving incoming calls from other endpoints. To receive notifications of incoming calls in a UCMA application, registering for calls of each type is necessary. An event handler will then be invoked whenever a call arrives. The application will have the option of accepting the call, declining it, or forwarding it to another destination.

This section covers all of these operations in detail.

The following code shows a class that establishes an application endpoint, registers for incoming audio calls, and accepts any audio calls that come in. The two important bits (highlighted in the code) are registering an event handler for incoming calls and accepting calls in the event handler. The following sections cover both.

```csharp
using System;
using System.Configuration;
using System.Threading;
using Microsoft.Rtc.Collaboration;
using Microsoft.Rtc.Collaboration.AudioVideo;
using Microsoft.Rtc.Signaling;

namespace TwoPartyCallControl
{
    public class AcceptIncomingAudioCallSample : ISampleComponent
    {
        ApplicationEndpoint _appEndpoint;
        AudioVideoCall _avCall;

        // A wait handle for startup and one for shutdown.
        // They are set to unsignaled to start.
        ManualResetEvent _startupWaitHandle =
            new ManualResetEvent(false);
        ManualResetEvent _shutdownWaitHandle =
            new ManualResetEvent(false);

        ILogger _logger;

        public AcceptIncomingAudioCallSample(
            ApplicationEndpoint endpoint, ILogger logger)
        {
            _appEndpoint = endpoint;
            _logger = logger;
        }

        public void Start()
        {
            // Register for incoming audio/video calls.
            _appEndpoint.RegisterForIncomingCall<AudioVideoCall>(
                OnIncomingAudioVideoCallReceived);
        }

        private void OnIncomingAudioVideoCallReceived(object sender,
```

```
        CallReceivedEventArgs<AudioVideoCall> e)
{
    _avCall = e.Call;

    try
    {
        // Accept the incoming call.
        _avCall.BeginAccept(ar =>
        {
            try
            {
                _avCall.EndAccept(ar);

                _logger.Log("Accepted incoming call.");
            }
            catch (RealTimeException rtex)
            {
                _logger.Log(
                    "Failed accepting incoming A/V call.",
                        rtex);
            }
        },
        null);
    }
    catch (InvalidOperationException ioex)
    {
        _logger.Log("Failed accepting incoming A/V call.",
            ioex);
    }
}

public void Stop()
{
    // Terminate the A/V call if necessary.

    if (_avCall != null &&
        _avCall.State != CallState.Terminating &&
        _avCall.State != CallState.Terminated)
    {
        try
        {
            _avCall.BeginTerminate(ar =>
            {
                try
                {
                    _avCall.EndTerminate(ar);
                }
                catch (RealTimeException rtex)
                {
                    _logger.Log("Failed terminating A/V call.",
                        rtex);
                }
            },
```

```
                    null);
            }
            catch (InvalidOperationException ioex)
            {
                _logger.Log("Failed terminating A/V call.", ioex);
            }
        }
    }
}
}
```

Code snippet TwoPartyCallControl\AcceptIncomingAudioCallSample.cs

Registering for Incoming Calls

When a new call arrives, in the form of a SIP INVITE message, at a Lync endpoint managed by a UCMA application, the endpoint must have an event handler registered for incoming calls of that modality in order to accept the call. If such an event handler is registered, the UCMA runtime will invoke the handler and provide a reference to the Call object in the event arguments.

If the endpoint has not been registered for incoming calls of the correct modality, UCMA will decline the call without any notice to the application.

Registering for Instant Messaging Calls

To register an event handler for incoming calls to an endpoint, call the RegisterForIncomingCall method. This method requires a type parameter, which should be the type of Call object the event handler is meant for. It also takes the event handler itself as a parameter.

The following snippet shows code that registers an event handler for instant messaging calls.

```
_appEndpoint.RegisterForIncomingCall<InstantMessagingCall>(
    OnIncomingInstantMessagingCallReceived);
```

Registering for Audio/Video Calls

Registering an event handler for audio/video calls is more or less the same as registering for instant messaging calls, as the following code snippet illustrates.

```
_appEndpoint.RegisterForIncomingCall<AudioVideoCall>(
    OnIncomingAudioVideoCallReceived);
```

Event Arguments in the Incoming Call Handler

When an incoming call event is invoked, looking at some of the context of the incoming call can be useful to help decide what to do with the call and whether to answer it.

Some of this context is available through the event arguments in the incoming call event handler, along with a reference to the Call object representing the incoming call.

Table 8-1 shows some of the more frequently used properties and what purpose they serve.

TABLE 8-1 Incoming Call Context

PROPERTY	PURPOSE
Call	Holds a reference to the `Call` object representing the incoming call.
CallToBeReplaced	If the incoming call is for a supervised transfer (also known as a call replacement), holds a reference to the `Call` object that is being replaced by the new incoming call. (More details on this appear later in the chapter.)
CustomMimeParts	If any custom MIME content is in the `INVITE` message, you can access it here.
DiversionContext	Holds an object that contains information on each diversion the call went through before reaching the endpoint.
IsConferenceDialOut	Tells whether the incoming call is a dial-out from a multi-point control unit (MCU), which is discussed in Chapter 11.
IsNewConversation	True if the incoming `INVITE` message is starting an entirely new conversation (as opposed to adding a new modality or replacing another call, for example).
RemoteParticipant	Holds an object with details on the Lync endpoint on the other end of the call.
RingBackDisabled	By default, when a SIP `INVITE` arrives for an endpoint that has registered an event handler for that modality, UCMA will automatically send `180 Ringing` messages at intervals until the call is answered, the caller gives up, or a timeout expires. Set this property to `true` to disable this behavior.
ToastMessage	Holds the toast message received with the incoming call, or null if there is no toast message.
TransferredBy	If the incoming call was transferred to the endpoint, this property holds the URI of the user that performed the transfer.

By inspecting these properties and determining its behavior according to their contents, your application can limit what types of calls it answers. For instance, an application can check the `IsNewConversation` property to allow new IM or audio calls, but not the addition of a new modality to an existing conversation. Likewise, an application might only accept calls that have been marked with a special type of MIME content in the SIP `INVITE`.

Receiving an Incoming Call

When receiving an incoming call, a UCMA application can deal with it in one of three general ways, based on the attributes of the call and the condition of the application:

- ➤ Accept the call
- ➤ Decline the call
- ➤ Forward the call to another destination

The following sections describe how to accomplish each of these with UCMA.

Inspecting the Properties of Incoming Calls

UCMA makes looking at the properties of an incoming call before accepting it quite easy. The event arguments object for the incoming call event handler has a Call property that references the Call object representing the incoming call. You can look at this (as well as the other event arguments) to determine who is calling, what type of call it is, whether it is a transfer, and numerous other pieces of information that may be helpful in determining what to do with the call.

DISABLING AUTOMATIC RINGING

By default, UCMA automatically sends 180 Ringing messages on behalf of your endpoint in response to an incoming call, for up to 10 minutes. If you prefer not to have those sent automatically (or you want to be tricky and send your own 180 Ringing messages manually) you can turn off this behavior by setting the RingBackDisabled property on the event arguments of the incoming call handler to true.

Accepting an Incoming Call

The code to accept an incoming call in UCMA is every bit as simple as the code to initiate a new outgoing call. Accepting a call requires a single asynchronous operation, represented by the methods BeginAccept and EndAccept.

 BeginAccept can only be called on a Call object that is in the Incoming state; calling the method in other situations will cause the Call to throw an exception.

When an application calls BeginAccept, the UCMA runtime responds to the INVITE message with a 200 OK response to accept the call. The 200 OK will contain any SDP content that is necessary for media negotiation. Essentially, the process is the same as the SIP handshake for an outgoing call, except that the roles are reversed: UCMA is reacting to an incoming SIP INVITE message rather than sending one.

Figure 8-2 shows the sequence of messages involved when an application accepts an incoming call.

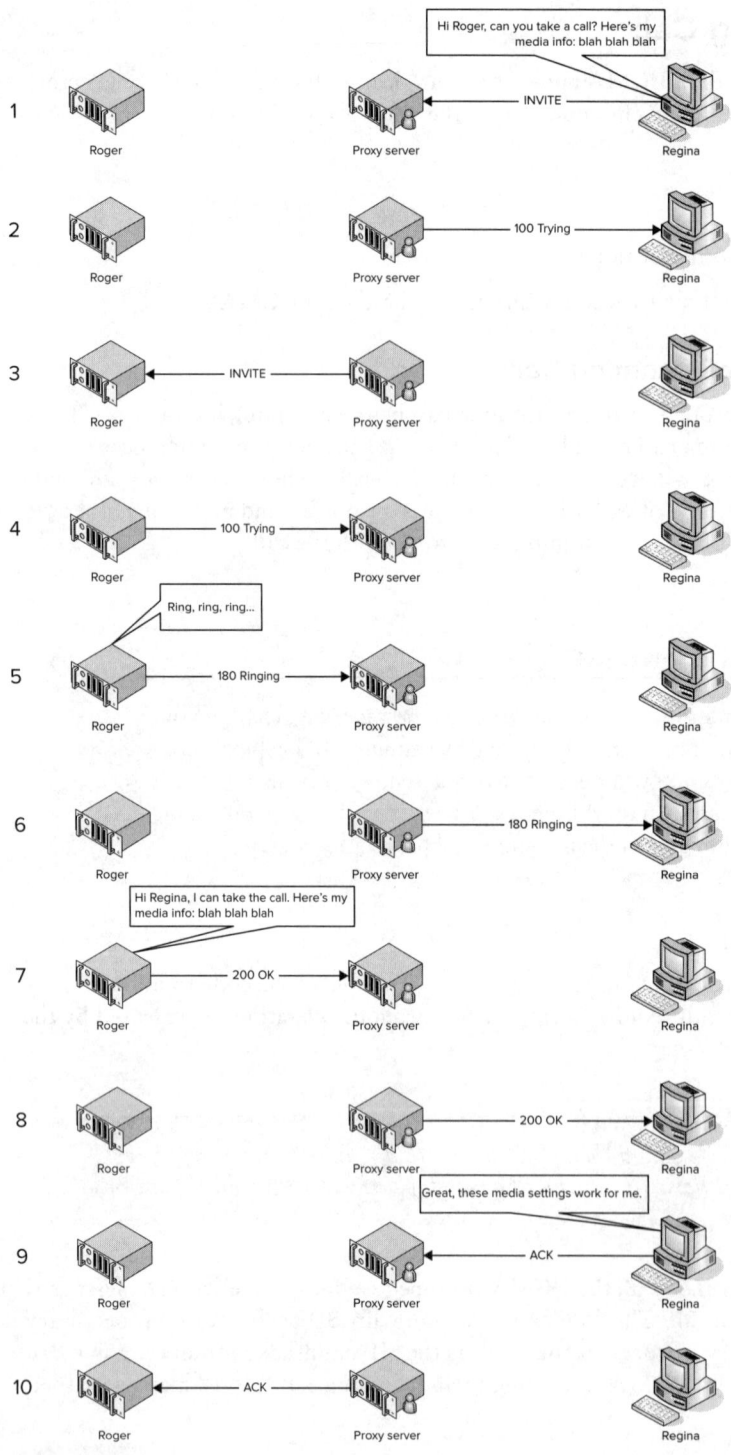

FIGURE 8-2

The following code snippet shows a typical example of the code to accept a call in UCMA.

Available for
download on
Wrox.com

```
private void OnIncomingAudioVideoCallReceived(object sender,
    CallReceivedEventArgs<AudioVideoCall> e)
{
    _avCall = e.Call;

    try
    {
        // Accept the incoming call.
        _avCall.BeginAccept(ar =>
        {
            try
            {
                _avCall.EndAccept(ar);

                _logger.Log("Accepted incoming call.");
            }
            catch (RealTimeException rtex)
            {
                _logger.Log(
                    "Failed accepting incoming A/V call.",
                    rtex);
            }
        },
        null);
    }
    catch (InvalidOperationException ioex)
    {
        _logger.Log("Failed accepting incoming A/V call.",
            ioex);
    }
}
```

Code snippet TwoPartyCallControl\AcceptIncomingAudioCallSample.cs

Declining an Incoming Call

An endpoint does not need to answer every single incoming call. As a gesture of politeness, an endpoint can let these rejected calls off easy by sending a SIP response to decline them. You can think of this as SIP etiquette. After the calling endpoint receives a decline response, it ends the SIP dialogue and goes about its business, or perhaps becomes moody and sulks if it has a problem with rejection.

To decline a call in UCMA, you can call the `Decline` method on the `Call` object. `Decline` only works on calls that are currently incoming. The following code snippet illustrates this.

Available for
download on
Wrox.com

```
using System;
using System.Configuration;
using System.Threading;
using Microsoft.Rtc.Collaboration;
using Microsoft.Rtc.Collaboration.AudioVideo;
```

```csharp
using Microsoft.Rtc.Signaling;

namespace TwoPartyCallControl
{
    public class DeclineIncomingAudioCallSample : ISampleComponent
    {
        ApplicationEndpoint _appEndpoint;
        InstantMessagingCall _imCall;

        // A wait handle for startup and one for shutdown.
        // They are set to unsignaled to start.
        ManualResetEvent _startupWaitHandle =
            new ManualResetEvent(false);
        ManualResetEvent _shutdownWaitHandle =
            new ManualResetEvent(false);

        ILogger _logger;

        public DeclineIncomingAudioCallSample(
            ApplicationEndpoint endpoint,
            ILogger logger)
        {
            _appEndpoint = endpoint;
            _logger = logger;
        }

        public void Start()
        {
            // Register for incoming audio/video calls.
            _appEndpoint.RegisterForIncomingCall<InstantMessagingCall>(
                OnIncomingInstantMessagingCallReceived);
            _appEndpoint.RegisterForIncomingCall<AudioVideoCall>(
                OnIncomingAudioVideoCallReceived);
        }

        private void OnIncomingInstantMessagingCallReceived(
            object sender,
            CallReceivedEventArgs<InstantMessagingCall> e)
        {
            _imCall = e.Call;

            try
            {
                // Accept the incoming call.
                _imCall.BeginAccept(ar =>
                {
                    try
                    {
                        _imCall.EndAccept(ar);

                        _logger.Log("Accepted incoming call.");
                    }
                    catch (RealTimeException rtex)
```

```
                    {
                        _logger.Log(
                            "Failed accepting incoming IM call.",
                            rtex);
                    }
                },
                null);
        }
        catch (InvalidOperationException ioex)
        {
            _logger.Log("Failed accepting incoming IM call.", ioex);
        }
}

private void OnIncomingAudioVideoCallReceived(object sender,
    CallReceivedEventArgs<AudioVideoCall> e)
{
    // Decline incoming A/V calls.

    try
    {
        e.Call.Decline();
    }
    catch (InvalidOperationException ioex)
    {
        _logger.Log("Failed declining incoming call.", ioex);
    }
}

public void Stop()
{
    // Terminate the IM call if necessary.

    if (_imCall != null &&
        _imCall.State != CallState.Terminating &&
        _imCall.State != CallState.Terminated)
    {
        try
        {
            _imCall.BeginTerminate(ar =>
            {
                try
                {
                    _imCall.EndTerminate(ar);
                }
                catch (RealTimeException rtex)
                {
                    _logger.Log("Failed terminating A/V call.",
                        rtex);
                }
            },
            null);
        }
        catch (InvalidOperationException ioex)
```

```
            {
                _logger.Log("Failed terminating A/V call.", ioex);
            }
        }
    }
  }
}
```

Code snippet TwoPartyCallControl\DeclineIncomingAudioCallSample.cs

 Unlike nearly every other method in UCMA, the Decline *method is synchronous. There are no* BeginDecline *and* EndDecline *methods — only* Decline.

If an endpoint does not accept an incoming call and simply leaves it alone, it will simply continue ringing. Depending on the limits set by the calling endpoint, this sad, futile ringing may go on for 30 seconds or more.

When you call the Decline method to decline an incoming call, the endpoint receiving the call sends a failure response to the originator of the call. The default response code is 603 Decline, but you can pass an instance of CallDeclineOptions into the Decline method to specify the exact response code to use. The following code sample shows this in action. If you substitute this code for the contents of the incoming audio/video call handler in the class shown earlier, it will decline calls with a 486 Busy Here response code instead of the default 603.

```
// Decline incoming A/V calls with a 486 response code.

CallDeclineOptions options = new CallDeclineOptions()
{
    ResponseCode = ResponseCode.BusyHere
};

try
{
    e.Call.Decline(options);
}
catch (InvalidOperationException ioex)
{
    _logger.Log("Failed declining incoming call.", ioex);
}
```

To set the response code you want to use, set the ResponseCode property of CallDeclineOptions to an integer between 400 and 699. This encompasses all the failure codes, but excludes non-failure codes such as 200 OK.

For the inveterate mischief-makers out there, that means you can't call Decline with 200 OK as the response code and wreak havoc in the Lync world. Sorry to disappoint you.

Selectively Accepting Calls

In some cases, declining incoming communications from certain contacts, or under certain conditions, is necessary. A UCMA application can look at several pieces of information when determining whether to accept a call.

To filter out calls based on the originator, for example, you can inspect the RemoteParticipant property on the event arguments.

The following code snippet shows a sample class that you can use to restrict incoming calls to those that come from the friendly authors of your favorite Unified Communications development book. The incoming call event handler inspects the URI of the remote participant and only accepts the call if the SIP URI is contained in a list of authorized participants. Otherwise, it declines the call with a 403 response code.

Available for download on Wrox.com

```csharp
using System;
using System.Configuration;
using System.Threading;
using Microsoft.Rtc.Collaboration;
using Microsoft.Rtc.Collaboration.AudioVideo;
using Microsoft.Rtc.Signaling;
using System.Collections.Generic;

namespace TwoPartyCallControl
{
    public class SelectivelyAcceptCallsSample : ISampleComponent
    {
        ApplicationEndpoint _appEndpoint;
        AudioVideoCall _avCall;

        // A wait handle for startup and one for shutdown.
        // They are set to unsignaled to start.
        ManualResetEvent _startupWaitHandle =
            new ManualResetEvent(false);
        ManualResetEvent _shutdownWaitHandle =
            new ManualResetEvent(false);

        ILogger _logger;

        public SelectivelyAcceptCallsSample(
            ApplicationEndpoint endpoint,
            ILogger logger)
        {
            _appEndpoint = endpoint;
            _logger = logger;
        }

        public void Start()
        {
            // Register for incoming audio/video calls.
            _appEndpoint.RegisterForIncomingCall<AudioVideoCall>(
                OnIncomingAudioVideoCallReceived);
        }

        private void OnIncomingAudioVideoCallReceived(object sender,
```

```
    CallReceivedEventArgs<AudioVideoCall> e)
{
    // Build a list with the authorized URIs.
    List<string> authorizedSipUris = new List<string>()
    {
        "sip:michaelg@fabrikam.com",
        "sip:georged@fabrikam.com"
    };

    if (authorizedSipUris.Contains(e.RemoteParticipant.Uri))
    {
        _logger.Log(
            "Call is from an authorized URI. Accepting.");

        AcceptCall(e.Call);
    }
    else
    {
        _logger.Log(
            "Call is not from an authorized URI. Declining.");

        CallDeclineOptions options = new CallDeclineOptions()
        {
            ResponseCode = ResponseCode.Forbidden
        };

        e.Call.Decline(options);
    }
}

private void AcceptCall(AudioVideoCall call)
{
    _avCall = call;

    try
    {
        // Accept the incoming call.
        _avCall.BeginAccept(ar =>
        {
            try
            {
                _avCall.EndAccept(ar);

                _logger.Log("Accepted incoming call.");
            }
            catch (RealTimeException rtex)
            {
                _logger.Log(
                    "Failed accepting incoming A/V call."
                    , rtex);
            }
        },
        null);
    }
```

```
        catch (InvalidOperationException ioex)
        {
            _logger.Log("Failed accepting incoming A/V call.",
                ioex);
        }
    }

    public void Stop()
    {
        // Terminate the A/V call if necessary.

        if (_avCall != null &&
            _avCall.State != CallState.Terminating &&
            _avCall.State != CallState.Terminated)
        {
            try
            {
                _avCall.BeginTerminate(ar =>
                {
                    try
                    {
                        _avCall.EndTerminate(ar);
                    }
                    catch (RealTimeException rtex)
                    {
                        _logger.Log("Failed terminating A/V call.",
                            rtex);
                    }
                },
                null);
            }
            catch (InvalidOperationException ioex)
            {
                _logger.Log("Failed terminating A/V call.", ioex);
            }
        }
    }
}
```

Code snippet TwoPartyCallControl\SelectivelyAcceptCallsSample.cs

Similarly, you can restrict calls based on such properties as the diversion context; the contact that transferred the call to your endpoint, if any; or custom MIME content in the INVITE message. Keep in mind that these headers may be relatively easy to fake, so if you want a high degree of security in your call filtering mechanism, you should probably use other measures as well.

Forwarding an Incoming Call to Another Endpoint

Declining an incoming call is not the only way of warding it away from an endpoint. You can also take the more subtle method of redirecting it to a different SIP URI, using the Forward method.

> *Like* Decline, *the* Forward *method only works on calls in the Incoming state. Calling it at other times causes the* Call *object to throw an* InvalidOperationException.

The following code shows the use of the Forward method.

```csharp
using System;
using System.Configuration;
using System.Threading;
using Microsoft.Rtc.Collaboration;
using Microsoft.Rtc.Collaboration.AudioVideo;
using Microsoft.Rtc.Signaling;

namespace TwoPartyCallControl
{
    public class ForwardIncomingAudioCallSample : ISampleComponent
    {
        ApplicationEndpoint _appEndpoint;

        // A wait handle for startup and one for shutdown.
        // They are set to unsignaled to start.
        ManualResetEvent _startupWaitHandle =
            new ManualResetEvent(false);
        ManualResetEvent _shutdownWaitHandle =
            new ManualResetEvent(false);

        ILogger _logger;

        public ForwardIncomingAudioCallSample(
            ApplicationEndpoint endpoint,
            ILogger logger)
        {
            _appEndpoint = endpoint;
            _logger = logger;
        }

        public void Start()
        {
            // Register for incoming audio/video calls.
            _appEndpoint.RegisterForIncomingCall<AudioVideoCall>(
                OnIncomingAudioVideoCallReceived);
        }

        private void OnIncomingAudioVideoCallReceived(object sender,
            CallReceivedEventArgs<AudioVideoCall> e)
        {
            // Forward incoming A/V calls.
            try
            {
                _logger.Log("Forwarding incoming call.");

                e.Call.Forward("sip:georged@fabrikam.com");
            }
```

```
        catch (InvalidOperationException ioex)
        {
            _logger.Log("Failed forwarding incoming call.", ioex);
        }
    }

    public void Stop()
    {
        // Nothing to do.
    }
  }
}
```

Code snippet TwoPartyCallControl\ForwardIncomingAudioCallSample.cs

The first parameter of Forward should be the SIP URI to which you want to redirect the incoming call. An optional second parameter takes an instance of CallForwardOptions. This class is very much like CallDeclineOptions and allows you to specify a response code which must be in the 300s. The default is 303.

Accepting a Transfer on a Connected Call

Later this chapter shows you how to transfer an active call to another destination. For some UCMA applications, though, accepting transfer messages from other endpoints may be important.

To understand what accepting a transfer message means, understanding the basics of how a transfer works in Lync is helpful. The transfer involves three endpoints, which, for clarity, we will call the transferring endpoint, the transferred endpoint, and the transfer-to endpoint. Figure 8-3 shows how a transfer occurs between these three characters. For simplicity, the proxy server is omitted in this diagram, but keep in mind that each of these messages is being routed through the proxy server.

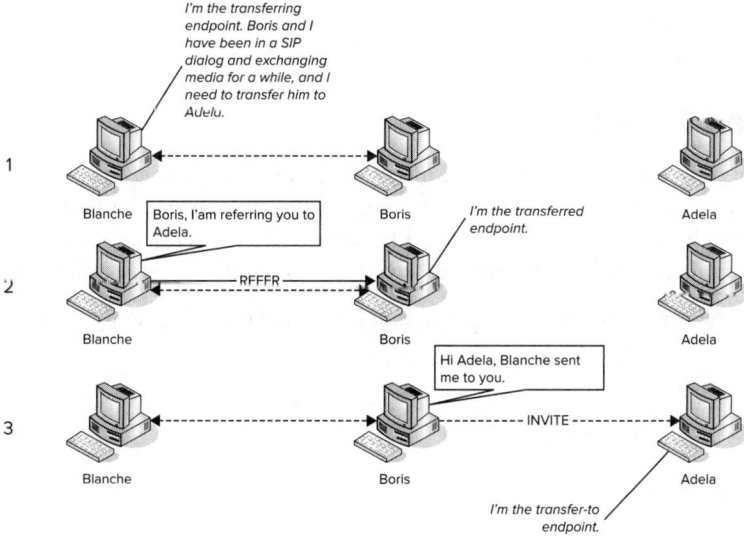

FIGURE 8-3

The gist of it is that the transferring endpoint sends a SIP REFER message to the transferred endpoint. This message says, in effect, "Go and place a call to this other person now." On receiving this message, the transferred endpoint places a new call to the transfer-to endpoint. After the call connects to the transfer-to endpoint (or sometimes before), the transferred endpoint terminates the call with the transferring endpoint and continues with the new call.

Out of the box, so to speak, a UCMA application does not know how to play the role of transferred endpoint. It will not accept REFER messages from other endpoints with which it has an active call. However, with an event handler for the TransferReceived event and a few more strategically placed lines of code, you can tell your application to accept these REFER messages and, after receiving them, deal with them appropriately by placing a new call to the transfer-to endpoint.

The following code sample shows a handler for the TransferReceived event that accepts the incoming transfer request and calls another method to place the new outgoing call.

Available for
download on
Wrox.com

```
private void OnTransferReceived(object sender,
    AudioVideoCallTransferReceivedEventArgs e)
{
    // Unregister the event handlers.
    _avCall.TransferReceived -= OnTransferReceived;
    _avCall.Forwarded -= OnCallForwarded;

    // Accept the REFER request with no special headers.
    e.Accept(null);

    ...
}
```

Code snippet TwoPartyCallControl\AcceptTransfersAndForwardsSample.cs

If you use the Conversation object provided in the event arguments, UCMA will automatically send notifications to the transferring endpoint to update it on the progress of the transfer. If you want to do this yourself, you can disable the automatic notifications by setting the ImplicitNotificationsDisabled property on the event arguments to true.

Handling the Accepted Transfer

On the surface you may think all you need to do with an incoming transfer request is call e.Accept in the event handler. If you do this by itself, your application will accept the transfer request from the transferring endpoint, but will make no attempt to place the new call to the transfer-to endpoint. You also need code to explicitly place a call to the SIP URI to which your call is being transferred.

The following code snippet shows an event handler that includes code for initiating a new call to the transfer-to endpoint.

Available for
download on
Wrox.com

```
private void OnTransferReceived(object sender,
    AudioVideoCallTransferReceivedEventArgs e)
{
    // Unregister the event handlers.
```

```
    _avCall.TransferReceived -= OnTransferReceived;
    _avCall.Forwarded -= OnCallForwarded;

    // Accept the REFER request with no special headers.
    e.Accept(null);

    // Create a new A/V call with the transfer-to URI using the
    // pre-initialized Conversation object.
    AudioVideoCall newCall = new AudioVideoCall(e.NewConversation);

    try
    {
        // Establish the call to the transfer-to endpoint.
        newCall.BeginEstablish(e.TransferDestination, null,
            ar =>
            {
                try
                {
                    newCall.EndEstablish(ar);
                }
                catch (RealTimeException rtex)
                {
                    _logger.Log("Failed establishing new call " +
                        "following transfer.", rtex);
                }
            },
            null
        );
    }
    catch (InvalidOperationException ioex)
    {
        _logger.Log("Failed establishing new call following transfer.",
            ioex);
    }
}
```

Code snippet TwoPartyCallControl\AcceptTransfersAndForwardsSample.cs

Accepting a Forward on an Outgoing Call

To handle a redirect response properly on an outgoing call, a UCMA application must register a handler for the `Forwarded` event on the `Call` object. Within the event handler, it must call the `Accept` method on the event arguments and then place a call to the new destination.

The following code snippet illustrates this.

Available for
download on
Wrox.com

```
private void OnCallForwarded(object sender,
    CallForwardReceivedEventArgs e)
{
    // Unregister the event handlers.
    _avCall.TransferReceived -= OnTransferReceived;
```

```
_avCall.Forwarded -= OnCallForwarded;

// Accept the forward response from the remote endpoint.
e.Accept();

// Change the destination to the new URI.
_destinationSipUri = e.ForwardDestination;

// Establish a new call to the forwarding destination.
EstablishCall();
}
```

Code snippet TwoPartyCallControl\AcceptTransfersAndForwardsSample.cs

The application can alternatively call the `Decline` method in the event arguments to refuse the
redirect.

TRANSFERRING AN ACTIVE CALL

A successful transfer involves three participants and a long sequence of SIP messages. With
UCMA, you can complete this entire procedure with two methods: `BeginTransfer` and
`EndTransfer`.

If you want the 10-second overview of how to execute a transfer in UCMA, you can take a look at the
following code snippet, which shows how to transfer an active audio/video call to another SIP URI.

Available for
download on
Wrox.com

```
try
{
    _avCall.BeginTransfer(_destinationSipUri,
        ar =>
        {
            try
            {
                _avCall.EndTransfer(ar);
            }
            catch (RealTimeException rtex)
            {
                _logger.Log("Failed transferring call.", rtex);
            }
        },
        null);
}
catch (InvalidOperationException ioex)
{
    _logger.Log("Failed transferring call.", ioex);
}
```

Code snippet TwoPartyCallControl\TransferCallSample.cs

Although you can transfer calls to your heart's content using nothing but this code, having at least a general sense of the SIP backdrop to this magical duo of methods pays off. The following sections describe the steps in this process and explain some of the options you can specify when executing a transfer.

The SIP Anatomy of a Transfer

A transfer on a Lync call starts with a SIP REFER message. The transferring endpoint sends the REFER message to the transferred endpoint while the two endpoints are participating in a call.

The SIP REFER Message

A REFER message generally looks something like this:

```
REFER sip:michaelg@fabrikam.com;opaque=user:epid:
    HDBxNZHKnV2aRq0Ta5HnuAAA;gruu SIP/2.0
From: <sip:outbound.sample@fabrikam.com>;epid=AE4D66EAD4;tag=814461b8ad
To: <sip:michaelg@fabrikam.com>;epid=330747cef7;tag=1bf0083fdf
CSeq: 1 REFER
Call-ID: f5c43ce0489e4874a65a1f2a32fa77f9
MAX-FORWARDS: 70
VIA: SIP/2.0/TLS 192.168.0.40:54520;branch=z9hG4bKd6f84186
ROUTE: <sip:CS-SE.fabrikam.com:5061;transport=tls;opaque=state:T:F;lr>
CONTACT: <sip:ts.fabrikam.com@fabrikam.com;gruu;opaque=srvr:
    outbound.sample:jRw31iBwA16ogIm8sXN68AAA>;automata;
    actor="attendant";text;audio;video;image
CONTENT-LENGTH: 0
EXPIRES: 600
REFER-TO: <sip:administrator@fabrikam.com>
REFERRED-BY: <sip:outbound.sample@fabrikam.com>;ms-identity="
    MIH5BgkqhkiG9w0BBwKggeswgegCAQExCzAJBgUrDgMCGgUAMAsGCSq
    GSIb3DQEHATGBYDCBxQIBATAjMBUxEzARBgNVBAMTCkZhYn
    Jpa2FtQ0ECCmEG7CcAAAAAAAYwCQYFKw4DAhoFADANBgkqhk
    iG9w0BAQEFAASBgD0VRH/QXh3spnYML3i9/n+PLRWBWlUqLl
    +I21mZWB4mO1NJ/1Pb4J1RMcY/rk9WaPCeQ06j210jWqKwmGw
    JzkGjtDG+9PdhmDHLxm92z6kKhzRG0Cd+HqVRz/Dccx1hzbx
    fjO6dk97VTARmI5qXfHyae88agW8RbhHCeCSfTyjd:
    Mon, 25 Oct 2010 03:11:14 GMT";ms-identity-info="
    sip:TS.fabrikam.com:12384;transport=Tls";
    ms-identity-alg=rsa-sha1
SUPPORTED: ms-dialog-route-set-update
SUPPORTED: gruu-10
USER-AGENT: RTCC/4.0.0.0 maximillian
P-ASSERTED-IDENTITY. "Outbound"<sip:outbound.sample@fabrikam.com>
Message-Body: -
```

The From header holds the URI of the transferring user, and the To header holds the URI of the transferred user. The transfer destination is sent in the Refer-To header.

Steps in a SIP Transfer

When it receives the REFER message, the transferred endpoint generally accepts it with a 200 OK. If for one reason or another it is not allowing transfers, it may decline the REFER with a failure response.

At this point, the transferred endpoint initiates a new SIP dialog with the transfer-to endpoint. The identity of the transferring endpoint is shown in the new INVITE message in the Transferred-By header.

If the transfer is being performed as an *unattended transfer* (see the next section, "Types of Transfers"), the transferred endpoint also ends the original call immediately by sending a BYE message. Otherwise, it continues communicating with the transferring endpoint, reporting the status of the new call with NOTIFY messages, and terminates the original call only when the new call is accepted and connects successfully. This allows the transferring endpoint to "rescue" the transferred endpoint if it never connects to the transfer-to endpoint.

Types of Transfers

Lync, and by extension UCMA, allows three different types of transfers, shown in the following list:

➤ Unattended transfer (also known as "blind" or "cold" transfer)

➤ Attended transfer (also known as "warm" transfer)

➤ Supervised transfer (or "call replacement")

The sequence of events in each type of transfer is different. The next few sections cover each type in detail.

Unattended Transfers

In an unattended transfer, the transferring endpoint washes its hands of the call as soon as it initiates the transfer and the transferred endpoint accepts the REFER message. The transferring endpoint does not receive any updates on the progress of the transfer, and has no way to reconnect to the transferred endpoint if the transfer-to endpoint does not answer or is unavailable.

Blind transfers have a bit of a stigma around them, because they are often associated with dismal customer service experiences. For instance, if you think back to the time you called to return that defective electronic toothpick dispenser, and the agent who answered after 10 minutes told you to hold on a second and then transferred you to 1-800-U-R-IDIOT, that was a blind transfer. In UCMA development, moreover, you usually want to confirm that a transfer has connected before abandoning the initial call. However, in some instances simply passing along the call to another destination is best.

Figure 8-4 illustrates an unattended transfer in action.

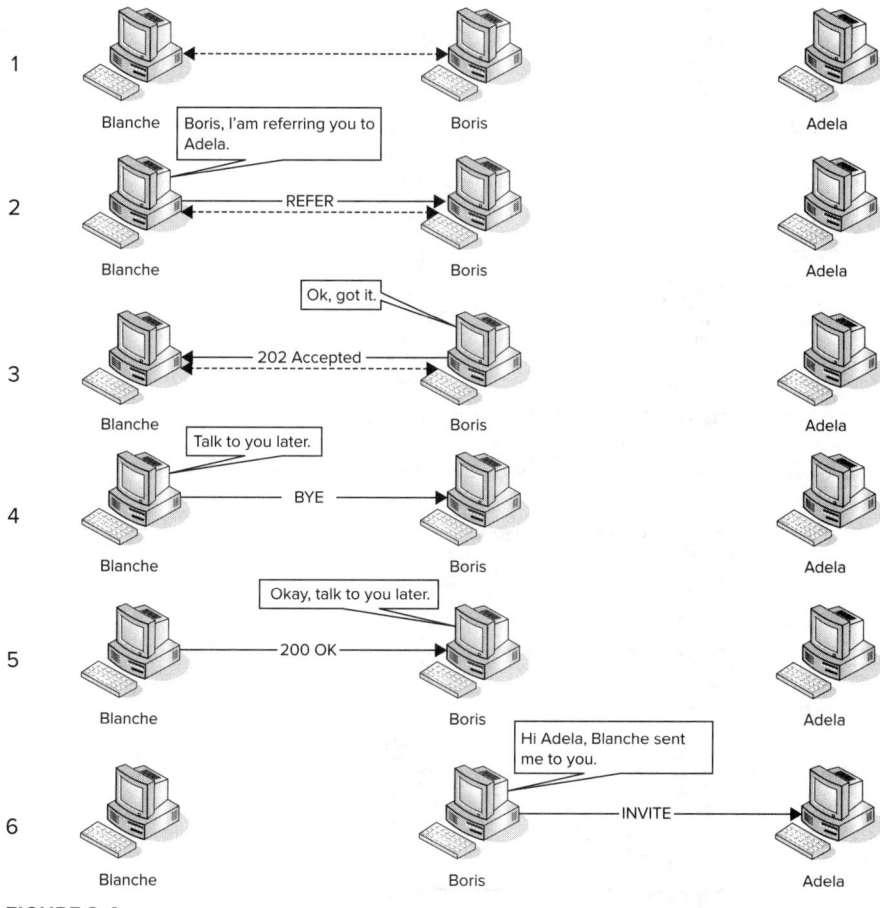

FIGURE 8-4

Attended Transfers

An attended transfer involves the transferring endpoint a bit more in the whole transfer process. In this type of transfer, the original call between the transferring and transferred endpoints remains in the Transferring state while the transferred endpoint is placing the new call to the transfer-to endpoint. Meanwhile, the transferred endpoint reports the progress of the transfer to the transferring endpoint in SIP NOTIFY messages.

Figure 8-5 shows the steps in an attended transfer.

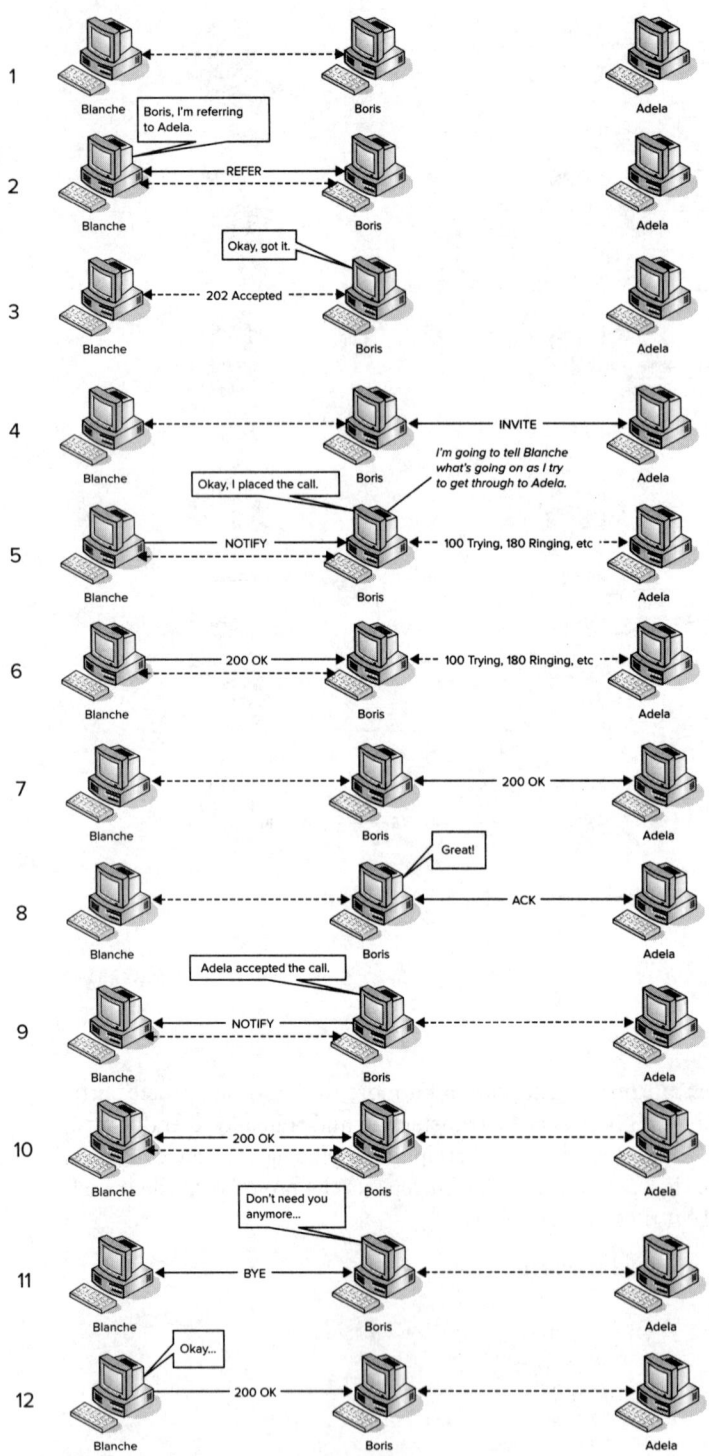

FIGURE 8-5

Attended transfer is the default when you do not specify a transfer type using the
`CallTransferOptions` class.

Supervised Transfers

The supervised transfer is the least intuitive of the transfer types. It is also referred to as *call
replacement*, because the transferred call takes the place of another already established call. The
first call is transferred to the remote participant on the second call and replaces the second call, in
effect bridging the remote participants on the two calls together.

In a supervised transfer, the SIP REFER message includes a `Replaces` component in the
`Refer-To` header, which identifies the call that should be replaced by the call being transferred.
This information is copied into a `Replaces` header in the INVITE message, and when the transfer-to
endpoint receives the INVITE, it uses this new incoming call as the continuation of the call that is to
be replaced.

Essentially, call replacement allows an endpoint that is on a call with Percival and on another call
with Victoria to slot Percival into its own place in the call with Victoria. Figure 8-6 illustrates this.

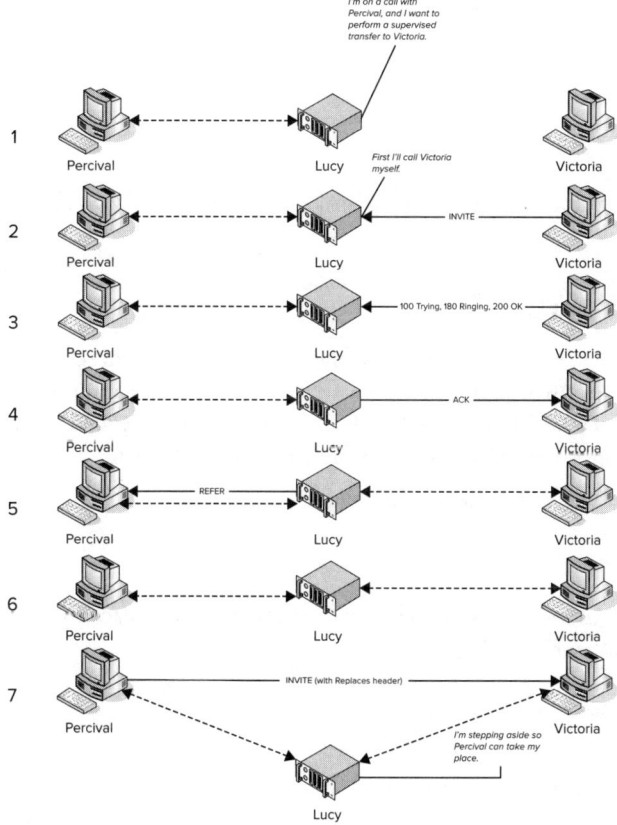

FIGURE 8-6

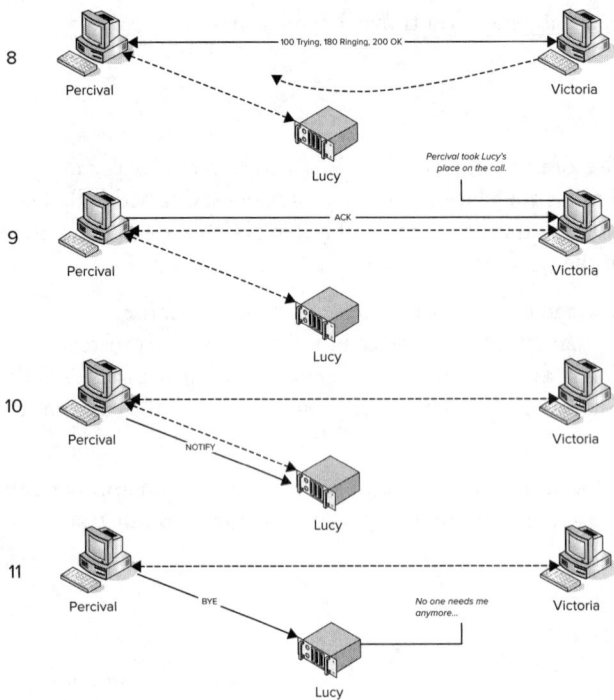

FIGURE 8-6 *(continued)*

UCMA applications can use call replacement as a simple way to broker a call between two other endpoints.

Initiating a Transfer with BeginTransfer

The same method, BeginTransfer, can be used to initiate any of the types of transfer described in the previous section. The transfer type is specified in an instance of CallTransferOptions, which can be passed in as a parameter to BeginTransfer. UCMA handles the intricacies of each transfer type behind the scenes. If no options are specified, UCMA performs an attended transfer by default.

The following sections illustrate how each type of transfer can be initiated in code.

Initiating an Unattended Transfer

The following code snippet shows the PerformUnattendedTransfer method, which uses the CallTransferOptions class to "blind transfer" a call.

Available for
download on
Wrox.com

```
private void PerformUnattendedTransfer()
{
    CallTransferOptions options =
        new CallTransferOptions(CallTransferType.Unattended);

    try
```

```
    {
        _avCall.BeginTransfer(_destinationSipUri, options,
            ar =>
            {
                try
                {
                    _avCall.EndTransfer(ar);
                }
                catch (RealTimeException rtex)
                {
                    _logger.Log("Failed transferring call.", rtex);
                }
            },
            null);
    }
    catch (InvalidOperationException ioex)
    {
        _logger.Log("Failed transferring call.", ioex);
    }
}
```

Code snippet TwoPartyCallControl\TransferCallSample.cs

Initiating an Attended Transfer

The following code snippet shows an attended transfer. Because this transfer type is the default, specifying it explicitly in code is not necessary, although you can if you choose.

Available for download on Wrox.com

```
private void PerformAttendedTransfer()
{
    try
    {
        _avCall.BeginTransfer(_destinationSipUri,
            ar =>
            {
                try
                {
                    _avCall.EndTransfer(ar);
                }
                catch (RealTimeException rtex)
                {
                    _logger.Log("Failed transferring call.", rtex);
                }
            },
            null);
    }
    catch (InvalidOperationException ioex)
    {
        _logger.Log("Failed transferring call.", ioex);
    }
}
```

Code snippet TwoPartyCallControl\TransferCallSample.cs

Replacing a Call with a Supervised Transfer

The following code snippet shows a supervised transfer. The application first creates a new outbound call to the transfer destination, then calls `BeginTransfer` on the original incoming call, passing in the new outbound call as the first parameter. UCMA transfers the original call to the remote participant on the new call, replacing that call.

```
private void PerformSupervisedTransfer()
{
    ConversationSettings settings = new ConversationSettings()
    {
        Subject = "Supervised transfer"
    };

    Conversation newConversation = new Conversation(_appEndpoint,
        settings);

    AudioVideoCall newCall = new AudioVideoCall(newConversation);

    try
    {
        newCall.BeginEstablish(_destinationSipUri, null,
            ar =>
            {
                try
                {
                    newCall.EndEstablish(ar);

                    ReplaceNewCallWithIncomingCall(newCall);
                }
                catch (RealTimeException rtex)
                {
                    _logger.Log("Failed establishing second call.",
                        rtex);
                }
            },
            null
        );
    }
    catch (InvalidOperationException ioex)
    {
        _logger.Log("Failed establishing second call.", ioex);
    }
}

private void ReplaceNewCallWithIncomingCall(AudioVideoCall newCall)
{
    // Transfer the original incoming call,
    // replacing the new call to the destination URI.
    try
    {
        _avCall.BeginTransfer(newCall,
            ar =>
            {
```

```
                try
                {
                    _avCall.EndTransfer(ar);

                    _logger.Log("Successfully replaced call.");
                }
                catch (RealTimeException rtex)
                {
                    _logger.Log("Failed replacing call.", rtex);
                }
            },
            null
        );
    }
    catch (InvalidOperationException ioex)
    {
        _logger.Log("Failed replacing call.", ioex);
    }
}
```

Code snippet TwoPartyCallControl\TransferCallSample.cs

Recovering from a Failed Transfer

If you are performing an attended transfer or supervised transfer, recovering the original call if your transfer fails is possible.

An easy way to get a transfer to fail is to specify a nonexistent SIP URI as the transfer destination in your test application. If you watch the resulting wreck in the Lync client, you will notice that when the transfer fails (and the asynchronous operation in the UCMA code ends with an exception), the original Lync conversation window is still there, but the call is on hold. When an application calls BeginTransfer and UCMA sends the REFER message to initiate the transfer, the original call is automatically placed on hold. To recover the original call after the transfer failure, all the application must do is take that call off of hold, and it can go about its merry way.

The following code shows an example of how to do this by adding code to retrieve the original call from hold in the catch block after the EndTransfer method is called. Chapter 12 covers the BeginRetrieve method and handling call hold states are discussed in more depth.

```
private void PerformAttendedTransfer()
{
    try
    {
        _avCall.BeginTransfer(_destinationSipUri,
            transferResult =>
            {
                try
                {
                    _avCall.EndTransfer(transferResult);
                }
                catch (RealTimeException rtex)
```

```
                        {
                            _logger.Log("Failed transferring call; " +
                                "retrieving it.", rtex);

                            RetrieveCallAfterTransferFailure();
                        }
                    },
                    null);
            }
            catch (InvalidOperationException ioex)
            {
                _logger.Log("Failed transferring call.", ioex);
            }
        }

        private void RetrieveCallAfterTransferFailure()
        {
            // Take the call off of hold after a transfer fails.

            try
            {
                _avCall.Flow.BeginRetrieve(retrieveResult =>
                {
                    try
                    {
                        _avCall.Flow.EndRetrieve(retrieveResult);

                        _logger.Log("Successfully retrieved call.");
                    }
                    catch (RealTimeException rtex)
                    {
                        _logger.Log("Failed retrieving call.", rtex);
                    }
                },
                null);
            }
            catch (InvalidOperationException ioex)
            {
                _logger.Log("Failed retrieving call.", ioex);
            }
        }
```

Code snippet TwoPartyCallControl\RecoverFailedTransferSample.cs

PARKING AND RETRIEVING CALLS

Some private branch exchange (PBX) systems, the phone systems used internally within a business, have a handy feature known as *call parking*. On these systems, if you are on a call and need to pass it along to someone, but you are not sure exactly where to transfer it, you can "park" the call on an unused extension, which anyone on the PBX can dial to "retrieve" it later.

The Call Park Server

Lync Server allows you to mimic the call parking functionality that is often found in PBX systems. If you have a call park server installed in your environment, you can use methods on the `AudioVideoCall` class to park and retrieve calls in your application.

Parking a Call

When you call the `BeginPark` method on an `AudioVideoCall`, the remote endpoint is disconnected from your application and "parked." The `EndPark` method returns a `CallParkResponseData` object; its `Orbit` property holds a `CallOrbit` object, which you can think of as the "bookmark" for the parked call. You will need the call orbit information to retrieve the call later.

Retrieving a Parked Call

To retrieve the parked call, create an entirely new `AudioVideoCall` and call `BeginEstablish`, passing in the `CallOrbit` object. If necessary, you can reconstruct the `CallOrbit` object using the orbit number or the orbit number and URI from the original object. This can be helpful if the call was originally parked by an endpoint not owned by your application.

The application will place a new call to the remote endpoint, retrieving the specified parked call.

MEDIA AND MESSAGES ON AN ACTIVE CALL

Establishing calls is all well and good, but a SIP dialog is not much use by itself unless you do something after it is established. Usually, this "something" is a type of media transfer. Managing the media transfer is the responsibility of the `MediaFlow` class and its modality-specific subclasses. Through these classes, UCMA allows you to manipulate the media in certain straightforward ways. Through the `Call` class itself, it also allows you to send and receive individual SIP messages on an existing SIP dialog.

Managing and manipulating audio media is a complex topic and involves quite a number of helper classes provided by UCMA. Chapter 12 covers audio media control in depth. The next few sections briefly describe some of the other media and messaging operations you can perform on active calls with UCMA.

Flow Classes for Media Management

The `MediaFlow` class and its subclasses (*flows* for short) represent the media session on an active call. UCMA has a set of classes called *media providers* that handle the sending and receiving of media; these classes are mostly internal and under normal circumstances a UCMA application does not need to deal with them directly. The media providers create flows to represent individual media sessions. One flow corresponds to a single media type on a single call. UCMA applications can interact with flow objects to control media settings and behavior.

It is possible to create new media types with customized media providers and media flows. This is only necessary in very advanced scenarios and is outside the scope of this book.

Sending Messages to a Remote Participant Using InstantMessagingFlow

After a SIP dialog is established, the participating endpoints can continue sending SIP messages back and forth to convey information or control the call state. Although the UCMA runtime takes care of some of these for you without assistance, you are also perfectly free to send and receive messages manually.

Instant messaging calls, in fact, use SIP messages for media transfer. In this case, the messaging is managed by the InstantMessagingFlow object, so that you do not need to worry about formatting the SIP messages yourself.

On an instant messaging call, each individual instant message is transferred via SIP by means of the somewhat redundantly named MESSAGE message. A typical MESSAGE message looks like this:

```
MESSAGE sip:michaelg@fabrikam.com;opaque=user:epid:
    HDBxNZHKnV2aRq0Ta5HnuAAA;gruu SIP/2.0
From: <sip:outbound.sample@fabrikam.com>;epid=C15B31BE9F;tag=8c4d16b3d2
To: <sip:michaelg@fabrikam.com>;epid=330747cef7;tag=568d26fb18
CSeq: 5 MESSAGE
Call-ID: 806dcacf-aa7e-4c30-85fa-824081b74c26
MAX-FORWARDS: 70
VIA: SIP/2.0/TLS 192.168.0.40:54394;branch=z9hG4bKa5262eb5
ROUTE: <sip:CS-SE.fabrikam.com:5061;transport=tls;
    opaque=state:T:F:Eu;lr>
CONTACT: <sip:ts.fabrikam.com@fabrikam.com;gruu;opaque=srvr:
    outbound.sample:jRw31iBwA16ogIm~CA
    8sXN68AAA>;automata;actor="attendant";text;audio;video;image
CONTENT-LENGTH: 38
SUPPORTED: ms-dialog-route-set-update
SUPPORTED: gruu-10
USER-AGENT: RTCC/4.0.0.0 maximillian
CONTENT-TYPE: text/plain; charset=utf-8
Message-Body: Jackdaws love my big sphinx of quartz.
```

To send a message on an instant messaging call, you can use the BeginSendMessage and EndSendMessage methods on the InstantMessagingFlow. You can also receive notifications of incoming instant messages by registering an event handler for the MessageReceived event on the InstantMessagingFlow.

The following class demonstrates how to send and receive instant messages on an active instant messaging call. It initiates a new outbound instant messaging call to a specified SIP URI and sends an initial message. It then waits for incoming messages, and repeats them back, replacing the letter "e" with the number "3."

```csharp
using System;
using System.Configuration;
using System.Threading;
using Microsoft.Rtc.Collaboration;
using Microsoft.Rtc.Collaboration.AudioVideo;
using Microsoft.Rtc.Signaling;

namespace TwoPartyCallControl
{
    public class SendInstantMessageSample : ISampleComponent
    {
        ApplicationEndpoint _appEndpoint;
        InstantMessagingCall _imCall;
        string _destinationSipUri;

        // A wait handle for startup and one for shutdown.
        // They are set to unsignaled to start.
        ManualResetEvent _startupWaitHandle =
            new ManualResetEvent(false);
        ManualResetEvent _shutdownWaitHandle =
            new ManualResetEvent(false);

        ILogger _logger;

        public SendInstantMessageSample(ApplicationEndpoint endpoint,
            ILogger logger)
        {
            _appEndpoint = endpoint;
            _logger = logger;
        }

        public void Start()
        {
            Console.Write("Enter destination URI: ");
            _destinationSipUri = Console.ReadLine();

            EstablishCall();
        }

        private void EstablishCall()
        {
            // Create a new Conversation.
            Conversation conversation = new Conversation(_appEndpoint);

            // Create a new IM call.
            _imCall = new InstantMessagingCall(conversation);

            try
            {
                // Establish the IM call.
```

```
            _imCall.BeginEstablish(_destinationSipUri,
                new CallEstablishOptions(),
                result =>
                {
                    try
                    {
                        // Finish the asynchronous operation.
                        _imCall.EndEstablish(result);

                        _imCall.Flow.MessageReceived +=
                            new EventHandler<
                                InstantMessageReceivedEventArgs>(
                            OnMessageReceived);

                        SendMessage("Jackdaws love my " +
                            "big sphinx of quartz.");
                    }
                    catch (RealTimeException ex)
                    {
                        // Catch and log exceptions.
                        _logger.Log("Failed establishing IM call",
                            ex);
                    }
                },
                null
            );
        }
        catch (InvalidOperationException ioex)
        {
            _logger.Log("Failed establishing IM call", ioex);
        }
    }

    private void OnMessageReceived(object sender,
        InstantMessageReceivedEventArgs e)
    {
        InstantMessagingFlow flow = sender as InstantMessagingFlow;

        if (e.HasTextBody)
        {
            SendMessage(e.TextBody.Replace("e", "3"));
        }
    }

    private void SendMessage(string message)
    {
        try
        {
            _imCall.Flow.BeginSendInstantMessage(message,
                ar =>
                {
                    try
                    {
```

```
                                _imCall.Flow.EndSendInstantMessage(ar);
                        }
                        catch (RealTimeException rtex)
                        {
                            _logger.Log("Failed sending IM.", rtex);
                        }
                    },
                    null
                );
            }
            catch (InvalidOperationException ioex)
            {
                _logger.Log("Failed sending IM.", ioex);
            }
        }

        public void Stop()
        {
            // Terminate the IM call if necessary.

            if (_imCall.State != CallState.Terminating &&
                _imCall.State != CallState.Terminated &&
                _imCall.State != CallState.Idle)
            {
                try
                {
                    _imCall.BeginTerminate(ar =>
                    {
                        try
                        {
                            _imCall.EndTerminate(ar);
                        }
                        catch (RealTimeException rtex)
                        {
                            _logger.Log("Failed terminating IM call.",
                                rtex);
                        }
                    },
                    null);
                }
                catch (InvalidOperationException ioex)
                {
                    _logger.Log("Failed terminating IM call.", ioex);
                }
            }
        }
    }
}
```

Code snippet TwoPartyCallControl\SendInstantMessageSample.cs

SENDING SIP INFO MESSAGES

For some advanced call control scenarios, you may need to send a specific type of SIP message, such as an INFO message, manually in your code.

The AudioVideoCall class provides a method, BeginSendMessage, which you can use to do this. In the parameters, you specify the type of SIP message, along with the content for the message body. You can also pass in an instance of CallSendMessageRequestOptions to specify custom SIP headers.

Manipulating Audio Media Using AudioVideoFlow

On an audio/video call, the AudioVideoFlow object handles the media stream. Properties and methods with this class give you some control over the media, and there are also several helper classes that can be attached to an AudioVideoFlow object to manipulate the audio on a call. Chapter 12 covers various possibilities in detail.

MONITORING CALL STATES

The Call object in UCMA exposes a number of events that allow applications to monitor the state of the call and its media flow, as well as the participants on the call. Applications can watch changes in these states in order to time call control actions, and they can also be useful in following the progress of a call for debugging purposes.

 When creating a new application, it is often a good practice to monitor the state of each call and write any state changes to a log or to the console. This can be extremely handy in figuring out what is happening when a call seems to be behaving oddly or is disconnecting prematurely.

Receiving Updates on Call State Changes

The StateChanged event on the Call object is invoked by UCMA whenever the State property of the Call changes. Table 8-2 lists the call states and their meanings.

TABLE 8-2: Call States

STATE NAME	MEANING
Idle	The call has been initialized as an outgoing call but has not been initiated (the INVITE has not yet been sent).
Incoming	The call is an incoming call that has not yet been accepted.
Establishing	The local endpoint is in the process of establishing the call with the remote endpoint.
Established	The SIP handshake has succeeded and the call is established with a remote endpoint.
Transferring	The local endpoint is sending a REFER message and the call is still in the process of being transferred.
Parking	The local endpoint is in the process of parking the call.
Terminating	The call is in the process of being terminated through a SIP BYE message.
Terminated	The call has been terminated and is no longer active.

In an event handler for the StateChanged event, a UCMA application can access both the previous state and the new state of the call. The following code shows an event handler that waits for an audio call to be established and then transfers it to another destination.

```
private void OnCallStateChanged(object sender,
    CallStateChangedEventArgs e)
{
    _logger.Log("Call state changed to {0}", e.State);

    // Check the new state of the call.
    if (e.State == CallState.Established)
    {
        AudioVideoCall call = (AudioVideoCall)sender;

        // If the call is established,
        // transfer it to the destination.
        call.BeginTransfer(_destinationSipUri,
            OnTransferCompleted, call);
    }
}
```

Receiving Updates on Flow State Changes

The StateChanged event on a MediaFlow object is invoked whenever the flow changes state. You can subscribe to this event to monitor changes in media transfer.

Table 8-3 lists media flow states and their meanings.

TABLE 8-3: Media Flow States

STATE NAME	MEANING
Idle	The media flow has not begun yet.
Active	The flow is active and media is being exchanged.
Terminated	The flow has been terminated and media is no longer being sent back and forth.

Receiving Quality of Service Data

The `AudioVideoCall` class has an event, `MediaTroubleshootingDataReported`, which allows UCMA applications to subscribe to quality of experience data reported by Lync Server. These data are provided as raw XML and are intended for debugging purposes. They are generally reported when the call terminates.

Chapter 13 describes how to use the quality of experience data reported through this event to assess the various factors that affect audio quality on Lync calls.

RETRIEVING INFORMATION ON REMOTE PARTICIPANTS

A two-party call has only one participant, which is either the endpoint your application has called or the endpoint that has called your application, so it is generally fairly obvious who is on the other end of the call. At times, though, looking up the identity or properties of the remote endpoint can be useful. The `Call` object provides a `RemoteParticipant` property for precisely this purpose.

The `RemoteParticipant` property holds a `ParticipantEndpoint` object with details on the remote endpoint. The `ParticipantEndpoint` object, in turn, has a `Participant` property, which holds a `Participant` object. The `Participant` object has information on the Lync *user*, whereas the `ParticipantEndpoint` object has information on the *user agent*, or endpoint.

You can see this for yourself by comparing the contents of `ParticipantEndpoint.Uri` and `Participant.Uri`. The former has a URI specific to the individual endpoint, whereas the latter has a SIP URI for the user, not tied to any one endpoint.

The following code shows an incoming audio call event handler that looks at the properties of the remote participant to determine whether the caller has a phone URI.

```
private void OnIncomingAudioVideoCallReceived(object sender,
    CallReceivedEventArgs<AudioVideoCall> e)
{
    // Only accept calls from callers with phone URIs.
    if (!string.IsNullOrEmpty(e.RemoteParticipant.PhoneUri))
    {
        e.Call.BeginAccept(OnAcceptCompleted, null);
    }
    else
```

```
        {
            e.Call.Decline();
        }
    }
```

The `Call` object also has a property called `RemoteEndpointProperties`, which holds information on the remote endpoint specific to the call. This includes information on whether the remote endpoint supports transfers and various other capabilities.

The following code snippet accesses `RemoteEndpointProperties` in order to determine whether the remote endpoint on a call accepts transfers before proceeding to transfer the call.

```
// Only transfer the call if the remote participant
// supports transfers. Otherwise, hang up in disgust.
if (_avCall.RemoteEndpointProperties.AllowTransfer)
{
    _avCall.BeginTransfer("sip:michaelg@fabrikam.com",
        OnTransferCompleted, null);
}
else
{
    _avCall.BeginTerminate(OnTerminateCompleted, null);
}
```

SUMMARY

In this chapter, you have seen how to initiate, accept, transfer, and terminate the various types of two-party calls. You have also learned about some other properties of the ubiquitous `Conversation` and `Call` classes. Understanding these topics is critical in building nearly any effective UCMA application.

The next chapter gives you a thorough introduction to another core area of UCMA — the APIs for publishing and querying presence information.

Presence with UCMA

WHAT'S IN THIS CHAPTER?

➤ Querying a user's presence

➤ Subscribing to a user's presence

➤ Publishing presence information automatically

➤ Publishing presence information on demand

➤ Publishing an "always-on" presence for an application

➤ Using the information from presence notifications

Unified Communications Managed API (UCMA) 3.0 allows you to retrieve and publish presence information in your applications with a minimal amount of code. Applications can retrieve presence on a one-time basis or create an ongoing presence subscription and can publish presence details for themselves in a number of ways. This chapter discusses the various methods of publishing, retrieving, and parsing presence information using UCMA.

A number of reasons exist as to why manipulating presence information is useful for Unified Communications applications, including the following:

➤ Some applications need to work with presence on behalf of individual users. A web client is an example; it needs to display the contact list that belongs to the user who is signed in.

➤ An application that provides a service may need to publish presence information to indicate to potential users whether it is available, what communication modalities it supports, and so forth.

➤ Some communication applications need to take action on the basis of other users' presence information. A contact center application, for instance, can perform "look-ahead routing" or "presence-based routing" by directing incoming calls only to agents who are in an available state.

UCMA makes each of these purposes simple to achieve by adding a layer of abstraction on top of the SIP messaging that makes presence work in Lync, and allowing developers to query, publish, and subscribe to presence with one asynchronous operation.

> *In the previous version of UCMA, although the SIP messaging was handled by the UCMA runtime, developers had to manipulate presence data in XML form. UCMA 3.0 adds data classes that allow developers to easily build the most common types of presence data without working directly with XML.*

The two samples from which most of the sample code in this chapter is drawn will help you to survive in an imaginary Unified Communications world that is dominated by intrigue and espionage. PresenceSpy keeps tabs on the availability changes of one or more users and reports back to you on their movements at the end of a monitoring session. As a countermeasure, PresenceCounterIntelligence publishes random presence changes for one or more users. Both sample applications are available on this book's website at www.wrox.com.

RETRIEVING PRESENCE INFORMATION FOR A REMOTE ENDPOINT

UCMA applications have two options for getting presence information about another user or application. (Incidentally, any entity that has presence information managed by Lync is known in Lync lingo as a *presentity*.) Option one is to make a one-time request for whatever presence information the application needs. This is called a *presence query* and is illustrated in Figure 9-1.

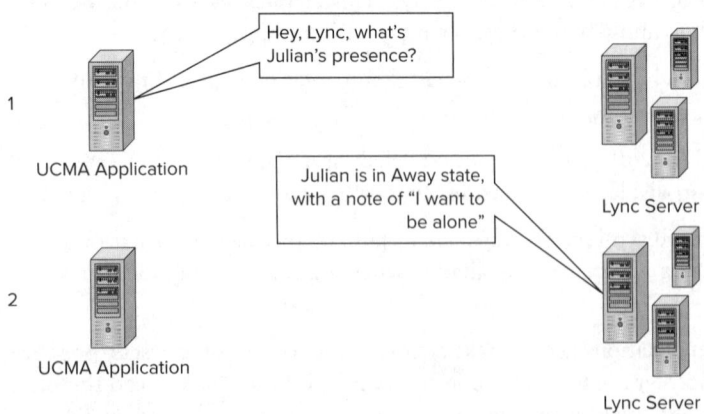

FIGURE 9-1

Presence queries are usually the best option for an application that needs to make a one-off decision based on a user's presence, but is not monitoring that user on a regular basis, or a service that needs to provide presence information in response to a specific request from a client.

Another option is to create a *presence subscription*. This means that the application asks Lync Server to notify it whenever new presence information is published for any of the users whom it is monitoring, as shown in Figure 9-2. The users whose presence the application subscribed to are referred to as the *subscription targets*.

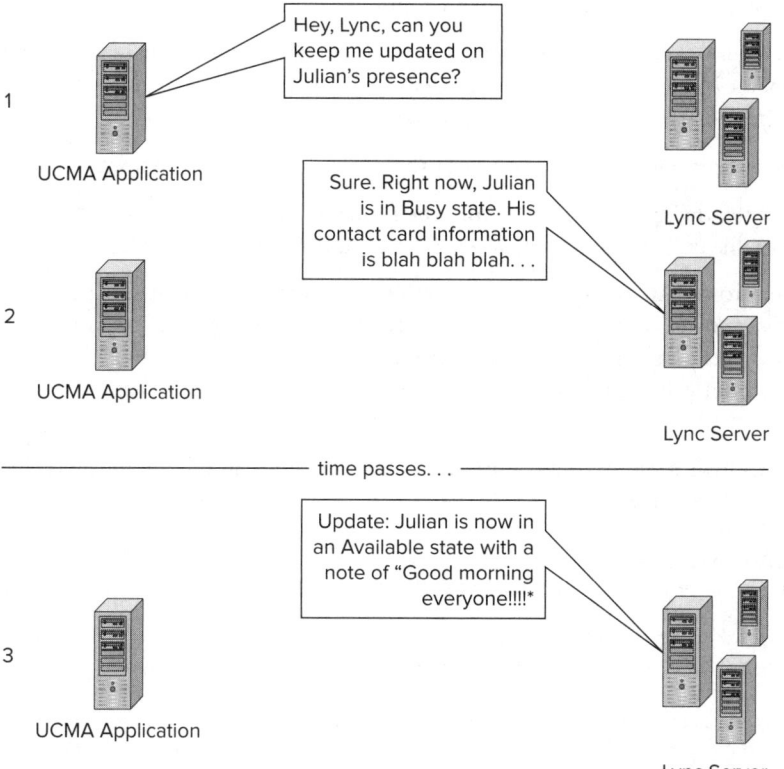

FIGURE 9-2

Presence subscriptions make the most sense for applications such as web-based clients that act on behalf of a number of users and need to have up-to-date information on the presence of everyone in a user's contact list. They are also often a good choice for applications that frequently refer to the presence of a group of users, such as a pool of customer service agents, to make routing decisions or control other behavior.

In either case, UCMA allows you to specify the presence categories you need. Presence categories, which are discussed in more detail in Chapter 6, distinguish the different types of information that Lync endpoints can publish with the enhanced presence model, such as availability, notes, contact information, phone information, and location. Creating custom presence categories is also possible — with a bit of work.

Querying a User's Presence

If an ongoing subscription to a user's presence is not necessary, an application can retrieve the user's presence on a one-time basis using a presence query.

The `ApplicationEndpoint` and `UserEndpoint` classes both have a `PresenceServices` property. This property holds a reference to an `ApplicationEndpointPresenceServices` or `UserEndpointPresenceServices` object, which gives developers access to some presence operations for an endpoint. The `BeginPresenceQuery` method on this object initiates a presence query to retrieve presence information for one or more users.

The users' SIP URIs are passed in as the first parameter, in the form of an enumerable collection of strings. The second parameter is an array of strings that represent the presence categories to query; see the "Parsing Presence Information" section later in this chapter for the possible choices.

An application can receive the presence information after the query completes in two ways:

➤ First, and most simply, the application can store the return value of `EndPresenceQuery`, which is an enumerable collection of `RemotePresentityNotification` objects.

➤ Alternatively, it can provide an event handler as the third parameter of `BeginPresenceQuery`; this event handler is invoked when the query results become available. This is handy if a presence notification event handler already exists elsewhere in the class that is used for presence subscriptions. The subscriptions and queries can happily share the same event handler with hardly any drama.

The following code snippet shows a method that initiates a presence query and handles the results returned by the `EndPresenceQuery` method.

```
private void HandlePresenceQueryInstantMessage(
    InstantMessagingCall call,      string toastMessage)
{

    // Extract the SIP URI from the toast message
    // by removing the text before "sip:".
    int sipUriStartPosition = toastMessage.IndexOf("sip:",
        StringComparison.OrdinalIgnoreCase);
    string sipUriToQuery = toastMessage.Remove(0,
        sipUriStartPosition);


    try
    {
        // Accept the incoming IM call containing the query command.
        IAsyncResult acceptCallAsyncResult =
            call.BeginAccept(
            ar =>
            {
                try
                {
                    call.EndAccept(ar);
                }
```

```
                catch (RealTimeException ex)
                {
                    _logger.Log("Failed accepting call.", ex);
                }
            },
        null);

    // Initiate the presence query for the state category only.
    _appEndpoint.PresenceServices.BeginPresenceQuery(
        new List<string>() { sipUriToQuery },
        new string[] { "state" },
        null,
        ar =>
        {
            try
            {
                // Retrieve the results of the query.
                IEnumerable<RemotePresentityNotification>
                    notifications =
                    _appEndpoint.PresenceServices.
                    EndPresenceQuery(ar);

                // Make sure the call has finished connecting.
                acceptCallAsyncResult.AsyncWaitHandle.WaitOne();

                // Grab the first notification in the results.
                RemotePresentityNotification notification =
                    notifications.FirstOrDefault();

                // Send an IM with the availability state name.
                SendMessageToInstantMessagingCallAndTerminate(
                    notification.AggregatedPresenceState.
                    Availability.ToString(),
                    call);
            }
            catch (RealTimeException ex)
            {
                _logger.Log("Presence query failed.", ex);
            }
        },
        null);

}
catch (InvalidOperationException ex)
{
    _logger.Log("Failed accepting call and querying presence.",
        ex);
}
}
```

Subscribing to Continuous Presence Updates Using RemotePresenceView

The `RemotePresenceView` class, new to UCMA 3.0, handles a single presence subscription on one or more remote users. It is associated with a single endpoint (either `ApplicationEndpoint` or `UserEndpoint`) and reports new presence notifications by invoking an event handler.

Creating and Registering a Presence Subscription

To create a presence subscription, first instantiate a `RemotePresenceView` object, passing in a reference to the endpoint in the constructor, as shown in the following snippet:

Available for
download on
Wrox.com

```
// Create a remote presence view.
_presenceView = new RemotePresenceView(_endpoint);
```

Code snippet PresenceSpy\PresenceSpySession.cs

Next, register an event handler for the `PresenceNotificationReceived` event on the `Remote PresenceView` object. The UCMA runtime will trigger this event any time the endpoint receives a new notification for one of its presence subscription targets. The event will also fire when the subscription is first established to report the current presence information for each subscription target.

 Always subscribe to the `PresenceNotificationReceived` event before starting the presence subscription. When the subscription request is sent to Lync Server, the server responds with an initial notification containing the current presence information for the subscription targets. If you have not already registered an event handler, your application may miss this initial notification or any other notifications that arrive very soon after the subscription starts.

The following code snippet illustrates registering an event handler to receive incoming presence notifications.

Available for
download on
Wrox.com

```
// Handle presence notification events.
presenceView.PresenceNotificationReceived +=
    new EventHandler<RemotePresentitiesNotificationEventArgs>(
        OnPresenceNotificationReceived);
```

Code snippet PresenceSpy\PresenceSpySession.cs

After an event handler is in place, start the presence subscription by calling `StartSubscribing ToPresentities` and passing in the presence targets (each one represented by a `RemotePresentity SubscriptionTarget` object) as an enumerable collection, as shown in the following code snippet. This is a synchronous method, and so it does not require a callback delegate or another method call to finish the operation.

```
// Create a list with only one subscription target.
List<RemotePresentitySubscriptionTarget> targets =
    new List<RemotePresentitySubscriptionTarget>();
targets.Add(new RemotePresentitySubscriptionTarget(_sipUri));

// Initiate the presence subscription.
_presenceView.StartSubscribingToPresentities(targets);
```

Code snippet PresenceSpy\PresenceSpySession.cs

When the application calls `StartSubscribingToPresentities`, the endpoint sends a SIP `SUBSCRIBE` message to Lync Server. The `SUBSCRIBE` message tells Lync Server to begin notifying the endpoint about new presence updates from the specified users in the specified categories. A typical message looks like the following. Both the `To` and `From` header contain the SIP URI of the subscribing endpoint, which makes sense as the message is handled by the Lync Front End Server and is not routed to any other users. The identity of the subscription target and the list of categories to which the endpoint wishes to subscribe are contained in an XML document in the message body. The URI of the subscription target is highlighted in the following code.

```
SUBSCRIBE sip:outbound.sample@fabrikam.com SIP/2.0
From: "Outbound"<sip:outbound.sample@fabrikam.com:13415;transport=Tls;
    ms-opaque=eddb24eaed385b26>;
    epid=68D3BA0FB8;tag=cf2482c9d5
To: <sip:outbound.sample@fabrikam.com>
CSeq: 4 SUBSCRIBE
Call-ID: e0dd562b219b413387106112f23ddd02
MAX-FORWARDS: 70
VIA: SIP/2.0/TLS 192.168.0.40:4317;branch=z9hG4bK613625f7
CONTACT: <sip:ts.fabrikam.com@fabrikam.com;gruu;opaque=srvr:
outbound.sample:jRw31iBwA16ogIm8sXN68AAA>;automata;
    actor="attendant";text;audio;video;image
CONTENT-LENGTH: 517
EVENT: presence
SUPPORTED: ms-dialog-route-set-update
SUPPORTED: com.microsoft.autoextend
SUPPORTED: ms-piggyback-first-notify
SUPPORTED: ms-benotify
SUPPORTED: eventlist
SUPPORTED: gruu-10
USER-AGENT: RTCC/4.0.0.0 PresenceSpy
CONTENT-TYPE: application/msrtc-adrl-categorylist+xml
REQUIRE: adhoclist,categorylist
Accept: application/msrtc-event-categories+xml,application/xpidf+xml,
    application/rlmi+xml, text/xml+msrtc.pidf,
    application/pidf+xml, multipart/related
Message-Body: <batchSub
    xmlns:xsi="http://www.w3.org/2001/XMLSchema-instance"
    xmlns:xsd="http://www.w3.org/2001/XMLSchema"
    xmlns="http://schemas.microsoft.com/2006/01/sip/batch-subscribe">
    <action name="subscribe"><adhocList>
    <resource uri="sip:michaelg@fabrikam.com" /></adhocList>
    <categoryList xmlns="http://schemas.microsoft.com/2006/
```

```
09/sip/categorylist"><category name="contactCard" />
<category name="state" /><category name="note" />
<category name="services" /><category name="calendarData" />
</categoryList></action></batchSub>
```

A few things are worth noting here. One is that the To header in the message does not contain the SIP URI of the subscription target; it contains the SIP URI of the user who is initiating the subscription. The SUBSCRIBE request itself is sent to the Lync Server and is not routed to any of the subscription targets. The URIs of the targets are sent in the message body, which contains an XML document with all the information necessary for Lync Server to process the presence subscription. The presence categories to which the user is subscribing are also contained in the XML document within the <categoryList> element.

After Lync Server has created the presence subscription, it responds with a 200 OK message. The body of this response includes initial presence information on each of the subscription targets. Here is an example:

```
SIP/2.0 200 OK
From: "Outbound"<sip:outbound.sample@fabrikam.com:13415;transport=Tls;
    ms-opaque=eddb24eaed385b26>;epid=68D3BA0FB8;tag=cf2482c9d5
To: <sip:outbound.sample@fabrikam.com>;tag=BB410080
CSeq: 4 SUBSCRIBE
Call-ID: e0dd562b219b413387106112f23ddd02
Contact: <sip:CS-SE.fabrikam.com:5061;transport=tls>
Content-Length: 2953
Via: SIP/2.0/TLS 192.168.0.40:4317;branch=z9hG4bK613625f7;
    ms-received-port=4317;ms-received-cid=1D0300
Expires: 33264
Require: eventlist
Content-Type: multipart/related; type="application/rlmi+xml";
    start=resourceList;
    boundary=fd7523dcba4842cf81d23498435ad925
Event: presence
subscription-state: active;expires=33264
ms-piggyback-cseq: 1
Supported: ms-benotify, ms-piggyback-first-notify
Message-Body:
--fd7523dcba4842cf81d23498435ad925
Content-Transfer-Encoding: binary
Content-ID: resourceList
Content-Type: application/rlmi+xml
<list xmlns="urn:ietf:params:xml:ns:rlmi"
    uri="sip:outbound.sample@fabrikam.com" version="0"
    fullState="false"/>
--fd7523dcba4842cf81d23498435ad925
Content-Transfer-Encoding: binary
Content-Type: application/msrtc-event-categories+xml
<categories xmlns="http://schemas.microsoft.com/2006/09/sip/categories"
    uri="sip:michaelg@fabrikam.com">
<category name="calendarData" instance="1440520487"
    publishTime="2010-11-20T21:20:07.490">
<calendarData xmlns="http://schemas.microsoft.com/
    2006/09/sip/calendarData" mailboxID="michaelg@fabrikam.com">
```

```
          freeBusy startTime="2010-11-19T08:00:00Z" granularity="PT15M"
          encodingVersion="1">AAAAAAAAAAAAAAAAAAAA
       AAAAAAAAAAAAAAAAAAAAAAAAAAAAAAAAAAAA
       AAAAAAAAAAAAAAAAAAAAAAAAAAAAAAAAAAAA
       AAAAAAAAAAAAAAAAAAAAAAAAAAAAAAAAAAAA</freeBusy>
          </calendarData>
    </category>
    <category name="contactCard" instance="0"
          publishTime="2010-11-11T21:12:55.053">
    <contactCard xmlns="http://schemas.microsoft.com/2006
          /09/sip/contactcard" >
    <identity >
    <name >
    <displayName >
    Michael Greenlee</displayName>
    </name>
    <email >
    michaelg@fabrikam.com</email>
    </identity>
    </contactCard>
    </category>
    <category name="contactCard" instance="4"
          publishTime="2010-11-20T21:19:59.480">
    <contactCard xmlns="http://schemas.microsoft.com/2006/
          09/sip/contactcard" isUCEnabled="true">
          </contactCard>
    </category>
    <category name="note"/>
    <category name="state" instance="1"
          publishTime="2010-11-21T02:31:15.890">
    <state xsi:type="aggregateState" xmlns:xsi="http://www.w3.org/2001/
          XMLSchema-instance" xmlns="http://schemas.microsoft.com/
          2006/09/sip/state">
          <availability>3500</availability><delimiter xmlns="http://schemas.microsoft.
          com/2006/09/sip/commontypes" />
          <device>computer</device>
          <end xmlns="http://schemas.microsoft.com/2006/
          09/sip/commontypes" /></state>
    </category>
    <category name="services" instance="0"
          publishTime="2010-11-21T02:31:15.890">
    <services xmlns="http://schemas.microsoft.com/2006/09/sip/service">
          <service uri="sip:michaelg@fabrikam.com"><capabilities>
          <text render="true" capture="true"
          deviceAvailability="3500" />
          <gifInk render="true" capture="false"
          deviceAvailability="3500" /><isfInk
          render="true" capture="false"
          deviceAvailability="3500" /><applicationSharing
          render="true" capture="true" deviceAvailability="3500" />
          <voice render="true" capture="true"
          deviceAvailability="3500" /><video render="true"
          capture="true" deviceAvailability="3500" />
          <contentWhiteboard render="true"
          capture="true" deviceAvailability="3500" />
```

```
<contentPoll render="true" capture="true"
deviceAvailability="3500" />
<contentPowerPoint render="true"
capture="true" deviceAvailability="3500" />
<contentNativeFile render="true"
capture="true" deviceAvailability="3500" />
</capabilities></service></services>
</category>
</categories>

--fd7523dcba4842cf81d23498435ad925--
```

This initial notification gives the UCMA application baseline information for each of the subscription targets to which it can apply subsequent updates.

Whenever an update occurs for one of the targets, Lync Server sends a SIP BENOTIFY message to the application. Later sections in this chapter discuss how to parse the information contained in these presence notifications.

Limitations on Presence Subscriptions

Lync Server limits the number of users who can subscribe to each presentity's presence to 200. In other words, if everyone in a company tries to subscribe to the CEO's presence, Lync Server will only allow the first 200 to initiate subscriptions.

This is problematic in a couple of cases. One is that certain services may need to receive presence updates on large numbers of contacts, regardless of how many other users are subscribing to their presence. The other problem is that a UCMA service application may be in the contact list of a very large number of users, quickly putting the number of subscribers over the limit of 200.

To solve the first problem, the RemotePresenceView class supports a "backup" mode of receiving presence updates using polling. In this mode, rather than initiating a subscription with Lync Server, it automatically queries the presence of each target at regular intervals. This gets around Lync Server's limit on the number of simultaneous presence subscribers.

By default, RemotePresenceView downgrades to the polling method if Lync Server rejects the initial SUBSCRIBE request. You can also tell RemotePresenceView to use polling from the outset using a RemotePresenceViewSettings object when creating an instance of RemotePresenceView. Set the SubscriptionMode on the RemotePresenceViewSettings object to determine which mode the endpoint uses to retrieve presence information. You can also set the polling interval using the PollingInterval property on RemotePresenceViewSettings. The following code snippet illustrates this:

```
// Set the presence view to poll every 30 seconds.
RemotePresenceViewSettings settings =
    new RemotePresenceViewSettings();
settings.SubscriptionMode =
    RemotePresenceViewSubscriptionMode.Polling;
settings.PollingInterval = new TimeSpan(0, 0, 30);

// Create a remote presence view.
_presenceView = new RemotePresenceView(_endpoint, settings);
```

To be notified when UCMA falls back on the polling method of receiving presence updates, subscribe to the `SubscriptionStateChanged` event on `RemotePresenceView`. The following code snippet contains a sample event handler for this event:

```
private void OnSubscriptionStateChanged(object sender,
    RemoteSubscriptionStateChangedEventArgs e)
{
    foreach (KeyValuePair<RealTimeAddress,
        RemotePresentityStateChange> pair
        in e.SubscriptionStateChanges)
    {
        Console.WriteLine(
            "Subscription for {0} changed to {1} state",
            pair.Key.Uri, pair.Value.State);
    }
}
```

For the second issue (dealing with the large numbers of users subscribing to a UCMA application's presence) UCMA allows you to mark an application endpoint as an "automaton" in the contact card presence category. This tells Lync Server that this presentity always has the same presence state, so users who subscribe to its presence do not need to receive updates. Consequently, the application will always appear as available in everyone's contact list. This option is discussed later in this chapter.

Parsing Presence Information

When a UCMA application receives a presence update notification, the new presence information is wrapped in `PresenceCategory` objects. Each `PresenceCategory` object corresponds to a single `<category>` element in the presence XML document, and the UCMA application has the option of reading the XML directly.

UCMA 3.0, however, also provides some category classes that derive from `PresenceCategory` and have strongly typed properties. With these classes, such as `PresenceState` and `ContactCard`, retrieving most of the commonly needed bits of presence information without writing XML-parsing code is possible.

The `RemotePresentityNotification` class, which contains all the presence category data for a single notification, gives access to the raw XML data through `PresenceCategory` objects and also has properties that hold the strongly typed presence category objects. This allows developers to choose which method they prefer.

 In the previous version of UCMA, presence updates were provided only in the form of raw XML. This made interpreting the presence updates somewhat burdensome. UCMA 3.0 introduced strongly typed presence category classes to make this process easier so developers can focus on solving business problems instead of writing XML parsing code.

Six presence categories are built into Lync, as shown in Table 9-1. By default, endpoints subscribe to updates in the first five categories.

TABLE 9-1: Built-in Presence Categories

CATEGORY	PURPOSE
State	Indicates how available the user is for communications, and whether the user is in a call or conference.
contactCard	Contains contact details for the user.
calendarData	Contains data from Exchange on the user's availability during the day.
services	Indicates which capabilities, such as video, audio, or instant messaging, a user currently supports.
note	Holds a plain-text status note, which is usually entered by the user in Communicator.
routing	Holds information about how calls for this user should be routed.

 UCMA applications cannot query or subscribe to the routing category for remote endpoints.

The State Category

The primary purpose of the information in the *state* category is to help users assess whether another contact is available to talk. It consists of two primary pieces of information: an integer availability value, which gives a numeric representation of how available the contact is currently (and also controls the color of the contact's "presence light" in Lync), and an activity token, which gives more detail on what the contact is currently doing and is the source of the text ("Available," "In a Call," or "In a Meeting," for instance) that appears next to a Lync presence icon in client applications.

NAMES FOR THE LITTLE COLORED THING THAT SHOWS LYNC PRESENCE

There is a long tradition of confusion concerning what to call the colored icon that shows the presence state of a Lync contact. The following list shows some of the prevailing choices:

➤ Presence icon (the most boring)

➤ Presence bubble (a holdover from Office Communications Server, in which the icon was circular)

➤ Presence light

➤ Presence chiclet

➤ Presenticon

➤ Tetrathorpe

Actually, we just made up those last two. We hope they catch on. (Read Chapter 12 to learn the definition of *octothorpe*.)

Availability values are generally between 3000 and 18500. Each range of values (an *availability class*) corresponds to one of the presence icons used in the Lync presence controls, as shown in Table 9-2.

TABLE 9-2: Availability Classes

RANGE OF VALUES	CLASS NAME	PRESENCE ICON
3000–4499	Online	Green
4500–5999	IdleOnline	Green/Yellow
6000–7499	Busy	Red
7500–8999	IdleBusy	Red/Yellow
9000–11999	DoNotDisturb	Dark Red with Dash
12000–14999	BeRightBack	Yellow
1500 –17999	Away	Yellow
>18000	Offline	Gray

Activity tokens usually correspond to ranges of availability values as well. However, which activity tokens go with which availability values varies depending on the type of presence state.

Four types of presence state exist. When endpoints publish state information, they publish one or more of these four types, which are user state, machine state, calendar state, and phone state. Table 9-3 shows the types of state information.

TABLE 9-3: Types of State Information

STATE TYPE	PURPOSE
User state	Holds state information manually chosen by the user, such as through the presence control on the Lync client.
Machine state	Holds state information determined by the current state of the device; for instance, whether the user has moved the mouse or typed anything recently.
Calendar state	Holds state information based on the user's Exchange calendar information; for instance, if the user has a meeting scheduled for the current time, the endpoint may publish calendar state data showing this.
Phone state	Holds state information based on whether any phone calls or conferences are currently active at the endpoint.

Lync Server receives the various pieces of state information from all endpoints where a given user is signed in and uses a set of rules to combine them into a single block of state information, which it then provides as *aggregate state* to any endpoints that request that user's presence. This process of combining the various state publications from one or more endpoints is called *presence aggregation*.

Aggregate presence state is available through the `AggregatedPresenceState` property on a `RemotePresentityNotification` object, as shown in the following code snippet, which retrieves the availability value and activity token string from a new presence notification. The availability value is translated into one of the values of the `PresenceAvailability` enumeration, whereas the activity token is turned into a `PresenceActivity` object, which contains the name of the activity in string form along with some other details.

```
// Get the new availability value.
PresenceAvailability newAvailability =
    notification.AggregatedPresenceState.Availability;

// Get the new activity token.
string newActivityToken =
    notification.AggregatedPresenceState.Activity.ActivityToken;
```

Code snippet PresenceSpy\PresenceSpySession.cs

The Contact Card Category

The *contact card* category holds contact information and other personal details for a user. Contact card information can be accessed through the `ContactCard` property on a `RemotePresentityNotification` object. This property contains a reference to a `ContactCard` object, which holds the various contact card fields in string properties.

As an example, the following code extracts a contact's display name and email address from a presence notification.

```
string displayName = notification.ContactCard.DisplayName;
string email = notification.ContactCard.EmailAddress;
```

The Note Category

The *note* category holds the text that a user enters in the Lync client or in an out-of-office message.

Both of these types of note are accessible through properties on the `RemotePresentityNotification` class. The `PersonalNote` property holds the note (if any) that the user has entered in the Lync client, and the `OutOfOfficeNote` property holds any out-of-office message that is currently in effect for the user. In both cases, the note is represented by an instance of the `Note` class, which holds the actual message in string format in its `Message` property.

The following code snippet shows how an application might access the text of the personal note in a presence notification.

```
// Get the new note.
stringnewNote =
    notification.PersonalNote.Message;
```

The Services Category

The *services* category holds information about a user's current communication capabilities. If the user is logged in at multiple endpoints, the capabilities across the different endpoints are combined.

Applications can access service information through the `ServiceCapabilities` property on the `RemotePresentityNotification` class, as shown in the following code snippet.

```
// Determine whether the user can handle audio and app sharing.
bool capableOfTakingSupportCalls =
    notification.ServiceCapabilities.AudioEnabled ==
        ServiceCapabilitySupport.Enabled &&
    notification.ServiceCapabilities.ApplicationSharingEnabled ==
        ServiceCapabilitySupport.Enabled;
```

The `ServiceCapabilites` property contains a reference to an instance of the `Services` class. This class has properties that indicate whether the user in question can support audio, video, application sharing, and instant messaging.

The `Services` class also has a property called `ServiceList`, which contains a list of `Service Capability` objects. Each of these objects represents a single capability of the user, and contains information on the availability state of the device that gives the user this capability. More capabilities exist than the four mentioned earlier; for example, users can have capabilities such as `contentWhiteboard` or `gifInk`.

Table 9-4 shows some of the capabilities that can appear in this list.

TABLE 9-4: Service Capabilities

CAPABILITY NAME	DESCRIPTION
text	Indicates that the endpoint can send and receive messages in text form.
voice	Indicates that the endpoint can participate in audio calls.
video	Indicates that the endpoint can participate in video calls.
calendar	Indicates that the endpoint can publish information from an Exchange calendar.
remoteCallControl	Indicates that the endpoint can perform remote call control operations.
CCCP	Indicates that the endpoint can handle Centralized Conference Control Protocol (CCCP) commands.
gifInk	Indicates that the endpoint can handle ink messages.
isfInk	Indicates that the endpoint can handle ink messages.
applicationSharing	Indicates that this endpoint can participate in application sharing calls.
contentWhiteboard	Indicates that the endpoint can handle whiteboard sharing sessions.
contentPowerPoint	Indicates that this endpoint can handle shared PowerPoint content.
contentNativeFile	Indicates that this endpoint can handle sharing arbitrary file content.
contentPoll	Indicates that this endpoint can participate in polls.

The following code snippet demonstrates how to use the `ServiceCapability` objects in the `ServiceList` property to determine the availability of a user's instant messaging device.

```
// Check that the user's IM device is in an available state.
ServiceCapability imDeviceServiceCapability =
    notification.ServiceCapabilities.ServiceList.FirstOrDefault(s =>
        s.CapabilityType == "text");
bool imDeviceReady = imDeviceServiceCapability != null &&
    imDeviceServiceCapability.DeviceAvailability ==
    PresenceAvailability.Online;
```

The Calendar Data Category

The *calendar data* category stores information that comes from a user's Exchange calendar. This is the information that enables you, for example, to see when someone is scheduled to be free in the Lync client.

Unlike the other presence categories, the calendar data category does not have a strongly typed class in UCMA 3.0. Applications that need to access the data from this presence category must parse the XML data manually.

PARSING PRESENCECATEGORYWITHMETADATA OBJECTS

If you find yourself in possession of a `PresenceCategoryWithMetaData` object that contains presence data you would have liked to read using one of the strongly typed presence category classes, all is not lost. Assuming you know the category of the information contained in the presence data, you can effect this magical transformation by passing the `PresenceCategoryWithMetaData` object into the constructor for the strongly typed presence class. The following code snippet shows how this works.

```
// Turn the wild, untamed presence state data into a tidy
// PresenceState object.
PresenceState stronglyTypedState =
    new PresenceState(mysteriousPresenceCategoryWithMetaData);
```

PUBLISHING PRESENCE FOR THE LOCAL ENDPOINT

The `LocalOwnerPresence` property on a `UserEndpoint` or `ApplicationEndpoint` exposes methods for publishing presence information. The process for publishing presence is slightly different depending on whether the endpoint is a user endpoint or an application endpoint: User endpoints can rely on the grammar-based method of publication, in which *instance IDs* and *container IDs* are automatically generated by Lync, whereas application endpoints must always supply these explicitly. This section describes both approaches in detail.

A UCMA endpoint can only publish presence information that belongs to the Lync user it represents. An application that needs to publish presence information for multiple users must create an endpoint for each user.

Presence containers, which are discussed in more depth in Chapter 10, are access control containers into which different types or amounts of presence information can be published, to control which other users have access to which information. When an endpoint publishes presence information, it publishes separate category items for each container that will hold the information. For instance, calendar information might be published to the Friends and Family, Workgroup, and Colleagues containers. User endpoints, when publishing presence, can simply provide the category data once, and the presence grammar will determine which containers should receive which pieces of information. Application endpoints, on the other hand, need to publish the category data once for each container, providing the ID of the container with each piece of category data.

Likewise, instance IDs, which uniquely identify a single presence publication, are automatically generated with the grammar-based publication method, but application endpoints must provide them manually. The instance ID is the same for each piece of presence category data published in one batch, so one publication might, for example, contain a `userState` category and a `note` category with container ID 400, and a `userState` category with container ID 300, all with an instance ID of 244.

Publishing Presence with a Presence Grammar

User endpoints can use the overload of `LocalOwnerPresence.BeginPublishPresence` that takes a collection of `PresenceCategory` objects as its first parameter. The objects in the collection can be instances of either the strongly typed presence category classes (such as `PresenceState`) or the `PresenceCategory` class itself (to publish presence information in raw XML form). The latter is necessary to publish presence information of a category that does not have a strongly typed class (such as the `routing` category, which contains information on call forwarding, team ring, and other such options).

The `PublishRandomStateAndNote` method, shown next, from the `PresenceCounterIntelligence` sample application, demonstrates the grammar-based method of publishing presence using the `BeginPublishPresence` method.

```
private void PublishRandomStateAndNote()
{
    _timer.Change(Timeout.Infinite, Timeout.Infinite);

    PresenceState newState = GetRandomNonStandardPresenceState();
    Note newNote = new Note(GetRandomNoteMessage());

    List<PresenceCategory> categories = new List<PresenceCategory>()
    {
        newState,
        newNote
```

```
    };
    try
    {
        _endpoint.LocalOwnerPresence.BeginPublishPresence(
            categories,
            ar =>
            {
                try
                {
                    _endpoint.PresenceServices.EndUpdatePresenceState(
                        ar);

                    _logger.Log("Published presence with state {0} " +
                        "and note {1}.",
                        newState.Availability, newNote.Message);
                    _timer.Change(GetRandomWaitMilliseconds(),
                        GetRandomWaitMilliseconds());
                }
                catch (RealTimeException ex)
                {
                    _logger.Log("Failed publishing presence.", ex);
                }
            },
            null);
    }
    catch (InvalidOperationException ex)
    {
        _logger.Log("Failed publishing presence.", ex);
    }
}
```

Code snippet PresenceCounterIntelligence\PresencePublishingSession.cs

AN EVEN EASIER WAY TO PUBLISH USER ENDPOINT STATE DATA

If your application needs to publish only state information for a user (for example, to mark a user as Busy) without any of the other categories, today is your lucky day. A method available in UCMA 3.0 makes these presence publications even easier than publishing presence with the BeginPublishPresence method.

The object referenced by the PresenceServices property on UserEndpoint has a method called BeginUpdatePresenceState. By calling this method, with an instance of PresenceState as the first parameter, you can publish a new state for the endpoint without bothering with creating a collection of PresenceCategory objects.

The PublishRandomState method (shown next) in the sample application illustrates this approach.

```
private void PublishRandomState()
{
    _timer.Change(Timeout.Infinite, Timeout.Infinite);

    PresenceState newState = GetRandomStandardPresenceState();

    try
    {
        _endpoint.PresenceServices.BeginUpdatePresenceState(
            newState,
            ar =>
            {
                try
                {
                    _endpoint.PresenceServices.
                        EndUpdatePresenceState(ar);

                    _logger.Log("Updated presence state to {0}.",
                        newState.Availability);
                    _timer.Change(GetRandomWaitMilliseconds(),
                        GetRandomWaitMilliseconds());
                }
                catch (RealTimeException ex)
                {
                    _logger.Log("Failed updating presence state."
                        , ex);
                }
            },
            null);
    }
    catch (InvalidOperationException ex)
    {
        _logger.Log("Failed updating presence state.", ex);
    }
}
```

Publishing Presence Without a Presence Grammar

Application endpoints do not have the luxury of using grammar-based presence publication. Instead, they must explicitly specify indicate which containers presence information should be published to, and must provide instance IDs when publishing presence information.

To provide these additional details when publishing presence using an application endpoint, pass instances of PresenceCategoryWithMetaData to LocalOwnerPresence.BeginPublishPresence. Each PresenceCategoryWithMetaData object wraps a single PresenceCategory instance (or an instance of one of the stronglytyped subclasses) along with an instance ID and container ID.

The following code snippet shows what the PublishRandomStateAndNote method would look like with non–grammar-based presence publication.

```
private void PublishRandomStateAndNoteWithMetaData()
{
    _timer.Change(Timeout.Infinite, Timeout.Infinite);

    PresenceState newState = GetRandomNonStandardPresenceState();
    Note newNote = new Note(GetRandomNoteMessage());

    // Create some presence category items with metadata.
    // Include the state and note data for friends/family only,
    // and just the state for workgroup and colleague contatcts.
    PresenceCategoryWithMetaData stateWithMetaDataForFriends =
        new PresenceCategoryWithMetaData(244, 400, newState);
    PresenceCategoryWithMetaData noteWithMetaDataForFriends =
        new PresenceCategoryWithMetaData(244, 400, newNote);
    PresenceCategoryWithMetaData stateWithMetaDataForWorkgroup =
        new PresenceCategoryWithMetaData(244, 300, newState);
    PresenceCategoryWithMetaData stateWithMetaDataForColleagues =
        new PresenceCategoryWithMetaData(244, 200, newState);

    List<PresenceCategoryWithMetaData> categories =
        new List<PresenceCategoryWithMetaData>()
    {
        stateWithMetaDataForFriends,
        noteWithMetaDataForFriends,
        stateWithMetaDataForWorkgroup,
        stateWithMetaDataForColleagues
    };

    try
    {
        _endpoint.LocalOwnerPresence.BeginPublishPresence(
            categories,
            ar =>
            {
                try
                {
                    _endpoint.PresenceServices.EndUpdatePresenceState(
                        ar);

                    _logger.Log("Published presence with state {0} " +
                        "and note {1}.",
                        newState.Availability, newNote.Message);
                    _timer.Change(GetRandomWaitMilliseconds(),
                        GetRandomWaitMilliseconds());
                }
                catch (RealTimeException ex)
                {
                    _logger.Log("Failed publishing presence.", ex);
                }
            },
            null);
    }
    catch (InvalidOperationException ex)
    {
```

```
            _logger.Log("Failed publishing presence.", ex);
        }
    }
```

RETRIEVING PRESENCE INFORMATION FOR THE LOCAL ENDPOINT

Before an application publishes presence information with an endpoint, the recommendation is that the application subscribe to local presence notifications for that endpoint using the `BeginSubscribe` method on the object referenced by the `LocalOwnerPresence` property. Unlike the presence subscriptions managed by instances of `RemotePresenceView`, the local presence subscription is for notifications about the endpoint's own presence. Table 9-5 shows the various types of information that an application can receive when the local presence subscription is active.

TABLE 9-5: Local Owner Presence Notifications

EVENT NAME	TYPE OF INFORMATION
ContainerNotificationReceived	Information on container membership for this user, if applicable.
DelegateNotificationReceived	Information on this user's delegates, if applicable.
PresenceNotificationReceived	Details of this user's presence information.
SubscriberNotificationReceived	Notification of a new subscription to this user's presence from a remote user.

The `PresenceCounterIntelligence` application subscribes to local owner presence for each user endpoint before using it to publish fake presence updates. The following code snippet shows the method in which the application initiates this subscription.

```
private void SubscribeToLocalPresence()
{
    _endpoint.LocalOwnerPresence.PresenceNotificationReceived +=
        new EventHandler<LocalPresentityNotificationEventArgs>(
            OnLocalPresenceNotificationReceived);

    try
    {
        // Subscribe to local presence notifications.
        _endpoint.LocalOwnerPresence.BeginSubscribe(ar =>
        {
            try
            {
```

```
                    _endpoint.LocalOwnerPresence.EndSubscribe(ar);

                    _timer = new Timer(OnTimerElapsed, null,
                        GetRandomWaitMilliseconds(),
                        GetRandomWaitMilliseconds());
                }
                catch (RealTimeException ex)
                {
                    _logger.Log("Failed subscribing to local owner presence"
                        , ex);
                }
            },
                null
                );
        }
        catch (InvalidOperationException ex)
        {
            _logger.Log("Failed subscribing to local owner presence", ex);
        }

    }
```

Code snippet PresenceCounterIntelligence\PresencePublishingSession.cs

On receiving the notifications, the sample application simply logs them. The possibilities, however, abound.

> ### WHEN PRESENCE MUST BE REPUBLISHED
>
> Endpoints need to refresh their registrations with Lync Server every so often, and once in a while the server will notify the endpoint that it needs to republish its presence information. Typically, this happens because for some reason the endpoint could not register with the same registrar as before, and needs to publish its presence information to the new registrar.
>
> To handle this situation, applications should subscribe to the `RepublishingRequired` event on each `UserEndpoint` or `ApplicationEndpoint` and publish its presence again in the event handler, particularly if the published presence information is crucial to the application's function.

MAKING AN APPLICATION AN AUTOMATON

With a few exceptions, the types of UCMA services that use application endpoints, such as "bots" and call routing applications, are meant to be always online and available. For applications like these, changing presence is completely unnecessary; they should always appear as "Available."

Because a limit exists on how many users can subscribe to presence updates for each endpoint, and because UCMA services may very well be used by many users, Lync allows services like these to identify themselves as "automatons," meaning their presence is not expected to change. Other users will not expect to receive presence updates for automatons, and will simply use the initial presence value or poll for any changes.

An attribute on the XML element for the `contactCard` category identifies a presentity as an automaton. You can control this using the `IsAutomatedService` property on the `ContactCard` class, which is set to true for automatons.

Publishing an Always-On Presence

UCMA 3.0 provides an easy way to publish an always-online presence state for an application when first establishing the endpoint. The following code snippet illustrates how to set an application endpoint to publish an always-online presence state using `ApplicationEndpointSettings`. The code first enables automatic presence publication for the endpoint, then sets the service capabilities of the endpoint, and then initializes and establishes the endpoint with those settings.

 The state information published by the application endpoint when automatic presence publication is turned on is accessible through the `PresenceState .PersistentOnline` static property, in case for some reason you ever need to publish it after establishing the endpoint.

Available for download on Wrox.com

```
// Set up the automatic presence publishing settings for the endpoint
ApplicationEndpointSettings settings =
    args.ApplicationEndpointSettings;
settings.AutomaticPresencePublicationEnabled = true;
settings.Presence.PresentityType = "automaton";

// Set the capabilities to be published for the endpoint
PreferredServiceCapabilities capabilities =
    settings.Presence.PreferredServiceCapabilities;
capabilities.InstantMessagingSupport = CapabilitySupport.Supported;
capabilities.AudioSupport = CapabilitySupport.UnSupported;
capabilities.ApplicationSharingSupport = CapabilitySupport.UnSupported;
capabilities.VideoSupport = CapabilitySupport.UnSupported;

_appEndpoint = new ApplicationEndpoint(_collaborationPlatform,
    settings);

_appEndpoint.BeginEstablish(OnApplicationEndpointEstablishCompleted,
    null);
```

Code snippet PresenceSpy\PresenceSpyUserAgent.cs

When `ApplicationEndpointSettings.AutomaticPresencePublicationEnabled` is set to true, the application endpoint will automatically publish presence upon startup with the automaton attribute set to true on the `contactCard` category, and with the `state` category indicating persistent availability.

Automatic Presence Publication for User Endpoints

Not to be outdone, the `UserEndpoint` class also has an automatic presence publication capability. The syntax is much the same as it is for `ApplicationEndpoint`, but for `UserEndpoint` it only sets the user's initial presence and does not leave the user in an "always-on" presence state. The following excerpt, from the `PresenceCounterIntelligence` sample application, demonstrates how it works.

```
UserEndpointSettings settings = new UserEndpointSettings(
    _sipUri,
    _proxyServerFqdn,
    TlsPort
    );

// Start out by automatically publishing Available presence.
settings.AutomaticPresencePublicationEnabled = true;
settings.Presence.UserPresenceState = PresenceState.UserAvailable;

_endpoint = new UserEndpoint(_platform, settings);
```

SUMMARY

In this chapter, you have seen how applications can retrieve and interpret presence data published by other users, and how they can publish presence information themselves, either when registering with Lync Server or on demand.

The next chapter covers another element of the collaboration capabilities in UCMA 3.0: the contact list APIs. Using these APIs, an application can access or modify the contact list of a Lync user.

10
Contact and Group Services in UCMA

WHAT'S IN THIS CHAPTER?

➤ Querying a contact list

➤ Adding, updating, and deleting contacts

➤ Adding, updating, and deleting groups

➤ Modifying access control settings

The contact list feature in Microsoft Lync Server 2010 allows each user to maintain a set of contacts, organized into groups, on the server so as to have access to it wherever the user logs in to Lync. When the Lync client connects to the server, it queries for contact list information, and then subscribes to the presence of all the contacts. Users can then make changes to their contact lists through Lync and can also modify access control settings for each contact.

UCMA provides an API for these same capabilities, through the `ContactGroupServices` class. This class is available through a property on `UserEndpoint`. Lync only maintains contacts for full-fledged users who are associated with a `User` object in Active Directory, so the `ApplicationEndpoint` class is left out of the running in this instance and does not have the `ContactGroupServices` property.

This is a sore point with the `ApplicationEndpoint`, so not bringing it up in conversation is best.

To help put the contact and group operations in context, this chapter shows code from a companion sample application, which is available on the website for this book. The sample application uses UCMA to perform a task that administrators who are deploying Lync for the first time often ask about: giving users in each department an initial contact list that contains the other users in that department.

All the code snippets in the following sections are taken directly from the sample application.

MANIPULATING CONTACTS IN THE CONTACT LIST

The first and most obvious task that you can accomplish with the contact list API in UCMA is adding, changing, or deleting contacts. The `ContactGroupServices` class has asynchronous methods to perform each of these tasks.

Querying a user's contact list is a bit less self-explanatory, because you do not simply call a method that performs the query. Instead, the application must initiate a contact and group subscription. After the subscription is initiated, the application receives a notification containing all current contacts and groups, and any changes that occur while the subscription is active will also generate notifications.

Subscribing to contacts before making any contact list changes is important for two reasons: One is that another endpoint could be making changes at the same time; another is that the subscription will allow the application to see the IDs that are assigned by Lync Server to any groups the application creates.

Querying a List of Contacts

To retrieve the full list of contacts and groups for a user, first attach an event handler to the `NotificationReceived` event on the `ContactGroupServices` instance, as shown in the following code snippet.

Available for download on Wrox.com

```
ContactGroupServices cgs = _userEndpoint.ContactGroupServices;
cgs.NotificationReceived +=
    new EventHandler<ContactGroupNotificationEventArgs>(
        cgs_NotificationReceived);
```

Code snippet ContactGroupMover\ContactGroupExporter.cs

Attaching this event handler before initiating a contact list subscription is important, because the event handler will be invoked almost immediately after the subscription starts.

After hooking up the event handler, call the `BeginSubscribe` method on `ContactGroupServices`. This method begins the process of subscribing to the user's contact list as an asynchronous operation. In the callback method for `BeginSubscribe`, call the `EndSubscribe` method to finish the asynchronous operation. Handle exceptions in whatever way you prefer.

The following code snippet shows how to initiate a contact list subscription.

Available for download on Wrox.com

```
try
{
    cgs.BeginSubscribe(ar =>
        {
            try
            {
                cgs.EndSubscribe(ar);
            }
            catch (RealTimeException rtex)
            {
```

```
                Console.WriteLine(rtex);
            }


        },
    null
    );
}
catch (InvalidOperationException ioex)
{
    Console.WriteLine(ioex);
}
```

Code snippet ContactGroupMover\ContactGroupExporter.cs

After the application subscribes to the user's contact list on Lync Server, the server sends an initial notification with the entire list of contacts and groups. The code in the event handler must process this information.

To identify the initial notification with the full list of contacts, check that `e.IsFullNotification` is set to `true`. The contacts and groups will be contained in `e.Contacts` and `e.Groups`, respectively. The following code snippet shows an excerpt from a notification handler that processes a full notification.

Available for
download on
Wrox.com

```
private void OnNotificationReceived(object sender,
    ContactGroupNotificationEventArgs e)
{
    Console.WriteLine("Received a contact update.");

    if (e.IsFullNotification)
    {
        _userEndpoint.ContactGroupServices.NotificationReceived -=
            OnNotificationReceived;

        ContactList list = new ContactList();
        list.Contacts = new List<ContactInfo>();
        list.Groups = new List<GroupInfo>();

        foreach (NotificationItem<Contact> item in e.Contacts)
        {
            Contact contact = item.Item;

            list.Contacts.Add(new ContactInfo()
            {
                Data = contact.ContactData,
                Name = contact.Name,
                GroupIds = contact.GroupIds,
                Extension = contact.ContactExtension,
                Uri = contact.Uri
            }
            );
        }

        foreach (NotificationItem<Group> item in e.Groups)
```

```
        {
            Group group = item.Item;

            list.Groups.Add(new GroupInfo()
            {
                Data = group.GroupData,
                Name = group.Name,
                Id = group.GroupId
            }
            );
        }

        XmlSerializer serializer = new XmlSerializer(typeof(ContactList));
        StreamWriter writer = File.CreateText(_filePath);
        serializer.Serialize(writer, list);

        try
        {
            _userEndpoint.ContactGroupServices.BeginUnsubscribe(ar =>
            {
                try
                {
                    _userEndpoint.ContactGroupServices.EndUnsubscribe(ar);
                }
                catch (RealTimeException rtex)
                {
                    Console.WriteLine(rtex);
                }
                finally
                {
                    _waitHandle.Set();
                }
            }, null);
        }
        catch (InvalidOperationException ioex)
        {
            Console.WriteLine(ioex);

            _waitHandle.Set();
        }
    }
}
```

Code snippet ContactGroupMover\ContactGroupDeleter.cs

If the application will be performing further contact list operations, or if it makes ongoing use of contact and group information, then keeping the subscription active and processing any additional notifications that arrive is a good idea. These will contain information on any changes that are made to the contact list.

Unsubscribing from contact list notifications is equally simple and can be done with the `BeginUnsubscribe` and `EndUnsubscribe` methods on the `ContactGroupServices` class. Remember to unregister the event handler for `NotificationReceived` as well. The following code snippet shows how to unsubscribe from contact list notifications.

Available for
download on
Wrox.com

```
try
{
    _userEndpoint.ContactGroupServices.BeginUnsubscribe(ar =>
    {
        try
        {
            _userEndpoint.ContactGroupServices.EndUnsubscribe(ar);
        }
        catch (RealTimeException rtex)
        {
            Console.WriteLine(rtex);
        }
        finally
        {
            ...
        }
    }, null);
}
catch (InvalidOperationException ioex)
{
    Console.WriteLine(ioex);

    ...
}
```

Code snippet ContactGroupMover\ContactGroupExporter.cs

The ContactGroupExporter class in the companion application for this chapter shows all the steps involved in obtaining a user's contact list from Lync Server. This class takes a UserEndpoint and a file path as parameters, subscribes to the user's contact list, and exports the resulting information as an XML file.

The following code shows the ContactGroupExporter class in its entirety.

Available for
download on
Wrox.com

```
using System;
using System.Collections.Generic;
using System.Linq;
using System.Text;
using Microsoft.Rtc.Collaboration;
using System.Threading;
using Microsoft.Rtc.Collaboration.ContactsGroups;
using Microsoft.Rtc.Signaling;
using System.Collections.ObjectModel;
using Microsoft.Rtc.Collaboration.Presence;
using System.Xml.Serialization;
using System.IO;

namespace ContactGroupMover
{
    internal class ContactGroupExporter
    {
        UserEndpoint _userEndpoint;
        string _filePath;
```

```
ManualResetEvent _waitHandle = new ManualResetEvent(true);
Collection<Contact> _contacts;
Collection<Group> _groups;
int i = 0;

internal WaitHandle WaitHandle
{
    get { return _waitHandle; }
}

internal ContactGroupExporter(UserEndpoint endpoint,
    string filePath)
{
    _userEndpoint = endpoint;
    _filePath = filePath;
}

internal void Export()
{
    _waitHandle.Reset();

    ContactGroupServices cgs =
        _userEndpoint.ContactGroupServices;
    cgs.NotificationReceived +=
        new EventHandler<ContactGroupNotificationEventArgs>(
            OnNotificationReceived);

    try
    {
        cgs.BeginSubscribe(ar =>
            {
                try
                {
                    cgs.EndSubscribe(ar);
                }
                catch (RealTimeException rtex)
                {
                    Console.WriteLine(rtex);
                }

            },
            null
            );
    }
    catch (InvalidOperationException ioex)
    {
        Console.WriteLine(ioex);
    }
}

private void OnNotificationReceived(object sender,
    ContactGroupNotificationEventArgs e)
{
    Console.WriteLine("Received a contact update.");

    if (e.IsFullNotification)
```

```
    {
        _userEndpoint.ContactGroupServices.NotificationReceived
            -= OnNotificationReceived;

        ContactList list = new ContactList();
        list.Contacts = new List<ContactInfo>();
        list.Groups = new List<GroupInfo>();

        foreach (NotificationItem<Contact> item in e.Contacts)
        {
            Contact contact = item.Item;

            list.Contacts.Add(new ContactInfo()
            {
                Data = contact.ContactData,
                Name = contact.Name,
                GroupIds = contact.GroupIds,
                Extension = contact.ContactExtension,
                Uri = contact.Uri
            }
            );
        }

        foreach (NotificationItem<Group> item in e.Groups)
        {
            Group group = item.Item;

            list.Groups.Add(new GroupInfo()
            {
                Data = group.GroupData,
                Name = group.Name,
                Id = group.GroupId
            }
            );
        }

        XmlSerializer serializer =
            new XmlSerializer(typeof(ContactList));
        StreamWriter writer = File.CreateText(_filePath);
        serializer.Serialize(writer, list);

        try
        {
            _userEndpoint.ContactGroupServices.
                BeginUnsubscribe(ar =>
            {
                try
                {
                    _userEndpoint.ContactGroupServices.
                        EndUnsubscribe(ar);
                }
                catch (RealTimeException rtex)
                {
                    Console.WriteLine(rtex);
```

```
                        }
                        finally
                        {
                            _waitHandle.Set();
                        }
                    }, null);
                }
                catch (InvalidOperationException ioex)
                {
                    Console.WriteLine(ioex);

                    _waitHandle.Set();
                }
            }
        }
    }
}
```

Code snippet ContactGroupMover\ContactGroupExporter.cs

Adding a Contact to the List

To add a contact to a user's contact list, use the `BeginAddContact` and `EndAddContact` methods on the `ContactGroupServices` class. The first parameter for `BeginAddContact` is the SIP URI of the user who is to be added to the contact list.

To specify additional information on the new contact, such as the contact's name, groups, or access control containers, create an instance of `ContactAddOptions` and pass it in as the second parameter to `BeginAddContact`.

The following excerpt from the `ContactGroupImporter` class in the sample application shows how to add a new contact:

Available for download on Wrox.com

```
private void AddContact(ContactInfo contactToAdd)
{
    UpdateContactGroupIds(contactToAdd);

    try
    {
        ContactAddOptions addOptions =
            new ContactAddOptions()
        {
            ContactData = contactToAdd.Data,
            ContactExtension = contactToAdd.Extension,
            ContactName = contactToAdd.Name
        };
        addOptions.GroupIds.AddRange(contactToAdd.GroupIds);_

        contactGroupServices.BeginAddContact(
            contactToAdd.Uri,
            addOptions,
            OnContactAddCompleted,
            null
        );
```

```
        }
        catch (InvalidOperationException ioex)
        {
            Console.WriteLine(ioex);
        }
    }

    private void OnContactAddCompleted(IAsyncResult result)
    {
        try
        {
            _contactGroupServices.EndAddContact(result);

            long remainingCount =
                Interlocked.Decrement(ref
                _contactCountLeftToAddOrModify);

            if (remainingCount == 0)
            {
                // All done.
                _waitHandle.Set();
            }
        }
        catch (RealTimeException rtex)
        {
            Console.WriteLine(rtex);
        }
    }
```

Code snippet ContactGroupMover\ContactGroupImporter.cs

Modifying an Existing Contact

The most common reason for modifying a contact in a user's contact list is to change the groups to which the contact belongs.

To change properties of a contact on the server, retrieving a cached record for the contact first using the BeginGetCachedContact and EndGetCachedContact methods is necessary. BeginGetCachedContact takes the SIP URI of the desired contact as its first parameter, and EndGetCachedContact returns a Contact object that contains the properties of the contact based on the most recent update from the server.

After changing the properties of the contact on the Contact object, call BeginUpdateContact, passing in the modified Contact object as the first parameter. Call EndUpdateContact to complete the asynchronous operation.

The following code snippet illustrates updating a contact on the server:

```
    private void UpdateContact(ContactInfo contactToUpdate)
    {
        UpdateContactGroupIds(contactToUpdate);

        try
```

```
        {
            // In order to update the contact,
            // it's necessary first to get the
            // cached contact from ContactGroupServices,
            // and make the changes to that object.

            _contactGroupServices.BeginGetCachedContact(
                contactToUpdate.Uri,
                OnGetContactCompleted,
                contactToUpdate
            );
        }
        catch (InvalidOperationException ioex)
        {
            Console.WriteLine(ioex);
        }
    }

    private void OnGetContactCompleted(IAsyncResult result)
    {
        ContactInfo newContactInfo =
            (ContactInfo)result.AsyncState;

        try
        {
            Contact contactObject =
                _contactGroupServices.EndGetCachedContact(result);

            try
            {
                contactObject.ContactData = newContactInfo.Data;
                contactObject.ContactExtension = newContactInfo.Extension;
                contactObject.Name = newContactInfo.Name;
                contactObject.GroupIds = newContactInfo.GroupIds;

                _contactGroupServices.BeginUpdateContact(
                    contactObject,
                    OnUpdateContactCompleted,
                    contactObject
                );
            }
            catch (InvalidOperationException ioex)
            {
                Console.WriteLine(ioex);
            }
        }
        catch (RealTimeException rtex)
        {
            Console.WriteLine(rtex);
        }
    }

    private void OnUpdateContactCompleted(IAsyncResult result)
    {
```

```
Contact contact =
    (Contact)result.AsyncState;

try
{
    _contactGroupServices.EndUpdateContact(result);

    ...
}
catch (RealTimeException rtex)
{
    Console.WriteLine(rtex);
}
}
```

Code snippet ContactGroupMover\ContactGroupImporter.cs

Deleting a Contact

Deleting a specific contact is quite simple with the BeginDeleteContact and EndDeleteContact methods. BeginDeleteContact takes the SIP URI of the contact that is to be deleted as its first parameter.

The following code snippet from the sample application illustrates deleting a contact.

Available for
download on
Wrox.com

```
private void DeleteContact(Contact contactToRemove)
{
    try
    {
        _contactGroupServices.BeginDeleteContact(
            contactToRemove.Uri,
            ar =>
            {
                try
                {
                    _contactGroupServices.EndDeleteContact(ar);

                    Interlocked.Decrement(ref _contactsToDelete);

                    CheckForCompletion();
                }
                catch (RealTimeException rtex)
                {
                    Console.WriteLine(rtex);
                }
            },
            null
        );
    }
    catch (InvalidOperationException ioex)
    {
        Console.WriteLine(ioex);
    }
}
```

Code snippet ContactGroupMover\ContactGroupDeleter.cs

MANIPULATING GROUPS IN THE CONTACT LIST

If you paid close attention during the previous section, you can probably take an excellent guess at how to add, update, and delete contact groups through UCMA.

Adding a Group to the List

To add a new group to a user's contact list, call `BeginAddGroup` and `EndAddGroup` on `ContactGroupServices`. The first parameter of `BeginAddGroup` is the name of the group; the second is group data.

The following code snippet, from the sample application, shows how to add a group.

```
private void AddGroup(GroupInfo groupToAdd)
{
    try
    {
        _contactGroupServices.BeginAddGroup(
            groupToAdd.Name,
            groupToAdd.Data,
            OnGroupAddCompleted,
            groupToAdd
        );
    }
    catch (InvalidOperationException ioex)
    {
        Console.WriteLine(ioex);
    }
}

private void OnGroupAddCompleted(IAsyncResult result)
{
    try
    {
        _contactGroupServices.EndAddGroup(result);
    }
    catch (RealTimeException rtex)
    {
        Console.WriteLine(rtex);
    }
}
```

Code snippet ContactGroupMover\ContactGroupImporter.cs

When the group is added to the contact list, an ID will be assigned to it. Unfortunately, the `EndAddGroup` method does not return this ID or any other information on the group, so the best way to determine the ID of the added group is to wait for a contact list change notification and check the information in the notification.

The following code snippet is an excerpt from the sample application that inspects contact list change notifications after the initial notification in order to find out the IDs assigned to added groups.

```csharp
void OnNotificationReceived(object sender, ContactGroupNotificationEventArgs e)
{
    Console.WriteLine("Received a contact update.");

    if (e.IsFullNotification)
    {
        ...
    }
    else
    {
        HandleAddedGroupNotification(e);
    }
}

private void HandleAddedGroupNotification(ContactGroupNotificationEventArgs e)
{
    IEnumerable<Group> addedGroups =
        e.Groups.Where(g => g.Operation == PublishOperation.Add).Select(n =>
            n.Item);

    foreach (Group group in addedGroups)
    {
        GroupInfo importedGroupInfo = _importedList.Groups.FirstOrDefault(
            g => g.Name == group.Name);

        if (importedGroupInfo != null)
        {
            // Store the ID of the added group that
            // matches the ID it had when it was imported.
            _addedGroupsByImportedGroupId.Add(importedGroupInfo.Id,
                group.GroupId);

            int groupsLeftToAdd =
                Interlocked.Decrement(ref _groupCountLeftToAdd);

            if (groupsLeftToAdd == 0)
            {
                // We don't need any more notifications,
                // so unsubscribe.
                _contactGroupServices.NotificationReceived -=
                    OnNotificationReceived;

                AddContacts();
            }
        }
    }
}
```

Code snippet ContactGroupMover\ContactGroupExporter.cs

Modifying an Existing Group

Modifying groups is perhaps the least useful ContactGroupServices operation, but it may come in handy if an application needs to rename existing groups without deleting and re-adding them.

To update a group, call `BeginUpdateGroup`, passing in the `Group` object with the desired changes. Call `EndUpdateGroup` to finish the asynchronous operation.

The following code snippet shows how to update a contact group.

```
try
{
    _contactGroupServices.BeginUpdateGroup(
        group,
        ar =>
        {
            try
            {
                _contactGroupServices.EndUpdateGroup(ar);
            }
            catch (RealTimeException rtex)
            {
                Console.WriteLine(rtex);
            }
        },
        null
    );
}
catch (InvalidOperationException ioex)
{
    Console.WriteLine(ioex);
}
```

Deleting a Group

Like deleting a contact from a user's contact list, deleting a group is quite simple. To delete a group, call `BeginDeleteGroup` and `EndDeleteGroup` on `ContactGroupServices`, as shown in the following code snippet.

```
private void DeleteGroup(Group groupToRemove)
{
    try
    {
        _contactGroupServices.BeginDeleteGroup(
            groupToRemove.GroupId,
            OnGroupDeleteCompleted,
            groupToRemove
        );
    }
    catch (InvalidOperationException ioex)
    {
        Console.WriteLine(ioex);
    }
}

private void OnGroupDeleteCompleted(IAsyncResult result)
{
    try
```

```
        {
            _contactGroupServices.EndDeleteGroup(result);

            ...
        }
        catch (RealTimeException rtex)
        {
            Console.WriteLine(rtex);
        }
    }
```

Code snippet ContactGroupMover\ContactGroupDeleter.cs

MANIPULATING PRESENCE ACCESS CONTROL USING CONTAINERS

Presence containers, discussed in the previous chapter, are access control containers that allow Lync users to restrict items of presence information to certain other users or categories of users.

The previous chapter described how to publish presence information to specific containers. This section explains the other side of the coin: how to control which users have access to which presence containers.

Three categories of container membership exist that you can add to or remove from a presence container. Table 10-1 shows these categories.

TABLE 10-1: Categories of Presence Container Membership

MEMBERSHIP CATEGORY	DEFINITION
Source network	The source of the contact — whether the contact is within the same enterprise, a federated contact, or from the public Internet.
SIP domain	The SIP domain associated with the contact; for example, wrox.com.
SIP URI	The SIP URI of an individual contact; for example, sip:bartholomew@wrox.com

Unlike the other contact operations described in this chapter, changing presence container membership does not involve the ContactGroupServices class. Instead, the LocalOwnerPresence class, described in the previous chapter, is responsible for container membership operations. This means that application endpoints as well as user endpoints can make changes to container memberships.

The LocalOwnerPresence class has an event, ContainerNotificationReceived, that is invoked whenever the endpoint receives an update to container membership from Lync Server. The following code snippet shows an event handler that stores the container membership data from an initial container notification.

```
void OnContainerNotificationReceived(object sender,
    ContainerNotificationEventArgs e)
{
    // Unsubscribe from the event so that only the initial
    // notification comes in.
    _userEndpoint.LocalOwnerPresence.ContainerNotificationReceived -=
        OnContainerNotificationReceived;

    // Initialize a data object to store the details.
    _membershipDetailsFromServer = new ContainerMembershipDetails();
    _membershipDetailsFromServer.Containers = new List<ContainerInfo>();

    foreach (ContainerMembership membership in
        e.ContainerList)
    {
        ContainerInfo info = new ContainerInfo()
        {
            ContainerId = membership.ContainerId,
            SipDomains = new List<string>(),
            SipUris = new List<string>()
        };

        // The source networks are stored in the ContainerMembership as
        // a flags enumeration.
        if ((membership.AllowedSourceNetworks & SourceNetwork.SameEnterprise) ==
            SourceNetwork.SameEnterprise)
        {
            info.SameEnterprise = true;
        }
        if ((membership.AllowedSourceNetworks & SourceNetwork.Federated) ==
            SourceNetwork.Federated)
        {
            info.Federated = true;
        }
        if ((membership.AllowedSourceNetworks & SourceNetwork.PublicCloud) ==
            SourceNetwork.PublicCloud)
        {
            info.PublicCloud = true;
        }

        foreach (string sipDomain in membership.AllowedSipDomains)
        {
            info.SipDomains.Add(sipDomain);
        }

        foreach (RealTimeAddress address in membership.AllowedSubscribers)
        {
            info.SipUris.Add(address.Uri);
        }

        _membershipDetailsFromServer.Containers.Add(info);
    }

    ...
}
```

Code snippet ContactGroupMover\ContainerMembershipHandler.cs

Adding Contacts to Presence Containers

The `BeginUpdateContainerMembership` method on the `LocalOwnerPresence` instance initiates an update to the membership of one or more presence containers. Its first parameter is a collection of `ContainerUpdateOperation` objects. Each `ContainerUpdateOperation` object represents changes (either additions or deletions) for a single presence container.

To indicate what additions should be made to a presence container, call the `AddSourceNetwork`, `AddSipDomain`, or `AddSipUri` method on the `ContainerUpdateOperation` object.

When the updates have been prepared, call `BeginUpdateContainerMembership`, passing in the collection of updates.

Removing Contacts from Presence Containers

To indicate deletions that should be made to the membership of a presence container, call the `DeleteSourceNetwork`, `DeleteSipDomain`, or `DeleteSipUri` method on the `ContainerUpdateOperation` object.

The following code snippet shows how container membership updates are prepared and then submitted using the `BeginUpdateContainerMembership` method.

```
List<ContainerUpdateOperation> updates =
    new List<ContainerUpdateOperation>();

foreach (ContainerInfo container in importedDetails.Containers)
{
    ContainerInfo containerFromServer =
        _membershipDetailsFromServer.Containers.FirstOrDefault(
        c => c.ContainerId == container.ContainerId);

    if (container.Equals(containerFromServer))
    {
        // No need for an update.
        continue;
    }

    ContainerUpdateOperation update =
        new ContainerUpdateOperation(container.ContainerId);

    if (container.SameEnterprise)
    {
        update.AddSourceNetwork(SourceNetwork.SameEnterprise);
    }
    else if (containerFromServer.SameEnterprise)
    {
        update.DeleteSourceNetwork(SourceNetwork.SameEnterprise);
    }

    if (container.Federated)
    {
        update.AddSourceNetwork(SourceNetwork.Federated);
```

```
        }
        else if (containerFromServer.Federated)
        {
            update.DeleteSourceNetwork(SourceNetwork.Federated);
        }

        if (container.PublicCloud)
        {
            update.AddSourceNetwork(SourceNetwork.PublicCloud);
        }
        else if (containerFromServer.PublicCloud)
        {
            update.DeleteSourceNetwork(SourceNetwork.PublicCloud);
        }

        if (containerFromServer != null)
        {
            IEnumerable<string> domainsToRemove =
                containerFromServer.SipDomains.Except(container.SipDomains);

            foreach (string domain in domainsToRemove)
            {
                update.DeleteDomain(domain);
            }
        }

        if (containerFromServer != null)
        {
            IEnumerable<string> urisToRemove =
                containerFromServer.SipUris.Except(container.SipUris);

            foreach (string uri in urisToRemove)
            {
                update.DeleteUri(uri);
            }
        }

        IEnumerable<string> domainsToAdd =
            container.SipDomains.Except(containerFromServer.SipDomains);

        foreach (string domain in domainsToAdd)
        {
            update.AddDomain(domain);
        }

        IEnumerable<string> urisToAdd =
            container.SipUris.Except(containerFromServer.SipUris);

        foreach (string uri in urisToAdd)
        {
            update.AddUri(uri);
        }

        updates.Add(update);
```

```
    }

    try
    {
        _userEndpoint.LocalOwnerPresence.BeginUpdateContainerMembership(
            updates,
            ar =>
            {
                try
                {
                    _userEndpoint.LocalOwnerPresence.EndUpdateContainerMembership(ar);
                }
                catch (RealTimeException rtex)
                {
                    Console.WriteLine(rtex);
                }
                finally
                {
                    Unsubscribe();
                }
            },
            null
        );
    }
    catch (InvalidOperationException ioex)
    {
        Console.WriteLine(ioex);
        Unsubscribe();
    }
```

Code snippet ContactGroupMover\ContainerMembershipHandler.cs

SUMMARY

In this chapter, you have seen how to use UCMA to retrieve and manipulate a Lync user's contact list, as well as make changes to presence container membership for access control.

The next chapter introduces the conferencing capabilities in UCMA, along with the many scenarios (some of them well outside the boundaries of traditional telephone conferencing) that they make possible.

11

Conference Services in UCMA

WHAT'S IN THIS CHAPTER?

➤ Creating and configuring Lync conferences

➤ Adding participants to a conference

➤ Controlling conferences with commands

➤ Providing services with trusted conference participants

In the simplest terms, a *conference* in Lync is a conversation that can include more than two participants. In a two-party conversation, the two participants can send media directly to each other. When a third participant comes into the picture, things quickly become complicated, because each one needs to receive media from all the others, and all participants need to be updated on any changes to the state of the conversation (such as one of the participants hanging up).

To coordinate all of these things, Lync brings in a handful of special server roles. The first is the *conference focus*, which is essentially a SIP traffic cop. The conference focus keeps track of the condition of the conference, who has access, who has joined, and so forth. The others are *multipoint control units* (MCUs), which are responsible for receiving media from all the conference participants, mixing it together, and sending it back out to each participant, so that everyone can hear (or see, or receive instant messages from, or share screens with) everyone else. A separate MCU exists for each modality; for instance, a conference that supports both instant messaging and audio must involve the instant messaging MCU and the audio/video MCU.

The most obvious use for a Lync conference is to allow more than two people to have a conversation. Note that one or more of the participants can be endpoints managed by a server application. These endpoints can manage, monitor, record, or provide extra services to a conference.

In some cases, however, only two human participants may be in the conference. This is common in applications that serve contact centers, help desks, or other teams that depend on advanced telephony capabilities. The conference in these situations allows a server application to participate in the conversation and send and receive media along with the two human participants.

These less obvious uses in areas other than conventional "conference calls" make conferences one of the most important tools in designing and building UCMA applications. At the same time, the way in which Lync manages conferences (and UCMA interacts with them) can be complex and at times confusing. Because of this, working with conferences in UCMA often presents challenges for developers. This chapter attempts to clarify how all the pieces involved in UCMA conference management fit together, while explaining the various UCMA conferencing operations and how to use them in custom Lync applications.

SETTING UP A CONFERENCE WITH UCMA

The first step in working with a conference in UCMA is to create the conference.

One of the most important points to remember when using the UCMA conference APIs is that although UCMA applications can create, control, join, and invite other users to a conference, the conference itself is not hosted by the UCMA application. The conference focus and the MCUs, which handle SIP signaling and media for the conference, respectively, are separate Lync services that are usually on a completely different server from the UCMA application. The UCMA application is only a participant in the conference, although it can be a conference owner or leader or even a "trusted participant" with special privileges (which are discussed later in the chapter).

This idea is a common source of confusion, so it bears reiterating in the form of diagrams. In Figure 11-1, a UCMA application has created a Lync audio conference and has invited two other participants. Each conference participant has its own separate SIP signaling session with the conference focus, while the audio media flows through the audio/video MCU. After the conference is in progress, the UCMA application does not have an active SIP session with the other conference participants. Instead, it communicates with them through the intermediaries of the focus and the MCU.

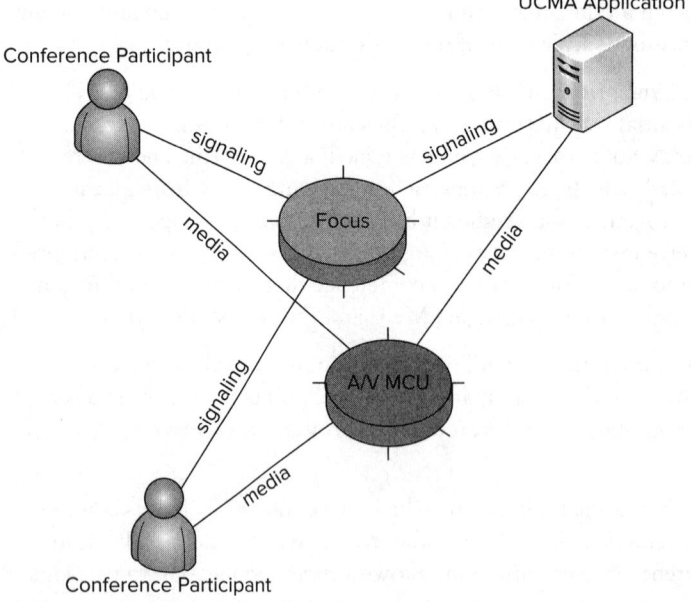

FIGURE 11-1

Later sections return to this point in more detail. For now, be sure to keep it in mind as you read.

 To be precise, the application does have a SIP signaling session with each MCU as well, which it uses to join the modality managed by that MCU in the conference. But the main signaling for the conference occurs with the conference focus.

So, when it needs to start a conference, the UCMA application must tell Lync Server to create one. The two ways in which it can go about this are to either explicitly "schedule" a conference with Lync Server, specifying options and an end time for the conference, or to create a conference "ad hoc" with some default options.

Using Scheduled Versus Ad-Hoc Conferences

To understand the difference between scheduled and ad-hoc conferences, think about the various options you have if you want to arrange a conference call through Lync. If you know that you will be having a conference call at a specific time, you can set up a conference in advance for that time through the Lync Outlook add-in. This is the equivalent of a scheduled conference.

If, on the other hand, you have just received an irate e-mail from a key customer whose shipment has not arrived, and you must simultaneously chew out everyone in the shipping department, you can simply invite the whole group to a new conversation. Lync will set up an audio conference for you on the spot, and you can leave it to the shipping folks to argue among themselves on how your customer's Christmas gifts were mistakenly sent to Rome, Italy, instead of Rome, Wisconsin. In UCMA, this would be an ad-hoc conference.

Scheduling a Conference Using ConferenceServices

To schedule a conference, call `BeginScheduleConference` on the `ConferenceServices` class. Each endpoint has an instance of `ConferenceServices`, which is accessible through a `ConferenceServices` property on the endpoint. As its first parameter, `BeginScheduleConference` takes a `ConferenceScheduleInformation` object; this object holds details (such as access settings, participants, and modalities) on the conference that is to be scheduled.

Specifying Settings Using ConferenceScheduleInformation

One of the primary reasons for scheduling a conference using `ConferenceServices` instead of using an ad-hoc conference is to exert more control over the behavior of the conference in areas such as access control. The `ConferenceScheduleInformation` class allows you to specify these settings when scheduling a conference.

Table 11-1 shows the various properties of `ConferenceScheduleInformation` that control the behavior of the conference. This chapter covers some of these properties in more detail later.

TABLE 11-1: ConferenceScheduleInformation Properties

PROPERTY	DESCRIPTION
AccessLevel	Determines what types of participants are admitted into the conference.
AttendanceAnnouncements Status	Controls whether the conference automatically makes announcements when participants join or leave the conference.
AutomaticLeaderAssignment	Determines which types of participants, if any, are automatically made into conference leaders on joining the conference.
ConferenceId	Indicates the unique ID of the conference.
Description	Contains a text description of the conference.
ExpiryTime	Indicates the time after which the conference may be deleted. The default is 8 hours after the conference is scheduled.
IsPasscodeOptional	If this is set to true, applications can elect not to prompt anonymous participants for the conference passcode.
LobbyBypass	Controls whether certain participants can bypass the "lobby" and be placed directly into the conference.
Mcus	Controls which MCUs the conference uses, and thus which modalities it supports.
OrganizerData	A string property for arbitrary XML data used by the conference organizer.
ParticipantData	Same as the preceding property, except that the XML data is sent to participants when they join the conference.
Participants	Contains information on authorized participants and their roles. Depending on the AccessLevel setting, some participants who are not in this list may also be admitted to the conference.
Passcode	Contains the passcode for the conference. Anonymous participants normally must enter this code to join the conference.
PhoneAccessEnabled	If this is true, participants can join the conference from a PSTN phone.
Subject	Contains a text subject for the conference. The subject will appear in the popup for the incoming conference invitation in the Lync client, as well as in the title bar of the conversation window.
Version	Contains a numeric revision number for the conference information.

CONFERENCE SCHEDULING TEMPLATES

Lync 2010 introduced a new feature in conference scheduling called scheduling templates. In a nutshell, the Lync administrator can configure a template with default settings. Users can then schedule conferences with this administrator-supplied template if they do not want to bother specifying their own settings.

The constructor for `ConferenceScheduleInformation` has an overload that takes a value from the `SchedulingTemplate` enumeration as its only parameter. Normally, a UCMA application supplies its own conference settings, so the default value (if you do not pass in this parameter) is `OrganizerSupplied`. If for some reason an application needs to schedule a conference with the administrator-supplied scheduling template, use this overload of the constructor and pass in `SchedulingTemplate.AdministratorSupplied`. In this case, Lync will use the settings from the administrator-supplied template and the application will not be able to supply any settings of its own.

Setting Access Control and Roles on a Conference

By specifying access control settings, applications can determine which users are admitted directly into a conference and which users must be approved first by a conference leader. Users who must be approved by a conference leader before being admitted are held in the *conference lobby*, where they hear hold music and cannot hear other conference participants or be heard, until they are either admitted or removed from the conference altogether.

Several forms of access control are available for conferences. The `AccessLevel` property on the `ConferenceScheduleInformation` object indicates generally which types of users may join the conference. Table 11-2 shows the options for the `AccessLevel` property and what they mean.

TABLE 11-2: Conference Access Level Options

ACCESSLEVEL VALUE	DESCRIPTION
`Locked`	No one can join the conference at all except for the organizer. Anyone else who tries to join will be held in the conference lobby. Anyone who is already in the conference will be able to stay, so this setting can be useful if you want to prevent anyone who is not already in from joining — perhaps to punish people who are late, or protect your quick pre-meeting gossip session.
`Invited`	Only users who have been specifically invited can join; others must wait in the conference lobby. Users can be pre-invited through the `Participants` property on `ConferenceScheduleInformation`, or a conference leader can invite them during the conference.

continues

TABLE 11-2 *(continued)*

ACCESSLEVEL VALUE	DESCRIPTION
SameEnterprise	Users from the same company as the organizer can join the conference, whereas others will be placed in the lobby.
Everyone	Any user, whether from the same company, a federated organization, or anonymous, will be able to join the conference.
None	This value means that the access level type is not set.

Providing a list of specific participants, along with their roles in the conference, is also possible through the `Participants` property on the `ConferenceScheduleInformation` class. This property contains a list of `ConferenceParticipantInformation` objects, each of which represents a single invited conference participant. The `ConferenceParticipantInformation` object identifies a participant as either a conference attendee or a conference leader, which determines whether the participant can perform conference control commands, such as locking the conference or removing users, while joined to the conference.

The following code snippet shows how to add a participant to the `Participants` collection for a conference that is to be scheduled.

```
// Add Galahad to the list of conference participants as an attendee.
scheduleInfo.Participants.Add(
    new ConferenceParticipantInformation("sip:galahad@wrox.com",
    ConferencingRole.Attendee));
```

To add a participant as a conference leader, simply change the second parameter in the constructor to `ConferencingRole.Leader`.

Last but not least, an application can specify whether PSTN users can join the conference, and what they must do to join. In order for PSTN users to join the conference at all, the `PhoneAccessEnabled` property must be set to `true` when the conference is being scheduled. Normally, these users are placed in the conference lobby until a conference leader approves them to join; however, the application can set the `LobbyBypass` property on the `ConferenceScheduleInformation` object to `LobbyBypass.EnabledForGatewayParticipants` to allow participants joining through a PSTN gateway to be placed directly into the conference.

 Participants can only join a conference through the PSTN if the necessary infrastructure components are present in the Lync environment to enable PSTN connectivity. Enabling phone access in a conference will have no effect if the application is deployed in an environment with no Mediation Server or PSTN gateway.

In any conference where the possibility exists for anonymous users to join, specifying a passcode in the `Passcode` property of the `ConferenceScheduleInformation` object is necessary. Anonymous users will then be prompted for the passcode when joining the conference. Some conference services, such as the Conferencing Auto-Attendant, will skip asking anonymous users for the passcode if the `IsPasscodeOptional` property is set to `true`.

The following code shows a `ConferenceScheduleInformation` object for a conference that is open to anyone within the same enterprise; others will be placed in the lobby. PSTN participants may join if they know the passcode, `123`. PSTN participants who enter the passcode correctly will be able to skip the lobby.

```
ConferenceScheduleInformation scheduleInfo = new ConferenceScheduleInformation();
scheduleInfo.AccessLevel = ConferenceAccessLevel.SameEnterprise;
scheduleInfo.PhoneAccessEnabled = true;
scheduleInfo.Passcode = "123";
scheduleInfo.LobbyBypass = LobbyBypass.EnabledForGatewayParticipants;
```

Specifying a Conference ID

Ordinarily, when a UCMA application schedules a conference, the conference is assigned a conference ID automatically. You can retrieve this conference ID through the `ConferenceId` property on the resulting `Conference` object. In some cases, however, having the application know the conference ID before the conference is scheduled is useful so that the application can provide the ID to other components. In these cases, the application can set the conference ID when creating the `ConferenceScheduleInformation` object.

The conference ID must fit a special format, and so the easiest way to generate valid IDs is to use the `ConferenceServices.GenerateConferenceId` static method. The following code snippet illustrates how to generate and set a conference ID in this manner.

```
// Generate a valid conference ID.
string generatedConferenceId = ConferenceServices.GenerateConferenceId();

// Use the conference ID for some other purpose ahead of time...
DoSomethingWithTheConferenceId(generatedConferenceId);

// Use the new conference ID to create the scheduling information.
ConferenceScheduleInformation scheduleInfo = new ConferenceScheduleInformation();
scheduleInfo.ConferenceId = generatedConferenceId;

// Schedule the conference, and so forth.
```

Scheduling a Conference Using BeginScheduleConference

After the `ConferenceScheduleInformation` object is created, schedule the conference using the `BeginScheduleConference` method on the `ConferenceServices` object that belongs to the endpoint. This begins the asynchronous operation to schedule the conference with Lync Server.

In the callback method, the application should call `EndScheduleConference`. This method returns a `Conference` object with details of the conference that has been scheduled. The `Conference` class has read-only properties (such as `AccessLevel`) that contain the conference settings specified in the `ConferenceScheduleInformation`. It also has several more properties (shown in Table 11-3) with details such as the conference URI that can be used to join the conference. Saving this `Conference` object somewhere after scheduling a conference so that the application has the information it needs to join the conference or invite other users to the conference later is a good idea.

TABLE 11-3: Conference Properties

PROPERTY	DESCRIPTION
ConferenceUri	The URI of the conference focus. This is the URI to which Lync endpoints can send an INVITE message to join the conference.
PhoneInformation	An object that contains details for PSTN access to the conference, including access numbers, the conference ID that PSTN users must enter to identify the conference, and alternative access numbers with covered regions and languages.
WebUrl	The URL that users can use to join the conference via the web.

The following code illustrates how an application can schedule a conference using
ConferenceServices and retrieve the conference URI and other access details from the resulting
Conference object.

```
private void ScheduleConference()
{
    try
    {
        // Create conference scheduling details for the conference.
        ConferenceScheduleInformation scheduleInfo =
            new ConferenceScheduleInformation();

        // Restrict the conference to invited users only.
        scheduleInfo.AccessLevel = ConferenceAccessLevel.Invited;

        // Don't automatically assign a leader.
        scheduleInfo.AutomaticLeaderAssignment =
            AutomaticLeaderAssignment.Disabled;

        // Add the A/V and IM MCUs.
        scheduleInfo.Mcus.Add(
            new ConferenceMcuInformation(McuType.AudioVideo));
        scheduleInfo.Mcus.Add(
            new ConferenceMcuInformation(McuType.InstantMessaging));

        // Add the caller as a participant.
        scheduleInfo.Participants.Add(
            new ConferenceParticipantInformation(
            _incomingAvCall.RemoteEndpoint.Participant.Uri,
            ConferencingRole.Attendee));

        // Set a subject for the conference.
        scheduleInfo.Subject = "Call Controller Session";

        // Schedule the conference.
        _endpoint.ConferenceServices.BeginScheduleConference(scheduleInfo,
            OnConferenceScheduleCompleted, null);
    }
```

```
        catch (InvalidOperationException ioex)
        {
            _logger.Log("Failed scheduling conference.", ioex);
        }
    }

    private void OnConferenceScheduleCompleted(IAsyncResult result)
    {
        try
        {
            _conference =
                _endpoint.ConferenceServices.EndScheduleConference(result);

            _logger.Log("Conference scheduled with URI {0} and web URL {1}",
                _conference.ConferenceUri,
                _conference.WebUrl);

            JoinConference();
        }
        catch (RealTimeException rtex)
        {
            _logger.Log("Failed scheduling conference.", rtex);
        }
    }
```

Code snippet CallController\CallControllerSession.cs

INVITING PARTICIPANTS TO A CONFERENCE

A Lync conference with only one participant is not particularly useful and can get quite lonely for the solitary UCMA application. With conference invitations, an application can easily provide other Lync users with the information they need to join the conference. For PSTN users, applications can tell the audio/video MCU to place an outbound call to a telephone number, bringing that number into the conference if the call is answered.

This section explains how conference invitations work and describes how to use them in a UCMA application.

Understanding the SIP Anatomy of a Conference Invitation

In SIP terms, inviting a Lync user to a conference is a multistep process. It involves at least three distinct SIP dialogs:

➤   Dialog between the inviter and the invitee, where the inviter provides the conference join information to the invitee.

➤   Dialog between the invitee and the conference focus, where the invitee joins the conference and gets conference information.

➤   Dialog between the invitee and the MCU, establishing a call of that modality between the invitee and MCU. (If the conference has multiple MCUs, this step will be repeated for each MCU.)

The most important point to note here is that the inviter is only involved in the first step, and after that the invitee itself is responsible for establishing communication with the Lync Server components that are managing the conference. Take a look at Figure 11-2 for the play-by-play.

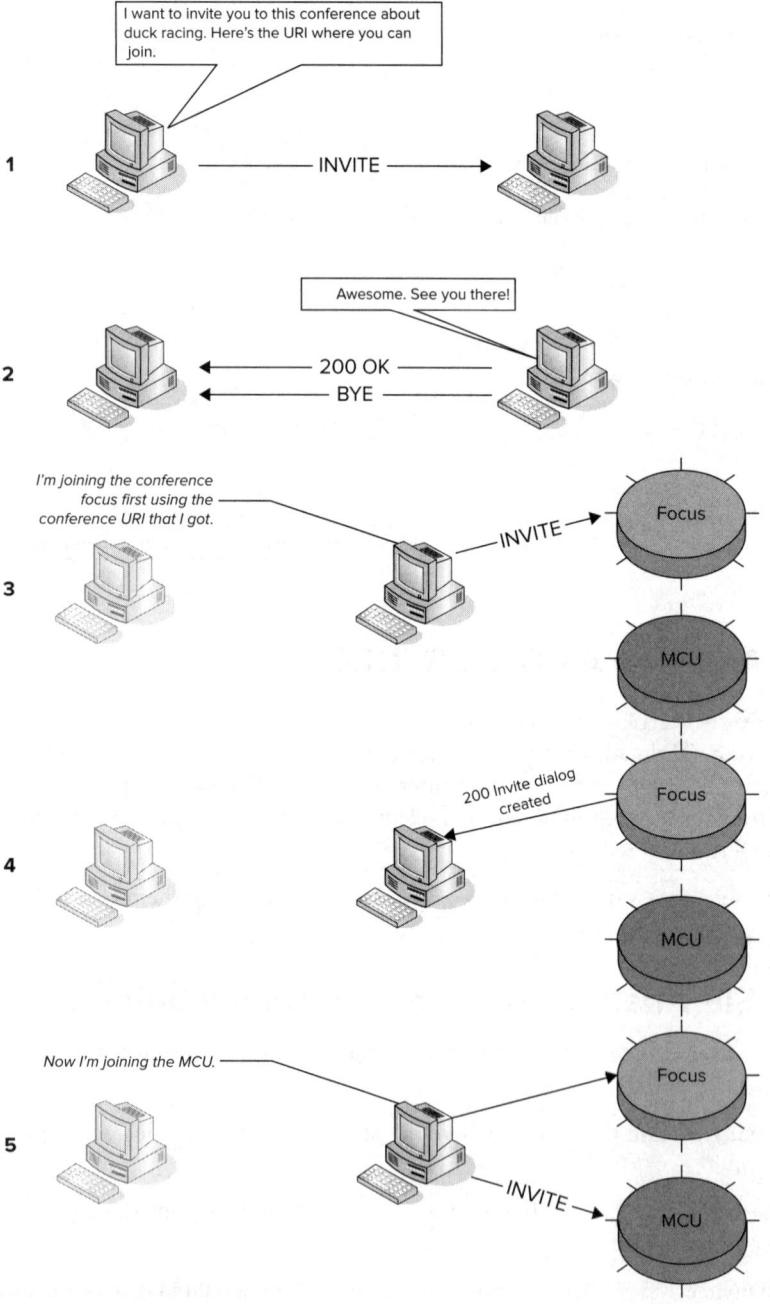

FIGURE 11-2

To deliver the conference invitation, the inviting user sends a special sort of SIP INVITE message to the user who is being invited. Instead of Session Description Protocol (SDP) content, this INVITE message has an XML document with conference details as its body. The invitee sends a 200 OK acknowledging this INVITE, and as soon as the SIP handshake has finished it immediately ends the SIP dialog with a BYE message. No media negotiation occurs, because no media is involved.

Here is an example of this initial INVITE message:

```
INVITE sip:adamb@fabrikam.com SIP/2.0
From: "Outbound"<sip:outbound.sample@fabrikam.com>;epid=B19FF086A2;tag=ce3cf06e2d
To: <sip:adamb@fabrikam.com>
CSeq: 10 INVITE
Call-ID: d39d8ad1-3ee8-4368-a47e-7bab825f1979
MAX-FORWARDS: 70
VIA: SIP/2.0/TLS 192.168.0.40:56775;branch=z9hG4bK45e83544
CONTACT: <sip:ts.fabrikam.com@fabrikam.com;gruu;opaque=srvr:outbound.sample:
    jRw31iBwA16ogIm8sXN68AAA>;automata;actor="attendant";
    text;audio;video;image
CONTENT-LENGTH: 241
SUPPORTED: ms-dialog-route-set-update
SUPPORTED: 100rel
SUPPORTED: gruu-10
USER-AGENT: RTCC/4.0.0.0 CallController
CONTENT-TYPE: application/ms-conf-invite+xml
ALLOW: ACK
Ms-Conversation-ID: 038f28d4fc984f74b9ff15022e669764
Allow: CANCEL,BYE,INVITE,PRACK,UPDATE
Message-Body: <Conferencing version="2.0">
<focus-uri>sip:outbound.sample@fabrikam.com;gruu;opaque=app:conf:focus:id:MIMC4N1L
    </focus-uri>
<subject />
<audio available="true" />
<im available="false">
<first-im />
</im>
</Conferencing>
```

Notice the XML message body, which contains the SIP URI at which the invited user can contact the conference focus, along with some other details.

On receiving the message with the conference invitation, a Lync endpoint generally handles it by contacting the conference focus, using the conference URI included in the invitation. This INVITE message looks similar to the following:

```
INVITE sip:outbound.sample@fabrikam.com;gruu;opaque=app:conf:focus:id:MIMC4N1L
    SIP/2.0
From: <sip:adamb@fabrikam.com>;tag=4ba7e31721;epid=aed0816a53
To: <sip:outbound.sample@fabrikam.com;gruu;opaque=app:conf:focus:id:MIMC4N1L>
CSeq: 1 INVITE
Call-ID: 9f70b5bbe25a4f7b9a8eed2064f89599
Via: SIP/2.0/TLS 192.168.0.20:62970
Max-Forwards: 70
Contact: <sip:adamb@fabrikam.com;opaque=user:epid:_bwZkhZM7Vq2VYySC_x9JQAA;gruu>
```

```
User-Agent: UCCAPI/4.0.7577.0 OC/4.0.7577.0 (Microsoft Lync 2010)
Supported: ms-dialog-route-set-update
Supported: timer
Supported: histinfo
Supported: ms-safe-transfer
Supported: ms-sender
Supported: ms-early-media
ms-keep-alive: UAC;hop-hop=yes
Allow: INVITE, BYE, ACK, CANCEL, INFO, UPDATE, REFER, NOTIFY, BENOTIFY, OPTIONS
ms-subnet: 192.168.0.0
Proxy-Authorization: TLS-DSK qop="auth", realm="SIP Communications Service",
    opaque="8ED7A1D7", targetname="CS-SE.fabrikam.com",
    crand="00bf43f6", cnum="39",
    response="cdbac682e708cbd2ce16322047da7a064fe25200"
Content-Type: application/cccp+xml
Content-Length: 953
Message-Body: <?xml version="1.0"?>
<request xmlns="urn:ietf:params:xml:ns:cccp" xmlns:mscp="
    http://schemas.microsoft.com/rtc/2005/08/cccpextensions"
    C3PVersion="1" to="sip:outbound.sample@fabrikam.com;
    gruu;opaque=app:conf:focus:id:MIMC4N1L"
    from="sip:adamb@fabrikam.com" requestId="0">
    <addUser><conferenceKeys confEntity="sip:outbound.sample@fabrikam.com;gruu;
    opaque=app:conf:focus:id:MIMC4N1L"/><ci:user
    xmlns:ci="urn:ietf:params:xml:ns:conference-info" entity="
    sip:adamb@fabrikam.com"><ci:roles><ci:entry>attendee</ci:entry>
    </ci:roles><ci:endpoint entity="{A958BD03-1340-48ED-A2D8-8DE597E97DE6}"
    xmlns:msci="http://schemas.microsoft.com/rtc/2005/08/confinfoextensions">
    <msci:clientInfo><cis:separator xmlns:cis="urn:ietf:params:xml:ns:
    conference-info-separator"></cis:separator><msci2:lobby-capable
    xmlns:msci2="http://schemas.microsoft.com/rtc/2008/12/confinfoextensions">
    true</msci2:lobby-capable></msci:clientInfo></ci:endpoint></ci:user>
    </addUser></request>
```

This second INVITE initiates a SIP handshake between the invitee and the conference focus. The content type of the message body in this case is application/cccp+xml, which identifies this as a *Centralized Conference Control Protocol* (CCCP, or C3P) message. In this case, the message is an addUser request from the user who is trying to join the conference. After the handshake completes successfully, the invitee is joined to the conference. Here is the response from the conference focus to the addUser request:

```
SIP/2.0 200 Invite dialog created
From: "Adam Barr"<sip:adamb@fabrikam.com>;tag=4ba7e31721;epid=aed0816a53
To: <sip:outbound.sample@fabrikam.com;gruu;opaque=app:conf:focus:id:MIMC4N1L>;
    tag=BE0B0080
CSeq: 1 INVITE
Call-ID: 9f70b5bbe25a4f7b9a8eed2064f89599
ms-keep-alive: UAS; tcp=no; hop-hop=yes; end-end=no; timeout=300
Record-Route: <sip:CS-SE.fabrikam.com:5061;transport=tls;opaque=state:
    T:F:Ci.R1353c11;lr;ms-route-sig=dzWuxbD3PmHOGqYhrrNSnK
    dwQZd1BMkU1MP9cVfHM46Fgax9vaaJOOVQAA>
Authentication-Info: TLS-DSK qop="auth", opaque="8ED7A1D7", srand="B8ACF915",
    snum="51", rspauth="17d9f63da197a604e25563a62f5b911a355e7859",
```

```
        targetname="CS-SE.fabrikam.com", realm="SIP Communications Service",
           version=4
Content-Length: 500
Via: SIP/2.0/TLS 192.168.0.20:62970;ms-received-port=62970;ms-received-cid=1353C00
Allow: INVITE, BYE, ACK, CANCEL, INFO, UPDATE
Contact: <sip:outbound.sample@fabrikam.com;gruu;opaque=app:conf:focus:id:MIMC4N1L>
           ;isfocus
Content-Type: application/cccp+xml
Session-Expires: 7200;refresher=uac
Require: timer
Supported: timer
Message-Body: <response xmlns="urn:ietf:params:xml:ns:cccp" xmlns:ci="
           urn:ietf:params:xml:ns:conference-info" requestId="0" C3PVersion="1"
           from="sip:outbound.sample@fabrikam.com;gruu;opaque=app:conf:focus:id:
           MIMC4N1L" to="sip:adamb@fabrikam.com" code="success">
<addUser>
<conferenceKeys confEntity="sip:outbound.sample@fabrikam.com;gruu;
           opaque=app:conf:focus:id:MIMC4N1L"/>
<ci:user entity="sip:adamb@fabrikam.com">
<ci:roles>
<ci:entry>attendee</ci:entry>
</ci:roles>
</ci:user>
</addUser>
</response>
```

Finally, the invitee sends an INVITE message to each of the MCUs, establishing a Lync call with each. Here is part of a SIP INVITE to the audio/video MCU:

```
INVITE sip:outbound.sample@fabrikam.com;gruu;opaque=app:conf:
           audio-video:id:9F8DDEK3 SIP/2.0
From: <sip:administrator@fabrikam.com>;tag=6f86cc820b;epid=8eb2b9887c
To: <sip:outbound.sample@fabrikam.com;gruu;opaque=app:conf:audio-video:id:9F8DDEK3>
CSeq: 1 INVITE
Call-ID: b37ca01fdc8f4396bc76465802b00354
Via: SIP/2.0/TLS 192.168.0.40:56842
Max-Forwards: 70
Contact: <sip:administrator@fabrikam.com;opaque=user:epid:h8Imu_x-s1GhF1VFS0UgtQAA
           ;gruu>
User-Agent: UCCAPI/4.0.7577.0 OC/4.0.7577.0 (Microsoft Lync 2010)
Supported: ms-dialog-route-set-update
Ms-Conversation-ID: a24ad16ad7304806acdfc52b53e594b8
Subject: Call Controller Session
Supported: timer
Supported: histinfo
Supported: ms-safe-transfer
Supported: ms-sender
Supported: ms-early-media
Supported: 100rel
ms-keep-alive: UAC;hop-hop=yes
Allow: INVITE, BYE, ACK, CANCEL, INFO, UPDATE, REFER, NOTIFY, BENOTIFY, OPTIONS
ms-subnet: 192.168.0.0
Accept-Language: en-US
ms-endpoint-location-data: NetworkScope;ms-media-location-type=Intranet
```

```
P-Preferred-Identity: <sip:administrator@fabrikam.com>
Supported: replaces
Supported: ms-conf-invite
Proxy-Authorization: TLS-DSK qop="auth", realm="SIP Communications Service",
    opaque="53EFA60D", targetname="CS-SE.fabrikam.com", crand="eb7267f3",
    cnum="46", response="f6dee046ed0e90590f3eea417093725fee265d9d"
Content-Type: multipart/alternative;boundary="----=_NextPart_000_001B_01CBB580.
    7BEF6900"
Content-Length: 3318
Message-Body: ------=_NextPart_000_001B_01CBB580.7BEF6900
Content-Type: application/sdp
Content-Transfer-Encoding: 7bit
Content-ID: <d109e8e8d6304cbaa203dbee85e40f80@fabrikam.com>
Content-Disposition: session; handling=optional; ms-proxy-2007fallback
v=0
o=- 0 0 IN IP4 192.168.0.40
s=session
c=IN IP4 192.168.0.40
b=CT:99980
t=0 0
m=audio 32882 RTP/SAVP 114 9 112 111 0 8 116 115 4 97 13 118 101
a=candidate:JZ8OXUUogdyo695Mmoj+SDCe6PzN4TIr4tcUUZS4BiM 1 PypC1fAlEb6jVK814pJzYQ
    UDP 0.830 67.104.203.240 3354
a=candidate:JZ8OXUUogdyo695Mmoj+SDCe6PzN4TIr4tcUUZS4BiM 2 PypC1fAlEb6jVK814pJzYQ
    UDP 0.830 67.104.203.240 3355
...
```

After the call is established between the invitee and the MCU, media can flow back and forth between the invitee and other conference participants via the MCU. The Lync client shows when a conference participant has successfully established communication with the MCU by lighting up the appropriate modality icon (phone, speech bubble, arrows, and so on) next to that participant's name in the conference roster.

Inviting Participants Using a ConferenceInvitation Object

The `ConferenceInvitation` object in UCMA handles sending a single conference invitation to a single Lync user. The `BeginDeliver` method of `ConferenceInvitation` essentially takes care of the first of the three SIP dialogs described in the previous section: It provides the conference join information to the user to whom it is directed. The asynchronous operation finishes after the user has accepted the invitation, and it is then up to the invited user to join the conference.

 The fact that a conference invitation has been delivered successfully does not guarantee that the invited user will join the conference. Even if the invitee accepts the invitation, it may experience a connectivity problem, for example, and fail to join. If your application needs to do something when the invited user actually joins the conference successfully, you must monitor the conference roster as described in the later section "Monitor Conference Events."

Creating a ConferenceInvitation Object

The `ConferenceInvitation` object picks up the information it needs about the conference from the `Conversation` object that is passed in to the constructor, as shown in the following code.

```
ConferenceInvitation inv = new ConferenceInvitation(conferenceConversation);
```

Alternatively, specify a conference ID and media types manually by including a `ConferenceInvitationSettings` object, as the following code illustrates.

```
ConferenceInvitationSettings settings = new ConferenceInvitationSettings();
settings.ConferenceUri = generatedConferenceId;
settings.AvailableMediaTypes.Add(MediaType.Message);

ConferenceInvitation inv =
    new ConferenceInvitation(conferenceConversation, settings);
```

Sending a Conference Invitation Using BeginDeliver

After the `ConferenceInvitation` object is initialized, send the invitation by calling `ConferenceInvitation.BeginDeliver`. The first parameter of `BeginDeliver` should be the SIP URI of the Lync user who is to be invited.

 Each `ConferenceInvitation` *object can only be used to invite a single user to the conference. Calling* `BeginDeliver` *again with a different SIP URI will result in an exception.*

The following code snippet shows a method that delivers conference invitations to a single Lync user.

Available for
download on
Wrox.com

```
private void InviteCallRecipient()
{
    ConferenceInvitation invitation =
        new ConferenceInvitation(_conferenceConversation);

    try
    {
        invitation.BeginDeliver(_callRecipientUri,
            deliverResult =>
            {
                try
                {
                    invitation.EndDeliver(deliverResult);
                }
                catch (RealTimeException rtex)
                {
                    _logger.Log("Failed inviting call recipient.",
                        rtex);
                }
            }, null);
}
```

```
catch (InvalidOperationException ioex)
{
    _logger.Log("Failed inviting call recipient.", ioex);
}
}
```

Code snippet CallController\CallControllerSession.cs

ACCEPTING AN INCOMING CONFERENCE INVITATION

Occasionally, a UCMA application must be designed to handle being invited to a conference. As an example, a conference recording application might register a contact that Lync users can invite to their conferences in order to have them recorded. By handling the ConferenceInvitationReceived event, an application can be notified of incoming conference invitations and can accept or decline them. The conference join information is provided to the application in the form of a ConferenceInvitation object.

For instant messaging conferences, UCMA provides an event on the ConferenceInvitation class called AutoAcceptNeeded, which fires when an invitation has been pending for long enough that it would be automatically accepted by the Lync client. (For an example of this, watch the behavior of the Lync client when an incoming instant message goes unanswered.) This event is mainly useful for middle-tier applications that provide a client interface for Lync users; the application can automatically accept the incoming conference invitation if the user has not already done so. Using some sort of synchronization mechanism is important so that the application does not accept the invitation on one thread at the same time that user input causes it to accept the invitation on another thread.

There is also a property on the ConferenceInvitation class, IsImmediateAutoAcceptNeeded, which is set to true in cases where the invitation should be accepted immediately by the application without prompting the user (where applicable).

The following code snippet shows an event handler for ConferenceInvitationReceived that handles incoming conference invitations by accepting them, unless the application is shutting down, in which case it declines incoming invitations.

```
private void OnConferenceInvitationReceived(object sender,
    ConferenceInvitationReceivedEventArgs e)
{
    ConferenceInvitation invitation = e.Invitation;

    lock (_sessionsSyncObject)
    {
        if (_draining)
        {
            // Don't accept invitations when shutting down.
```

```
                        invitation.Decline();
                }
                else if (invitation.AvailableMediaTypes.Contains(
                    "message"))
                {
                    // Accept only invitations for conferences that
                    // include the instant messaging modality.
                    ConferenceMonitorSession session =
                        new ConferenceMonitorSession(invitation,
                        _logger);
                    session.StateChanged += OnSessionStateChanged;

                    _sessions.Add(session);

                    session.Start();
                }
                else
                {
                    // Decline the invitation if the IM modality is
                    // not included.
                    invitation.Decline();
                }
            }
        }
```

Code snippet ConferenceMonitor\ConferenceMonitorUserAgent.cs

Inviting Participants Using Audio MCU Dial-Out

The ConferenceInvitation method of adding conference participants does not work very well with PSTN contacts, because telephones do not speak SIP, and so, as Figure 11-3 shows, they do not have any particularly good way to receive the conference information and communicate with the conference focus.

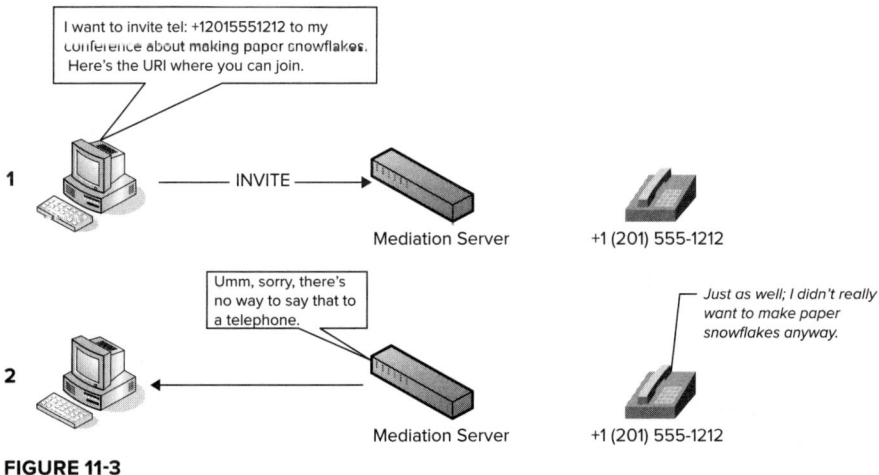

FIGURE 11-3

Because plenty of reasons exist as to why one might want to invite someone to a conference through a PSTN phone (for example, an employee on the road using a mobile phone), the audio/video MCU has the ability to call a contact directly to bring it into the conference's audio MCU session. UCMA applications can tell the audio/video MCU to do this by calling the `BeginDialOut` method on the `AudioVideoMcuSession` object associated with the conference. The `AudioVideoMcuSession` object, which later sections cover in more detail, is accessible through the `AudioVideoMcuSession` property on the `ConferenceSession` class.

The `BeginDialOut` method causes UCMA to send a command to the audio/video MCU, telling it to dial out to the specified URI.

Adding PSTN Participants Using BeginDialOut Method

The following code snippet shows how to add a PSTN participant to a conference by having the MCU dial out.

```csharp
private void DialOut(string sipUri)
{
    try
    {
        ConferenceSession confSession =
                _conferenceConversation.ConferenceSession;
        AudioVideoMcuSession mcuSession =
            confSession.AudioVideoMcuSession;

        // Send the dial out command to the MCU.
        mcuSession.BeginDialOut(sipUri,
            dialOutResult =>
            {
                try
                {
                    mcuSession.EndDialOut(dialOutResult);
                }
                catch (RealTimeException rtex)
                {
                    _logger.Log("Failed dialing out from MCU.", rtex);
                }
            },
            null);
    }
    catch (InvalidOperationException ioex)
    {
        _logger.Log("Failed dialing out from MCU.", ioex);
    }
}
```

Code snippet CallController\CallControllerSession.cs

The first parameter of the `BeginDialOut` method is the URI (usually a "tel" URI) of the destination. Specifying options using the `McuDialOutOptions` or `AudioVideoMcuDialOutOptions` classes as additional parameters is also possible.

The "tel" URI scheme, for telephone numbers, is described in RFC 3966. Lync allows endpoints to place calls to PSTN numbers through the mediation server using "tel" URIs, although Lync expresses phone numbers internally in a slightly different format, like the following:

```
sip:+12015551212@wrox.com;user=phone
```

This type of phone URI is what typically appears in UCMA properties as the SIP URI of a Lync conversation participant that is connected through the mediation server.

Handling Dial-Outs to the Lync Client

Although PSTN phones can't handle conference invitations and need to be coddled with a personal call from the MCU instead, the Lync client objects to audio/video MCU dial-outs. In a peculiar display of passive-aggressive behavior, it rejects the dial-out call, grabs the conference URI, and turns around and calls into the conference itself, picking up from step 2 in the process described earlier in "The SIP Anatomy of a Conference Invitation." Because of this, using the `ConferenceInvitation` class with Lync contacts whenever possible, and reserving MCU dial-outs for PSTN participants, is generally better. If you do need to dial out to a Lync user for some reason, expect slightly odd behavior: The dial-out operation will fail with an exception, but the invited user will join the conference anyway.

Transferring a Call into the Conference

In addition to dialing out to bring new participants into a conference, the MCU has the ability to transfer an existing call to the MCU in order to seamlessly bring the remote participant from a two-party call into the conference.

As an alternative to inviting a user to the conference directly, an application can place a new outbound two-party call to the user, and after the call is established it can direct the MCU to transfer the two-party call into the conference. This can be particularly useful as a way of bringing incoming calls to the application into a conference, as shown in the following code sample.

```
private void TransferIncomingCallIntoConference()
{
    try
    {
        AudioVideoMcuSession avMcu =
            _conferenceConversation.ConferenceSession.AudioVideoMcuSession;

        // The incoming call has already been accepted. Now, direct
        // the MCU to transfer it into the conference.
        avMcu.BeginTransfer(_incomingAvCall, null,
            transferResult =>
            {
```

```
        try
        {
            avMcu.EndTransfer(transferResult);

            InviteCallRecipient();
        }
        catch (RealTimeException rtex)
        {
            _logger.Log(
                "Failed transferring call into conference.",
                rtex);
        }
    }, null);
}
catch (InvalidOperationException ioex)
{
    _logger.Log("Failed transferring call into conference.", ioex);
}
}
```

Code snippet CallController\CallControllerSession.cs

ESCALATING AN INSTANT MESSAGE CALL TO A CONFERENCE

Instant messaging calls cannot be transferred, but another way exists to turn a two-party IM call into a conference. This is the `BeginEscalateToConference` method on the `Conversation` class. This method, when called on a `Conversation` object that already has an active IM call associated with it, will seamlessly bring the participants on that call into a conference.

To perform an escalation, first join a conference using the same `Conversation` object by calling `Conversation.ConferenceSession.BeginJoin`. After this is done, call `Conversation.BeginEscalateToConference` to bring the call participants into the newly joined conference. When the operation completes, the call will have been converted into a conference.

`BeginEscalateToConference` does not work with audio calls, but the `BeginTransfer` method on `AudioVideoMcuSession` generally serves well enough for those cases.

JOINING A CONFERENCE

To join a Lync conference, an endpoint must establish two or more signaling sessions: one with the conference focus, and one with each MCU. In UCMA, all of these signaling sessions are tied to a single instance of the `Conversation` class, and the details of the SIP messages are hidden so that developers can write code on the level of `Conversation` and `Call` objects.

Managing Conference Communication Using the ConferenceSession Object

The ConferenceSession class encapsulates all communication with the conference focus. Each Conversation object comes with a ConferenceSession instance already attached to it, and developers can call the BeginJoin method on ConferenceSession in order to have the endpoint that owns the Conversation join a conference.

If the Conversation object involved has come from a conference invitation that the application has accepted, or if a conference URI is provided as the first parameter to BeginJoin, the UCMA endpoint joins the existing conference. Otherwise, it joins an *ad-hoc conference*, as described later in this chapter.

The following code shows an example of how to use the ConferenceSession.BeginJoin method. In this case, the application is joining a conference for which it has received an invitation.

```csharp
private void JoinConference()
{
    _conferenceConversation = _invitation.Conversation;

    try
    {
        _conferenceConversation.ConferenceSession.BeginJoin(
            new ConferenceJoinOptions(),
            joinResult =>
            {
                try
                {
                    _conferenceConversation.ConferenceSession.
                        EndJoin(
                        joinResult);

                    JoinInstantMessagingMcu();
                }
                catch (RealTimeException rtex)
                {
                    _logger.Log("Failed joining conference.",
                        rtex);
                }
            },
            null);
    }
    catch (InvalidOperationException ioex)
    {
        _logger.Log("Failed joining conference.", ioex);
    }
}
```

Code snippet ConferenceMonitor\ConferenceMonitorSession.cs

After a UCMA endpoint has joined a conference through a `Conversation`, it appears in the conference roster. However, it isn't able to send or receive any media until it establishes communication with the MCUs. (In the Lync client, it would show up in the list of conference participants, but none of the modality icons next to it, such as the phone and the speech bubble, would be highlighted.) To connect to the MCUs, the application must establish a call within the `Conversation` for each modality it is going to join.

Clarifying a few points here is important, because handling conferences in UCMA can be a bit confusing at first. Each `Conversation` object in UCMA really always represents a communication session between two parties, as shown in Figure 11-4. The "local" end of this communication session is always one of the endpoints controlled by the application. The conversation can have multiple modalities, with each modality being represented by a separate signaling session and a separate media stream (as shown in the diagram), but those separate sessions are tied together, share the same conversation ID, and involve the same two participants.

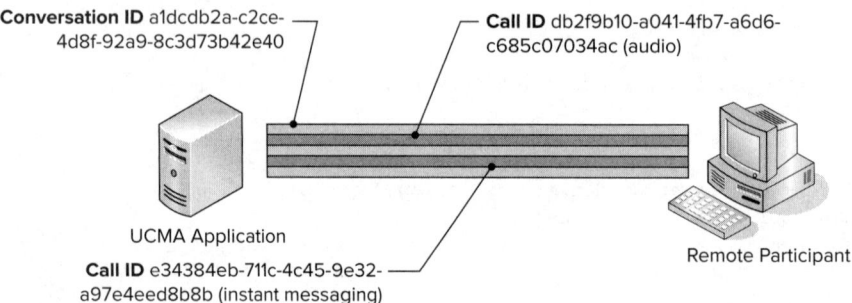

FIGURE 11-4

When an endpoint managed by a UCMA application joins a conference, the `Conversation` object is still, under the covers, handling a two-party communication session. In this case, however, the communication is between the UCMA endpoint and the conference, and shown in Figure 11-5. Each other conference participant has its own communication session with the conference focus and MCUs.

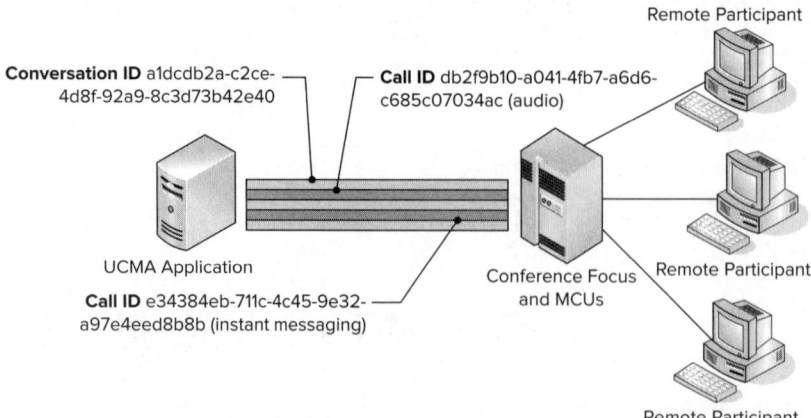

FIGURE 11-5

> *Technically, the focus and the various MCUs have different SIP URIs, but they are all part of a single conference, and so for purposes of explanation thinking of them as one conversation participant makes sense.*

Thinking of the focus session and the MCU sessions as separate modalities in the conversation may be helpful. The important thing to note, though, is that when a UCMA endpoint joins a conference, it is, to put it in general terms, calling the conference rather than calling all the other participants at once.

It's very much like the experience of calling into a conference bridge from a PSTN telephone. You place a call to a conference number, and then other participants also dial into the number, at which point you can hear one another.

Going back to the subject of establishing calls, after an endpoint has joined a conference through `Conversation.ConferenceSession.BeginJoin`, it must establish at least one call within the same `Conversation` in order to send and receive media. When it does this, it is essentially "calling in" to that MCU. Because, at this point, UCMA already knows the SIP URIs it needs to call from the conference focus, no need exists to specify a SIP URI in the `Call.BeginEstablish` method. The following code sample shows this in action with a call to the instant messaging MCU.

```
private void JoinInstantMessagingMcu()
{
    try
    {
        _imCall = new InstantMessagingCall(
            _conferenceConversation);

        _imCall.BeginEstablish(establishResult =>
            {
                try
                {
                    _imCall.EndEstablish(establishResult);

                    SubscribeToEvents();
                    this.State =
                        ConferenceMonitorSessionState.Started;
                }
                catch (RealTimeException rtex)
                {
                    _logger.Log("Failed establishing IM call.",
                        rtex);
                }
            }, null);
    }
    catch (InvalidOperationException ioex)
    {
        _logger.Log("Failed establishing IM call.",
            ioex);
    }
}
```

A behind-the-scenes look at the messaging involved in this operation would show that the endpoint first establishes a SIP session with the conference focus, then another SIP session with the IM MCU. Figure 11-6 offers a visualization of these different signaling sessions and where the other participants come into the picture.

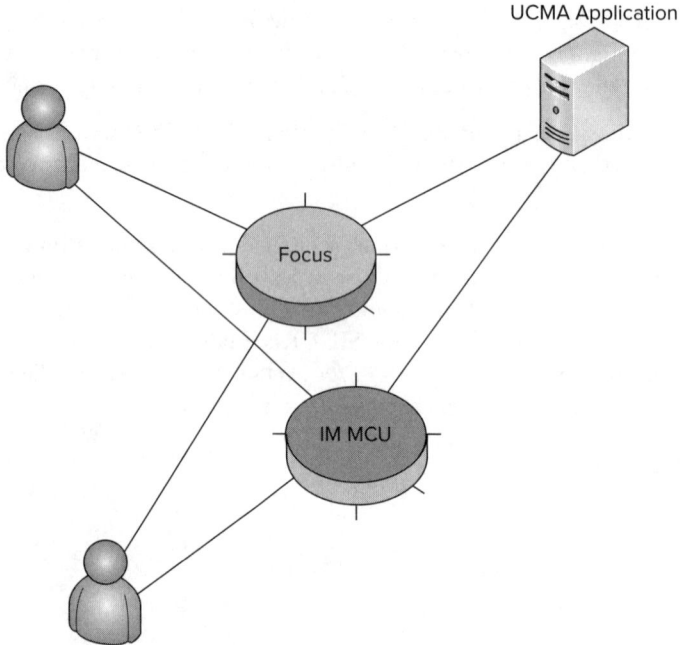

FIGURE 11-6

Specifying Conference Joining Details with the ConferenceJoinOptionsClass

The primary piece of information that is needed to join a conference is the conference URI. In some cases, though, an application must specify other settings when joining a conference. UCMA applications can use the ConferenceJoinOptions class to set these options.

The most common use of ConferenceJoinOptions is to indicate that an application should join a conference as a trusted participant. Trusted participants in conferences are discussed later in this chapter. The other options that ConferenceJoinOptions controls have to do with the conference lobby, where participants that have not been authorized to join the conference are kept until a conference leader admits them or ejects them.

Joining an Ad-Hoc Conference

Often, an application needs to start up a conference on the fly and can manage with a default set of options. In these cases, UCMA applications can use an *ad-hoc conference*. Instead of scheduling a conference, obtaining the new conference's URI, creating a new Conversation object, and then calling `Conversation.ConferenceSession.BeginJoin` with that conference URI, the application can call `Conversation.ConferenceSession.BeginJoin` on a new `Conversation` without any conference URI. UCMA will automatically schedule a new conference with an expiry time eight hours ahead and with all possible MCUs, and join this new conference, all in one operation.

The following code sample shows how to perform an ad-hoc conference join.

```
// Create an entirely new conversation.
_conferenceConversation = new Conversation(_endpoint);

// Start an ad hoc conference join with the conversation.
_conferenceConversation.ConferenceSession.BeginJoin(
        new ConferenceJoinOptions(),
        joinResult =>
              {
                  try
                  {
                      _conferenceConversation.ConferenceSession.EndJoin(
                          joinResult);

                      JoinAudioVideoMcu();
                  }
                  catch (RealTimeException rtex)
                  {
                      _logger.Log("Failed joining conference.", rtex);
                  }
              }, null);
```

BEGINJOIN AND THE CONFERENCE LOBBY

If an endpoint belonging to a UCMA application is joining a conference where it is not an invited participant (or a trusted participant), it will be placed in the conference lobby. The `State` property of both the `Conversation` and `ConferenceSession` objects will change to `InLobby`, and the asynchronous conference join operation will not complete until the endpoint is admitted or denied access. This means that if a callback was passed into `BeginJoin`, or the code is waiting on the wait handle of the `IAsyncResult` returned by `BeginJoin`, these will wait until the endpoint is out of the lobby.

PROVIDING SERVICES WITH TRUSTED CONFERENCE PARTICIPANTS

At times, a UCMA application must provide some type of service to other participants on a conference or a call. This service might be a feature controlled by the participants (such as a conference attendant that allows PSTN participants to mute themselves by dialing a tone on the phone keypad) or might even be invisible to the participants (as in call monitoring systems that randomly record a percentage of calls or allow supervisors to listen in silently).

To support scenarios like these, UCMA allows application endpoints to join a conference in a special mode which makes them *trusted conference participants*. This trusted mode has two main effects:

➤ The participant can perform special privileged operations, such as modifying audio MCU routing settings, or sending conference commands on behalf of other users.

➤ The participant is not visible to other participants in the conference roster.

These two things allow applications to control conferences in useful ways without the application being visible as a (potentially confusing) conference participant.

User endpoints, shady characters that they are, cannot join conferences in trusted mode.

If you think about it, user endpoints really get the short end of the stick in UCMA. Application endpoints get to have all the fun impersonating other identities, while user endpoints are the ones that are not trusted.

Joining a conference in trusted mode is as simple as setting the `JoinMode` property on an instance of `ConferenceJoinOptions`, which can then be passed into `BeginJoin` as a parameter. For a trusted join, the `JoinMode` property should be set to `TrustedParticipant`.

The next few sections describe some of the more common uses of trusted conference participants. Chapter 12 describes some of the capabilities of trusted participants in more detail.

USING TRUSTED JOIN TO PROVIDE SERVICES ON TWO-PARTY CALLS

Although plenty of opportunities exist for putting trusted participants to use in conferences, it may not be immediately obvious that this feature can also be useful when only two participants are involved. In certain more complex scenarios, such as in contact centers, various special services need to be available for audio calls and other communications. These might include recording, reporting on-call statistics such as average handle time, and silent monitoring by supervisors, among other things.

With a normal two-party Lync call, providing these services is not possible for a UCMA application. Chapter 12 discusses this conundrum in more detail in the sections on the `BackToBackCall`, but in a nutshell, the reason is that a

UCMA application has neither visibility nor control of a call in which it is not a participant, as illustrated in Figure 11-7.

One solution is to set up a two-party call in a case like this as a conference with three participants: the two original participants, plus the UCMA application as a trusted participant. Because the application is a trusted participant, it doesn't appear in the roster, and it seems to the two other participants as if they are on a two-party call. Meanwhile, the application has complete freedom to control or monitor the conference because it is a participant.

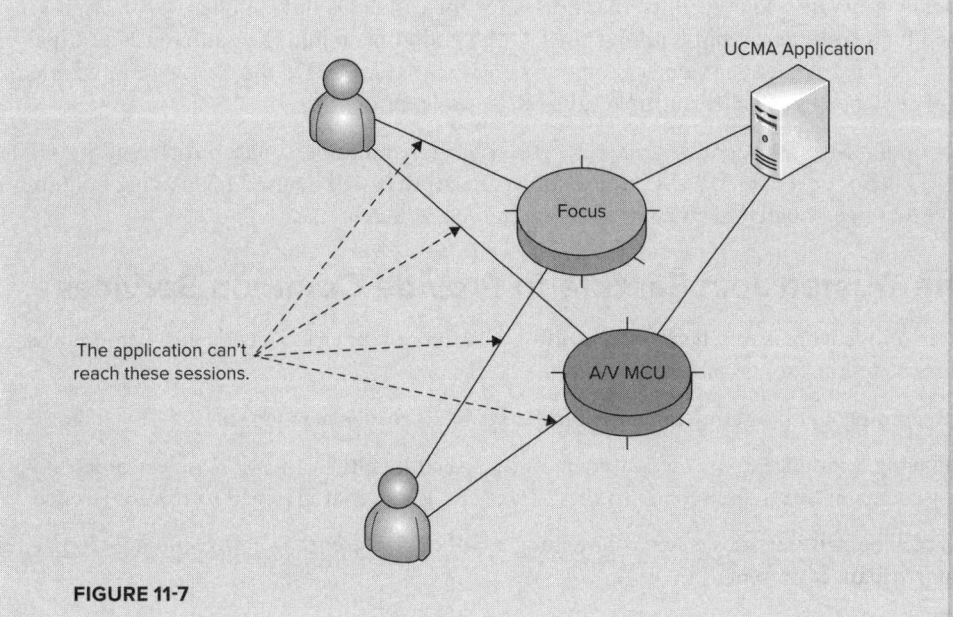

FIGURE 11-7

Avoiding Problems with the Trusted Conference Join Feature

Developers should know about two things that are not immediately obvious about trusted conference participants when using the trusted join feature.

One is that instant messages from trusted participants exhibit some strange behavior. Generally, instant messages from a trusted participant "expose" the participant, making the participant's name suddenly appear in the roster — unless no instant messages have been sent in the conference, in which case the instant messages from the trusted participant may simply not appear.

Because of this, not using trusted participants to send instant messages is best. If an application needs to join a conference as a trusted participant and also send instant messages into the conference, it can join the conference twice, using two separate calls with different identities, one trusted and one not.

Secondly, note that when joining a conference multiple times from the same endpoint (such as to provide multiple services to a call) a conference will only allow each user to join the conference once. In other words, a single SIP URI cannot be in the conference twice.

You can circumvent this limitation in two ways. One is that the `AudioVideoCallEstablishOptions` class has a property, `UseGeneratedIdentityForTrustedConference`, which causes UCMA to automatically generate a fake identity that it uses for the call. This only applies to calls that are established for a conference, but it allows the UCMA endpoint to join the conference multiple times using multiple `AudioVideoCall` objects on one `Conversation`. This is the only case in which a `Conversation` object can share multiple calls of the same modality.

The other option is to use separate `Conversation` objects, and impersonate a different SIP URI on each one. This can be a fake SIP URI; for instance, a call that will be used for playing hold music could have an impersonated identity of holdmusic@*yourdomain*.com.

Using the Trusted Join Feature to Provide Common Services

The trusted join feature is excellent for providing a variety of services to calls and conferences. Some of the more common uses include:

➤ Recording a call or conference without a visible recorder participant

➤ Playing announcements on conferences, by attaching either a `Player` object or a `SpeechSynthesisConnector` to the `AudioVideoCall` that is joined to the conference

➤ Tracking call statistics, such as how long a call or conference is active and how long each participant is present

➤ Playing hold music

➤ Changing audio routing settings so that certain participants cannot hear certain others

Chapter 12 describes many of the media control features mentioned here in much more detail.

CONTROLLING CONFERENCE ATTENDANCE WITH CONFERENCE COMMANDS

Conference leaders, the conference organizer, and trusted participants can send commands to the conference focus to control the conference and its participants. In UCMA, these commands can be sent through the `ConferenceSession` class.

> A UCMA application can only send these conference control commands if it is
> acting as a conference leader or if it is a trusted participant. If it is merely an
> attendee, the commands will return an error.

Terminating a Conference

To terminate a conference immediately and remove all participants, call the
`BeginTerminateConference` method on `ConferenceSession`. The following code shows how to
terminate a conference using this method.

Available for
download on
Wrox.com

```
private void TerminateConference()
{
    try
    {
        ConferenceSession confSession =
            _conferenceConversation.ConferenceSession;

        confSession.BeginTerminateConference(
            terminateResult =>
            {
                try
                {
                    confSession.EndTerminateConference(terminateResult);
                }
                catch (RealTimeException rtex)
                {
                    _logger.Log("Failed terminating conference.", rtex);
                }
            },
            null);
    }
    catch (InvalidOperationException ioex)
    {
        _logger.Log("Failed terminating conference.", ioex);
    }
}
```

Code snippet CallController\CallControllerSession.cs

Note that calling `BeginTerminateConference` on the `ConferenceSession` class is different from
calling `BeginTerminate` on the `Conversation` class and has entirely different effects. Calling
`Conversation.BeginTerminate` simply ends the communication between the UCMA endpoint and
the conference, whereas `ConferenceSession.BeginTerminateConference` shuts down the whole
conference. See Figure 11-8 for an illustration of the differences.

Terminate Conversation

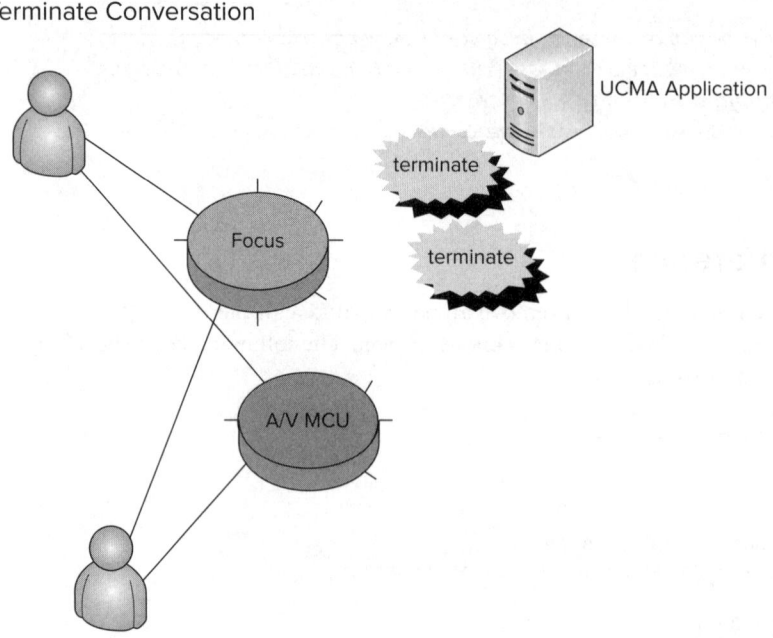

Terminate Conference

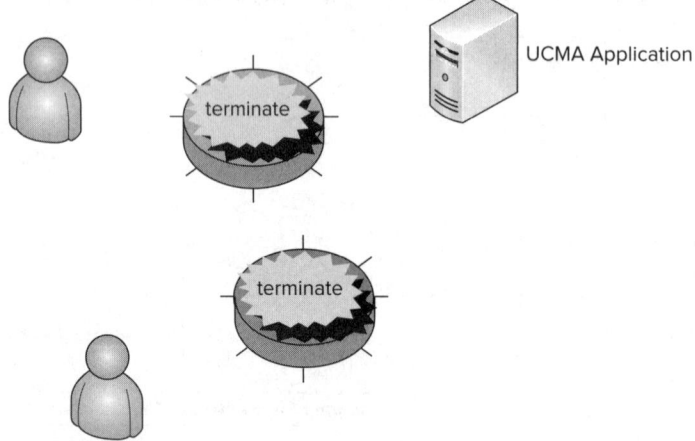

FIGURE 11-8

Ejecting a Conference Participant

One never knows when a previously friendly and docile conference participant may take on a nasty disposition and begin acting troublesome. For such situations, the BeginEject method of ConferenceSession is invaluable. It directs the conference focus to remove a specific participant from the conference.

The following code shows the usage of BeginEject.

```csharp
private void Eject(string sipUri)
{
    try
    {
        ConferenceSession confSession =
                _conferenceConversation.ConferenceSession;

        // Get a list of conference participant endpoints.
        Collection<ParticipantEndpoint> participants =
            confSession.GetRemoteParticipantEndpoints();

        // Look for the specified participant in the list.
        ParticipantEndpoint endpointToEject =
            participants.FirstOrDefault(p => p.Participant.Uri == sipUri);

        if (endpointToEject != null)
        {
            // Get the ConversationParticipant object to pass to
            // BeginEject.
            ConversationParticipant participantToEject =
                endpointToEject.Participant;

            // Eject the participant.
            confSession.BeginEject(participantToEject,
                ejectResult =>
                {
                    try
                    {
                        confSession.EndEject(ejectResult);

                        // See you later!
                    }
                    catch (RealTimeException rtex)
                    {
                        _logger.Log("Failed ejecting participant.", rtex);
                    }
                },
                null);
        }
    }
    catch (InvalidOperationException ioex)
    {
        _logger.Log("Failed ejecting participant.", ioex);
    }
}
```

Code snippet CallController\CallControllerSession.cs

 You can also have a participant ejected from a specific MCU only by calling the
BeginEject *method on the corresponding* McuSession *class.*

Locking or Unlocking a Conference

Locking a conference prevents any new participants from joining besides the organizer. To tell the conference focus to lock the conference, call the `BeginLockConference` method on `ConferenceSession`, as shown in the following code.

```
private void LockConference()
{
    try
    {
        ConferenceSession confSession =
            _conferenceConversation.ConferenceSession;

        confSession.BeginLockConference(
            lockResult =>
            {
                try
                {
                    confSession.EndLockConference(lockResult);
                }
                catch (RealTimeException rtex)
                {
                    _logger.Log("Failed locking conference.", rtex);
                }
            },
            null);
    }
    catch (InvalidOperationException ioex)
    {
        _logger.Log("Failed locking conference.", ioex);
    }
}
```

Code snippet CallController\CallControllerSession.cs

To unlock a conference, call the `BeginUnlockConference` method, as shown in the following code.

```
private void UnlockConference()
{
    try
    {
        ConferenceSession confSession =
            _conferenceConversation.ConferenceSession;

        confSession.BeginUnlockConference(
            unlockResult =>
            {
                try
                {
                    confSession.EndUnlockConference(unlockResult);
                }
                catch (RealTimeException rtex)
```

```
                {
                    _logger.Log("Failed unlocking conference.", rtex);
                }
            },
            null);
    }
    catch (InvalidOperationException ioex)
    {
        _logger.Log("Failed unlocking conference.", ioex);
    }
}
```

Code snippet CallController\CallControllerSession.cs

Modifying Conference Configuration or Participants' Roles

The settings for a conference and the roles of participants can be set in the
ConferenceScheduleInformation class when a conference is first being scheduled. If a
change becomes necessary, however, or if the conference was originally created as an ad-hoc
conference, the BeginModifyRole and BeginModifyConferenceConfiguration methods of the
ConferenceSession class can come in handy.

Call BeginModifyConferenceConfiguration to change the access level, lobby bypass setting, or
automatic leader assignment policy for the conference. Each of these settings has the same effect
that it has when set in ConferenceScheduleInformation.

Call BeginModifyRole to change a conference participant from an attendee to a leader or vice
versa. This method takes a ConversationParticipant object as its first parameter, much like
BeginEject. The second parameter is the new role that will be assigned to the participant.

MANAGING ACCESS WITH THE CONFERENCE LOBBY

The *conference lobby* is a new concept in Lync Server 2010. Prior to Lync (in Office
Communications Server 2007 R2 and earlier versions) users who tried to join a conference to which
they had not been invited or from which they were excluded by the conference's access level were
simply blocked from joining. This created some difficulties in managing conference attendance: No
way existed to see users who were trying to join and decide whether or not to admit them. All users
had to be authorized before they could join at all.

The conference lobby allows users to join the conference and be held in a virtual "waiting room"
where they cannot hear other participants or be heard. Conference leaders can see who is in the
lobby and can admit those participants to the conference or deny them entry and remove them
altogether. Essentially, users can be "screened" as they are trying to join rather than in advance.

UCMA applications, when acting as conference leaders or as trusted participants, can also watch
for lobby participants and can admit or reject them.

Requiring Participants to Enter Via the Lobby

The lobby only comes into play when a user joins a conference but has not yet been authorized to do so. If the user is included through the access level (for instance, if the conference has an access level of `SameEnterprise` and the user is from the same organization) or if the user has been explicitly specified as a conference participant, he or she can skip the lobby and join the conference directly. So, to require certain participants to join via the lobby and be screened, ensure that the conference's access level is set at a restrictive-enough level to exclude those participants from being admitted immediately.

To watch for new lobby participants, subscribe to the `LobbyParticipantAttendanceChanged` event on the `Conversation` class, as shown here:

Available for
download on
Wrox.com

```
_conferenceConversation.LobbyParticipantAttendanceChanged +=
    OnLobbyParticipantsChanged;
```

Code snippet CallController\CallControllerSession.cs

When a user attempts to join the conference and is placed in the lobby, this event handler will be invoked. The application can then admit or reject the new lobby participants.

> *An application can join a conference without lobby management capabilities if the* `CanManageLobby` *property on* `ConferenceJoinOptions` *is set to* `false`*. The default is* `true`*.*

Allowing Participants into the Conference from the Lobby

Applications can admit or reject lobby participants using the `LobbyManager` class. Each `ConferenceSession` instance has an instance of this class, which can be accessed through the `LobbyManager` property.

To admit a lobby participant into the conference, call `BeginAdmitLobbyParticipants` on `LobbyManager`. The first parameter should be an enumerable collection of `ConversationParticipant` objects. These can be retrieved either from the event arguments of the `LobbyParticipantAttendanceChanged` event, or from the `GetLobbyParticipants` method of the `Conversation` class.

The following code sample shows the usage of `BeginAdmitLobbyParticipants`.

Available for
download on
Wrox.com

```
private void OnLobbyParticipantsChanged(object sender,
    LobbyParticipantAttendanceChangedEventArgs e)
{
    LobbyManager lobbyManager =
        _conferenceConversation.ConferenceSession.LobbyManager;

    // Wait for one second and then admit the added lobby participants.
```

```
Thread.Sleep(1000);

try
{
    lobbyManager.BeginAdmitLobbyParticipants(e.Added,
        admitResult =>
        {
            try
            {
                lobbyManager.EndAdmitLobbyParticipants(admitResult);
            }
            catch (RealTimeException rtex)
            {
                _logger.Log("Failed admitting lobby participants.",
                    rtex);
            }
        },
        null);
}
catch (InvalidOperationException ioex)
{
    _logger.Log("Failed admitting lobby participants.", ioex);
}
}
```

Code snippet CallController\CallControllerSession.cs

To reject and remove lobby participants, follow the same procedure, but use the
BeginDenyLobbyParticipants method.

CONTROLLING MEDIA USING THE MCUSESSION CLASSES

The multipoint control units, or MCUs, control the flow of media in a conference. By sending
messages that contain commands to the MCU, a UCMA application can perform actions in a
conference that affect the handling of media.

 *Although the MCU ultimately handles media commands in a conference, the
messages are directed to the conference focus, which then forwards them to
the appropriate MCU.*

In audio conferences, a need often exists for an application to mute one or more of the participants;
the mute command is therefore one of the most useful MCU commands. The audio/video MCU is
also capable of placing outbound calls to potential conference participants, as well as transferring
calls that have already been established *into* the conference, which can be useful as a method of
turning a two-party audio call into a conference. These last two capabilities are discussed earlier in
this chapter.

Receiving Instant Messages in a Conference

Developers who are beginning to work with Lync conferences in UCMA might be surprised not to find a `MessageReceived` event on the `InstantMessagingMcuSession` class, and might wonder how to receive incoming instant messages in a conference (if it includes the IM modality).

Actually, receiving instant messages from a conference is no different from receiving instant messages in an ordinary two-party call. The application can subscribe to the `MessageReceived` event on the `InstantMessagingFlow` just as it would for a two-party call. (The `InstantMessagingFlow` it should use is the one from the instant messaging call that the application has established for the conference.)

Remember that this call is actually a two-party call between the application and the instant messaging MCU. Any new instant messages in the conference will find their way to the application through the dialog between the application and the MCU.

Muting a Participant

Anyone who has ever led or participated in a Lync conference has had occasion to use the mute feature. For participants, being able to prevent other participants from hearing chewing sounds, off-color remarks, or traffic is handy. Conference leaders, meanwhile, can exert their power over fellow participants by silencing heavy breathing or contrary opinions.

UCMA applications can mute themselves or other participants in an audio conference in much the same way, by sending a mute command to the audio/video MCU. To have the MCU mute a participant, call `BeginMute` on the `AudioVideoMcuSession` object associated with the conference. The first parameter of `BeginMute` is a `ParticipantEndpoint` object, which identifies the participant that should be muted. Generally, the easiest way to retrieve this object is to call `GetRemoteParticipantEndpoints` on the `AudioVideoMcuSession` object, which will return a collection of `ParticipantEndpoint` objects. The matching `ParticipantEndpoint` can then be retrieved from the collection by SIP URI.

 If the application needs to mute itself, call `GetLocalParticipantEndpoints` *instead of* `GetRemoteParticipantEndpoints` *to get a collection that includes the local endpoint.*

The following code sample demonstrates muting a participant through the audio/video MCU. It first retrieves the collection of `ParticipantEndpoint` objects from the `AudioVideoMcuSession` object and takes the first one that matches the provided SIP URI. It then passes this `ParticipantEndpoint` instance into the `AudioVideoMcuSession.BeginMute` method.

```
private void Mute(string sipUri)
{
    try
    {
        ConferenceSession confSession =
            _conferenceConversation.ConferenceSession;
```

```
            AudioVideoMcuSession mcuSession =
                confSession.AudioVideoMcuSession;

            // Get a list of conference participant endpoints.
            Collection<ParticipantEndpoint> participants =
                confSession.AudioVideoMcuSession.GetRemoteParticipantEndpoints();

            // Look for the specified participant in the list.
            ParticipantEndpoint endpointToMute =
                participants.FirstOrDefault(p => p.Participant.Uri == sipUri);

            if (endpointToMute != null)
            {
                // Eject the participant.
                mcuSession.BeginMute(endpointToMute,
                    muteResult =>
                    {
                        try
                        {
                            mcuSession.EndMute(muteResult);
                        }
                        catch (RealTimeException rtex)
                        {
                            _logger.Log("Failed muting participant.", rtex);
                        }
                    },
                    null);
            }
        }
        catch (InvalidOperationException ioex)
        {
            _logger.Log("Failed muting participant.", ioex);
        }
    }
```

Code snippet CallController\CallControllerSession.cs

Unmuting a participant is equally easy. To do this, call BeginUnmute on AudioVideoMcuSession, passing in a ParticipantEndpoint object as with BeginMute.

```
    private void Unmute(string sipUri)
    {
        try
        {
            ConferenceSession confSession =
                    _conferenceConversation.ConferenceSession;
            AudioVideoMcuSession mcuSession =
                confSession.AudioVideoMcuSession;

            // Get a list of conference participant endpoints.
            Collection<ParticipantEndpoint> participants =
                confSession.AudioVideoMcuSession.GetRemoteParticipantEndpoints();
```

```
        // Look for the specified participant in the list.
        ParticipantEndpoint endpointToUnmute =
            participants.FirstOrDefault(p => p.Participant.Uri == sipUri);

    if (endpointToUnmute != null)
    {
        // Eject the participant.
        mcuSession.BeginUnmute(endpointToUnmute,
            unmuteResult =>
            {
                try
                {
                    mcuSession.EndUnmute(unmuteResult);
                }
                catch (RealTimeException rtex)
                {
                    _logger.Log("Failed unmuting participant.", rtex);
                }
            },
            null);
    }
}
catch (InvalidOperationException ioex)
{
    _logger.Log("Failed unmuting participant.", ioex);
}
}
```

Code snippet CallController\CallControllerSession.cs

MONITORING CONFERENCE EVENTS

UCMA applications that work with Lync conferences generally need to monitor some of the conference events in order to keep up with state and participant changes. Because participants join the conference focus and the MCU sessions separately, the `ConferenceSession` class and the `McuSession` class have separate events to report participant changes. By subscribing to these events, applications can be notified when users join the conference focus and when they begin participating in the various media sessions. Applications can also subscribe to conference state change events to keep track of changes in the condition of the conference.

One of the slightly counterintuitive points about inviting Lync users to a conference is that the invitation process itself does not give the application any feedback on whether the invited user actually joins the conference. It is possible (although discouraged) for a Lync endpoint to accept a conference invitation but not make any effort to join the conference at all. This is one of the reasons why it is important for applications that work with Lync conferences to monitor conference participation changes.

Receiving Notifications of Conference Participant Changes

Subscribing to notifications of participant changes from the conference focus is not particularly complicated. The `ConferenceSession` class, which more or less handles the application's interaction with the conference focus, has a `ParticipantEndpointAttendanceChanged` event that fires whenever anyone joins or leaves the conference focus. An application can subscribe to this event as shown in the following code snippet:

```
confSession.ParticipantEndpointAttendanceChanged +=
    OnConferenceAttendanceChanged;
```

In the event handler, the event argument class has two properties, `Joined` and `Left`, which contain all the participants who have either joined or left, respectively. The list of participants in each is in the form of a collection of key/value pairs, with the key being a `ParticipantEndpoint` object and the value being a `ConferenceParticipantEndpointProperties` object. The former has details on the participant such as the SIP URI; the latter has information specific to the conference, such as the participant's role and whether he or she is in the lobby.

The following code shows a handler for the `ConferenceSession.ParticipantEndpoint`
`AttendanceChanged` event that writes to the log each time a user joins or leaves the conference.

Available for download on Wrox.com

```
private void OnConferenceAttendanceChanged(object sender,
    ParticipantEndpointAttendanceChangedEventArgs<
    ConferenceParticipantEndpointProperties> e)
{
    foreach (KeyValuePair<ParticipantEndpoint,
        ConferenceParticipantEndpointProperties>
        pair in e.Joined)
    {
        _logger.Log(
            string.Format("{0} joined the conference.",
            pair.Key.Participant.Uri));
    }

    foreach (KeyValuePair<ParticipantEndpoint,
        ConferenceParticipantEndpointProperties>
        pair in e.Left)
    {
        _logger.Log(
            string.Format("{0} left the conference.",
            pair.Key.Participant.Uri));
    }
}
```

Code snippet ConferenceMonitor\ConferenceMonitorSession.cs

Receiving Notifications of Media Participant Changes

The participation change events on the `McuSession` classes are nearly identical to the ones on the `ConferenceSession` class. The following code snippet shows how an application can subscribe to this event on an `InstantMessagingMcuSession` object.

```
mcuSession.ParticipantEndpointAttendanceChanged +=
    OnMcuAttendanceChanged;
```

The following code shows an example of an event handler for this event. Again, everything is much the same as for the `ConferenceSession.ParticipantEndpointAttendanceChanged` event, except that there is a different object with MCU-related properties as the value component of the key/value pairs.

```
private void OnMcuAttendanceChanged(object sender,
    ParticipantEndpointAttendanceChangedEventArgs<
    InstantMessagingMcuParticipantEndpointProperties> e)
{
    foreach (KeyValuePair<ParticipantEndpoint,
        InstantMessagingMcuParticipantEndpointProperties>
        pair in e.Joined)
    {
        _logger.Log(
            string.Format("{0} joined the IM MCU.",
            pair.Key.Participant.Uri));
    }

    foreach (KeyValuePair<ParticipantEndpoint,
        InstantMessagingMcuParticipantEndpointProperties>
        pair in e.Left)
    {
        _logger.Log(
            string.Format("{0} left the IM MCU.",
            pair.Key.Participant.Uri));
    }
}
```

Code snippet ConferenceMonitor\ConferenceMonitorSession.cs

These MCU participation change events are invoked when a Lync user joins an MCU session associated with a particular conference. This happens after (usually almost immediately after) the user joins the conference focus. Applications may need to monitor these events to know when a user who has been invited to the conference is actually able to receive media, or when to perform MCU actions on the user, like muting the user or modifying MCU audio routes (as discussed in Chapter 12). These actions will fail if the user has not yet connected to the relevant MCU.

Tracking Conference States

Applications can monitor the current state of the connection to a conference using the `State` property on `ConferenceSession`. Note that these states are not the state of the conference itself, but of the signaling session with the conference. By monitoring this property, applications can be notified when an endpoint has lost connectivity with a conference and is reconnecting, when a conference session has terminated, or when an endpoint is being held in the conference lobby.

Each `McuSession` class also has a `State` property that applications can use to monitor the condition of each media session. For instance, the `State` property on an `McuSession` object changing to `Retrying` indicates that a connectivity problem has occurred and the endpoint is trying to reestablish the connection with the MCU.

WORKING WITH THE CONVERSATION CONTEXT CHANNEL

You learned in Chapter 4 how to use the Lync Extensibility Window context to host a Silverlight application in the Lync conversation window. In a conference scheduling and management application similar to the sample application included with this chapter, you can use such a Silverlight application to provide additional call control and monitoring capabilities to presenters in the conference.

The `ConversationContextChannel` class introduced in UCMA 3.0 provides the functionality to establish a context channel with a Silverlight application hosted in the Lync conversation window. The `Conversation` class in the Lync API exposes a `BeginSendContextData` method and `ContextDataReceived` event to allow the conversation to interact with the UCMA 3.0 application via the context channel.

Establishing a Context Channel

To establish a context channel between the UCMA application and an existing conversation, create an instance of the `ConversationContextChannel` class and specify the conversation and participant to establish the channel with.

After creating the context channel, wire up its `StateChanged` and `DataReceived` events to track when the state of the context channel changes, and when the UCMA application receives contextual data across the channel from the conversation.

Before establishing the context channel, create an instance of `ConversationContextChannelEstablishOptions` to specify the name of the contextual application and conversation to send the context to — this ensures that the context data is sent to the correct Lync conversation window.

Finally, call the `ConversationContextChannel.BeginEstablish` method to begin establishing the context channel.

Available for
download on
Wrox.com

```
// Create a new context channel with the remote endpoint.
// Create a new context channel with the remote endpoint.
ConversationContextChannel contextChannel =
    new ConversationContextChannel(
        _conferenceConversation,
        participantEndpoint);

// Subscribe to incoming data from the channel.
contextChannel.DataReceived += OnContextChannelDataReceived;

try
{
```

continues

(continued)

```
        var options =
            new ConversationContextChannelEstablishOptions();
        options.ApplicationName = "Fabrikam Agent Dashboard";
        options.RemoteConversationId =
            _conferenceConversation.Id;

        // Establish the context channel.
        contextChannel.BeginEstablish(
            new Guid("DF518B8D-068D-4CB7-B42B-078E8BDEBBE4"),
            options,
            establishResult =>
            {
                try
                {
                    contextChannel.EndEstablish(establishResult);

                    // Send some initial context...
                }
                catch (RealTimeException rtex)
                {
                    _logger.Log("Failed opening context channel."
                        , rtex);
                }
            },
            null);
    }
    catch (InvalidOperationException ioex)
    {
        _logger.Log("Failed opening context channel.", ioex);
    }
```

Code snippet CallController\CallControllerSession.cs

Sending Context from the UCMA Application

After the context channel is established, you can send context data to the conversation on the other side of the context channel. Use the `BeginSendData` method of the `ConversationContextChannel` class to send context data to the conversation.

To send context data to the conversation, you must specify the MIME type of the context and an encoded byte array containing the context data to send. The encoded context data can't be larger than 4kB.

You can send the context data as a simple string; however, you should encapsulate the context data in a custom class that you serialize and send as XML. The application on the other side of the context channel can deserialize the XML and process the contained object in order to take action on the context data.

```
    var initialContext = new InitialContextItem()
    {
        CustomerId = "4815162342",
        CustomerName = "Dharma",
        CustomerSipUri =
            _incomingAvCall.RemoteEndpoint.Participant.Uri
    };

    var serializedContext = SerializationHelper.SerializeObject<
        InitialContextItem>(initialContext);

    contextChannel.BeginSendData(
        new System.Net.Mime.ContentType("text/plain"),
        new System.Text.UTF8Encoding().
            GetBytes(serializedContext),
        sendDataResult =>
        {
            try
            {
                _logger.Log("Initial context sent: {0}",
                    serializedContext);
                contextChannel.EndSendData(sendDataResult);
            }
            catch (RealTimeException)
            {
                throw;
            }
        },
        null);
```

Processing Context in the Silverlight Application

With the context channel established between the UCMA application and the
Silverlight application running in the Lync conversation window, the Silverlight
application can process any context sent by the UCMA application, and also send
context back to the UCMA application.

In order for the Silverlight application to process context from the UCMA
application, it needs to handle the `ContextDataReceived` event of the
`Conversation` class — you can wire it up in the `Loaded` event of the Silverlight
application.

```
    void Page_Loaded(object sender, RoutedEventArgs e)
    {
        _lyncClient = LyncClient.GetClient();
        _self = _lyncClient.Self;

        _conversation = LyncClient.GetHostingConversation()
            as Conversation;

        if (_conversation != null)
```

continues

(*continued*)

```
        {
            _conversation.InitialContextReceived +=
                new EventHandler<InitialContextEventArgs>
(Conversation_InitialContextReceived);
            _conversation.ContextDataReceived +=
                new EventHandler<ContextEventArgs>
(Conversation_ContextDataReceived);
        }
    }
```

In the handler for the `InitialContextReceived` event, use the instance of `InitialContextEventArgs` to retrieve the context data sent by the UCMA application. This is transmitted as a string, so your application needs to know the correct way to handle this data; for example, if an XML string containing a serialized instance of a class comes across the context channel.

```
    void Conversation_InitialContextReceived(object sender,
        InitialContextEventArgs e)
    {
        var initialContext = SerializationHelper.
            DeserializeObject<InitialContextItem>(
                e.ApplicationData);

        if (initialContext != null)
        {
            _customerSipUri = initialContext.CustomerSipUri;

            Dispatcher.BeginInvoke(
            new Action(() =>
            {
                tbCustomerId.Text = initialContext.CustomerId;
                tbCustomerName.Text =
                    initialContext.CustomerName;
            }));
        }
    }
```

The Silverlight application can use the `ContextDataReceived` event to handle recurring context data from the UCMA application.

```
    void Conversation_ContextDataReceived(object sender,
        ContextEventArgs e)
    {
        // do something with the context data in e.ContextData
    }
```

The Silverlight application can also send context back to the Silverlight application using the `BeginSendContextData` method of the `Conversation` class.

When sending context, you need to specify the GUID representing the contextual application to send context to, a string representing the type of context to send, and the context itself. For example, you can serialize an instance of a custom `CallControlAction` class that allows you to take an action on a participant in the conference and send the context to the UCMA application, which in turn deserializes it and takes action.

```
private void btnMute_Click(object sender, RoutedEventArgs e)
{
    var callControlActionItem = new CallControlActionItem()
    {
            Action = CallControlAction.Mute,
            SipUri = _customerSipUri
    };

    SendContextData(callControlActionItem);
}

private void SendContextData(
    CallControlActionItem callControlActionItem)
{
    if (_conversation != null)
    {
        _conversation.BeginSendContextData(
            _applicationGuid,
            "text/plain",
            SerializationHelper.SerializeObject<
                CallControlActionItem>(
                    callControlActionItem),
            result => { _conversation.EndSendContextData(
                result); },
            null);
    }
}
```

Receiving Context Data in the UCMA Application

The `DataReceived` event of the `ConversationContextChannel` class is raised when the UCMA application receives context data from the Silverlight application across the context channel.

The application can retrieve the context data using the instance of `ConversationContextChannelDataReceivedEventArgs` in the event handler. After retrieving the context data, the UCMA application can process it and take the corresponding action.

```
private void OnContextChannelDataReceived(object sender,
    ConversationContextChannelDataReceivedEventArgs e)
{
    var callControlActionItems =
        SerializationHelper.DeserializeObject<
            CallControlActionItem>
```

continues

```
(continued)
        (e.ContentDescription.ToString());

            _logger.Log("Action: {0} SIP URI: {1}",
                callControlActionItems.Action,
                callControlActionItems.SipUri);

    }
```

SUMMARY

In this chapter, you have learned how to create conferences using UCMA, join those conferences from UCMA endpoints, and invite other users to conferences. In addition, you have seen how UCMA applications can exert control over conferences by sending commands to the conference focus and MCUs, and by acting as trusted participants.

The next chapter expands on some of the concepts introduced in this chapter and Chapter 8 by introducing the media control features in UCMA. In combination with the concepts in the last few chapters, the media control APIs make building complex voice applications such as automatic call distributors, auto-attendants, and call recording systems possible.

12
Advanced Media Control in UCMA

WHAT'S IN THIS CHAPTER?

➤ Playing music, sounds, or speech on calls

➤ Recording call audio

➤ Recognizing speech input

➤ Playing and recognizing dual-tone multi-frequency (DTMF) tones

➤ Changing hold or mute state of a call

➤ Maintaining control over calls between other parties

➤ Controlling conference audio

➤ Creating "sub-conferences" within a conference

Of all the new functionality in this latest release of UCMA, the added media control capabilities generate perhaps the most excitement, and with good reason. Although they may seem obscure and complicated, features such as back-to-back calls and manual audio routing in conferences allow unified communications developers to replicate in Lync Server environments what were once exclusive and expensive features of high-end contact center and PBX platforms. A few examples are:

➤ Silent monitoring of calls by a supervisor.

➤ Playing customized hold music and messages to waiting callers.

➤ Providing messages or voice menus to only one conference participant (such as the organizer or leader).

➤ Managing a two-party call between two other users, or tracking it for billing purposes.

➤ "Whisper" mode where two participants in a conference can have a private conversation that others cannot overhear.

➤ Playing strange noises that others cannot hear to specific conference participants until they think they are crazy ("Did anyone else hear that? No, I *definitely* heard a frog noise!").

On second thought, you might not want to try that last item.

PLAYING OR RECOGNIZING DTMF TONES

Dual-tone multi-frequency (or DTMF) tones are those lovely sounds that are produced when you push the buttons on your phone keypad. In addition to allowing you to dial calls, they have many varied uses, including navigating phone menus, annoying telemarketers, and annoying your sister. Thanks to the `ToneController` class in UCMA, using them for fun and profit in Lync Server applications is also possible.

Attaching the ToneController

A `ToneController` instance can handle both sending and receiving DTMF tones on a single audio call. Before it can do either of these, it must be attached to the call's `AudioVideoFlow`, as shown in the following code:

```
// Create a new ToneController.
_toneController = new ToneController();

// Attach it to the flow of an existing audio call.
_toneController.AttachFlow(_avCall.Flow);
```

Code snippet AdvancedMediaControl\ToneControllerSample.cs

Sending DTMF Tones

Once attached, the `ToneController` can send DTMF tones into the audio call. The `Send` method tells it to play a specific tone, which you can specify either as an integer or using the `ToneId` enumeration. A second, optional parameter specifies the volume as a percentage of the maximum. The following code demonstrates the `Send` method by sending the tones 4, #, and 7 in sequence.

```
// Send the 4 tone.
toneController.Send(4);

// Send the pound tone.
toneController.Send(ToneId.Pound);

// Send the 7 tone at 80% of max volume.
toneController.Send(ToneId.Tone7, 80);
```

Code snippet AdvancedMediaControl\ToneControllerSample.cs

> *The pound sign (#) is also called an* octothorpe. *This piece of information makes excellent fodder for small talk at parties.*

Receiving DTMF Tones

To have the `ToneController` recognize incoming DTMF tones, you can attach an event handler to its `ToneReceived` event, as shown in the following:

Available for
download on
Wrox.com

```
toneController.ToneReceived +=
    new EventHandler<ToneControllerEventArgs>(OnToneReceived);

private void OnToneReceived(object sender, ToneControllerEventArgs e)
{
    ToneController toneController =
        sender as ToneController;

    // Calculate a tone two notes above,
    // looping around to the bottom if necessary.
    int playbackTone = e.Tone + 2;
    if (playbackTone > 15)
    {
        playbackTone -= 16;
    }

    // Play back the higher tone.
    toneController.Send(e.Tone + 2);
}
```

Code snippet AdvancedMediaControl\ToneControllerSample.cs

On receiving any DTMF tone, the code shown here will send back a tone two notes higher, enabling callers to play beautiful DTMF duets with the UCMA application.

Detecting Fax Tones

Intelligent though it is, the `ToneController` does not speak Fax. However, it does expose an event, `IncomingFaxDetected`, which you can use to determine when incoming tones on an audio call are not ordinary DTMF tones at all, but part of an attempt to fax something to your UCMA application. The following code shows how to subscribe to this event.

Available for
download on
Wrox.com

```
toneController.IncomingFaxDetected +=
    new EventHandler<IncomingFaxDetectedEventArgs>(OnIncomingFaxDetected);
```

Code snippet AdvancedMediaControl\ToneControllerSample.cs

Unfortunately, you can't do much with the incoming fax from a UCMA application, but this event at least makes it possible to recognize the nature of the strange sounds on the call, and perhaps redirect it to a real fax machine that can properly receive the fax. It also makes it easier for contact center or reporting applications to exclude fax calls from statistics.

HOW LYNC SERVER SENDS DTMF TONES

The three generally accepted ways of sending DTMF tones on a VoIP call are:

➤   **In-band** — The tone sounds are included directly in (uncompressed) RTP audio. This does not work if the audio is compressed.

➤   **RFC 2833** — The tones are sent in a special type of event within the RTP.

➤   **SIP INFO** — Tones are sent as individual SIP INFO messages, not in the RTP stream.

Lync Server uses the second method, which can be useful to know when debugging issues with DTMF tones. If you are having trouble sending or receiving tones on PSTN calls, you may want to look at the configuration of your media gateway or SIP trunk, because it could be set to use one of the other two methods.

PLAYING MUSIC, SOUNDS, OR SPEECH

Given that humans have been communicating by speech since long before the computer keyboard made its appearance; there is something very natural about having a computer talk to you. It should therefore come as no surprise that Lync Server can be extended to create services that talk to you on audio calls. Moreover, it can play music and sounds just as well as any touch-screen MP3 player.

The two classes that make all of this magic possible are `Player` and `SpeechSynthesisConnector`. The `Player` class loads in an audio file in WMA format and plays it into the audio stream of one or more audio calls, even repeating it over and over automatically if you so desire. The `SpeechSynthesisConnector` class connects to one or more `AudioVideoFlow` instances and exposes a stream into which audio can be fed from a `SpeechSynthesizer` object, which generates the text-to-speech audio.

Playing Music and Sounds with the Player Class

Three pieces fit together to make audio playback happen on a call:

➤   The media source

➤   The `Player` object

➤   The `AudioVideoFlow` for the call

A single `Player` instance can play the same audio at the same time to multiple flows. This is useful when an application needs to play hold music to multiple callers. Likewise, playing the same audio to several calls independently is also possible by using multiple `Player` instances with a single media source. This may be necessary if the timing of a message or sound will be different depending on the call, such as with on-hold messages that repeat after a certain number of seconds of wait time.

The Media Source

Although the `Player` class can use any subclass of `MediaSource` as the source of the audio, UCMA only includes a single implementation, `WmaFileSource`. As the name suggests, this class takes audio from a WMA file based on a path provided in the constructor.

The first step in creating a media source is to instantiate it with a file path. Keep in mind that the path will be relative to the working directory of the UCMA application.

Before the media source can be used with a `Player` instance, it must be prepared in an asynchronous operation with the `BeginPrepareSource` method. It can be prepared in one of two modes: buffered mode or unbuffered mode. In buffered mode, the media source caches the audio after it has been encoded into a given audio codec, so that the encoding does not need to be repeated every time the audio is played to a call. This can improve the performance of the application, particularly if there is a lot of audio playback.

 It is important to note that, when prepared in buffered mode, the media source will not pick up any changes to the underlying media file. Buffered mode is only appropriate if the content of the media file generally does not change.

The following code creates a new `WmaFileSource` instance using a WMA file in the working directory and prepares it in buffered mode. When the asynchronous operation completes, it calls another method (defined elsewhere in the class) to create the `Player`.

Available for
download on
Wrox.com

```
WmaFileSource fileSource = new WmaFileSource("music.wma");
fileSource.BeginPrepareSource(MediaSourceOpenMode.Buffered,
    ar =>
    {
        try
        {
            fileSource.EndPrepareSource(ar);

            CreatePlayer(fileSource);
        }
        catch (RealTimeException rtex)
        {
            Console.WriteLine(rtex);
        }
    },
    null);
```

Code snippet AdvancedMediaControl\PlayerSample.cs

After the media source is ready, you can use it to create one or more `Player` classes.

Creating and Preparing the Player Instance

Setting up an instance of `Player` is straightforward. The basic setup requires only two lines of code — one to create the `Player` instance and another to set the media source it will use:

```
Player player = new Player();
player.SetSource(fileSource);
```

Code snippet AdvancedMediaControl\PlayerSample.cs

At this point, the `Player` is ready to be attached to an `AudioVideoFlow` to send audio to a call.

UNATTACHED PLAYERS

Like the proverbial tree in the forest, if a `Player` plays audio in a UCMA application, but no `AudioVideoFlows` are attached to hear it, does it actually make a sound?

As a matter of fact, this is controlled by the mode of the `Player`. The `Player` class has two modes that control its behavior when it is not attached to any `AudioVideoFlows`. The default is automatic mode, in which playback of the audio will stop automatically if the `Player` is no longer attached to any `AudioVideoFlows`. In some cases, however, having the `Player` continue to play even if no `AudioVideoFlows` are attached to receive the audio is necessary. In this case, you can set the `Player` to manual mode by means of the `SetMode` method.

```
player.SetMode(PlayerMode.Manual);
```

Code snippet AdvancedMediaControl\PlayerSample.cs

A `Mode` property is also on the `Player` class, but it is read-only, so using the `SetMode` method to change the mode of the `Player` is necessary.

The `AttachFlow` method on the `Player` attaches an `AudioVideoFlow` to the `Player` so that the audio from the `Player` will go to that call. This method can be called multiple times to attach more than one flow to a `Player`. (No, that's not why it's called the `Player` class.) Keep in mind that if the playback of the audio has already started when the flow is attached, only the audio from that point forward will go to the call. So if you attach the flow when the `Player` is halfway through that stirring rendition of "Twinkle, Twinkle, Little Star," the caller may miss some of the good parts. Sorry.

A corresponding `DetachFlow` method exists for when one of the `Player`'s attached flows has terminated or no longer needs the services of the `Player`. Detaching the flows of calls that have terminated is important, so that those resources can be garbage collected.

Yes, sometimes it's best for a `Player` to let go.

Starting the Player and Controlling Playback

Starting and stopping playback is as easy as calling the `Start` or `Stop` method on the `Player` class. The following code shows how you might use a single `Player` referenced in an instance variable to play audio to any calls that come in to the endpoint. The code attaches an event handler to the `AudioVideoFlow.StateChanged` event, which it uses to detach the flow from the `Player` when the call terminates, and then accepts the call. After the call is accepted, it attaches the call's `AudioVideoFlow` to the `Player` instance and starts the `Player` if it is not already playing.

```
private void OnAudioVideoCallReceived(object sender,
    CallReceivedEventArgs<AudioVideoCall> args)
{
    try
    {
        _logger.Log("Accepting call.");

        // Accept the call.
        args.Call.BeginAccept(
            ar =>
            {
                try
                {
                    // Attach an event handler to monitor audio flow state.
                    args.Call.Flow.StateChanged += new
                        EventHandler<MediaFlowStateChangedEventArgs>(
                            Flow_StateChanged);

                    args.Call.EndAccept(ar);

                    _logger.Log("Accepted call.");

                    AttachToPlayer(args.Call.Flow);
                }
                catch (RealTimeException ex)
                {
                    _logger.Log("Failed to accept call.", ex);
                }
            },
            null);
    }
    catch (InvalidOperationException ex)
    {
        _logger.Log("Failed to accept call.", ex);
    }
}

private void AttachToPlayer(AudioVideoFlow flow)
{
    try
    {
        // Attach the flow to the player.
        _player.AttachFlow(flow);

        _logger.Log("Attached flow to the player.");
    }
```

```
            catch (OperationFailureException ofex)
            {
                _logger.Log("Failed to attach flow to player.", ofex);
            }
            catch (InvalidOperationException ioex)
            {
                _logger.Log("Failed to attach flow to player.", ioex);
            }

            // Start the player if it is not already started.
            if (_player.State != PlayerState.Started)
            {
                try
                {
                    _player.Start();
                }
                catch (OperationFailureException ofex)
                {
                    _logger.Log("Failed to start player.", ofex);
                }
                catch (InvalidOperationException ioex)
                {
                    _logger.Log("Failed to start player.", ioex);
                }
            }
        }

        private void Flow_StateChanged(object sender, MediaFlowStateChangedEventArgs e)
        {
            AudioVideoFlow flow = sender as AudioVideoFlow;

            if (e.State == MediaFlowState.Terminated)
            {
                // Detach the flow from the player if
                // the flow has terminated.
                _player.DetachFlow(flow);

                // Remove the event handler for the flow.
                flow.StateChanged -= Flow_StateChanged;
            }
        }
```

Code snippet AdvancedMediaControl\PlayerSample.cs

A number of other options are available for controlling playback. One is that the `Player` has a `PlaybackSpeed` property that you can use to set the `Player` to play the audio faster or slower than normal speed. For example, add the following code snippet to the `CreatePlayer` method to tell the `Player` to play its audio 75 percent faster than normal.

```
// Make people in the recording sound like chipmunks.
_player.PlaybackSpeed = PlaybackSpeed.OneAndThreeQuarters;
```

Code snippet AdvancedMediaControl\PlayerSample.cs

Pausing playback using the `Pause` method and then resuming it later from the same point by calling `Start` again is also possible, as shown in the following code snippet:

```
// Pause the player temporarily.
_player.Pause();

// Do some things....
Thread.Sleep(1000);

// Resume playback from where it left off.
_player.Start();
```

Code snippet AdvancedMediaControl\PlayerSample.cs

Finally, the `Skip` method causes the `Player` to skip forward or backward a specified number of milliseconds in the media source. For example, the following code shows an event handler for the `ToneReceived` event on a `ToneController`, which might appear in a personal assistant application that plays back recorded voice mail messages. If the application receives the tone corresponding to 4 on the phone keypad, it skips backward by one second; if it receives the 6 tone, it skips forward one second.

```
void OnToneReceived(object sender, ToneControllerEventArgs e)
{
    if (e.Tone == (int)ToneId.Tone4)
    {
        // Skip backward.
        _player.Skip(-1000);
    }
    else if (e.Tone == (int)ToneId.Tone6)
    {
        // Skip forward.
        _player.Skip(1000);
    }
}
```

Code snippet AdvancedMediaControl\PlayerSample.cs

Playing Continuous Hold Music

One of the more common uses of the `Player` class is to play a continuous loop of hold music to multiple calls. In this case, having the `Player` simply repeat the audio over and over regardless of how many `AudioVideoFlow`s are attached to it may be desirable.

The following code sample shows one way of accomplishing this. The `CreatePlayer` method creates a new instance of `Player` and supplies it with a media source, then switches the `Player` to manual mode, which will prevent it from automatically stopping playback if the last `AudioVideoFlow` is detached or terminated. Next, it attaches an event handler to the `StateChanged` event. When the `Player` changes to the `Stopped` state, the event handler immediately starts it again. When the application is ready to shut down the hold music, the event handler can be removed so that the `Player` stops without being restarted.

```
private void CreatePlayer(WmaFileSource fileSource)
{
    _player = new Player();
    _player.SetSource(fileSource);
    _player.SetMode(PlayerMode.Manual);
    _player.StateChanged += new
        EventHandler<PlayerStateChangedEventArgs>(OnPlayerStateChanged);
    _player.Start();
}

private void OnPlayerStateChanged(object sender, PlayerStateChangedEventArgs e)
{
    if (e.State == PlayerState.Stopped)
    {
        _player.Start();
    }
}
```

Text-to-Speech with the SpeechSynthesisConnector

The SpeechSynthesisConnector class allows audio from an instance of SpeechSynthesizer (from the foreign Microsoft.Speech namespace) to be pumped into the AudioVideoFlow of an active audio call. It does this by exposing a stream to which the output from the SpeechSynthesizer can be directed.

The SpeechSynthesisConnector, unlike the Player, can only be attached to a single AudioVideoFlow. After it is attached, it must be started before the speech synthesis begins, and stopped after the speech has finished.

The following code shows a class that uses a SpeechSynthesizer with a SpeechSynthesisConnector to speak a welcome message into all incoming calls.

Available for
download on
Wrox.com

```
using System;
using Microsoft.Rtc.Collaboration;
using Microsoft.Rtc.Collaboration.AudioVideo;
using Microsoft.Rtc.Signaling;
using Microsoft.Speech.AudioFormat;
using Microsoft.Speech.Synthesis;

namespace AdvancedMediaControl
{
    public class SpeechSynthesisSample : ISampleComponent
    {
        ApplicationEndpoint _endpoint;
        ILogger _logger;

        internal SpeechSynthesisSample(ApplicationEndpoint endpoint,
            ILogger logger)
        {
            _endpoint = endpoint;
            _logger = logger;
```

```
        }

        public void Start()
        {
            _endpoint.RegisterForIncomingCall<AudioVideoCall>(
                OnAudioVideoCallReceived);
        }

        private void OnAudioVideoCallReceived(object sender,
            CallReceivedEventArgs<AudioVideoCall> args)
        {
            try
            {
                _logger.Log("Accepting call.");

                // Accept the call.
                args.Call.BeginAccept(
                    ar =>
                    {
                        try
                        {
                            // Attach an event handler to monitor
                            // flow state.
                            args.Call.Flow.StateChanged += new
                                EventHandler<
                                MediaFlowStateChangedEventArgs>(
                                Flow_StateChanged);

                            args.Call.EndAccept(ar);

                            _logger.Log("Accepted call.");

                            SpeakMessage(args.Call.Flow, string.Format(
                                "Hello, {0}. Thanks for calling. " +
                                "Your SIP URI is {1}",
                                args.Call.RemoteEndpoint.
                                Participant.DisplayName,
                                args.Call.RemoteEndpoint.
                                Participant.Uri));
                        }
                        catch (RealTimeException ex)
                        {
                            _logger.Log("Failed to accept call.", ex);
                        }
                    },
                    null);
            }
            catch (InvalidOperationException ex)
            {
                _logger.Log("Failed to accept call.", ex);
            }
        }

        private void SpeakMessage(AudioVideoFlow flow, string message)
```

```
    {
        SpeechSynthesizer synth = new SpeechSynthesizer();
        SpeechAudioFormatInfo formatInfo =
            new SpeechAudioFormatInfo(16000,
            AudioBitsPerSample.Sixteen,
            Microsoft.Speech.AudioFormat.AudioChannel.Mono);
        SpeechSynthesisConnector connector =
            new SpeechSynthesisConnector();

        synth.SetOutputToAudioStream(connector.Stream, formatInfo);

        connector.AttachFlow(flow);
        connector.Start();

        synth.SpeakCompleted += new
            EventHandler<SpeakCompletedEventArgs>(
            (sender, args) =>
            {
                connector.Stop();
                synth.Dispose();
            });

        synth.SpeakAsync(message);
    }

    private void Flow_StateChanged(object sender,
        MediaFlowStateChangedEventArgs e)
    {
        AudioVideoFlow flow = sender as AudioVideoFlow;

        if (e.State == MediaFlowState.Terminated)
        {
            if (flow.SpeechSynthesisConnector != null)
            {
                flow.SpeechSynthesisConnector.DetachFlow();
            }

            // Remove the event handler for the flow.
            flow.StateChanged -= Flow_StateChanged;
        }
    }

    public void Stop()
    {
        _endpoint.UnregisterForIncomingCall<AudioVideoCall>(
            OnAudioVideoCallReceived);
    }
    }
}
```

Code snippet AdvancedMediaControl\SpeechSynthesisSample.cs

The code attaches an event handler to each call, which it uses to detach the SpeechSynthesisConnector after the call has finished. It creates the SpeechSynthesizer and SpeechSynthesisConnector, and sets the output from the synthesizer to the stream exposed by the connector, also supplying a definition of the audio format.

Next, it attaches the connector to the AudioVideoFlow and starts the connector. To perform the speaking as an asynchronous operation, it first attaches an event handler, using a lambda expression for convenience. It then tells the SpeechSynthesizer to speak the message.

RECORDING CALLS AND CONFERENCES

Because many organizations have auditing and monitoring requirements, recording is one of the most compelling features of UCMA for developers building new communications solutions. Thanks to the UCMA Recorder class, capturing audio from a call is extremely simple.

The code in this section shows the relevant methods from an application that receives incoming calls and immediately begins recording them. It also listens for the pound tone, which causes it to pause the recording, or if it is already paused, to start the recording again. It saves all recordings in WMA format to the path C:\recordings\, using the call ID as the name of the file.

```csharp
private void OnAudioVideoCallReceived(object sender,
    CallReceivedEventArgs<AudioVideoCall> args)
{
    try
    {
        _logger.Log("Accepting call.");

        // Accept the call.
        args.Call.BeginAccept(
            ar =>
            {
                try
                {
                    // Attach an event handler to monitor audio flow state.
                    args.Call.Flow.StateChanged += new
                        EventHandler<MediaFlowStateChangedEventArgs>(
                            Flow_StateChanged);

                    args.Call.EndAccept(ar);

                    _logger.Log("Accepted call.");

                    // Create a new recorder.
                    Recorder recorder = new Recorder();

                    // Use the call ID as the filename and create a media sink.
                    string fileName = string.Format("C:\\recordings\\{0}.wma",
                        args.Call.CallId);
                    WmaFileSink fileSink = new WmaFileSink(fileName);

                    // Set the recorder to use the media sink and attach
```

```
                          // it to the flow.
                          recorder.SetSink(fileSink);
                          recorder.AttachFlow(args.Call.Flow);

                          _logger.Log("Prepared and attached recorder.");

                          // Start recording.
                          recorder.Start();

                          _logger.Log("Started recording.");

                          // Attach a tone controller to listen for the # tone.
                          ToneController toneController = new ToneController();
                          toneController.ToneReceived += new
                              EventHandler<ToneControllerEventArgs>(
                                  toneController_ToneReceived);
                          toneController.AttachFlow(args.Call.Flow);

                          _logger.Log("Attached tone controller.");
                      }
                      catch (RealTimeException ex)
                      {
                          _logger.Log("Failed to accept call.", ex);
                      }
                  },
                  null);
        }
        catch (InvalidOperationException ex)
        {
            _logger.Log("Failed to accept call.", ex);
        }
    }

    void OnToneReceived(object sender, ToneControllerEventArgs e)
    {
        ToneController toneController = sender as ToneController;

        // If the # key is recognized, switch the state
        // of the recorder.
        if (e.Tone == (int)ToneId.Pound)
        {
            Recorder recorder = toneController.AudioVideoFlow.Recorder;

            if (recorder.State == RecorderState.Started)
            {
                recorder.Pause();
                _logger.Log("Paused recording.");
            }
            else
            {
                recorder.Start();
                _logger.Log("Started recording.");
            }
        }
```

```
    }

    private void Flow_StateChanged(object sender, MediaFlowStateChangedEventArgs e)
    {
        AudioVideoFlow flow = sender as AudioVideoFlow;

        if (e.State == MediaFlowState.Terminated)
        {
            // Clean up the recorder and tone controller.
            if (flow.Recorder != null)
            {
                flow.Recorder.DetachFlow();
                _logger.Log("Detached recorder.");
            }

            if (flow.ToneController != null)
            {
                flow.ToneController.DetachFlow();
                _logger.Log("Detached tone controller.");
            }

            // Remove the event handler for the flow.
            flow.StateChanged -= Flow_StateChanged;
        }
    }
```

Code snippet AdvancedMediaControl\RecorderSample.cs

Like the `Player`, `SpeechSynthesisConnector`, and `ToneController`, the `Recorder` must be attached to an `AudioVideoFlow` to function. It also needs a `MediaSink` instance associated with it. The `MediaSink` receives the output of the recorder. The only `MediaSink` instance that comes with UCMA is the `WmaFileSink`, which outputs the media to a WMA file at a supplied path.

Starting, Stopping, and Pausing Recording

Starting the recording is as easy as calling the `Start` method on the `Recorder` object. Calling the `Stop` method ends the recording and causes the file to be written out. If you call the `Start` method again after calling `Stop`, the `Recorder` will begin an entirely new recording.

To temporarily pause the recording without ending it altogether, you can use the `Pause` method. Calling the `Start` method while the `Recorder` is paused will resume the recording at the point where it left off.

 The `Pause` method is new in UCMA 3.0. In the previous version of the API, no way existed to stop and resume during a single recording. The only option was to make multiple recordings in separate files.

Recording a Conference

You can only attach the `Recorder` to a single `AudioVideoFlow`, but recording multiple people at once by attaching the `Recorder` to an `AudioVideoFlow` that is associated with a call to a conference is possible (and common). The `Recorder` will pick up all the mixed audio coming from the audio/video multipoint control unit (MCU).

Detecting Speech on a Call

No one wants to listen to a recording of a call with long silences, and thankfully, the `Recorder` class in UCMA 3.0 makes this unnecessary by providing an event, `VoiceActivityChanged`, that is triggered whenever someone starts or stops speaking. You can think of it as the equivalent of the little curvy lines that appear next to the phone icon in Lync when someone on an audio conference is speaking.

The following code shows an event handler for the `VoiceActivityChanged` event that uses the voice activity state to pause the recording when no one on the call is speaking.

```
// Subscribe to voice activity changes.
recorder.VoiceActivityChanged +=
    new EventHandler<VoiceActivityChangedEventArgs>(OnVoiceActivityChanged);

...

private void OnVoiceActivityChanged(object sender, VoiceActivityChangedEventArgs e)
{
    Recorder recorder = sender as Recorder;

    if (e.IsVoice && recorder.State == RecorderState.Paused)
    {
        // If the recorder is paused and someone
        // speaks, start recording.
        recorder.Start();
    }
    else if (!e.IsVoice && recorder.State == RecorderState.Started)
    {
        // If the recorder is going and no one
        // is talking, pause it.
        recorder.Pause();
    }
}
```

Code snippet AdvancedMediaControl\RecorderVoiceActivitySample.cs

RECOGNIZING SPEECH

To anyone steeped in the wonders of modern technology, the `ToneController`, which recognizes those tones that allow you to play "Mary Had a Little Lamb" on your phone keypad, and to "push one for customer service" when you call your local bank branch, may seem a bit passé.

Thankfully, UCMA provides for recognition of much more than tones in the form of the `SpeechRecognitionConnector`. This delightful class exposes an audio stream that you can feed into the `SpeechRecognitionEngine` in the `Microsoft.Speech` namespace, allowing applications to recognize spoken commands and statements.

> *Unfortunately, the* `RotaryPhonePulseController` *class never made it into UCMA, which may be another indication that it's time to get rid of that old rotary phone from 1953 — just a thought.*

The following code shows a class, `SpeechRecognitionSample`, which takes an `AudioVideoCall` in the `Incoming` state, answers it, and then uses the `SpeechRecognitionConnector` and `SpeechRecognitionEngine` to listen for the words "yes," "no," "hello," and "goodbye." When it hears any of those words, it writes the word out to the log and stops listening.

When the `AudioVideoFlow` terminates, the class calls the `Dispose` method on the `SpeechRecognitionConnector`, the `SpeechRecognitionEngine`, and the `SpeechRecognitionStream` to release unmanaged resources.

```csharp
using System;
using System.Collections.Generic;
using System.Linq;
using System.Text;
using Microsoft.Rtc.Collaboration.AudioVideo;
using Microsoft.Speech.Recognition;
using Microsoft.Rtc.Collaboration;
using Microsoft.Rtc.Signaling;
using Microsoft.Speech.AudioFormat;

namespace AdvancedMediaControl
{
    public class SpeechRecognitionSample : ISampleComponent
    {
        private ApplicationEndpoint _endpoint;
        private AudioVideoCall _call;
        private ILogger _logger;
        private SpeechRecognitionStream _stream;
        private SpeechRecognitionConnector _connector;
        private SpeechRecognitionEngine _engine;

        internal SpeechRecognitionSample(ApplicationEndpoint endpoint,
            ILogger logger)
        {
            _endpoint = endpoint;
            _logger = logger;
        }

        public void Start()
        {
```

```csharp
    _endpoint.RegisterForIncomingCall<AudioVideoCall>(
        OnAudioVideoCallReceived);
}

private void OnAudioVideoCallReceived(object sender,
    CallReceivedEventArgs<AudioVideoCall> args)
{
    _call = args.Call;

    try
    {
        _logger.Log("Accepting call.");

        // Accept the call.
        _call.BeginAccept(OnAcceptCompleted, null);
    }
    catch (InvalidOperationException ex)
    {
        _logger.Log("Failed to accept call.", ex);
    }
}

private void OnAcceptCompleted(IAsyncResult result)
{
    try
    {
        _call.EndAccept(result);

        _logger.Log("Accepted call.");

        // Attach an event handler to detect the
        // flow termation.
        _call.Flow.StateChanged += new
            EventHandler<MediaFlowStateChangedEventArgs>(
            OnFlowStateChanged);

        // Create a new connector and engine.
        _connector = new SpeechRecognitionConnector();
        _engine = new SpeechRecognitionEngine();

        // Build a grammar for the engine based on
        // a list of recognized words, and load the grammar.
        Choices choices = new Choices(
            new string[] { "yes", "no", "hello", "goodbye" }
        );
        Grammar grammar = new Grammar(new
            GrammarBuilder(choices));
        _engine.LoadGrammarCompleted += new
            EventHandler<LoadGrammarCompletedEventArgs>(
            OnLoadGrammarCompleted);
        _engine.LoadGrammarAsync(grammar);
    }
    catch (RealTimeException ex)
    {
        _logger.Log("Failed to accept call.", ex);
```

```
        }
    }

    void OnLoadGrammarCompleted(object sender,
        LoadGrammarCompletedEventArgs e)
    {
        // When the grammar is loaded, attach the
        // connector to the flow and start it.
        _connector.AttachFlow(_call.Flow);
        _stream = _connector.Start();

        // Provide the audio stream from the connector to
        // the recognition engine, along with format details.
        SpeechAudioFormatInfo audioFormat =
            new SpeechAudioFormatInfo(16000,
            AudioBitsPerSample.Sixteen,
            Microsoft.Speech.AudioFormat.AudioChannel.Mono);
        _engine.SetInputToAudioStream(_stream, audioFormat);

        // Begin recognition.
        _engine.RecognizeCompleted += new
            EventHandler<RecognizeCompletedEventArgs>(
            OnRecognizeCompleted);
        _engine.RecognizeAsync(RecognizeMode.Single);
    }

    void OnRecognizeCompleted(object sender,
        RecognizeCompletedEventArgs e)
    {
        // Log the recognized word.
        _logger.Log("Recognized {0}", e.Result.Text);
    }

    void OnFlowStateChanged(object sender,
        MediaFlowStateChangedEventArgs e)
    {
        if (e.State == MediaFlowState.Terminated)
        {
            // These resources need to be released to prevent
            // memory leaks.
            if (_connector != null)
            {
                _connector.Stop();
                if (_connector.AudioVideoFlow != null)
                {
                    _connector.DetachFlow();
                }
                _connector.Dispose();
            }
            if (_stream != null)
            {
                _stream.Dispose();
            }
            if (_engine != null)
```

```
                {
                    _engine.Dispose();
                }
            }
        }

        public void Stop()
        {
            _endpoint.UnregisterForIncomingCall<AudioVideoCall>(
                OnAudioVideoCallReceived);
        }
    }
}
```

Code snippet AdvancedMediaControl\SpeechRecognitionSample.cs

The `SpeechRecognitionConnector`, like the `Recorder`, may only be attached to one `AudioVideoFlow` at a time.

SPEECHRECOGNITIONCONNECTOR OR WORKFLOW SDK?

In most cases, using the UCMA Workflow software development kit (SDK) to build an application or component that uses speech recognition is easier than building the same components using the SpeechRecognitionConnector. This is especially true for interactive voice response (IVR) systems, which take different paths of execution based on spoken responses to questions. For a comprehensive overview of the UCMA Workflow SDK, see Chapter 14.

For some scenarios, however, the Workflow SDK is not appropriate. For instance, a server application that listens for specific voice commands in an audio conference would be quite difficult to build with the Workflow SDK. Using a `SpeechRecognitionConnector` to provide the conference audio to a `SpeechRecognitionEngine` would be simpler.

CONTROLLING HOLD AND MUTE STATES

Through the `AudioVideoFlow` class, UCMA applications can manipulate the mute or hold status of active audio calls. This is chiefly useful on two-party calls when the application is sending or receiving audio from a remote endpoint, using one of the classes described in previous sections.

Holding or Retrieving an Audio Call

You can put an audio call on hold in a UCMA application using the `BeginHold` and `EndHold` methods on the `AudioVideoFlow`. You must specify the type of hold, which can be any of the following:

➤ `None` — The call is put on hold, but audio continues flowing back and forth.

➤ `BothEndpoints` — The call is put on hold and audio stops flowing.

➤ `RemoteEndpoint` — The call is put on hold and any audio coming from the remote endpoint is ignored. Audio continues flowing to the remote endpoint from the application.

➤ `RemoteEndpointMusicOnHold` — Same as the preceding point, and the remote endpoint is specifically told to expect hold music. The application must supply the music itself, usually by using a `Player` object.

The `BothEndpoints` option has the same effect as putting a call on hold in Lync. The others still put the call on hold, causing the hold indicator to appear if the remote participant is using Lync, but change the audio in different ways.

The following code puts an audio call on hold, muting both endpoints:

```csharp
try
{
    audioVideoCall.Flow.BeginHold(HoldType.BothEndpoints,
        ar =>
        {
            try
            {
                audioVideoCall.Flow.EndHold(ar);
            }
            catch (RealTimeException ex)
            {
                _logger.Log("Failed holding call.", ex);
            }
        },
        null
    );
}
catch (InvalidOperationException ex)
{
    _logger.Log("Failed holding call.", ex);
}
```

Code snippet AdvancedMediaControl\HoldMuteSample.cs

To take a call off of hold, use the `BeginRetrieve` and `EndRetrieve` methods, as shown in the following code sample.

```csharp
try
{
    audioVideoCall.Flow.BeginRetrieve(
        ar =>
        {
            try
            {
                audioVideoCall.Flow.EndRetrieve(ar);
            }
            catch (RealTimeException ex)
```

```
                    {
                        _logger.Log("Failed retrieving call.", ex);
                    }
                },
                null
            );
        }
        catch (InvalidOperationException ex)
        {
            _logger.Log("Failed retrieving call.", ex);
        }
```

Code snippet AdvancedMediaControl\HoldMuteSample.cs

 Don't be fooled by the naming — the EndHold *method does not take a call off of hold. Its purpose is to end the asynchronous operation that puts a call on hold. Use* BeginRetrieve/EndRetrieve *to take a call off of hold.*

Muting or Unmuting the Audio Flow

If you want to interrupt the flow of audio on a call without actually putting it on hold, you can simply mute the audio using the AudioControl class, which is accessible in the Audio property on the AudioVideoFlow. The Mute method (one of the few in UCMA 3.0 that is not asynchronous) stops audio from flowing in the direction you specify. The mute direction can be any of the following:

➤ None (no change)

➤ Send

➤ Receive

➤ SendReceive (both send and receive)

The direction you specify is the one that is muted. For instance, the following code will stop sending outbound audio.

```
// Mute the outgoing audio.
audioVideoCall.Flow.Audio.Mute(MuteDirection.Send);
```

Code snippet AdvancedMediaControl\HoldMuteSample.cs

You can reverse the mute with the Unmute method. As with Mute, you must specify the direction that is to be unmuted, as shown in the following.

```
// Unmute the outgoing audio.
audioVideoCall.Flow.Audio.Unmute(MuteDirection.Send);
```

Code snippet AdvancedMediaControl\HoldMuteSample.cs

Finally, you can determine the current mute state by examining the `DirectionMuted` property:

```
// Unmute the audio if it is muted.
if (audioVideoCall.Flow.Audio.DirectionMuted != MuteDirection.None)
{
    audioVideoCall.Flow.Audio.Unmute(MuteDirection.SendReceive);
}
```

Code snippet AdvancedMediaControl\HoldMuteSample.cs

 Note that calling Mute *with a direction of* None *does not unmute the audio; it has no effect at all. To unmute, you need to actually call the* Unmute *method.*

STAYING ON THE SIGNALING PATH WITH BACK-TO-BACK CALLS

At first glance, you might think that the term *back-to-back call* refers to those annoying situations where someone schedules an important call with you for 1:00 p.m. to 2:00 p.m., and someone else schedules an equally important call for 2:00 p.m. to 3:00 p.m., leaving you no time for an afternoon nap under your desk. As a matter of fact, the `BackToBackCall` class in UCMA has nothing whatsoever to do with overscheduling, and because its function (mediating the SIP messaging between two remote endpoints) is a bit abstract and difficult to fathom, this section takes some time to explain what a back-to-back call does and why a unified communications developer might want to use one.

The Straight and Narrow Signaling Path

Write an application in UCMA that takes an incoming call and transfers it to another user is quite easy. The code to handle the incoming call might look something like the following:

```
private void OnAudioVideoCallReceived(object sender,
    CallReceivedEventArgs<AudioVideoCall> args)
{
    _logger.Log("Accepting call...");

    AudioVideoCall incomingCall = args.Call;

    incomingCall.StateChanged += new
        EventHandler<CallStateChangedEventArgs>(OnCallStateChanged);

    try
    {
        incomingCall.BeginAccept(
            ar =>
            {
                try
                {
                    incomingCall.EndAccept(ar);
                }
                catch (RealTimeException ex)
                {
```

```
                        _logger.Log("Failed accepting call.");
                    }

                    _logger.Log("Accepted call.");

                    _logger.Log("Transferring call...");

                    try
                    {
                        incomingCall.BeginTransfer("sip:galahad@wrox.com",
                            OnTransferCompleted, incomingCall);
                    }
                    catch (InvalidOperationException ioex)
                    {
                        _logger.Log("Failed initiating transfer.", ioex);
                    }
                },
                null
            );
        }
        catch (InvalidOperationException ioex)
        {
            _logger.Log("Failed initiating accept.");
        }
    }

    private void OnCallStateChanged(object sender, CallStateChangedEventArgs e)
    {
        _logger.Log("Call state changed from {0} to {1}.", e.PreviousState, e.State);
    }

    private void OnTransferCompleted(IAsyncResult result)
    {
        AudioVideoCall incomingCall =
            result.AsyncState as AudioVideoCall;

        try
        {
            incomingCall.EndTransfer(result);
        }
        catch (RealTimeException ex)
        {
            _logger.Log("Failed transferring call.", ex);
        }
    }
```

This incoming call event handler accepts every incoming audio/video call and immediately transfers it to `sip:galahad@wrox.com`. If you were to watch the status of the `AudioVideoCall` object during this process, you would see it go through the following statuses in quick succession:

➤ Incoming

➤ Establishing

➤ Established

> ➤ Transferring

> ➤ Terminating

> ➤ Terminated

In other words, as soon as the transfer is successfully transferred to the other endpoint, the original call terminates. The application is not a participant on the new call. It has been left out.

Figure 12-1 shows the sequence of events. The call from the first user, Frederick, goes to the application, which accepts the call and refers Frederick to Galahad. Frederick accordingly places a new call to Galahad, and as soon as this call connects, the call with the application terminates. This means that the application has no control over the call between Frederick and Galahad; the SIP messages go directly between their two endpoints, and the application is not on the signaling path at all.

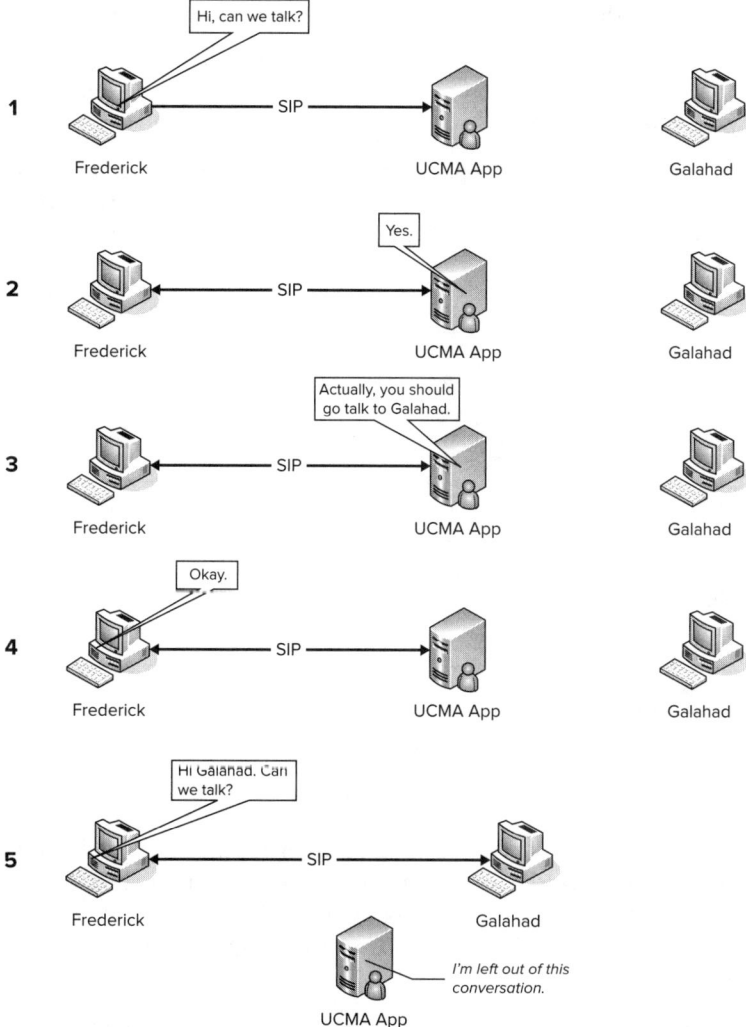

FIGURE 12-1

If the aim of the application is merely to bounce the call over to another endpoint and forget about it, this is not necessarily a problem. Several situations can occur, though, in which an application might need to stay in the middle of a two-party call between two other endpoints:

➤ A call billing application might need to keep track of when the call ends so it knows the amount that should be invoiced.

➤ A web-based call control application might need to terminate, transfer, or otherwise manipulate calls after connecting them when the user issues commands through the web interface.

➤ A helpdesk might want to mask the identity of the individual phone representative that answers a helpdesk call.

A contact center or other application might need to manage a call internally as a conference to allow for multiple participants, while making it appear as a normal two-party call to the caller

The `BackToBackCall` class makes all of these scenarios possible by keeping the application on the signaling path for the call.

How the Back-to-Back Call Works

In SIP terms, the `BackToBackCall` allows a UCMA application to act as a *back-to-back user agent* (often abbreviated B2BUA). A back-to-back user agent mediates SIP messages between two other endpoints, while allowing the media streams to flow directly back and forth between the endpoints. Figure 12-2 gives a visualization of how this works.

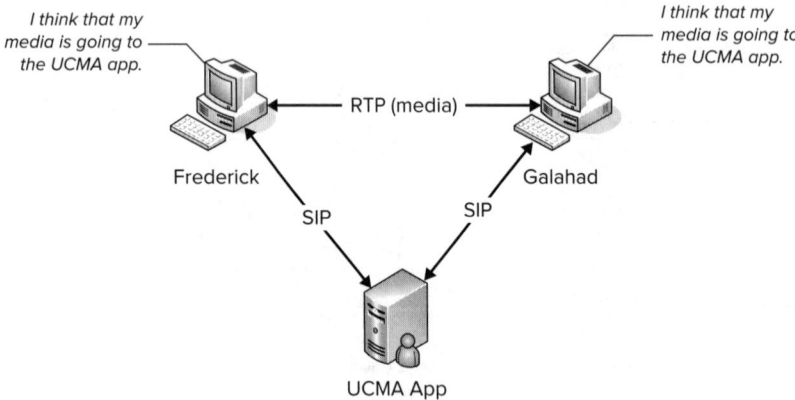

I think that my media is going to the UCMA app.

I think that my media is going to the UCMA app.

RTP (media)

Frederick

Galahad

SIP

SIP

UCMA App

FIGURE 12-2

If you dissect a back-to-back call, you find that it is actually made up of two distinct SIP dialogs (often referred to as the *call legs*): one between the first endpoint and the application, and another between the application and the second endpoint. Both remote endpoints (Frederick and Galahad in Figure 12-2) are sending SIP messages to the application, and from the perspective of those two user agents they are both on calls with the application itself.

However, when an application that is acting as a back-to-back user agent constructs the Session Description Protocol (SDP) information to negotiate the media delivery for the two calls, it does something tricky. Instead of providing its own IP address to Frederick and Galahad when telling them where to send the RTP stream carrying the audio for the call, it gives Frederick's IP address to Galahad and gives Galahad's IP address to Frederick! The result is that Frederick thinks he is in an audio call with the application, but his audio is actually going to Galahad, while Galahad also thinks he is in an audio call with the application, and his audio is going to Frederick. Figure 12-3 shows how this plays out on a back-to-back call.

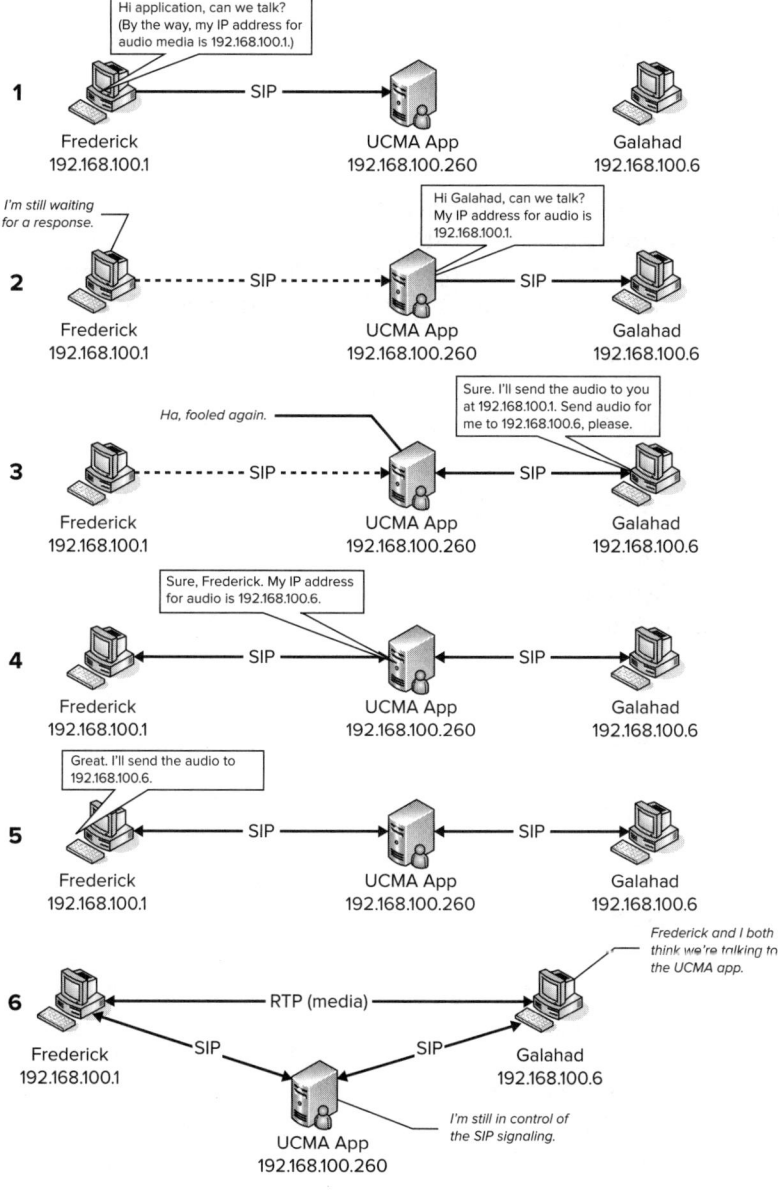

FIGURE 12-3

The whole arrangement seems eerily reminiscent of a bad romantic comedy where the heroine wants to set up her two friends, Joe and Jane, who hate each other, so she creates a fake secret admirer for each of them, sends each one love letters from the imaginary admirer for a while until they are hooked, and then arranges for Joe and Jane both to meet their "secret lovers" at the same place.

The `BackToBackCall` class, however, actually works in real life.

Initiating a Back-to-Back Call

A back-to-back call requires two call legs, in one of two configurations:

➤   An idle call and an incoming call

➤   Two idle calls

Establishing a back-to-back call in either case involves creating a new `BackToBackCall` instance, and providing the `Call` objects for the two call legs. A `BackToBackCallSettings` object wraps each of the `Call` objects. It also has a property for a SIP URI so that the destination can be specified if the `Call` object is in the `Idle` state. The following code snippet shows this in action.

```
BackToBackCallSettings settings1 = new BackToBackCallSettings(incomingCallLeg);
BackToBackCallSettings settings2 = new BackToBackCallSettings(outgoingCallLeg,
    "sip:galahad@wrox.com");

BackToBackCall b2bCall = new BackToBackCall(settings1, settings2);
```

At this point, the back-to-back call is ready to be established asynchronously with the `BeginEstablish` method. The code to establish a back-to-back call looks almost identical to the code for establishing an ordinary two-party call:

```
try
{
    _logger.Log("Establishing back to back call...");

    b2bCall.BeginEstablish(
        ar =>
        {
            try
            {
                b2bCall.EndEstablish(ar);

                _logger.Log("Established back to back call.");
            }
            catch (RealTimeException ex)
            {
                _logger.Log("Failed establishing a back to back call.", ex);
```

```
                    }
                },
                null);
    }
    catch (InvalidOperationException ioex)
    {
        _logger.Log("Failed initiating a back to back call.", ioex);
    }
```

Behind the scenes, UCMA mediates the SIP messaging between the two endpoints and sets them up to send the media directly to each other.

Back-to-Back with an Incoming and an Outgoing Call

The back-to-back call is useful for services such as "hunt groups" or automatic call distributors that take inbound calls and seamlessly connect them to individual agents for answering. With a back-to-back call, the application can keep the identity of the individual who answers the call concealed and can perform call control operations, such as terminating or transferring the call.

The following code shows an incoming call event handler that connects an incoming call to an agent using a back-to-back call.

```
private void OnAudioVideoCallReceived(object sender,
    CallReceivedEventArgs<AudioVideoCall> args)
{
    _logger.Log("Incoming call.");

    AudioVideoCall incomingCall = args.Call;

    // Create a new call leg for the agent.
    Conversation agentCallLegConversation = new Conversation(_endpoint);
    AudioVideoCall agentCallLeg = new AudioVideoCall(agentCallLegConversation);

    // The incoming call will serve as the other call leg.
    AudioVideoCall incomingCallLeg = args.Call;

    // Create the settings for the back to back call.
    BackToBackCallSettings settings1 = new BackToBackCallSettings(incomingCallLeg);
    BackToBackCallSettings settings2 = new BackToBackCallSettings(agentCallLeg,
        _destinationSipUri);

    // Create and establish the back to back call.
    BackToBackCall b2bCall = new BackToBackCall(settings1, settings2);

    try
    {
        _logger.Log("Establishing back to back call...");

        b2bCall.BeginEstablish(
            ar =>
```

```
        {
            try
            {
                b2bCall.EndEstablish(ar);

                _logger.Log("Established back to back call.");
            }
            catch (RealTimeException ex)
            {
                _logger.Log("Failed establishing a back to back call.", ex);
            }
        },
        null);
    }
    catch (InvalidOperationException ioex)
    {
        _logger.Log("Failed initiating a back to back call.", ioex);
    }
}
```

Code snippet AdvancedMediaControl\BackToBackIncomingOutgoingSample.cs

Back-to-Back with a Call That Is Already Established

Establishing a back-to-back call becomes a bit more difficult when one of the call legs is a call that is already established. This is often the case, for example, in helpdesk or call center applications, where some initial processing may be done on a call before it is routed to an agent. In these applications, the application typically accepts the call and either plays a message, places it into an interactive voice response (IVR) menu, or collects information in some other manner. When this is done, the call generally needs to be routed to an agent. Another common scenario occurs in outbound dialing campaigns or "click-to-call" applications where both ends of the call must be established by the application. Unfortunately, an established call cannot be used as a call leg for a back-to-back call. A call routing trick known as the "self-transfer" helps with this conundrum. In UCMA, a self-transfer looks more or less like the following code:

```
    _call.BeginTransfer(_call, OnSelfTransferCompleted, null);
```

Essentially, it is a call replacement (or "supervised") transfer in which the call being transferred and the call being replaced are the same call. In something rather like a SIP enactment of a snake biting its own tail, the application transfers a call to itself, causing the remote party to "restart" the call from the beginning as an incoming call. Figure 12-4 shows the steps in a self-transfer.

Because this new call is in the Incoming state, the back-to-back call can use it as one of its call legs.

An important advantage of the self-transfer is that the Call object for the new incoming call exposes a reference to the old (replaced) call. The application can store state from the communication session with the caller in the ApplicationContext property on the original call and can then access it after the self-transfer. This allows for continuity even though the incoming call is, in SIP terms, an entirely new signaling session.

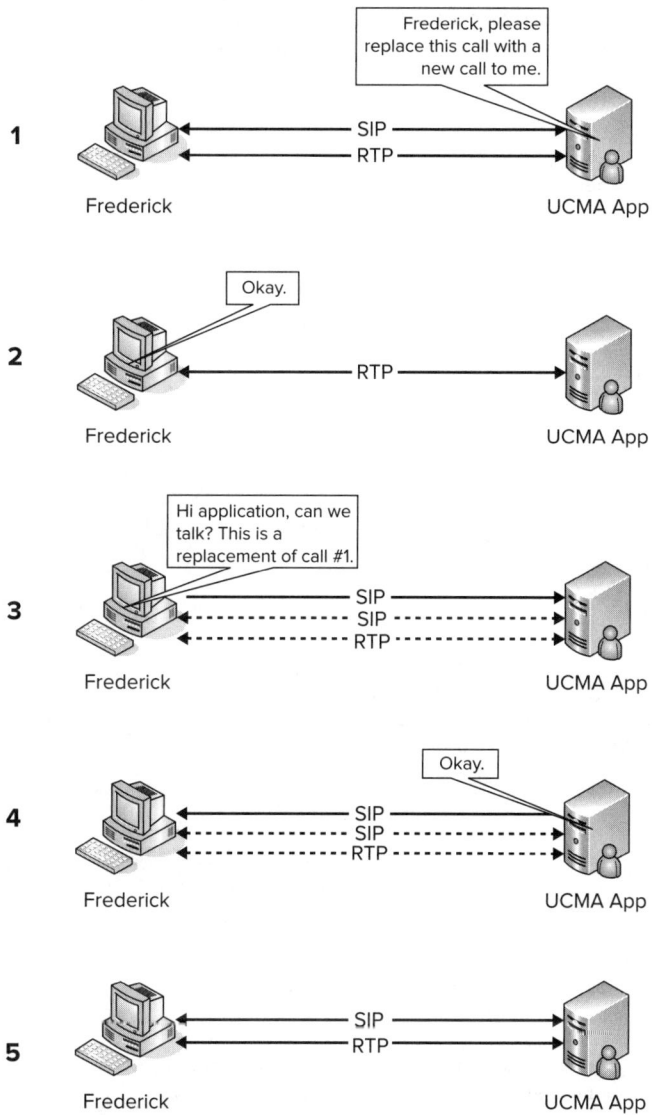

FIGURE 12-4

The following code shows this technique in action. In a very simplified version of a helpdesk application, the code answers new incoming calls and passes them to a new instance of the CallSession or ConferenceCallSession class for handling. The CallSession class listens for the pound tone, and when the caller presses it, it stores a SIP address for an agent in an instance variable and self-transfers the call.

Meanwhile, when the application receives a call that is replacing another call, it checks the ApplicationContext property on the replaced call to see whether it contains a reference to a

CallSession instance. If so, it passes the new call into that CallSession object, allowing it to resume where it left off and create a back-to-back call with the responding agent.

Here is the incoming call handler:

```csharp
private void OnAudioVideoCallReceived(object sender,
    CallReceivedEventArgs<AudioVideoCall> args)
{
    _logger.Log("Incoming call.");

    AudioVideoCall incomingCall = args.Call;

    if (args.CallToBeReplaced == null)
    {
        _logger.Log("Receiving new call...");

        if (_useConference)
        {
            // Create a new ConferenceCallSession to handle the call.
            ConferenceCallSession newSession = new ConferenceCallSession(args.Call,
                _destinationSipUri, _logger);
            newSession.Start();
        }
        else
        {
            // Create a new CallSession to handle the call.
            CallSession newSession = new CallSession(args.Call,
                _destinationSipUri, _logger);
            newSession.Start();
        }
    }
    else
    {
        if (args.CallToBeReplaced.ApplicationContext is CallSession)
        {
            // This is a self-transfer from a CallSession.
            // Let the CallSession pick up where it left off.
            _logger.Log("Receiving self-transfer...");
            CallSession originalCallSession =
                (CallSession)args.CallToBeReplaced.ApplicationContext;
            originalCallSession.HandleSelfTransfer(args.Call);
        }
        else if (args.CallToBeReplaced.ApplicationContext is ConferenceCallSession)
        {
            // This is a self-transfer from a CallSession.
            // Let the CallSession pick up where it left off.
            _logger.Log("Receiving self-transfer...");
            ConferenceCallSession originalCallSession =
                (ConferenceCallSession)args.CallToBeReplaced.ApplicationContext;
            originalCallSession.HandleSelfTransfer(args.Call);
        }
        else
        {
```

```
                // This is not a proper self-transfer; decline.
                args.Call.Decline();
                _logger.Log("Declined invalid transfer.");
            }
        }
    }
```

Code snippet AdvancedMediaControl\BackToBackEstablishedSample.cs

The following code demonstrates the CallSession class.

```csharp
using System;
using System.Collections.Generic;
using System.Linq;
using System.Text;
using Microsoft.Rtc.Collaboration.AudioVideo;
using Microsoft.Rtc.Collaboration;
using Microsoft.Rtc.Signaling;

namespace AdvancedMediaControl
{
    internal class CallSession
    {
        AudioVideoCall _call;
        ILogger _logger;
        ToneController _toneController;
        string _agentSipUri;

        internal CallSession(AudioVideoCall call,
            string agentSipUri,
            ILogger logger)
        {
            _call = call;
            _agentSipUri = agentSipUri;
            _logger = logger;
        }

        internal void Start()
        {
            _call.StateChanged +=
                new EventHandler<CallStateChangedEventArgs>
                    (OnCallStateChanged);

            // Accept the incoming call.
            try
            {
                _logger.Log("Accepting call...");

                _call.BeginAccept(
                    ar =>
                    {
                        try
                        {
```

```
                    _call.EndAccept(ar);

                    _logger.Log("Accepted call.");

                    // Attach a tone controller.
                    _toneController = new ToneController();
                    _toneController.ToneReceived += new
                        EventHandler<ToneControllerEventArgs>
                            (OnToneReceived);
                    _toneController.AttachFlow(_call.Flow);

                    // Other things could happen here,
                    // such as an IVR.

                    _logger.Log("Attached tone controller.");
                }
                catch (RealTimeException ex)
                {
                    _logger.Log("Failed accepting call.", ex);
                }
            },
            null
        );
    }
    catch (InvalidOperationException ex)
    {
        _logger.Log("Failed accepting call.", ex);
    }
}

internal void HandleSelfTransfer(AudioVideoCall call)
{
    // The incoming call will serve as the first call leg.
    AudioVideoCall incomingCallLeg = call;

    // Create a second call leg for the agent.
    Conversation agentCallLegConversation =
        new Conversation(call.Conversation.Endpoint);
    AudioVideoCall agentCallLeg =
        new AudioVideoCall(agentCallLegConversation);

    // Create the settings for the back to back call,
    // using the SIP URI previously stored for the agent.
    BackToBackCallSettings settings1 =
        new BackToBackCallSettings(incomingCallLeg);
    BackToBackCallSettings settings2 =
        new BackToBackCallSettings(agentCallLeg, _agentSipUri);

    // Create and establish the back to back call.
    BackToBackCall b2bCall =
        new BackToBackCall(settings1, settings2);

    try
    {
```

```
            _logger.Log("Establishing back to back call...");

            b2bCall.BeginEstablish(
                ar =>
                {
                    try
                    {
                        b2bCall.EndEstablish(ar);

                        _logger.Log("Established back to back.");
                    }
                    catch (RealTimeException ex)
                    {
                        _logger.Log(
                            "Failed establishing back to back.",
                            ex);
                    }
                },
                null);
    }
    catch (InvalidOperationException ioex)
    {
        _logger.Log("Failed initiating a back to back call.",
            ioex);
    }
}

private void OnToneReceived(object sender,
    ToneControllerEventArgs e)
{
    if (e.Tone == (int)ToneId.Pound)
    {
        // Store this class as the application context for the
        // call so it can be retrieved after the transfer.
        _call.ApplicationContext = this;

        // Self-transfer the call.
        try
        {
            _logger.Log("Self-transferring call...");

            _call.BeginTransfer(_call,
                ar =>
                {
                    try
                    {
                        _call.EndTransfer(ar);

                        _logger.Log(
                            "Completed self-transfer.");
                    }
                    catch (RealTimeException ex)
                    {
```

```
                                    _logger.Log("Self-transfer failed.",
                                        ex);
                        }
                    },
                    null
                );
            }
            catch (InvalidOperationException ex)
            {
                _logger.Log("Failed initiating self-transfer.",
                    ex);
            }
        }
    }

    private void OnCallStateChanged(object sender,
        CallStateChangedEventArgs e)
    {
        _logger.Log("Call state changed from {0} to {1}.",
            e.PreviousState, e.State);
    }
  }
}
```

Code snippet AdvancedMediaControl\CallSession.cs

Back-to-Back Calls with Conferences

Back-to-back calls are equally useful with conferences. Using a back-to-back call, a UCMA application can essentially broker a connection between a remote user agent and the conference, retaining control over the SIP signaling on that connection. This allows for several useful scenarios, such as:

➤ Joining a user to a conference invisibly

➤ Seamlessly transferring a remote user from a conference into a two-party call

➤ Allowing domain users to join a conference anonymously

When building UCMA applications that deal with conferences, keeping in mind that the application does not manage the conference itself is important. The conference focus and multipoint control units (MCUs) are located elsewhere, generally on another server. (Refer to Chapter 11 for more details on how Lync Server conferences work.)

When a UCMA application joins an ad hoc conference or a conference that it has scheduled, it becomes one of the participants in that conference. Assuming it joins as a conference leader or as a trusted participant, it can control the conference by sending commands to the conference focus or to an MCU, but it is not in the signaling path of the SIP sessions between the *other* conference participants and the focus and MCUs. Figure 12-5 illustrates this configuration. Not being on the signaling path of those calls from the other participants into the conference, the application cannot exert any control over the SIP messaging in order to, for instance, make them join as trusted participants.

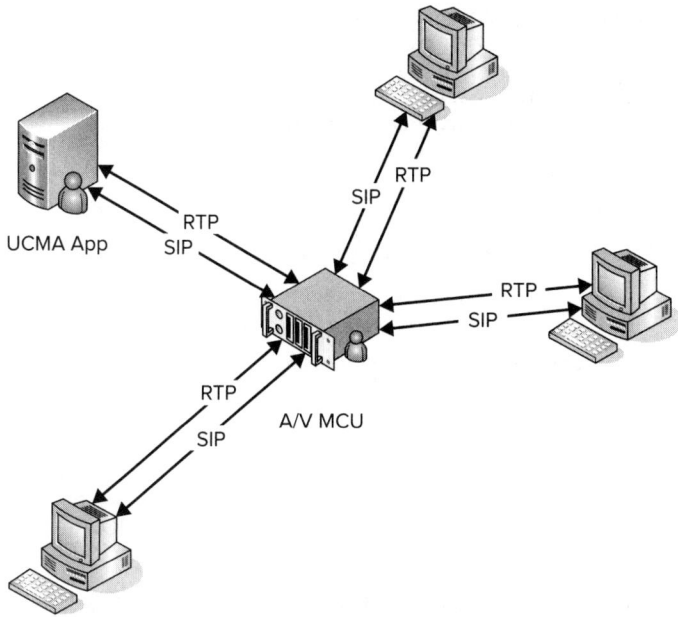

FIGURE 12-5

A back-to-back call can resolve this problem. Using a back-to-back call, the application can mediate calls from remote endpoints into the conference it has created, retaining control over the SIP signaling.

The following code illustrates this with a modified version of the CallSession class from the previous section. This ConferenceCallSession class serves the same purpose as CallSession, but instead of connecting the caller with a single agent via a back-to-back call, it connects the caller with a conference that could contain multiple agents, or even services provided by the application. (Methods that are unchanged have been omitted.)

```
internal class ConferenceCallSession
{
    ...

    internal void HandleSelfTransfer(AudioVideoCall call)
    {
        // The incoming call will serve as the first call leg.
        AudioVideoCall incomingCallLeg = call;

        // Create a second call leg for the call into the conference.
        Conversation conferenceCallLegConversation =
            new Conversation(call.Conversation.Endpoint);

        // Use a fake SIP URI when joining the conference.
```

```
        conferenceCallLegConversation.Impersonate("sip:customer@fabrikam.com",
            null, null);

        // Join the conference as a normal participant.
        ConferenceJoinOptions joinOptions = new ConferenceJoinOptions()
        {
            JoinMode = JoinMode.Default
        };

        // Join the ad hoc conference, creating the SIP dialog
        // with the new conference focus.
        try
        {
            conferenceCallLegConversation.ConferenceSession.BeginJoin(
                joinOptions,
                ar =>
                {
                    try
                    {
                        conferenceCallLegConversation.ConferenceSession.EndJoin(
                            ar);

                        // Create an AudioVideoCall for the call to the A/V MCU.
                        AudioVideoCall conferenceCallLeg =
                            new AudioVideoCall(conferenceCallLegConversation);

                        InitiateBackToBackCall(incomingCallLeg, conferenceCallLeg);
                    }
                    catch (RealTimeException ex)
                    {
                        _logger.Log("Failed joining ad hoc conference.", ex);
                    }
                },
                null
            );
        }
        catch (InvalidOperationException ex)
        {
            _logger.Log("Failed joining ad hoc conference.", ex);
        }
    }

    private void InitiateBackToBackCall(AudioVideoCall incomingCallLeg,
        AudioVideoCall conferenceCallLeg)
    {
        // Create the settings for the back to back call.
        // There's no need to provide a SIP URI for the outgoing call
        // since the conversation is already associated with the conference.
        BackToBackCallSettings settings1 = new BackToBackCallSettings(
            incomingCallLeg);
        BackToBackCallSettings settings2 = new BackToBackCallSettings(
            conferenceCallLeg);

        // Create and establish the back to back call.
```

```
BackToBackCall b2bCall = new BackToBackCall(settings1, settings2);

try
{
    _logger.Log("Establishing back to back call...");

    b2bCall.BeginEstablish(
        ar =>
        {
            try
            {
                b2bCall.EndEstablish(ar);

                _logger.Log("Established back to back call.");
            }
            catch (RealTimeException ex)
            {
                _logger.Log("Failed establishing a back to back call.",
                    ex);
            }
        },
        null);
}
catch (InvalidOperationException ioex)
{
    _logger.Log("Failed initiating a back to back call.", ioex);
}
}

...
}
```

Code snippet AdvancedMediaControl\ConferenceCallSession.cs

The back-to-back call works in much the same way as it does with two-party calls; in fact, the SIP session with the audio/video MCU is really just a type of two-party call, albeit one in which the audio from the remote end is mixed from a number of other conference participants. The only significant code difference is that the application doesn't need to supply a SIP URI for the outgoing call leg, because the conference is already associated with the Conversation object, and so UCMA can figure out the SIP URI it needs to call on its own.

CONTROLLING WHO CAN HEAR WHAT

A conventional audio conference attempts to simulate being in the same room as the other conference participants; all the conference participants can hear one another equally. In a Lync Server audio conference, the audio/video MCU accomplishes this by taking all the incoming audio streams from the various participants and mixing them, creating an outgoing audio stream for each participant that combines the incoming audio from all *other* participants. Figure 12-6 shows this mixing in action.

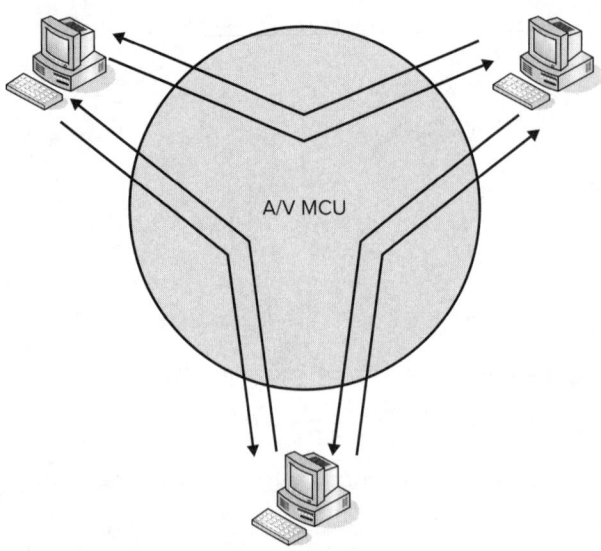

FIGURE 12-6

Sometimes, though, an application needs to exert finer-grained control over the routing of audio between a group of endpoints. For instance, a supervisor may need to listen to calls without being heard, perhaps occasionally saying something to an employee that the customer cannot hear, or an application may need to play hold music to the participants on a call while also preventing them from hearing each other.

Even though these situations don't quite fit the profile of an ordinary conference call, by bringing all the endpoints into a Lync Server audio conference, the application can use the audio/video MCU's mixing capabilities to manage who should hear what.

UCMA 3.0 gives developers two ways of changing the audio mixing performed by the MCU:

➤ UCMA applications can send a command to the MCU telling it to remove a specific participant from the default audio routing, meaning that it will no longer get the standard mix of audio from all other participants.

➤ Applications can specify custom audio routing for any call to the MCU they control.

Adding or Removing Participants from the Default Audio Mix

By default, the audio/video MCU sends each conference participant an audio stream that combines the audio from every other participant, as shown earlier in Figure 12-6. To provide the MCU with customized audio routing rules for a given participant, you must first remove that participant from the default audio routing.

Removing a participant from the default audio routing has two effects:

➤ Audio from the removed participant is no longer sent to other participants.

➤ The removed participant no longer receives any audio from any other participants.

You can manually define audio routes for a participant who has been removed from the default routing, but until these manual routes are in place, the removed participant will effectively be isolated from the rest of the audio conference, as shown in Figure 12-7.

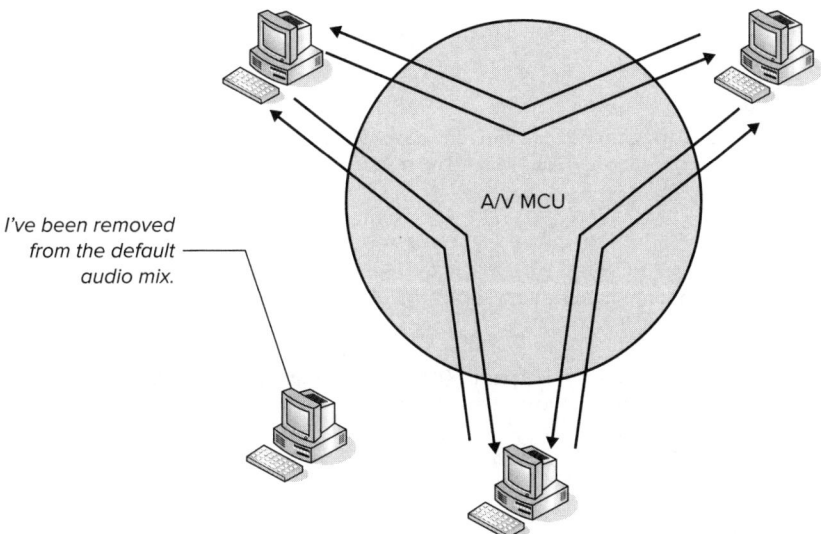

I've been removed from the default audio mix.

A/V MCU

FIGURE 12-7

Removing a Participant from the Default Routing

To remove a participant from the default audio routing, call the `BeginRemoveFromDefaultAudioRouting` method. This causes your application to send a special command to the audio/video MCU. Only trusted conference participants are authorized to send this command; if the application sends the command as an ordinary conference leader, it gets an error message in response. In this way, the command to remove a participant from default audio routing is different from the various other MCU commands applications can send. It's also not an operation that conference leaders can perform through Lync.

The following code demonstrates removing participants from the default audio routing using the `BeginRemoveFromDefaultAudioRouting` method. It gets a collection containing references to all participants in the audio portion of the conference, and removes each one from the default audio routing for 60 seconds.

Available for download on Wrox.com

```
// Get a handle to the MCU session.
AudioVideoMcuSession mcuSession =
    conferenceConversation.ConferenceSession.AudioVideoMcuSession;

// Get a collection of the endpoints participating in the conference.
Collection<ParticipantEndpoint> participants =
    mcuSession.GetRemoteParticipantEndpoints();

// Set the duration of the removal to 60 seconds.
```

```
    // The participants will be returned to default routing after then.
    RemoveFromDefaultRoutingOptions options = new RemoveFromDefaultRoutingOptions()
    {
        Duration = new TimeSpan(0, 1, 0)
    };

    foreach (ParticipantEndpoint participant in participants)
    {
        try
        {
            // Remove each participant from the default audio routing.
            mcuSession.BeginRemoveFromDefaultRouting(participant, options,
                ar =>
                {
                    try
                    {
                        mcuSession.EndRemoveFromDefaultRouting(ar);

                        _logger.Log(
                            "Removed participant {0} from default audio routing.",
                            participant.Participant.Uri);
                    }
                    catch (RealTimeException ex)
                    {
                        _logger.Log(
                            "Failed removing participant from default audio routing.",
                                ex);
                    }
                },
                null
            );
        }
        catch (InvalidOperationException ex)
        {
            _logger.Log("Failed removing participant from default audio routing.", ex);
        }
    }
```

Code snippet AdvancedMediaControl\RemoveFromDefaultRoutingSample.cs

The effect of this code will be to prevent every conference participant from hearing or being heard by any other participant for one minute — perhaps a useful effect if you need to defuse an argument on a conference call. In practice, it is not much different from muting each conference participant, except that they will not appear as muted in the conference roster. However, you can combine it with manual audio routes, as described shortly, to create more complex audio routing arrangements.

Keep in mind that an application can join the same conference several times by using different `Conversation` instances. To call `BeginRemoveFromDefaultAudioRouting`, the application must use a `Conversation` with which it has joined as a trusted participant. The following code illustrates this.

```
// Create two conversations: one for normal join, the other for trusted join.
Conversation joinedAsNormalParticipantConversation = new Conversation(
    _appEndpoint);
Conversation joinedAsTrustedParticipantConversation = new Conversation(
    _appEndpoint);

// Join the conference normally on the first conversation.
ConferenceJoinOptions normalOptions = new ConferenceJoinOptions()
{
    JoinMode = JoinMode.Default
};

try
{
    joinedAsNormalParticipantConversation.ConferenceSession.BeginJoin(
        normalOptions,  OnNormalJoinCompleted, null);
}
catch (InvalidOperationException ex)
{
    _logger.Log("Failed joining conference.", ex);
}

// Join as a trusted participant on the second conversation.
ConferenceJoinOptions trustedOptions = new ConferenceJoinOptions()
{
    JoinMode = JoinMode.TrustedParticipant
};

try
{
    joinedAsTrustedParticipantConversation.ConferenceSession.BeginJoin(
        trustedOptions,  OnTrustedJoinCompleted, null);
}
catch (InvalidOperationException ex)
{
    _logger.Log("Failed joining conference.", ex);
}

// This will throw an exception.
joinedAsNormalParticipantConversation.ConferenceSession.
    AudioVideoMcuSession.BeginRemoveFromDefaultRouting(
    endpointToRemove, OnRemoveComplete, null);

// This will work fine.
joinedAsTrustedParticipantConversation.ConferenceSession.
    AudioVideoMcuSession.BeginRemoveFromDefaultRouting(
    endpointToRemove, OnRemoveComplete, null);
```

Because of this, any call managed by your application that needs custom audio routing must be joined to the conference using the trusted participant join mode.

Removing a Call from Default Audio Routing Automatically

Many cases exist in which an endpoint participating in a conference should be excluded from the default audio mixing from the very beginning. For instance, supervisors who are silently monitoring conversations do not need to be put into the default audio routing at all when first joining the conference. UCMA 3.0 allows you to specify when establishing a new call to an audio conference that the endpoint involved should be excluded from the default audio routing. To do this, create a `CallEstablishOptions` instance for the call, set `CallEstablishOptions` `.AudioVideoMcuDialInOptions.RemoveFromDefaultRouting` to true, and pass the `CallEstablishOptions` object as a parameter to the `BeginEstablish` method, as shown in the following code snippet.

```
// Specify that the call should be excluded
// from default audio routing.
AudioVideoCallEstablishOptions options = new AudioVideoCallEstablishOptions();
options.AudioVideoMcuDialInOptions.RemoveFromDefaultRouting = true;

// Establish the call using the CallEstablishOptions.
_call.BeginEstablish(options, OnEstablishCompleted, null);
```

As with `BeginRemoveFromDefaultAudioRouting`, this approach will only work if your application has joined the conference as a trusted participant on the conversation it is using for this call.

You can use a similar property on the `McuDialOutOptions` class, which defines options for an audio/video MCU dial-out, to keep new participants out of the default audio routing when dialing out to them directly from the MCU.

```
// Specify that the call should be excluded
// from default audio routing.
McuDialOutOptions options = new McuDialOutOptions();
options.RemoveFromDefaultRouting = true;

// Dial out using the McuDialOutOptions.
_mcuSesson.BeginDialOut(destinationUri, options, OnDialOutCompleted, null);
```

Adding a Participant Back into the Default Audio Routing

To return a participant back to the default audio routing, you can use the `BeginAddToDefaultAudioRouting` method. An endpoint that is added back to the default audio routing can once again hear and be heard by other participants in the audio conference. No way exists to specify a duration when adding a participant to the default audio routing, as there is when removing a participant.

The following code adds back a single participant who has previously been removed from default audio routing.

```
try
{
    // Add each participant to the default audio routing.
    mcuSession.BeginAddToDefaultRouting(participant,
        ar =>
        {
            try
            {
```

```
                    mcuSession.EndAddToDefaultRouting(ar);

                    _logger.Log("Added participant {0} to default audio routing.",
                        participant.Participant.Uri);
                }
                catch (RealTimeException ex)
                {
                    _logger.Log(
                        "Failed adding participant to default audio routing.", ex);
                }
            },
            null
        );
    }
    catch (InvalidOperationException ex)
    {
        _logger.Log(
            "Failed adding participant to default audio routing.", ex);
    }
```

Code snippet AdvancedMediaControl\RemoveFromDefaultRoutingSample.cs

 If the application has defined any custom audio routes for the participant, those must also be removed, as described in the next section. Adding a participant back into the default audio mix does not automatically clean up the manual audio routes.

Creating Custom MCU Audio Routes

Lync Server allows a trusted participant in an audio conference to supply a set of specific audio routing rules that the MCU will use to mix audio for that participant endpoint. These rules can control the mixing of both the outgoing audio from the endpoint and the incoming audio to the endpoint from other participants.

UCMA 3.0 provides access to these manual audio routes through the AudioVideoMcuRouting class. An AudioVideoMcuRouting object belongs to a single AudioVideoCall and can be referenced through the AudioVideoCall.AudioVideoMcuRouting property. It can only be used with an AudioVideoCall that is associated with a conference; it will not work with two-party calls.

Each modification of an audio routing rule is represented by an instance of AudioRoute .AudioRoute has two subclasses: IncomingAudioRoute is for changing the routing from other conference participants to the local participant; OutgoingAudioRoute is for changing the routing from the local participant to other conference participants.

Figure 12-8 illustrates the effect of a manual audio route. In the first section of the diagram, Guinevere has been removed from the default audio mix and cannot hear or be heard by the other participants, Dudley and Vernon. Note that Guinevere is a trusted conference participant, so she will not appear to the other participants in the conference roster.

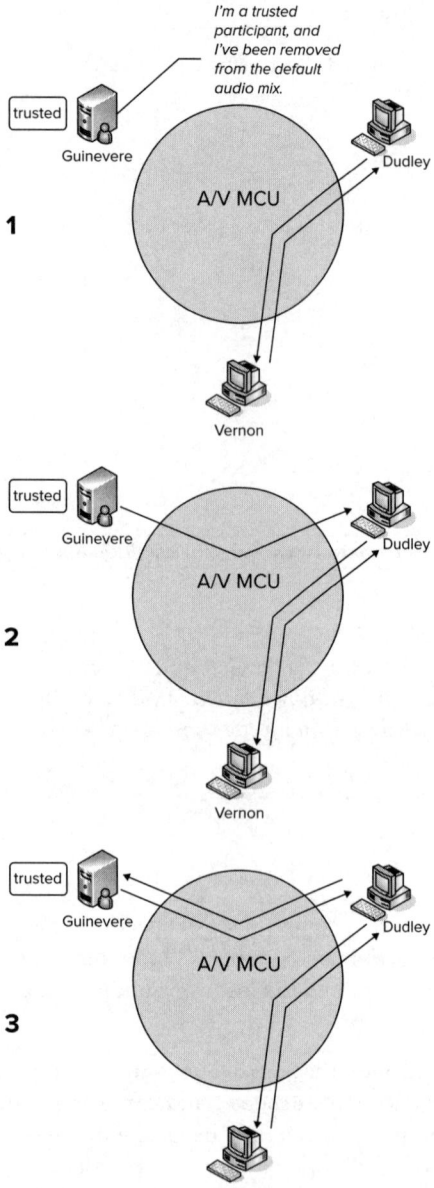

FIGURE 12-8

In the second section, an outgoing audio route has been added from her to Dudley, meaning that Dudley can hear Guinevere, but Guinevere cannot hear Dudley.

In the third section, an incoming audio route has also been added to Guinevere from Dudley. Now Guinevere and Dudley can hear each other, but Vernon still cannot hear Guinevere and Guinevere cannot hear Vernon.

If more than one conference participant provides manual audio routes, there can be routes that are redundant. For example, if Dudley adds an outgoing route to Guinevere, the effect is the same as if Guinevere adds an incoming route from Dudley.

Adding Manual Audio Routes

If long class names were less of a nuisance, calling the `AudioRoute` classes `IncomingAudioRouteOperation` and `OutgoingAudioRouteOperation` might have been more accurate, because they actually represent commands to the audio/video MCU to either add or remove incoming or outgoing audio routing rules. The following code initializes the `AudioRoute` objects to add incoming and outgoing routes to Dudley's endpoint in an audio conference.

```
private void AddRoutesToAndFromDudley(AudioVideoCall callToConference)
{
    AudioVideoMcuSession mcuSession =
        callToTheConference.Conversation.ConferenceSession.AudioVideoMcuSession;

    // Find the ParticipantEndpoint object that represents Dudley.
    ParticipantEndpoint dudleyParticipantEndpoint =
        mcuSession.GetRemoteParticipantEndpoints().FirstOrDefault(p =>
            p.Participant.Uri == "sip:dudley@wrox.com");

    if (dudleyParticipantEndpoint == null)
    {
        _logger.Log("Dudley not found in the conference.");
        return;
    }

    // Create an outgoing route to Dudley.
    OutgoingAudioRoute outgoingRoute =
        new OutgoingAudioRoute(dudleyParticipantEndpoint);
    outgoingRoute.Operation = RouteUpdateOperation.Add;

    // Create an incoming route from Dudley.
    IncomingAudioRoute incomingRoute =
        new IncomingAudioRoute(dudleyParticipantEndpoint);
    incomingRoute.Operation = RouteUpdateOperation.Add;

    // Still need to send the routes to the MCU...
}
```

To actually send the audio routing updates to the MCU, you must call the `BeginUpdateAudioRoutes` method on the audio call's `AudioVideoMcuRouting` class, as shown next.

Available for download on Wrox.com

```
private void AddRoutesToAndFromDudley(AudioVideoCall callToTheConference)
{
    AudioVideoMcuSession mcuSession =
        callToTheConference.Conversation.ConferenceSession.AudioVideoMcuSession;

    // Find the ParticipantEndpoint object that represents Dudley.
```

```
ParticipantEndpoint dudleyParticipantEndpoint =
    mcuSession.GetRemoteParticipantEndpoints().FirstOrDefault(p =>
        p.Participant.Uri == _dudleySipUri);

if (dudleyParticipantEndpoint == null)
{
    _logger.Log("Dudley not found in the conference.");
    return;
}

// Create an outgoing route to Dudley.
OutgoingAudioRoute outgoingRoute =
    new OutgoingAudioRoute(dudleyParticipantEndpoint);
outgoingRoute.Operation = RouteUpdateOperation.Add;

// Create an incoming route from Dudley.
IncomingAudioRoute incomingRoute =
    new IncomingAudioRoute(dudleyParticipantEndpoint);
incomingRoute.Operation = RouteUpdateOperation.Add;

try
{
    // Send the audio route updates to the MCU.
    callToTheConference.AudioVideoMcuRouting.BeginUpdateAudioRoutes(
        new List<OutgoingAudioRoute>() { outgoingRoute },
        new List<IncomingAudioRoute>() { incomingRoute },
        ar =>
        {
            try
            {
                callToTheConference.AudioVideoMcuRouting.EndUpdateAudioRoutes(
                    ar);
            }
            catch (RealTimeException ex)
            {
                _logger.Log("Failed updating audio routes.", ex);
            }
        },
        null
    );
}
catch (InvalidOperationException ex)
{
    _logger.Log("Failed updating audio routes.", ex);
}
}
```

Code snippet AdvancedMediaControl\ManualAudioRoutesSample.cs

Making the update through a command on the AudioVideoMcuSession object is not possible; the updates are specific to a single AudioVideoCall.

Removing Manual Audio Routes

If you need to remove the manual audio routes — before returning the endpoint to the default audio mix, for instance — you can simply change the `Operation` property on the `AudioRoute` objects, like so:

```
// Remove the outgoing route to Dudley.
OutgoingAudioRoute outgoingRoute =
    new OutgoingAudioRoute(dudleyParticipantEndpoint);
outgoingRoute.Operation = RouteUpdateOperation.Remove;

// Remove the incoming route from Dudley.
IncomingAudioRoute incomingRoute =
    new IncomingAudioRoute(dudleyParticipantEndpoint);
incomingRoute.Operation = RouteUpdateOperation.Remove;

try
{
    // Send the audio route updates to the MCU.
    callToTheConference.AudioVideoMcuRouting.BeginUpdateAudioRoutes(
        new List<OutgoingAudioRoute>() { outgoingRoute },
        new List<IncomingAudioRoute>() { incomingRoute },
        ar =>
        {
            try
            {
                callToTheConference.AudioVideoMcuRouting.EndUpdateAudioRoutes(ar);
            }
            catch (RealTimeException ex)
            {
                _logger.Log("Failed updating audio routes.", ex);
            }
        },
        null
    );
}
catch (InvalidOperationException ex)
{
    _logger.Log("Failed updating audio routes.", ex);
}
```

Code snippet AdvancedMediaControl\ManualAudioRoutesSample.cs

You should explicitly remove any custom audio routes when returning an endpoint to the default audio routing. They will not be removed automatically.

For convenience, you may want to store the `IncomingAudioRoute` *and* `OutgoingAudioRoute` *objects somewhere after you use them to add the custom routing rules so that you can use them later when removing the routing rules again, by flipping the* `Operation` *property on each one to* `Remove`.

Unfortunately, the `AudioVideoMcuRouting` *class does not provide any way to look up the routing rules currently active on the MCU, so maintaining this information locally is easiest.*

Manipulating Audio Routing for Remote Participants

Because the manual audio route updates are sent to the MCU through the `AudioVideoMcuRouting` instance, which belongs to a local `AudioVideoCall`, an application can only modify the audio routing rules for local participants. In other words, it needs to control the call between that participant and the audio/video MCU. For a reminder of how this works, take a look at Figure 12-9.

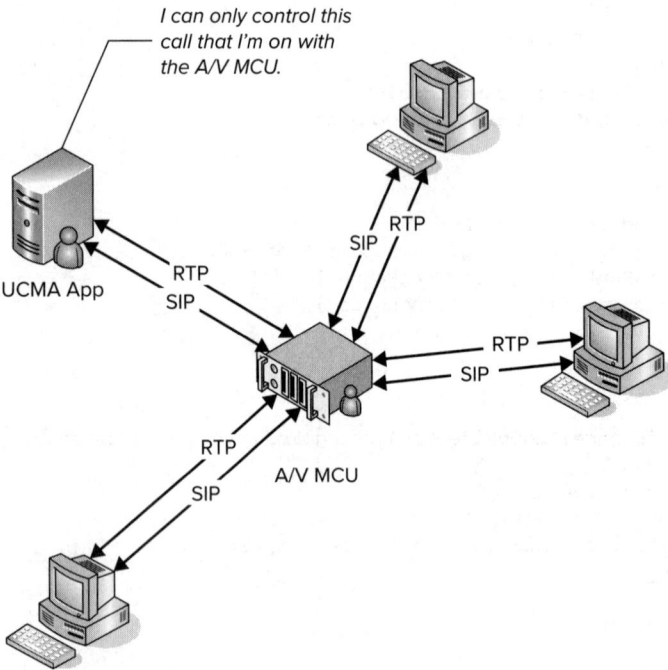

FIGURE 12-9

A UCMA application that joins a conference has its own audio call with the audio/video MCU that controls the conference. The other conference participants have their own calls with the audio/video MCU, which the UCMA application does not control.

You may be wondering whether a certain class from earlier in this chapter could be applied here. If so, your suspicions are correct. This is a perfect mission for the `BackToBackCall` class. Using a `BackToBackCall`, the UCMA application can broker the calls between remote participants and the audio/video MCU, and can then continue to rule over the SIP signaling on those calls with an iron fist — or at least specify manual audio routing rules for them. Figure 12-10 shows how a number of participants can all be connected with the audio conference through back-to-back calls.

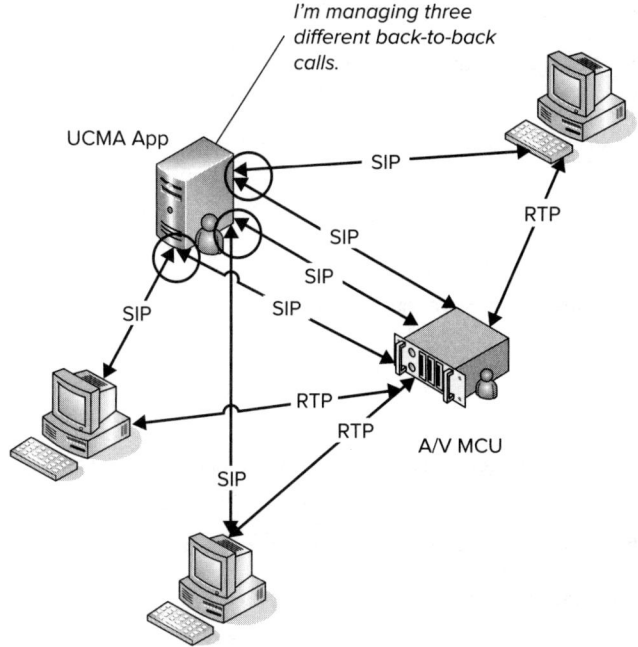

FIGURE 12-10

Keep in mind that the participants must still join the conference as trusted participants in order to have manual audio routes specified. This means that the call leg that connects to the conference must be joined to the conference with the join mode set to TrustedParticipant. Otherwise, the audio routing changes will not work.

The following code shows an incoming audio call handler that allows supervisors to silently and invisibly monitor a specific participant in a conference. The code creates a back-to-back call using the incoming call and a new call to the audio conference. On the outgoing call leg, it uses the identity of the original caller to join the conference, but joins as a trusted participant. It then adds an incoming audio route from the monitored participant to the supervisor. The effect is that the supervisor can hear only the monitored participant and cannot be heard or seen in the roster by any participants.

```
private void OnAudioVideoCallReceived(object sender,
    CallReceivedEventArgs<AudioVideoCall> args)
{
    AudioVideoCall incomingAudioCall = args.Call;

    // Create a new conversation for the call leg to the conference.
    Conversation conferenceLegConversation = new Conversation(_endpoint);

    // Impersonate the calling user when joining the conference.
    conferenceLegConversation.Impersonate(args.Call.RemoteEndpoint.Participant.Uri,
        args.Call.RemoteEndpoint.Participant.PhoneUri,
```

```
            args.Call.RemoteEndpoint.Participant.DisplayName);

// Must be a trusted participant for manual audio routes.
ConferenceJoinOptions joinOptions = new ConferenceJoinOptions()
{
    JoinMode = JoinMode.TrustedParticipant
};

try
{
    // Join the conference.
    conferenceLegConversation.ConferenceSession.BeginJoin(_conferenceUri,
        joinOptions,
        joinResult =>
        {
            try
            {
                conferenceLegConversation.ConferenceSession.EndJoin(
                    joinResult);

                // Create the audio call for the outgoing call leg.
                AudioVideoCall conferenceCallLeg =
                    new AudioVideoCall(conferenceLegConversation);

                BackToBackCallSettings incomingCallSettings =
                    new BackToBackCallSettings(incomingAudioCall);
                BackToBackCallSettings outgoingCallSettings =
                    new BackToBackCallSettings(conferenceCallLeg);

                // Remove the enpdoint from the default routing initially.
                AudioVideoCallEstablishOptions options = new
                    AudioVideoCallEstablishOptions();
                options.AudioVideoMcuDialInOptions.RemoveFromDefaultRouting =
                    true;

                outgoingCallSettings.CallEstablishOptions = options;

                // Initialize a back to back call.
                BackToBackCall b2bCall =
                    new BackToBackCall(incomingCallSettings,
                        outgoingCallSettings);

                EstablishBackToBackCall(b2bCall);
            }
            catch (RealTimeException ex)
            {
                _logger.Log("Failed joining conference.", ex);
            }
        },
        null
    );
}
catch (InvalidOperationException ex)
{
```

```
                _logger.Log("Failed joining conference.", ex);
        }
}

private void EstablishBackToBackCall(BackToBackCall b2bCall)
{
    try
    {
        // Begin establishing the back to back call.
        b2bCall.BeginEstablish(
            establishResult =>
            {
                try
                {
                    b2bCall.EndEstablish(establishResult);

                    // Create an incoming route from the participant
                    // that is being monitored to this endpoint.
                    IncomingAudioRoute incomingRoute =
                        new IncomingAudioRoute(_participantToMonitor);
                    incomingRoute.Operation = RouteUpdateOperation.Add;

                    AudioVideoCall conferenceCallLeg =
                        b2bCall.Call2 as AudioVideoCall;

                    try
                    {
                        // Update the audio routing with the new incoming route.
                        conferenceCallLeg.AudioVideoMcuRouting.
                            BeginUpdateAudioRoutes(
                            null,
                            new List<IncomingAudioRoute>() { incomingRoute },
                            routeResult =>
                            {
                                try
                                {
                                    conferenceCallLeg.AudioVideoMcuRouting.
                                        EndUpdateAudioRoutes(routeResult);
                                }
                                catch (RealTimeException ex)
                                {
                                    _logger.Log("Failed updating audio routes.",
                                        ex);
                                }
                            },
                            null
                        );
                    }
                    catch (InvalidOperationException ex)
                    {
                        _logger.Log("Failed updating audio routes.", ex);
                    }
                }
                catch (RealTimeException ex)
```

```
                    {
                         _logger.Log("Failed establishing call.", ex);
                    }
                },
                null
            );
        }
        catch (InvalidOperationException ex)
        {
            _logger.Log("Failed establishing call.", ex);
        }
    }
```

Code snippet AdvancedMediaControl\ManualAudioRoutesBackToBackSample.cs

You can join as many users as necessary to the conference through back-to-back calls in your application, as long as the application uses a different SIP URI each time it joins.

SUMMARY

In this chapter you have seen the many options UCMA provides for controlling media on audio calls. This advanced functionality allows developers to create complex communication management services such as automatic call distributors and virtual assistants.

In building and deploying such complex applications, developers inevitably run into confusing errors and challenging debugging situations. The asynchronous nature of UCMA and its dependencies on an intricate server infrastructure only compound the difficulty. The next chapter presents some techniques to aid troubleshooting and debugging, as well as some common problems that developers run into with UC development.

13

Debugging UCMA Applications

WHAT'S IN THIS CHAPTER?

➤   Using Lync Server Debugging Tools

➤   Interpreting SIP Message Logs

➤   Using Quality of Experience Metrics

➤   Troubleshooting Common UCMA Issues

Two factors make troubleshooting a particularly important topic for UCMA development. One is that because UCMA takes the low-level work of managing connections and Session Initiation Protocol (SIP) messaging away from the developer, putting together a working application often takes very little time. Another is that because UCMA applications have so many dependencies on the surrounding Lync and network infrastructure, many possible sources of trouble exist outside of the application's own code. Because of these two factors together, UCMA developers can expect to spend a large percentage of their time on troubleshooting, and must be relatively proficient in digging out the causes of problems even when they arise from the environment rather than the application itself.

Building simple UCMA applications without any knowledge of SIP or of Lync Server infrastructure and configuration is quite possible. However, the authors believe that, in order to be successful at developing full UCMA applications meant for production use, developers must understand at least the basics of what is going on "under the covers." This chapter, therefore, has two aims: one is to detail the best practices for creating stable UCMA code that is easy to debug and for troubleshooting some of the most common issues that UCMA applications experience; the other is to show what in the process *causes* these issues and what they look like at the level of SIP signaling, so that developers have the necessary tools to debug more obscure issues on their own.

USING LOGS AND SERVER TRACES

The first line of defense in the UCMA developer's debugging arsenal is the venerable `OCSLogger` `.exe` tool, still named for Lync's predecessor, Office Communications Server. This tool controls the collection of the various logs generated by Lync Server. A second source of logs is the Lync client, which you can set to write log messages both to the Windows Event Log and to a separate plain-text log file.

Using Lync Server Logs

The main benefit of Lync server logs in troubleshooting issues with UCMA applications is that the server logs can show the SIP messages that are sent back and forth between the application's endpoints and other Lync endpoints. Looking at the flow of SIP messages can often elucidate problems that would otherwise be completely bewildering. These problems may be environmental (issues with the configuration of Lync Server or the application server, for example) or in the code of the application (incorrect use of UCMA).

Getting into the habit of collecting logs from the Lync front-end server whenever troubleshooting an issue with a UCMA application, after verifying that it does not stem from an obvious code problem, is a good idea. This section explains how to collect these logs with the OCSLogger tool and how to read the logs for information that can help with debugging and troubleshooting.

 On many SIP-based communication platforms, it is common to use a network sniffer such as Wireshark to gather information for troubleshooting. Because Lync uses transport-layer security (TLS) by default, network sniffers are usually not useful.

If you want to use Wireshark or another sniffer to examine SIP traffic, it is possible to switch the Lync client to use TCP rather than TLS. To do this, go to the Options dialog box, Personal section, and clicking the Advanced button. In the resulting dialog box, it is possible to make manual changes to the server settings, including using TCP instead of TLS.

Collecting Logs with the Logging Tool

On any Lync server, the default install location for the logging tool is `Program Files\Common` `Files\Micrsosoft Lync Server 2010\Tracing\OCSLogger.exe`. When opened, the logging tool displays the window shown in Figure 13-1. The options in the Components list will vary depending on the server where the tool is running.

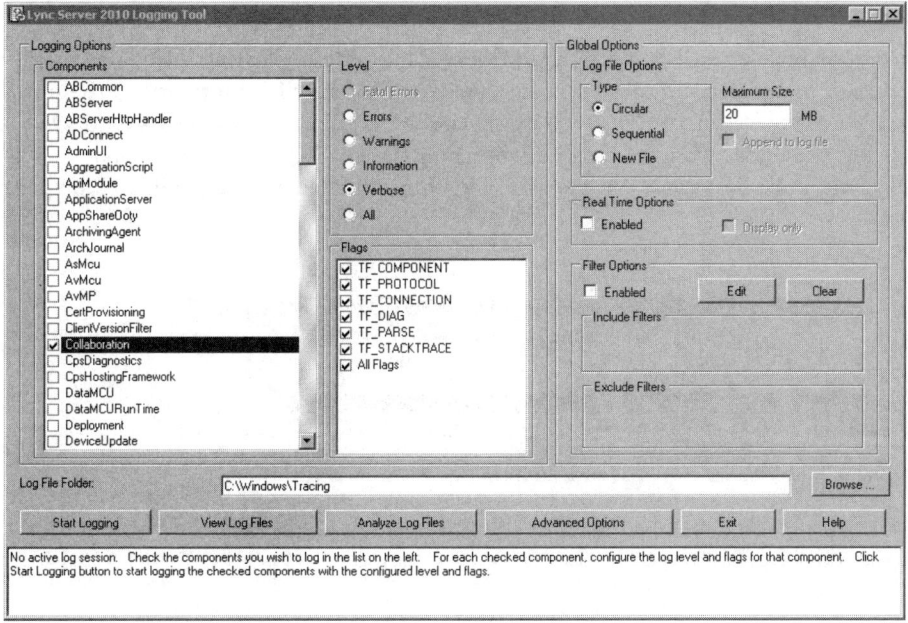

FIGURE 13-1

Before starting the logging, first choose one or more types of activity to log using the Components list. Generally, the most useful items to select when debugging UCMA applications are SIPStack, Collaboration, and S4 (or the latter two on application servers, where SIPStack is generally not available).

 To select an item in the Components list, click it once to select it and then click it again to mark the checkbox. The items are not marked with a check on the first click, which can be confusing.

For each item in the Components list, setting additional logging options using the Level and Flags settings is also possible. For the most part, the defaults are fine when doing UCMA troubleshooting. Depending on the amount of traffic on the server, increasing the maximum size of the log file may be helpful.

To begin logging, click Start Logging at the bottom of the window. While logging is active, perform whatever operation needs to be logged, and then click Stop Logging to end the logging session.

Viewing Lync Server Logs

Two options are available for reading through Lync Server logs after collecting them. The first is to output the log details to a text file, which you can then search for specific information. To do this, click View Log Files at the bottom of the OCSLogger window. A dialog box appears with a list of the components for which logs were collected, as shown in Figure 13-2. Select the ones that should appear in the text file, and click View. The generated log file will open automatically in Notepad.

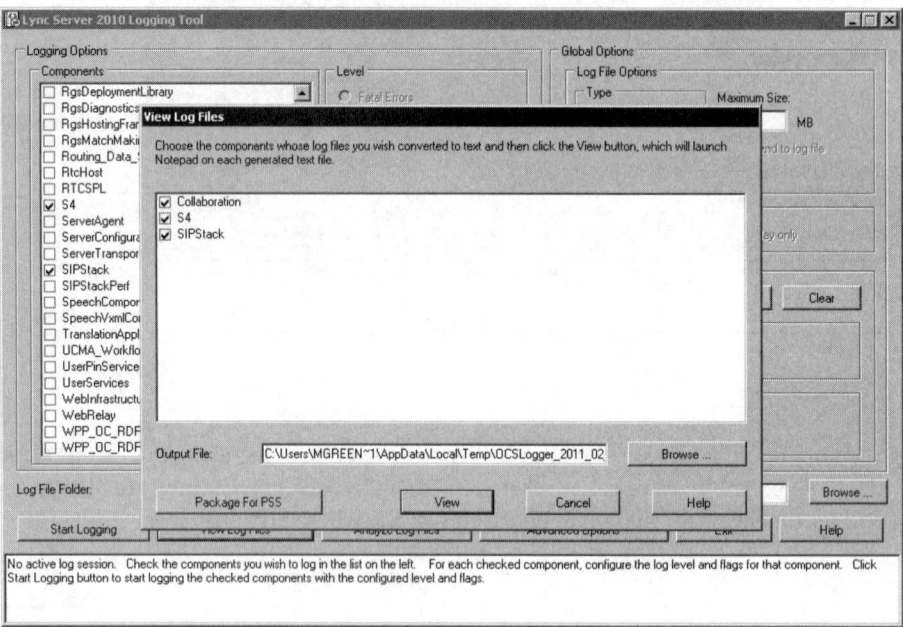

FIGURE 13-2

Although Notepad can be quite adequate for browsing small log files or for searching for specific items, following the sequence of events in a longer log file simply by reading through the generated text can be quite challenging. Where a more readable view is necessary, the `Snooper.exe` tool can be invaluable.

Snooper is included in a package of tools known as the Microsoft Lync Server 2010 Resource Kit Tools. The Resource Kit Tools are available for download on Microsoft's website at `www.microsoft.com/downloads/en/details.aspx?FamilyID=80cc5ce7-970d-4fd2-8731-d5d7d0829266`. After the Resource Kit Tools are installed, you can open a log in Snooper automatically by clicking Analyze Log Files in the OCSLogger window.

Snooper displays log data in a more graphical form, as shown in Figure 13-3. It breaks down the log messages into a list, showing individual SIP messages or events along with the timestamp and From and To addresses, if applicable. Clicking on an item in the list causes the full contents of the message or event to be shown in the pane on the right-hand side. In addition, when a message that is part of a larger SIP dialog is selected in the list, other messages related to that dialog are highlighted, so that you can more easily follow the full sequence of events without being distracted by unrelated messages.

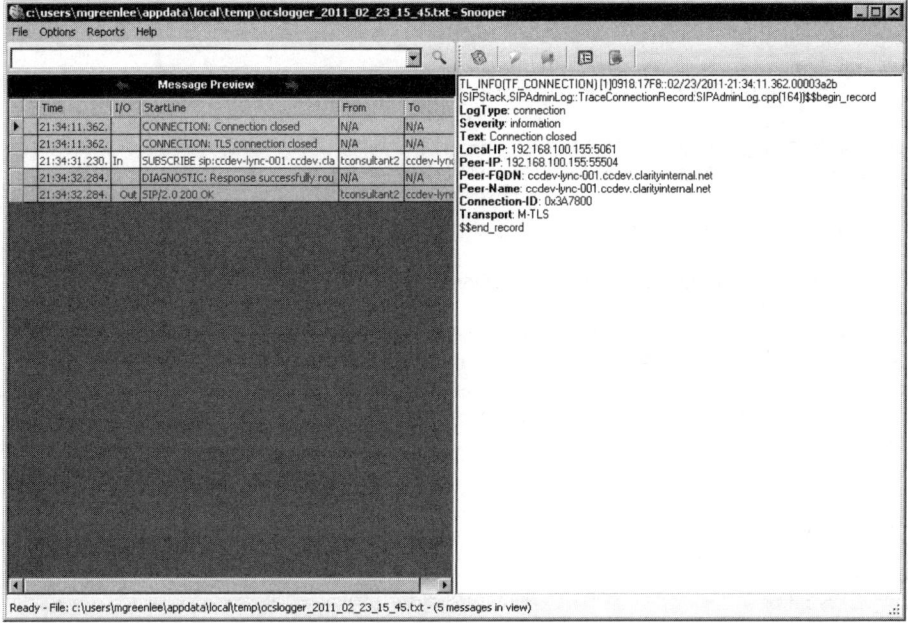

FIGURE 13-3

Whenever possible, the authors recommend viewing log data in Snooper rather than trying to sift through the logs in text format in Notepad.

Interpreting SIP Messages in Server Logs

Particularly where troubleshooting is concerned, we believe that the best way to learn is by doing. For learning how to read the logs of SIP messages between servers, no substitute exists for simply reading lots of logs. This section, however, aims to accelerate this process a bit by presenting log files that show some common scenarios and walking through the SIP messages step by step.

Rest assured that after you have gained a basic level of familiarity with interpreting the SIP messaging in Lync server logs, it will be one of the most useful tools in troubleshooting Lync issues.

The following samples use scenarios from the sample applications used in earlier chapters.

Reading SIP Requests

The SIP messages contained in logs can, at a first glance, look overwhelmingly complicated. Understanding the purpose of the different pieces is helpful. Take a look at the following message, which is a typical request message; this one is for an INVITE request.

```
TL_INFO(TF_PROTOCOL) [1]0B1C.0134::02/26/2011-19:06:25.589.00012892
(SIPStack,SIPAdminLog::TraceProtocolRecord:SIPAdminLog.cpp(125))
$$begin_record
Trace-Correlation-Id: 2287832666
Instance-Id: 00026800
Direction: incoming
Peer: ts.fabrikam.com:31732
Message-Type: request
Start-Line: INVITE sip:michaelg@fabrikam.com SIP/2.0
From: "Outbound"<sip:outbound.sample@fabrikam.com>;epid=531E0B2242;
tag=125787b6d0
To: <sip:michaelg@fabrikam.com>
CSeq: 3 INVITE
Call-ID: 4a8b77c4-4be2-4403-896a-94e1c7e6a9c3
MAX-FORWARDS: 70
VIA: SIP/2.0/TLS 192.168.0.40:31732;branch=z9hG4bK83dda982
CONTACT: <sip:ts.fabrikam.com@fabrikam.com;gruu;
opaque=srvr:outbound.sample:jRw31iBwA16ogIm8sXN68AAA>;
automata;actor="attendant";text;audio;video;image
CONTENT-LENGTH: 146
EXPIRES: 600
PRIORITY: Normal
SUPPORTED: ms-dialog-route-set-update
SUPPORTED: timer
SUPPORTED: ms-delayed-accept
SUPPORTED: ms-sender
SUPPORTED: gruu-10
USER-AGENT: RTCC/4.0.0.0 maximillian
CONTENT-TYPE: application/sdp
ALLOW: ACK
P-ASSERTED-IDENTITY: "Outbound"<sip:outbound.sample@fabrikam.com>
Content-ID: f2952165-0d4c-40df-84b2-20fa019f156b
Ms-Conversation-ID: fcce26bdf97845d4b4762abc08559857
Session-Expires: 1800
Min-SE: 90
Allow: CANCEL,BYE,INVITE,MESSAGE,INFO,SERVICE,
OPTIONS,BENOTIFY,NOTIFY,UPDATE
Message-Body: v=0
o=- 835763695 835763695 IN IP4 67.104.203.240
s=session
t=0 0
m=message 5060 sip null
a=accept-types:text/plain application/ms-imdn+xml
$$end_record
```

The first few lines identify it as a SIP message and indicate the beginning of the message record. Most importantly, they also show the date and time stamp, as shown in the following snippet.

```
TL_INFO(TF_PROTOCOL) [1]0B1C.0134::02/26/2011-19:06:25.589.00012892
(SIPStack,SIPAdminLog::TraceProtocolRecord:SIPAdminLog.cpp(125))
$$begin_record
```

The next few lines contain some background information on the message. Again, several simple pieces of information are in here that can come in handy. The `Direction` line indicates whether the message came into the server where the log was run, or was sent out from it. The `Peer` line shows the address and port that the message came from or was sent to, and the `Message-Type` line shows whether this message is a request or a response.

```
Trace-Correlation-Id: 2287832666
Instance-Id: 00026800
Direction: incoming
Peer: ts.fabrikam.com:31732
Message-Type: request
```

The `Start-Line` label indicates the beginning of the actual SIP message. Everything following this, up to $$end_record at the bottom of the log record, is part of the SIP message itself.

In a request, the first line of the message contains the method name (in this case, `INVITE`), the destination of the message, and the protocol, as shown in the following snippet.

```
INVITE sip:michaelg@fabrikam.com SIP/2.0
```

Table 13-1 shows SIP methods and in which cases you will most commonly see them.

TABLE 13-1: SIP Methods and UCMA Operations

METHOD	RELEVANT UCMA OPERATIONS
INVITE	Establishing a call
	Sending a conference invitation
	Connecting to a conference focus
	Connecting to a multipoint control unit (MCU)
BYE	Ending a call
REFER	Transferring a call
SUBSCRIBE	Subscribing to presence
	Watching a transfer's progress in an attended transfer
REGISTER	Establishing an endpoint
NOTIFY	Receiving presence updates
BENOTIFY	Receiving updates on a transfer in progress
INFO	Sending conference control commands
SERVICE	Publishing presence

The next two headers are fairly self-explanatory: From identifies the source of the message, and To identifies the destination.

```
From: "Outbound"<sip:outbound.sample@fabrikam.com>;epid=531E0B2242;
tag=125787b6d0
To: <sip:michaelg@fabrikam.com>
```

The extra stuff on the end of the SIP URI in the From header helps identify this specific endpoint — keep in mind that a user can be signed in at multiple endpoints using the same SIP URI.

The CSeq header gives a sequence number for the request; for example, 3 INVITE means that this is the third INVITE sent by the endpoint.

```
CSeq: 3 INVITE
```

The next header, Call-ID, uniquely identifies this particular call or SIP dialog. This header maps to the CallId property on the Call class.

```
Call-ID: 4a8b77c4-4be2-4403-896a-94e1c7e6a9c3
```

Further along in the headers is the Ms-Conversation-ID header, which corresponds to the Id property on the Conversation class. This ID ties together messages from the same conversation, whether it includes one or more calls.

```
Ms-Conversation-ID: fcce26bdf97845d4b4762abc08559857
```

The message has quite a few other headers, but going into detail on each one is not necessary, because many of them are less useful in troubleshooting.

The body of the message, however, is often worth examining. The CONTENT-TYPE header identifies what is contained in the body. In this case, for example, application/sdp identifies the message body as information in Session Description Protocol (SDP), which is used for media negotiation:

```
CONTENT-TYPE: application/sdp
```

Before delving in to the various types of content that can be found in SIP message bodies, it is worth mentioning a few points about the structure of SIP responses.

Reading SIP Responses

A response to a SIP request looks relatively similar in structure to a SIP request, but a few key differences exist. The following is a typical SIP response, a 100 Trying response to an INVITE.

```
TL_INFO(TF_PROTOCOL) [1]0B1C.0134::02/26/2011-19:06:25.600.000128b0
(SIPStack,SIPAdminLog::TraceProtocolRecord:SIPAdminLog.cpp(125))
$$begin_record
Trace-Correlation-Id: 2287832666
Instance-Id: 00026801
Direction: outgoing;source="local"
Peer: ts.fabrikam.com:31732
```

```
Message-Type: response
Start-Line: SIP/2.0 100 Trying
From: "Outbound"<sip:outbound.sample@fabrikam.com>;epid=531E0B2242;
tag=125787b6d0
To: <sip:michaelg@fabrikam.com>
CSeq: 3 INVITE
Call-ID: 4a8b77c4-4be2-4403-896a-94e1c7e6a9c3
Via: SIP/2.0/TLS 192.168.0.40:31732;branch=z9hG4bK83dda982;
ms-received-port=31732;ms-received-cid=B0FC00
Server: http%3A%2F%2Fwww.microsoft.com%2FLCS%2FDefaultRouting
Content-Length: 0
Message-Body: -
$$end_record
```

The start line of a SIP response is slightly different from the start line of a request, beginning with SIP/2.0 to identify the protocol, and then the response code, 100 Trying. Another important point to note is that the From and To headers reflect the source and destination of the *request*, not this response. In this case, for example, the response itself is going from sip:michaelg@fabrikam.com back to sip:outbound.sample@fabrikam.com, but the From header shows sip:outbound.sample @fabrikam.com because that is the source of the original request.

Responses, like requests, can have a message body, or, as in this case, the body can be empty.

Reading a Session Description Protocol Message Body

Session Description Protocol, commonly known as SDP, is defined in RFC (Request for Comments) 4566 from the Internet Engineering Task Force (IETF). Lync uses SDP to communicate information about how media can be sent and received while establishing a call. An elementary understanding of SDP can be helpful for troubleshooting problems with media, such as:

➤ Calls failing after the recipient picks up

➤ Calls with no audio

➤ One-way audio

➤ Instant messages not reaching their destination after a call is established

This section explains what the various sections of a typical SDP message mean. You can find further details in Microsoft's protocol document at http://msdn.microsoft.com/en-us/library/cc245962%28v=prot.10%29.aspx.

The subsequent explanations refer to the following sample SDP message from an audio call:

```
v=0
o=- 1 0 IN IP4 192.168.0.40
s=session
c=IN IP4 192.168.0.40
b=CT:3000000
t=0 0
m=audio 14594 RTP/SAVP 112 111 0 8 116 4 13 118 97 101
c=IN IP4 192.168.0.40
a=rtcp:14595
a=candidate:2qSHSQ/8dAz9eZzHkU3Sw5fnzGo2G2pII+qAvnEYCcY
```

```
1 zOV7tDyAvVsb7AdLZk3x7g UDP 0.840 192.168.0.40 14594
a=candidate:2qSHSQ/8dAz9eZzHkU3Sw5fnzGo2G2pII+qAvnEYCcY
2 zOV7tDyAvVsb7AdLZk3x7g UDP 0.840 192.168.0.40 14595
a=label:main-audio
a=cryptoscale:1 client AES_CM_128_HMAC_SHA1_80
inline:bOBFVN0YiwxaDRVdMCRYkyOxwRqSIcnhEzvkqXQ5|2^31|1:1
a=crypto:2 AES_CM_128_HMAC_SHA1_80 inline:
CxmLl7y+FaMLXhjYA6AfKXJfu3nRTnP
vprl46Lwr|2^31|1:1
a=crypto:3 AES_CM_128_HMAC_SHA1_80 inline:
LAWG4gX4qhf51ajsGZMQo0BlEZ+b32rbpQsNO5hm|2^31
a=rtpmap:112 G7221/16000
a=fmtp:112 bitrate=24000
a=rtpmap:111 SIREN/16000
a=fmtp:111 bitrate=16000
a=rtpmap:0 PCMU/8000
a=rtpmap:8 PCMA/8000
a=rtpmap:116 AAL2-G726-32/8000
a=rtpmap:4 G723/8000
a=rtpmap:13 CN/8000
a=rtpmap:118 CN/16000
a=rtpmap:97 RED/8000
a=rtpmap:101 telephone-event/8000
a=fmtp:101 0-16,36
--27chH1tS8EX9p0ksH4Kw2mgfokIFmrGh
```

The first few lines of the message are not particularly important for troubleshooting, and mostly contain boilerplate items like the version of SDP (always 0) and the IP address from which the message originates:

```
v=0
o=- 1 0 IN IP4 192.168.0.40
s=session
c=IN IP4 192.168.0.40
b=CT:3000000
t=0 0
```

The next line, beginning with m=, identifies a media type, in this case audio:

```
m=audio 14594 RTP/SAVP 112 111 0 8 116 4 13 118 97 101
```

After the media type is a port number, followed by the protocol. For audio calls, this is usually RTP/SAVP, which denotes Secure Real-time Transport Protocol, or SRTP. This means that media streams for this call are encrypted. RTP/AVP denotes ordinary (unencrypted) Real-time Transport Protocol.

Instant message calls use a value of message for the media type, and sip for the protocol, because the media (in this case, text) is conveyed using additional SIP messages. The message excerpt below illustrates this: It indicates that IM messages will be conveyed via SIP messages on port 5060.

```
m=message 5060 sip null
```

The next item of interest (in audio calls only) is the section containing *media candidates*. Media candidates offer options for locations where media can be routed and are used in the media negotiation process:

```
a=candidate:2qSHSQ/8dAz9eZzHkU3Sw5fnzGo2G2pII+qAvnEYCcY
1 z0V7tDyAvVsb7AdLZk3x7g UDP 0.840 192.168.0.40 14594
a=candidate:2qSHSQ/8dAz9eZzHkU3Sw5fnzGo2G2pII+qAvnEYCcY
2 z0V7tDyAvVsb7AdLZk3x7g UDP 0.840 192.168.0.40 14595
```

The last few items on each media candidate line show the protocol (TCP or UDP), IP address, and port where media can be routed. For the call to succeed, at least one of these must be reachable from the remote endpoint. In this example, for instance, both media candidates contain internal IP addresses that would not be routable from the public Internet. Sometimes, because of DNS configuration issues, contacts outside the local network will be given media candidates that are not routable from the public Internet, leading to call failures. Troubleshooting these issues is outside the scope of this book, but you can identify them through a quick look at the media candidates.

Using Lync Client Logs

To enable logging in the Lync client, open the Options window in Lync, go to the General section if it is not already selected, and select "Turn on Logging in Lync" and "Turn on Windows Event Logging for Lync." Figure 13-4 shows the Options window with these two options selected.

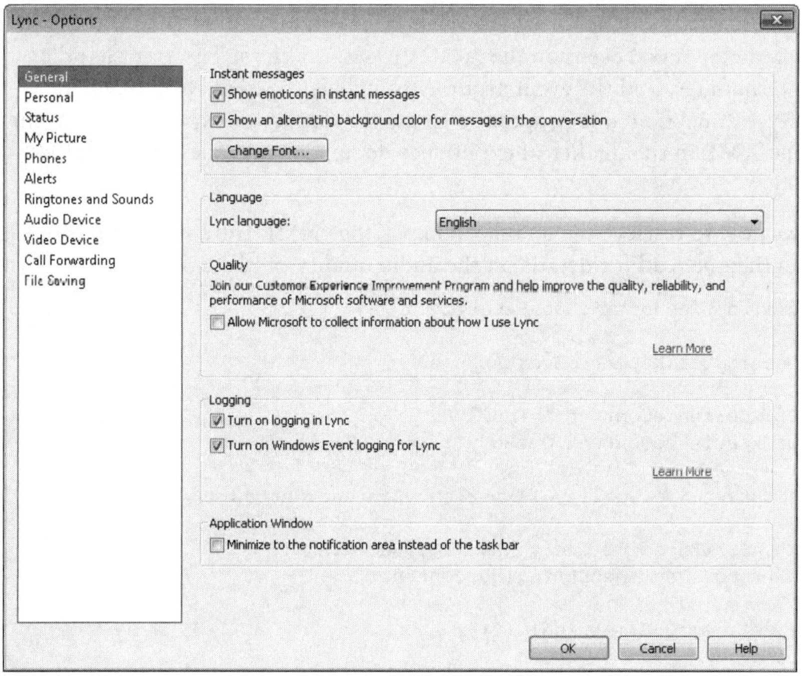

FIGURE 13-4

After Lync client logging is enabled, Lync will write trace files within the `%userprofile%\Tracing` directory.

The easiest of these files to use are the ones with a `.uccapilog` extension. Open these files in a text editor to see log entries from the Lync client, including SIP messages sent and received. Most of the time, you can find this same information more easily in the Lync server logs, but occasionally the client logs can be handy in figuring out what messages are reaching the Lync client and at what time.

USING QUALITY OF EXPERIENCE METRICS IN UCMA

Because the audio on a Lync call must be processed and transmitted in real time, performance issues either on the client or the server side can lead to degradation in the audio quality. Although most of the time these effects, when they appear, are simply annoying, they can occasionally make conversation impossible.

Troubleshooting audio quality problems within a Lync server environment is not usually a developer responsibility and is beyond the scope of this book. However, statistics on audio quality and network conditions during calls can be helpful in backing up reports of audio issues with concrete data, or in identifying the source at a high level. In addition, in deploying UCMA applications, collecting statistics on call quality to ensure that the environment can support the expected load without audio degradation can sometimes be helpful.

For these purposes, UCMA offers a way for applications to receive reports of audio quality metrics on the termination of each audio call.

To receive quality of experience data, an application can subscribe to the `MediaTroubleshootingDataReported` event on the `AudioVideoCall` class. The event handler is invoked when the call terminates, and the event arguments include the quality of experience data in the (`QualityOfExperienceContent` property). To use the quality of experience data, the application must parse the XML in the quality of experience document to retrieve the specific statistics that it needs.

The following code shows how to retrieve the quality of experience XML from the event arguments. This XML document can then be read for details on the audio quality on the call.

```
private void OnMediaTroubleshootingDataReported(
    object sender,
    MediaTroubleshootingDataReportedEventArgs e)
{
    if (e.QualityOfExperienceContent != null &&
        e.QualityOfExperienceContent.GetBody() != null)
    {
        byte[] qoeContent = e.QualityOfExperienceContent.GetBody();

        System.Text.ASCIIEncoding enc = new ASCIIEncoding();
        string qoeString = enc.GetString(qoeContent);

        Console.WriteLine("QoE metrics: {0}",
            qoeString);
    }
}
```

TROUBLESHOOTING COMMON UCMA ISSUES

A large share of the issues developers encounter when testing or deploying their UCMA applications are the result of a few underlying causes. Understanding these underlying problems can save developers a good deal of frustration, especially when starting out in UCMA development. This section covers several of these common problems and their solutions.

Troubleshooting TLS Exceptions

Almost every developer starting out with UCMA has encountered and been bewildered by a `TlsException`. This exception indicates that UCMA is having trouble with transport layer security (TLS), which the majority of UCMA applications use to communicate with other Lync servers in a secure manner.

Lync makes extensive use of mutual transport-layer security (MTLS) in establishing secure connections between Lync servers. Each server authenticates itself to the other using private key certificates. In the case of a UCMA application, this means that the Lync front-end server verifies the identity of the UCMA application server and the application server also checks the identity of the front-end server.

Most often, a `TlsException` occurs because of a problem with the certificates that Lync uses for MTLS. The next few sections cover the typical causes of such certificate problems.

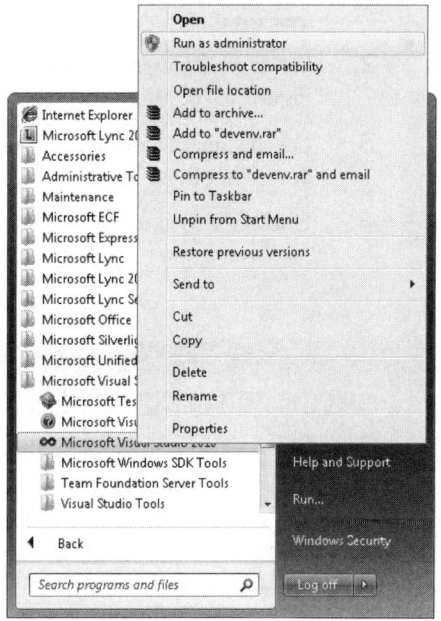

Fixing TLS Exceptions in Visual Studio

New UCMA developers most commonly encounter their first `TlsException` when debugging UCMA applications in Visual Studio. The reason is usually that the Visual Studio process does not have the necessary permissions to access the private key certificate that UCMA needs to authenticate itself to the Lync front-end server. The solution to a `TlsException` in this case is to close Visual Studio and reopen it with administrator privileges. You can do this by right-clicking in Visual Studio and selecting Run As Administrator from the menu, as shown in Figure 13-5.

FIGURE 13-5

Handling TLS Exceptions When Running an Application

TLS exceptions occur because an application that is trying to connect to Lync Server using TLS either does not supply a certificate for the collaboration platform or supplies a certificate that is not trusted by Lync Server. This can happen for a number of reasons:

➤ No TLS certificate is installed on the application server.

➤ A TLS certificate is installed, but it does not have the correct subject name (the fully qualified domain name of the application server).

➤ A TLS certificate exists, but it is not issued by a certification authority (CA) that is trusted by Lync.

➤ The TLS certificate installed on the Lync Front End Server is not issued by a CA that is trusted by the application server.

➤ The UCMA application is running under a user account that does not have permission to access the certificate private key.

➤ The UCMA application is not retrieving the certificate correctly from the certificate store.

When an application is throwing a `TlsException` on startup, first check that it is running with the proper credentials. Running the application as an administrator is a quick way to check whether permissions are the problem. The later section "Resolving Certificate Permission Issues" discusses how to fix TLS exceptions that are caused by insufficient permissions.

If this does not seem to be the issue, quickly verifying that a TLS certificate is installed on the server whose subject name is the FQDN of the server is worth the time. To do this, follow these steps:

1. Open Microsoft Management Console (MMC) by clicking Start ➪ Run and entering `mmc.exe`.

2. When MMC opens, choose File ➪ Add/Remove Snap-in. Select Certificates, as shown in Figure 13-6, and click Add to add the Certificates snap-in.

3. On the Select Computer dialog box that appears, choose Computer account, click Next, and then click Finish.

4. Click OK to exit the Add/Remove Snap-ins dialog box.

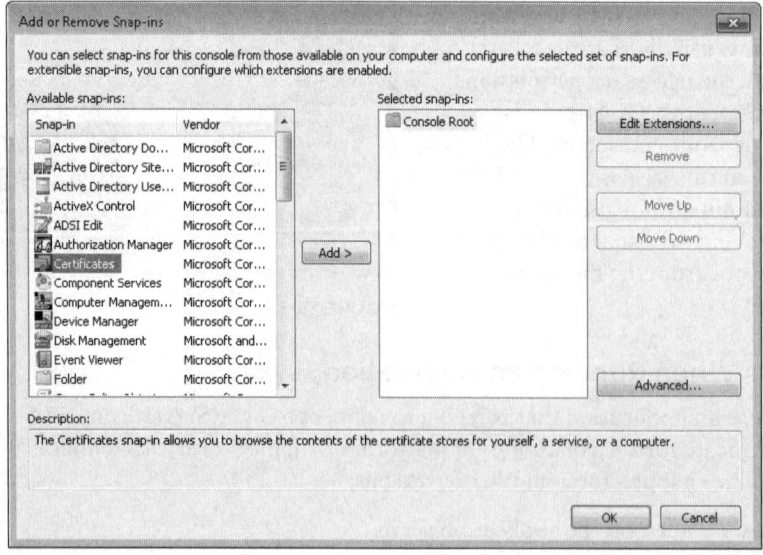

FIGURE 13-6

5. After the Certificates snap-in loads, expand the items on the left side of the window to locate the Certificates folder within the Personal folder, as shown in Figure 13-7, and verify that the TLS certificate is present.

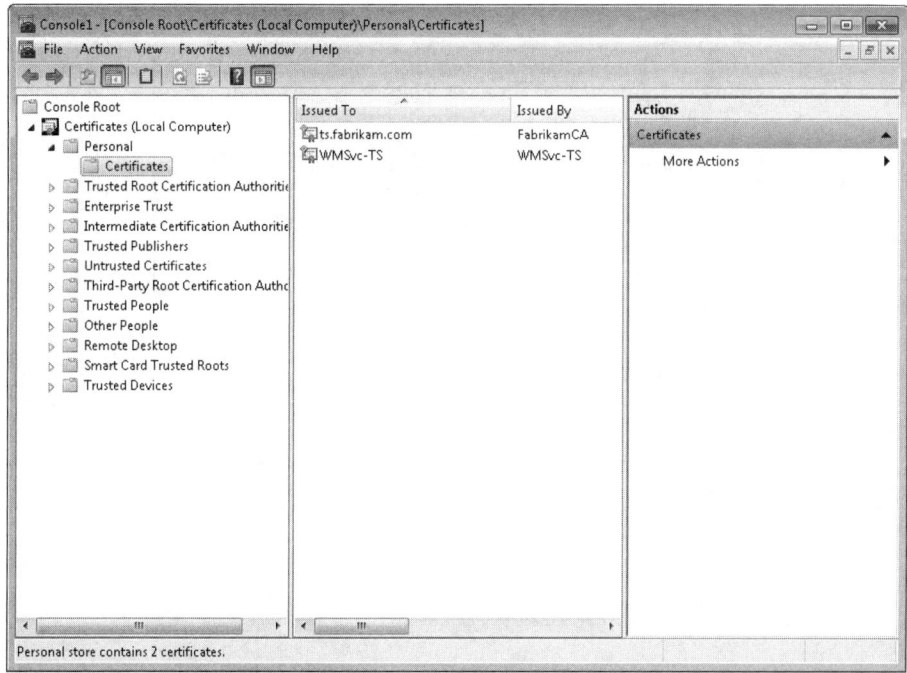

FIGURE 13-7

The later section "Fixing Certificate Setup Problems" details what to do if the certificate is not present or is not configured properly.

Resolving Certificate Permission Issues

To use the TLS certificate on the application server, a UCMA application must be running with a Windows identity that has permission to access the certificate's private key. If the application is running using a service account, granting that service account access to the private key may be necessary.

To do this, follow these steps:

1. Open MMC by clicking Start ⇨ Run and entering `mmc.exe`.

2. Add the Certificates snap-in as described in the "Handling TLS Exceptions When Running an Application" section and find the TLS certificate within the Personal folder — the subject name will match the FQDN of the application server.

3. Right-click on the certificate and choose All Tasks ⇨ Manage Private Keys, as shown in Figure 13-8.

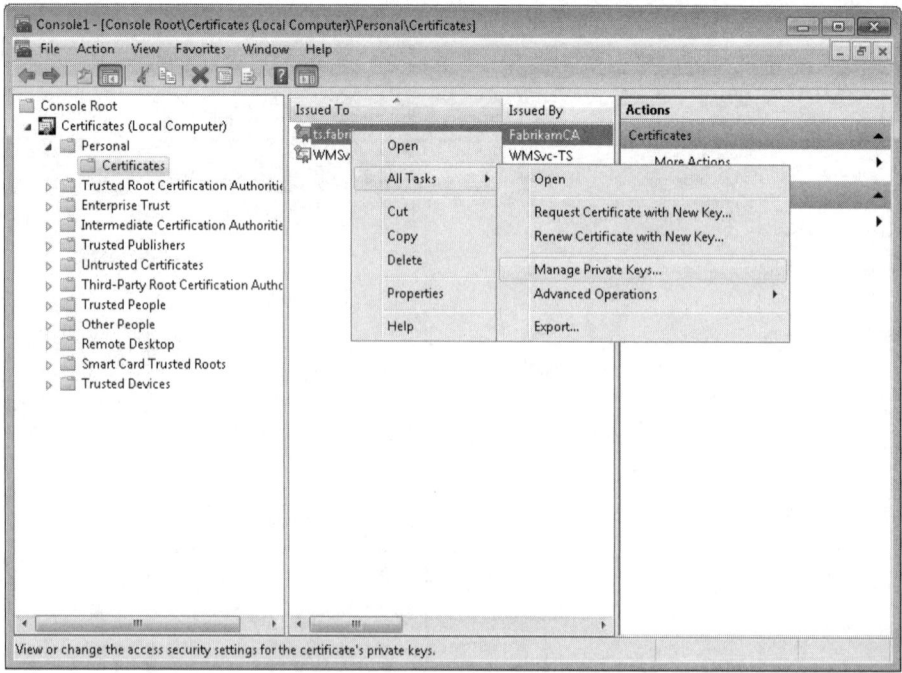

FIGURE 13-8

The resulting window allows you to change permissions for the certificate private keys.

4. To grant the service account permission to access the private key, click Add, enter the username, click OK, and select the Read permission for the newly added user under the Allow column.

CERTIFICATE PERMISSIONS AND IIS

For a UCMA application using TLS to run successfully in Internet Information Services (IIS), the application pool must be using an identity that has access to the certificate private key. To find out what identity the application pool is using, or to change it, select the application pool in the Application Pools section of the IIS Manager console, and click Advanced Settings on the right side of the window.

Fixing Certificate Setup Problems

If a TLS certificate is installed on the application server and the UCMA application has access to it, but it is still not working, check that the certificate is set up correctly. Its subject name must be the fully qualified domain name (FQDN) of the application server. Typos in the subject name are a common source of problems. The certificate should be installed in the local computer certificate store, and must have a private key. Verify that all of these are the case if a UCMA application does not seem to be retrieving the certificate.

 Certificate subject names are not case-sensitive (nor are SIP URIs). This means that there is usually no need to worry about case differences in subject names when troubleshooting. However, it is important to ensure that any application code that looks up the certificates is also not case-sensitive.

The certificate used by a UCMA application must also be designated for both client authentication and server authentication. Recall from Chapter 6 that a Lync endpoint acts as both a user agent client and a user agent server. In both cases, it needs to be able to prove its identity.

Troubleshooting "The Connection Was Forcibly Closed by the Remote Host"

On occasion, an application will fail to start and will throw a `ConnectionFailureException` with the message "The connection was forcibly closed by the remote host." Though not a TLS exception, this exception is generally caused by a certificate trust problem.

Typically, this type of error occurs when the UCMA application has found a certificate to use for TLS, but the Lync front-end server does not accept the certificate for authentication. If this error occurs, verify that the subject name of the certificate matches the fully qualified domain name (FQDN) of the application server. If the application server is part of a trusted application pool, the pool FQDN must also be a subject alternate name. The certificate must also be issued by a certification authority that is trusted by the front-end server.

Handling a "Failed to Listen On Port Specified" Error

When a UCMA application is provisioned in Active Directory using the Lync PowerShell cmdlets, as discussed in Chapter 7, it is assigned a listening port. Lync Server uses this listening port to send SIP messages to the application. When the application starts up a collaboration platform, it reserves that listening port so that it can receive incoming messages from the Lync front-end server. If for whatever reason it cannot reserve this port, it will fail with an exception that says "Failed to listen on port or address specified." These exceptions are quite common and, although frustrating, are usually quite easy to fix.

Fixing Port Conflicts

By far the most common reason why an application cannot use its listening port is that another instance of the application on the same server has already reserved it. When an error of this kind occurs, the first thing to check is that the UCMA application is not already running, either as a console application, a Windows service, or in some other form. Check processes run by other users on the same server by going to Task Manager, switching to the Processes tab, and clicking "Show processes from all users."

Eliminating Port Conflicts When Using IIS

Sorting out listening port conflicts can be particularly dicey if the UCMA code is hosted by Internet Information Services (IIS). This is because of the way in which IIS recycles worker processes by default. To help minimize downtime when, for instance, updates to a website are being deployed, IIS creates a new worker process, waits for it to start up, and then shuts down the old worker process.

For UCMA applications, this situation creates problems, because only one instance of the application can use the listening port. When updates to the application are deployed, the new instance generally fails to start because the listening port is already reserved by the old instance.

To fix this problem, changing IIS's recycling behavior for the application pool in which the UCMA application is running is necessary. To do this, follow these steps:

1. Open IIS, go to the Application Pools section of the control panel, and select the appropriate application pool.

2. Click Advanced Settings on the right side of the window to open the settings dialog box.

3. Scroll down to the Recycling section, and set the Disable Overlapped Recycle property to True.

4. Click OK to save the settings. After saving, you can now deploy changes to the application without encountering problems at startup.

Figure 13-9 shows the application pool settings dialog box with overlapped recycling disabled.

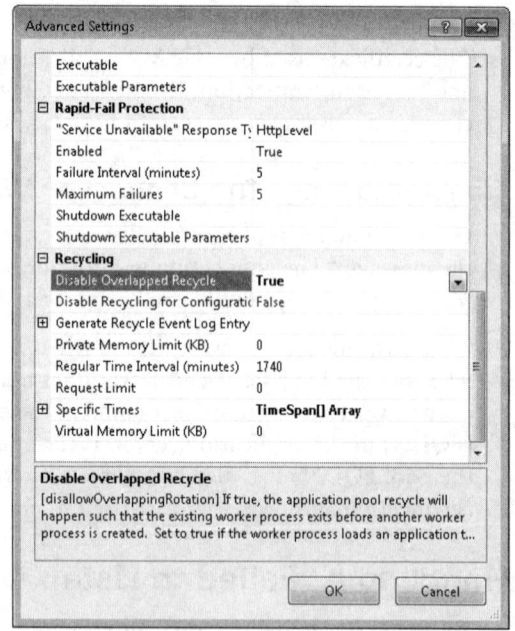

FIGURE 13-9

Resolving Problems with Auto-Provisioning

The auto-provisioning method of retrieving collaboration platform and endpoint settings requires a few items to be in place that are not required to create a collaboration platform and endpoint by manually specifying provisioning settings. If application startup fails with auto-provisioning but works fine when you specify the settings manually, these dependencies are prime suspects.

Checking Management Store Replication

Auto-provisioning depends on a local management store, which is replicated from the central management store. If this management store replication is not in place, auto-provisioning will not work properly. If an application fails at startup with an exception when using auto-provisioning, check that management store replication is enabled using the `Get-CsManagementStoreReplicationStatus` PowerShell cmdlet.

See Chapter 7 for instructions on using the `Get-CsManagementStoreReplicationStatus` cmdlet as well as how to enable replication if it is not already enabled.

Checking Service Account Group Membership

If on startup an application using auto-provisioning complains about not having access to the "xds" database, you must add the Windows identity that is being used to run the application to the group on the local computer called RTC Component Local Group. Alternatively, you can run the application using a local administrator account.

Troubleshooting Incoming Calls

Occasionally, a UCMA application that has just been deployed seems not to receive its incoming calls. Calls to an endpoint owned by the application ring endlessly, but the incoming call event handler is not invoked. This is one of the most frustrating problems to encounter in application deployment.

Thankfully, more often than not the problem stems from one of two causes: Either the application is listening on the wrong port, or a firewall or other application is blocking incoming communications on the listening port so that they do not reach the application.

Identifying Listening Port Problems

The simplest explanation for calls that do not reach the application is that the application has the listening port wrong. Whenever Lync Server tries to route a SIP `INVITE` to the application, it will send it to the application server on the listening port that was assigned to that application during provisioning. If the application starts its collaboration platform using manual settings, and provides a different listening port with the settings, the application will not receive any of these messages from Lync Server.

Consequently, the first thing to check if your application uses manual settings and is not receiving calls is that the listening port assigned to the application matches the listening port specified in the `ServerPlatformSettings` object that is used by the collaboration platform. For instructions on configuring the listening port and other provisioning settings, see Chapter 7.

Identifying Firewall Issues

Even if the application is using the correct listening port, the possibility exists for an overzealous firewall (or some other application) to interfere with the messages coming in on that port. When calls are not reaching your application, check that a firewall is not blocking incoming connections on the application's listening port. If the server is already protected by another firewall, turning off Windows Firewall often solves the problem.

 Make sure that your server is adequately protected — don't remove necessary firewall protection simply to get a UCMA application working.

Troubleshooting Transfers

Transfers in Lync are relatively complex operations, and as such they can go wrong in a number of different places. Describing every possible cause of a failed transfer in this chapter is not feasible, but this section explains some of the most common causes and how to solve them.

The most important point to consider when investigating a transfer failure is that, in order to complete the transfer, the *transferee* (the transferred endpoint) must place a new call to the *transfer destination*. Accordingly, the transferee must be able to reach the transfer destination, taking into account things like dial plans, external access policies, and so forth. It does not help if the *transferor* can route a call to the transfer destination; if the transferee cannot, then the transfer will fail.

To discover issues with call routing from the transferred endpoint to the transfer destination, run OCSLogger during the transfer and inspect the SIP messages. Look for the REFER message from the transferor to the transferee, which will indicate the beginning of the transfer operation, and then find the INVITE message from the transferee to the transfer destination. This SIP dialog between the transferee and the transfer destination must succeed for the transfer to complete. An error response, such as a 404 or 504, generally indicates why the transfer is failing.

Solving Issues with Referenced Assemblies

For a UCMA application to run, either the UCMA SDK or the UCMA runtime (available for download at www.microsoft.com/downloads/en/details.aspx?FamilyID=418cc593-f31e-48be-957c-d3c9020c6b01) must be installed on the server where the application is running. For applications that use speech recognition or speech synthesis, including UCMA Workflow applications, language packs are also necessary. You can download them at www.microsoft.com/downloads/en/details.aspx?FamilyID=47ffd4e5-e682-4228-8058-dd895252a3c3&displaylang=en.

If these prerequisites are installed, but the UCMA application seems not to be finding them, check the target platform to which the application is being compiled. This must be set to x64 or Any CPU. If the target platform is set to x86, the application will look for nonexistent 32-bit versions of the referenced assemblies, often leading to an extremely frustrating session of troubleshooting.

INSPECTING SIP RESPONSES IN CODE

Most of the time, letting UCMA handle the SIP messaging without trying to intervene is best. Once in a while, however, looking at the details of a SIP response message and taking action depending on its contents may be useful.

Most of the *EndMethodName* methods in UCMA return an instance of the SipResponseData class. This object has properties that correspond to the various SIP headers discussed earlier in this chapter, as well as to other components of the message such as the response code. The following code shows an example of inspecting the SIP response data from a UCMA operation and taking action on the basis of the contents:

```
SipResponseData response =
    _appEndpoint.EndEstablish(result);

if (response.ResponseCode == ResponseCode.NotFound)
{
    // Handle a not found response.
}
else if (response.ResponseCode ==
    ResponseCode.NotAcceptableHere)
{
    // Handle a not acceptable here response.
}
```

For debugging and for handling specific error conditions, having access to these particulars of the response can be handy.

SUMMARY

This chapter has covered some of the highlights of effective troubleshooting of problems with UCMA applications. A good deal more information is available on this topic, but the material in this chapter should serve as a foundation for additional learning, much of which you can gain only through experience.

The next chapter offers an introduction to UCMA's cousin API, UCMA Workflow.

14

Building Communications-Enabled Business Processes with the UCMA 3.0 Workflow SDK

WHAT'S IN THIS CHAPTER?

➤ Building communications workflows with the UCMA 3.0 Workflow SDK

➤ Working with workflow activities, communications events, and communications commands

➤ Building workflow activity prompts

➤ Constructing grammars to validate input from the caller

➤ Processing the output of a communications workflow

➤ Building custom workflow activities

The Unified Communications Managed API (UCMA) 3.0 Workflow software development kit (SDK) is used to build communications-enabled workflow solutions such as Interactive Voice Response (IVR) systems and personal virtual assistants. In a call center scenario, the UCMA 3.0 Workflow SDK can be used to build an IVR that captures information from the caller before the call center software connects him or her with an agent possessing the necessary skills to assist them. The UCMA 3.0 Workflow SDK can also be used to build a personal virtual assistant such as a conference room reservation system. Employees call into the conference room reservation system, authenticate using their PIN, specify the building they would like to find a conference room in, and let the system find available conference rooms for them to choose from and reserve.

Using the UCMA 3.0 Workflow SDK, you can visually construct communications-enabled workflows by dragging workflow activities onto a design service; arranging, configuring, and connecting them to form the workflow solution. Workflows can be constructed to accept audio or instant message calls, or both. In the case of audio calls, input from the user can be in the form of Dual-Tone Multi-Frequency (DTMF) tones, speech recognition, or both. The text-to-speech engine, available in 26 different languages, is used to convert text to prompts that the caller hears during different activities of the workflow. Professionally recorded audio prompts can also be substituted to give the IVR a more polished feel.

The UCMA 3.0 Workflow SDK consists of a collection of communications-enabled Windows Workflow 3.0 activities. Under the covers, all of the workflow activities are implemented using UCMA. You can use custom UCMA code to replicate any of the functionality in the UCMA 3.0 Workflow SDK workflow activities or even build your own custom activities.

In this chapter, you learn how to build communications workflow solutions with the UCMA 3.0 Workflow SDK. You also learn how to build custom communications workflow activities, host a UCMA 3.0 Workflow SDK communications workflow in a Windows Service, and initiate and collect the output of a communications workflow from a UCMA application.

SETTING UP YOUR DEVELOPMENT ENVIRONMENT

Microsoft has made a set of virtual machines (VMs) available for companies and developers to evaluate Microsoft Lync Server 2010. All the VMs are based on Windows Server 2008 R2 64-bit Standard Edition. One of the VMs is configured as a development machine; you can use these VMs for your development, or you can build your own Microsoft Lync Server 2010 VM environment. You can download these VMs at Microsoft.com.

If you are working in your own Lync Server environment — or building a new one from scratch — you must install the UCMA 3.0 SDK on your development server and configure it to host a UCMA 3.0 Trusted Application Pool. Chapter 7 has detailed instructions for installing the UCMA 3.0 SDK and creating a Trusted Application Pool.

Requirements for Developing with the UCMA 3.0 Workflow SDK

The UCMA 3.0 Workflow SDK includes Visual Studio project templates that you can use to create inbound and outbound communications workflow projects. You can also install additional language packs to allow the communications workflow to provide speech recognition and text-to-speech capabilities in different languages.

Visual Studio Support

You can use Visual Studio 2008 SP1 or Visual Studio 2010 targeting .NET Framework 3.5 to build UCMA 3.0 Workflow SDK applications. You can't develop UCMA 3.0 workflows that target the .NET Framework 4.0.

Windows Workflow Foundation Support

The UCMA 3.0 Workflow SDK is largely unchanged from the 2.0 version, so it will not work with Windows Workflow Foundation 4.0. However, you can use workflow activities from Windows Workflow Foundation 3.0 and 3.5 when developing communications workflows with the UCMA 3.0 Workflow SDK.

Installing the UCMA 3.0 Workflow SDK

The UCMA 3.0 Workflow SDK is installed as part of the UCMA 3.0 SDK installation process. The UCMA 3.0 SDK can only be installed on 64-bit versions of Windows Server.

The UCMA 3.0 Workflow SDK is installed to `C:\Program Files\Microsoft UCMA 3.0\SDK\Workflow`. You can find the necessary assemblies, SDK documentation, and sample applications in this folder.

Assemblies

If you're not creating your Visual Studio project from one of the Communications Workflow project templates, you can reference `Microsoft.Rtc.Workflow.dll` from `C:\Program Files\Microsoft UCMA 3.0\SDK\Workflow\Bin`, or directly from the GAC.

Visual Studio Project Templates

When creating a new project in Visual Studio, the New Project dialog allows you to choose the version of the .NET Framework that your application should target. You simply change the target to .NET Framework 3.0 or 3.5 and click on the Communications Workflow section.

You can use the following Visual Studio project templates to create communications workflow applications with the UCMA 3.0 Workflow SDK, as shown in Figure 14-1:

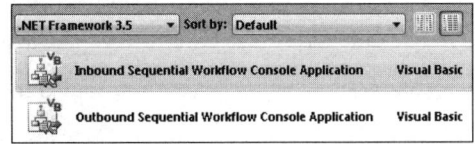

➤ Inbound Sequential Workflow Console Application

FIGURE 14-1

➤ Outbound Sequential Workflow Console Application

A communications workflow created using the Inbound Sequential Workflow Console Application project template handles incoming audio and instant message calls. This is suitable for a personal virtual assistant scenario; for example, an employee calling in to reserve a conference room using a voice-enabled conference room scheduler.

On the other hand, a communications workflow created using the Outbound Sequential Workflow Console Application project template will initiate audio or instant message calls to users. You can use these types of communications workflows in a customer service scenario, where you would follow up with customers and ask them to take a short survey about their experience.

In the companion project available with this chapter, the code created in `Program.cs` *by the Visual Studio project template is encapsulated into a new class called* `WorkflowInitiator`. *The* `Program` *class is responsible for calling into the* `WorkflowInitiator` *class to start the workflow. Separating the workflow startup logic into the* `WorkflowInitiator` *class allows you to start the workflow from a project other than a console application; for example, a Windows Service. Later in this chapter, you learn how to deploy a UCMA 3.0 Workflow SDK communications workflow into a Windows Service.*

Installing Additional Language Packs

After installing the UCMA 3.0 SDK, you can install additional language packs that your communications workflow application can use to provide speech recognition and text-to-speech functionality in a particular locale.

Separate downloads are available for speech recognition and text-to-speech language packs. The text-to-speech packs are often referred to by the character name; for example, Helen for en-US.

Language packs are available for the locales listed in Table 14-1.

TABLE 14-1: UCMA 3.0 Language Packs

LOCALE	LANGUAGE (COUNTRY)	VOICE NAME
ca-ES	Catalan (Spain)	Herena
da-DK	Danish (Denmark)	Helle
de-DE	German (Germany)	Hedda
en-AU	English (Australia)	Hayley
en-CA	English (Canada)	Heather
en-GB	English (United Kingdon)	Hazel
en-IN	English (India)	Heera
en-US	English (United States)	Helen
es-ES	Spanish (Spain)	Helena
es-MX	Spanish (Mexico)	Hilda
fi-FI	Finnish (Finland)	Heidi
fr-CA	French (Canada)	Harmonie
fr-FR	French (France)	Hostense
it-IT	Italian (Italy)	Lucia

LOCALE	LANGUAGE (COUNTRY)	VOICE NAME
ja-JP	Japanese (Japan)	Haruka
ko-KR	Korean (Korea)	Heami
nb-NO	Norwegian (Norway)	Hulda
nl-NL	Dutch (The Netherlands)	Hanna
pl-PL	Polish (Poland)	Paulina
pt-BR	Portuguese (Brazil)	Heloisa
pt-PT	Portuguese (Portugal)	Helia
ru-RU	Russian (Russia)	Elena
sv-SE	Swedish (Sweden)	Hedvig
zh-CN	Chinese (China)	HuiHui
zh-HK	Chinese (Hong Kong SAR)	HunYee
zh-TW	Chinese (Taiwan)	HanHan

You may have noticed that the majority of the language pack voice names start with the letter H. This is in reference to the underlying technology: HMM-based Speech Synthesis. HMM stands for Hidden Markov Model, which is a form of a Bayesian learning network commonly used for pattern recognition. After the network is trained for a specific language, it can be used for speech recognition.

CREATING YOUR FIRST COMMUNICATIONS WORKFLOW

The code accompanying this chapter contains a simple Help Desk communications workflow application that demonstrates using the UCMA 3.0 Workflow SDK to build an inbound audio-enabled communications workflow.

In this workflow, an employee calls in and authenticates by entering his PIN number. The workflow then retrieves a list of open Help Desk tickets that were created by the caller and prompts him to choose one. The workflow checks to see whether the Help Desk support agent assigned to the ticket is available, and transfers the call to the agent. In this chapter, you learn how this communications workflow was constructed. You can download the completed code at www.wrox.com.

Creating a New Communications Workflow Project

Now you will learn how to create a new Inbound Sequential Workflow project using the Visual Studio project template available with the UCMA 3.0 Workflow SDK. After creating the communications workflow project, you will see how the workflow accepts and disconnects the incoming call, arranges workflow activities into a communications sequence, and handles global communications commands and events.

To create a new communications workflow project, open Visual Studio 2010 and create a new Inbound Sequential Workflow Console Application project (this project template is available in the Communications Workflow Installed Templates section under C# or VB.NET). Make sure you target .NET Framework 3.5 or you won't see the project template in the New Project dialog.

The Inbound Sequential Workflow Console Application Visual Studio project template hosts the UCMA 3.0 Workflow SDK workflow in a console application, providing you with a convenient way to develop and test the workflow. Later in this chapter, you learn how to host a communications workflow in a Windows Service.

You are first prompted to choose a language for the workflow; any language packs that you have installed in your development environment will be available for you to choose from, as shown in Figure 14-2. You can choose only one language for the workflow.

`Workflow1.xoml` opens in the workflow designer after you create the project. You can see the activities that were automatically added to the workflow in Figure 14-3.

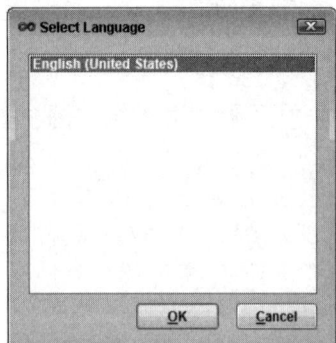

FIGURE 14-2

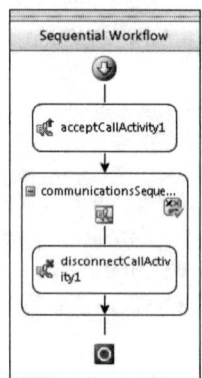

FIGURE 14-3

You can also see the code-behind of the workflow by opening `Workflow1.xoml.cs`. The code-behind of the workflow typically contains event handlers for the various workflow activities and other business logic on which the workflow relies.

Before you starting adding activities to the workflow, notice that it only consists of an `AcceptCall` activity and a `CommunicationsSequence` activity, which contains a `DisconnectCall` activity. If you were to run this workflow and call into it, it would pick up the call and hang up immediately.

Accepting and Disconnecting Audio Calls and Instant Messages

The `AcceptCall` activity is the first workflow activity in an inbound communications workflow; it is responsible for accepting the incoming audio or instant message call and passing the workflow execution flow on to the `CommunicationsSequence` activity.

The `DisconnectCall` activity will disconnect the current audio or instant message call, ending the workflow execution.

 Instead of continuing to distinguish between the two, the term call *is used interchangeably to refer to either an audio or instant message conversation.*

Communications Sequences

The `CommunicationsSequence` activity acts as a container for workflow activities; the workflow activities in a `CommunicationSequence` activity are executed in sequence. This activity is created by default when you create a communications workflow project and cannot be deleted.

A UCMA 3.0 Workflow SDK communications workflow is obviously intended to handle multiple concurrent calls. The `CommunicationsSequence` activity knows which call to execute the workflow sequence for based on its `CallProvider` property, which is set by default to an instance of the `AcceptCall` activity representing a call into the workflow as shown in Figure 14-4.

A communications workflow must have at least one `CommunicationSequence` activity. Using multiple `CommunicationSequence` activities in a communications workflow allows you to separate specific pieces of the workflow logic.

The `CommunicationsSequence` activity also provides scope for communications events and commands. You can access the communications events and commands for a `CommunicationsSequence` activity by choosing View Commands or View CommunicationsEvents from the context menu of the activity, as shown in Figure 14-5.

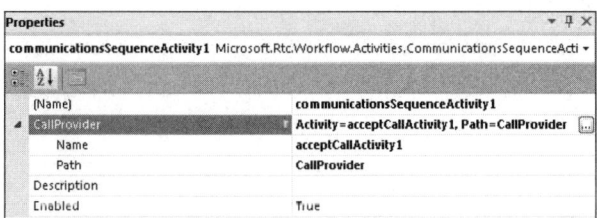

FIGURE 14-4

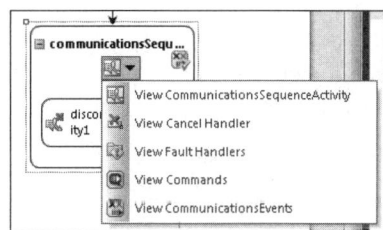

FIGURE 14-5

Commands

Commands provide a global mechanism for handling commands from the caller at any point in the communications sequence. A command can be something as simple as the caller saying "Help" or pressing 0 to get help during the workflow. Commands can also be used to recognize specific words from callers regardless of where they are in the workflow sequence; for example, by listening for profanity to recognize whether the caller is upset or frustrated.

You can access the `Commands` activity by selecting View Commands from the context menu of the `CommunicationsSequence` activity shown in Figure 14-5. This opens the `Commands` activity in the designer as shown in Figure 14-6.

You can drag activities into the `Commands` activity and build a simple communications sequence of workflow activities that execute when the specific command is prompted.

For example, you can drag a `SpeechHelpCommand` activity into the `Commands` activity, as shown in Figure 14-7, and add workflow activities that execute when the Help command triggers.

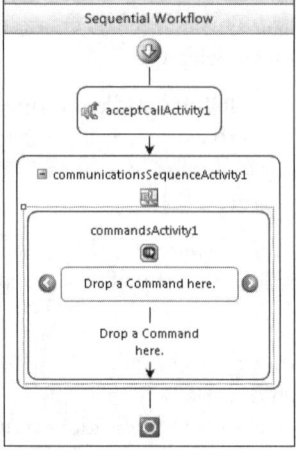

FIGURE 14-6

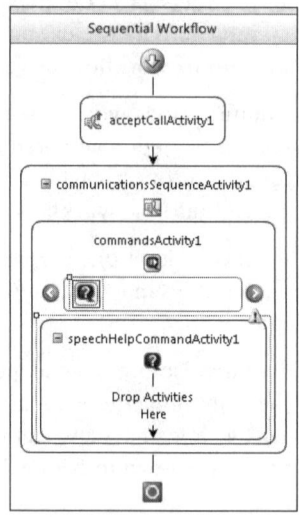

FIGURE 14-7

The following command activities are available in the UCMA 3.0 Workflow SDK:

➤ `SpeechCommand`

➤ `SpeechHelpCommand`

➤ `SpeechRepeatCommand`

You learn more about these activities later in this chapter.

Communications Events

Communications events enable the workflow to react to global events, such as the caller entering incorrect input several times. You can access the `CommunicationsEvents` activity by selecting View CommunicationsEvents from the context menu of the `CommunicationsSequence` activity. A `CallDisconnected` event is added by default to the `CommunicationsEvents`, as shown in Figure 14-8, to perform logic that handles disconnecting the call.

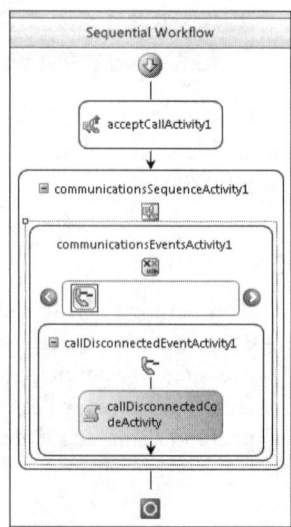

FIGURE 14-8

You can drag other activities into the `CommunicationsEvents` activity and build a simple communications sequence of workflow activities that execute when the specific event fires. For example, you can drag a `ConsecutiveNo RecognitionsSpeechEvent` activity into the `Communications Events` activity, as shown in Figure 14-9, and add workflow activities to transfer callers to a customer agent when they provide invalid input a configurable number of consecutive times during the workflow.

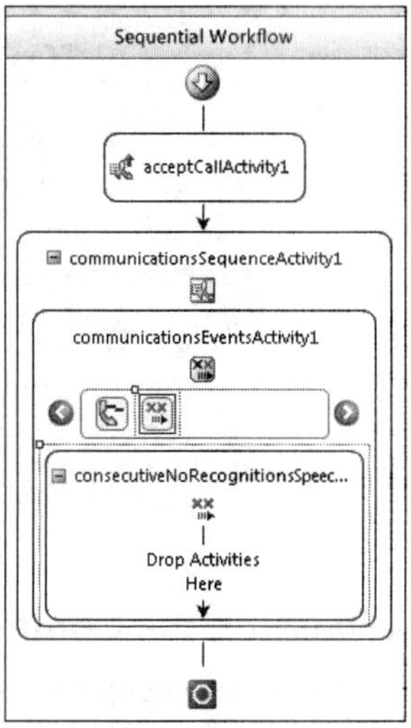

The following communications event activities are available in the UCMA 3.0 Workflow SDK:

➤ `CallDisconnectedEvent`

➤ `CallOnHoldEvent`

➤ `CallOnHoldTimeoutEvent`

➤ `CallRetrievedEvent`

➤ `ConsecutiveNoInputsSpeechEvent`

➤ `ConsecutiveSilencesSpeechEvent`

➤ `ConsecutiveNoRecognitionsSpeechEvent`

➤ `ConsecutiveNoInputsInstantMessagingEvent`

➤ `ConsecutiveSilencesInstantMessagingEvent`

➤ `ConsecutiveNoRecognitionsInstantMessagingEvent`

You learn more about these activities later in this chapter.

FIGURE 14-9

Starting the Communications Workflow

Open `WorkflowInitiator.cs`. The code starts the UCMA `CollaborationPlatform` and creates an `ApplicationEndpoint` on which the application can receive calls. When the endpoint receives the call, it executes the handler for the specific type of call and starts the workflow. You're already familiar with most of this code from the Chapter 7, so this section will focus instead on configuring the endpoint to handle calls and starting the communications workflow.

The `WorkflowInitiator` class in the Help Desk IVR project isn't created by default as part of the Visual Studio project template for an inbound or outbound communications workflow. Moving this logic into its own class and simply calling into it from the console application's `Main` method is helpful. This allows you to separate the workflow startup code in such a way that it can be called by a Windows Service (or other host process) project that references the workflow project.

> ### USING AUTO PROVISIONING IN THE WORKFLOW STARTUP CODE
>
> The Visual Studio project templates for inbound and outbound communications workflows are unchanged from the UCMA 2.0 Workflow SDK, so they don't take advantage of the new Auto Provisioning functionality in UCMA 3.0. A recommendation is that you replace the startup code that is created by default as part of the Visual Studio project template and replace it with the code from Chapter 7.
>
> Refer to the companion project available with this chapter for an example of integrating the workflow startup code with the collaboration platform startup code that takes advantage of Auto Provisioning.

Initializing the Communications Workflow

Before wiring up the workflow to accept and handle calls, the code in the project template initializes the Windows Workflow Foundation workflow runtime and configures it to run the UCMA 3.0 Workflow SDK services that the communications workflow will use.

The code first creates an instance of System.Workflow.Runtime representing an instance of the Windows Workflow Foundation runtime to be used as a runtime engine for workflows.

Two UCMA 3.0 Workflow SDK services are then added to the workflow runtime: Communications WorkflowRuntimeService and TrackingDataWorkflowRuntimeService.

The workflow runtime is then started by calling StartRuntime():

```
_workflowRuntime = new WorkflowRuntime();
_workflowRuntime.AddService(new CommunicationsWorkflowRuntimeService());
_workflowRuntime.AddService(new TrackingDataWorkflowRuntimeService());
_workflowRuntime.StartRuntime();
```

Code snippet HelpDeskIVR\WorkflowInitiator.cs

CommunicationsWorkflowRuntimeService allows the workflow runtime to control the underlying UCMA call and endpoint objects. TrackingDataWorkflowRuntimeService allows the workflow runtime to track the usage of various activities within the workflow.

Wiring Up AudioVideoCallReceived and InstantMessagingCallReceived

After the collaboration platform startup process is completed and the application endpoint setting configured, use the RegisterForIncomingCall<T> method on ApplicationEndpoint to register for an incoming call. To register for an AudioVideoCall, specify that as the type of call and provide a delegate to execute when a call of that type is received:

```
_endpoint.RegisterForIncomingCall<AudioVideoCall>(AudioVideoCallReceived);
```

Code snippet HelpDeskIVR\WorkflowInitiator.cs

The handler accepts two parameters: the sender and an instance of `CallReceivedEventArgs<T>`:

```
private static void AudioVideoCallReceived(object sender,
CallReceivedEventArgs<AudioVideoCall> e)
```

Code snippet HelpDeskIVR\WorkflowInitiator.cs

You can also use a lambda expression instead of specifying a separate handler:

```
_endpoint.RegisterForIncomingCall<AudioVideoCall>(
    (s, e) =>
        {
            // Insert code to run when the AudioVideoCall is received
        });
```

To register for an incoming instant message, specify `InstantMessagingCall` as the type of call:

```
_endpoint.RegisterForIncomingCall<InstantMessagingCall>
    (InstantMessagingCallReceived);
```

Provide a handler to execute when the endpoint receives an instant messaging call:

```
private static void InstantMessagingCallReceived(object sender,
CallReceivedEventArgs<InstantMessagingCall> e)
```

Starting the Communications Workflow Runtime Service and Loading the Workflow Instance

The instance of `CallReceivedEventArgs` in the call received handler contains the UCMA `Call` object representing the incoming call that will be attached to the instance of the communications workflow.

The `StartWorkflow` function creates an instance of the workflow and then initializes the `CommunicationsWorkflowRuntimeService` for the instance, as shown in the following:

```
WorkflowInstance workflowInstance =
    _workflowRuntime.CreateWorkflow(typeof(Workflow1));
var communicationsWorkflowRuntimeService = (CommunicationsWorkflowRuntimeService)
    workflowRuntime.GetService(typeof(CommunicationsWorkflowRuntimeService));
```

Code snippet HelpDeskIVR\WorkflowInitiator.cs

As shown in the following code, `EnqueueCall` is called on the `CommunicationsWorkflow RuntimeService` instance to attach the call to the instance of the workflow. `SetEndpoint` is then called to attach the workflow instance to the application endpoint. Finally, `SetWorkflowCulture` is called to set the language that the workflow will use (the language is chosen when initially creating the workflow project. The workflow engine now begins processing the activities in the communications sequence.

```
communicationsWorkflowRuntimeService.EnqueueCall
    (workflowInstance.InstanceId, call);
communicationsWorkflowRuntimeService.SetEndpoint
    (workflowInstance.InstanceId, _endpoint);
communicationsWorkflowRuntimeService.SetWorkflowCulture
    (workflowInstance.InstanceId, new CultureInfo("en-US"));
```

Code snippet HelpDeskIVR\WorkflowInitiator.cs

The call is terminated if an error occurs during this process. The error-handling code in the `StartWorkflow` function block is skipped for brevity.

Trusted Application and Trusted Application Endpoint

As with a UCMA application running in a console application or Windows Service, a UCMA 3.0 Workflow SDK workflow must be associated with a trusted application endpoint, which in turn is associated with a trusted application.

The trusted application endpoint is the contact that users will call from Microsoft Lync; for example, users would call the Help Desk at `sip:helpdesk@fabrikam.com`. A phone number can also be exposed so that users can call the Help Desk from a device such as a mobile phone or other non-Lync device.

In the companion Help Desk IVR project, the `app.config` file contains two configuration keys: `ApplicationId` and `TrustedContactURI`, representing the trusted application and trusted application endpoint.

Refer to Chapter 7 for instructions on how to create a trusted application and trusted application endpoint.

WORKING WITH COMMUNICATIONS WORKFLOW ACTIVITIES

At the core of any communications workflow is the ability to communicate with callers and get information from them. The UCMA 3.0 Workflow SDK includes a collection of Windows Workflow Foundation 3.0– and 3.5–compatible workflow activities that you can add to a communications workflow. These activities are accessible via the Visual Studio Toolbox in the Unified Communications Workflow section. The toolbox also contains Windows Workflow v3.0 and Windows Workflow v3.5 sections, which contain more general workflow activities that you can add to a communications workflow.

This chapter focuses on using speech-enabled workflow activities. However, the following sections also describe the equivalent instant messaging activities where applicable and draw parallels between using both types.

Interacting with Callers with Statement Activities

You can use statement activities to send audio or instant message prompts to the caller during the execution of the communications workflow. Statements activities are one-way; they don't accept any input from the caller.

SpeechStatement Activity

You can use the `SpeechStatement` activity to allow the communications workflow to synthesize and read a prompt to the caller, or to play a professionally recorded prompt. This activity doesn't accept any input from the caller; the workflow runtime will immediately move on to processing the next activity in the communications sequence.

Drag a `SpeechStatement` activity into the communications sequence in the workflow designer surface. As you can see in Figure 14-10, a yellow exclamation mark is on the top right of the activity.

The yellow exclamation mark indicates that the workflow activity is missing a piece of information necessary for it to execute. When you hover over the exclamation mark, you see the following message: "Please specify the main prompt used by this activity. The main prompt is used on the first turn."

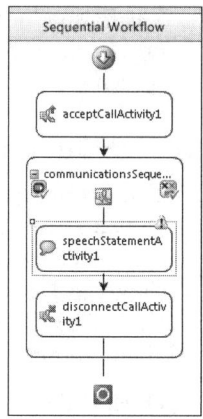

FIGURE 14-10

Open the properties of the `SpeechStatement` activity and set the value of the `MainPrompt` property to `"Welcome to the Help Desk"` as shown in Figure 14-11.

Notice that the yellow exclamation mark no longer appears on the `SpeechStatement` activity. When the workflow runtime gets to this activity, it uses the text-to-speech engine in the `en-US` language back to synthesize the text of the `MainPrompt` property and read it back to the caller.

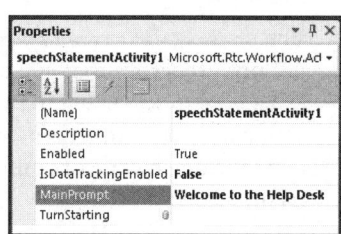

FIGURE 14-11

InstantMessagingStatement Activity

The `InstantMessagingStatement` activity is identical to the `SpeechStatement` activity except that it communicates with the caller via instant messaging. It also contains a `MainPrompt` property that you must set to the text that will be sent to the caller when the workflow runtime executes the activity.

Querying Callers with Question/Answer Activities

The usefulness of a communications workflow would be very limited if it weren't for the ability to collect input from the caller. The `SpeechQuestionAnswer` and `InstantMessagingQuestionAnswer` activities are used to gather speech and instant messaging input from the caller.

This section starts by providing a high-level overview of these activities. Later in this chapter, you learn how to configure more advanced properties of the activities, such as speech and DTMF grammars to enable them to accept complex input from the caller.

InstantMessagingQuestionAnswer Activity

You can use the `InstantMessagingQuestionAnswer` to prompt the caller for input via instant message. Other than the obvious, the only difference between this activity and the `SpeechQuestionAnswer` activity is that it doesn't expose some of the same timeout properties that the `SpeechQuestionAnswer` activity does.

The reason for this is that detecting the end of an instant messaging communication — the caller presses Enter or clicks Send — is a lot simpler for the workflow runtime than detecting the end of speech input from the caller.

SpeechQuestionAnswer Activity and Its Properties

You use the `SpeechQuestionAnswer` activity to prompt the caller for input. Drag a `SpeechQuestionAnswer` activity onto the design surface; you will notice again that a yellow exclamation mark is visible on the top right of the activity, as shown in Figure 14-12. You need to set the `MainPrompt` property of the activity and define the grammars that it will use to validate input. You learn more about grammars later in this chapter.

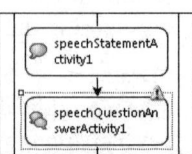

FIGURE 14-12

Open and explore the properties of the `SpeechQuestion Answer` activity, as shown in Figure 14-13.

Prompts

The `SpeechQuestionAnswer` activity has a number of prompt properties that you can configure. In this section, you learn how to set these prompts in the property dialog of the activity. Later in this chapter, you learn to set these prompts dynamically in code or configure them to use professionally recorded audio prompts.

FIGURE 14-13

➤   `MainPrompt`: Set the value of the `MainPrompt` property to the text that the activity will read to the caller when the activity executes; for example, **Please enter your PIN code**.

➤   `NoRecognitionPrompt`: Set the value of the `NoRecognitionPrompt` property to the prompt that the activity will play when it can't recognize the input provided by the caller. Input is not recognized by the activity when it doesn't match the rules specified in the `ExpectedDtmfInputs`, `ExpectedSpeechInputs`, `DtmfGrammars`, or `Grammars` properties of the activity.

➤   `EscalatedNoRecognition`: If you set a value for the `EscalatedNoRecognitionPrompt` property, the activity will play the prompt when the caller enters invalid input two or more times.

➤   `SilencePrompt`: Set the value of the `SilencePrompt` property to a prompt to play if the timeout set in the activity's `InitialSilenceTimeout` property has elapsed without the caller providing any input.

➤   `EscalatedSilencePrompt`: If you set a value for the `EscalatedSilencePrompt` property, the activity will play the prompt when the user stays silent two or more times in a row.

➤   `HelpPrompt`: Set the value of the `HelpPrompt` property to a prompt to play if the user input matches the grammar specified by the Help command in scope to the communications sequence. You learn how to configure the workflow Help command later in this chapter.

➤ RepeatPrompt: Set the value of the RepeatPrompt property to a prompt to play if the user input matches the grammar specified by the Repeat command in scope to the communications sequence. You learn how to configure the workflow Repeat command later in this chapter.

Timeouts

The SpeechQuestionAnswer activity has a number of timeout properties that you can configure.

 You may find that the default value of some of the timeout properties might be too short for practical use. Recommended values are described next.

➤ CompleteTimeout: This property refers to the length of silent time required following user input before the recognizer finalizes the result. This is set by default to 00:00:00.5000000; however, increasing this to 00:00:01 or more gives the caller more time when providing more complex input.

➤ IncompleteTimeout: This property refers to the length of time after user input that recognition is complete. This is set by default to 00:00:01; you can experiment with this value and increase it if appropriate depending on the input that the SpeechQuestionAnswer activity is expecting.

➤ InitialSilenceTimeout: This property refers to the length of time before which the user has to provide input or recognition fails. This is set by default to 00:00:03; which is enough for most cases.

CanBargeIn

Setting CanBargeIn to True indicates that the caller can start providing input to the activity before the activity has completed playing the prompt. For example, if the activity is listing a number of choices for the caller to pick from, the caller would be able to say or input his choice before all of them have been provided. Conversely, setting CanBargeIn to False ensures that recognition does not start until the end of the prompt.

ExpectedSpeechInputs and ExpectedDTMFInputs

You can configure the SpeechQuestionAnswer activity to accept both speech and DTMF input from the caller. When the input that the activity expects is limited or simple, you can describe it in the ExpectedDtmfInputs and ExpectedSpeechInputs of the property.

Drag another SpeechQuestionAnswer activity onto the design surface to prompt the user for the action he would like to take. Set the MainPrompt to: **Please say or enter 1 to check on the status of a Help Desk ticket, or say or enter 2 to speak with a Help Desk agent.**

Editing the ExpectedDtmfInputs or ExpectedSpeechInputs properties in the properties dialog of the SpeechQuestionAnswer activity brings up a string collection editor in which you can enter a set of strings that the activity will expect.

To provide the values for the expected DTMF inputs, enter each on a separate line, as shown in Figure 14-14.

If you only want the caller to say the number of the choice, set the value of the `ExpectedSpeechInputs` property to the same value as the `ExpectedDtmfInputs` property. Otherwise, edit the expected speech inputs property of the activity to enter the appropriate string that the speech recognition engine will attempt to match against, as shown in Figure 14-15.

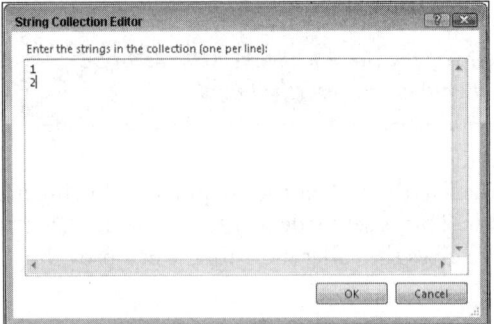

FIGURE 14-14

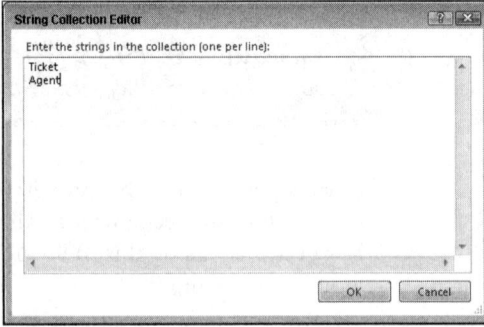

FIGURE 14-15

Note that the accuracy of speech recognition may suffer if your strings are complex; you might want to adjust your prompt to something like, `Please say Ticket or enter 1 to check on the status of a Help Desk ticket, or say Agent or enter 2 to speak with a Help Desk agent`.

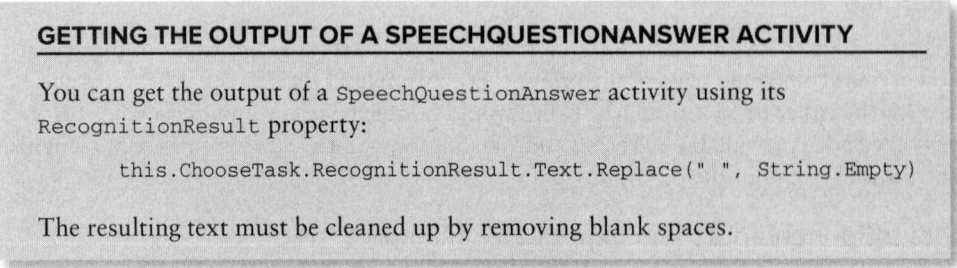

GETTING THE OUTPUT OF A SPEECHQUESTIONANSWER ACTIVITY

You can get the output of a `SpeechQuestionAnswer` activity using its `RecognitionResult` property:

```
this.ChooseTask.RecognitionResult.Text.Replace(" ", String.Empty)
```

The resulting text must be cleaned up by removing blank spaces.

Other Communications Workflow Activities

The Unified Communications Workflow section of the Toolbox contains several other workflow activities that you can use in a communications workflow. Two of the more commonly used activities are `GetPresence` and `BlindTransfer`; consult the UCMA 3.0 Workflow SDK documentation for information about other activities.

The GetPresence Activity

You use the `GetPresence` activity to get the presence of a contact or multiple contacts with specified SIP URIs, as shown in Figure 14-16.

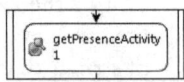

FIGURE 14-16

As shown in the following code, you can specify the `Targets` property in the property dialog of the activity or set its value in the code-behind of the workflow by setting the property to a `List<RealTimeAddress>`. Make sure to add a `using` statement for `Microsoft.Rtc.Signaling` to be able to use `RealTimeAddress` in your code.

```
this.GetAgentPresence.Targets.Add(
        new RealTimeAddress(this.TicketAssignedTo));
```

Code snippet HelpDeskIVR\Workflow1.xoml.cs

> *The `GetPresence` activity doesn't have an event handler or code-behind in which you can set the `Targets` property. Instead, set the value of the `Targets` property in the `ExecuteCode` event handler of the `Code` activity available with Windows Workflow Foundation 3.0. Make sure to set the `Targets` property of the `GetPresence` activity before it is executed.*

Use the `Results` property of the `GetPresence` activity to get the presence of the SIP URIs specified in the `Targets` property. `Results` returns a `Dictionary<RealTimeAddress, PresenceResult>`. You will most likely execute some branching logic based on the results of this operation. Make sure to add a `using` statement for `Microsoft.Rtc.Workflow.Common` to be able to use `PresenceResult`.

The BlindTransfer Activity

The `BlindTransfer` activity, shown in Figure 14-17, performs a blind transfer to the contact specified in its `CalledParty` property.

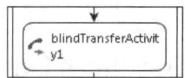

FIGURE 14-17

In a blind transfer, the workflow runtime will hand off call control back to the Microsoft Lync Server 2010 infrastructure and disconnect itself from the call. The drawback of this approach is that, as the developer, you won't be able to take any action based on the result of the transfer; for example, the called party didn't pick up.

Later in this chapter, you learn how to use custom UCMA code to perform an attended call transfer, only handing off call control when the called party has picked up the call.

Adding Windows Workflow Foundation Activities

The Windows Workflow v3.0 section in the Toolbox contains several activities that you may find useful when building communications workflows. This section describes how you can use the `Code` and `IfElse` activities to interact with the UCMA 3.0 Workflow SDK activities in a communications workflow. Consult the Windows Workflow Foundation documentation for information about the other workflow activities.

The Code Activity

Use the `Code` activity, shown in Figure 14-18, to execute custom code at any time during the workflow. The most common use case for the `Code` activity is to perform pre- and post-processing for the other UCMA 3.0 Workflow SDK

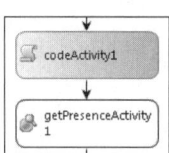

FIGURE 14-18

activities in the workflow; for example, to set the `Targets` property of a `GetPresence` activity and retrieve its results afterwards.

Double-click the `Code` activity in the workflow designer to generate its `ExecuteCode` event handler in the code-behind of the workflow.

The IfElse Activity

Use the `IfElse` activity, as shown in Figure 14-19, to perform conditional branching during the workflow. For example, different workflow logic will execute depending on the user's choice: check on the status of a ticket, or speak to an agent.

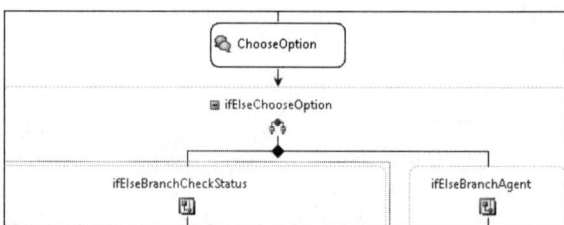

FIGURE 14-19

There are two ways to define a condition for the `IfElse` activity: using a *declarative rule condition* or using a *code condition*. When using a declarative rule condition to validate an `IfElse` activity, you have to specify a validation expression in the Rule Condition Editor window. The rule is stored in the workflow markup, not in the code-behind file. On the other hand, when using a code condition, you specify a function in the workflow's code-behind whose purpose is to return `true` or `false` values indicating the validity of the condition. Unlike with a declarative rule condition, you can put a breakpoint in the function and debug it as the workflow is running. If the condition logic defined in a code condition is reusable, you can apply it to other `IfElse` activities in the workflow.

Setting a Declarative Rule Condition

In the properties dialog of the `IfElse` activity, set the value of the `Condition` property to `Declarative Rule Condition`, as shown in Figure 14-20, and give the condition a name. Edit the `Expression` property to write the condition.

In the Rule Condition Editor window, enter the following code, which describes the condition for the rule to be true. Check the `RecognitionResult` property of the `ChooseOption` `SpeechQuestionAnswer` activity and create a condition based on the caller's input. The condition is true if the caller enters "1" or says "ticket."

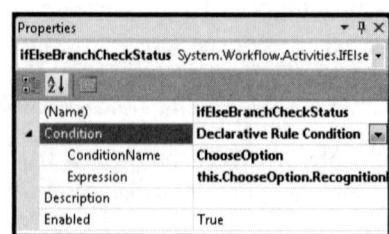

FIGURE 14-20

Available for download on Wrox.com

```
this.ChooseOption.RecognitionResult.Text.Replace(" ", string.Empty) == "1"
|| this.ChooseOption.RecognitionResult.Text.Replace
    (" ", string.Empty).ToLower() == "ticket"
```

Code snippet HelpDeskIVR\Workflow1.rules

The Rule Condition Editor will validate your code before saving it (see Figure 14-21).

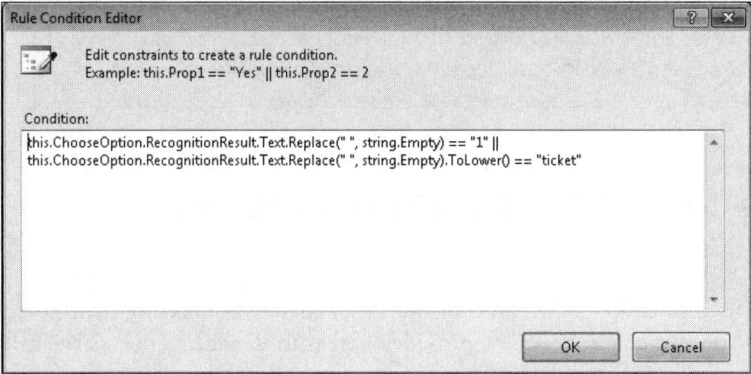

FIGURE 14-21

Setting a Code Condition

To configure the IfElse activity to use a code condition instead of a declarative rule condition, create a function in the workflow's code-behind with the following signature:

```
private void ConditionName(object sender, ConditionalEventArgs e)
```

For example, the following code condition function checks to see whether the agent assigned to the selected ticket is online:

Available for download on Wrox.com

```
private void IsAgentOnlineCondition(object sender, ConditionalEventArgs e)
{
    if (this.GetAgentPresence.Results
        [new RealTimeAddress(this.TicketAssignedTo)].PresenceStatus
            == PresenceAvailability.Online)
    {
        e.Result = true;
    }
    else
    {
        e.Result = false;
    }
}
```

Code snippet HelpDeskIVR\Workflow1.xoml.cs

In the property dialog of the IfElse activity, change the condition type to a code condition and select IsAgentOnlineCondition as the condition to use, as shown in Figure 14-22.

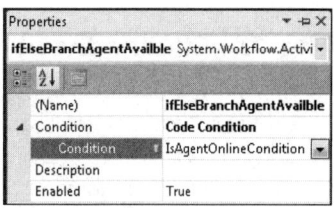

FIGURE 14-22

If your condition code is the slightest bit complex, the author recommends using a code condition instead of a declarative rule condition. Not only are debugging and testing the condition easier when you can step through it in the code-behind of the workflow, but they also help to keep your business logic organized in one place.

USING PROMPTS TO CREATE A NATURAL DIALOG WITH THE CALLER

An IVR system is commonly used to collect information from callers before connecting them to an agent. Information collected from the caller is used to provide context to the agent such as the caller's account number and what he is calling about. IVRs are also extensively used for self service; for example, to retrieve information about an airline's arrivals and departures, or to provide access to the caller's bank or credit card account information. In both scenarios, the goal is to ensure customer satisfaction by servicing the caller's request accurately, and in the shortest amount of time possible. Well-constructed IVR prompts help create a natural dialog with callers, enabling them to effectively interact with and navigate through the IVR.

You learned earlier how to set the various prompt properties of the `SpeechStatement` and `SpeechQuestionAnwer` activities in their properties dialog. Although these prompts are suitable for "Hello World" applications, you will find that to create natural-sounding prompts, you will want to construct them dynamically. Instead of welcoming the caller with a simple "Hello," wouldn't it be much more personal to say, "Good morning, George"?

In this section, you learn how to use the `PromptBuilder` to build prompts dynamically. Sometimes, the text-to-speech engine needs a gentle nudge in the right direction in order to properly synthesize text such as a date; you will learn how to use speech hints to guide it during synthesis. If you don't want to use speech synthesis, this section shows you how to integrate professionally recorded prompts into your IVR.

Building Prompts Dynamically

You are limited to static prompts when setting an activity's prompts in the workflow designer. Static prompts are rarely enough for a communications workflow to provide a natural and personalized dialog with the caller. To achieve that, you need to set the text of the prompt at runtime, for example, when personalizing the prompt to include the caller's name. This section describes using the `TurnStarting` event handler of the `SpeechStatement` or `SpeechQuestionAnswer` activities to construct their prompts at runtime.

The TurnStarting Event Handler

When the workflow engine processes a `SpeechStatement` or `SpeechQuestionAnswer` activity, it is said to take a *turn* through the activity. Both the `SpeechStatement` and `SpeechQuestionAnswer` activities expose a `TurnStarting` event handler that executes before the workflow engine processes the activity. This provides a perfect extensibility point for setting the activity's prompts at runtime.

You generate the `TurnStarting` event handler for a `Speech Statement` or `SpeechQuestionAnswer` activity by right-clicking the activity in the workflow designer and choosing Generate Handlers. Open the activity's Properties dialog; you will see the event handler name as the value of the `TurnStarting` property, as shown in Figure 14-23.

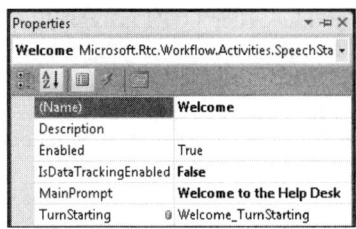

The handler is generated in the workflow's code-behind. You can now set the activity's various prompts in the handler body; for example, use `AppendText` to set the `MainPrompt` of the `Welcome` `SpeechStatement`activity:

FIGURE 14-23

Available for
download on
Wrox.com

```
private void Welcome_TurnStarting(object sender,
    Microsoft.Rtc.Workflow.Activities.SpeechTurnStartingEventArgs e)
{
    this.CallerUri =
communicationsSequenceActivity1.CallProvider.Call.RemoteEndpoint.Participant.Uri;

    this.Welcome.MainPrompt.ClearContent();
    this.Welcome.MainPrompt.AppendText(
        "Welcome {0}. I can help you manage your Help Desk tickets",
        GetUserDisplayName(this.CallerUri));
}
```

Code snippet HelpDeskIVR\Workflow1.xoml.cs

In this example, set `MainPrompt` to greet the caller by name — you can implement a function to get the caller's display name from Active Directory to provide a personalized greeting. `AppendText` has several overloads that enable you to customize how the text is synthesized by the text-to-speech engine. You can set the synthesized text's emphasis, the rate or speech at which it is played by the workflow engine, and its volume.

Before setting an activity's prompts in the `TurnStarting` handler, call `ClearContent` on the prompt to clear its value. The workflow engine can take several turns through a `SpeechStatement` or `SpeechQuestionAnswer` activity. If you don't clear the prompt, the `TurnStarting` handler will simply keep appending text to the prompt: "Hello George. Hello George. Hello George."

 If you set the value of a prompt both in the activity's Properties dialog and its `TurnStarting` *handler, the workflow will use both. Make sure to use* `ClearContent` *to ensure that only the text you set in the* `TurnStarting` *handler is appended to the prompt.*

Getting the Caller's Identity in the TurnStarting Handler

The `TurnStarting` handler of the `WelcomeSpeechStatement` activity is a great place to capture the identity of the caller. You can use the caller's URI to look up his name in Active Directory and greet him by name.

The caller's URI is available from the `Uri` property of the `Participant` object on the `Call`'s endpoint:

```
this.CallerUri =
communicationsSequenceActivity1.CallProvider.Call.RemoteEndpoint.Participant.Uri;
```

Code snippet HelpDeskIVR\Workflow1.xoml.cs

Now that you know the caller's URI, you can look up his display name in Active Directory using this function:

```
private string GetUserDisplayName(string sipUri)
{
    try
    {
        DirectorySearcher ds = new DirectorySearcher();

        ds.SearchRoot = new DirectoryEntry("");
        ds.Filter = string.Format("msrtcsip-primaryuseraddress={0}", sipUri);
        ds.PropertyNamesOnly = false;
        ds.ServerTimeLimit = new TimeSpan(0, 10, 0);

        SearchResult result = ds.FindOne();

        string userPrincipalName = result.Properties["displayName"][0].ToString();
        return userPrincipalName;
    }
    catch (Exception)
    {
        return String.Empty;
    }
}
```

Code snippet HelpDeskIVR\Workflow1.xoml.cs

Make sure you reference `System.DirectoryServices.dll` and add a `using` statement for `System.DirectoryServices`.

Using the PromptBuilder Class to Construct Prompts

Use the `PromptBuilder` class to construct a complex prompt piece by piece just as you would use a `StringBuilder` to construct a string by appending strings to it. You're already using the `PromptBuilder` behind the scenes when calling `AppendText` or `AppendBreak` (or any of the other *append* functions on a prompt). The only difference is that using the `PromptBuilder` class, you construct the prompt first, and then attach it to the activity.

Take a look at an example of setting the `NoRecognitionPrompt` of the `EnterPIN` activity using a `PromptBuilder`. First, clear the prompt. Create an instance of `PromptBuilder` and append the no-recognition prompt text to it. After appending a medium-length break, append the text of the `MainPrompt`, essentially repeating the instructions to the caller.

After the `PromptBuilder` has been constructed, call `AppendPromptBuilder` on the `NoRecognitionPrompt` of the `EnterPIN` activity and pass in the `PromptBuilder` instance as a parameter:

```
this.EnterPIN.Prompts.NoRecognitionPrompt.ClearContent();

var noRecPrompt = new PromptBuilder();
noRecPrompt.AppendText("Sorry, I didn't get that");
noRecPrompt.AppendBreak(PromptBreak.Medium);
noRecPrompt.AppendText(this.EnterPIN.MainPrompt.ToString());
this.EnterPIN.Prompts.NoRecognitionPrompt.AppendPromptBuilder(noRecPrompt);
```

Code snippet HelpDeskIVR\Workflow1.xoml.cs

Using Speech Hints to Improve Speech Synthesis

You can use speech hints to give the text-to-speech engine a hint on how the text should be synthesized. For example, if you append a date to a prompt, the text-to-speech engine will attempt to synthesize it phonetically unless you let it know that the text represents a date.

In the Help Desk IVR example, the IVR lists the Help Desk tickets created by the caller and the date they were created on. To present the choices to the caller, the `MainPrompt` of the `ChooseTicket` activity is constructed in a `for` loop in its `TurnStarting` handler. The loop iterates through the tickets created by the caller and appends the `MainPrompt` with the `Description` and `DateCreated` of the ticket. Use `AppendTextWithHint` to specify a `SayAs` hint; in this case using `SayAs.Date` to instruct the text-to-speech engine to synthesize the text as a date:

```
private void ChooseTicket_TurnStarting(object sender,
    Microsoft.Rtc.Workflow.Activities.SpeechTurnStartingEventArgs e)
{
    this.ChooseTicket.MainPrompt.ClearContent();
    this.ChooseTicket.MainPrompt.AppendText(
        "Please choose one of the following open tickets:");
    this.ChooseTicket.MainPrompt.AppendBreak(PromptBreak.Medium);

    foreach (var ticket in _tickets)
    {
        this.ChooseTicket.MainPrompt.AppendText("Ticket " + ticket.Id);
        this.ChooseTicket.MainPrompt.AppendBreak(PromptBreak.Small);
        this.ChooseTicket.MainPrompt.AppendText(ticket.Description);
        this.ChooseTicket.MainPrompt.AppendBreak(PromptBreak.Small);
        this.ChooseTicket.MainPrompt.AppendText("created on");
        this.ChooseTicket.MainPrompt.AppendTextWithHint(
            ticket.DateCreated.ToShortDateString(), SayAs.Date);
        this.ChooseTicket.MainPrompt.AppendBreak(PromptBreak.Medium);
    }
}
```

Code snippet HelpDeskIVR\Workflow1.xoml.cs

The SayAs enum is available in the Microsoft.Speech.Synthesis namespace and contains the following values:

- SpellOut
- NumberOrdinal
- NumberCardinal
- Date
- DayMonthYear
- MonthDayYear
- YearMonthDay
- YearMonth
- MonthYear
- MonthDay

- DayMonth
- Year
- Month
- Day
- Time
- Time24
- Time12
- Telephone
- Currency
- Text

Using AppendTextWithHint in conjunction with the Microsoft.Speech.Synthesis.SayAs enum gives you the ability to ensure that text is synthesized in the manner that you intend it to be; for example, using SpellOut to spell out some text, or Time24 to synthesize the time in 24-hour format.

Other Prompt Customizations

The PromptBuilder class (or default PromptBuilder exposed by the prompts of the SpeechStatement and SpeechQuestionAnswer activities) provides some more ways of customizing your activities' prompts.

Emphasis, Rate, and Volume

You can use different overloads of AppendText to append text to a prompt with a specific emphasis or at a certain rate or volume.

If you want to emphasize a certain piece of text, choose one of the values of the Microsoft .Speech.Synthesis.PromptEmphasis enum to override the default prompt emphasis:

- Strong
- Moderate
- Reduced

Choose one of the values of the `Microsoft.Speech.Synthesis.PromptRate` enum to tell the text-to-speech engine to synthesize the prompt text at a specific rate:

➤ ExtraFast

➤ Fast

➤ Medium

➤ Slow

➤ ExtraSlow

To synthesize prompt text at a particular volume, use the `Microsoft.Speech.SpeechSynthesis .PromptVolume` enum:

➤ ExtraSoft

➤ Soft

➤ Medium

➤ Loud

➤ ExtraLoud

Prompt Styles

Individual overloads of `AppendText` are available to synthesize text with a particular emphasis, rate, or volume. However, you can combine any or all three into a `PromptStyle` definition and use `StartStyle` and `EndStyle` to define bounds of for the style:

```
this.EnterPIN.Prompts.NoRecognitionPrompt.ClearContent();
var noRecPrompt = new PromptBuilder();
noRecPrompt.StartStyle(
    new PromptStyle()
    {
        Emphasis = PromptEmphasis.Strong,
        Rate = PromptRate.ExtraFast,
        Volume = PromptVolume.ExtraLoud
    });
this.EnterPIN.Prompts.NoRecognitionPrompt.AppendText(
    "Sorry, I did not hear that!");
this.EnterPIN.Prompts.NoRecognitionPrompt.EndStyle();
```

Sentences and Paragraphs

If your workflow contains longer prompts, you can divide them into paragraphs and sentences using `StartParagraph`, `StartSentence`, `EndParagraph`, and `EndSentence`.

Working with Professionally Recorded Prompts

Professional IVR systems typically use professionally recorded audio prompts instead of relying on synthesized text. Although audio prompts provide a much more polished — and human — feel to the IVR, pre-recording every piece of text that you expect to use in your prompts might be impossible. You might find that you need to mix audio prompts with synthesized text to achieve the result you need.

 Audio prompts should be recorded using the WAV format.

Adding Recorded Prompts to the Workflow Project

Add individual .wav files of your recorded prompts into a folder in your Visual Studio workflow project; for example, `audioprompts`. For it to be accessible by the workflow runtime, set the Build Action on each file to Content, and Copy to Output Directory to Copy Always.

Constructing Audio Prompts

Incorporating audio prompts into your activities is really simple; just call `AppendAudio` on a prompt or `PromptBuilder` instance and provide the path to the recording to use:

```
this.Welcome.Prompts.MainPrompt.AppendAudio(@"audioprompts\welcome.wav");
```

WORKING WITH GRAMMARS

If the input expected by a `SpeechQuestionAnswer` activity is too complex (or you just don't know it at design time) to be described in the `ExpectedDtmfInputs` or `ExpectedSpeechInputs` properties, you can specify a grammar against which the input will be validated. When you know in advance the various combinations of input that needs to be validated, you can define the validation rules in a GRXML grammar file. If the input you need to validate is more complex, you can use the objects in the `Microsoft.Speech.Recognition.SrgsGrammar` namespace to create a grammar dynamically at runtime.

Using GRXML Grammars to Validate Input

In the Help Desk IVR, the caller's PIN is a five-digit number. Before incurring the processing cost of validating the PIN against a back-end system, the workflow can at least verify that it is in the correct format. You can use a GRXML grammar to define the rules for validating a five-digit number.

Building a Simple Grammar File

A GRXML file is just an XML file that references the http://www.w3.org/2001/06/grammar namespace. The file contains rules that collectively define the grammar. You can use a grammar to validate both DTMF and voice input — the caller can say her PIN or enter it using the Lync keypad:

```
<grammar xmlns="http://www.w3.org/2001/06/grammar"
         version="1.0"
         tag-format="properties-ms/1.0"
         xml:lang="en-US"
         root="validPIN">
  <rule id="digit" scope="public">
    <one-of>
      <item>0</item>
      <item>1</item>
      <item>2</item>
      <item>3</item>
      <item>4</item>
      <item>5</item>
      <item>6</item>
      <item>7</item>
      <item>8</item>
      <item>9</item>
    </one-of>
  </rule>
  <rule id="validPIN" scope="public">
    <one-of>
      <item repeat="5">
        <ruleref uri="#digit"/>
      </item>
    </one-of>
  </rule>
</grammar>
```

Code snippet HelpDeskIVR\PINGrammar.grxml

 To specify that a grammar should only be used to validate DTMF or Voice input, set its mode *attribute; for example,* mode="dtmf" *or* mode="voice".

Creating Rules

The PIN grammar contains two rules: digit and validPIN. The digit rule specifies that in order for the input that the rule processes to be considered valid, it needs to be <one-of> the listed <item>s.

The validPIN rule references the digit rule and specifies that valid input should consist of a sequence of five items that satisfy the digit rule. For example, 123e5 would be considered invalid, whereas 12345 would be considered valid input.

Specifying a Default Rule

The rule specified in the grammar's `root` is the rule that is used to process input. As you can see in the example of the PIN grammar, the root rule can reference other rules in the grammar.

Associating a Grammar File with a Workflow Activity

To associate a GRXML grammar with a workflow activity, set the `DtmfGrammars` or `Grammars` property of the activity, as shown in Figure 14-24.

In order for it to be accessible by the workflow runtime, set the Build Action on each grammar file packaged with the workflow to Content, and Copy to Output Directory to Copy Always, as shown in Figure 14-25.

FIGURE 14-24

FIGURE 14-25

Building Grammars Dynamically in Code

In the Help Desk IVR, the `ChooseTicket` activity in the workflow doesn't know until runtime how many open tickets are available for the caller. If the caller only has two open tickets, an input of three when prompted to choose the ticket should be considered invalid. The ability to set the expected inputs for the activity at design time — or use a GRXML grammar — isn't sufficient to validate the caller's input in this case. You must construct a grammar dynamically based on the number of open tickets.

Before creating the new grammar, clear out the activity's `ExpectedDtmfInputs` and `Expected SpeechInputs` properties.

The number of choices to present to the caller is the number of open tickets from the caller. Create a `string[]` of choices based on the IDs of the open tickets.

Create an instance of the `SrgsDocument` class to define the grammar. Add a new rule to the grammar by creating a new `SrgsRule`. Similarly to how you defined a `<one-of>` rule declaratively in the GRXML file, you can create that rule in code by creating an instance of `SrgsOneOf` and providing the `string[]` of choices, and adding it to the rule.

Add the rule to the grammar's `Rules` collection and then set it as the grammar's `Root` rule.

Finally, clear the activity's `DtmfGrammars` and `Grammars` collections and add the new grammar to each collection, as shown in the following code.

Remember that because this code might be executing in the `Turn_Starting` *handler of an activity, clearing these properties before setting them is important; otherwise, the new grammar will be added again to the Grammars collection of the activity every time the* `Turn_Starting` *handler executes.*

Available for download on Wrox.com

```
this.ChooseTicket.ExpectedDtmfInputs = null;
this.ChooseTicket.ExpectedSpeechInputs = null;

var choices = new string[_tickets.Count];
choices = (from t in _tickets select t.Id.ToString()).ToArray();

var grammar = new SrgsDocument();

var rule = new SrgsRule("Items");
var oneOf = new SrgsOneOf(choices);
rule.Elements.Add(oneOf);
grammar.Rules.Add(rule);
grammar.Root = rule;

this.ChooseTicket.DtmfGrammars.Clear();
this.ChooseTicket.DtmfGrammars.Add(new Grammar(grammar));
this.ChooseTicket.Grammars.Clear();
this.ChooseTicket.Grammars.Add(new Grammar(grammar));
```

Code snippet HelpDeskIVR\Workflow1.xoml.cs

You can also optionally specify the grammar's mode by setting the `Mode` *property of the* `SrgsDocument` *to a value of the* `Microsoft.Speech.Recognition.SrgsGrammar` *enum, for example:*

```
grammar.Mode = SrgsGrammarMode.Dtmf;
```

Other Tools to Build GRXML Grammars

Unfortunately, the UCMA 3.0 Workflow SDK doesn't contain any tools specifically intended for authoring GRXML grammars. Developers familiar with Microsoft Speech Server 2007 will recall that it contains tools for authoring GRXML grammars. Many IVR developers still rely on the tools available with Speech Server 2007 to author GRXML grammars intended for use in a UCMA 3.0 Workflow SDK communications workflow.

The sample applications installed as part of the UCMA 3.0 Workflow SDK contain some helpful examples of more complex GRXML grammars. You can find these sample applications at `C:\Program Files\Microsoft UCMA 3.0\SDK\Workflow\Sample Applications`.

The Microsoft Speech Platform SDK installed as part of the UCMA 3.0 SDK also contains very helpful sample GRXML grammars. You can find these at `C:\Program Files\Microsoft Speech Platform SDK\Samples\Sample Grammars`.

COMMUNICATIONS EVENTS AND COMMANDS

Communications events and commands add another dimension to a communications workflow in that they provide a global way to handle workflow events and react to workflow commands from the caller. Events and commands are scoped to a communications sequence; you can access them from the context menu of the `CommunicationsSequence` activity by selecting View Commands or View CommunicationsEvents.

Handling Global Workflow Events

The metaphor for integrating communications event activities into your workflow is the same regardless of the activity. Open the `CommunicationsEvents` activity of the communications sequence by selecting View CommunicationsEvents from the context menu of the `CommunicationsSequence` activity. Drag an event activity into the `CommunicationsEvents` activity and configure its properties if applicable. Finally, create the workflow activities that will execute with the event is triggered.

ConsecutiveNoRecognitionsSpeechEvent

Use the `ConsecutiveNoRecognitionsSpeechEvent` activity to define a workflow sequence that executes when the caller's input into a `SpeechQuestionAnswer` activity isn't recognized after a configurable number of attempts. For example, in the Help Desk IVR, you might want to transfer the caller to an agent if she enters an invalid PIN three times.

Drag a `ConsecutiveNoRecognitionsSpeechEvent` activity into the `CommunicationsEvents` activity. Open the properties of the activity and set the value of `MaximumNoRecognitions` to 3, as shown in Figure 14-26.

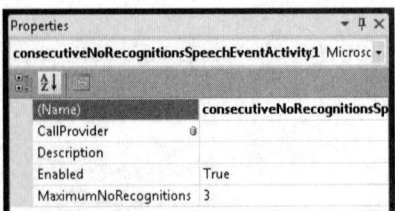

FIGURE 14-26

Drag a `SpeechStatement` activity into the `ConsecutiveNo RecognitionsSpeechEvent` activity, as shown in Figure 14-27, to let the caller know that he is going to be transferred to an agent. Set the `MainPrompt` property of the `SpeechStatement` activity to: **It looks like you need help, let me transfer you to an agent**.

Drag a `BlindTransfer` activity into the `CommunicationsEvents` activity, as shown in Figure 14-27, to perform a blind transfer of the call to an agent.

In a real IVR system, you will want to do something more sophisticated than blindly transferring the call to someone; for example, forward the call to an Automatic Call Distributor that will queue the call and wait for an available agent.

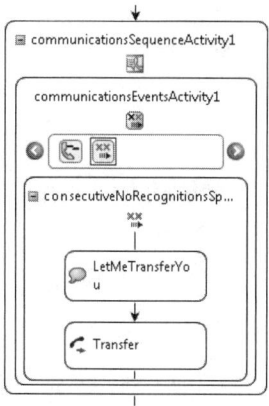

FIGURE 14-27

Other Communications Event Activities

Here are the other communications event activities and the configurable properties you can set for each.

➤ `CallDisconnectedEvent`: A `CallDisconnectedEvent` activity is added by default to every workflow. Use this activity to execute custom logic after the caller disconnects the call.

➤ `CallOnHoldEvent`: The `CallOnHoldEvent` activity executes when the caller is placed on hold.

➤ `CallOnHoldTimeoutEvent`: The `CallOnHoldTimeoutEvent` activity executes when the caller has been on holder for longer than the time specified in the `CallOnHoldTimeout` property.

➤ `CallRetrievedEvent`: The `CallRetrievedEvent` activity executes when the caller is taken off hold.

➤ `ConsecutiveSilencesSpeechEvent`: The `ConsecutiveSilencesSpeechEvent` activity executes when the caller is silent a number of times in a row specified in the `MaximumSilences` property. When no input is provided within the time specified in the `InitialSilenceTimeout` of a `SpeechQuestionAnswer` activity, it is treated as silence.

➤ `ConsecutiveNoInputsSpeechEvent`: The `ConsecutiveNoInputsSpeechEvent` activity executes when the caller fails to provide input a number of times in a row specified in the `MaximumNoInputs` property.

Each no-recognition or silence event counts as a no-input event. The `ConsecutiveNoInputs SpeechEvent` activity is thus able to handle a mix of no-recognition and silence events and act accordingly.

For example, set the `MaximumNoInputs` property of the `ConsecutiveNoInputsSpeechEvent` activity to 3. Set the `MaximumNoRecognitions` property of the `ConsecutiveNoRecognitionsSpeechEvent` activity to 3, and set the `MaximumSilences` property of the `ConsecutiveSilencesSpeechEvent` activity to 3, as well.

Consider the following input sequence from the caller in response to the `EnterPIN` activity (see Table 14-2):

TABLE 14-2: User Prompt Sequence

SEQUENCE	DESCRIPTION
Prompt	Please enter your PIN.
Caller Response	Silence
Prompt	Sorry, I did not hear that. Please enter your PIN.
Caller Response	123e4
Prompt	I didn't get that. Please enter your PIN.
Caller Response	Silence

At this point, neither the `ConsecutiveNoRecognitionsSpeechEvent` nor `ConsecutiveSilences` `SpeechEvent` activities have reached the threshold defined in the `MaximumNoRecognitions` and `MaximumSilences` properties, respectively. However, in this sequence, three no-inputs have occurred. This causes the `ConsecutiveNoInputsSpeechEvent` activity to execute.

These event activities function identically to their speech counterparts:

➤ `ConsecutiveSilencesInstantMessagingEvent`

➤ `ConsecutiveNoRecognitionsInstantMessagingEvent`

➤ `ConsecutiveNoInputsInstantMessagingEvent`

Implementing Global Workflow Commands

Workflow commands provide a global mechanism for a communications workflow to process commands from the user such as "Help," or "Operator." The `SpeechHelpCommand` and `SpeechRepeatCommand` are closely tied to the `HelpPrompt` and `RepeatPrompt` prompt properties of the `SpeechQuestionAnswer` activity. They trigger those prompts to play on the `SpeechQuestionAnswer` activity that the caller is currently on. The `SpeechCommand` is a more powerful workflow command since a caller can trigger it regardless of the `SpeechQuestionAnswer` activity that he is on.

To add workflow commands to the `Commands` activity of the communications sequence, open the `Commands` activity by selecting View Commands from the context menu of the `CommunicationsSequence` activity. Drag a command activity into the `Commands` activity and configure its properties if applicable. Finally, create the workflow activities that will execute when the caller triggers the command.

SpeechHelpCommand

The `SpeechHelpCommand` activity is used to provide the caller with a mechanism to request help during the workflow. Set the `ExpectedDtmfInputs` and `ExpectedSpeechInputs` properties of

`SpeechHelpCommand` activity. When the workflow is processing any `SpeechQuestionAnswer` activity in the workflow, if the user provides input that matches the grammars defined for the `SpeechHelpCommand`, the caller will hear the `RepeatPrompt` of that activity.

Drag a `SpeechHelpCommand` activity into the `Commands` activity as shown in Figure 14-28.

Open the Properties of the `SpeechHelpCommand` activity and set its `ExpectedDtmfInputs` to "0" and `ExpectedSpeechInputs` to "Help" as shown in Figure 14-29. When the caller enters 0 or says Help, he will hear the `RepeatPrompt` of the activity he is on.

You can drag other workflow activities into the `SpeechHelpCommandActivity`; for example, to acknowledge to the caller that he asked for help, as shown in Figure 14-30.

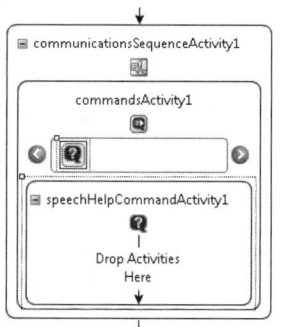

FIGURE 14-28

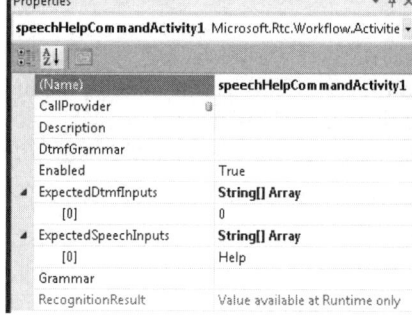

FIGURE 14-29

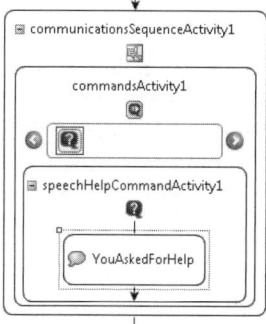

FIGURE 14-30

More importantly, set the value for `HelpPrompt` for the various activities in the workflow so that they are equipped to handle the Help command. For example, set the `HelpPrompt` of the `EnterPIN` activity to: **I need your PIN so I can log you in to the Help Desk.** A good technique is to append some text to the activity's `HelpPrompt`, and then append the value of the `MainPrompt`, effectively offering some explanation to the caller and then repeating the instructions.

SpeechRepeatCommand

The `SpeechRepeatCommand` activity is almost identical to the `SpeechHelpCommand`, except that it is tied to the `RepeatPrompt` of `SpeechQuestionAnswer` activities in the workflow. Define the `ExpectedDtmfInputs` and `ExpectedSpeechInputs` properties of the activity. When the caller provides input that matches those grammars, they will hear the `RepeatPrompt` of the activity he is on.

SpeechCommand

The `SpeechCommand` activity is a very flexible command activity that you can configure via its `ExpectedDtmfInputs` and `ExpectedSpeechInputs` properties to recognize and act upon specific input from the caller.

A frustrated caller might begin to repeatedly say, "Operator" or "Agent." Configuring a `SpeechCommand` to recognize this and act on it is critical to providing a good experience for the caller, perhaps transferring him to a priority customer service queue with a shorter hold time.

CALLING UCMA CODE FROM A COMMUNICATIONS WORKFLOW

When working with the UCMA 3.0 Workflow SDK, you will quickly realize that the built-in workflow activities are only enough for basic communications scenarios. For example, it's unlikely that you will ever use the `BlindTransfer` activity in a production IVR application. When transferring a call, you will typically want to perform an attended transfer, where the application only disconnects from the call after the called party picks up. No built-in workflow activity to perform an attended transfer exists. However, there is nothing stopping you from including custom UCMA code to perform an attended transfer in your workflow solution.

When the caller chooses a ticket in the Help Desk IVR application, instead of performing a blind transfer of the call to the agent that the ticket is assigned to, the application should perform an attended transfer of the call to the agent. This section describes how to use a `Code` activity to call custom UCMA code that performs an attended transfer of the call to the agent.

In an attended transfer, the original call is only disconnected when the called party picks up the call. This allows you to add some business logic to the call transfer process to deal with any errors that may occur during the transfer, or if the person who the call is being transferred to declines the call or doesn't pick up within a set amount of time.

Creating a Code Activity to Perform the Attended Transfer

To perform an attended call transfer, you need to write UCMA code to impersonate the caller, create a new call, and then transfer the call. You can implement this logic in a `Code` activity.

Add a `Code` activity, as shown in Figure 14-31, that will contain the code used to perform the attended call transfer.

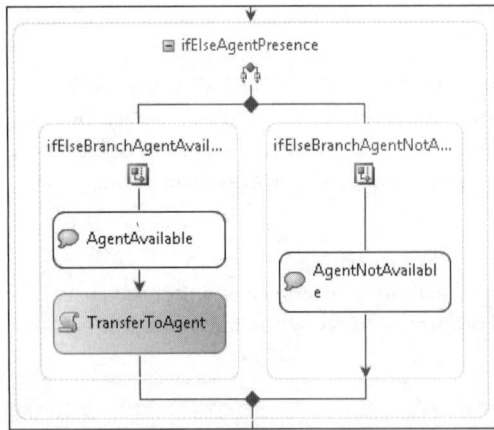

FIGURE 14-31

In the `ExecuteCode` handler of the `Code` activity, get a handle to the conversation endpoint and create a new `Conversation` on the endpoint, as shown in the following code. You will use this new `Conversation` object to establish a new `AudioVideo` call to the agent that the ticket is assigned to.

```
private void TransferToAgent_ExecuteCode(object sender, EventArgs e)
{
    // Get the local endpoint
    var endpoint =
        communicationsSequenceActivity1.CallProvider.Call.Conversation.Endpoint;

    // Create a new conversation on the endpoint
    var conversation = new Conversation(endpoint);

    ...
}
```

Code snippet HelpDeskIVR\Workflow1.xoml.cs

Impersonating the Caller

When you transfer the call to the agent, it will appear to come from the URI of the trusted application endpoint by default, as shown in the following code. However, you can use impersonation so that the call appears to come from the person who initially called into the Help Desk IVR.

```
...

// Impersonate the caller
conversation.Impersonate(
    communicationsSequenceActivity1.CallProvider
        .Call.RemoteEndpoint.Participant.Uri,
    null,
    null);

...
```

Code snippet HelpDeskIVR\Workflow1.xoml.cs

Call the `Impersonate` method on the `Conversation` object and provide the SIP URI of the contact to impersonate. In this case, use the SIP URI of the person who called the Help Desk IVR.

Creating a New AudioVideo Call

You're now ready to write the logic to transfer the call to the agent that the ticket is assigned to. Create a new `AudioVideoCall` on the `Conversation` instance as shown in the following code.

This code chains the calls to the `AudioVideoCall`'s `BeginEstablish` and `EndEstablish` methods to run the code synchronously. If you run this code asynchronously, the workflow runtime will continue to execute and may reach the workflow's `DisconnectCall` activity before beginning the call transfer process.

The `BeginEstablish` method accepts a destination SIP URI and an instance of `AudioVideoCall` `EstablishOptions`. Use the `MaximumEstablishTime` property of `AudioVideoCallEstablish` `Options` to specify that the call should be established within 60 seconds.

```
...

// Create a new AudioVideoCall
var avCall = new AudioVideoCall(conversation);

try
{
    // Establish the call synchronously
    avCall.EndEstablish(
        avCall.BeginEstablish(
            this.TicketAssignedTo,
            new AudioVideoCallEstablishOptions()
            {
                MaximumEstablishTime = new TimeSpan(0, 0, 60)
            },
            null,
            null));
}
catch (RealTimeException exEstablish)
{
    throw exEstablish;
}

...
```

Code snippet HelpDeskIVR\Workflow1.xoml.cs

Transferring the Call

With the new `AudioVideo` call established, you can now perform an attended transfer of the original call to the agent. The original call is the call that was initially made by the caller to the Help Desk IVR. Get a reference to the original call via the `Call` property of the `CallProvider` in the communications sequence activity, and cast it to an `AudioVideoCall` object.

Call `BeginTransfer` synchronously, specifying the call to replace and an instance of `CallTransferOptions` that indicates that the transfer type is `CallTransferType.Attended`:

```
...

try
{

    var initialCall =
        communicationsSequenceActivity1.CallProvider.Call
```

```
    as AudioVideoCall;

        initialCall.EndTransfer(
            initialCall.BeginTransfer(
                avCall,
                new CallTransferOptions(CallTransferType.Attended),
                null,
                null));
    }
    catch (OperationFailureException ofe)
    {
        Console.WriteLine
    ("The agent declined or did not answer the call: {0}",
     ofe.Message);

    }
    catch (RealTimeException exTransfer)
    {
        throw exTransfer;
    }

    ...
```

Code snippet HelpDeskIVR\Workflow1.xoml.cs

Catch the `OperationFailureException` when transferring the call. This exception is thrown if the person to whom the call was transferred declines or doesn't answer the call.

BUILDING YOUR OWN WORKFLOW ACTIVITIES

You can build your own Windows Workflow Foundation activities to use in your communications workflow solution; for example, an activity that sends an email to a user given her address, or an activity that looks up the Active Directory display name for a user given her SIP URI. In this section, you learn how to create a custom workflow activity to perform an attended call transfer.

The UCMA 3.0 Workflow SDK activities use classes from the `Microsoft.Speech` *namespace to perform speech synthesis and text-to-speech processing. In UCMA, the* `Player` *and* `Recorder` *classes in the* `Microsoft.Rtc.Collaboration` *namespace are used to play and record media from various sources. The* `Player` *and* `Recorder` *classes implement optimizations for working with real-time media; however, the classes in the* `Microsoft.Speech` *namespace don't implement these optimizations. When building applications with the UCMA 3.0 Workflow SDK activities designed for audio calls, you may notice some media-related performance issues since the activities have to use the un-optimized classes in the* `Microsoft.Speech` *namespace to handle media. If you are concerned about audio performance under high load, you can consider creating custom workflow activities that play audio files on a call using the* `Player` *class. This will allow you to take full advantage of the optimizations for real-time media.*

Creating the Custom Activity

If you are building custom activities that you intend to use across multiple communications workflow solutions, you will typically put them in their own assembly. In this example, create the custom workflow activity directly in the communications workflow project for simplicity.

Add a new activity to the Visual Studio project. You can find the Activity project item type in the Workflow section of the Add New Item dialog, as shown in Figure 14-32. Call the new activity `AttendedTransferActivity.cs`.

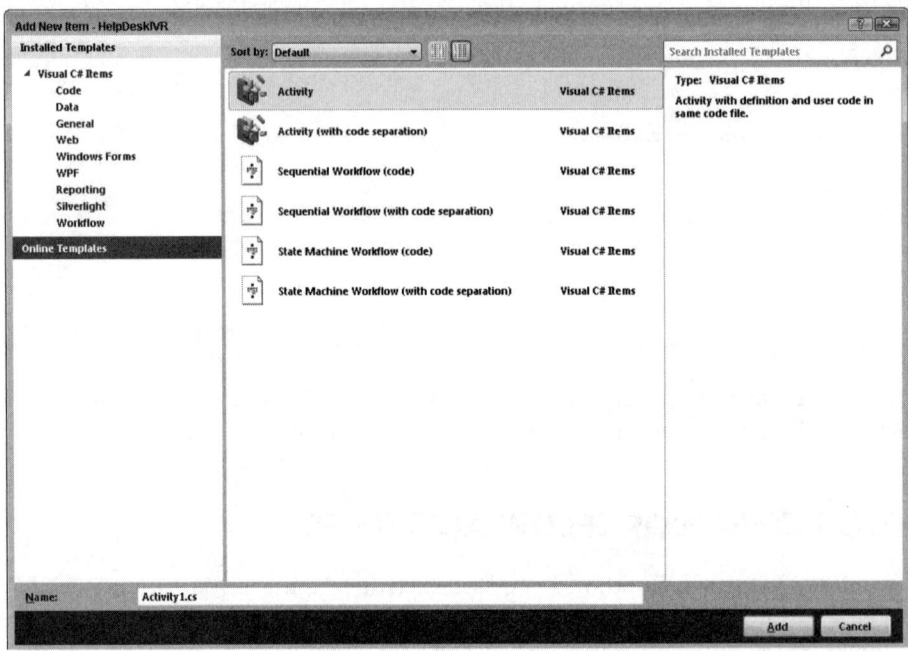

FIGURE 14-32

This creates a workflow activity of type `System.Workflow.Activities.SequenceActivity`. This type of activity is similar to the `CommunicationsSequence` activity in that it can contain other activities. This isn't the desired type of activity for the attended call transfer call activity; change the type of the activity to `System.Workflow.ComponentModel.Activity`.

Double-click `AttendedTransferActivity.cs` in the Solution Explorer window to open the activity in design view, as shown in Figure 14-33.

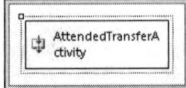

FIGURE 14-33

Defining the Custom Activity's Properties

When working with the other workflow activities in the UCMA 3.0 Workflow SDK, you saw that they expose properties that you can set in the workflow designer or in the code-behind. The custom workflow activity that you will be building will expose a `CalledParty` property that you can set to specify the contact that the activity will perform an attended transfer to. This section describes how to define the CalledParty and other properties of the custom workflow activity.

Switch the code view of the activity. You need to define the properties of the custom activity that you can set in the workflow designer. For example, the SIP URI of the contact to perform an attended transfer to should be a parameter of the custom activity.

Define a CalledParty dependency property in the custom activity. Dependency properties are commonly used in Silverlight and WPF to define properties that will be used in data binding. Later when you add the AttendedTransfer activity to the design surface of the communications workflow, you will be able to set its CalledParty property in its Properties dialog and bind it to a variable in the workflow project.

A dependency property definition should also include a property accessor to get and set the values of the property. The CalledParty property accessor is decorated with a [ValidationOption (ValidationOption.Required)] attribute to indicate that it is required:

```
public static DependencyProperty CalledPartyProperty =
    DependencyProperty.Register(
        "CalledParty",
        typeof(string),
        typeof(AttendedTransferActivity));

[ValidationOption(ValidationOption.Required)]
public string CalledParty
{
    get
    {
        return (string)base.GetValue(CalledPartyProperty);
    }
    set
    {
        base.SetValue(CalledPartyProperty, value);
    }
}
```

Code snippet HelpDeskIVR\AttendedTransferActivity.cs

Also define a dependency property called WorkflowCall representing the initial call that was made into the workflow, as shown in the following code. The Call provides access to several items required by the code to perform an attended transfer: the endpoint, the SIP URI of the caller, and the call itself.

```
public static DependencyProperty WorkflowCallProperty =
    DependencyProperty.Register(
        "WorkflowCall",
        typeof(Call),
        typeof(AttendedTransferActivity));

[ValidationOption(ValidationOption.Required)]
public Call WorkflowCall
```

```
    {
        get
        {
            return (Call)base.GetValue(WorkflowCallProperty);
        }
        set
        {
            base.SetValue(WorkflowCallProperty, value);
        }
    }
}
```

Code snippet HelpDeskIVR\AttendedTransferActivity.cs

Implementing the Activity Logic

Having defined the properties of the custom activity that you can set in the workflow designer or in the code-behind, you can now implement the code that will execute when the activity is processed by the workflow runtime. To do this, you will override the `Execute` method of the `System.Workflow.Activities.SequenceActivity` class and provide the code implementation to perform the attended call transfer.

Implement the workflow logic in the overridden `Execute` method as shown in the following code. The method returns a value of the `System.Workflow.ComponentModel.ActivityExecutionStatus` enum representing the execution status of the workflow.

This code is almost identical to the attended transfer code from the previous exception; the only different is that it references the `CalledParty` and `WorkflowCall` dependency properties of the activity instead of referencing a module level variable for the SIP URI and properties of `communicationsSequenceActivity1` directly.

If the code throws an exception, the function returns `ActivityExecutionStatus.Faulting`, otherwise it returns `ActivityExecutionStatus.Closed`, indicating success.

```
protected override ActivityExecutionStatus
    Execute(ActivityExecutionContext executionContext)
{
    try
    {
        // Get the local endpoint
        var endpoint = this.WorkflowCall.Conversation.Endpoint;

        // Create a new conversation on the endpoint
        var conversation = new Conversation(endpoint);

        // Impersonate the caller
        conversation.Impersonate(
            this.WorkflowCall.RemoteEndpoint.Participant.Uri,
            null,
            null);

        // Create a new AudioVideoCall
```

```csharp
        var avCall = new AudioVideoCall(conversation);

        try
        {
            // Establish the call synchronously
            avCall.EndEstablish(
                avCall.BeginEstablish(
                    this.CalledParty,
                    new AudioVideoCallEstablishOptions()
                    {
                        MaximumEstablishTime = new TimeSpan(0, 0, 60)
                    },
                    null,
                    null));
        }
        catch (RealTimeException exEstablish)
        {
            throw exEstablish;
        }

        try
        {
            var initialCall = this.WorkflowCall as AudioVideoCall;

            initialCall.EndTransfer(
                initialCall.BeginTransfer(
                    avCall,
                    new CallTransferOptions(CallTransferType.Attended),
                    null,
                    null));
        }
        catch (OperationFailureException ofe)
        {
            Console.WriteLine(
                "The agent declined or did not answer the call: {0}",
                ofe.Message);

        }
        catch (RealTimeException exTransfer)
        {
            throw exTransfer;
        }
    }
    catch (Exception)
    {
        return ActivityExecutionStatus.Faulting;
    }

    return ActivityExecutionStatus.Closed;
}
```

Code snippet HelpDeskIVR\AttendedTransferActivity.cs

Adding the Custom Activity to the Workflow

The custom activity is now ready to be used in a communications workflow project. If you are building a library of custom workflow activities, it is better to place them in their own assembly and reference that assembly from your communications workflow project. The custom activities will appear in the Visual Studio Toolbox so that you can add them to the communications workflow.

In this example, the custom activity is defined directly in the communications workflow project and will be available in the Toolbox after compiling the project. Compile the project. You should now see the `AttendedTransfer` activity in the Visual Studio Toolbox, as shown in Figure 14-34.

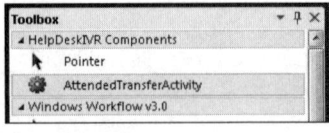

FIGURE 14-34

Drag an `AttendedTransfer` activity onto the workflow design surface, as shown in Figure 14-35. You can disable the `Code` activity that you previously used to perform the attended call transfer.

Open the Properties dialog of the `AttendedTransfer` activity to set the values of the `CallParty` and `WorkflowCall` properties of the activity, as shown in Figure 14-36. Because these properties are defined as dependency properties, you can bind them to other variables in the communications workflow.

Bind the `CalledParty` property of the `AttendedTransfer` activity to the `TicketAssignedTo` property of the communications workflow, as shown in Figure 14-37.

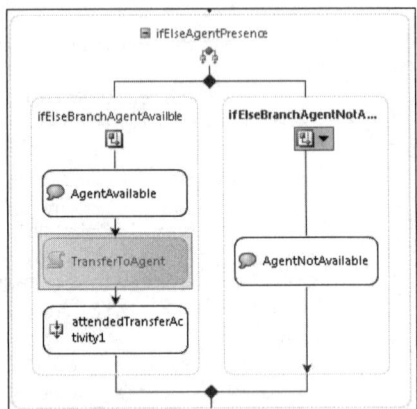

FIGURE 14-35

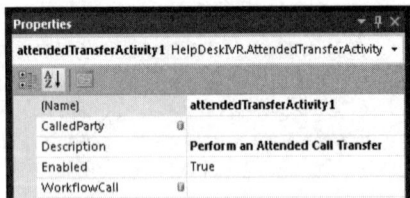

FIGURE 14-36

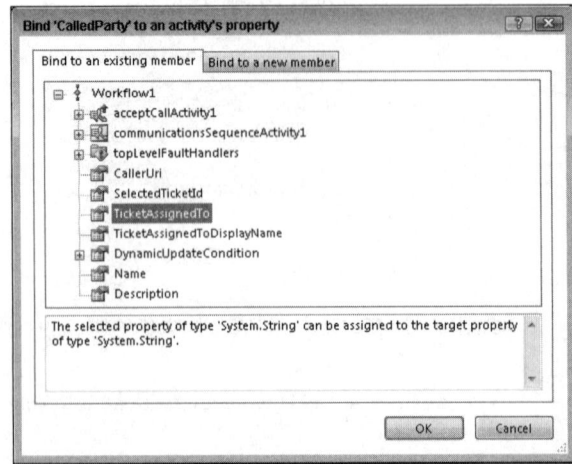

FIGURE 14-37

Bind the `WorkflowCall` property of the `AttendedTransfer` activity to the `Call` property of the `CallProvider` instance exposed by `communicationsSequenceActivity1`, as shown in Figure 14-38.

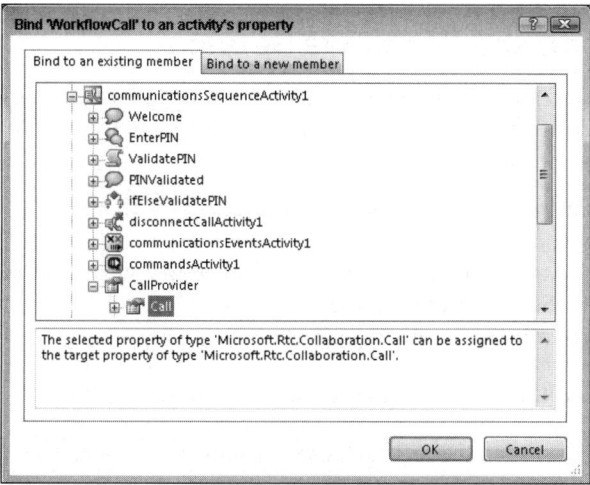

FIGURE 14-38

The `AttendedTransfer` custom workflow activity now completely encapsulates the functionality to perform an attended call transfer.

DEPLOYING A COMMUNICATIONS WORKFLOW IN A WINDOWS SERVICE

In a production environment, you will typically deploy a UCMA 3.0 Workflow SDK communications workflow as part of a Windows Service. Running the workflow in a Windows Service provides the support for the long-running process that the communications workflow is intended to be, as well as the tools necessary to manage the lifecycle of the service.

In this section, you learn how to create a Windows Service project intended to host the UCMA 3.0 Workflow SDK communications workflow. You also learn how to start and stop the communications workflow from the Windows Service project, and also how to install and configure the Windows Service on a Windows server.

Adding a Windows Service Project to the Solution

In this section, you will add a Windows Service project to the solution containing your communications workflow. The service will reference the workflow project and is responsible for starting and stopping the workflow.

From the Visual Studio Solution Explorer window, right-click the solution and choose Add ➪ New Project. In the Add New Project dialog window, under Visual C#, select Windows, and choose Windows Service to create a new Windows Service project and add it to the solution. Give the new project the name HelpDeskIVR.Service.

Add a project reference from the HelpDeskIVR.Service project to the HelpDeskIVR project. This will allow you to call into the workflow project's `WorkflowInitiator` class to start and stop the communications workflow.

Setting the Current Directory for the Windows Service

When you package files such as grammars and audio prompts with the communications workflow as Content / Copy Always, the Windows Service hosting the workflow expects to find these files in the same location as the service's compiled executable.

However, if you don't set the service's current directory, this location defaults to `C:\Windows\System32`. The Windows Service obviously won't find these files in `C:\Windows\System32`. Use `SetCurrentDirectory` to instruct the service to use the directory that it is installed in as its current directory. Open `Program.cs` in the Windows Service project and add the following code snippet to the body of the `Main` function to set the current directory of the service.

Available for download on Wrox.com

```
Directory.SetCurrentDirectory(System.AppDomain.CurrentDomain.BaseDirectory);
```

Code snippet HelpDeskIVR.Service\Program.cs

Use `System.IO.Directory.SetCurrentDirectory` to set the current directory of the Windows Service, where `System.AppDomain.CurrentDomain.BaseDirectory` is the directory where the Windows Service executable is running from.

> *When you reference the workflow project from the Windows Service project, some files from the workflow project are not copied automatically into the output of the Windows Service project; for example, the* `app.config` *file, or recorded prompt files. You need to create a copy of these files in the Windows Service project. Alternatively, you can create them as Solution Items and then add them as linked items to both the communications workflow project and the Windows Service project.*

Starting and Stopping the Communications Workflow from the Windows Service

When deploying a communications workflow inside a Windows Service, the communications workflow should start when the service starts and stop when the service stops. The HelpDeskIVR.Service project references the HelpDeskIVR project, allowing the service to call methods in the `WorkflowInitiator` class of the workflow project to start and stop the communications workflow. This section describes how the Windows Service starts and stops the communications workflow.

Open `Service1.cs` in the Windows Service project and add a `using` statement to the top of the class definition to reference the communications workflow project namespace.

Create a module-level variable representing an instance of the `WorkflowInitiator` class from the HelpDeskIVR project. You will use this to start and stop the communications workflow from within the `OnStart` and `OnStop` methods in `Service1`. In the `OnStart` method, create an instance of the `WorkflowInitiator` class and call `Initialize` to initialize and start the communications workflow. In the `OnStop` method, call `Cleanup` on the instance of `WorkflowInitiator` to stop the communications workflow and tear down the corresponding UCMA application endpoint and collaboration platform, as shown in the following code.

```csharp
public partial class Service1 : ServiceBase
{
    WorkflowInitiator _initiator;

    public Service1()
    {
        InitializeComponent();
    }

    protected override void OnStart(string[] args)
    {
        _initiator = new WorkflowInitiator();
        _initiator.Initialize();
    }

    protected override void OnStop()
    {
        _initiator.Cleanup();
    }
}
```

Code snippet HelpDeskIVR.Service\Service1.cs

Adding an Installer to the Windows Service

You can add an installer class to a Windows Service project to package directly into the project information about how to configure and run the service. This information is then available to a service installation utility such as InstallUtil .exe when installing the service. This section describes adding an installer class to the Windows Service project to set the display name when the service is listed in the Server Manager and to define the security context under which the service will run.

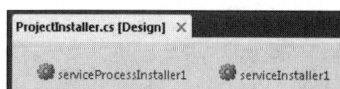

FIGURE 14-39

Open `Service1` in design view, right-click on the design surface and select Add Installer. This adds an installer item called `ProjectInstaller` to the project. As shown in Figure 14-39, `ServiceInstaller` and `ServiceProcessInstaller` installation components are automatically added to the design surface.

Open the properties of `serviceInstaller1`; here you can set the service's display name, as shown in Figure 14-40.

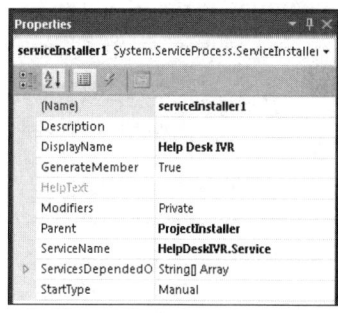

FIGURE 14-40

Open the properties of `serviceProcessInstaller1`; here you can set the security context in which the service will run, as shown in Figure 14-41.

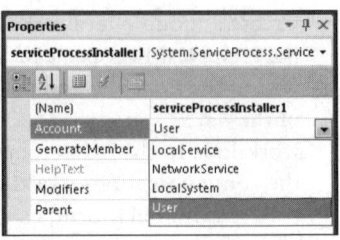

You can set `Account` to one of the following:

➤ `LocalService`

➤ `NetworkService`

FIGURE 14-41

➤ `LocalSystem`

➤ `User`

Set the value of the Account property to `User`. You will most likely want to run the service under a specific account identity. You configure that as part of the service installation process or in the Server Manager after installing the service.

Installing the Windows Service Using InstallUtil

You're now ready to deploy the Windows Service so that you can manage it from the Server Manager.

Compile the Windows Service project and copy the project output to a folder on the server where you will configure the service to run from. For example, create a folder at `C:\HelpDeskIVR` on the server and copy all the contents of `...\HelpDeskIVR.Service\bin\Release` from your development environment into `C:\HelpDeskIVR on the server`. Any files that you marked as Content / Copy Always will automatically be copied into the Windows Service project output directory when you compile it; for example, your grammar files and audio prompts.

Use the `InstallUtil` utility to install the Windows Service; you can find `InstallUtil.exe` in the .NET 2.0 installation directory; for example, `C:\Windows\Microsoft.NET\Framework\v2.0.50727` or `C:\Windows\Microsoft.NET\Framework64\v2.0.50727`.

 Use the appropriate version of `InstallUtil` to install the service as a 32- or 64-bit service. Be sure to set the Platform Target of your communications workflow and Windows Service projects appropriately.

Assuming that the Help Desk IVR service executable is at `C:\HelpDeskIVR\HelpDeskIVR.Service.exe`, use the following command to install the Windows Service:

```
InstallUtil.exe
C:\HelpDeskIVR\HelpDeskIVR.Service.exe
```

As shown in Figure 14-42, you are immediately prompted to set the account identity that the service will run under. Enter the credentials that the service will use.

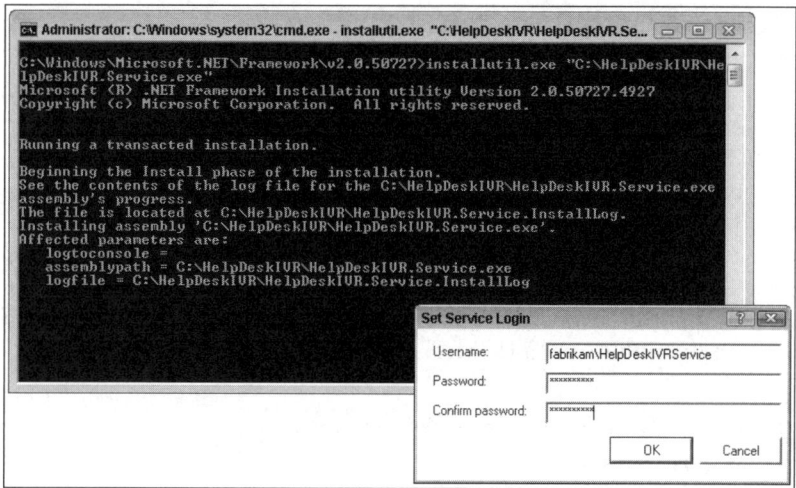

FIGURE 14-42

After the installation is completed, an installation log file is created in the service directory. The file contains details of about the events that occurred during the installation process.

Use the /u switch to uninstall the service, for example:

```
InstallUtil.exe /u
C:\HelpDeskIVR\HelpDeskIVR.Service.exe
```

Configuring and Starting the Service

If the service installation succeeded, you will see the service listed in the Services Control Manager in the Server Manager, as shown in Figure 14-43. Here you can configure which account to use as the identity of the service and also start and stop the service.

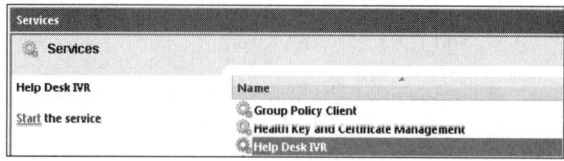

FIGURE 14-43

Because the service StartType was set to Manual in the service installer, the Help Desk IVR service isn't started by default. Start the service. If any errors occur during startup, you will be able to see them in the server's Event Viewer.

 To debug a Windows Service, you must attach to its process from Visual Studio. Note than when you use this technique you can't debug any logic in the service's OnStart *method.*

HOSTING A COMMUNICATIONS WORKFLOW IN A UCMA APPLICATION

A complex communications-enabled application such as a Contact Center or Automatic Call Distributor will usually include one or more workflow components. In a call center, the caller is routed through an IVR to capture the reason for their call; for example, a New Order. The output from the IVR is captured and the caller is placed on hold while an agent with the right skills becomes available. Unlike the simple examples in this chapter where the workflow begins with an `AcceptCall` activity and ends with a `DisconnectCall` activity, the communications workflow is only a small part of the overall application. In this section, you learn how to integrate a UCMA 3.0 Workflow SDK communications workflow into a UCMA application.

Integrating a Communications Workflow XOML Into a UCMA Application

The code accompanying this chapter includes a console-based UCMA application that accepts an incoming audio call, walks the user through a very simple workflow to gather some input, and displays the selected caller input in the console application. Although this is a very simplistic example, it demonstrates the ability to integrate a sequential workflow XOML into a UCMA application, start the workflow, and use the output of the workflow in the UCMA application.

Adding a Sequential Workflow to a UCMA Application

When you create a UCMA 3.0 Workflow SDK communications workflow project, it automatically includes a sequential workflow project time (a XOML file and its code-behind). You won't be able to add this project item type to a console application project, so you have to create it in another project and copy it into the console application project. After adding the XOML and its rules and code-behind file to your project, adjust the namespace of the file to match your project.

Also add the following references:

➤   `Microsoft.Rtc.Workflow`

➤   `Microsoft.Speech`

➤   `System.Workflow.Activities`

➤   `System.Workflow.ComponentModel`

➤   `System.Workflow.Runtime`

➤   `System.WorkflowServices`

Configuring the Workflow's Call Provider

When integrating a UCMA 3.0 Workflow SDK communications workflow into a UCMA application, the UCMA application becomes responsible for accepting and disconnecting the call from the user. The `AcceptCall` and `DisconnectCall` activities in the communications workflow are no longer required. Deleting these activities from the communications workflow also means that the `CommunicationsSequence` activity in the workflow needs a new call provider. This section describes deleting the `AcceptCall` and `DisconnectCall` activities from the communications workflow and exposing a new `CallProvider` property that you can set when starting the workflow from the UCMA application.

Delete the `AcceptCall` and `DisconnectCall` activities from the workflow so that it looks like the workflow shown in Figure 14-44. The console application that hosts the workflow, not the workflow itself, will be responsible for connecting and disconnecting the call.

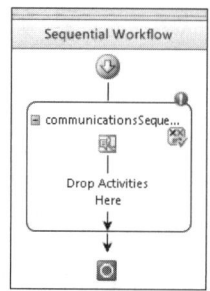

You can see in Figure 14-44 that the `CommunicationsSequence` activity has a red warning exclamation mark on it. The `CallProvider` property of the `CommunicationsSequence` activity was set to the `AcceptCall` activity that no longer exists in the workflow.

Add a public property of type `CallProvider` to the workflow's code-behind class. You will pass a value into the workflow instance for the call provider that the workflow will use:

FIGURE 14-44

Available for
download on
Wrox.com

```
public CallProvider CallProvider { get; set; }
```

Code snippet GetInputFromCaller\GetCallerChoice.xoml.cs

In the workflow designer, set the `CallProvider` property of the `CommunicationsSequence` activity to the `CallProvider` property from the workflow's code-behind as shown in Figure 14-45.

Implementing the Workflow Logic

A typical use case for hosting a UCMA 3.0 SDK Workflow communications workflow in a UCMA application is to gather some input from the caller — such as their account number and reason for their call — and then connect them with an agent to help them. The output from the communications workflow can be used to provide the agent with some information about the customer; for example, if the customer provided an account number, the customer's account is loaded in the CRM system running on the agent's desktop.

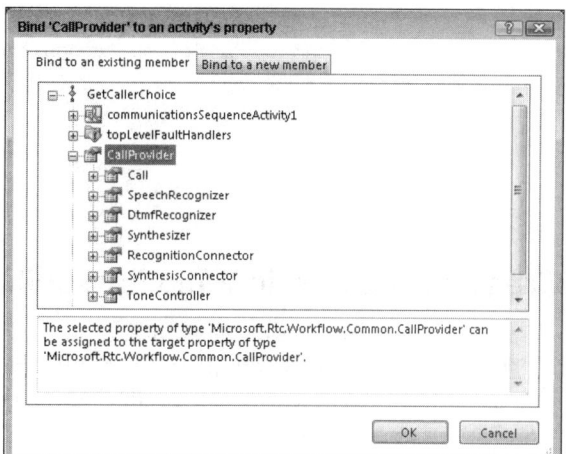

FIGURE 14-45

This section describes a simple example of collecting input from the caller and then exposing it as output from the communications workflow, thereby making it available to the UCMA application that is hosting the communications workflow.

Add a `SpeechQuestionAnswer` activity to the workflow and configure its `ExpectedDtmfInputs` and `ExpectedSpeechInputs` properties to prompt the caller to choose option 1, 2, or 3 (see the following code). In the `Turn_Starting` handler of the activity, build a prompt to ask the user to choose one of the options.

```
private void ChooseOption_TurnStarting(object sender,
    Microsoft.Rtc.Workflow.Activities.SpeechTurnStartingEventArgs e)
{

    this.ChooseOption.MainPrompt.ClearContent();
    this.ChooseOption.MainPrompt.AppendText("Please say or choose option");
    this.ChooseOption.MainPrompt.AppendTextWithHint("1", SayAs.NumberCardinal);
    this.ChooseOption.MainPrompt.AppendTextWithHint("2", SayAs.NumberCardinal);
    this.ChooseOption.MainPrompt.AppendText("or");
    this.ChooseOption.MainPrompt.AppendTextWithHint("3", SayAs.NumberCardinal);
}
```

Code snippet GetInputFromCaller\GetCallerChoice.xoml.cs

Add a `Code` activity to capture the caller's choice and record it in a module-level variable. Because it is marked as public, the `SelectedOption` property will automatically be exposed in the workflow's output parameter collection:

```
public string SelectedOption { get; set; }

private void SetSelectedOption_ExecuteCode(object sender, EventArgs e)
{
    if (this.ChooseOption.RecognitionResult != null)
    {
        this.SelectedOption =
            this.ChooseOption.RecognitionResult.Text.Replace
(" ", string.Empty);
    }
}
```

Code snippet GetInputFromCaller\GetCallerChoice.xoml.cs

Creating a Generic Workflow Initiator

You can use a generic workflow initiator in your UCMA application to start various workflows. The workflow initiator is responsible for initializing the workflow runtime and starting the appropriate workflow with the specified arguments.

Initializing the Workflow Runtime

You can maintain one instance of the `WorkflowInitiator` class in your UCMA application and use it to start workflows as needed. In the constructor of the `WorkflowInitiator` class, initialize the workflow runtime. Wire up an event handler for the `WorkflowCompleted` event of the `WorkflowRuntime`. You will use the event handler to capture the output of the workflow:

```
public WorkflowRuntime WorkflowRuntime { get; set; }

public WorkflowInitiator()
{
    this.WorkflowRuntime = new WorkflowRuntime();
    this.WorkflowRuntime.AddService(new CommunicationsWorkflowRuntimeService());
```

```
        this.WorkflowRuntime.AddService(new TrackingDataWorkflowRuntimeService());
        this.WorkflowRuntime.StartRuntime();
    }
```

Code snippet GetInputFromCaller\WorkflowInitiator.cs

Starting a Workflow from the Workflow Initiator

The `WorkflowInitiator` class exposes a `StartWorkflow` method that accepts the following parameters:

➤ `localEndPoint`: The application endpoint for the UCMA application.

➤ `call`: The call to start the workflow on.

➤ `requestData`: An instance of `SipRequestData` that contains information about the incoming SIP request. This is available from the `CallReceivedEventArgs` from the call made to the UCMA application.

➤ `workflowType`: The type of the workflow to start.

➤ `namedArgumentValues`: A `Dictionary<string, object>` of parameters to pass into the workflow instance.

This is similar to the workflow startup code that you're already familiar with. The code creates a new `CallProvider` on the `Call` instance and adds it to the workflows arguments. This matches up to the public property of the workflow called `CallProvider` and will be set as the call provider for the workflow's `CommunicationsSequence` activity.

The workflow instance is then created using an overload of the `CreateWorkflow` function that accepts a list of arguments and values to provide to the workflow. In this example, you're only passing in the call provider that the workflow will use. However, you can pass in any other information to the workflow, such as the values for prompts that some of the workflow's activities will use.

```
public Guid StartWorkflow(
    LocalEndpoint localEndpoint,
    Call call,
    SipRequestData requestData,
    Type workflowType,
    Dictionary<string, object> namedArgumentValues)
{
    var callProvider = new CallProvider(call, new CultureInfo("en-US"));
    namedArgumentValues.Add("CallProvider", callProvider);

    var workflowInstance = this.WorkflowRuntime.CreateWorkflow
    (workflowType, namedArgumentValues);

    var communicationsWorkflowRuntimeService =
        (CommunicationsWorkflowRuntimeService)
        this.WorkflowRuntime.GetService
```

```
            (typeof(CommunicationsWorkflowRuntimeService));

    var dataTrackingService =
        (TrackingDataWorkflowRuntimeService)
        this.WorkflowRuntime.GetService
            (typeof(TrackingDataWorkflowRuntimeService));

    communicationsWorkflowRuntimeService.SetEndpoint
        (workflowInstance.InstanceId, localEndpoint);

    communicationsWorkflowRuntimeService.SetWorkflowCulture
        (workflowInstance.InstanceId, new CultureInfo("en-US"));

    workflowInstance.Start();
    return workflowInstance.InstanceId;
}
```

Code snippet GetInputFromCaller\Program.cs

Starting a Workflow from the UCMA Application

A UCMA application typically implements an `AudioVideoCallReceived` event handler that executes when the trusted application endpoint associated with the application receives a call. With a call now established with the user, you can use the methods exposed by the workflow's `WorkflowInitiator` class to start the UCMA 3.0 Workflow SDK communications workflow from the UCMA application.

Starting the Workflow using the WorkflowInitiator

To start the workflow, you need to provide values for any required input parameters, and wire up an event handler that will execute when the workflow completes executing. If any output is available from the workflow, you can collect it in that event handler. Next you will start the communications workflow from the UCMA application.

Create an instance of the `WorkflowInitiator` class and a `Dictionary<string, object>` of input parameters to provide to the workflow.

Wire up an event handler for the `WorkflowCompleted` event of the `WorfklowRuntime` — you will use this to access the output parameters collection of the workflow.

Call `StartWorkflow` to start a specific workflow type by providing the `typeof` the workflow to start. The `StartWorkflow` function returns a `Guid` representing the instance ID of the workflow that was just started. Store this `Guid` in a `Dictionary<Guid, string>`, which will be used to store the output from the specific workflow instance.

```
var workflowInitiator = new WorkflowInitiator();
workflowInitiator.WorkflowRuntime.WorkflowCompleted +=
    new EventHandler<WorkflowCompletedEventArgs>
(WorkflowRuntime_WorkflowCompleted);
```

```
var namedArgumentValues = new Dictionary<string, object>();

Guid instanceId =
    workflowInitiator.StartWorkflow(
        _applicationEndpoint,
        e.Call,
        e.RequestData,
        typeof(GetCallerChoice),
        namedArgumentValues);

_workflowOutput.Add(instanceId, string.Empty);
```

Code snippet GetInputFromCaller\Program.cs

Capturing the Output of the Workflow

The WorkflowCompleted event of the WorkflowRuntime fires when the workflow is completed. You can capture the output of the workflow in the event handler.

Any public property exposed by the workflow is returned in the OutputParameters object of type Dictionary<string, object> that is exposed by WorkflowCompletedEventArgs.

Get the instance ID of the workflow that was just completed by getting a reference to the WorkflowInstance in the WorkflowCompletedEventArgs and querying its InstanceId property. The OutputParameters object contains the SelectedOption representing the caller's choice.

Available for
download on
Wrox.com

```
static void WorkflowRuntime_WorkflowCompleted(object sender,
WorkflowCompletedEventArgs e)
{
    Console.WriteLine("Workflow instance {0} completed",
        e.WorkflowInstance.InstanceId);

    _workflowOutput[e.WorkflowInstance.InstanceId] =
        e.OutputParameters["SelectedOption"].ToString();

    Console.WriteLine("You selected option: {0}",
        e.OutputParameters["SelectedOption"].ToString());
}
```

Code snippet GetInputFromCaller\Program.cs

In a real application, you will take a specific action based on the caller's selection, such as transferring him to an agent queue based on his choice. In this example, simply write the output of the workflow to the console.

Because your application will most likely be handling multiple concurrent calls from users, you need to be able to match up the workflow instance to a specific call. This simple example uses a Dictionary<Guid, string> to match the workflow instance ID to the output of the workflow.

SUMMARY

The UCMA 3.0 Workflow SDK gives you the tools to build communications-enabled workflow solutions such as IVRs and personal virtual assistants. Use the different available prompts to create a natural dialog with the caller. Communications events and commands allow you to build functionality into the workflow to handle global events and also commands from the caller, such as asking for help. You can call UCMA code from within the workflow and even build your own custom workflow activities to use in your communications workflows.

INDEX